MASTERING THE GRILL

MASTERING THE GRILL

THE OWNER'S MANUAL FOR OUTDOOR COOKING

BY ANDREW SCHLOSS AND DAVID JOACHIM / PHOTOGRAPHS BY ALISON MIKSCH

CHRONICLE BOOKS
SAN FRANCISCO

Library of Congress Cataloging-in-Publication Data available.

ISBN-10: 0-8118-4964-3
ISBN-13: 978-0-8118-4964-7

Manufactured in China.

Design and typesetting by Barretto-Co.

The photographer wishes to thank her parents for their ardent support
and generous spirit, which infuse her life and work.

Distributed in Canada by Raincoast Books
9050 Shaughnessy Street
Vancouver, British Columbia V6P 6E5

10 9 8 7 6 5 4 3 2 1

Chronicle Books LLC
680 Second Street
San Francisco, California 94107
www.chroniclebooks.com

DEDICATION

FOR **RON JOACHIM** (1945-2003),
A MASTER OF FIRE

ACKNOWLEDGMENTS

Three years ago, we started researching and writing about the science of grilling. Since then, so many people have fanned the flames, it's difficult to know where to begin thanking everyone. Initial sparks came from our agent Lisa Ekus and editor Bill LeBlond, who encouraged the notion of us writing a book together. Thank you both for your support and insight every step of the way. To Amy Treadwell, huge thanks for lending your intelligent and creative mind to our sprawling manuscript. Barretto-Co., we can't thank you enough for making a mountain of information so easily accessible with your simple, bold design. Thanks also to Arthur Mount for your detailed illustrations and to Rebecca Pepper for razor-sharp copyediting.

We spent 18 months testing recipes and would like to thank everyone who test-drove, sampled, and critiqued the recipes in this book, especially Tara Mataraza Desmond and Meera Malik for offering plenty of down-to-earth suggestions during long days at the grill, as well as Christine Bucher; August and Maddox Joachim; Bonnie Joachim; Jon, Michelle, Jonathan, and Michael Joachim; Bill, Mary, Leah, and Brian Joachim; Chris and Lisa Neyen; Tom Villa; Kurt Larson; Paul Dellapa; Dave Pryor; Selene Yeager; Tom Aczel; Michelle Raes; Andrew and Kim Brubaker; Doug Ashby; Danielle Lubene; Bill, Beth, and Natalie Strickland; Mark Bowman; Mark Taylor; Röbi Eugster; Dale and Cindy Mack; Bill and Bridget Doherty; Cathy, Ken, Tomias, Nick, and Tessa Peoples; Kathy, Dan, Elizabeth, and Natalie Shollenberger; Karen, Dana, Ben, and Isaac Schloss; Ned and Debby Carroll; Topher Desmond; Mary and Allen Frankel; Diane Zilka; Karen Mauch; Joan and Burton Horn; Deborah Shain; and Murray Silberman.

Throughout the recipe testing and photography, we cooked with food from a huge array of food merchants and purveyors. Thanks in particular to John and Sukey Jamison of Jamison Farm for outstanding lamb; Bill's Poultry at the Allentown Farmer's Market for quail and other birds; and the many farmers at the Emmaus Farmer's Market, especially Rod Wieder of Backyard Bison and George and Melanie DeVault of Pheasant Hill Farm.

We took on this book's photography ourselves and are indebted to the talented photography team that created such stunning photographs over months and months of shooting, including photographer extraordinaire Alison Miksch, food stylist and papaya connoisseur Michael Pedersen, assistant food wizard Donna Land, photography assistant and scarf aficionado Jada Vogt, and tireless prop stylist Erika Ellis. We also thank Asa and Olivia Fritz and Donna and Ed Land for graciously allowing us to set up camp in your fields and fireplaces for various photo shoots. Big thanks to Phillip Shulman; Carol Moore; Christine Bucher; August and Maddox Joachim; Bill, Beth, and Natalie Strickland; Sharon, Walter, and Tess Sanders; and Sean and Morgan O'Rourke for modeling during these photo shoots. To Susan Pollack, a special thank-you for taking some very cool shots of us hamming it up at the grill.

For trumpeting our book title and roadside assistance during book promotion, thanks to Jennifer Tomaro and Peter Perez at Chronicle Books. Thanks also to the behind-the-scenes staff at Chronicle for helping us bring this book to life, including Tera Killip, Doug Ogan, and Evan Hulka.

Lastly, big hugs to our wives Christine and Karen for gracefully enduring yet another book and making room in our homes for more grills, smokers, and knives.

CONTENTS

PART II: THE GRILLMASTER'S RECIPES

If you have ever sacrificed a rack of ribs to the incendiary powers of a backyard grill, or tried to convince yourself that "black and crusty" is exactly how you like your chicken, then you know firsthand the ambiguous art of cooking over an open flame. The problem is not always a lack of skill; it may be a lack of understanding. Many of us operate under the delusion that grilling is little more than throwing the desired number of edible items over a blaze and sitting back until they heat through. However, cooking outdoors, without the high-tech benefits of things like thermostats and heavy-gauge saucepans, requires greater vigilance and knowledge than anything demanded from indoor cooking.

The first step in mastering live fire is figuring out what it's all about. Many grill books and many food science texts are available, but very few cookbooks venture into the science behind grilling. That's the focus of our book. We aim to explain how grilling works, how to make grills work better, and how to use simple flavoring and cooking techniques to cook delicious grilled foods. We don't go overboard with trendy food science wizardry. We use no test tubes, vials, centrifuges, or *sous-vide* (French for "under pressure"). Our tools are the ones most grill lovers are comfortable and familiar with: tongs, spatulas, and knives. But we'll occasionally employ something offbeat if it is useful, such as a marinade injector or a grill skillet.

Likewise, our main ingredients are the usual four-legged animal meats like beef, pork, and lamb, as well as fish and fowl of every sort, plus some game meats here and there. We also devote an entire chapter to vegetables and another to fruits, doughs, and cheese. We grill everything from whole animals to primal cuts to retail cuts to parts and pieces. Our grilling techniques range from the expected to the adventurous. For instance, we prefer to cook some food directly in the hot coals rather than on a grill grate, such as Sweet Potatoes in the Coals with Lime-Cilantro Butter (page 287). We also cook some foods in roasting pans on the grill grate when it makes sense (see Clambake on the Grill, page 237). We also use brines, marinades, sauces, glazes, mops, dips, pastes, and spice rubs to enhance flavors. And our recipes can be grilled with gas, charcoal, or wood as the fuel.

All of this should be fairly familiar to most grill lovers. So what's new here? In this book, we approach the grill from the perspective of science and mechanics. Our goal is to impart an understanding of what happens during grilling, so that you can make better-tasting grilled food. Great grilling and barbecuing involve more than following accepted techniques and endless ingredient jockeying. Grilling is more than an art. It's simply not enough to say that grilling is an "inexact science," as many grill books do. After all, baking was an inexact science before we understood the structure of flour, the browning properties of sugar, the alchemy of leaveners, and the tenderizing effects of fat. Just like bakers, tinkering grill cooks want to know more about the medium and the method. They want to know what's going on when raw food meets live fire. They want to know when to use a dry rub and when to marinate, what meats should be brined and which foods take best to mops, sops, and sauces. They want to know why a strip steak sometimes browns nicely, while at other times it burns inedibly. And they want the holy grail of grilling—to know how to make a simple, tender grilled hamburger rather than a charred hockey puck. We believe that just as baking science has allowed bakers to hone their craft, knowing the science of live-fire cooking will allow backyard grill lovers to vastly improve their flair with the flames.

This book tells you exactly how various grills, pit barbecues, and smokers work. It explains the physics of fire, the chemistry of dry-heat cooking, and the mystery of this most primal cooking method. It's also an owner's manual to virtually all of the equipment that home cooks will encounter when grilling and barbecuing. We explain not just how to use various types of grills but how they work mechanically, how to maintain them, and how to repair them. You'll also learn about the science of heat transference and how different fuels affect this fundamental process. You'll marvel at the physical and chemical transformations that govern all live-fire cooking, from the gradual magic of slow, low-heat barbecuing to the brisk alchemy of fast, high-heat grilling.

Then we move on to ingredients, discussing in lay terms the basic molecular makeup of meat, poultry, game, fish, shellfish, vegetables, fruits, cheese, eggs, and doughs—and, most importantly, what happens when these foods react with flame.

Our goal is to help you understand the hows of grilling: how a hot grill fire quickly melts and caramelizes the sugars in vegetables, increasing their sweetness and taming their bitterness; how the low, wood-fueled heat of a smoky pit barbecue slowly melts the fat in meat, which in turn acts as a natural basting liquid; and how the intense flavor of a grilled steak with a crisp crust results from the accelerated browning that occurs when the compound sugars on the surface of the meat quickly caramelize over a hot flame.

With this grounding in the fundamentals, you can be confident about the whens and whys of grilling: when and why to marinate, brine, rub, baste, mop, glaze, and sauce to achieve the optimal flavor and texture of various grilled and barbecued foods. We give you the knowledge you need to grill without following recipes. After all, the fun of grilling is participating directly in the cooking process as it occurs—and, ultimately, influencing that process. Let's face it: Live fire is inspiring. And grilling is the most basic enactment of the principle that cooking = food + heat. We simply explain what's going on during grilling so that you can play more freely at the fire and experiment with the variables of tools, fuels, time, temperature, ingredients, flavors, and go-withs.

But this is not a book just for grilling extremists. We recognize that some cooks want to be experts, while others just want to make dinner. The bulk of the book is filled with recipes. From basic Steakhouse Burgers (page 93) to a fire-roasted Honey-Glazed Roast Suckling Pig (page 239), the more than 300 recipes in this book demonstrate basic grilling principles and fabulous grilled flavor. Rib-Eye Steaks with Fragrant Chile Rub and Salsa Butter (page 141) shows how a tender cut of meat achieves optimal taste and texture from a dry rub, with a final flourish of flavored butter. Apple-Sage Barbecued Turkey Legs (page 197) demonstrates that low heat and slow cooking can bring out the best flavor of even relatively lean meats. And Fennel-Brined Trout Grilled with Bacon and Herbs (page 178) shows how to infuse flavor through brining while improving mouth-feel with the natural basting power of bacon.

Every recipe has the straightforward layout of the assembly directions in an owner's manual. Starting with the setup for gas, charcoal, and wood grills, each recipe then lists all of the grilling tools and ingredients needed, approximate timing, and concise directions. Plenty of useful information and recipe variations surround the actual recipes. Even if you never consult the first few chapters (where we explain most of the science), you will have all the information in any given recipe necessary for mastering that particular dish.

We believe that the ultimate goal of mastering the grill is confidence and freedom: the confidence to solve problems as they arise (and they inevitably will) and the freedom to play with your food. There are countless reasons why you should learn how to use your grill more efficiently and completely. For one, you've got to eat, so you might as well eat well. But more important, in a world where there are numerous ways to get a meal on the table, the main reason to grill it yourself is because it's fun. The act of cooking with fire is inherently exciting. We hope that this book will give you a level of mastery that allows you to create your own recipes, improvise your own techniques, and rediscover the excitement every time you step up to the grill.

CHAPTER 1

MASTERING YOUR EQUIPMENT

Grilling equipment runs the gamut from the most primitive wooden stick to the most industrialized gas-fired, stainless-steel grill. Impale a piece of food on a stick, hold it over a flame, and you are grilling. Strictly speaking, you don't even need the stick. You can grill a steak or chop directly on hot coals, with no equipment whatsoever: no firebox, no grill grate, not even a set of tongs (see the recipe for Scotch Steak in the Coals with Stilton Butter on page 145). If you're crazy or quick enough, you can even turn the steak with your fingers.

But most grillers love their tools. And the majority of modern grills do make it easier to cook with fire, containing the flames and providing better heat control. When we talk about grills, we mean any box, bowl, barrel, or other physical structure designed to contain and control fire for the purpose of cooking food. There are two basic elements to any grill: the firebox (or hearth) where the fire burns, and the grilling grate on which the food cooks. You'll find these two elements at work in the simplest campfire grills and in the most complex electric-ignition, mixed-fuel, rotisserie-equipped, smoker-ready, high-capacity outdoor kitchen grills.

Different grills have different purposes. No doubt, there is a grill out there that's built just for you, but it's also possible that you will see the benefits in more than one model. Three things distinguish most grills from one another:

THE FUEL SOURCE. Typically, the fuel will be gas, charcoal, wood, or a combination.

THE GRILL'S MATERIAL. A grill can be constructed from stone, ceramic, aluminum, steel, or almost any other inflammable material. The material's density and heat conductivity partially determine the grill's overall cooking characteristics.

THE GRILL'S DIMENSIONS. Size and shape may range from just a few inches to several yards in width, depth, or length. Dimensions primarily determine the available cooking space and the grilling techniques for which the grill is best suited. See Chapter 2 for information on various grilling techniques.

If you're in the market for a grill, consider all three factors. Also think about how often you grill and the amount of food you typically cook at any given time. The grill you buy should have ample cooking space for your average grilling session. Whole turkeys, leg of lamb, prime rib, and other large roasts are best grilled on a cooking area of at least 600 square inches or 22 inches in diameter, preferably more. Smaller roasts, steaks, chops, fish fillets, and shellfish can be grilled on a cooking area as small as 150 square inches or 14 inches in diameter. A larger grill allows you to cook both small and big foods.

The ideal grill for you also depends on your budget and whether you prefer the convenience of gas or the more intense heat of charcoal. The debate over gas versus charcoal rages on (see sidebar at left for features to look for in each). You may find that one gas grill and one charcoal grill satisfies all of your grilling needs. Maybe you'd like an indoor grill as well. Either way, it helps to know about the various types of grills available so you can master grilling on each and every one. Here's a look at the most widely used types of grills—from the simplest to the most complex.

01. CAMPFIRE GRILL

These inexpensive grills ($10 to $50) consist mainly of a cast-iron or steel cooking grate designed to sit over a wood-burning fire. The adjustable-height grate is attached to a stake or two T-shaped legs to suspend the grate over the fire. As with all grills, the best models are sturdy, stable, and durable, but campfire grills should also be easily portable. Heat is controlled by the amount of coals you rake beneath the cooking grate and by adjusting the grate up or down.

02. FIREPLACE GRILL

Similar to campfire grills, fireplace grills (also known as Tuscan grills) are designed to fit into the more confined area of a fireplace. These grills don't always have adjustable grill grates, so be sure the grate will be elevated at least 4 to 6 inches above the coals of your fireplace.

03. HIBACHI

Here's where the all-important firebox comes into play. While campfire and fireplace grills rest over an open fire on a flat surface, every other grill confines the flame to a firebox that's elevated above the ground. Used for millennia in Japan, a hibachi looks like a deep, heavy-duty tray with a grill grate on top. The best models provide heat control with adjustable grill grates, air vents on the sides of the firebox, and an elevated fire grate to allow oxygen to flow beneath the coals. Most hibachis are charcoal fired, but some modern versions are gas fired or electric. The cooking space is usually limited to 100 to 200 square inches, so hibachis are best for vegetables, burgers, kebabs, steaks, and bone-less chicken parts over direct heat. They provide inexpensive ($20 to $75), portable, tabletop grilling for decks, patios, and balconies. You can buy or rent very large versions, known as table grills. These oversized hibachis rest on tall legs that elevate the firebox to roughly counter height and provide plenty of grill space for cooking dozens of burgers or steaks at once. Some models also come with a rotisserie setup for whole birds and roasts. You'll see table grills most often at outdoor festivals where big quantities of quickly grilled foods are served.

04. FIRE BOWL

A modern cross between a campfire ring (a circular enclosure for a fire) and a hibachi, a fire bowl is designed for enjoy-ing a contained wood fire as well as cooking over it. It consists of a large, shallow metal bowl (usually cast iron or copper) about 20 to 40 inches in diameter, with short legs to prop the bowl off the ground. Cooking grates often cover only half of the bowl so that the fire can easily be refueled from one side and hot coals can be raked to the other side for cooking. Like hibachis, fire bowls are best for quick grilling on decks and patios, but they are not as portable and cost a bit more.

05. KETTLE GRILL

This bowl-shaped grill has become the icon of charcoal grilling in America. The Weber-Stephen Products Company, which originated the design, also trademarked it, but several other manufacturers make similar grills. The kettle grill has one key advantage over hibachis and fire bowls: its lid. Without the lid, a kettle grill functions much like a tall fire bowl or like a large, round hibachi with added cooking space (the high sides of the deep bowl shape also help to protect the coals from wind). But with the domed lid in place, a kettle grill can function more like an oven than a grill. Put on the lid and you can contain the heat in an enclosed environment so that it surrounds the food rather than just coming up from the bottom. And if you put the hot coals on one side of the firebox and the food on the other (known as indirect grilling), you can "grill-roast" whole birds and large cuts of meat so that they cook through to the center and brown beautifully on the surface without burning.

Most kettle grills don't have adjustable-height grill grates, so heat is controlled by the thickness of your coal bed, the air vents on the bottom of the firebox (or fire bowl, really), and the air vents in the lid. Again, the lid is key because it allows you to position the lid's air vents on the opposite side of the fire bowl's air vents so that heat and smoke are drawn up from the bottom, across the food, and then out the lid on the opposite side. It also permits you to add pieces of wood to the hot coals in a kettle grill, increasing the smoke and transforming the grill into something closer to a smoker (see page 16). For the money, a charcoal kettle grill remains one of the most versatile outdoor cookers avail-able today. Some models are also available with a "gas-assist" feature that quickly ignites the charcoal with a burst of gas but uses the coals for cooking the food. The cooking area ranges from 14 to 24 inches in diameter, with prices ranging from $50 to $350.

06. BARBECOOK GRILL

This stainless-steel charcoal grill looks like a shiny kettle grill on a pedestal. It has many of the same features as a kettle grill, with the advantage of a built-in chimney starter (see page 27) to quickly light the coals with newspaper. It's among the most popular charcoal grills in Europe and costs anywhere from $200 to $800.

07. CERAMIC GRILL-OVEN

Modern ceramic grills are modeled on two ancient designs: the Indian tandoor and the Japanese *kamado.* These are both charcoal-fired clay ovens, but the bell-shaped tandoor is open at the top, while the egg-shaped *kamado* has a tight lid. The charcoal and heat-retaining clay in a tandoor generate intense heat (up to 700°F) that quickly sears food. In a *kamado,* the heat-retentive property of the clay and the lid are used for slowly roasting food at low temperatures (as low as 200°F). Modern versions of these charcoal grill-ovens are made of thick, heavy ceramic and are shaped like an egg, similar to the *kamado.* The heat-retentive ceramic makes an efficient slow-cooker, allowing you to use very few coals and generating low heat for long periods of time. The airtight lid traps heat and moisture, creating exceptionally juicy whole birds and roasts. Add wood as fuel, and these cookers become efficient smokers. Ceramic grills usually have a cooking area of 10 to 20 inches in diameter, but vertical space allows you to add a second grill grate below the first. Two popular brands are Primo and Big Green Egg.

08. PIT GRILL OR SMOKER

Notice that our description of various wood and charcoal cookers has progressed from "grill" to "grill-oven" to "grill or smoker." There's a big gray area between grilling and smoking, but here's the primary difference: Grills cook food quickly, using relatively high, direct heat, and smokers cook food slowly, using relatively low, indirect heat and lots of wood smoke. A pit grill or smoker is expressly designed for smoking (or barbecuing), in which food is cooked not so much by the radiant heat of the coals as by the relatively cool heat of the wood smoke generated by those coals. To achieve this, the firebox on a pit grill or smoker is often located in a separate chamber offset from the cooking chamber. The cooking chamber is often shaped like a horizontal barrel, as these cookers were originally made (and continue to be made) from steel barrels. But any deep shape (pit) that allows heat to circulate around the food can be used as a smoker.

Some pit grills and front-loading grills allow for both grilling over direct heat and smoking via indirect heat. The available cooking space on these grill-smokers usually hovers between 500 and 800 square inches, but barbecue caterers may use huge rigs with three to four times that much cooking space. A typical backyard steel-barrel smoker burns charcoal or wood, costs $200 to $500, and has enough grill space for several beef briskets or racks of pork ribs or a whole suckling pig. As on a kettle grill, heat is adjusted with the lid and air vents. We should mention here that some water smokers not meant for grilling can be fired by electricity instead of wood or charcoal. These dedicated smokers are usually manufactured in a vertical cylindrical shape and include a water pan for keeping food moist as it smokes.

09. GAS GRILL

A single feature distinguishes gas grills from all other types: the fuel. Gas ignites instantly, emits a clean flame (no smoke or ashes), maintains a consistent yet variable temperature, and can be shut down easily. These conveniences have made gas grills the most popular grills in America, according to the Hearth, Patio & Barbecue Association. Gas grills are typically constructed of durable steel, from the firebox to the burners, and include a hinged lid. Other features vary widely, creating a huge price range from about $250 to upward of $10,000. If you're in the market for a gas grill, see the "What Makes a Good Gas or Charcoal Grill?" sidebar on page 14. Also, turn to page 18 to understand how a gas grill works.

10. ELECTRIC GRILL

Instead of a flame, a metal coil serves as the heat source for these inexpensive grills ($50 to $100). Otherwise, electric grills usually resemble hibachis and are designed for the same purpose: quickly cooking small amounts of small or tender foods over direct heat. Some models have lids and can be used outdoors, but most are designed for simple, indoor grilling. The heating coil typically rests below the cooking grate, but on newer models the heating element is built into the cooking grate, which limits flare-ups and smoke. Heat is easily controlled with a knob that increases or decreases the flow of electricity. Almost any food that is grilled over direct heat on a charcoal or gas grill can be cooked on an electric grill, including the recipes throughout this book. For that matter, most grill recipes using direct heat will work under a broiler as well (minus the grill marks).

11. CONTACT GRILL OR GRILL PAN

Another option for the indoor cook, contact grills and grill pans dispense with the firebox altogether. A contact grill looks like an electric waffle iron with grill grids. The George Foreman Grill is a popular model. Preheat the grids, add food, and close the top, and the hot grids on the top and bottom create nice grill marks in your food. Grill pans have the same effect, although they cook only from the bottom and are heated by the burners of your stove top. The flavor and texture of foods "grilled" on a contact grill or grill pan are quite different from those of foods cooked on outdoor charcoal and gas grills because the heat is not as intense, there is no smoke flavor, and moisture remains on the cooking surface as the food cooks, creating a hybrid cooking method somewhere between grilling, sautéing, and steaming. Contact grills and grill pans range in price from $20 to $120.

All grills work by generating intense heat that sears food and creates intense flavors through deep browning (grill marks). Known as "Maillard reactions," these browning reactions are partly responsible for the bold, complex taste of grilled food. Smoke generated by burning wood or charcoal or by fat dripping onto the heat source also contributes to the characteristic flavor of grilled food.

The higher the heat in a grill, the more browning reactions you will get. For this reason, a grill's fuel or heat source is by far the biggest determining factor in how it works, although a grill's material and dimensions also play a role. Fuel is so important because different fuels require different amounts of energy to ignite and different amounts of oxygen to become combustible at a rate suitable for cooking. Once a grill's fuel source is burning, however, all grills cook food through a combination of radiant heat from the fire, conduction of heat through the metal grill grate and food, and, when indirect grilling, convection of hot air around the food. See page 34 for more on the science of heat transference. Here's a glimpse into the inner workings of the two most common grills: charcoal and gas.

CHARCOAL

Natural lump charcoal and briquettes are both forms of burned wood that has already expended more than half its potential energy. That's why charcoal fires don't burn as hot as wood fires. It's also why many people swear by grilling over wood rather than charcoal or gas for the most intense heat and the best browning (and most complex flavor) in grilled food. However, charring wood makes it easier to ignite so that its heat can be more readily harnessed for cooking. Not everyone can start a wood fire every time they want to grill.

When wood is preburned to make charcoal, most of the wood's volatile organic compounds are burned off in the form of smoke. What's left behind is carbon, which produces the heat in glowing coals, and ash, which is made up of minerals left behind after the carbon has burned off. This explains why charcoal fires (and wood fires that have burned down to coals) don't emit much visible smoke.

Charcoal ignites at roughly 600°F, and matches, paper, or lighter fluid all get the job done. Once charcoal has ignited, its carbon combines with available oxygen to produce carbon dioxide, which results in heat. The ratio of charcoal to oxygen determines how hot the fire will get. The air vents on the firebox and lid of a charcoal kettle grill allow you to increase or decrease the flow of oxygen to speed up or slow down the combustion rate and, consequently, raise or lower the grill's heat. An elevated fire grate also improves airflow, allowing for easier temperature adjustment. With no lid, as on a hibachi, a charcoal grill also receives oxygen from above, but it's more difficult to control that oxygen flow. A gust of wind can fan the flames and instantly raise or lower the grill's temperature.

WHY GAS GRILLS CAN'T SEAR AS WELL AS CHARCOAL

To get a good sear on a steak, you need a raging hot fire and dry surfaces on the meat and the grill grate (oil on the grate is okay). With those two constants, you might think the fuel is irrelevant, but grill aficionados always claim that you can't turn out as good a grilled steak from a gas grill as you can from a charcoal grill. Well, they're right. Here's why: Charcoal burns drier than gas. When charcoal or wood burns, it produces primarily carbon dioxide, but when propane or natural gas burn, they produce carbon dioxide and vaporized water. Gas is about 30 percent moisture. That means $1/2$ to 1 cup of water is released during every 10 minutes of cooking on most gas grills. The moisture is delivered to the surface of the grill grate and the surface of the food, adding steam to the cooking process and preventing the temperature from rising as high as it does in a charcoal grill. Consequently, a gas grill can't produce the same sort of thick, crusty steak that you get when grilling over the high and dry heat of charcoal.

Steel is the most common construction material for charcoal grills such as kettle grills and hibachis. Steel is a good conductor of heat, so it heats up and cools down relatively quickly. But it doesn't retain heat very well, and so metal grills generally require more fuel because the heat is lost more easily through the grill's firebox. Ceramic charcoal grills, on the other hand, don't conduct heat as quickly but are far superior at retaining heat. Ceramic grills run more efficiently, requiring less fuel because heat is retained in the grill's firebox.

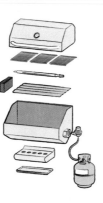

GAS

BENEFITS OF A CLEAN BLUE FLAME
When burned with an optimal mix of fuel and oxygen, both propane and natural gas emit a clear blue flame with no smoke. A clear blue flame indicates that only harmless water vapor and carbon dioxide (CO_2) are formed during burning. A yellow flame indicates insufficient oxygen for complete combustion of the fuel to take place. A small amount of yellow at the tip of a blue flame isn't hazardous, but a complete yellow flame will emit a bit more carbon monoxide (CO), a colorless, odorless toxic gas. You should be concerned only if the yellow-flaming grill is in a very confined area with poor ventilation. But you may want to improve your grill's efficiency by checking for leaks or cleaning the burners to achieve a clear blue flame (see "Grill Cleaning, Maintenance, and Repair," facing page).

Charcoal grills can be as simple as a metal box and a metal grill grate, but even a single-burner gas grill is much more complex. You still have the basics: fuel, ignition source, and oxygen. But the difference in fuel changes everything, because vaporous gas has a relatively narrow range of flammability.

A gas grill's fuel, whether a tank of propane (LP gas) or a direct line of natural gas (methane), is delivered to the grill burners through a main fuel hose. After you open the valve at the fuel source, the temperature knobs on the grill adjust the amount of fuel that reaches the burners.

Before combustion takes place at the burners, the fuel must be ignited. Unlike the simple fire starters for charcoal grills (matches and paper, lighter fluid, or an electric heating-coil starter), gas grills typically use an ignition system based on electricity generated by pressure, called piezoelectricity. Some crystalline substances, like quartz, generate an electric polarity under pressure, which sends a high-voltage spark across the face of the crystal. When you push the ignition button or turn the starter knob on your grill, the hammering sound you hear is just that–a small hammer applying pressure to a crystal (usually quartz) so that it generates a spark. You could also light the burners on a gas grill with a match or other flame, but piezoelectric igniter buttons are easier to use when they are working properly.

Once you generate a spark, in order for combustion to take place, both propane and natural gas require a very precise ratio of oxygen to fuel. This ratio (5 to 1) is regulated by the size and shape of the grill's burners. If the ratio is off, combustion is incomplete and the flame appears more yellow than blue (see the sidebar at left for details on the blue flame). Each burner mixes fuel and oxygen in the proper ratio and spreads it out over the burner's surface area, where it is emitted as flame through small holes or ports. Better gas grills have separately controlled stainless-steel burners for more precise and variable heat adjustment across the grill's cooking area. They also have evenly spaced burners that run from one side of the firebox to the other to distribute the heat evenly over the entire cooking area with fewer hot and cold spots.

Most gas grills also include some sort of heat diffuser over the burners to evenly distribute and retain the heat as well as protect the burners from dripping fat and juices. Metal plates, lava rock, and ceramic briquettes are the most common diffusers. Once the heat is diffused, it's delivered to the food on the grill grates through a combination of radiant heat, conduction, and convection (when the lid is down), as with charcoal grills.

C. GRILL CLEANING, MAINTENANCE, AND REPAIR

Most grills fail or need repair because they are rarely cleaned. But you don't need to scrub your grill until it gleams like a sports car. After several uses, a grill naturally develops a light patina on the grill grates and firebox that gives it character and doesn't negatively affect performance.

Of course, if you have a 1/4-inch-thick layer of soot and carbonized food on the grill grates, firebox, or lid, you may want to consider cleaning the grill more often. It all depends on how much you use your grill. Cleaning doesn't have to mean disassembling the entire grill and then putting it back together. You can do some brief cleaning every time you grill and more extended cleaning about once a season, depending on usage. Think of the annual cleaning as an opportunity to get under the hood, check out the parts of your grill, and make sure everything is working optimally. Cleaning will help your grill perform better and extend its life. On a gas grill, turn off the gas supply before extended cleaning.

EVERY TIME YOU GRILL

· Clean the grill grate. We regularly clean our grill grates twice with a stiff wire grill brush: once before adding food and once after removing food. If you brush the grill grate only once, do it while the grate is hot; a hot grate cleans easier than a cold one. After scraping the grate, close the lid and turn off the gas on a gas grill or close the vents on a charcoal grill to shut down the grill until cool.

· Check the grease catcher or ash catcher. If either one is full, empty it before beginning to grill.

· Wipe down the side tables. Some side tables develop nasty stains when left dirty for long periods of time. Regularly wipe down the tables with warm, soapy water, just as you would wipe down a countertop.

· Keep it dry. Moisture + oxygen + metal = rust. Dry any wet surfaces of the grill with a clean cloth to prevent rusting.

ONCE A YEAR

· Check the heat diffuser (gas only). Metal heat diffusers will develop a buildup of food debris. Simply scrape it off with an old spatula or metal bristle brush.

· Clean the lid and firebox. Remove the grill grate and fire grate of a charcoal grill and shovel any ashes from the fire box. On a gas grill, after removing the heat diffuser, scrape away any debris from the firebox. Wash the lid and firebox with warm, soapy water. For heavy soot buildup on the interior, use a heavy-duty grill cleaner. If you see what looks like peeling paint hanging from the interior of the grill lid, don't panic, and whatever you do, don't grab a paint brush. The flakes are baked-on grease that has turned to carbon; you can remove them by wiping them with a damp paper towel.

· Check the burner tubes (gas only). If your grill's flame is more yellow than blue, there may be cracks or obstructions in the burner tubes, preventing the optimal mix of oxygen and fuel (see page 30). Spiders sometimes nest in tubes that are not in use. Check the tubes for visible cracks or holes (other than the port holes). If you see any cracks, replace the tubes according to the manufacturer's directions, which is usually a simple matter of detaching the old holes (ports) with a pin. Be careful not to enlarge the ports, as their original diameter provides an optimal fuel-oxygen mix.

· For interior cleaning of the burner tubes, follow the manufacturer's directions. All burner tubes are constructed a little differently. If you can't find your grill manual, the following cleaning method works well for most tubes: Remove the tubes from the firebox and shine a flashlight into the orifices at the ends of the tubes. Clean the tube interiors with a long, narrow, flexible brush, a pipe cleaner, or a straightened metal coat hanger. You can also shoot a stream of water through the tubes with a garden hose. If you clean the burners at the beginning of your typical grilling season, thoroughly dry the burner tubes and reaffix them to the grill's firebox. If you clean at the end of your typical grilling season and will be storing the grill, coat the burners in vegetable oil and wrap them in foil to keep insects out during storage.

There are two ways of detecting a gas leak. Although propane and natural gas are odorless, ethyl mercaptan is added to these fuels to give them a detectable odor. Mercaptan reeks of rotten eggs. If you smell this persistent odor, do a leak check to locate the source of the leak. Mix a 1-to-1 ratio of dish soap and water. Turn on the fuel supply at the fuel source only (the propane tank or the natural gas line), but don't open the temperature control knobs on the grill's control panel. Brush the soapy water over the hose(s) and connections between the fuel supply, fuel valve, and temperature control knobs. Anywhere that bubbles appear indicates a gas leak. Inspect the hose(s) and connections for cracks or worn areas (grease sometimes attracts rodents, who may chew through the hoses). Next, brush the soapy water onto the welds around the propane tank, its supply valve, and the bottom ring of the tank and check for bubbles. Tighten all connections and immediately replace the hoses, valves, or fuel tank as necessary. The same bubble test should be performed on newly installed hoses, valves, and fuel tanks to confirm a tight seal with no gas leaks.

- Check the hoses (gas only). Make sure all connections are tight and that the hoses have no holes, cracks, or excessively worn areas. Follow the manufacturer's directions to replace any cracked or worn hoses, again a simple matter of removing old hoses and attaching new hoses.
- Check the control panel (gas only). Spray lubricant into any sticky control knobs. Brush away any spiderwebs under the control panel, using a small stiff brush. Spot-check the exterior of the grill and remove any spiderwebs.
- Check the igniter (gas or gas-assist only). If it isn't working, scrub the tip of the electrode with rubbing alcohol. Some electric igniters also require small batteries (such as AA). Replace old batteries as necessary.
- Check for corrosion. Scrub away any white spots or corrosion with a mixture of 1 part vinegar and 1 part water. To repaint your grill's exterior (only portions that are not porcelain enameled), clean it, sand it lightly, and coat with one to three coats of heat-resistant grill paint. Let the paint dry completely before using.
- Keep it dry. Dry any wet surfaces to prevent rusting. Most grills are coated in enamel to prevent rusting, but it pays to keep your grill dry anyway.

D. GRILL STORAGE

The lucky among us are able to grill outside year-round in a fair climate. Others may need to store their grills and equipment to protect them from foul weather. We live in the northeastern United States, where year-round grilling is possible, but grill storage (or covering) helps to prolong the life of a grill during the cold and rainy months.

To store a charcoal grill constructed of metal (such as a kettle grill), clean out any remaining ashes from the firebox before storage; residual ashes will attract moisture, which can lead to rust. Close the air vents in the fire bowl and lid to prevent small animals from nesting inside the grill. A tarp or grill cover also helps to protect your grill from the elements so that it will last longer before succumbing to rust and entropy.

To store a gas grill, turn off all valves and control knobs, especially the valves at the fuel source, such as the propane tank. Disconnect the propane tank and cover it with the safety cap supplied on the tank. Store the tank in an open yet secluded area, away from children. Avoid storing a propane tank in a garage, shed, or other enclosed area, which poses a safety hazard due to heat buildup.

Store tools and utensils inside on a pot rack or pegboard or in a drawer to shield them from the corrosive effects of moisture. Or store them outside in a sealed storage container or tackle box. If your grill has utensil hooks and/or cabinets, you can store your tools there, but be aware that they may still be exposed to moisture outside if the grill is not well covered.

E. GRILL TOOLS AND ACCESSORIES

Grill tools are like toys for fire lovers. Some have practical purposes, but others are just fun to play with. The "essential" tools will vary according to the type and amount of grilling you do. We think our heatproof silicone grill gloves are essential, but you may find them frivolous if you rarely need to pull a large, hot roast or roasting rack off the grill. Here's a list of tools that make it easier (or at least more fun) to manage your grill, your food, and your flavors.

TOOLS FOR THE GRILL

GRILL BRUSHES, SCRAPERS, AND SCRUBBERS. Basic cleaning tools, grill scrapers come in a variety of styles. Look for brushes with long handles and a large head of stiff bristles for easy cleaning of grill grates. Stainless steel should be cleaned only with a brass-bristled brush, since a steel brush can scratch its surface; iron grates can be scrubbed with any metal brush. Many brushes have metal scrapers at the tip of the head to remove stubborn debris. A V-shaped brush or scraper makes it easier to clean individual bars on a grill grate. Scrubbers resemble scouring pads and are designed to clean the firebox and lid (or the grill grate).

GRILL LAMP. Have you ever shone a flashlight onto your grill to check the food? If so, get a grill lamp to free up your hands. These lamps clamp to the side of your grill and often have adjustable necks to position the light where you need it. Some require an outlet and/or extension cord, while others are battery powered. You could also use an inexpensive work lamp from a hardware store. Or look for a handle lamp, which replaces the handle on your gas grill with one that has a built-in light.

GRILL GLOVES. Grilling means working with intense heat. Insulated heat-resistant gloves will protect your hands. Leather makes a good choice, but we prefer silicone gloves, which are waterproof and heat resistant to about 500°F. Wear them and you can grab a hot grill grate, grill rack, or roasted turkey right off the grill.

COAL RAKE. Use this to quickly rake coals into beds of varying thicknesses and varying heat levels. Most stiff garden rakes are too long and large for the typical kettle grill. A children's garden rake is just the right size.

COAL SHOVEL. A small shovel lets you easily shovel hot or spent coals and ashes from the firebox. Again, a child-size metal garden shovel works best for backyard grills. But the bigger the grill, the bigger the coal shovel should be.

COAL POKER. This is not strictly necessary, but you might like one if you grill in a wood-burning grill, over a campfire, or in a fireplace. Look for a coal poker that's long, metal, and curved at the end to easily hook coals and logs for repositioning.

DISPOSABLE ALUMINUM PANS. A disposable aluminum pan has multiple uses on the grill: a drip pan to catch grease; a roasting pan to retain juices for making a pan sauce; a sauté pan for simmering foods in liquid, such as boiled shrimp or brats in beer; a warming container for grilled food; and a soaking container for wood chips or chunks or bamboo skewers. Keep several sizes on hand.

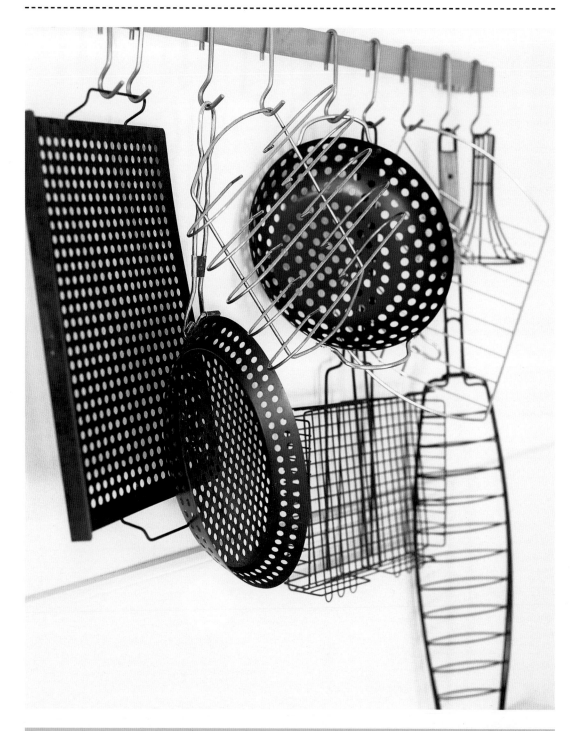

TONGS. These are perhaps the most important item in your grilling toolbox. Basic grill tongs should have long, sturdy handles, be spring-loaded so that the tongs close only with pressure, and have scalloped ends to get a better grip on foods. Avoid tongs with thin handles; they tend to bend when pressed, rendering them useless for grabbing food. Some practical variations on the theme: Fish tongs have extremely wide ends to match the dimensions of fish and make it easier to handle small whole fish or fillets. Tongulas have a flat spatula on one end of the tongs and a typical scalloped end on the other. A hybrid of tongs and a spatula, a good tongula can be used to both grab a steak and flip a burger.

SPATULA. Another key grill tool, a spatula excels at flipping small, delicate foods like burgers and fish fillets. Look for a stiff, long-handled spatula with a wide blade and beveled edge to easily reach beneath foods without mangling them. An offset grill spatula is the most ergonomic, and most have slats to prevent steam buildup while handling grilled food. A few also have a jagged edge on one side of the blade to tenderize meat and a bottle opener in the handle to release the carbonation of frosty beverages.

SKEWERS. Keep a few types on hand for kebabs and satays: metal, bamboo, and two-pronged. Flat metal skewers help to keep the food from spinning around the skewer. Two-pronged skewers do a slightly better job but may not evenly pierce small foods such as cherry tomatoes. Bamboo skewers make a more authentic presentation of Asian, Middle Eastern, and South American kebabs. But decorative metal skewers may be more your style. Almost any long, thin, stiff object will do the job: Try thick rosemary stems or even long twigs. Soak any wooden skewer in water for 30 minutes before grilling to keep it from burning.

GRILL TRAYS, GRATES, AND SCREENS. Often made of enameled metal, these perforated grill toppers allow you to cook small or delicate foods such as cut vegetables, meat chunks, and shrimp or scallops without letting them fall into the fire and without the use of skewers. They often include handles on both sides and can also be used to cook doughs right on the grill (see Grilled Rosemary and Prosciutto Focaccia, page 337). Grill purists may scoff, but these grill toppers expand the possibilities of your grill.

GRILL SKILLET AND WOK. Similar to vegetable grill trays, these perforated pans also include a long handle on one side. Often the handle is foldable so that you can close the grill lid without the handle sticking out. Grill skillets and woks allow you to replicate stovetop cooking on the grill, but with the addition of live fire and smoke. They're great for quickly cooking small pieces of food, but they also put another layer of metal between the food and the heat, which brings the cooking method further away from grilling.

GRILL FORK. We prefer not to use grill forks because they poke holes in food, especially the skins of poultry and sausage. A relatively insignificant amount of fat and juices escape, but it's often enough to cause flare-ups. And they feel awkward to use on the grill. Forks are for the table. Sturdy tongs or heat-resistant silicone gloves can do the job of most grill forks. But you may like to have a grill fork on hand for the odd roast that turns best when stabbed. Some models feature a built-in instant-read thermometer.

GRILL BASKET. This long-handled tool encloses food between two hinged wire grids, creating a shallow basket. Lift the basket by the handle and you can easily flip the food without it sticking or falling apart. It's very useful for grilled sandwiches, fish, and other delicate foods that are prone to sticking or falling apart on the grill. For the best protection against sticking (and the best searing), preheat and oil the basket in the same way you would preheat and oil the grill grate. Put food into a hot basket rather than a cold one.

RIB RACK. A rack is essential for grilling lots of ribs on a small grill. This simple metal accessory positions four racks of ribs parallel to one another on their long edges. With two of these tools, you can simultaneously grill eight racks of ribs on a standard charcoal kettle grill.

V-SHAPED ROASTING RACK. These resemble oven roasting racks and help roasts hold their shape during grilling.

VERTICAL ROASTING RACK. Excellent for chicken and other poultry, these racks hold birds in an upright position so that they cook and brown evenly and drain fat easily. They're available in various sizes for small to large birds.

THERMOMETER. Instant-read thermometers give you the precise internal temperature of foods within seconds of inserting the probe. They're unbeatable for judging the doneness of thick meats and roasts. Available in digital or analog models.

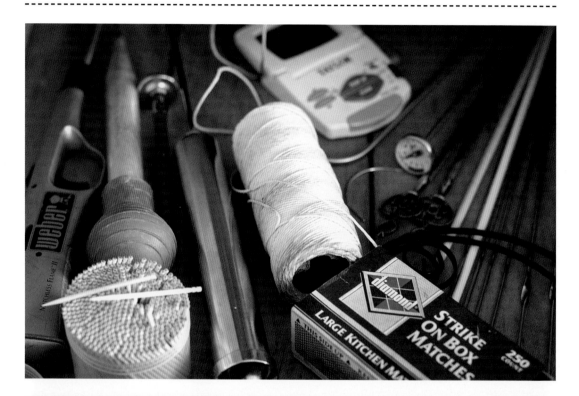

TOOLS FOR FLAVOR

BASTING BRUSH. Need flavor on the surface of your food? Brush it on with a basting brush, whether it's a baste, a glaze, or a sauce. Natural bristle brushes won't melt on the grill as nylon will, and they work well with all bastes, glazes, and sauces. Silicone brushes work best with thicker sauces because thinner bastes tend to slip right off the silicone bristles. Long-handled basting brushes protect your hands, but we often baste with short-handled natural bristle paintbrushes from the hardware store.

GRILL MOP. Resembling a diminutive kitchen mop, this tool is useful for dabbing or drizzling thin mop sauces onto large pieces of meat without brushing off any seasonings that may already be there. Barbecue caterers, restaurateurs, and competitors actually use full-size kitchen mops to accommodate their larger quantities of food; hence the name.

SPRAY BOTTLE. These standard, readily available plastic bottles filled with a nozzle and hand pump are handy for spraying flavored liquids onto slow-cooking foods to keep them moist and deepen their flavor.

INJECTOR. A marinade injector (also known as a kitchen syringe) looks like a large hypodermic needle. There's no easier way to inject flavor deep into the muscle tissue of meats. Any flavored liquid can be used, but those with no solids work best because they don't clog the needle. Metal ones tend to last longer than plastic models.

F. GRILL FUELS AND FIRE STARTERS

Your grill's fuel source determines its cooking characteristics more than any other factor. Understanding how that fuel is manufactured and exactly what it's made of will help you to master cooking with it. All fuels need to be ignited for combustion to occur, so we'll take a look at various fire starters as well. They all work a bit differently.

FUELS

PROPANE. The most popular grills in America are fueled by propane. Propane and natural gas are similar but different fuels. The hoses on a gas grill will tell you which fuel the grill uses, because propane hoses are about half the diameter of natural gas hoses. Why? Because propane gas has the ability to be compressed into a liquid, reducing its volume and making it suitable for storage in a portable tank. Propane, properly termed LP gas or liquid petroleum gas, comes from the refining of crude oil and natural gas. Liquid petroleum gas is composed of 90 to 95 percent propane and smaller amounts of propylene, butane, and butylene. It's colorless and odorless, but ethyl mercaptan is added so you can smell it easily for safety purposes. Inside the container, LP gas is in two states of matter: liquid and vapor. The liquid falls to the bottom and the vapor remains on top. Most propane tanks are filled to about 80 percent capacity, leaving about 20 percent for the vapor to expand during ambient temperature fluctuations. Propane tanks also come with an overfill protection device, or OPD, to prevent hazardous overfilling of the tank. When you open the gas valve and withdraw pressurized liquid propane from the tank, it reverts from its liquid state back to a gaseous state. Propane (C_3H_8) has three carbon atoms and eight hydrogen atoms. Unlike solid fuels such as lump charcoal, gaseous fuels like propane emit water vapor when burned, due to their hydrogen atoms, meaning that they don't burn as hot or as dry as coals.

NATURAL GAS. Another petroleum product, natural gas is similar to liquid propane gas but is composed of 90 to 95 percent methane and smaller amounts of ethane and propane, as well as ethyl mercaptan for odor detection. Methane (CH_4) is a natural gas produced by decaying matter. Grills fueled by natural gas are connected directly to the gas line so that you don't have to bother refilling a small tank, as you do with propane—a convenience that more and more grill aficionados opt for, especially those with outdoor kitchens or grills that remain outside in fair weather year-round.

CHARCOAL BRIQUETTES. Charcoal comes in two ready-made forms: briquettes and lump charcoal. Briquettes burn steadily and evenly, but some brands are made with cheap scrap wood, sawdust, borax to bind it all together, nitrate and petroleum products to help the briquettes ignite, and lime to whiten the ash so you'll know when the coals are ready for cooking over. When using briquettes, we find that national brands tend to perform more consistently and produce better flavor than store brands.

LUMP CHARCOAL. This type of charcoal is closer to real wood in its natural state, and we prefer it. No binders or other additives are used to make lump charcoal. Whole logs are burned and then broken into rough pieces that resemble the charred wood left after a campfire. All charcoal is essentially charred wood made by burning wood with intense heat (about 1,000°F) in the absence of oxygen to drive off the wood's water, its volatile compounds such as methane and hydrogen, and its tars such as benzo(a)pyrene. What's left is carbon, trace volatile compounds, and ash. Because charcoal is mostly carbon, it lights more easily than raw wood and produces less smoke. But about 60 percent of the fuel's potential energy is spent during this charring process, so charcoal fires don't burn as hot or as long as wood fires. One exception is bincho-tan, a dense Japanese hardwood charcoal made from oak that burns at 1,100° to 1,200°F. Most other charcoal burns at 700° to 800°F.

A MAKESHIFT FIRE STARTER
Manufactured fire starters come in many forms, from lighter fluid and paraffin cubes to compressed blocks of sawdust (see page 27 for more). But any easily combustible material, such as dry leaves, paper, or a candle, can be used to start a fire. To make a simple fire starter for fireplace fires or campfires, wad up a paper towel and set it in a paper cup. Pour in cooking oil to almost fill the cup. Saturate the paper but leave an inch or so of the tip exposed out of the cooking oil to act as a wick. Put the makeshift candle beneath your fuel (wood or charcoal) and light the wick. The candle will completely burn itself up, igniting the other fuel in the process.

WOOD. Logs, branches, twigs, chunks, and chips of wood all produce smoke when burned. That's the primary advantage of this fuel source for grill and barbecue lovers, because wood smoke infuses foods with its alluring aromas. Wood smoke aromas vary from tree to tree. As grill fanatics, we are fortunate to have hardwood trees in our backyards, including oak, pear, and apple trees. When branches fall off the trees, we use them as fuel or to provide wood smoke in our grills. Large wood chunks or split logs (or whole logs, for that matter) can be used as the sole fuel source in wood-burning grills. Large pieces, branches, or chunks can be used for smoking and as a secondary fuel source in charcoal grills. Wood chunks and chips are also widely available at hardware stores, home improvement centers, and online grill gear stores. You may also find wood pellets and sawdust that can be wrapped in foil or put in a metal container for smoking. Wood planks, yet another form of wood for grilling, are used primarily for flavor and convenience, not fuel. Planks ease the handling of thin, delicate foods such as fish fillets on the grill and add the smoky aromas of the wood itself. You can buy wood planks for grilling at hardware stores and home centers, or you can use untreated cedar shingles. For that matter, you can use any untreated 1/4-inch-thick plank of wood.

Note that freshly cut wood is about 50 percent water and doesn't burn easily. It slowly smolders and smokes instead of quickly burning up. "Seasoning" the wood or letting it dry out reduces the water content to about 20 percent so that it burns more easily. See "Adding Smoke" on page 37 for directions on how to use wood chips and chunks for fuel and flavor when grilling.

FIRE STARTERS

LIGHTER FLUID. Made with liquid butane, lighter fluid ignites easily and speeds the combustion of charcoal. Some charcoal is impregnated with a form of lighter fluid so that you don't have to squirt it on. We prefer not to use lighter fluid or impregnated charcoal because petroleum products can lend an off flavor to foods. But the truth is that if you use lighter fluid carefully, squirting it only onto your fuel source, the petroleum will burn off by the time the coals are ready. We resort to lighter fluid only for large mounds of coals in big grills. If you use it, be careful not to squirt any on the sides of your grill because petroleum fumes will burn off more slowly there and may give your food a distasteful aroma.

LONG-STEM LIGHTER. Another form of contained butane, long-stem butane lighters make it easy to light wood fires and chimney starters full of coals. Keep at least one on hand for easy fire-starting.

CHIMNEY STARTER. Resembling a big, perforated coffee can, a chimney starter makes charcoal grilling incredibly easy without the need to resort to lighter fluid. The starter allows the coals to ignite quickly (15 to 20 minutes) due to the upward draft of oxygen. See page 32 for directions on how to use a chimney starter.

PARAFFIN LIGHTER CUBES. Resembling white ice cubes or big white dice with no dots, these fire starters can be used instead of paper to light a wood fire, pyramid of coals, or chimney starter full of coals. They leave no aftertaste.

SAWDUST STARTER. Like paraffin cubes, compressed blocks of sawdust make convenient fire starters for wood and charcoal fires. They look somewhat like small blocks of particle board.

ELECTRIC COAL STARTER. Plug this fire starter into an outlet (with an extension cord if necessary), and then plunge it into the center of a mound of coals. The electric heating coil will ignite the coals in about the same time it takes to use a chimney starter.

HEAT DIFFUSER. These don't ignite a fire, but they do spread out the heat and reduce hot and cold spots so that food cooks more evenly. Heat diffusers are used mostly in gas grills above the burner tubes, and they typically come in the form of lava stones, ceramic briquettes, or metal bars. Ceramic briquettes are available with small bits of wood infused into the ceramic to impart a wood smoke flavor to foods cooked on a gas grill.

CHAPTER 2

MASTERING YOUR TECHNIQUE

Fire is raw energy that results when oxygen unites rapidly with another substance. Usually, oxygen bonds with materials so slowly that combustion doesn't occur. For instance, when oxygen unites with iron, you get rust (no flames there). But when the same union occurs with gasoline or another petroleum distillate, fire and intense heat are given off. Anything with the potential of bonding rapidly with oxygen in this way is called fuel.

In order for combustion to take place, three things have to be present: fuel, an ignition source, and plenty of oxygen. In a gas grill, these elements are mostly automated and controlled by the fuel knobs or valves, an electric igniter, and a regulated mixture of fuel and oxygen. Lift the lid, open the valves, and push the igniter button (or insert a flame into the match hole), and a gas grill will light instantly.

In a charcoal grill, on the other hand, the essential elements are less regulated. The fuel is often some form of wood: paper, sawdust, twigs, branches, logs, or charred wood (charcoal). Depending on the form of the wood, the amount of energy required from the ignition source to reach the fuel's ignition temperature varies. In order for a fuel to ignite, its molecules must be moving fast enough to pass into a gaseous phase, so the easier it is to turn a solid fuel source into a gas, the less energy it takes to start a fire.

Paper (wood pulp) takes very little energy to flame; a match will do the trick. Sawdust (ground wood) needs a little more energy; a match still works, but it must be held against the wood longer for combustion to take place. Solid wood is harder still to combust, although smaller pieces require less energy than thicker ones. All of this explains why a wood fire that will last long enough to cook food must happen in stages. The first stage is paper or dry leaves, which ignite easily and spend themselves quickly. They are best used as tinder to create enough energy to ignite second-stage kindling (small twigs, etc.), which in turn must burn hot enough and long enough to light third-stage branches, followed by fourth-stage logs (see the illustrations on facing page). The denser and larger the wood, the harder it is to ignite, but the longer and hotter it will burn. Sometimes a distilled petroleum product, like lighter fluid, is soaked into hard-to-ignite solid fuels in order to start their combustion more quickly. The following chart shows the approximate amount of energy it takes to ignite common fuels.

IGNITION POINTS

Fuel	Temperature (F)
Lighter fluid	300°
Match heads	325°
Carbon dust	350°
Paper	435°
Wood shavings	500°
Charcoal	600°
Solid wood	800°

Preburning (charring) wood makes it easier to ignite. To make charred wood or natural lump charcoal, wood is burnt until it is reduced to carbon. At that point, about 60 percent of its potential energy has been spent, so a charcoal fire will burn out faster than a wood fire. It's a trade-off, but one that is advantageous to most of us who don't have hours to nurse a wood fire until it turns into a thick, glowing bed of coals.

01. STARTING A WOOD FIRE

Three things happen when wood burns: Water in the wood evaporates, the wood smokes, and the wood gradually burns down to hot coals. Freshly cut logs are about 50 percent water and don't burn easily. Seasoned or dried wood is about 20 percent water and burns more easily because less energy (heat) is required to evaporate the water.

The goal is to light a wood fire quickly so that it produces minimum smoke and maximum combustion. For this, you need dry wood and an initial burst of heat from a match or other fire starter. There are dozens of ways to construct a wood fire. We'll discuss only the two primary ones: the bottom-up method and the top-down method. In both methods, the dry fuel is layered from most to least combustible, and then it is lit. The fuel can be layered on a flat surface, such as the cleared ground in a pit or fire ring, on a fireplace floor, or on the floor of a grill. Preferably, it will be layered on an elevated grate. Elevating the wood allows for better airflow and faster, more complete combustion. If you don't have a fire grate, put two or three medium-large logs on the flat surface and layer the fuel on top of this makeshift log grate.

BOTTOM-UP METHOD Clear the area and put down a layer of crumpled paper, dry leaves, or another easily combustible fuel (crumpling the paper helps air to reach all of its surfaces). Next put on a layer of small twigs, lath, or other thin wood, followed by increasingly thicker branches and small or split logs. Then ignite the paper at the bottom with a flame or other fire starter. The wood ignites from the bottom up. Save the largest logs to add to the fire after it is well established. This method works best with a tepee construction, layering each type of fuel in a cone shape. If you're on soft ground, it helps to drive a single branch into the ground in the center of the tepee to help hold up the sides. As the wood burns, the cone will burn and eventually fall as hot coals, at which point larger logs can be tossed onto the coals. Because the cone is rather tall at first and then falls, the bottom-up method is best suited for campfires or fire bowls where there is no limit to the vertical space and plenty of room for falling embers.

TOP-DOWN METHOD Less popular but more impressive, the top-down method is the bottom-up method in reverse. Put your largest logs on the bottom, followed by layers of increasingly combustible split logs, branches, twigs, and other kindling. Paper or dry leaves go on the top. Light the top and, believe it or not, the fire ignites from the top to the bottom. This method works best with a box or crisscross construction made by positioning two large logs on the bottom parallel to one another. Position smaller or split logs on top of and perpendicular to the large ones to create a box shape. Continue crisscrossing layers of increasingly combustible small branches, twigs, lath, and finally paper or dry leaves on top. Because the box is more stable and shorter than the cone, this method works well in fireplaces and shallow grills where there is limited vertical space in the firebox. A top-down fire is also less likely to collapse and smother itself.

Whichever method you choose, allow the wood fire to burn down to a bed of brightly glowing embers before cooking over them. If the embers start to lose their heat, add more wood to the fire. For fireplace and campfire cooking, it helps to create two areas of the fire—a refueling area at the back or side and a cooking area at the front or other side. Add fresh wood to the refueling area and rake hot coals into the cooking area to create a level bed of embers.

02. STARTING A CHARCOAL FIRE

Charcoal is wood that's already been burned. It may come in the form of briquettes or lump charcoal (see page 25 for more on each type). The easiest way to light charcoal is to stack it up so that oxygen can quickly and easily travel upward through the coals. You can also use lighter fluid or another petroleum distillate, but most grilling aficionados avoid lighter fluid, claiming that it gives food a petroleum aftertaste. The truth is that once lighter fluid has burned off and the coals are glowing orange-red, there is no petroleum left. That is, unless you happen to squirt some lighter fluid onto the side of the grill, where it will very slowly emit petroleum fumes that can become infused in your food. If you choose to quick-start a fire with lighter fluid (which may be the easiest way if you're facing a huge mound of coals to light for a sizable grill), just be sure to squirt only the coals and let them burn to a glowing orange before you start cooking over them.

To ignite charcoal without petroleum, you have three basic options: Stack the coals in a pyramid, use a chimney starter, or use an electric starter. A pyramid of charcoal takes 30 to 40 minutes to burn down to a red-orange glow worthy of cooking over. Using an elevated fire grate and layering the pyramid with sheets of newspaper helps somewhat. But a chimney starter (our favorite method) cuts lighting time nearly in half because it increases the oxygen flow to the coals. The coals also light more evenly than with the pyramid method, and you don't need lighter fluid. Chimney starters look like large, tall coffee cans with a divider near the bottom, holes on the sides, and a handle. See the next section for instructions on how to use one. If using an electric starter, insert the metal loop of the starter into the bottom of a pyramid of coals, then plug in the starter (use an extension cord if necessary). The hot metal ignites the coals and they, in turn, ignite each other. Remove the starter when it is surrounded by glowing orange coals. The pyramid of coals should be ready for cooking in 30 to 40 minutes.

LIGHTING COALS IN A CHIMNEY STARTER

Crumple up two or three sheets of newspaper and stuff them into the bottom (smaller compartment) of the chimney starter. Avoid packing in any more newspaper. Too much paper will restrict the oxygen flow and slow down the lighting. Instead of paper, you could use another fire starter such as paraffin starter cubes (see "Fire Starters" on page 27 for more options). In that case, set the fire starter on cleared ground or beneath an elevated fire grate.

Set the newspaper-stuffed chimney starter on cleared ground or on a fire grate such as the one in the typical kettle grill. Fill the top of the starter with charcoal and light the paper (or your fire starter) with a match or other flame. Depending upon the design of your chimney starter, it may help to tilt it so you can light the paper from the bottom.

Oxygen will flow upward through the tall column of coals, igniting them quickly and evenly. Let the coals burn in the starter until they are glowing orange. If the weather is cold or the charcoals seem stubborn, you can stuff one or two more pieces of paper into the bottom of the starter after the first pieces have burned up. Once the coals are glowing, grab the handle of the starter (wear grill gloves) and invert the hot coals into your grill. For direct grilling (see page 36), rake the coals into an even bed or a bed with a high side and a low side. For indirect grilling (see page 36), either split the coals to opposite sides of the grill or rake them to one high side, leaving an empty unheated space. You should get 45 minutes to 1 hour of firepower from the coals.

03. HOW TO MAINTAIN A LIVE FIRE

We call charcoal and wood fires "live" fires because they are not as controlled as the flame produced by a gas grill. Getting a live fire to ignite is one thing; keeping it burning is another. Remember: The life of a fire is dependent on having enough oxygen to bond with the amount of fuel on hand. If there is only a small amount of oxygen, a fire may start, but it won't last long, which means the art of fire tending requires a constant flow of oxygen to the flames. To create that flow, there must be air all around the fire, which is why fires are built on grates to raise them above solid ground.

In a kettle grill, the fire grate is suspended about halfway between the grill floor and the grill grate, leaving ample air space under the fire. Vents on the bottom and on the lid of the kettle also allow air to flow to the fire, even when the grill is covered. In a box grill, or hibachi, the fire grate is much closer to the floor of the grill, but there are air vents on the sides and bottom; and because hibachis are not lidded there is ample oxygen entering from above.

With a wood fire, using an elevated grate improves access to air from underneath. Start with a tepee or box construction for the best airflow (see the illustrations on page 31). As the fire burns, adjust the position of the logs to maintain ample air space around each log. Eventually, the wood will oxidize enough so that it no longer contains enough fuel to flare, at which point it will have reduced to glowing embers and will no longer need a steady supply of oxygen.

Be sure to refuel the fire before it gets too low. For a wood fire, add dry, seasoned wood to the hot coals while the coals are glowing red and hot enough to ignite the wood. To increase airflow around a fresh log, it may help to prop it up on a half-burned log rather than simply laying it over the top. In a charcoal grill, you can add fresh charcoal or pre-lit charcoal using a chimney starter (see facing page).

If necessary, you can force air onto the fire to increase the oxygen flow and help the fire light more quickly and evenly. We've tried everything, from blowing air through our mouths to using a bellows, waving a magazine, positioning the fire toward the wind, using a hair dryer, and blasting the fire with a leaf blower. All of these methods work, but those that force the most oxygen the most quickly onto the fire work best. In our experiments, the leaf blower won.

Even if you supply sufficient air, a piece of wood will never burn completely. There will always be elements within the wood that cannot bind with oxygen. These incombustible particles become ash if they are large, and if they are small enough to become airborne, they form most of the visual and aromatic components of smoke. The amount and type of incombustible particles in the wood determines the quality of its smoke. Because lump charcoal and charcoal briquettes are almost pure carbon, they combust more completely than wood, leaving less (but finer) ash behind and producing less aromatic smoke. Soot, a black residue that can be left on grilled food or around the edges of a fire, is not a by-product of burnt wood; rather, it is unburned carbon, and its presence indicates that there was insufficient oxygen for the amount of fuel. Check your grill lid for black soot. Typically, you'll find more soot buildup when you grill with the lid down or via indirect heat, because these methods restrict the oxygen supply.

Even the best-built fire will do you no good if the heat doesn't get to the food. There are three methods of heat transference that take place during grilling. Understanding them is basic to mastering all grilling techniques.

01. CONDUCTION

Heat makes molecules move faster. The faster they move, the more likely it is that they will bump into an adjacent molecule and transfer heat from one molecule to the other. This straightforward interchange of energy is called *conduction.* It is the basic way that heat moves from the fire to the surface of the grill grate, through the grill grate, and, finally, into a piece of food.

Although conduction is at play in all areas of the grilling process, the way heat moves through a metal grate is different than how it moves through a slab of meat, for instance. Metals are particularly good heat conductors because, even though most of their molecules are tightly bound, they contain electrons that jump easily from one atom to another. This mobility of electrons moves heat quickly through metal grilling equipment. But meat and other grilled ingredients don't heat through as efficiently.

Before a steak even touches the grill, the grill grate should be thoroughly heated, which ensures that the surface of the meat gets a blast of energy at the onset of cooking. That's why most grilled steak recipes direct you to preheat the grill. For direct grilling, a hot grill grate is necessary to force heat deeply into the meat as quickly as possible; once the heat moves from the highly conductive metal grate into a less conductive steak, the heat transference slows down dramatically. The surface of grilling meat continues to receive the bulk of the available heat energy throughout the cooking process, passing it along very gradually, which allows us to produce a thick crust on the surface of a steak while keeping the interior moist and rare.

The amount of heat coming from the fire itself has little effect on how fast that heat transfers through the meat; a hotter fire simply makes the surface crustier. So the more well-done you like your meat, the lower the temperature must be to ensure that the center cooks through without scorching the surface. Likewise, large, thick roasts need to be grilled away from direct heat to give heat traveling through the meat enough time to reach deep into the center.

02. CONVECTION

While conduction moves heat to food through the metal grill grate (and throughout the food itself), *convection* moves heat around food. As the fire heats air inside a closed grill, the molecules in the air move faster. Moving molecules take up more space than still ones, which makes the hot molecules rise. Air currents develop, circulating hot air toward the top of the grill, which forces cooler air down toward the fire, where it is heated, causing it to rise, and so on. Convection is not a primary method of heat transference in grilling (especially with no grill lid), but it does account for some of the cooking that takes place in indirect grilling, in which food does not come into direct contact with a hot grill grate or a radiating flame.

03. RADIANT HEAT

Radiation is harder to understand than conduction or convection, because this type of heat never touches the food, yet it is the principal form of heat transference in grilling. The best way to grasp the process of radiant heat is to think of the sun. The sun's heat radiates through space to the earth, warming the planet. Along the way, it doesn't heat up the void of outer space, as it would if convection were taking place, and there are no metal wires traveling from the sun to the earth, conducting the heat to us. In radiation, energy is passed from one atom to another in the form of pure energy, until it comes in contact with a convecting fluid (like our atmosphere, in the case of solar energy) or a conducting solid (like a hamburger, in the case of grilling), where its energy manifests itself as heat.

Radiant heat is invisible (a good reason why it's hard to visualize). It is one of many forms of radiant energy that are used extensively in everyday life: Radio waves, TV waves, microwaves, visible light, and X-rays are all forms of radiant energy with different strengths. Their relative strengths, called frequencies, are measured on the electromagnetic spectrum, as shown in the following figure.

Radio	TV	Microwave Cell Phones	Infrared (Heat)	Visible Light	Ultra-Violet	X-Rays	Gamma Rays
0	10^5	10^{10}		10^{15}		10^{20}	

Frequency (cycles per second)

Radio and TV waves are so weak (10^5 to 10^9 cycles per second) that they need metal antennas to speed up their movement in order to be transmitted or received. Microwaves are strong enough (10^9 to 10^{11} cycles per second) to affect polar molecules (like water), and since most food is largely water, microwaves can be used in cooking. Infrared heat (10^{11} to 10^{14} cycles per second) is the only section of the spectrum that feels hot; the waves in this section are strong enough to melt fat, coagulate protein, caramelize sugar, and gelatinize starch, as well as boil water. Visible light is stronger (10^{14} to 10^{15} cycles per second) than heat radiation; it is powerful enough to change the pigments in our skin and cause fats to become rancid. Ultraviolet rays (10^{15} to 10^{18} cycles per second) can burn our skin, damage our DNA, and cause the development of malignancies. X-rays and gamma rays (more than 10^{18} cycles per second) ionize molecules by stripping electrons from them; they are strong enough to kill microbes, making them a useful form of radiation in industrial sterilization processes.

Visible light (the only form of radiant energy that we can see) occupies a small area of the spectrum and can be divided into seven wavelengths, which appear to our eye as different colors; red is the weakest and violet is the strongest. Radiant heat energy that is weaker than visible light is called infrared (below red). Ultraviolet (beyond violet) is what we call radiation that is stronger than visible light. The colors of fire correspond to this energy spectrum, ranging from orangey red to blue-violet. Obviously, flames are visible, but we have already said that radiant heat is invisible. Does that mean that fire isn't really hot? Sort of. The colorful parts of a flame are stronger forms of radiant energy than the invisible heat rising from them, but the area of heat surrounding a flame is hotter than the flame itself.

Although the principles of conduction, convection, and radiant heat help us to understand how grilling works, in actual practice these principles are not as clear-cut. They all occur simultaneously. The flow of heat from fire to grill grate is radiation. The heating of the grate itself is conduction. The heating of the food's surface is a combination of conduction from the grill grate, radiation from the heat flowing between the bars of the grate, and convection of the air around the food (especially when the grill is covered). As heat moves through the interior of the food, it is being transferred from one molecule to another by conduction and by convection as heated juices begin to circulate through the ingredient. To visualize these principles at work, see the illustration below.

1. Convection
2. Conduction
3. Radiation

Most grilling techniques were developed long before the science of heat transference was understood. But even a basic understanding of the science behind cooking food over an open flame will help you to master the techniques of grilling.

Grilling and barbecuing are two distinct methods of dry-heat cooking. Grilled food is cooked quickly over direct, high heat. Barbecued food is cooked slowly via indirect, low heat with plenty of smoke. Several other grilling methods fall somewhere between these two extremes, including indirect grilling, rotisserie grilling or spit-roasting, smoking on a grill, and grilling right on the coals. Here's how to master each technique.

A HOT, CLEAN, WELL-OILED GRILL

Think of your grill grate as an open sauté pan. Just like a sauté pan, it should be clean, hot, and lubricated before adding any food. A hot, clean, well-oiled grill gives you the best browning, deepest grill marks, and purest flavors.

Preheating. A hot grill grate helps to sear foods and create deep grill marks. It also prevents sticking. We recommend preheating the grill grate for at least 10 minutes on high heat, preferably with the lid down. Once the grate is as hot as a branding iron, adjust the grill's temperature as necessary. If you want to create attractive crosshatch grill marks, let the food grill for at least 3 to 5 minutes, and then rotate the food 45 degrees from its original position and grill for another 3 to 5 minutes. Finish cooking on a cooler part of the grill.

Lubricating. As another safeguard against sticking (and for a bonus of darker grill marks), oil the grill grate just before adding food. Our favorite method is to wad up a paper towel, dip it in oil with tongs, and wipe the oily towel over the hot grill grate. The oily paper towel greases the grill grate and cleans off any remaining residue from your last grilling session. Keep some oil and a roll of paper towels near the grill, and the process is simple. You could also lube the grill grate with another kind of fat, like a chunk of trimmed beef or pork fat. Or you could spray the rack with oil spray, but first remove the grill grate from the grill to avoid flare-ups. Regular lubricating and preheating helps to season your grill grate and develop an increasingly nonstick surface.

Cleaning. To keep your grill grate as clean as possible, scrape it twice with a stiff wire grill brush—before adding food and after removing food. If you brush the grill only once, do it immediately after removing food. A hot rack cleans more easily than a cold rack, and you will already be at the grill anyway. If you wait until later, any food residue will only dry out, harden, and become more difficult to remove.

01. DIRECT GRILLING

This method is probably familiar to you. You cook food directly over a fire (charcoal, wood, or gas) on a hot grill grate that's set 2 to 6 inches above the flame. Direct grilling is similar to broiling, except that the heat comes from below instead of above and the hot grill grate creates dark marks on the food's surface. Use this method for foods that will sear on the surface and cook through to the center in less than 30 minutes, including hamburgers, hot dogs, sausages, steaks, chops, poultry parts, fish fillets and steaks (and small whole fish), shellfish, vegetables, fruits, doughs, and other small or tender foods. Larger or more dense foods may burn on their surface before the interior is cooked. Save these for another grilling method.

To set up a gas grill for direct grilling, simply heat it to the desired temperature, which is usually medium-high heat (about 450°F). Make it easier to control the heat by setting up two or three areas on the grill for high, medium, and low heat. On a charcoal grill, rake the hot coals into a bed that's 3 to 4 inches thick on one side and 1 to 2 inches thick on the other. Use the higher-heat area to sear meats and grill vegetables or other quick-cooking foods. Move foods to the lower-heat area if they start to burn or to finish cooking them. You can also use the lower-heat area for toasting breads. See the Direct-Grilling Guide on page 41 for more details on setting up charcoal or wood grills for various heat levels.

Closing the grill lid traps heat and smoke, which speeds the cooking and infuses the food with more smoke flavor. For these reasons, we usually close the lid when direct grilling. (If your grill doesn't have a lid, improvise by covering the food with a disposable aluminum pan.) At times, however, the food cooks so quickly that there's little reason to close the lid. Leave the lid off for thin, small, or very tender foods that cook in less than 5 minutes, such as sliced summer squash, boneless chicken breasts, shrimp, and thin fish fillets.

02. INDIRECT GRILLING

This method works best with bigger or denser foods that take more than 30 minutes to cook, including beef brisket or whole beef tenderloin, pork shoulder or loin roasts, whole chickens and turkeys, and large whole fish. Instead of putting food directly over the heat, you keep the food away from the heat so that it has time to cook through to the center without burning on the surface.

To set up a charcoal grill for indirect grilling, make a split charcoal bed by splitting the coals on opposite sides of the firebox and leaving a large, empty space in the middle. Or you can rake the coals to one side and leave the other side empty. We find that a split charcoal bed provides more even heating because the heat surrounds the food. But if your grill is small, you may get a larger unheated area (for larger roasts) by raking the coals to one side instead of two. Either way, put the food over the unheated part of the grill and close the lid. The indirect heat of the coals becomes trapped in the grill, surrounding the food and slowly cooking it, similar to the way roasting works in a conventional oven.

For fatty cuts of meat, like brisket and pork shoulder, it helps to put a disposable aluminum drip pan under the food between the coals, to catch dripping fat and minimize flare-ups. When indirectly grilling lean or low-moisture foods like skinless poultry roasts or pork tenderloins, we sometimes pour flavored liquid into the pan, such as beer, wine, stock, or citrus juice mixed with seasonings. As the liquid heats, the rising steam keeps these foods moist and infuses them with subtle flavors.

If your grill doesn't have a lid but does have an adjustable grill grate (as on a flat charcoal grill or open wood-burning pit), set the grill up for indirect grilling by raising the grill grate 1 to 3 feet above the coals. You won't be able to trap heat or smoke, so plan on increasing the cooking time and losing some smoke flavor.

A single chimney starter (see page 27) full of coals will burn out after 45 minutes to 1 hour of indirect grilling. Add fresh coals by lighting a new batch of coals as the old ones begin to die down. Pour the new hot coals right over the old ones and continue cooking. If you don't have a chimney starter, put fresh unlit coals over the old hot coals and leave the lid off the grill until the new coals begin to ash over.

Many charcoal grill grates come with hinged sides, so you can easily add fresh coals to each side. If your grate doesn't have hinges, lift off the entire hot rack and the food with well-insulated or heatproof grill gloves. Put the hot rack of food over foil on the ground or another heatproof surface, add your fresh coals, and then return the racked food to the grill.

Indirect grilling is similar on a gas grill, except that you light some of the burners but leave the others off. If your gas grill has two burners, light one burner and put your food over the unlit burner. If your grill has three or more burners, light the outside burners and put the food over the middle unlit burners. When using indirect grilling for fatty cuts of meat on a gas grill, make sure the grease catcher is empty or put a drip pan beneath the roast.

The grill lid is a key element of most indirect grilling. It traps heat and smoke, increasing the temperature inside the grill and infusing food with smoke flavor. Keep the lid down as much as possible. Every time you lift the lid, heat escapes, lowering the temperature inside the grill and lengthening the cooking time. See the Indirect-Grilling Guide on page 41 for a summary of setting up charcoal or wood grills for various levels of indirect heat.

03. ROTISSERIE GRILLING

A form of indirect grilling, rotisserie cooking positions food on a spit above or in front of the heat, where the food slowly rotates. This method produces incomparably moist and evenly browned whole birds, roasts, and ribs. As the meat turns, the external fat gradually melts and rolls around the meat, basting the meat and keeping it moist. Rotisserie-grilled meats are, in effect, self-basting; but if you notice any dry spots on the meat, brush a little oil over the area to ensure even browning.

Rotisseries are available for most gas and charcoal grills. Each one works a little differently; set yours up according to the manufacturer's directions. In most cases, that means sliding the food onto the spit of the rotisserie and then securing the food with the rotisserie skewers. Be sure to push the skewers firmly into opposite sides of the food to fasten it to the spit rod. Then you put the skewered food into the rotisserie assembly. The food should be suspended 6 to 12 inches away from direct heat and turn freely as the rotisserie rotates. You may need to remove your grill grate to allow room for the food to rotate unobstructed.

Spit-roasting is another name for rotisserie grilling, but it's usually done on a larger scale with primal cuts of meat or whole animals. Most often, spit-roasting refers to animals suspended several feet over burning coals and slowly turned by hand or a motor. For example, see Spit-Roasted Whole Spring Lamb Overcome by Garlic on page 243. For simpler rotisserie recipes, turn to Three-Ginger Rotisserie Chicken (page 190) or Bedouin Leg of Lamb on a Spit (page 242).

04. ADDING SMOKE

Many people associate the aroma of wood smoke with grilled foods. But gas grilling adds no wood smoke flavor, and charcoal adds only a wisp. It's true that you get some smokiness from dripping fat in a gas grill, but if you really want to get smoking, you need to burn wood. The traditional way is to build a wood fire (see page 31). The modern way is to add wood chunks or chips to your gas or charcoal grill.

Wood chunks and chips work best when using indirect grilling to cook large or thick foods that will need at least 30 minutes of cooking time. That gives the food time to absorb the smoky aromas. But you can also infuse smoke flavor into small, thin, or delicate foods by smoking them over the unheated area of your grill and then moving them to the heated area to cook through. For an example, see Smoked Jerk Tofu on page 296.

Dry wood chips and chunks ignite quickly and incinerate when placed on hot coals. To extract the maximum amount of smoke, slow down the rate of combustion by soaking the chips in water for at least 30 minutes, preferably 1 hour. The longer you soak wood chips and chunks, the longer they'll smolder before burning up. Soaking also helps to maintain a steady temperature in your grill. Even though you are adding fuel to the grill in the form of wood, the reduced combustion rate caused by soaking prevents the fuel from igniting and raising the grill temperature. Wood chips or chunks can be soaked in a bucket, a bowl, a heavy-duty plastic bag, or almost any pool of water. For subtle aromas, use a flavored liquid such as beer instead of water.

FLARE-UPS AND HEALTH

Flare-ups are the bane of a grillmaster's existence. They happen when fat drips onto your heat source. Flare-ups make food taste sooty, and the smoke can send potentially harmful molecules (called poly-cyclic aromatic hydrocarbons, or PAHs) back to your food. According to the American Institute for Cancer Research, scientists haven't determined a safe level for these substances in our diet, so they recommend erring on the side of caution. To avoid these potential carcinogens, the best recommendation is to keep fat off the grill. Choose lean cuts of meat, and trim visible fat before grilling. Cut meats into small pieces or grill them over medium-high heat so they cook quickly and have less time to drip fat onto the coals. Or when grilling fattier cuts like beef brisket and pork shoulder, use indirect heat (see page 36) to avoid flare-ups.

It also helps to keep fat in marinades to a minimum. But studies show that it's a good idea to marinate or brine because these flavoring methods can reduce another potential carcinogen called hetero-cyclic amines, or HCAs. According to the American Institute for Cancer Research, marinades may provide a barrier between the meat and the heat; or the citrus juice, oils, and herbs in marinades may provide some anticancer protection. Even so, keep a spray bottle of water handy to douse any flare-ups that may occur.

On a charcoal grill, drain the soaked wood and put about 1 cup of chips or two to four wood chunks directly onto the hot coals; if using a split charcoal bed, split these amounts between the two sides. Wait until the wood smokes, about 5 to 10 minutes, then add the food to the grill and close the lid to trap the smoke. Position the lid so that the upper vents on the lid are on the opposite side of the lower vents on the firebox. This draws the maximum amount of smoke over the food. See the illustration on the facing page.

Soaked chips and chunks should last nearly as long as charcoal, which means you'll need to add more wood after about 45 minutes to 1 hour of indirect grilling. Chunks will last slightly longer than chips. For several hours of indirect grilling, keep extra soaked chips or chunks on hand.

On a gas grill, the process is similar, with a few exceptions. You can't put the wood directly onto the burner, so you need to contain it somehow. If your gas grill has a smoker box, simply fill the box with soaked wood chips or chunks. If you don't have a smoker box or tray, make a smoking packet or smoker tray with aluminum foil. For a flat smoking packet, wrap a single layer of soaked wood in foil; the single layer exposes more surface area of the wood to the heat and creates more smoke. Poke several large holes in the top of the packet to allow smoke to escape. For an open smoker tray, crimp the foil into a makeshift rectangular pan or tray and fill it with a layer of chips. Put the smoker box, packet, or tray directly over one of your grill burners under the grill grate, or over the dedicated smoker burner if your grill has one. Heat the burner to high. Wait until you see smoke, about 10 to 15 minutes, and then adjust the heat for the food you are cooking. Cook with the lid down to trap the smoke, and replenish the wood chips or chunks when the old ones die out, about once every hour.

The aromas in wood smoke vary from tree to tree. Mesquite and hickory woods produce a thick, heavy smoke that pairs well with robust foods such as beef and pork. Oak, maple, alder, and pecan give off a medium-bodied smoke that goes well with pork, poultry, game, and fish. Fruit woods such as apple and cherry emit a lighter, sweeter smoke that gently flavors more delicate foods like poultry, shellfish, and vegetables. The flavor differences are subtle, so use whatever wood is available in your area. We like to use a light hand when grilling with smoke, because a heavy smoke flavor can easily overpower the flavor of the grilled food itself.

05. BARBECUING

Smoking on a grill begins to tread into the domain of barbecue, another culinary arena with its own techniques and traditions. As we mentioned earlier, grilling uses high, direct heat and barbecuing uses low, indirect heat. But the hallmarks of barbecue are billows of thick wood smoke and long cooking times—up to 24 hours in some cases. Here's a quick look at barbecuing, which is mostly outside the scope of this grilling book.

Traditionally, barbecued foods are cooked in a pit or smoker with a separate (offset) firebox. With the heat in one chamber and the food in another, the food cooks by the relatively cool heat of smoke generated by the wood rather than by the radiant heat of burning coals. In the cooking chamber, the temperature remains very low (200° to 225°F) throughout the entire cooking time. This low temperature allows foods to cook very slowly without burning, which is a key factor in dissolving the tough connective tissue that surrounds the muscle fibers in relatively tough meats such as brisket and ribs. It simply takes time for these connective tissues to gradually dissolve and add moisture to the meat. If brisket, for instance, were cooked quickly over high heat, it would be leathery and unpalatable. But when barbecued low and slow, it becomes meltingly tender and succulent. Cooking slowly by the indirect heat of smoldering wood also infuses the meat with deep, smoky aromas.

06. COOKING IN THE COALS

Here's a nifty grilling technique. Dispense with your grill grate altogether and put the food directly on the hot coals. Steaks and chops cooked this way quickly develop a thick crust and amazing flavor due to the deep browning created by the intense heat right on the surface of the burning embers. This method also works well for dense foods with thick skins, such as root vegetables and tubers.

To grill steaks and chops in the coals, you have to use lump charcoal, wood chunks, or logs, all of which create relatively large ashes. Avoid briquettes, which burn down to such a fine ash that the ashes stick to the meat and make it taste sooty. Before adding food to hot coals, you have to blow off the excess ashes. Rake the coals to a somewhat flat bed, and then blow off the ashes with a leaf blower, a hair dryer, a portable fan, or a magazine and a strong arm. Put the meat directly on the coal bed and cook until nicely crusted, about 3 to 5 minutes per side. Season the meat as you turn it, then remove it from the coals and pick off any loose ash. See Scotch Steak in the Coals with Stilton Butter (page 145) for an example.

To grill root vegetables in the coals, bury the unpeeled vegetables in the hot embers and cook until tender when pricked with a fork or knife, 40 to 60 minutes, depending upon the size and density of the vegetable. The skin will char to an inedible blackness, but the flesh inside will be tender, moist, and smoky. And you'll win raves from whoever sees you pull off this feat of grillmastery. For an example, see Sweet Potatoes in the Coals with Lime-Cilantro Butter (page 287).

07. WRAPPING

Food can be wrapped in lotus leaves, grape leaves, banana leaves, corn husks, aluminum foil, or almost any other wrapper that will stand up to the heat of the grill. It's a useful technique for delicate foods like fish or loose foods like ground meat that can crumble easily during grilling. Complete wrapping also traps moisture inside the wrapper so that food steams, cooks more quickly, and becomes infused with the subtle flavor of the wrapper. Most wrappers are soaked in water before wrapping to prevent them from burning. Use the technique of wrapping with direct or indirect grilling. For some examples, see Turkey Sausages in Vine Leaves (page 111), Fish Stuffed with Five-Treasure Jasmine Rice Roasted in a Lotus Leaf (page 233), and Grilled Brie Wrapped in Grape Leaves (page 345).

08. COOKING ON A PLANK

Thin, delicate foods such as fish fillets can stick to the grill, break apart, and become difficult to serve. A wood plank solves these problems and adds smoky flavors to the food. It also allows delicate foods to cook more gently and gradually because the wood forms a barrier between the food and the flame. This technique is used most often with salmon fillets (try Mustard-Glazed Planked Salmon with Horseradish-Dill Sauce, page 175), but can be applied to other fish fillets or delicate foods such as fruit, cheese, vegetables, and ground meats.

To grill on a plank, choose a relatively thin (about $1/4$ inch thick) plank of wood that is wide and long enough to accommodate the food you are grilling. Cedar and alder are the most common wood planks used for grilling, but fruit woods such as apple and cherry also work well. Soak the wood plank in water for at least 30 minutes—and preferably for 1 hour—so that the wood smokes and smolders instead of igniting on the grill. Put the food on the plank, brush with a glaze or add other seasonings, and then put the planked food on the grill grate and close the lid. When cooked through, remove the planked food to the table and serve. The bottom and edges of the plank will be charred, so you may prefer to put the planked food on a cutting board or large platter rather than directly on the table. Serve the food from the plank, dividing it into portions as necessary. For more information on wood planks, see page 27.

Instead of using a solid wood plank, you can try using wood "paper." These thin, pliable sheets of wood are wrapped around the food, which allows you to turn the food for more even heating and delivers the woodsy aromas to all surfaces of the food. Sheets of wood need to soak for only 5 to 10 minutes, instead of 30 minutes to 1 hour. They make a good choice for individual or smaller pieces of food.

D. MASTERING TEMPERATURE

The temperature of any fire is determined by its ratio of fuel to oxygen. Add plenty of both fuel and oxygen and the fire gets blazing hot. Increase the fuel but restrict the oxygen, and the fire burns slowly. Increase the oxygen but restrict the fuel, and the fire burns quickly. The outside air temperature and wind can also increase or decrease the temperature of the fire.

Finding the right temperature for the food you're grilling is easy on a gas grill because the fuel-to-oxygen ratio is largely predetermined by the gas flow. Your variables here are the knobs and the lid (and the weather, but there isn't much you can do about that). For the highest heat on a gas grill, crank the knobs on full blast and put the lid down to trap the heat. For the lowest heat, set the knobs to low and close the lid. For varying heat levels, set one burner to high, set the second to low, and if you have three burners or more, set the others to medium. You can also use the upper warming rack for low heat.

With a charcoal or wood fire, you still manage the fuel-to-oxygen ratio, but you have a few added variables: The type of fuel (denser woods burn hotter than less dense woods), the thickness of the coal bed, the amount of potential energy remaining in the burning coals (which is roughly determined by their appearance), and the vents on the firebox and lid of the grill. Adjusting the temperature is a matter of making a thicker or thinner coal bed and managing the airflow with the grill lid and vents. If you spread a fresh layer of hot coals to about a 4-inch thickness, you'll have a blazing hot fire at roughly 650°F. As the coals burn and turn to ash in a wood fire, their color will change from bright orange to dull red, with increasing amounts of gray ash. Regulate the temperature by raking the coals into a thick or thin bed (for high or low heat), adding fresh coals, and opening, partially opening, or closing the grill vents and lid. Opening the vents and lid raises the temperature by increasing oxygen flow. Closing them lowers the temperature by cutting off the oxygen supply. The charts that follow explain how to create varying levels of heat for both direct and indirect grilling with charcoal or wood.

DIRECT-GRILLING GUIDE

Heat	Temperature (F)	Coal Appearance	Coal-Bed Thickness	Grate Height	Vents	Counting by Thousands*
High	450°–500°	Red-hot glow	4 inches	2 inches	100% open	2 times
Medium-high	400°–450°	Orange glow; light ash	3 to 4 inches	3 inches	80% open	4 times
Medium	350°–400°	Medium ash; visible glow	3 inches	4 inches	70% open	6 times
Medium-low	300°–350°	Medium ash; faint glow	2 inches	5 inches	60% open	8 times
Low	250°–300°	Thick ash; spotty faint glow	1 1/2 inches	6 inches	50% open	10 times

INDIRECT-GRILLING GUIDE

Heat	Temperature (F)	Coal Appearance	Coal-Bed Thickness	Grate Height	Vents	Counting by Thousands*
High	400°–450°	Red-hot glow	4 inches; split bed	2 inches	100% open	4 times
Medium-high	350°–400°	Orange glow; light ash	3 to 4 inches; split bed	3 inches	80% open	5 times
Medium	300°–350°	Medium ash; visible glow	3 inches; split bed	4 inches	70% open	8 times
Medium-low	250°–300°	Medium ash; faint glow	2 inches; split bed	5 inches	60% open	10 times
Low	225°–250°	Thick ash; spotty faint glow	1 1/2 inches; split bed	6 inches	50% open	11 times

*At this temperature, you should be able to hold your hand (palm down) about 4 inches above the grill grate and count, saying "one thousand" after each number ("1 one thousand, 2 one thousand, . . ."), the number of times listed in the chart without having to withdraw your hand.

The two parts of a muscle—muscle fiber and connective tissue (see page 46)—cook differently. As meat heats, the protein in the muscle fibers becomes firmer and more opaque, and the collagen in the connective tissue melts. We can use either of these changes to determine the doneness of a piece of meat, and the one you use depends on the meat you're cooking.

Tender meat tends to have very little connective tissue. Most steaks are soft enough to bite into when raw, which allows us to judge their degree of doneness solely on the changes that happen to the protein in the muscle fibers as they heat. Raw meat protein is wet, translucent, brightly colored, and soft. As it gets warmer it becomes drier, more opaque, browner, and firmer. The hotter the meat gets, the more these physical changes manifest themselves, which allows us to equate the look and feel of a piece of cooked meat with specific temperatures. For instance, at 120° to 125°F, the center of a porterhouse steak is juicy, bright red, glistening, and tender; we call that rare. At 135° to 140°F, the center is moist, pink, matte, and resilient; we call that medium-done. Raise the interior temperature to over 165°F and the meat becomes dry, tan, dull, and firm—in other words, well-done.

When judging the doneness of tough meat that has a lot of connective tissue, we do not have the luxury of using the changes in muscle fibers as our guide. Tough meat is done cooking when it is tender (period!); there is no such thing as a rare, medium-rare, or medium-done brisket. Tough cuts, like brisket or chuck, are finished cooking when (and only when) the collagen in the connective tissue has melted enough to make the meat tender enough so that you can pierce it easily with fork. For that reason you don't need to take the temperature of a tough meat to test its doneness; if it is tender, it is ready. Since collagen starts to dissolve at around 160°F, tough meats will not show signs of tenderness until they are in the medium-well to well-done stage. The other element necessary to tenderize collagen is moisture, which is why tough meats are grilled slowly and basted frequently with a mopping liquid.

Grinding tough meat automatically tenderizes it by breaking the connective tissue into small pieces, but that doesn't mean you can cook it less than its tougher whole-muscle counterpart. During grinding, the surface and interior of a piece of meat are mixed together, causing bacteria on the surface to become dispersed throughout the batch, which is why it is not advisable to eat any ground meat that is not cooked to a temperature of at least 145°F. The U.S. Department of Agriculture (USDA) recommends 160°F to ensure that all areas of the food have reached a temperature of 140°F or higher, but we have found that at that temperature all of the moisture is gone as well. We prefer to stop the cooking of beef burgers at an internal temperature of 150°F; the meat will be slightly pink in the center and still relatively juicy. If you have any reason to doubt the safety of the ground beef you are using, you are welcome to cook your burgers a bit longer, but as long as the interior is above 140°F all harmful bacteria should be neutralized.

MEAT DONENESS

Meat	Blue	Rare	Medium-Rare	Medium	Medium-Well	Well-Done
Beef steak	120°F	125°F	135°F	145°F	155°F	170°F
Beef roast	115°F	125°F	135°F	145°F	155°F	170°F
Beef tough cuts	–	–	–	–	155°F	170°F
Ground beef	–	–	–	–	150°F	160°F
Pork chops	–	–	–	145°F	155°F	170°F
Pork roast	–	–	–	145°F	155°F	170°F
Pork shoulder	–	–	–	–	165°F	170°F
Ground pork	–	–	–	–	155°F	165°F
Lamb chops	120°F	125°F	135°F	145°F	155°F	170°F
Lamb roasts	115°F	125°F	135°F	145°F	155°F	170°F
Lamb shoulder	–	–	–	–	155°F	170°F
Ground lamb	–	–	–	–	150°F	160°F
Veal chops	–	–	135°F	145°F	155°F	170°F
Veal roasts	–	–	135°F	145°F	155°F	170°F
Veal shanks	–	–	–	–	155°F	170°F
Ground veal	–	–	–	–	150°F	160°F
Poultry	–	–	–	–	170°F	180°F
Fish	–	–	–	140°F	150°F	160°F

Grilled vegetables and fruits develop wonderful flavor due to their high sugar content. The sugar quickly caramelizes on the grill, creating complex flavors that are impossible to achieve by moist-heat cooking methods such as boiling or steaming. Judging produce doneness, however, is primarily a matter of texture. Most fruits and vegetables are done grilling when they are hot, crisp-tender, and lightly grill-marked. By crisp-tender, we mean that the plant tissues have retained enough cellular structure and moisture to be somewhat crisp, yet the cell walls are weak enough to be tender and palatable. When a plant is heated, its cell walls begin to break down and lose structure and moisture, becoming increasingly soft. As the internal temperature rises, the texture of grilled produce goes from firm and crisp to crisp-tender to soft and mushy and finally to dry and carbonized. That middle stage of crisp-tenderness is often the best-tasting for grilled produce.

Most fruits and ripe vegetables taste crisp-tender when raw, so take care not to overcook these delicate foods on the grill. Tender vegetables can quickly go from juicy and nicely grill-marked to limp and overly charred. When in doubt, err on the side of undercooking produce. Brief grilling over medium-high or high heat is usually all it takes to soften plant tissues to the crisp-tender stage. Denser vegetables with tough fibers, particularly root vegetables such as beets, should be cooked until fully tender when tested with a fork.

Like other ingredients, fruits and vegetables can be grilled to tenderness using a variety of methods: Direct heat, indirect heat, in the coals, or wrapped in foil. See the Vegetable-Grilling Guide on page 260 and the Fruit-Grilling Guide on page 306 for detailed information on how to grill specific types of produce.

03. JUDGING DOUGHS' DONENESS

Flatbreads like those for pizza and naan grill up beautifully. The doughs for these thin breads cook quickly (1 to 3 minutes) and develop a wide area of crisp crust. We prefer to grill flatbreads directly on a hot grill grate to expose the dough to as much flame as possible. But you can also use a perforated grill rack, which acts more like a baking sheet. To grill topped flatbreads like pizza, you grill the dough on one side before adding the toppings. Then you flip the dough, put the toppings on the grilled side, and slide the dough back onto the grill to brown the underside. Covering the grill is essential to bring heat to the cheese on top so it will melt. You can also grill thicker flatbreads like focaccia without flipping them. The process is more like grill-baking because you use a perforated baking sheet and cover the grill to trap the heat, as in an oven.

The high heat of the grill rapidly vaporizes the moisture in flatbread dough, creating air bubbles that puff up the dough. Grilled flatbreads are done when puffed, lightly grill-marked, and matte rather than shiny on the surface. Untopped flatbreads such as naan will form several bubbles across the surface, while topped flatbreads like pizza will puff up where there are no toppings, such as at the edges.

Yeasted bread loaves can't be baked on a grill, but slices can be toasted. Bread slices are often used to make grilled sandwiches such as panini. These breads are usually toasted over medium to medium-high heat and are done when lightly browned and crisp on the surface. The same goes for toasting cakes and pastries, although the higher sugar content can cause cakes and pastry to brown more quickly, so we usually toast these over medium to medium-low heat.

04. RESTING

As foods cook on the grill, they lose moisture and become dry. This process begins on the surface of the food (which is closest to the heat) and gradually progresses toward the center. Moisture either evaporates or is driven toward the center of the food. So when any food is removed from the grill, it is less juicy on the surface than it is at the core. Letting the food rest before cutting allows moisture to redistribute from the center back toward the surface. If you cut into steak immediately after grilling, the moisture will be unevenly distributed: The surfaces will be drier than the center. Immediate cutting also drains excess juices at the center because the saturated muscle tissues cannot hold the extra juices that were driven there.

For the juiciest-tasting grilled food, allow it to rest after grilling and before cutting. The thicker the food, the longer it should rest. The juices in a 1-inch to 2-inch-thick steak will redistribute after 5 to 8 minutes. The juices of a thick roast or small whole bird will redistribute in 10 to 20 minutes. Large birds such as turkeys and whole animals like lambs and hogs should rest for 30 minutes after grilling.

CHAPTER 3

MASTERING YOUR INGREDIENTS

Meat is the edible part of an animal. Although countless factors (where an animal lived, what it ate, how it was slaughtered, its grade, and its cut) influence the characteristics of a piece of meat, at a structural level, the quality of any meat depends on the balance of three components: protein, water, and fat. The amount of each and its properties determine whether a meat is flavorful or bland, tender or tough, moist or dry.

01. PROTEIN

Animals are built of protein. The protein can be either in muscle fibers, which are the red, bulky parts of meat, or in connective tissue, which is the transparent membrane that surrounds the fibers and the muscles themselves.

As a muscle is exercised, its fibers take on protein, making the muscle bigger, redder, and more flavorful. At the same time, its connective tissue—which is mostly collagen—thickens and becomes more elastic, which makes the muscle harder and tougher. So when meat is taken from an older animal or an exercised muscle group, it will have lots of flavor, a dark red color, and a tendency to be tough.

The first rule of choosing meat, then, is to look at the protein, or the lean parts. What color are they? Paler specimens have less flavor but are more tender. For instance, veal (infant beef) is blander than mature beef, but it is soft enough to cut with a fork. The bottom line: Less-exercised muscles are paler, more tender, and milder in flavor. More-exercised muscles are darker, tougher, and more flavorful.

A word of caution: You can compare color only within one type of meat. Tender beef is darker and redder than tough pork. Toddler-age grass-fed veal has a rosier hue than milk-fed baby veal, but it is paler and tougher than a rack of spring lamb. That's because the animals are raised differently.

The second rule of choosing meat is to look at texture. Large, tough muscle fibers will make the surface of a piece of tough meat look rough, like terrycloth. On the other hand, small, undeveloped fibers are barely visible, giving tender meat a sleek, silken appearance. The thickness of the connective tissue surrounding the fibers magnifies such differences. Thicker connective tissue makes a rough surface look even rougher. Undeveloped connective tissue is hardly noticeable.

Don't confuse the opaque white veins that web the surface of most meats with connective tissue. These are veins of fat; connective tissue is transparent.

The third element to consider is the ratio of water to protein in any given piece of meat. Water is what makes meat juicy. Held within the muscle fibers, it will remain in the meat as long as the fibers stay intact. What makes a piece of meat juicy is the ratio of water content to protein content. The following chart gives relative percentages of water and protein for the most commonly butchered meats.

PERCENTAGES OF WATER AND PROTEIN IN MEAT

Meat	Percentage of Water	Percentage of Protein
Fish	70	20
Chicken	65	30
Beef	60	18
Turkey	58	20
Lamb	16	16
Pork	12	12

As you can see, pork has the lowest ratio of water to protein, which helps to explain why an unwatched grilled pork chop can dry up in a matter of minutes. But it's also why pork is a good candidate for curing and smoking: These techniques concentrate the flavors in meat by reducing its moisture content. With less moisture to reduce, the flavors of pork concentrate easily.

Fish have a similar problem. They, too, can lose moisture instantaneously during cooking, but it happens for the opposite reason. Fish have the highest ratio of water to protein, but their protein is weak. When the protein filaments break, as they do when a fish overcooks, the juices easily flow out and the flesh becomes dry.

02. FAT

Fat is by far the most controversial element in meat. Cursed as a harbinger of obesity and heart disease, fat is the demon that most meat producers try to exorcise. For instance, today's pork is about 31 percent leaner than it was twenty years ago, according to the National Pork Board. But by scrambling to rid their product of the unmentionable, meat marketers have done little to help consumers understand that fat is the key element that makes meat palatable.

Fat is the way animals store energy. The bulk of the fat is held in specialized cells, called adipose tissue, which are concentrated under the skin and around the outside of muscle groups. Adipose fat does not permeate meat; rather, it borders the lean sections and is often trimmed away during butchering. Except as a means of self-basting a roast or for rendering, adipose fat has little culinary benefit.

Only marbling, the barely visible veins of fat webbed throughout the lean parts of meat, affects palatability. Marbling makes meat more tender, more flavorful, and perceptibly moister. Here's how it works: When an animal eats more calories than it needs, the excess is stored as adipose fat. If the animal continues to eat to excess, the adipose cells eventually become overfilled. The overflow is rerouted directly into the organs and muscles themselves, causing the muscles to become marbled and flabby, a trait that does not serve the health of the animal, but works wonders for its meat.

Marbling tenderizes meat in two ways. First, it stretches the connective tissue into thin sheets, making it more likely to soften during cooking, but more importantly, it isolates one muscle fiber from another, helping them to separate into tiny, easily chewed packets.

Much of the flavor of meat is in its fat. Because fat cells are essentially energy storage containers, any fat-soluble substance eaten by an animal can end up stored in its fat. This means that the content of fat tissue varies from animal to animal, depending on the species, where it lived, and what it ate. These variations in the fat give each piece of beef, lamb, chicken, or pork its unique flavor.

Unlike surface fat, which bastes only the outside of meat, marbled fat melts into the fibers individually, spreading its flavor impact into every bite. Fat itself has flavor, but it also plays an essential role in the perception of all aromatic flavors. So the marbling in a piece of meat doesn't just make the meat taste better; it also helps to carry the impact of the seasonings and sauces on the meat.

As we mentioned before, juiciness comes from the water content of meat. But really, the sensation of juiciness happens on two levels. The first comes from actual moisture held in meat fibers that is released when the fibers are broken during chewing. The secondary perception of juiciness is due to saliva flow stimulated by the presence of fat in the mouth. That is why a well-marbled meat will taste juicy even when it has been cooked relatively dry, while a bite of veal (too young to be thickly marbled) may start out moist and tender, but will dry out in the mouth before it's swallowed. Fat is necessary to carry flavor.

When buying meat, look for pieces with a minimum of exterior fat (about $1/4$ to $1/2$ inch) but a good degree of marbling. It isn't necessary to have large globs of fat striated through the lean protein, but neither should you seek out fat-free pieces of meat. If fat and cholesterol are dietary concerns, the best option is to limit your quantity of meat, but don't sacrifice the quality and succulence of the small amount of meat your diet allows.

03. GRASS-FED, GRAIN-FED, AND ORGANIC

As we mentioned earlier, an animal's diet and lifestyle affect the flavor of its meat. Completely grass-fed animals tend to have stronger-flavored meat and less consistent flavor than those fed a regulated diet of grain for part of their lives. Since the 1950s, almost all animals raised for meat in the United States develop at least 30 percent of their weight by being grain-fed in feed lots for 100 to 200 days before slaughter, which allows meat producers to standardize flavor (through a consistent diet), tenderness (by discouraging exercise), and the time it takes to bring an animal to market (by maximizing calorie expenditure and minimizing energy expenditure).

In other countries, raising an animal completely on grass is the norm. Pasture-fed Argentinean beef is world famous, and grass-feeding has gained popularity in England since the outbreak of mad cow disease there. But in the United States the movement against grain-feeding is still small. Typically, feed-lot cattle are grazed for at least a year

1. Marbling
2. Adipose fat

KILLING WITH KINDNESS

The techniques used for slaughtering are those that produce the best-tasting meat. Fortunately, they are also the most humane. Animals have a small amount of glycogen (animal starch) stored in their muscle fiber, which is used for quick bursts of energy, especially when an animal feels threatened. If an animal senses danger during slaughtering, its glycogen stores will be used up, a phenomenon that can ruin its meat. That's because muscle cells continue to live after an animal has been killed, deriving energy from any glycogen that is present. One of the by-products of the metabolism of available glycogen is lactic acid, which reduces the activities of enzymes in muscle tissue, slows the growth of microbes that cause spoilage, and causes some moisture to migrate from within the cells out to the surface of the meat, giving it a moist appearance. If the glycogen is depleted before slaughter by the animal becoming stressed or fearful, the accumulation of lactic acid never occurs, and the resulting meat will be dry, tough, dark colored, and easily spoiled. This phenomenon is known as "dark-cutting meat" and has been observed and avoided since the 1700s.

To keep from traumatizing an animal that is about to be slaughtered, it is surreptitiously stunned, usually with an electric charge to the head. Then it is hung by its legs, the major blood vessels in the neck are opened, and the animal is drained of about half its blood, which decreases the risk of spoilage. After bleeding, the hide is stripped, the carcass is opened, the organs are removed, and the carcass is chilled.

Within 2 1/2 hours of slaughter for beef (1 hour or less for smaller animals), the muscles clench in rigor mortis. If cut and cooked before that time, the meat will be tender, but once rigor mortis starts the meat cannot be handled until the rigor passes, about 24 hours for beef.

Hanging the carcass by its hind legs during slaughtering stretches the muscles to their maximum length at the time rigor mortis occurs. If this was not done and the protein filaments were overlapping when rigor mortis began, the muscle filaments would bond to one another, and the meat would become exceptionally tough.

As the meat hangs, protein-digesting enzymes continue to soften the muscle structure, and the meat texture relaxes. At this point, the carcass can be sectioned and sold. It is also the beginning of the aging process, which can be encouraged for up to a month when producing ultra-high-quality aged beef (see "Aged Beef," page 53).

READING A MEAT LABEL
The names for a particular cut of meat change by region, culture, and marketing incentives. To help with the confusion, the National Livestock and Meat Board has created a standardized meat label that most supermarkets use. The label tells you the type of meat, its primal cut, its retail cut, how it is trimmed, how fresh it is, its weight, its price per pound, and what you end up paying. For ground meat, it will also include the percentage of lean meat.

before being finished with grain. The opponents of this system argue that keeping an animal on grass throughout its life gives its meat a more complex flavor, a sweeter aroma, and a meatier texture. But even though a steak from a grass-fed steer can be excellent, grass-fed beef tends to be inconsistent in quality, reminiscent of the early days of organic produce, when tough fibers and a gnarled appearance had to be overlooked for the sake of purity.

The popularity of grass-fed meat is growing, and demand currently surpasses supply. More and more prominent chefs are serving grass-fed beef in their restaurants, and if more consumers jump on the bandwagon, meat producers may find it profitable to become grass growers rather than grain importers, in which case grass-fed meat could become as mainstream, and as quality driven, as organic produce.

Don't confuse grass-fed meat with meat labeled "organic." Some organic meats are grass-fed, but it's not a requirement. Certified organic meat must only meet the USDA National Organic Program standards, ensuring that it is

· Fed on 100 percent organic feed (vitamin and mineral supplements are allowed).
· Given neither hormones to promote growth nor antibiotics.
· Given access to pasture if it is a ruminant, such as cattle (organic beef can be fed on grain in feed lots, but for no more than 200 days, and its feed must be organic).

04. CUTS OF MEAT

Knowing what part of the animal a piece of meat comes from can be a shortcut in determining its quality. As we've already discussed, the amount of exercise a particular muscle gets has a lot to do with its flavor, and with how tough or tender it will be. Meat that is cut from a part of the body that moves a lot will have more flavor, and it will also be tougher. Meat from a relatively unused part of the body will be milder and more tender.

Regardless of whether you are buying beef, veal, pork, or lamb, the exercised sections of a four-legged animal are always the same—the shoulder, the hips, the chest, the groin, and the legs. Tender meat lies along the center of the back, in the ribs, and in the loin, the area that lies between the ribs and the hips. The charts in the following pages show the relative tenderness of cuts from various animals.

If you're having a hard time imagining this, get down on your hands and knees and start crawling around. Pretend you're a cow. What's moving? Bend down and graze. Do you feel your abdomen contract? That's your flank. Move around. Feel the roll of your shoulders and the sway of your hips. Meat butchered from those areas will be relatively tough. Feel your thigh. Do you feel that the inside of your thigh is softer than the back of it? The inside is your top round; the back is your bottom round. Which do you think would produce more-tender meat?

The large muscle groups of four-legged animals are called primal cuts. Although the cuts are the same in all types of meats, the names vary by animal (see the chart below). Carcass diagrams of individual animals are included in the sections on beef (page 51), veal (page 55), pork (page 57), and lamb (page 60).

PRIMAL CUTS (THE DARKER THE SHADING, THE TOUGHER THE CUT)			
Beef	**Veal**	**Pork**	**Lamb**
Chuck	Chuck	Shoulder	Shoulder
Brisket and plate	Breast and foreleg	Belly	Breast and foreleg
Rib	Rack	Loin	Rack
Loin	Loin	Loin	Loin
Sirloin	Loin	Loin	Loin
Round	Leg	Leg	Leg

Primal cuts are large. For instance, a primal rib of beef can weigh more than 40 pounds, a primal chuck more than 100 pounds. You will usually be buying subprimal or secondary cuts. A 3-rib rib roast of beef, trimmed of excess bone and fat, will typically weigh about 6 pounds and feed six people; the primal rib, after trimming, will serve about fourteen.

The price of meat is set by supply and demand. Because every animal yields the same cuts, an increased demand for sirloin steaks, without a corresponding need for chuck, raises the price of sirloin and lowers chuck prices.

The main factor that has traditionally influenced the popularity of one cut of meat over another is tenderness (which is at odds with the primary flavor component of meat, its fat, as explained on page 47). A carcass has a lot more tough meat than tender meat. That disparity has made filet mignon sell for the same price per ounce that budget meats cost per pound. It's what makes T-bone more expensive than round and tenderloin pricier than sirloin. These meats do not taste any better than cheaper cuts, but they can be sliced with a butter knife. And for that tenderness alone, many diners are willing to blow the budget.

Although tender cuts are generally preferred for grilling, it is possible to grill tougher cuts by cooking them low and slow. Barbecued chuck is delicious; it just takes three to four times as long to grill as the same size rib roast, and eight times longer than a tenderloin.

Why do you need to know whether a cut of meat is tender or tough? Because a meat's texture determines which cooking method will yield the best results. When meat cooks, two things happen: (1) the protein in the fibers becomes more firm and opaque, and (2) the collagen melts (as long as there is some moisture present). This is why tough meat becomes tender only if it is cooked with liquid—that is, stewing, braising, or barbecuing. Tender meats with sheer fibers of collagen don't need moist cooking (in fact, they can be ruined by it); they are best cooked with a dry, direct heating method like grilling. That is why steaks and chops from the loin, rib, and tenderloin are often grilled, while shoulder and leg steaks are typically barbecued. For more detailed information on specific cooking methods, see Chapter 2, "Mastering Your Technique."

05. GROUND MEAT

Ground meat is another story. Grinding pulverizes collagen, nullifying any toughness it once imparted. When a tough cut of meat is ground, you get the flavor of a well-exercised muscle with none of its toughness. The cuts of meat that are most often ground are chuck (shoulder), sirloin (where the back meets the hips), and round (leg). Each brings different amounts of flavor and slight variations in texture to the table. A shoulder that moved every time a steer took a step is going to develop more flavor and toughness than a back muscle that lay farther away from a joint.

Because the structural integrity of meat is destroyed by grinding, most of the natural moisture it once held is released as it sits. The small amount that remains evaporates quickly during cooking. Once the moisture is gone, the perception of juiciness depends on the meat's fat content, which is why ground beef with a fat content of less than 10 percent will yield unpalatably dry results, a 10 to 15 percent fat content will taste lean and juicy, a 15 to 20 percent fat content will taste richer, and burgers with more than 20 percent fat will have full flavor, a fatty mouth feel, and a glistening surface when hot. It is unusual for the fat content of ground meat to exceed 22 percent.

Commercially ground meats are made by combining a percentage of lean meat with a percentage of fat. If you are grinding meats at home, the exact fat percentage is difficult to determine unless you take the trouble to separate all of the fat from the lean, weigh them separately, and calculate the percentage. We have recently seen ground beef packages that list the cut of beef, but not the lean percentage, on the label. The only way to judge the fat content of the beef packaged this way is to look at the color: the paler the red, the higher the fat content.

A note on the doneness of ground meat: We believe that you should cook ground meat thoroughly but not overcook it (for details, see "Judging Meat Doneness" on page 42). Here's why. Most harmful bacteria are destroyed by temperatures in excess of 140°F. Because these bacteria live largely on the surface of a piece of meat, cooking processes like roasting, grilling, frying, and boiling are sufficient to destroy the surface bacteria, even if the interior temperature of the meat does not reach 140°F. However, if the meat is ground, the bacteria live throughout all parts of the meat, not just the surface. So you should take care to cook ground meats to an internal temperature of more than 145°F.

06. GRADING

All meat that is slaughtered in the United States is inspected for sanitary handling and wholesomeness by the USDA, but only the most expensive meat is graded. Grading determines quality and yield, not safety, and whether a meat producer decides to have a carcass graded or not is purely voluntary.

Although any animal can be graded, graded beef is the most widespread, followed by pork. For several reasons, less and less meat is graded in this country. First of all, grading is an added expense in bringing meat to market, and for all but the most luxurious cuts (rib, loin, and tenderloin) a high grade will not increase the retail price by much. What's more, the qualities that consumers say they want in their meat (less fat and more lean) are contrary to the criteria used by the grading system.

The amount of marbling, the webbing of fat deep within the lean muscle of well-fed animals, is the primary factor that determines a high-quality grade. Other criteria, such as the age of the animal and its musculature, are considered in determining grade, but they have less effect on the flavor and texture of the meat, and they are given less weight in determining the final grade.

Most of the meat sold in supermarkets is "No Roll," which means not graded. After meat is graded, the USDA grade stamp is marked on the carcass in blue ink with a roller that imprints the grade on each primal cut. If the carcass is not graded, it doesn't get rolled with the stamp; hence the name. Grading information for specific meats can be found in the sections on beef (page 50) and pork (page 59).

<section type="sidebar">
GROUND RULES

Millennia before the hamburger helped to reset the parameters of quick cooking in America, the ancient Romans, Greeks, and Phoenicians knew that ground meat was the ultimate convenience food. Not only did it cook up faster than bullock on a spit, but it could also be preserved and flavored effortlessly just by mixing it with spices.

Today, we often forget the versatility of ground meat, resorting to it for easy, unimaginative meals that anyone will eat but no one relishes. Part of the problem is that the relative ease and speed of cooking have bred neglect of flavor and texture. But like all seemingly simple preparations, there is a hidden depth that must be understood by anyone who wants to master the burger.

All but a fraction of the ground meat sold is beef. Of the three cuts of beef most commonly ground, the most flavorful is chuck (from the well-exercised shoulder), followed by bottom round and sirloin. If a smooth texture is of great importance, ground sirloin is the best bet. But if you want flavor, make your burgers from chuck. Round is for those who want to tread the middle ground (or grind).

If your butcher looks at you oddly when you ask for ground pork, veal, or lamb, it is because they likely don't get much call for these items. Instruct them to run the desired variety of stew meat through a grinder twice. Of course, if you have a meat grinder at home, you can grind the stew meat yourself, a practice that can save money and ensure freshness. (Ground meat is quite perishable.) Although it is possible to use a food processor for chopping meat, the machine will not grind, and can result in a flaccid, unpleasantly textured purée if you're not careful.

Ground turkey is the most commonly available ground poultry, although ground chicken is on the rise. Usually, ground poultry is made from a combination of dark and white meats, as dark meat improves the overall texture and flavor. Poultry is much lower in fat than beef and other four-legged meats, and for that reason it tends to make drier, blander burgers. To boost flavor, turkey and chicken burger recipes typically include spices and condiments.

The key thing to keep in mind when cooking burgers is this: As protein heats, it contracts, and any juices that it once held are squeezed out. The result is a dry burger. The fat in beef burgers helps to counteract this dryness, but in low-fat burgers, like those made with poultry, the loss of moisture is disastrous. An easy way to help retain juiciness is to include something in the burger mix that absorbs moisture, usually fresh breadcrumbs. Fresh breadcrumbs work better than dry ones, because they are less absorbent, thereby leaving some of the juices in liquid form. Burgers made with dry commercial breadcrumbs tend to make a burger that is soft but not juicy.
</section>

Because most mass-marketed meat is not graded, meat producers and supermarket butchers have devised brand names to distinguish their products from the competition. Some companies identify their meat as "pure" or "natural," terms the government has defined simply as using minimal processing and avoiding artificial ingredients. Some companies go a step further, producing meats that are free of hormones and antibiotics. And some brands are specific to certain breeds, like Certified Black Angus and Certified Hereford Beef.

Many supermarkets label meat with very little marbling "extra-lean" and charge a premium price for it. The USDA defines extra-lean beef as having less than 5 percent fat and less than 2 percent saturated fat, which would place it at a middle to low level on the grading scale. Not only is it not worth the high price, but it is easily destroyed by overcooking.

07. BEEF

Cattle are huge animals, weighing well over 1,000 pounds and yielding more than 500 pounds of edible meat per carcass. Almost all of the cattle raised for meat in the United States are hybrids. The longhorn of cowboy ballad and cattle drive fame, the breed that established the beef industry in North America, was stringy and tough, and they all but died out as a source of meat in the late nineteenth century, when they were replaced by blockier, meatier, British breeds, such as Hereford and Durham, and the Scottish breed Angus. These animals were bred with drought-resistant humped breeds from Asia, particularly Brahmans, to create a stock that was resistant to environmental hardships and disease but possessed large musculature, good marbling, and tender meat. These qualities became the hallmark of American beef.

Tastes have changed since the high point of American beef consumption in the 1950s and '60s. Beef producers responded to declining beef sales and health concerns over dietary fat by shortening the amount of time that animals were fattened in feed lots, and by breeding leaner and larger European cattle into the American hybrid. Now breeds like Chiangus, a mix of Angus beef and Chianina, the giant cattle of central Italy, have become premium beef in the United States, because they are both very lean and very tender, a sensory combination that could not have been attained a generation ago.

Beef producers categorize cattle by gender and sexual maturity. Male cattle tend to be larger and yield more meat per carcass, but the meat tends to be stringier and tougher than meat from female animals. Female animals yield finer-textured, more tender meat, but their muscle groups are smaller and give a poorer yield per carcass. As you can see, neither male nor female cattle have all of the characteristics the industry wants—tender, fine-textured meat, and large, high-yielding muscles.

In order to raise cattle with both maximum yield and maximum tenderness, male cattle are castrated. Intact males (bulls) tend to be large and aggressive. They run around, fight with other males, and are difficult to fatten in feed lots. But castrate them at a young age, and they will grow in size but their musculature will stay soft and tender—everything one wants in cattle designed for the plate.

The best-quality beef comes from either younger females or castrated males. Mature females are classified as cows, and females that have not yet calved are called heifers. Males are either bulls, steers (castrated bulls), or bullocks (young steers). Bulls are not generally sold as meat, and only steers, bullocks, and heifers produce beef of the highest quality.

There are eight quality grades for beef: prime, choice, select, standard, commercial, utility, cutter, and canner. All of the beef that is sold at retail markets falls within the top three grades.

Prime beef has the highest degree of marbling, but since only about 2 percent of the beef produced in the United States is graded prime, and almost all of that is exported or sold to restaurants, it is unlikely that you will ever see it at your local supermarket. A good butcher may be able to get you prime beef, but usually only loin steaks and roasts. Cheaper cuts don't sell for enough money to warrant offering them as prime. They're out there, though. Only whole carcasses can be graded, which means that for every prime rib roast, there is a prime chuck roast and a prime brisket coming from the same steer. Most butchers don't cut from whole carcasses or sides any longer, but if you can find one who does, you may be able to get a prime brisket or prime short ribs, which should be much juicier than what is usually available.

Sixty-seven percent of the beef that is graded is graded choice. Don't be led astray by this figure. Remember that most beef is not graded at all, and if it were, the vast amount would receive the select grade. Because choice is such a large grade, it is broken into subcategories, the best-known of which is top choice. Within the choice category, the USDA permits marbling ranging from small (4 percent—hardly any visible marbling) to moderate (8 percent—the lean meat is striated with visible fat). Because prime beef is so hard to come by (and has an average marbling of 9.5 percent), top choice is as close to prime as most of us are able to purchase.

Select grade beef can have as little as 3 percent marbling, which is barely visible, and it dries out easily when overcooked. Since most of the beef you buy would be tagged select if it were graded, it is preferable to cook supermarket steaks and roasts to medium (145°F) or rarer.

As we discussed earlier, the amount of exercise a particular muscle gets determines the flavor and tenderness of the meat it produces. So knowing where on the cattle your steak or roast comes from tells you a lot about how you should cook it and what results you can expect.

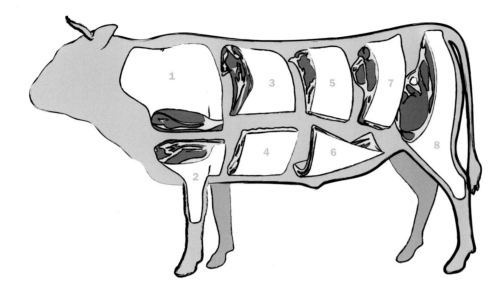

BEEF PRIMAL CUTS
1. Chuck
2. Brisket
3. Rib
4. Plate
5. Short loin
6. Flank
7. Sirloin
8. Round

Cattle carcasses are divided into eight primal cuts, which are sold to retail butchers, who divide them further into steaks, chops, roasts, and ground beef. Tender cuts come from the muscle groups that get the least amount of exercise, which run along the back of the body—the rib, short loin, and sirloin. Tougher meats are from the areas that move or support the body—the chuck, brisket, plate, flank, and round.

Arranged from most tender at the top to the toughest at the bottom, the cuts of beef that you can grill are listed in the following chart.

CUTS OF BEEF FOR GRILLING, FROM MOST TENDER TO TOUGHEST	
Primal Cuts	**Retail Cuts**
Short loin	Tenderloin T-bone Porterhouse Strip steak
Rib	Rib roast Rib steak
Sirloin	Sirloin steak Tri-tip
Plate	Skirt steak Hanger steak
Flank	Flank steak
Round	Top round London broil
Chuck	Chuck roast
Brisket	Brisket

SHORT LOIN The tenderest and most expensive cut of beef is the tenderloin (also known as fillet roast, fillet steak, filet mignon, and châteaubriand). It is a long, tapered muscle (shaped like a baseball bat) that runs along the spine. There is one attached to either side of the vertebrae; the wider end nestles into the hip and tapers as it approaches the rib cage. Its anatomical function is to make the back arch upward, something cattle never do. Since obsolescence breeds tenderness, you can cut beef tenderloin with a fork, which is why people will pay as much for an ounce of it as they will pay for a pound of a more-exercised muscle.

The tenderloin lies on the underside of the spine. The loin muscle runs parallel to it, on the top side of the spine. Steaks that are cut from the back therefore each have a piece of loin and a piece of tenderloin, with a T-shaped bone in between, which is a cross section of the spine. When a steak is cut from the area that is closer to the hip (porterhouse), the circumference of the tenderloin (or filet) piece will be larger; when it's cut closer to the ribs (T-bone), the section of filet is smaller. Both steaks are delicious; you just get a bigger filet on a porterhouse than on a T-bone. If the tenderloin is removed and sold separately as a fillet steak or fillet roast, the remaining piece is sold as a strip steak (also known as New York strip or Kansas City strip).

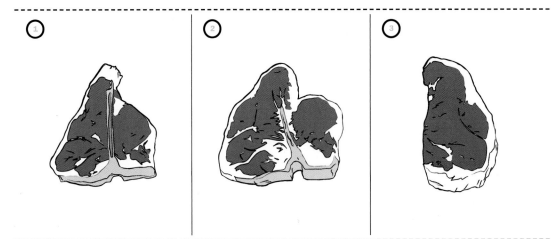

PRIMAL RIB A beef primal rib contains a section of seven ribs running between the exercised (and tough) muscles of the chuck and the unexercised, very tender short loin. The chuck end is larger, composed of several muscle groups, including the eye, surrounded by a wide flap of relatively lean blade meat. The other muscles in the rib are the rib-eye cap and the deckle.

The rib can be divided into roasts or steaks. Rib roasts are sold by number of ribs; a 3-rib roast will serve six people. When the ribs are left long (about 6 inches), the roast is said to be a "standing rib roast" because the arch of the ribs acts as a rack for holding the meat upright on the grill. This presentation is often referred to erroneously as prime rib, which technically refers only to beef that has been graded prime. A regular rib roast is trimmed to have shorter bones (about 3 inches long); the pieces that are removed are sold as short ribs.

Rib steaks may be cut from any rib in the primal cut, with or without a bone. Often steaks cut from the loin end are sold trimmed down to the eye muscle, in which case they are sold as rib-eye steaks or Delmonico steaks. A rib steak taken from the center, or ninth rib, is called an entrecôte.

The rib is one of the most succulent cuts to grill. Though not as tender as steaks and roasts from the short loin, it is more much more flavorful. If you are concerned about toughness, ask your butcher to cut from the loin end or small end.

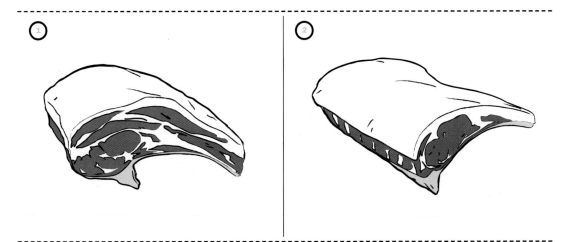

SIRLOIN The sirloin is not one of the largest cuts of beef, but it is one of the most diverse. The sirloin traverses the hip, so at one end it is very close to a high-priced super-tender porterhouse, and at the other end it is just a hairline away from rump or round. If a bone is present, you can tell roughly where in the sirloin your steak came from by the shape of the bone. At the porterhouse end the bone

SHORT LOIN
1. T-bone
2. Porterhouse
3. Boneless strip steak

PRIMAL RIB
1. Chuck end
2. Loin end

will look like a broken T-bone (see the steak labeled 1 below). As you move deeper into the hip, the top of the "T" will thicken into a square, and the tail will become wider and curvy (see steak 2). Eventually, at the opposite end, the sirloin will have a circular bone, which is a cross-cut of the leg bone (see steak 3), indicating that the steak comes from the most exercised part of the cut.

Because of this variety, sirloin is usually priced to sell, and for the most part it is a good value, with little waste. Since some pieces of sirloin can tend toward toughness, it is a good idea to look for visible marbling in the lean, and if you purchase sirloin that is very lean, try not to overcook it.

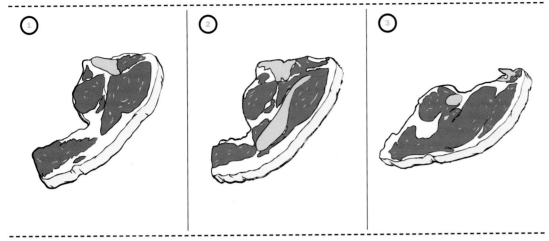

SIRLOIN STEAKS:
From loin end to round end

PLATE AND FLANK Of the tough cuts, the ones that can be grilled most easily come from the underside of the cattle, in the plate and flank primal cuts. The retail cuts from these sections that are best for grilling are skirt steak, hanger steak, and flank steak. Unlike meat from the shoulders and hips, these muscle groups are not used for movement; rather they support the internal organs. Accordingly, they have long, thick muscle fibers running parallel to one another (similar to a hammock), which are easier to chew when cut in thin slices against the grain.

Flank steak was the original London broil, named because it was a tough, flavorful cut that could be grilled (or broiled) like more expensive steaks. Now it's more common to see London broil cut from the round. However, because the muscle fibers are not parallel in a round steak, it is impossible to make every slice against the grain of the meat, which is why London broil made from the round is always inconsistent in texture (see page 143 for more on London broil).

TOUGH CUTS: CHUCK, BRISKET, AND ROUND Roasts and steaks from the tough cuts need special attention on the grill. They can be partially tenderized through marinating (see page 86), but this will not soften them completely. The chuck and brisket must be cooked slowly over indirect heat, and they benefit from frequent basting with a mop sauce or marinade (see pages 84 and 86).

A round of beef is huge, composed of four large muscle groups that vary greatly in tenderness. Only the top round, which comes from the soft inner thigh, is suitable for grilling, and only if it is marinated and cooked slowly via indirect heat.

AGED BEEF Like cheese and wine, beef benefits from a period of aging, during which it becomes more tender and more flavorful. Although most meat is aged only incidentally for the few days it takes to ship it from the packing plant to the butcher's counter, a small amount of prime grade beef is aged for a month or more. Dry-aged beef is rare, usually found only in expensive steak houses and at specialty butchers, but it is distinctive enough that you should be aware of it.

Dry aging is done with a combination of refrigeration (at 34° to 38°F/1° to 3°C) and high humidity (70 to 80 percent). Under these conditions, muscle enzymes in the meat remain active, breaking down large proteins into smaller, more flavorful amino acids, and breaking down glycogen into sweet sugars and fat into aromatic fatty acids. Other enzymes attack the connective tissue and contracted muscle fibers, causing them to relax and tenderizing the meat. This has two effects: It makes the collagen gelatinize more quickly during cooking, allowing the meat to be more tender at rarer temperatures, and it decreases the pressure of the connective tissue so that it squeezes out less juice as the meat cooks. The result: tender, juicy meat that can be served quite rare.

During the aging process, a substantial amount of dehydration takes place, which concentrates the meat's flavor. Mold also grows on the surface, which must be trimmed and results in a weight loss of up to 20 percent; hence the high price.

Although less than 1 percent of the meat in the United States is dry aged, a good percentage goes through a process that the meat industry calls "wet aging." Wet-aged meat is vacuum-packed in plastic and kept under refrigeration for between 4 days and 2 weeks. During that time, the same muscle enzymes activated in dry aging help to tenderize the meat and improve its flavor, but because the sealed plastic doesn't permit any dehydration, the rich concentration of flavor that is the hallmark of dry-aged beef never occurs.

Retail Cut	Primal Cut	Other Names	Description	How to Grill
Bottom sirloin	Sirloin	Ball tip, flap	Lean, medium grain	Kebab, direct, medium-high heat
Brisket first-cut	Brisket	Brisket flat	Flat, rough rectangle; long, medium-coarse grain	Marinate, indirect, medium-low heat
Chuck roast or steak	Chuck	Pot roast, chuck eye roast, blade steak	Large, lots of connective tissue, coarse grain running in different directions	Marinate, indirect, medium-low heat
Flank steak	Flank	London broil	Lean, flat rectangle; long, coarse, even parallel grain	Marinate, direct, medium-high heat
Ground beef	Chuck, round, sirloin	Hamburger, ground (primal cut)	Pink to red, uniform texture, sold by percentage of lean to fat	Direct, medium-high heat
Hanger steak	Plate	Butcher's steak, hanging tender	Dark red, lean, shaped like a long "V," membrane running down middle	Direct, medium-high heat
Rib roast	Rib	Prime rib	Fine-grained eye topped by coarse-grained "lifter" section, striated with fat	Indirect, medium heat
Rib steak	Rib	Delmonico, rib-eye	Fine grained, fat on one side	Direct, medium-high heat
Short ribs	Chuck, rib, plate	Crosscut ribs	Medium-coarse grain, striated with fat	Indirect, medium heat
Skirt steak	Plate	Fajita steak	Rectangular, flat, lean, coarse grained	Marinate, direct, medium heat
Sirloin	Strip steak	New York strip, Kansas City, club	Rectangular, medium grain, layer of fat and gristle on one side	Direct, medium-high heat
Short loin	T-bone/porterhouse	—	T-shaped bone separates strip (medium-fine grain) from filet (fine grain)	Direct, medium-high heat
Short loin	Tenderloin	Filet, filet mignon, châteaubriand	Baseball bat shaped, yields round steaks, velvety texture, lean	Direct, medium-high heat
Sirloin	Tri-tip	Sirloin triangle	Medium-coarse grain, triangular shape	Marinate, indirect, medium heat

VEAL PRIMAL CUTS
1. Shoulder
2. Shank
3. Rib
4. Breast
5. Loin
6. Leg

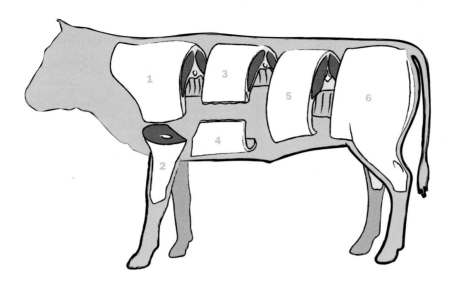

Technically, veal is baby beef slaughtered before 9 months of age, but most veal actually comes from animals less than 4 months old. Its meat is pale, tender, and lean, although these characteristics vary widely depending on how the calf was raised and how it was fed. Veal older than 5 months is usually classified as calf or baby beef and will have a rosy color, a firmer texture, and some marbling.

Many cooks erroneously believe that the younger the veal, the better the meat. Although youth ensures tenderness and mild flavor, it also means a minimum of marbling, which can cause the meat to toughen and dry as it cooks. Veal slaughtered before 8 weeks will certainly have this problem.

Veal quality is more dependent on feed and exercise than on age. The tenderest veal is milk-fed or formula-fed and raised in stalls. Many people object to eating veal that spends the entirety of its short life confined to a stall. Grass-fed and range-fed veal is an option if you are concerned. This type of veal is a deeper color than formula-fed veal, and it has a beefier flavor. If you are a classicist (culinarily speaking), you might object to these qualities, but many contemporary Americans prefer the flavor of grass-fed veal.

Veal carcasses vary greatly in size, from 50 pounds to over 300 for large Dutch formula-fed veal (also known as Provimi) that yield large cuts of meat with exceptional tenderness. Because veal is young beef, it has the same body parts, but there are fewer primal cuts. The sirloin is included with the leg, and the plate, flank, and brisket are all included in the breast. The same distribution of tender and tough cuts applies, but because veal is younger than beef, more of the cuts are tender enough to grill.

Arranged from the most tender at the top to the toughest at the bottom, the cuts of veal that you can grill are shown in the following chart.

CUTS OF VEAL FOR GRILLING, FROM MOST TENDER TO TOUGHEST

Primal Cuts	Retail Cuts
Loin	Veal loin
	Loin chops
	Medallions
Rib	Veal rack
	Rib chops
Leg	Cutlets
	Veal leg
Shoulder	Shoulder chop
	Veal shoulder
Shank	Osso buco

LOIN The veal loin is most commonly divided into chops, but it can also be roasted whole or boned. It includes a T-shaped bone that separates the loin-eye muscle from a small tenderloin muscle. It looks very similar to a T-bone beef steak (see the illustration on page 52). The tenderloin can be separated and sold cut into veal medallions, or high-grade scaloppine.

If the loin is separated from the leg before the tenderloin is removed, the smaller half will be included in the loin. The larger butt-tenderloin will then be included in the top half of the leg.

RIB A rack of veal ribs corresponds to a standing rib roast in beef. Like beef, it consists of seven ribs, and it is frequently sold "frenched," meaning that $1\frac{1}{2}$ inches of each bone is cleaned of all meat and fat, which allows it to be used as a handle to facilitate gnawing or carving.

More commonly, the rack is sliced and sold as chops. Veal rib chops are the most sought after and highest priced of all cuts of veal. They consist of a tender fine-grained eye surrounded by layers of fat and cap muscles. When chops come from the end of the rack closest to the shoulder, the diameter of the chop is larger, but the eye muscle is smaller. You will get more lean meat and less fat per pound by buying rib chops from the loin end, but the chops will be smaller. Because they are so lean, it is best to grill veal chops that are at least 1 inch thick.

LEG A leg of veal has five muscles (top round, bottom round or heel, sirloin tip or knuckle, top sirloin butt, and shank), which can be grilled separately or rolled and tied together. As with beef, the top round is the most tender, but all of the parts are delicious grilled with medium, indirect heat. Because the leg is relatively lean, it benefits from brining or marinating.

SHOULDER, BREAST, AND SHANK Like a chuck of beef, veal shoulders account for about one-third of the weight of a carcass. They include the clod (main muscle); the blade; the chuck tender, which lies between the shoulder blade and the spine; and the first four ribs. Chops and roasts can be cut from any part of the shoulder, and although all are tender enough to grill, their texture can be improved by marinating or brining.

Veal shanks, especially the cross sections sold as osso buco, can be grilled. They are very flavorful, but decidedly tough. You can tenderize them deliciously by grilling over the lowest possible indirect heat and basting them frequently with an herbed marinade.

The veal breast corresponds to the brisket and plate sections of beef. Although it can be grilled like shanks, it is better left to pot roasting.

CUTS OF VEAL FOR GRILLING

Retail Cut	Primal Cut	Other Names	Description	How to Grill
Ground veal	Trimmings	Veal burger	Pale pink, lean, mild	Direct, medium heat
Leg	Leg	Round, rump, scaloppine	Mild, medium-fine grain, lean	Indirect, medium heat
Loin chop	Loin	Veal chop	Pale, fine grained, fat cap, T-bone	Direct, medium-high heat
Loin roast	Loin	Short loin	Pale, fine grained, fat cap	Indirect, medium heat
Rack	Rib	Veal rib roast	Pale, fine grained, fat cap, rib bone	Indirect, medium heat
Ribs	Chuck, breast	Spareribs	Coarse grained, striated with fat	Indirect, medium heat
Rib chop	Loin	Veal chop	Pale, fine grained, fat cap, rib bone	Direct, medium-high heat
Shank	Shank	Osso buco	Coarse grain, small muscle groups surrounded by fat and connective tissue, marrow bone	Indirect, medium-low heat

Shoulder chop	Chuck	Shoulder steak, blade steak	Coarse grain, a lot of connective tissue, long bone	Marinate, indirect, medium heat
Shoulder roast	Chuck	Blade roast, shoulder clod	Coarse grain, a lot of connective tissue, blade and rib bones	Marinate, indirect, medium-low heat

09. PORK

Although the demand for lean meat has changed how all livestock is raised and fattened, the raising of pork has changed the most dramatically. Thirty years ago a full-grown pig typically weighed more than 300 pounds. Now the top weight is closer to 240, which yields a carcass of about 180 pounds and a little more than 100 pounds of edible meat. Today's pig has less fat (about an inch along the back, compared to several inches in the old days) and larger, leaner muscles.

All of these changes have made lean cuts of pork very similar to chicken in overall fat content, saturated fat, cholesterol, and calories. But this leanness has made cooking pork much more difficult. As we discussed earlier (see pages 46–47), pork is very low in moisture. What made it juicy in the past were abundant deposits of fat dispersed within its lean parts. Now that these are gone, modern pork dries out, with inedible results, if cooked at too high heat or for too long.

Pork can harbor trichina, the parasite responsible for trichinosis. The threat of trichinosis compelled old pork recipes to recommend cooking all pork to 180°F, a temperature at which all of its moisture is long gone. Although at one time trichinosis was a worry, it has been all but eradicated from pork sold commercially today. In 1950, there were 400 recorded cases of trichinosis in the United States. From 1983 to 1989, there were fewer than 30, and most of these were traced to home-grown pigs that were not inspected, or to hunted animals, like wild boar and bear.

Trichinae are killed at 140°F. The National Pork Board advises cooking pork to 160°F, but most chefs (us included) recommend cooking lean, tender cuts like chops, loins, and tenderloins to between 150°F and 155°F (still slightly pink in the center), and fattier large cuts, like shoulders and fresh hams, to between 160°F and 165°F.

1. Store Name   **6.** Freshness
2. Kind of meat   **7.** Weight
3. Preparation   **8.** Pound Price
4. Retail Cut   **9.** You Pay
5. Primal Cut

The names for a particular cut of meat change by region, culture, and marketing incentives. To help with the confusion, the National Livestock and Meat Board has created a standardized meat label that most supermarkets use. The label tells you the type of meat, its primal cut, its retail cut, how it is trimmed, how fresh it is, its weight, its price per pound, and what you end up paying. For ground meat, it will also include the percentage of lean meat.

PORK PRIMAL CUTS
1. Shoulder
2. Foreleg
3. Loin
4. Belly
5. Leg

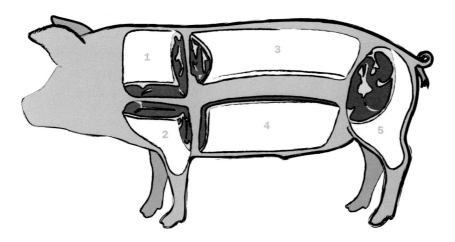

The cuts of pork are simpler than those of beef or veal. There are only five primals: shoulder, foreleg, loin, belly, and leg, and all of them are small enough to be sold whole. Baby pigs, weighing between 20 and 30 pounds, can be grilled intact on most home grills. Adult pigs (whole hogs) need special equipment such as a spit-roaster or large barrel smoker.

All parts of a pig are tender enough to grill. The cuts, ranging from most tender to toughest, are shown in the chart on page 58.

Primal Cuts	Retail Cuts
Loin	Pork loin roast
	Loin chops
	Center-cut chops
	Tenderloin
	Back ribs
	Country-style ribs
	Veal leg
Leg	Ham
	Ham steaks
Belly	Pork belly
	Spareribs
Shoulder	Boston butt
	Picnic ham
Foreleg	Hocks

LOIN The loin of pork is cut extra long to maximize the number of cuts that can be derived from this, the tenderest part of the pig. It runs between the shoulder and the leg and includes four areas from which chops are taken: blade end, ribs, loin, and sirloin, plus the tenderloin. Blade chops are made up of several muscle groups striated with fat and punctuated with multiple bones (see Chop 1 below). They can be fairly chewy unless they are marinated or brined. When blade chops are split open, they are sold as country-style ribs. Chops cut from the rib section are called "center cut"; they have a large, uninterrupted eye that is ideal for stuffing, and an arched rib bone (see Chop 2). Loin chops are similar except that they have a T-bone separating a smaller eye from a section of tenderloin (see Chop 3). Pork sirloin chops have more bones, more fat layers, and slightly tough meat, although they are still tender enough to grill (see Chop 4).

PORK LOIN CHOPS
1. Blade
2. Center-cut rib
3. Loin
4. Sirloin

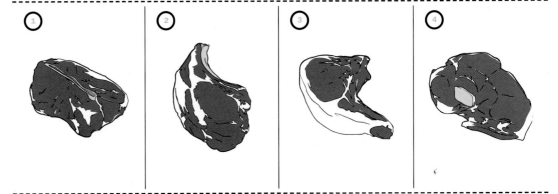

A pork tenderloin is small, usually just large enough to serve two people. Like other tenderloins, it is buttery soft and expensive, although pork tenderloin is not nearly as pricey as beef or veal. The ribs from the loin are also diminutive, and consequently are called "baby back." They are meaty and leaner than spareribs from the belly.

LEG A leg of pork comprises the ham (thigh) and the shank (lower leg). A whole fresh ham can weigh from 14 pounds to more than 26 pounds and yields 6 to 12 pounds of meat. It is composed of three muscle groups, which can be sold separately as inside round, outside round, and knuckle.

BELLY Pork belly is a flavorful cut that is laden with fat, best known as the cut from which bacon is made. Its bones are sold as spareribs. There are at least 11 ribs in a rack of spareribs, and the cut includes portions of breast meat, the sternum, and the diaphragm. When these sections are trimmed, the rack takes on a rectangular shape and is sold as St. Louis ribs.

SHOULDER Pork shoulder is a tough and fatty cut that is best for making pulled pork barbecue. It is composed of two sections, either of which makes delicious pulled pork. The upper shoulder, the Boston butt, is the larger of the two. The meat from the arm is sold as picnic ham.

Retail Cut	Primal Cut	Other Names	Description	How to Grill
Baby back ribs	Loin	Loin ribs	Small, meaty ribs; striated with fat; medium-coarse grain	Indirect, medium heat
Ham	Leg	Fresh ham, inside round	Medium grain, well marbled	Indirect, medium heat
Ground pork	Trimmings	Burger	Pale, mild, rich, smooth texture	Direct, medium heat
Loin chops	Loin	Center-cut chop	Pale, fine grained, fat cap, T-bone	Direct, medium-high heat
Loin roast	Loin	Center-cut loin roast	Pale, fine grained, fat cap	Indirect, medium heat
Rib chops	Loin	Center-cut chop	Pale, fine grained, fat cap, rib bone	Direct, medium-high heat
Rack	Loin	Pork rib roast, crown roast	Pale, fine grained, fat cap, rib bone	Direct, medium-high heat
Shoulder	Shoulder	Boston butt, picnic	Fatty, coarse grained, several muscles run in different directions, best for pulled pork	Indirect, medium-low heat
Spareribs	Belly	St. Louis ribs	Meaty, rectangular rack of ribs; coarse grained; striated with fat	Indirect, medium-low heat
Country spareribs	Shoulder	Blade-end ribs	Lots of meat and fat with several small bones, medium-coarse grain	Indirect, medium-low heat
Suckling pig	Whole	Whole pig, piglet	Whole baby pig weighing 20 to 25 pounds, pale, tender, succulent, crisp skin	Indirect, medium-low heat
Tenderloin	Loin	Pork filet	Fine grained, very pale, very tender, very lean	Indirect, medium-high heat

GRADES OF PORK Pork grades are simpler than beef grades. Labeled 1 through 4, they are an evaluation of the ratio of lean meat to fat, with number 1 yielding the highest proportion of lean. Almost all of the pork sold to consumers is number 1 grade.

10. LAMB

The average meat-eating person in the United States consumes only a little more than 1 pound of lamb per year, yet it is the most popular meat in Mediterranean countries, which makes it an essential meat for any American who loves to cook. Most people expressing distaste for lamb complain that it has a strong flavor and a musky aroma, which can be said about the meat of mature sheep (mutton) but not the delicate young lamb that is sold today.

Lamb comes from animals that are between 5 and 12 months old, although the majority of the lamb sold in supermarkets is from the young end of that spread. Lamb older than 12 months (called yearling) is rarely seen, and mutton (sheep older than 2 years) is usually available only through halal butchers or in communities with a voracious Anglophilic palate.

New Zealand, Australia, China, and Iceland all export lamb to the United States. Domestically, all of the states raise some lamb, and several states (Texas, Colorado, California, Wyoming, South Dakota, and Utah) produce enough to export lamb across the country. American lambs are larger than their European and Pacific Rim counterparts, yielding chops and roasts that are nearly twice the weight of imported lamb.

Suckling or spring lamb, which is exceptionally mild and tender, can be grill-roasted whole on a spit (see page 243). Spring lambs usually weigh between 20 and 35 pounds and yield about half of their weight in meat. Although the seasonal name used to indicate lambs that were born in the spring, suckling lambs are now available year-round due to improved husbandry practices. A good source is Jamison Farm in Latrobe, Pennsylvania (jamisonfarm.com), which produces hormone-free lamb and will ship anywhere in the country.

LAMB PRIMAL CUTS
1. Shoulder
2. Breast and foreleg
3. Rack
4. Loin
5. Leg

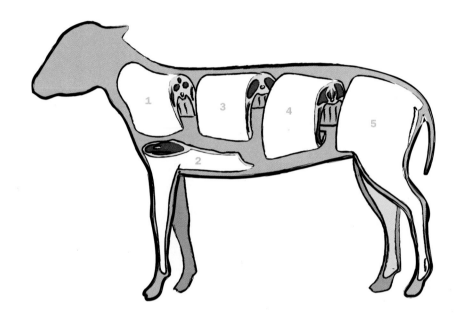

All cuts of lamb are tender enough to be grilled, although the shoulder and breast benefit from frequent basting with a marinade or sauce. The cuts of lamb, from most tender to toughest, are shown in the following chart.

CUTS OF LAMB FOR GRILLING, FROM MOST TENDER TO TOUGHEST	
Primal Cuts	**Retail Cuts**
Loin	Loin chops
	Loin roasts
	Medallions / noisettes
Rack	Rack of lamb
	Rib chops
Leg	Whole leg
	Half leg
	Leg roasts
	Leg steaks
	Cubed leg meat
Shoulder	Shoulder chop
	Lamb shoulder
Breast and foreleg	Ribs / riblets
	Shank

LOIN Lamb loin chops have the same configuration as a T-bone steak of beef or a loin chop of veal or pork. The loin is also sold as a roast, most regally with both sides attached, which is called a saddle of lamb. When the saddle is cut into chops, they are called double loin chops and look like two T-bone steaks fused together. Crosscuts of a boneless loin are called medallions or noisettes.

RACK A rack of lamb corresponds to a standing rib roast of beef. It consists of 8 ribs that run from the shoulder to the loin down one side of the spine; the eye of the rack is a continuation of the main muscle in the loin. When the rib bones are trimmed of meat and fat, leaving just the eye and cap of meat, the rack is said to be "frenched." A foresaddle of lamb consists of both sides of the rack still attached to one another, and a crown roast consists of two or three sides tied together with their ribs arching outward to resemble a crown.

LEG Unlike the legs of larger animals, a primal leg of lamb is sold with the hip bone still attached, which gives the roast a dramatic shape but can be problematic for carving. Most of the time you will want the aitchbone (hipbone) removed. The hip half and leg half are also sold separately, and either can be bought boneless, in which case they are usually rolled and netted. If you're grill-roasting a boneless leg, ask your butcher to tie the leg rather than net it, because it's difficult to remove the net after cooking over an open fire. A cross section of leg is sold as center-cut leg chops or steaks (these have a round bone) or as lamb sirloin chops or steaks (these have several oddly shaped bones); both grill well.

TOUGH CUTS: SHOULDER, BREAST, AND SHANK The tougher cuts are delicious grilled over indirect low heat. They need time for their fibers to soften, but because they are well marbled they never dry out. A period of marinating helps to add flavor and tenderize the meat.

CUTS OF LAMB FOR GRILLING

Retail Cut	Primal Cut	Other Names	Description	How to Grill
Ground lamb	Trimmings	Burger	Red, aromatic, rich, smooth texture	Direct, medium heat
Loin chops	Loin	Center-cut chop	Red, fine grained, fat cap, T-bone	Direct, medium-high heat
Loin roast	Loin	Center-cut loin roast	Red, fine grained, fat cap	Indirect, medium heat
Rib chops	Rib	Center-cut chop	Red, fine grained, fat cap, rib bone	Direct, medium-high heat
Rack	Rib	Crown roast	Red, fine grained, fat cap, rib bone	Direct, medium-high heat
Shoulder	Shoulder	Shoulder roast or shoulder chops	Fatty, coarse grained, several muscles run in different directions	Indirect, medium-low heat
Shank	Foreleg	—	Coarse grain, small muscle groups surrounded by connective tissue, usually whole	Indirect, medium-low heat
Sirloin	Loin	Sirloin roast or steak	Medium-fine grain, often attached to leg	Direct, medium heat
Riblets	Breast	Spareribs	Fatty, medium grain, flavorful	Indirect, medium heat
Spring lamb	Whole	Baby lamb	Whole baby lamb weighing 30 to 35 pounds, pale, tender, succulent, crisp skin	Indirect, medium-low heat
Tenderloin	Loin	Filet, tender	Silken texture, very tender, lean	Direct, medium-high heat

The anatomy of wild animals is the same as that of other animals raised for meat. By comparing a wild animal to its domesticated counterpart, you will know its primal cuts, its relative flavor, and the best ways to grill it. The principal differences will be in texture and flavor.

Contrary to their succulent image in folklore and film, game meats are usually drier and tougher than meat bred for food. This makes sense when you think about the factors that make meat tender and juicy. Wild animals get lots of exercise, making their muscles tough and flavorful, and unlike livestock they don't spend their last months in a feed lot gorging on high-calorie grain, so their muscles have little marbling.

The majority of game meats sold commercially is not wild. Venison, bison, rabbit, alligator, duck, pheasant, and quail are all farm raised, an agriculture that breeds animals to be close to their wild roots, fed on the kinds of foods found in the wild, and given a maximum of exercise, all within confines that permit the producer to control the quality of the finished product. Farm-raised game meats are more consistent than their wild counterparts, and can be raised to have particular culinary qualities, but they will never develop the depth of flavor of an animal that runs free.

You can substitute wild meats in recipes designed for their domestic brethren by marinating or brining, shortening the cooking time to compensate for the lack of fat, and lowering the temperature to help the meat tenderize.

The following chart lists the most commonly available game meats, their choicest cuts, and how to grill them.

GAME AND SPECIALTY MEATS FOR GRILLING

Meat	Primal Cut	Retail Cut	Description	How to Grill
Alligator (farm raised)	Tail	Medallions	White meat, lean, flavor like chicken or rabbit, fishy aftertaste, slightly watery	Direct, medium heat
Alligator (farm raised)	Rib	Ribs	Pale pink meat, marbled, full flavored	Marinate, indirect, medium-low heat
Beefalo Bison	Rib, loin, sirloin	Steaks	Deep red meat, very lean, like beef but coarser, best cooked rarer than beef	Marinate, direct, medium-high heat
Boar (preferably young)	Rib, loin, ham	Roasts	Red meat, relatively lean, mild if young, cook like pork or venison	Marinate, indirect, medium-low heat
Goat (preferably kid)	Whole, shoulder, leg	Roasts	Light colored, mild, lean, cook like lamb	Marinate, indirect, low heat
Goat (preferably kid)	Rib, loin	Chops, steaks	Light colored, mild, lean, cook like lamb	Direct, medium heat
Rabbit	Whole	Whole	White meat, mild, lean, cook like veal	Marinate or brine, indirect, medium heat
Venison (farm raised)	Rib, loin, sirloin	Roasts	Dark red, lean, fine grained, moist, cook similar to beef but rarer	Marinate, indirect, medium heat
Venison (farm raised)	Rib, loin, sirloin	Steaks	Dark red, lean, fine grained, moist, cook similar to beef but rarer	Marinate, direct, medium-high heat

Chickens are odd birds. Their puny wings have no more chance to lift their girth in prolonged flight than a human's arms do. Their legs are those of a sumo wrestler, and their Mae West breasts are better suited to take to a sauce than the skies. Bred away from their ornithological roots, chickens, turkeys, and geese are now primarily culinary animals.

Commercial poultry is raised to develop at lightning speed on minimum feed. Currently it takes only 8 pounds of feed to grow a chicken to 4 pounds in just 6 weeks—a supreme feat of animal husbandry that results in meat that is remarkably consistent and inevitably bland, due to the fact that the animals spend their brief lives packed into cages where they get hardly any exercise. When you add in the fact that poultry raised under these conditions must be pumped with antibiotics to keep its meat wholesome, it's easy to understand the groundswell of popularity for free-range poultry. Although the term brings forth images of chickens and turkeys gamboling through fields, "free-range" technically means only that the birds have access to an open pen for a few hours a day. Unfortunately, most chickens and turkeys, being hopeless underachievers, fail to take advantage of this opportunity.

All poultry is inspected by the USDA to ensure that it is free of disease and safe for consumption. Inspected poultry is wholesome, but it is not sterile. It still contains bacteria that can cause illness, and so the USDA requires that all poultry be labeled with safe-handling procedures, which include storage methods (refrigerated or frozen), thawing directions (refrigerator or microwave), cleaning advice (sterilizing work surfaces after preparation), cooking process (minimum temperature of 170°F), and how to store leftovers (refrigeration).

Unlike meats, where only the best carcasses are graded for quality, almost all poultry sold in the United States is graded. Grading is voluntary, but most poultry companies opt in, and practically all of the poultry sold—including whole birds and parts—is graded "A." It indicates that the bird has rounded, heavy muscles, a layer of fat under the skin, and is free of unsightly defects, like rips in the skin, broken bones, and surface discoloration.

Poultry is classified by species (chickens, turkeys, duck, etc.) and then divided into classes based on the characteristics of their meat, which is determined mostly by the age and sex of the bird. The classes of poultry for grilling are described in the following chart.

CLASSES OF POULTRY FOR GRILLING

Poultry	Description	How to Grill
Chicken		
Cornish game hen	Immature, less than 5 weeks, either sex, 2 pounds or less	Whole: indirect, medium heat Split: direct, medium heat
Broiler/fryer	Young, less than 10 weeks, either sex, flexible breastbone tip	Whole or split: indirect, medium heat Parts: direct, medium heat
Roaster	Young, less than 12 weeks, either sex, less flexible breastbone tip	Whole or split: indirect, medium heat Parts: direct, medium heat
Turkey		
Fryer/roaster	Immature, less than 12 weeks, either sex, flexible breastbone tip	Indirect, medium heat
Young	Less than 6 months, either sex, less flexible breastbone tip	Indirect, medium heat

Poultry	Description	How to Grill
Turkey (continued)		
Yearling	Fully matured, less than 15 months, either sex (can be identified)	Indirect, medium heat
Mature hen or tom	Adult turkey, more than 15 months, either sex (usually identified)	Indirect, medium-low heat
Duck		
Duckling	Young, less than 8 weeks, either sex, soft bill and soft windpipe	Whole or split: indirect, medium heat Parts: direct, medium heat
Roaster	Young, less than 16 weeks, either sex, bill not completely hardened, windpipe easily dented	Whole or split: indirect, medium heat Parts: direct, medium heat

01. POULTRY CUTS

Poultry can be sold whole, halved, or cut into parts. The parts can be sold individually by the pound, or the separate parts of a single bird can be packaged together. In that case all of the parts must come from the same bird; if they don't, it should be noted on the label. Chickens and turkeys can be divided into five-, six-, or eight-part cuts. Ducks and geese are most often sold whole, or the breast is sold alone.

POULTRY PARTS

1. Five-Part Cut
a. Wing
b. Full breast
c. Full leg

2. Six-Part Cut
a. Wing
b. Breast half
c. Full leg

3. Eight-Part Cut
a. Wing
b. Breast half
c. Thigh
d. Drumstick

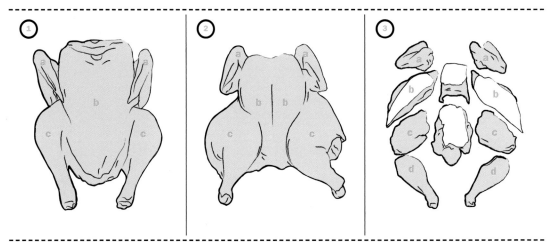

Anyone who has been asked, as the bird is being carved, "White or dark?" knows that chicken and turkey meat comes in two colors. The breast is paler, drier, and leaner; the legs are darker, moister, and richer; and the wings lie somewhere in between. But have you ever wondered why?

Although animal behavior is diverse, the movement of animals can be divided simply into two broad categories: fast, sudden movement, as when a bird is startled, and deliberate, persistent movement, as when a chicken pecks for food in the yard or cattle stand grazing in a field.

Two types of muscle fibers are associated with these two forms of movement. White muscle fibers are used for quick, sudden movements, and darker-pigmented red muscle fibers control slower and more prolonged movement. Each type of fiber uses a different energy supply, which accounts largely for the difference in color.

White muscle fibers are fueled by glycogen, a small supply of carbohydrate stored directly in the muscle fiber. When an animal gets a sudden urge to bolt, the glycogen can be rapidly converted into energy by enzymes right in the muscle cells, delivering energy to a muscle almost instantaneously. Normally, white muscle cells use oxygen to help metabolize glycogen. But when energy is needed faster than oxygen can be delivered by the blood, these cells have the capability to use glycogen without the presence of oxygen. When that happens, a waste product, lactic acid, builds up in the muscle cells, which limits the muscle's endurance. Eventually, the excess lactic acid is removed and the glycogen is replaced, but that requires rest. That is why white muscle fibers are used for short bursts of energy followed by a period of recuperation.

Red muscle fibers are fueled by fat, which definitely needs oxygen in order to be metabolized. Red fibers are fairly thin, allowing them easy access to oxygen and fat (in the form of fatty acids) from the blood circulating around them. They also contain their own supply of fat and the ability to break that fat down into energy. In order to function properly, this mechanism is dependent on myoglobin, a pigment that gives red muscle fibers their color. Myoglobin receives oxygen from the blood and passes it on to fat-oxidizing proteins in the muscle fiber, similar to the way its relative, hemoglobin, carries oxygen through the blood. Both myoglobin and hemoglobin are red due to the presence of iron. The more a red muscle fiber is exercised, the greater its oxygen needs will be, and the more myoglobin it will contain.

Because most of the muscles in an animal perform a mixture of rapid and slow movements, they are built from both white and red muscle fibers. The ratio of white to red depends on the muscle's genetic design and how it is used during the animal's life. So chickens and turkeys, which tend to flap their wings rapidly for short periods of time when agitated, will have a predominance of white muscle fibers in their breasts and wings, while their legs, which are used for prolonged periods of walking and standing, will have a higher concentration of red muscle fibers, giving the muscles in those parts a darker hue. Cattle, which rarely startle and bolt, are red-meated throughout, and game birds that fly steadily for long distances tend to have wing and breast meat that is quite dark.

02. FAT AND SKIN

Unlike four-legged livestock, poultry is sold with its skin on. This helps to keep the meat moist while cooking, both by forming a protective layer that inhibits drying and by sheathing it in a layer of fat that melts into the meat as it grills. For that reason, it's a good idea to grill poultry with the skin on, even if you are planning to serve it without the skin.

If you want to decrease the amount of fat, cut away all visible pockets before cooking. When preparing particularly fatty poultry, like duck and goose, for grilling, you need to melt the fat, either by scalding the bird under a stream of boiling water prior to cooking or by starting the cooking over high heat to get the fat moving and then reducing the heat to cook the meat through. A drip pan should always be used with fatty poultry to keep the fat from dripping directly into the fire and causing flare-ups.

C. MASTERING SEAFOOD

Seafood is the largest source of edible wildlife in the world. For most of us, eating wild animals is rare. The animals we eat have been bred away from their wild state over generations, to a standard of tenderness and flavor that we have come to expect as normal. So the chicken you purchase in July tastes very much the same as the one you bought in January.

Meat from wild animals, on the other hand, is subject to numerous changing variables. The quality of most seafood is dependent on factors such as the time of year it was caught, where the animal lived, what its diet was like, and how the animal was processed after it was killed. All of which means that when you are dealing with seafood or any wild meat, its quality can vary from season to season—or from day to day—even when sold in the same market.

01. FISH

The fishing industry has tried to control some of the vagaries of the wild by farming the most popular varieties of fish, like salmon, trout, sea bass, turbot, mahimahi, yellowfin, and tuna. Like other meats, farmed fish grow faster than their counterparts in the wild, and they are often more tender and richer tasting. They are harvested without suffering the stress and damage of being hooked or netted, and they are processed closer to the time when and nearer to the place where they are caught.

But the aquaculture story is not all positive. Raising fish in ocean pens has contaminated nearby water with waste products, food, and antibiotics. There have been cases of genetically modified farmed fish escaping into the environment, where they infiltrate the diversity of the surrounding wild population, and some studies have shown that fish meal, which is the primary component of aquaculture feed, contains elevated levels of environmental toxins, particularly PCBs, that accumulate in the flesh of farmed salmon.

How a fish lived determines most of its culinary attributes (some people think farmed fish taste bland and fatty; others think they are mild and rich), which makes it imperative that consumers become familiar not just with the signs of wholesomeness but with the qualities of particular fish families before purchasing.

CLASSES OF FISH

Fish are categorized in a number of ways. The broadest classification is the one made between fish that live in freshwater and fish that live in the sea. Saltwater fish make up the bulk of the fish available in coastal areas. Except for mass-produced farmed fish, most freshwater fish are available only in the regions where they were caught.

Saltwater fish are broadly classified by body shape into two groups, round fish and flatfish, of which round fish is the larger classification. Round fish are about as wide from side to side as they are from back to belly, giving them a rounded silhouette when cut in cross section. They include such common fish as cod, trout, bass, and perch. Flatfish, on the other hand, are usually no more than an inch or two in depth from side to side but can be several feet wide from the dorsal fin on their back to the pelvic fin on their belly side. They have an oblique silhouette in cross section and include 200 species of flounder, sole, and halibut.

FISH TYPE
1. Round fish body shape
2. Flatfish body shape

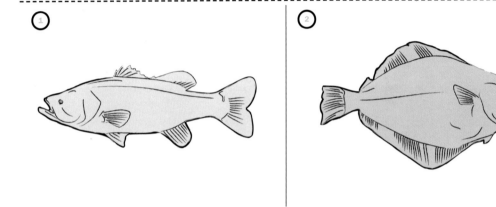

Round fish can be further categorized into lean and fat fish. Lean fish have a fat content of between 0 and 5 percent of their body weight. Since most of this fat is concentrated in the liver, which is removed when the fish is dressed, the actual edible portion of fat is even lower. Lean fish tend to have pale, dry flesh and a subtle, unassertive flavor. Fat fish can have a body fat content of anywhere from 5 to 35 percent, and unlike lean fish, the fat is distributed throughout the entire body. Fat fish have moist, assertively flavored flesh, which is generally dark in color and dense in structure. Incidentally, all flatfish are lean.

The chart on the facing page lists the most common fish, classified by body shape and fat content, including a description and how we like to grill them.

Fish	Shape	Description	How to Grill
Bluefish	Round	Soft, dark meated, fatty, strong flavor, vary in size	Large: indirect, medium-high heat Small: direct, medium-high heat
Catfish	Round	Freshwater, pale flesh, meaty, firm, sweet	Fillet: direct, medium-high heat
Cod	Round	Large, lean, firm flesh, white meat, large flakes, mild	Steaks: indirect, medium-high heat
Dolphin (mahimahi)	Round	Firm, lean, large flakes, white meat, sweet flavor	Direct, medium-high heat
Eel	Round	Fatty, fine flake, rich	Skinned: direct, medium heat
Flounder	Flat	White, lean, delicate flake, mild	Direct, medium-high heat
Halibut	Flat	Large flounder	Direct, medium-high heat
Herring	Round	Rich, delicate flake, dark, assertive flavor	Boneless fillet: direct, high heat
Mackerel	Round	Rich, delicate flake, dark, assertive flavor	Fillet: direct, medium-high heat
Monkfish	Round	Only eat tail, meaty, white flesh, sweet flavor	Indirect, medium-high heat
Pompano	Round	Mild, flaky, sweet flavor	Direct, medium heat
Red snapper	Round	White meat, sweet, large flakes, mild	Indirect, medium-high heat
Salmon	Round	Red to pink flesh, rich, assertive flavor, wild has less fat than farm raised	Whole: indirect, medium heat Fillet or steak: direct, medium-high heat
Shad	Round	Rich, delicate flake, dark, assertive flavor	Boneless fillet: direct, medium-high heat
Shark	Round	Firm, meaty, strong tasting	Steaks: direct, medium heat
Striped bass (rockfish)	Round	White, large flakes, mild, sweet	Indirect, medium-high heat
Sturgeon	Round	Very large, firm flesh, rich, meaty	Medallions: direct, medium heat
Swordfish	Round	Dark meat, firm, meaty, assertive flavor	Steaks: direct, medium heat
Tuna	Round	Dark red, meaty, firm, assertive	Steaks: direct, medium-high heat; cook only to rare
Turbot	Flat	Large flounder	Direct, medium-high heat
Trout	Round	Freshwater, meaty, tender, whole fish	Direct, medium-high heat

Because of the perishability of most fish, they should be cooked and eaten as close to the time of purchase as possible. However, if it becomes necessary to store fish for a day or two, here are a few tricks that will prolong its freshness:

- Remove the guts from any fish before it is stored. The organs of a fish harbor its largest source of bacterial contamination. Once they are removed, the degree and speed of decay are greatly diminished. Also, digestive enzymes in fish are very powerful. If permitted to remain in the belly of the fish long after it has been caught, these enzymes will eat away at the walls of the body cavity, making the interior flesh prone to bacterial decay.
- Compared to other meats, the muscle tissue of most fish is relatively weak, making it an easy mark for bacteria living on the surface of the fish or those in the air. To inhibit bacterial growth, it's a good idea to rinse a fish off in lightly salted water before it is stored. This will destroy any surface bacteria and inhibit more from growing. About 1 teaspoon of salt in 1 cup of water will help keep fish fresher without altering its flavor.
- Keep fish cold. It is best to keep fish under refrigeration packed in ice, but this is good only if the fish is in a perforated container so that water from the melting ice can drip away. The perforated container could be a large colander or a vegetable grill tray. Never store fish directly in water. If you don't have a perforated container, wrap the fish loosely in a plastic bag and place it over ice. Change the ice as needed. Even with these precautions, fish should be used within one to two days of purchase.
- It is never preferable to freeze fish. Freezing breaks down the tissue of all foods, and if that tissue was weak to begin with, as it is in fish, the damage can be drastic. However, if you must freeze fish, make sure it is as fresh as possible. An old fish will not become fresher in the freezer. Clean it well and wrap it tightly in plastic and then in a layer of paper or foil. Freeze the fish quickly; the faster it freezes solid, the less damage will be done. In fact, if you know before you buy it that you will have to freeze a fish, either delay buying it or buy it already frozen. Commercially frozen fish are processed immediately after they are caught, and they are flash frozen to a solid state, so the results will be better than those you can achieve at home.

Regardless of the type of fish you are buying, all fresh fish have certain standard qualities:

- Fresh fish have firm flesh. Poke the side of a fish in its thickest portion. The imprint of your finger should spring right back. If it leaves an impression, it is an indication that the flesh has begun to decompose.
- A fresh fish will have clear, clean eyes that bulge outward slightly. Reject specimens with sunken or cloudy eyes.
- Lift the gill flaps at the back of the head and look at the spongy gills inside. They should be bright red or pink, without hints of brown or gray.
- The skin of the fish should have a full covering of scales that are firmly attached. The characteristic skin color should be bright and should have no blemishes or reddish patches under its surface.
- Perfectly fresh fish has no odor whatsoever, except possibly the faint aroma of seawater. Any fishy odor is an indication of decay. In fact, this smell test is a fairly accurate way of choosing a fish store. When a store smells fishy, something's not right behind the counter.

Once you have chosen your fish, you can prepare it in a number of ways, depending on how it is to be cooked. Here are some definitions.

WHOLE DRESSED. The fish has been scaled and gutted, and its gills have been removed. Its head and tail will still be on. Whole dressed fish are suitable for indirect grilling (and are wonderful stuffed). If the fish is 2 inches or less in thickness, it can be grilled with direct heat.

PAN DRESSED. The fish has been scaled and gutted, with the head removed. It can be cooked in the same way as whole dressed fish.

SCORED. The whole dressed or pan-dressed fish has been slashed on the sides to allow heat to permeate the flesh more quickly. Scoring is usually done by the consumer, not the fishmonger.

FILLET. The term "fillet" refers to the sides of a fish cut lengthwise free from its backbone. The rib cage can be removed or not. A fillet cut does not mean the piece of fish is boneless, only that the central spine and its attached ribs have been separated from the meat. When the fillets of a fish are left jointed at the backside, it is called a butterfly fillet. When it is cut along the back and left jointed at the belly, as is done for some stuffed dishes, the fillet is called a kited fillet.

SPLIT. The fish has been cut into two fillets; usually the head and tail all removed. In this presentation, the central bone can be removed or not. It is typically used for stuffing a fish before cooking it.

STEAK. This cut is a cross section of a round-bodied fish that has been scaled and gutted. A portion of the backbone is left on to help hold the meat together. When a steak has a horseshoe shape, it is from the section nearest the head and is said to be center cut. If the steak is an oval shape, it is from the section closer to the tail, or the loin. Steaks are great for grilling, because the meat will not tear if it should stick.

02. SHELLFISH

Unlike fish that swim, shellfish don't have an internal skeleton, and consequently they don't move around much. There are two main groups: crustaceans and mollusks. Crustaceans include lobsters, crabs, crayfish, and shrimp. Mollusks are made up of single-shelled animals like abalone; double-shelled animals like mussels, clams, oysters, and scallops; and animals that have internalized their shells, namely squid and octopus.

CRUSTACEANS

Crustaceans are part of the largest phylum or group, *Arthropoda,* which includes most insects. Like insects, crustaceans have segmented exoskeletons that protect and support their muscles and organs, as well as several

---

appendages adapted to swimming, walking, and hunting. Crustaceans are composed of two sections. The head, or cephalothorax, is forward and corresponds to our head and torso; the tail, or abdomen, is usually the larger part, composed of a strong, meaty muscle used for swimming. The exception to this structure is the crab, which has a large cephalothorax, but because it doesn't swim, its abdomen consists of a thin plate that tucks under the thorax.

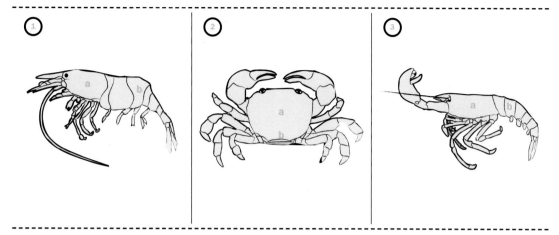

CRUSTACEAN BODY STRUCTURES

1. Shrimp
a. Cephalothorax (head)
b. Abdomen (tail)

2. Crab
a. Cephalothorax (head)
b. Abdomen (tail)

3. Lobster
a. Cephalothorax (head)
b. Abdomen (tail)

In order for crustaceans to grow, they must periodically molt or shed their shells. To make the transition, the animal forms a tough cuticle over its body, crawls from its shell, and pumps itself up with water (up to twice its original body weight) to stretch the cuticle to its maximum size. Gradually, the cuticle mineralizes and hardens, forming a new shell with enough room for growth.

Molting means that the flesh of wild crustaceans varies seasonally, with large, dense muscles right before molting and meat that is more than half water immediately afterward. In general, crustaceans are considered inedible once they've shed their shells, except for soft-shell crabs, which are watched carefully and removed from the water as soon as they shed their shells, to ensure that the new cuticle does not have a chance to harden.

Crustaceans are highly perishable, spoiling within hours of death. For that reason, lobsters and crabs are always sold alive or cooked. Shrimp are beheaded (which removes the part of the animal that spoils quickest) and the tail meat is frozen. Shrimp that are sold with the head on need more careful handling (frequent icing) and are more perishable than headless shrimp. Shrimp freeze exceptionally well, and all shrimp are frozen as close to harvesting as possible. Even when you purchase "fresh" shrimp, they have been previously frozen and then thawed in the store. This means that frozen shrimp are actually closer to fresh than the shrimp labeled "fresh" in the fish case.

SHRIMP are sold by "count," which is the number of shrimp in a pound. The lower the count, the larger the shrimp. Shrimp that are very large are often called "prawns" in the States, although in the rest of the world a prawn is a different crustacean altogether. The following chart lists industry shrimp counts and the retail names that are usually assigned to them. Shrimp that are larger than 26–30 are best for grilling. Any shrimp larger than U-10 should be butterflied (split lengthwise and opened like a book) to help them cook evenly.

SHRIMP COUNTS

Count per Pound	Weight per Shrimp	Retail Name
Under 10 (U-10)	1.60 oz or more	Extra colossal
10–15 (U-15)	1.25 oz	Colossal
16–20	1.00 oz	Extra jumbo
21–25	0.73 oz	Jumbo
26–30	0.57 oz	Extra large
31–35	0.50 oz	Large
36–40	0.42 oz	Medium large
41–50	0.35 oz	Medium
51–60	0.28 oz	Small
61–70	0.24 oz	Extra small (titi)

SPLITTING A LOBSTER FOR GRILLING

1. Put the live lobster on a rimmed baking sheet. Uncurl the tail and lay it out flat. Insert a sharp knife just behind the head and cut the shell of the thorax in half lengthwise.

2. Turn the lobster onto its back. Insert your knife into the abdomen of the lobster right where the tail meets the thorax, with the edge of the blade facing the head. In one motion, bring the knife down the center line of the body, splitting the front end of the lobster in half.

3. Now reverse directions and split the posterior end in the same way. Separate the two halves by pressing lightly on them. Remove the sand sac from the head and discard. Remove the light green tomalley from the body cavity and, if present, the long sac of dark green roe that runs down the back of the lobster. These can be saved and used to flavor a stuffing or thicken a sauce. The lobster is now ready for grilling, or it can be separated into claw and tail sections.

Although more than 300 species of commercial shrimp are fished from all over the world, almost all of the shrimp in the U.S. market are warm-water shrimp, which are categorized by the color of their shells when raw: white, brown, pink, and black tiger.

- White shrimp have grayish white shells when raw that turn pink when cooked. The flesh is white to pink.
- Brown shrimp have tan shells when raw that become coral when cooked. The meat is white with coral streaks.
- Pink shrimp have pink shells that turn deep pink after cooking. The flesh is white with pink overtones.
- Tiger shrimp are the fastest-growing farmed shrimp and are often lower priced than other types. Their shells are black-and-gray striped and turn bright red when cooked. The meat is white with a red skin.

To clean a shrimp, remove the shell. If the shrimp are large and you are not tossing them with other ingredients, you can leave the end of the tail on; otherwise, remove it. The "vein" in the crevice running along the outside curve of the shrimp is the tail end of the digestive tract. It can be filled with sand and grit and should be removed, especially if it is dark in color. Frozen cleaned and shelled shrimp are available, but they tend not to be as fresh as shrimp that have been frozen intact.

LOBSTER There are two orders of lobster: Atlantic lobsters, which live in seawater, and crayfish, which live in fresh-water. Both are similarly structured, with large tails and enlarged pincers on their forelegs. Spiny and rock lobsters are their distant clawless relatives. They are usually sold for their tail meat alone and are the principal source for frozen lobster tail.

Unlike shrimp, lobsters must be sold alive or cooked. Choose live lobsters that are active and feisty; they will keep well for a day in the refrigerator covered with damp newspaper or seaweed. It is dangerous to cook a dead lobster, unless it succumbs before your eyes and you cook it immediately. This is due mostly to enzymes in the midgut gland (tomalley or liver), a creamy, pale green mass located in the thorax of the lobster, which are released as soon as a lobster dies and will start to break down its meat within hours. To keep this from happening, you can remove the tail and claw sections and discard the thorax. The tail and claw meat can then be stored in the refrigerator for a day or so without ill effect.

Since putting a live lobster on a hot grill is not an option (unless you ascribe to the Marquis de Sade school of cooking), you must kill the lobster before you grill it. There are two sides to consider before you kill for food. One is ethical and the other is technical. Ethically, we must come to terms with the fact that the killing is necessary, and technically we have to know how to do it as efficiently as possible.

The question asked most frequently when discussing this subject is, "Does the animal feel any pain?" We have been told repeatedly by experienced cooking teachers and chefs that shellfish feel no pain when they are killed. Yet whenever we drop a crab into a pot or split a lobster for grilling, the flailing of legs and claws is as good an imitation of pain as we have seen.

It is our belief that death hurts, and that those who tell themselves their victims feel no pain are only trying to ease their own discomfort. Yet if we are going to cook with shellfish we must kill them. The question then becomes not whether a lobster can feel pain (no one really knows how much pain a lobster feels; it doesn't have a central nervous system, and its brain receives input only from its antennae and eyes), but how to perform the killing quickly and efficiently so the animal does not suffer unnecessarily.

Most people prefer to boil lobster, probably because it requires a minimum of hand-to-hand combat. To boil lobsters, bring enough seasoned liquid to a boil to cover all of the shellfish by an inch. The liquid can be salted water, a combination of wine or beer with water, or a complex brew of spices and herbs. Drop the lobster into the rapidly boiling water and cover the pot. When the pot returns to a boil the lobster has ceased living, and you can finish cooking it on the grill.

This is fine, except that the results taste more boiled than grilled. For a more authentic grilled flavor, we prefer to cook lobster totally over the fire, which means splitting and dividing the animal before cooking (see the sidebar at left).

MOLLUSKS

Mollusks are a weird bunch of critters. The group is large and diverse. It hardly seems possible that an oyster and an octopus could be related, and because most mollusks are covered by shell and lack distinguishable body parts, to the casual observer they may appear more like rocks than food. The key to their diversity is the adaptability of their three main body parts: (1) a tough, muscular foot for moving; (2) a nonsegmented visceral mass that includes the sensing, circulatory, digestive, and sexual organs; and (3) the mantle, an extension of the body wall that is responsible for excreting a shell and supporting the eyes and small tentacles that detect food or danger.

Mollusks that can be grilled fall into three classes: gastropods, bivalves, and cephalopods. Each combines the same body parts in a unique way. Abalone is the only gastropod that can be grilled. It has a single broad, shallow shell that covers a wide, muscular foot, which is the part we eat. Because abalone is tough, it should be marinated and grilled just until browned and heated through. Overcooking will make it inedibly tough.

Clams, mussels, oysters, and scallops are bivalves. They have two shells, hinged on one side. Clams have a large foot, which they use to burrow deep into sand, and a siphon that can be extended up to the sand surface and used to suck in passing food. Their mantle has diversified into a mechanism that helps them open and close their shells. A ligament on the narrow side of the shells attaches the shells and pulls them together, causing the other side to open up. If a predator should approach, clams can close their shells suddenly and tightly (clam up) by constricting two tough muscles that extend between the shells. These adductor (from the Latin *adducere,* "to bring together") muscles are the main reason that clams are a commercial food source. If it weren't for them, clams would dehydrate quickly after being drawn from the sea, but because the adductors keep them tightly closed, clams can stay alive under refrigeration for days. If the shell of a raw clam is open, the clam has probably died and should not be eaten. To make sure, tap on the shell firmly; if the clam closes, it is fine but should be cooked as soon as possible.

Some clams don't follow this model. Their siphons extend beyond the rims of their shells, making it impossible to close them up. These "soft-shell" clams are highly perishable and need to be cooked as close to purchase as possible.

Mussels are similar to clams, except that they attach their feet permanently to rocks, where they can filter food from water that passes between their shells. They have no need for a siphon, and one adductor muscle is always larger than the other. Oysters also attach themselves to rocks but have much thicker, heavier shells than mussels, with a single large adductor muscle at their center.

Clams, mussels, and oysters are easy to grill. Start by scrubbing the shells clean. Any of them, but especially clams, benefit by being immersed in ice-cold salt water (1 tablespoon salt per 3 cups water) for several hours, which will help them expel sand and grit. To cook them, after checking that all are tightly closed, put the shellfish in a metal pan (a disposable aluminum one is fine) with seasoning, cover, and grill over medium direct heat until the mollusks open. As soon as they open they are done. Discard any that are still closed.

Scallops neither burrow nor attach themselves to rocks. They sit freely on the ocean floor, and when a predator approaches they use their adductor muscles to open and close their shells, propelling themselves away. Scallops cannot clamp shut, and because of that they are very susceptible to dehydration when they are caught. In fact, they are so perishable that only the single large adductor muscle, which is less prone to spoilage, is commonly sold.

Did you ever wonder why a scallop doesn't look anything like a clam, mussel, or oyster? Adductor muscles have two functions—they close the shells, and they hold them closed. The portion of the muscle that closes the shell is made up of quick-responding white muscle fiber that is very tender; the part that keeps the shells closed, on the other hand, is one of the strongest and toughest muscles known. These clamping muscle fibers are abundant in the adductors of other mollusks, but in scallops they are relatively tiny. You will notice them on most scallops as a tiny rubbery flap attached to one side. Be sure to remove this flap before cooking, or it will make the scallop incredibly tough.

Squid and octopuses are mollusks turned inside out. The remnant of the shell forms an internal bony support, and the mantle forms a sheet of muscle that expands and contracts, creating jet propulsion that powers the animal through the water. The body sac and the tentacles of squid and small octopuses can be grilled. Once they are cleaned, there is no special technique, other than doing everything in one's power to get them brown before they overcook. As soon as they are firm, they are done, which means they are best grilled over the highest possible flame for the shortest possible time.

D. MASTERING PRODUCE

Vegetables vary greatly. Some are leaves. Some are roots. Some are stems. Some can even be fruits. The same vegetable can go by several names, and the same plant can produce a number of distinct vegetables, which is why judging vegetable quality is such a complex issue.

Looking, smelling, and poking are not enough. It helps to know what you're looking at. It helps to know that although white and purple eggplant may look different, once you get them peeled and diced they cook up and taste exactly the same. It's good to know that a Jerusalem artichoke is not anything like the more commonly seen globe artichoke, and that kale, cabbage, collard, broccoli, cauliflower, kohlrabi, and brussels sprouts are all different members of the same plant family.

It would be impossible to detail all the idiosyncrasies of every vegetable in the space we have here, nor is it necessary. To understand vegetables, just look at their interconnections.

Spinach and lettuce might be unrelated, but they're both leaves and therefore have similar traits. Cauliflower and mushrooms have nothing to do with one another botanically, but they demand the same precautions in cooking because they're both white. New potatoes share more culinary characteristics with spring peas than they do with mature potatoes, because both are young. The part of the plant from which a vegetable comes, its color, its age, and how it has been stored are what determine a vegetable's qualities.

01. ROOTS

Let's start at the bottom and work our way up the plant. Roots hold the plant in the ground, from which they absorb nutrients and store them as starch and sugar. Like all storage units, roots need strong walls and lots of space. Plant fibers are rigid and contain within their walls large storage chambers (vacuoles). As the plant matures, the vacuoles pack in more sugar and get bigger; at the same time, their walls thicken and get harder. The quality of a root vegetable is therefore a delicate balance between sweetness and toughness. Harvest it too soon and it will be puny and lack flavor; wait too long and its fibers will turn wooden.

This is why the quality of root vegetables is best judged by their size. Small = mild and tender. Medium = crunchy and sweet. Large = tough and tasty. In any bunch of beets or carrots, it's likely that you'll get vegetables of different sizes. The larger ones may need to be cooked briefly in liquid to tenderize them before grilling; smaller roots can be grilled directly.

Working our way up, let's look at tubers, such as white potatoes, water chestnuts, Jerusalem artichokes, and yams. Botanically, these are underground stems, not root vegetables. But because they look like roots, grow like roots, store starch the same way roots do, and are cooked like other roots, culinarily they are considered root vegetables.

02. STEMS

Stems do two things. First, they hold up the plant, lifting the leaves toward the sun. Second, they act as a nutrient throughway: Stems contain the veins through which nutrients stored in the root move up to the leaves, fruits, and flowers, and through which sugars manufactured in the leaves descend back down for storage in the roots. To perform these functions, stems are structured a lot like roots. They have rigid support fibers interspersed with hollow veins, but unlike roots, stem fibers are not tough enough to do the job alone. They must be helped by a steady flow of fluid in the veins in order to have the snap (a brief resistance followed by a burst of juice) that indicates quality in a stem vegetable. If the vascular tissue dehydrates, the stem will lose its crispness, and the vegetable will become limp.

In some stem vegetables, like celery or fennel, crispness can be restored by submerging the stalks in ice water. This forces water back into the dehydrated veins. But other stem produce, like asparagus and broccoli, needs to be peeled before it can be revived. These vegetables have a water-resistant skin that delays water loss but also inhibits the ability of the vegetable to regain crispness after it dries out.

03. FRUITS AND VEGETABLES

Fruit is the part of a plant that protects and nourishes the seed until it is ready to grow into a new plant. As the seed matures, the fruit ripens, until it is fully colored, loaded with sugar, and bursting with juice, qualities that make it attractive to animals, who hopefully will eat the fruit and scatter the seed, thus helping the plant species to flourish.

According to this description, apples, pears, peaches, cherries, tomatoes, cucumbers, squashes, eggplant, bell peppers, and avocados are all fruits. So why do we call some of these fruits "vegetables"? There are two definitions of "fruit." The one we discussed already is the botanical definition, the role that fruit plays in the life cycle of a plant. But the common use of the word is based on a culinary understanding, which says that fruits are sweet. So any botanical fruit that we don't like to taste sugary (tomatoes, cucumber, squashes, etc.) we call a "vegetable." For the purpose of this discussion, let's call them "fruit-vegetables."

Sweetness develops as a fruit ripens, and for some fruit-vegetables, like tomatoes or corn, that sweet flavor is desirable, but for others, like cucumber or zucchini, ripeness is akin to rottenness. Think about the signs of ripeness—yielding flesh, sweet flowing juice, a potent perfume—is this what you want in a cucumber? Ripe cucumbers are yellow and squishy. Ripe zucchini are flaccid and slimy with seeds. In these fruit-vegetables we want other qualities–firmness, crispness, greenness, and a clean, fresh smell. So go ahead and judge the quality of fruit-fruits by how ripe they are, but choose your fruit-vegetables by the opposite criterion.

Roots, stems, vegetables, and fruits can all be grilled. A few leaf vegetables such as romaine, endive, radicchio, and cabbage can also be deliciously transformed by a short sojourn over a fire. However, the main attraction of moist, delicate leaves in a grilled meal is their ability to refresh the palate after it has been overcome by a plate of spicy barbecue or saturated by the rich juices of a grilled porterhouse.

04. LEAVES

Leaves produce energy for a plant by transforming sun and air into sugar (photosynthesis). To do their job, leaves are broad and flat so that they can capture the maximum amount of sunlight and water. Inside, they have a network of air pockets to help the flow of carbon dioxide and oxygen through the cell walls where photosynthesis takes place. This aerated framework makes leaves much more susceptible to dehydration and bruising than other vegetables. Although they are the most delicate part of a plant, some leaves are heartier than others, and these hearty ones are the best choice for grilling. Cabbage, Brussels sprouts, Belgian endive, radicchio, and romaine all grill beautifully.

05. FLOWERS

The final vegetable form, flowers, are not typically eaten, and only three of them are ever grilled. Broccoli (the buds of cabbage flowers), cauliflower (the sterile curd of the same plant), and artichokes (a thistle encasing a flowery "choke") are all enhanced by grilling, but none of them are fully blooming flowers.

The following chart lists the most appropriate produce for grilling. It includes signs of quality and storage information. For preparation and grilling information, see pages 260 and 306.

PRODUCE FOR GRILLING

Vegetable	Signs of Quality	Storage
Apples	Hard, unblemished	Refrigerate; weeks
Apricots	Tender, bright orange, fragrant	Room temperature; 2 days
Artichoke	Heavy, full, closed, packed, no brown	Refrigerate; 4 days
Asparagus	Closed buds, firm, no wrinkles, dry	Refrigerate; 2 days
Bananas	Firm, yellow skin, little brown	Room temperature; 3 days
Beets	Small, round, no scales, crisp greens	Refrigerate; 1 week
Broccoli	Dark color, closed buds, no yellow	Refrigerate; 4 days
Brussels sprouts	Tight, round heads; small; pale	Refrigerate; 4 days
Cabbage	Heavy for size, tight head, fresh smell, no yellow	Refrigerate; 1 week
Carrots	Whole, uniform, bright, unsprouted	Refrigerate; 2 weeks
Cauliflower	White, tight curd, no spots, fresh leaves	Refrigerate; 4 days
Citrus	Firm, fragrant, full color	Refrigerate; 1 week
Corn	Summer; full ears; heavy, full kernels; dry silks	Don't
Eggplant	Full color, heavy for size, firm, small	Refrigerate; 2 days
Endive (curly, Belgian, escarole, radicchio)	Firm, hearty leaves; no wilting; pale color (except radicchio)	Refrigerate; 2 days
Fennel	Full, round bulb; short ribs; dry leaves; no scars	Refrigerate; 4 days
Figs	Fragrant, yielding, not soft	Refrigerate; 2 days
Garlic	Firm, round, heavy for size, white to purple skin	Cool, dark, dry; 2 weeks
Grapes	Firm, bright color, tight skin	Refrigerate; 4 days
Leeks (and scallions)	Long white section; bright, crisp green leaves; no yellow; small is better	Refrigerate; 2 days
Mangoes	Yielding, bright color	Room temperature; 2 to 3 days
Mushrooms	White to brown, button to plate-size, firm, dry	Refrigerate; 1 to 2 days
Onions	Heavy for size, firm, dry	Cool, dark, dry

Vegetable	Signs of Quality	Storage
Papayas	Yielding, bright color	Room temperature; 2 to 3 days
Parsnips	Uniform, firm, off-white, not brown	Refrigerate, unpeeled; 4 days
Peaches	Fragrant, firm but yielding, no soft spots	Room temperature; 2 to 3 days
Peppers, sweet or hot	Bright, firm, no soft spots	Refrigerate; up to 1 week
Pineapple	Fragrant, no dark spots or off aroma	Room temperature; 2 days
Potatoes, new	Very small, crisp, uniform, dry	Refrigerate; 1 week
Potatoes, russet	Large, long, thick skin, firm	Cool, dark, dry; several weeks
Romaine	Closed heads, assertive flavor, sturdy leaves	Refrigerate; 5 days
Squash, summer (yellow, zucchini)	Bright color, tender, small, firm, no hard or soft spots	Refrigerate; 3 weeks
Squash, winter (acorn, butternut, etc.)	Hard, shiny skin; bright color; smooth; no breaks	Cook, dark, dry; 2 weeks
Sweet potatoes or yams	Orange, red, yellow, or white; hard; no soft spots; uniform	Refrigerate; 1 week
Tomatoes	Bright, not too ripe, no soft spots, aromatic	Room temperature; 2 days

E. GRILLED CHEESE

Cheese is made by separating milk into solid curd and liquid whey. The whey is drained off and the remaining curd (largely a concentrate of the protein and fat that were in the milk) is pressed into a perforated form where it solidifies, after which it is ripened and aged. Depending on the type of animal (cow, sheep, goat, etc.) that the milk came from, what the animal recently ate, and where it lived, the composition of the curd will be different. Depending on how long and under what conditions the curd is aged, the resulting cheese could be hard or soft, pungent or mild, creamy or crumbly, surface-ripened or blue-veined.

All these variables mean that there are literally thousands of cheeses, and most of them will never come close to a grill. There is only one reason to ever grill cheese—to melt it. Here's what you need to know to melt cheese.

Cheese is mostly protein and fat. Dairy fat begins to melt at about 90°F, which causes the cheese to soften slightly and form small beads of liquid fat on the surface. As it gets hotter, the bonds that hold the protein together begin to collapse, and the cheese will slump, eventually pooling into a thick liquid. The ease with which a cheese melts has to do with its moisture content. Creamy, moist cheese, like Brie, will melt when barely warm (about 130°F); firm cheeses like Cheddar or Swiss start to flow at about 150°F; and hard, dry grating cheese such as Parmesan won't show any signs of softening until it gets over 180°F. Some cheeses, like fresh goat cheese, *queso blanco,* and *paneer,* will not melt at all, which means they will not lose their shape during grilling.

F. GRILLED DOUGH

Although it is possible to bake on a grill, the process is problematic and the results are often unpredictable. The only exceptions are flat-breads, like pizza, pita, and naan, which are the right dimension to cook through without scorching, are firm enough to balance on a grill grate, and have the right textural stretch to benefit from a crispy skin speckled with char.

Like all dough, flatbread dough is a mixture of flour and liquid. Flour is composed of two elements—starch and protein. When you add liquid to wheat flour (the principal flour used in baking), the starch expands, giving the dough bulk, and the protein activates, giving the dough structure. The longer you mix the dough, the greater the activity of the protein (called gluten) and the sturdier the finished baked good will be.

The development of gluten can be positive or negative, depending on what you are baking. In bread baking, gluten is essential. It gives bread a chewy consistency and traps gases produced by yeast, which make the bread rise. To encourage gluten development, bread bakers follow three basic guidelines:

· Use high-protein, low-starch flour (bread flour).
· Move the dough as much as possible to encourage the formation of protein bonds.
· Don't add fat or anything else that will interfere with protein bonding.

Glutinous dough stretches well and holds its shape. When it is placed over a fire (direct medium heat for flatbreads), gases trapped in the layers of gluten will expand, causing the dough to bubble and rise. The rim of grilling pizza dough rises higher than the center because it is not held down by sauce, cheese, and other heavy ingredients. Thin flatbreads, like pita, will tend to form a pocket in the center, because their thinness allows for only a few bands of gluten. As the trapped air bubbles expand, there is no place to go, so they merge into an inflated central pocket. Thicker grilled flatbread, like naan (page 343), will have a more even distribution of bubbles.

Although cakes and pastries can't be baked on a grill, they can be warmed and toasted. Because these products tend to be sweet, it is best to use medium-low or medium heat to keep them from burning. It may also be helpful to toast delicate cakes and pastries on a grill screen or some other perforated pan to keep them from crumbling while still exposing them to flame.

CHAPTER 4

MASTERING YOUR FLAVORS

Most recipes are identified by their seasoning, such as (you fill in the blanks) "lemon-rosemary grilled _____," "_____ with fragrant chile rub," and "_____ with wasabi butter." Yet the way a dish is flavored is its most superficial and mutable aspect. A burger is a burger is a burger—that is, until it becomes a burger with Szechwan peppercorns, a mole burger with spicy black beans, or a blue cheese burger flamed in brandy. Nothing has changed about the ground beef in these burgers, how they are formed, the way they are grilled, or the temperature at which they are done cooking. Ninety-nine percent of what makes them hamburgers has remained unchanged, but what a difference that 1 percent of flavor makes.

Most seasoning comes from the aromatic parts of plants. We call them "aromatic" because the bulk of flavor perception comes through the nose. The perception of flavor comes from two areas of receptors. Taste receptors in the mouth receive five components of flavor: sweet, salt, sour, bitter, and savory (umami). Everything else is aromatic, captured through odor receptors deep inside the nose (deep enough that we actively sniff in air when we want to perceive an aroma).

The importance of aroma to the perception of flavor is evident to anyone with a stuffed nose. In fact, with your nose held shut, it is difficult to tell the difference between foods that have the same texture. If you have any doubt, hold your nose and take a bite each of apple and pear. They both feel wet and crisp, and they both taste sweet and tart. But release your nose and they immediately distinguish themselves. You can try the same thing with an onion to an even greater dramatic effect. Hold your nose and take a small bite of onion. Most people perceive no flavor at all (a few perceive sweetness). Now release your nose and you will be enveloped in a cloud of onion-ness.

The reason aromatic chemicals in plants are so smelly is that they are volatile, meaning they are small and light enough to evaporate from food, fly through the air, and travel up your nose. Since all molecules travel faster when they are heated, cooking food causes more of the volatile aromatic chemicals to escape, which is why cooked and cooking food is so much more fragrant than raw food, and why hot food often tastes better than the same food cold.

So why do some parts of a plant have more flavor than other parts? The parts of plants that we use for seasoning are those with the most concentrated aromatic elements, which make up the defense system of the plant. A plant's leaves, bark, seeds, and roots are designed to irritate and possibly sicken any animal that comes into contact with the plant, in the botanical hope that the aroma alone will keep predators away. In small amounts, these powerful aromatics can also make our food more alluring. Herbs are the leaves, either fresh or dried, of a plant. Spices are the bark, seeds, and roots.

You probably have never tasted a spice alone; if you do, you will find that it is far from a pleasurable experience. Raw clove anesthetizes anything it touches, oregano is unpleasantly bitter, and unadulterated pepper feels as if it is burrowing a cavity into your tongue. All of these reactions (the reason behind the medicinal reputations of many herbs and spices) come from the potent concentration of volatile substances in a seasoning. But if you dilute a spice or herb, let's say a few milligrams of oregano in several pounds of tomatoes, what was once unpleasantly bitter (and toxic) becomes mildly aromatic (and safe).

The flavorful components in a seasoning are more soluble in oil than they are in water, which is why the presence of fat or oil in a food increases its aromatic properties. The alcohol and acetic acid in vinegar, which are related to fat molecules in structure, can also dissolve the aromatics in a seasoning; that is why they are standard parts of the structure of marinades and brines.

Although spices and herbs have their own distinct flavors, most of them fall into a few families of plants, as shown in the following chart. Within each family, the spices tend to have a similar flavor profile, giving you a framework from which you can begin to make pairings. Keep in mind that many classic spice blends span families, such as ginger, allspice, nutmeg, clove, and cinnamon.

FAMILIES OF HERBS AND SPICES

Mint Family	Carrot Family	Chile Family (Capsaicin)	Pepper Berries
Basil	Anise		Black peppercorns
Lavender	Caraway		(dried ripe berry)
Lemon balm	Celery seed	Bell pepper	
Marjoram	Chervil	Cayenne	Green peppercorns
Mint	Cilantro	Habanero	(dried or preserved
Oregano	Coriander	Jalapeño	unripe berry)
Rosemary	Dill	New Mexican paprika	
Sage	Dill seed	Pimento	Pink (rose) pepper
Savory	Fennel	Scotch bonnet	(preserved ripe berries)
Thyme	Fennel seed	Serrano	
	Fennel pollen	Tabasco	White peppercorns
	Lovage		(dried hulled berry)
	Parsley		

Ginger Family	Mustard Family	Nutmeg Family	Myrtle Family	Cinnamomum Family
Cardamom	Horseradish			
Galangal	Mustard	Mace	Allspice	Cassia
Ginger	Wasabi	Nutmeg	Clove	Cinnamon
Turmeric				

If you have a question about the compatibility of two or more seasonings, smell them side by side. If the combined aromas are pleasant, the flavors will work together. Likewise, if you want to know whether a recipe would benefit from the addition of another seasoning, take a bite and, with the food still in your mouth, sniff some of the seasoning. You will instantly know what the additional flavoring will do to the recipe.

Although there are resemblances between some seasonings within a family that are close enough to allow one herb or spice to be substituted for another (fennel and anise, mace and nutmeg, allspice and clove), the ability to interchange one seasoning for another depends more on their balance of primary flavor components.

The flavors of all seasonings are built from a complex of chemical compounds. Sometimes a single compound provides the entire flavor. Anise, for instance, owes its sweet, floral, licorice-like flavor to the chemical anethole. The flavor of clove comes largely from eugenol, and mustard and horseradish both get their pungency from thiocyanate compounds. But the flavor architecture of most herbs and spices is far more complex, built from an interplay of many chemical compounds.

The following chart gives you the general flavor structure of common herbs and spices. If two seasonings have many flavor components in common, chances are they will substitute for one another easily, especially if they have the same distinctive flavor components. Keep in mind that any substitution will make a difference in flavor, but when two seasonings are similarly structured that difference should not be large or unpleasant.

FLAVOR COMPONENTS OF SEASONINGS

Seasoning Herb (H) / Spice (S)	Sweet	Freshness	Citrus	Floral	Licorice	Pine	Wood	Intensity	Key Flavor Component
Allspice (S)	x	x		x			x		Cineole
Anise (S)	x		x	x	x				Anethole
Basil (H)	x	x		x	x	x		x	
Bay (H)		x				x	x	x	
Caraway (S)			x				x		D-carvone
Cardamom (S)	x		x	x			x	x	Cineole
Chile (S)								x	Capsaicin
Cilantro (H)	x	x	x	x				x	Decenal
Cinnamon (S)	x	x		x			x	x	Cinnamaldehyde
Clove (S)	x			x			x	x	Eugenol
Coriander (S)	x	x	x	x			x		
Cumin (S)						x	x	x	Cuminaldehyde
Dill (H)		x	x			x			
Dill seed (S)		x	x			x	x		D-carvone
Fennel seed (S)			x		x	x		x	Anethole
Galangal (S)	x	x		x		x		x	Cineole
Ginger (S)	x	x	x				x	x	Cineole
Horseradish (S)		x						x	Thiocyanates
Juniper (H)	x					x	x		Pinene
Lemongrass (H)			x	x					Citral
Lemon verbena (H)			x	x					Citral
Mace (S)	x			x			x		Sabinene
Marjoram (H)	x	x	x	x			x		
Mint (H)	x	x	x			x		x	Menthol
Mustard (S)							x	x	Thiocyanates
Nutmeg (S)	x		x	x			x	x	Sabinene, cineole
Oregano (H)				x	x	x	x		Carvacrol
Parsley (H)	x	x							
Peppercorn (S)				x			x	x	Piperine
Rosemary (H)	x	x		x			x	x	Pinene
Sage (H)		x				x		x	Thujone
Szechwan pepper (S)		x	x	x				x	Gerianiol
Star anise (S)	x		x	x	x		x		Anethole
Tarragon (H)	x	x		x	x	x		x	Pinene, estragole
Thyme (H)		x	x	x		x		x	Thymol
Turmeric (S)		x	x	x			x		Cineole
Wasabi (S)		x						x	Thiocyanates

People cook with what they have, imprinting the flavors and ingredients that grow in their land, and the cooking techniques that come from their history, into their food. European cuisines generally have more herbs than spices, because most herbs grow in a temperate climate and most spices are tropical. Mexican food has a large Spanish influence, stemming from the Spanish invasion in 1521, but it is much spicier than the food of Spain because of the chiles that were native to the New World from before the Spanish arrived. Spanish food is spicier than French food because the Spanish were influenced by their connection to Mexico. However, it is not as spicy as the food of the Far East, where chiles caught on when they were brought there by Spanish and Portuguese traders in the seventeenth century, probably because the flavor of chiles was reminiscent of native pepper berries.

Because every part of the world has its own geography, climate, and history, it has developed a cuisine and a system of flavors specific to those conditions. There are overlaps because of interchanges between cultures (Spain and Mexico), geographic proximity (Thailand and Vietnam), and similar climatic conditions (southeastern France and northern California), but speaking in the broadest terms, people of a particular culture prepare their food with a palate of seasonings that defines their cuisine and separates it from all other cuisines in the world.

The following chart roughly outlines the general seasoning components in regional cuisines, starting from the southern shore of the Mediterranean and traveling westward around the world, ending on the European side of the Mediterranean.

SEASONINGS USED IN REGIONAL CUISINES

Flavors	Region
Cumin, coriander, cinnamon, ginger, chile, mace	Morocco
Garlic, cumin, mint	North Africa
Mint, lemon, parsley, sumac, thyme, flower petals	Middle East
Coriander, cardamom, cumin, cinnamon, clove, ginger	Northern India
Coriander, cumin, mustard seed, tamarind, chile	Southern India
Ginger, garlic, turmeric	Burma
Coriander, cumin, ginger, chile, fish sauce	Thailand
Fish sauce, coconut, chile	Laos
Fish sauce, lemon, chile, cilantro	Vietnam
Soy sauce, sugar, peanut, chile	Indonesia
Soy sauce, ginger, garlic, sesame	Peking
Soy sauce, ginger, vinegar, sugar, pepper	Szechwan
Soy sauce, ginger, garlic	Canton
Soy sauce, sugar, seaweed	Japan
Soy sauce, sugar, sesame, chile	Korea
Tomato, citrus, chile, cinnamon, Mexican oregano	Mexico
Olive oil, onion, pepper, tomato, garlic	Spain
Olive oil, thyme, rosemary, sage	Southern France
Wine, butter, tarragon, parsley, thyme, chervil, onion	Northern France
Olive oil, garlic, oregano	Southern Italy
Olive oil, garlic, basil, parsley	Northern Italy
Olive oil, lemon, oregano	Greece
Dill, paprika, caraway	Eastern Europe

PEPPER

There are two types of pepper. Black pepper is native to Asia, spreading west about 3,500 years ago; chile peppers are native to South America and traveled around the world during the sixteenth century. Today, both families of peppers are eaten everywhere, but tropical cuisines tend to gravitate more toward chiles, while black pepper has become the preeminent pepper in Europe and North America.

The active agent in chiles, capsaicin, is so potentially irritating that one would expect that anyone who wanted to avoid pain would shun it. Paul Rozin, professor of psychology at the University of Pennsylvania, has postulated that the experience of eating chiles gives us excitement because it exposes us to pain that we know won't really hurt us. Like bungee jumping, eating chiles allows us to experience danger within safe limits. It's also likely that the sensation of pain from chiles may cause the brain to release pain-relieving chemicals that remain in our system after the heat sensation of the chiles has passed, leaving us with a mild sense of euphoria. Whatever the reason, the present-day consumption of capsaicin peppers compared to black pepper is 20 to 1, and it is a principal flavor component of the cuisines of Central and South America, Southeast Asia, India, the Middle East, North Africa, and the Szechwan and Hunan provinces of China.

The amount of capsaicin in a chile depends on its genetics, its growing conditions (hot, dry conditions increase the amount), and its ripeness (with the capsaicin peaking just when the green fruit starts to turn color). Capsaicin is concentrated in the placenta of the chile, the white internal membrane that holds the seeds. From there, it migrates into the seeds and along the inner walls of the pepper, where it is found in lesser amounts. For that reason, you can manipulate the amount of capsaicin in your cooking by cutting away all or part of the core and seeds. When you do this, or when you handle any chile, make sure to protect your skin with disposable rubber gloves. Or hold the uncut chile by its stem as you prepare it (you can safely cut the flesh from the core while holding the stem with your ungloved fingers). Either way, avoid getting any capsaicin oil on your skin. It's hard to wash away, so washing your hands doesn't do much good.

The amount of capsaicin in a chile is measured in Scoville units, a measurement invented by Wilbur Scoville, a chemist working for the Parke Davis pharmaceutical company, in around 1912. One drop of pure capsaicin in 1 million drops of water is equal to 15 Scoville units. Sweet bell pepper measures 0 on the Scoville scale, and pure capsaicin measures 16,000,000 units. The following chart gives the relative amounts of capsaicin for common chiles. Variables in growing conditions and ripeness of individual peppers account for the range within each chile variety.

SCOVILLE UNITS FOR CHILE VARIETIES

Chile	Scoville Units
Habanero	100,000–350,000
Scotch bonnet	100,000–325,000
Jamaican	100,000–200,000
Thai	50,000–100,000
Chiltepin	50,000–100,000
Piquin	40,000–58,000
Cayenne	30,000–50,000
Tabasco	30,000–50,000
De árbol	15,000–30,000
Manzano	12,000–30,000
Serrano	5,000–23,000
Chipotle	5,000–10,000
Jalapeño	2,500–8,000
Guajillo	2,500–5,000
Pasilla	1,000–2,000
Ancho	1,000–2,000
Poblano	1,000–2,000
Anaheim	500–1,200
New Mexico	500–1,000
Pepperoncini	100–500
Bell pepper	0

Black pepper is the dried berry of a climbing vine in the genus *Piper*. Its active agent is piperine, which increases as the skin ripens from green to red, peaking just as the fruit starts to turn color. During drying, the skin of a ripe pepper berry turns dark brown to black, giving dried black peppercorns their distinctive appearance. Most of the piperine and aromatic oils are contained in the skin (the interior of a peppercorn is largely starch), which is why polishing the skin in order to make the peppercorn white rids it of most of its aroma and heat. Green peppercorns are harvested before ripening, and pink pepper (not to be confused with pink peppercorns, which come from another plant entirely) is made from fruit that is picked just as it is changing color and preserved in brine instead of being dried.

SALT

Salt is like no other seasoning. It is a mineral (the only one we eat in its pure form), an essential nutrient (without it, the osmotic pressure that supports your cells would collapse), one of the basic tastes (your tongue has specialized taste receptors to help you perceive the presence of salt), a preservative (it discourages the growth of bacteria that spoil food and also allows flavor-producing salt-friendly bacteria to flourish), and a flavor enhancer (it enhances the aroma of foods and suppresses bitter sensations). With salt, seasoning is easy; without it, a cook needs an arsenal of flavor enhancers to take its place.

The expansive role that salt plays in the production of food comes from its chemical structure. Composed of a positively charged sodium ion bound to a negatively charged chlorine ion, salt breaks into its component parts when dissolved in water. The tiny fast-moving ionic atoms penetrate food easily, where they react with proteins, opening them up so that they can readily absorb seasonings and other flavorful components in a recipe. They also draw moisture out of food, which concentrates flavors, solidifies textures, and makes raw protein turn opaque. These changes, which replicate the effects of cooking, are why foods like gravlax and prosciutto are said to be "cooked" in salt. The same reaction is responsible for salt's ability to draw bitter juices from vegetables, like eggplant or cucumbers, and it is why we cure meats with salt before smoking (excess water in meat would resist the absorption of smoked flavors, which are oil based).

About half of the salt in the world is extracted from sea water, and the other half is mined from rock. The flavor of a particular salt (other than saltiness) comes from traces of minerals such as magnesium chloride, sulfate, calcium sulfate, and clay, and from plant material like algae, which may be present in the source material. Unrefined salt is about 98 percent sodium chloride; highly refined table salt is about 99.7 percent.

Humans seem to be hard-wired to like the flavor of salt, due undoubtedly to the fact that we need to take in some salt every day. But even though salt is an essential nutrient, the amount of salt that is preferred varies widely from culture to culture and from person to person. There is evidence that the ability to perceive salt diminishes with age. Most young adults can detect the presence of salt in a 0.05 percent solution, while adults who are over 60 don't perceive saltiness until the concentration is twice that level. This could be part of the reason that many adults consume more salt than they need nutritionally, exacerbating hypertension.

Most of our recipes call for specific amounts of salt. At times the amount is determined by the need for a certain chemical or physical reaction, as in brines or cures, but when the salt is just for flavor we want you to feel free to adjust the amount to your taste. We tried to keep the level in most recipes moderate, but if you know you like very little salt or you are on a salt-restricted diet, you should start with less and add more to taste.

FLAVORING METHODS

Although there are thousands of seasonings and seasoning blends, there are only four methods of infusing flavors into solid food:

- Rubs are a way to flavor the outside of an ingredient by literally rubbing a dry seasoning mixture into its surface.
- Brines are a mixture of salt, water, and flavoring that use the power of salt (see above) to open up the physical structure of an ingredient, allowing it to form chemical bonds that infuse its fibers with moisture and flavor.
- Marinades are similar to brines except that acid is the active ingredient. Although marinades have a reputation for tenderizing as well as flavoring, they really affect only the surface of the ingredient.
- Injection physically saturates the interior of a food with flavored fluid. Injecting brine or marinade will increase their ability to affect the interior of an ingredient, but it is easy to overdo it, so be careful; too much will cause the interior to pickle, dehydrate, and toughen.

B. RUBS

Traditionally, rubs were made for barbecue preparations to create an intensely flavored, crispy crust that would contrast with the moist, meaty interior developed through hours of slow cooking and constant basting. But now you are just as likely to see them on quick-cooking steaks, chops, burgers, and boneless poultry as a speedy way to surround them with intense flavor.

Most rubs contain a significant amount of salt and sugar, as much as 25 percent. The salt attacks the protein in meats, opening up the structure of the amino acids so that they are better able to absorb the flavors in the rub. At the same time, the sugar combines with the amino acids, creating a structure that breaks down quickly into hundreds of flavorful compounds when it hits the heat of the grill. These reactions of sugars and proteins, known as the Maillard reaction (after Louis Maillard, the French chemist who discovered them), is why browned meat tastes so good (see page 17 for more on browned meat and the Maillard reaction).

Resting a rubbed ingredient for 10 minutes while the grill is heating helps the salt and sugar to do their jobs, but it will not help the rub to permeate more than skin-deep, which is not a bad thing. One of the interesting dynamics of flavor perception is that we perceive flavors in sequence. Take sweet and sour, for example. When you eat something seasoned with sweet and sour flavors, rather than meshing into a single flavor, the pair refuses to combine. Instead the two flavors vibrate: sweet/sour/sweet/sour. As soon as we try to commit our palates to one of them, the other flavor appears, wiping its predecessor away. This phenomenon of taste perception, called layering, is a golden opportunity for anyone who cooks. Because we perceive flavors sequentially, rather than all rolled up together, it is possible to concoct highly sophisticated flavor juxtapositions, crusting a spicy rub over a steak that has been infused with a savory brine and then lacquering it with a sweet-and-sour dipping sauce at the table.

C. MOPS

A mop is a flavorful fluid that is a cross between a marinade (see page 86) and a brine (see page 85). By balancing sour and salty flavors, mops have an effect on meats similar to that of brines and marinades, but they minimize the risk of skewing the flavor too far in either direction. Typically, mops are brushed or drizzled onto meats as they grill; hence the name.

D. BRINES

The primary role of brining is to add moisture to food. The intense heat needed for direct grilling tends to dehydrate foods like pork chops and chicken breasts that have delicate fibers and little interior fat. That makes pork chops and chicken breasts prime candidates for brining. Soaking in a brine that is around 5 percent salt by weight for as little as 1 hour before grilling can make meat noticeably juicier and preserve its tenderness.

Brine works in two ways. Salt dissolves the protein in contracting muscle filaments, making them looser and therefore more tender. It also increases the capacity of muscle cells to bond with water, causing them to absorb water from the brine, which increases their weight by as much as 10 percent. As the water infuses into the meat, any flavor components from herbs, spices, or flavorful liquids are also absorbed, making brines an effective way to season meats beneath the surface. When meat cooks, it naturally loses moisture (about 20 percent), but by bulking up the moisture in meat through brining before it goes on the grill, you can effectively cut the net loss of juices by half.

The biggest disadvantage in using a brine is that the drippings from the meat tend to be too salty to use as a base for a sauce. This is a problem only when you are grill-roasting a turkey or other large poultry for which you might want to prepare gravy. Otherwise, a separate sauce, salsa, or chutney works beautifully with brined meats.

The best meats for brining are those that tend to dry out on the grill. Lean cuts of pork, chicken, and turkey benefit greatly from brining, but so do some fattier cuts. Spareribs, for instance, which have a good amount of fat but tend to toughen during grilling, are transformed by the tenderizing effects of brine.

Since brining works from the outside in, the meat fibers closest to the surface are the ones that reap most of the benefits, and since these are the parts that tend to dry out most during cooking, even a short period of soaking can produce noticeable benefits.

Incomplete brining will give you less than optimum moisture retention, but prolonged brining can oversaturate a food with brine, especially when the muscle tissue is delicate, like that of fish. Optimal brining time depends on a number of factors, including the density of the ingredient, its size, its shape, and the strength of the brine. Use the following chart as a general guideline.

BRINING GUIDE

Food	Brining Time
Small seafood and thin fish (less than 1 inch)	About 30 minutes
Thick fish (more than 1 inch) and boneless poultry	About 1 hour
Bone-in poultry pieces, chops, and steaks	2 to 3 hours
Roasts (less than 3 pounds) and ribs	3 to 6 hours
Large roasts or whole birds (up to 6 pounds)	4 to 8 hours
Whole large birds, such as turkeys	8 hours to overnight

Marinades are similar to brines in most ways: They are liquid, they are flavorful, and they infuse their flavors into solid ingredients by opening up tightly wound proteins. The big difference is that their active ingredient is acid, rather than salt. The acid can be almost anything—vinegar, citrus, fruit juice, wine, buttermilk, yogurt, tea, or coffee—and although each brings a different flavor to the mix, they all work in the same way.

Keep in mind that the atoms of all substances are in flux. The formula for water is H_2O, and most of the molecules in a cup of water are in that form. But at any given moment, there is a small percentage of molecules that break into positively charged hydrogen ions (H^+) and negatively charged hydroxyl groups (OH^-). The free H^+ atoms could join with an OH^- and form back into water, or they could bond to another water molecule, forming a positively charged H_3O molecule. Under normal conditions, very little of this is going on, but if enough H^+ ions start floating around, the whole mixture and anything in its vicinity could become unstable. Our bodies are designed to keep this from happening, so we have developed the ability to recognize any substance that releases H^+ ions into the environment. We taste them as sour, and we call them acids. The more positive ions an acid releases, the stronger it is.

Substances that do the opposite of acids (accept positive ions) are called bases, or alkalis. The relative strength of acids and bases is measured on a pH scale, which runs from 0 to 14, with purified water at the neutral center of 7. Anything with a pH below 7 is an acid, and anything above 7 is considered alkaline.

The following chart lists the pH of some common substances. Notice that almost all foods are acidic (only egg white and baking soda are alkaline) and that ingredients that we don't taste as sour at all, like fresh milk, are only a few pH points away from ingredients that taste quite sour, like vinegar. That's because a decrease in pH of just 1 point indicates a tenfold increase in the concentration of hydrogen ions.

pH OF COMMON SUBSTANCES

	Concentration of Hydrogen Ions	pH	Examples
Acid	10,000,000	0	Battery acid (0.5)
Acid	1,000,000	1	Stomach acid (1.3)
Acid	100,000	2	Lemon juice (2.2)
Acid	10,000	3	Orange juice (3), vinegar (3)
Acid	1,000	4	Tomato juice (4), yogurt (4.5)
Acid	100	5	Black coffee (5.2)
Acid	10	6	Tap water (6.4), milk (6.9)
Neutral	1	7	Pure ionized water (7)
Base	1/10	8	Egg white (8)
Base	1/100	9	Baking soda (8.8)
Base	1/1,000	10	Milk of magnesia (10.5)
Base	1/10,000	11	Household ammonia (11.9)
Base	1/100,000	12	Soapy water (12.4)
Base	1/1,000,000	13	Bleach (13.3)
Base	1/10,000,000	14	Drain cleaner (14)

Just as salt does (see the discussion on page 83), acids alter the structure of animal proteins and plant cells by disrupting their chemical bonds. A piece of fish or meat, submerged in an acidic marinade, begins to break apart; its fibers tenderize, it takes on moisture, and it forms bonds with flavorful elements in the marinade. Because acids release only positive ions, and salt breaks into both positive (Na^+) and negative (Cl^-) ions, brines are more effective than marinades at accomplishing these tasks. Unless you inject a marinade deep into the interior of an ingredient, it is difficult for it to have any tenderizing effect deeper than a fraction of an inch without making the finished dish overly sour. Adding sweet ingredients or dairy products to a marinade can help counteract its sourness.

F. GLAZES AND SAUCES

Glazes are sweet, and because of that they burn easily. Brush them onto grilling foods to add a caramelized sheen, but don't expect the flavor of a glaze to penetrate past the surface. A glaze is most effective as a flavorful and textural counterpoint when used in conjunction with a brine or marinade.

Sauces, salsas, chutneys, and other accompaniments are best used as table condiments with grilled meats. When paired with the right marinade or rub, they can make a grilled meal sing. But if you want to cook with sauces, use them like a glaze—only during the last few minutes of cooking—and then serve more for dipping at the table. There are hundreds of bottled barbecue sauces on the market and many are produced regionally, following the style of their region. For more information on regional styles of barbecue sauce, see the sidebar on page 391.

CHAPTER 5

MASTERING BURGERS AND OTHER QUICK MEALS

MASTERING TECHNIQUE

BASIC BURGER OR CHEESEBURGER 90
BASIC KEBAB 90

RECIPES

GRILL TOOLS AND EQUIPMENT
· Long-handled spatula

TIP
· For more information on making and serving burgers, see "Burger Guidelines" on page 92.

MASTERING TECHNIQUE
BASIC BURGER OR CHEESEBURGER

There is something novel in this burger—ice water. As discussed in the section on ground meats (page 49), grinding forces most of the moisture out of the meat. Adding more fat helps to restore some of the perception of juiciness, but for those who want less fat in their hamburger this is not an option. We opt for using burger with a moderate amount of fat (15 percent) plus some water. As the burger cooks, the fat melts and the water steams, helping the burger to cook through faster. The reason for using ice-cold water is to keep the meat chilled, and if you choose to eat your burgers rare, the cold water will migrate toward the center, resulting in a burger so juicy at its core that you will have to reach for a second napkin.

THE GRILL

Gas: Direct heat, medium-high (425° to 450°F)
Clean, oiled grate

Charcoal: Direct heat, light ash
12-by-12-inch charcoal bed (about 3 dozen coals)
Clean, oiled grate on lowest setting

Wood: Direct heat, light ash
12-by-12-inch bed, 3 to 4 inches deep
Clean, oiled grate set 2 inches above the fire

INGREDIENTS (MAKES 6 SERVINGS)

2 pounds ground beef chuck, 85% lean
5 tablespoons ice-cold water
1/2 teaspoon kosher salt, or more to taste
1/4 teaspoon ground black pepper, or more to taste

Oil for coating grill grate
12 slices good-quality American, provolone,
   or Cheddar cheese (optional)
6 hamburger buns, split

DIRECTIONS

1. Heat the grill as directed.

2. Using your hands, mix the beef, water, salt, and pepper in a bowl until well blended; do not overmix. Using a light touch, form into 6 patties no more than 1 inch thick. Refrigerate the burgers until the grill is ready.

3. Brush the grill grate and coat it with oil. Put the burgers on the grill, cover, and cook for 7 minutes, flipping after about 4 minutes, for medium-done (150°F on an instant-read

thermometer inserted into the thickest part, slightly pink). Add a minute per side for well-done (160°F).

4. If you are making cheeseburgers, put 2 slices of cheese on each burger 1 minute before the burgers are going to be done.

5. To toast the buns, put them cut-sides down directly over the fire for the last minute of cooking.

6. If serving the burgers directly from the grill, serve on the buns. If the burgers will sit, even for a few minutes, keep the buns and burgers separate until just before eating.

GRILL TOOLS AND EQUIPMENT
· 4 long, flat skewers or
  two-pronged skewers
· Long-handled tongs

TROUBLESHOOTING KEBABS
Trouble 1: Potato takes longer to cook through than steak, and a cherry tomato will turn to mush long before a wedge of onion loses its crunch. What's a kebab maker to do? There are several strategies for lessening the disparities between skewer mates.
· Cut harder, longer-cooking ingredients
  into smaller pieces.

MASTERING TECHNIQUE
BASIC KEBAB

Grilling small pieces of meat on a skewer has its advantages:
· The seasoning reaches all parts of every bite.
· Small pieces cook faster.
· Everything is bite-size, eliminating the need for excessive cutlery at the table.
· You can grill a whole meal (meat, vegetable, and starch) on a single skewer.
· Kebabs can be beautiful, juxtaposing vegetables, fruits, and meats of different colors, shapes, and textures.

It also has its disadvantages:
· Everything on a skewer has to cook at the same rate.
· Where pieces touch they will not brown.
· Turning skewers can be tricky.

As you can see, the advantages outweigh the disadvantages, and all of the potential pitfalls are avoidable (see "Troubleshooting Kebabs," facing page). The big advantage of the skewer is speed; from the absorption of flavor, through cooking time, to plating and serving, everything is streamlined.

Use this basic recipe as a template. Add flavor with a brine or marinade (pages 85–86), replace the salt and pepper in the recipe with a spice rub (see page 84), brush the cooked kebab with glaze, and/or serve them with a dipping sauce (see page 87).

TROUBLESHOOTING KEBABS, CONTINUED

· Place faster-cooking ingredients near the ends of the skewers, where they are more likely to sit at the cooler perimeter of the fire.

· Precook tough ingredients so that they finish grilling at the same time as other ingredients on the skewer.

· Cook one type of ingredient per skewer. Obviously, the disadvantage of this is that you won't be able to serve a skewer to each person.

Trouble 2: All food leaches moisture as it cooks. If there is not ample space for it to evaporate, as when two pieces of meat are packed together on a skewer, the moisture will get trapped, causing the meat to steam rather than grill. That is why there must be at least $1/4$ inch of space between the items on a skewer.

Trouble 3: As ingredients lose moisture during cooking, they shrink, causing them to pull away from the skewer and creating a gap. If your skewer is round, when you turn it, the ingredient will spin rather than turn with the skewer, making it cumbersome to get all of the ingredients to brown evenly. You can prevent this from happening by using flat skewers, two-pronged skewers, or twisted skewers, all of which grip the pieces in various ways.

Kebab baskets are long, narrow grilling baskets that allow you to line up precut ingredients as if they were on a skewer and cook them evenly by turning the basket as each side browns. Although they work well, to serve these "kebabs," you have to empty the contents of the baskets before bringing the food to the table, which means you could have cooked everything on a large grill screen, gotten the same results, and dirtied far less equipment.

THE GRILL

Gas:	Direct heat, medium-high (425° to 450°F) Clean, oiled grate	**Wood:**	Direct heat, light ash 12-by-12-inch bed, 3 to 4 inches deep Clean, oiled grate set 2 inches above the fire
Charcoal:	Direct heat, light ash 12-by-12-inch charcoal bed (about 3 dozen coals) Clean, oiled grate on lowest setting		

INGREDIENTS (MAKES 4 SERVINGS)

1 pound trimmed sirloin steak, boneless chicken breasts, or pork loin, cut into 16 cubes

$1/2$ teaspoon kosher salt

$1/4$ teaspoon ground black pepper

1 tablespoon canola oil

Oil for coating grill grate

DIRECTIONS

1. Heat the grill as directed.

2. Toss the meat, salt, pepper, and 1 tablespoon oil in a large bowl until uniformly coated.

3. Arrange 4 pieces of meat on each skewer, leaving space between them.

4. Brush the grill grate and coat it with oil. Put the prepared skewers on the grill, cover, and cook until browned on both sides and the pieces feel firm, 8 to 10 minutes, turning them halfway through. Serve 1 skewer per person.

THE GREAT AMERICAN HAMBURGER AND CHEESEBURGER

What makes a burger great? Let us count the ways. The meat must be flavorful, the fat content sufficient but moderate, and the seasoning apparent but not overt. The patty has to hold together but not be compacted. The bun should be soft enough so that it does not require greater biting pressure than the contents it holds, but not so fluffy that it soaks up burger juices like a sponge. The cut surface of the bun must be toasted, and the garnishes should be kept simple: The cheese barely melted, vegetables cold and crisp, and condiments applied by the eater, not the cook. If all these guideposts are met, you shall never eat better, my child.

TIMING

Prep: 5 minutes
Grill: 7 minutes

GRILL TOOLS AND EQUIPMENT

· Long-handled spatula

THE GRILL

Gas:	Direct heat, medium-high (425° to 450°F) Clean, oiled grate	**Wood:**	Direct heat, light ash 12-by-12-inch bed, 3 to 4 inches deep Clean, oiled grate set 2 inches above the fire
Charcoal:	Direct heat, light ash 12-by-12-inch charcoal bed (about 3 dozen coals) Clean, oiled grate on lowest setting		

BURGER GUIDELINES

- Wet your hands with cold water when mixing the meat and when forming burgers. It will keep the meat from sticking to your hands.
- If using ground beef that is more than 85 percent lean, brush the surface of your burgers with oil before grilling to keep them from sticking and to help them brown.
- How well done you like burgers is not just a matter of taste. While roasts, chops, and steaks can be cooked to rare without raising food safety fears, burgers cannot. It is simply not safe to eat burgers cooked to less than 150°F. (For a full discussion of meat safety, see page 42.) At that temperature, a burger will be very slightly pink in the center and will feel springy to the touch. For a precise temperature reading, insert an instant-read thermometer through the side of a burger into its center.
- The best garnishes are classic: a slice of ripe beefsteak tomato, a mound of sautéed onions, a leaf of romaine lettuce, a dollop of coleslaw, or a few slices of dill pickle.
- Try substituting kaiser rolls (or another crusty round roll) for hamburger rolls.

INGREDIENTS (MAKES 6 SERVINGS)

2 pounds ground beef chuck, 85% lean

5 tablespoons ice-cold water

1 teaspoon ketchup

$^1/_2$ teaspoon kosher salt

$^1/_4$ teaspoon ground black pepper

Oil for coating grill grate

12 slices good-quality American, provolone, or Cheddar cheese (optional)

6 hamburger buns, split

DIRECTIONS

1. Heat the grill as directed.

2. Using your hands, mix the beef, water, ketchup, salt, and pepper in a bowl until well blended; do not overmix. Using a light touch, form into 6 patties no more than 1 inch thick. Refrigerate the burgers until the grill is ready.

3. Brush the grill grate and coat it with oil. Put the burgers on the grill, cover, and cook for 7 minutes, flipping after about 4 minutes, for medium-done (150°F, slightly pink). Add a minute per side for well-done (160°F).

4. If you are making cheeseburgers, put 2 slices of cheese on each burger 1 minute before the burgers are going to be done.

5. To toast the buns, put them cut-sides down directly over the fire for the last minute of cooking.

6. If serving the burgers directly from the grill, serve on the buns. If the burgers will sit, even for a few minutes, keep the buns and burgers separate until just before eating.

Photo: The Great American Cheeseburger

STEAKHOUSE BURGERS

TIMING
Prep: 5 minutes
Grill: 7 minutes

Steak sauce, that classic amalgam of Worcestershire, mustard, and tamarind, has the power to transubstantiate a humble burger to steakhouse eminence. In this recipe, the sauce not only flavors the meat, it also adds moisture and helps to increase the perception of juiciness even when the burger is cooked to well-done.

GRILL TOOLS AND EQUIPMENT
· Long-handled spatula

GETTING CREATIVE
· Because these burgers have so much flavor, it is best to keep your garnishes simple: a slice of ripe beefsteak tomato, a mound of sautéed onions, a leaf of romaine lettuce, a dollop of coleslaw, or a few slices of dill pickle.
· If you want to add cheese, make it something assertive: an imported Swiss, some crumbled blue, or a smear of Brie would work well.
· Substitute about 3/4 cup chopped sweet onion (such as Vidalia) for the scallions.

THE GRILL

Gas: Direct heat, medium-high (425° to 450°F)
Clean, oiled grate
Charcoal: Direct heat, light ash
12-by-12-inch charcoal bed (about 3 dozen coals)
Clean, oiled grate on lowest setting

Wood: Direct heat, light ash
12-by-12-inch bed, 3 to 4 inches deep
Clean, oiled grate set 2 inches above the fire

INGREDIENTS (MAKES 6 SERVINGS)

2 pounds ground beef chuck, 85% lean
1/3 cup bottled steak sauce
2 teaspoons jarred horseradish
1/2 teaspoon kosher salt

1/4 teaspoon coarsely ground black pepper
4 scallions, roots trimmed, cut into 1/2-inch pieces
Oil for coating grill grate
6 hamburger buns, split

DIRECTIONS

1. Heat the grill as directed.
2. Using your hands, mix the beef, steak sauce, horseradish, salt, pepper, and scallions in a bowl until well blended; do not overmix. Using a light touch, form into 6 patties no more than 1 inch thick. Refrigerate the burgers until the grill is ready.
3. Brush the grill grate and coat it with oil. Put the burgers on the grill, cover, and cook for 7 minutes, flipping after about

4 minutes, for medium-done (150°F, slightly pink). Add a minute per side for well-done (160°F).
4. To toast the buns, put them cut-sides down directly over the fire for the last minute of cooking.
5. If serving the burgers directly from the grill, serve on the buns. If the burgers will sit, even for a few minutes, keep the buns and burgers separate until just before eating.

SZECHWAN SCALLION BURGERS

TIMING
Prep: 5 minutes
(plus 5 minutes for Szechwan salt)
Grill: 7 minutes

GRILL TOOLS AND EQUIPMENT
· Long-handled spatula

Szechwan peppercorns are rust colored with rough skin that splits open to reveal a brittle black seed. The spice mainly consists of the empty husks, which give it a rosy hue when ground. Szechwan pepper has a floral fragrance, and even though the food of the Szechwan province can be fiery, the peppercorn itself is not very hot. This burger is half pork, which gives it a smooth texture and a pleasant sweetness.

THE GRILL

Gas: Direct heat, medium-high (425° to 450°F)
Clean, oiled grate
Charcoal: Direct heat, light ash
12-by-12-inch charcoal bed (about 3 dozen coals)
Clean, oiled grate on lowest setting

Wood: Direct heat, light ash
12-by-12-inch bed, 3 to 4 inches deep
Clean, oiled grate set 2 inches above the fire

1 pound ground beef chuck, 85% lean

1 pound ground pork

1/3 cup soy sauce

3 cloves garlic, minced

1 tablespoon finely grated peeled gingerroot

1 teaspoon Sesame Szechwan Salt (page 380)

1 tablespoon sriracha hot pepper sauce

4 scallions, roots trimmed, cut into thin slices

Oil for coating grill grate

6 hamburger buns, split

DIRECTIONS

1. Heat the grill as directed.

2. Using your hands, mix the beef, pork, soy sauce, garlic, ginger, Szechwan salt, hot pepper sauce, and scallions in a bowl until well blended; do not overmix. Using a light touch, form into 6 patties no more than 1 inch thick. Refrigerate the burgers until the grill is ready.

3. Brush the grill grate and coat it with oil. Put the burgers on the grill, cover, and cook for 7 minutes, flipping after about 4 minutes, for medium-done (150°F, slightly pink). Add a minute per side for well-done (160°F).

4. To toast the buns, put them cut sides down directly over the fire for the last minute of cooking.

5. If serving the burgers directly from the grill, serve on the buns. If the burgers will sit, even for a few minutes, keep the buns and burgers separate until just before eating.

WHOLE-GRAIN MUSTARD BURGERS

The mustard seeds in these hearty, pungent burgers are soaked in balsamic vinegar, which softens their skins, giving them a resiliency that makes them pop between the teeth with every bite. The horse-radish in the mixture underscores the mustard flavor, and the concentrated sugars in the balsamic vinegar naturally counter the slightly bitter aftertaste of the mustard seed. See the sidebar on page 105 for more information on mustard.

THE GRILL

Gas: Direct heat, medium-high (425° to 450°F)
Clean, oiled grate

Charcoal: Direct heat, light ash
12-by-12-inch charcoal bed (about 3 dozen coals)
Clean, oiled grate on lowest setting

Wood: Direct heat, light ash
12-by-12-inch bed, 3 to 4 inches deep
Clean, oiled grate set 2 inches above the fire

INGREDIENTS (MAKES 6 SERVINGS)

2 teaspoons mustard seeds

2 tablespoons balsamic vinegar

2 pounds ground beef chuck, 85% lean

2 tablespoons spicy brown mustard

2 teaspoons jarred horseradish

1/2 teaspoon kosher salt

Oil for coating grill grate

6 hamburger buns, split

DIRECTIONS

1. Heat the grill as directed.

2. Combine the mustard seeds and vinegar in a small bowl and set aside to soak for about 10 minutes.

3. Using your hands, mix the beef, soaked mustard seeds, mustard, horseradish, and salt in a bowl until well blended; do not overmix. Using a light touch, form into 6 patties no more than 1 inch thick. Refrigerate the burgers until the grill is ready.

4. Brush the grill grate and coat it with oil. Put the burgers on the grill, cover, and cook for 7 minutes, flipping after about 4 minutes, for medium-done (150°F, slightly pink). Add a minute per side for well-done (160°F).

5. To toast the buns, put them cut-sides down directly over the fire for the last minute of cooking.

6. If serving the burgers directly from the grill, serve on the buns. If the burgers will sit, even for a few minutes, keep the buns and burgers separate until just before eating.

HORSERADISH, CHEDDAR, AND APPLE BURGERS

TIMING
Prep: 5 minutes
Grill: 7 minutes

Horseradish is related to the mustard family, which is probably why it works so well in this burger inundated with Cheddar and apple. If horseradish makes you wince, you can substitute spicy mustard, but the effect won't be nearly as exciting.

THE GRILL

Gas: Direct heat, medium-high (425° to 450°F)
Clean, oiled grate

Charcoal: Direct heat, light ash
12-by-12-inch charcoal bed (about 3 dozen coals)
Clean, oiled grate on lowest setting

Wood: Direct heat, light ash
12-by-12-inch bed, 3 to 4 inches deep
Clean, oiled grate set 2 inches above the fire

INGREDIENTS (MAKES 6 SERVINGS)

2 pounds ground beef chuck, 85% lean

3 tablespoons jarred horseradish

1/2 teaspoon kosher salt

1/4 teaspoon coarsely ground black pepper

4 ounces Cheddar cheese, shredded (1 cup)

1/2 apple, peeled, cored, and finely chopped

1/3 cup apple juice or apple cider

6 hamburger buns, split

DIRECTIONS

1. Heat the grill as directed.

2. Using your hands, mix the beef, horseradish, salt, pepper, cheese, apple, and apple juice in a bowl until well blended; do not overmix. Using a light touch, form into 6 patties no more than 1 inch thick. Refrigerate the burgers until the grill is ready.

3. Brush the grill grate and coat it with oil. Put the burgers on the grill, cover, and cook for 7 minutes, flipping after about

4 minutes, for medium-done (150°F, slightly pink). Add a minute per side for well-done (160°F).

4. To toast the buns, put them cut-sides down directly over the fire for the last minute of cooking.

5. If serving the burgers directly from the grill, serve on the buns. If the burgers will sit, even for a few minutes, keep the buns and burgers separate until just before eating.

GRILL TOOLS AND EQUIPMENT
· Long-handled spatula

GETTING CREATIVE
· Because these burgers are sweet and pungent, they can be complemented with a wide variety of garnishes, from fruit (a few slices of apple or pear) to a selection of mustards (something aromatic and whole grain) or a garden vegetable, like a slice of sweet onion, a leaf of romaine lettuce, a dollop of coleslaw, or a few slices of dill pickle.

· If you want to add cheese, make it something that goes well with apple; an imported Swiss, some crumbled blue, or a slice of Cheddar all work well.

· Substitute pear for the apple.

SPICY BLACK BEAN BURGERS

TIMING
Prep: 5 minutes
 (plus 5 minutes for rub)
Grill: 7 minutes

Like all ground-meat dishes, burgers benefit from some filler. Fillers add flavor and creaminess, and because most contain some starch, and starch absorbs moisture, burgers containing a purée of beans, or bread or cereal, keep their juices better than plain old unadulterated naked ground beef alone. In this burger, the filler is bean dip, which adds a little heat and the fragrance of cumin as well as moisture.

THE GRILL

Gas: Direct heat, medium-high (425° to 450°F)
Clean, oiled grate

Charcoal: Direct heat, light ash
12-by-12-inch charcoal bed (about 3 dozen coals)
Clean, oiled grate on lowest setting

Wood: Direct heat, light ash
12-by-12-inch bed, 3 to 4 inches deep
Clean, oiled grate set 2 inches above the fire

GRILL TOOLS AND EQUIPMENT
· Long-handled spatula

GETTING CREATIVE
· The spicy character of these burgers goes well with fresh tomatoes, caramelized onions, assertive greens like spinach or arugula, or a few slices of crisp cucumber.

· If you want to add cheese, make it something you'd add to a chili, like aged Cheddar, Monterey Jack, or smoked Gouda.

· If you can't find corn cakes (such as Thomas'), substitute kaiser rolls (or another crusty round roll).

· Substitute rehydrated powdered black beans or refried beans for the bean dip.

INGREDIENTS (MAKES 6 SERVINGS)

2 pounds ground beef chuck, 85% lean

1/4 cup finely chopped *jalapeño en escabèche* (canned jalapeño), drained

1/2 teaspoon Cajun Blackening Rub (page 373)

1/2 cup jarred black bean dip

Oil for coating grill grate

6 store-bought corn cakes

2 tablespoons butter, melted

DIRECTIONS

1. Heat the grill as directed.

2. Using your hands, mix the beef, jalapeño, Cajun rub, and bean dip in a bowl until well blended; do not overmix. Using a light touch, form into 6 patties no more than 1 inch thick. Refrigerate the burgers until the grill is ready.

3. Brush the grill grate and coat it with oil. Put the burgers on the grill, cover, and cook for 7 minutes, flipping after about

4 minutes, for medium-done (150°F, slightly pink). Add a minute per side for well-done (160°F).

4. To toast the corn cakes, brush with butter and toast directly over the fire for the last minute of cooking.

5. If serving the burgers directly from the grill, serve each on top of a corn cake. If the burgers will sit, even for a few minutes, keep the corn cakes and burgers separate until just before eating. Serve with a fork and knife; these are not hand-held.

ROASTED PEPPER–MOLE BURGERS

Mole is the most elaborate of the Mexican sauces. Made by grinding and simmering cooked chiles, toasted spices, ground nuts, chopped fruit, and broth, even a simple mole can take more than a day to prepare. As a time-saver, several Hispanic food manufacturers market prepared mole paste, which includes all of the flavorful ingredients you would add to a mole, precooked and ready to go. In this burger, we use mole paste like ketchup or mustard, to add instant flavor and complexity.

THE GRILL

Gas: Direct heat, medium-high (425° to 450°F)
Clean, oiled grate

Charcoal: Direct heat, light ash
12-by-12-inch charcoal bed (about 3 dozen coals)
Clean, oiled grate on lowest setting

Wood: Direct heat, light ash
12-by-12-inch bed, 3 to 4 inches deep
Clean, oiled grate set 2 inches above the fire

INGREDIENTS (MAKES 6 SERVINGS)

2 pounds ground beef chuck, 85% lean

1 roasted red bell pepper, stemmed, seeded, and finely chopped (about 1/2 cup)

2 tablespoons jarred mole paste

1/4 teaspoon ground chipotle chile

1/2 teaspoon kosher salt

1/4 teaspoon ground black pepper

Oil for coating grill grate

6 kaiser rolls, split

DIRECTIONS

1. Heat the grill as directed.

2. Using your hands, mix the beef, bell pepper, mole paste, chipotle, salt, and pepper in a bowl until well blended; do not overmix. Using a light touch, form into 6 patties no more than 1 inch thick. Refrigerate the burgers until the grill is ready.

3. Brush the grill grate and coat it with oil. Put the burgers on the grill, cover, and cook for 7 minutes, flipping after about

4 minutes, for medium-done (150°F, slightly pink). Add a minute per side for well-done (160°F).

4. To toast the rolls, put them cut-sides down directly over the fire for the last minute of cooking.

5. If serving the burgers directly from the grill, serve on the rolls. If the burgers will sit, even for a few minutes, keep the rolls and burgers separate until just before eating.

TIMING

Prep: 5 minutes

Grill: 8 to 10 minutes

GRILL TOOLS AND EQUIPMENT

· Long-handled spatula

GETTING CREATIVE

· The spicy character of these burgers goes well with fresh tomatoes, caramelized onions, assertive greens like spinach or arugula, or a few slices of crisp cucumber.

· If you want to add cheese, make it something you'd add to a chili, like aged Cheddar, Monterey Jack, or smoked Gouda.

BUFFALO BLUE CHEESE BURGERS

TIMING
Prep: 5 minutes
Grill: 7 minutes

The buffalo in this recipe refers to the magic mixture of hot sauce and butter that brought the city of Buffalo, New York, culinary fame, not the noble beast that roamed the Western plains. The burgers are studded with blue cheese and seasoned with celery seed, echoing the blue cheese dressing and celery sticks that are standard accompaniments to all things Buffalo. If you enjoy a pun and revel in redundancy, there is no reason you couldn't make these burgers with beefalo and have some fun.

GRILL TOOLS AND EQUIPMENT
· Long-handled spatula

NOTE:
These burgers don't need any garnish, not even a bun, but if you just don't like to eat your burgers with a knife and fork, we recommend serving them on a crusty flat-bread, like ciabatta, rather than a soft bun.

THE GRILL

Gas: Direct heat, medium-high (425° to 450°F)
Clean, oiled grate on lowest setting

Charcoal: Direct heat, light ash
12-by-12-inch charcoal bed (about 3 dozen coals)
Clean, oiled grate on lowest setting

Wood: Direct heat, light ash
12-by-12-inch bed, 3 to 4 inches deep
Clean, oiled grate set 2 inches above the fire

INGREDIENTS (MAKES 6 SERVINGS)

2 pounds ground beef chuck, 85% lean
$1/2$ teaspoon celery seed
$1/3$ cup finely chopped onion
1 tablespoon minced garlic

1 cup crumbled blue cheese
3 tablespoons butter
$1/4$ cup mild hot sauce, such as Durkee Red Hot
Oil for coating grill grate

DIRECTIONS

1. Heat the grill as directed.
2. Using your hands, mix the beef, celery seed, onion, garlic, and blue cheese in a bowl until well blended; do not overmix. Using a light touch, form into 6 patties no more than 1 inch thick. Refrigerate the burgers until the grill is ready.
3. Melt the butter in a small saucepan. Mix in the hot sauce with a whisk; keep warm.

4. Brush the grill grate and coat it with oil. Put the burgers on the grill, cover, and cook for 7 minutes, flipping after about 4 minutes, for medium-done (150°F, slightly pink). Add a minute per side for well-done (160°F).
5. Put the burgers in the hot sauce mixture and turn to coat. Serve with forks and knives.

BACON-PARMESAN BURGERS

TIMING
Prep: 5 minutes
Grill: 7 minutes

This doesn't look like your typical bacon burger. There are no sodden bacon strips, nor do they have crusty caps of cheese. You won't see a slab of hothouse tomato or rings of red onion garnishing the patty. There's nothing to see because everything is mixed into the burger, and what a difference a little invisibility makes. With all the flavorful ingredients distributed within the ground beef, every bite gets invaded with flavor.

GRILL TOOLS AND EQUIPMENT
· Long-handled spatula

THE GRILL

Gas: Direct heat, medium-high (425° to 450°F)
Clean, oiled grate

Charcoal: Direct heat, light ash
12-by-12-inch charcoal bed (about 3 dozen coals)
Clean, oiled grate on lowest setting

Wood: Direct heat, light ash
12-by-12-inch bed, 3 to 4 inches deep
Clean, oiled grate set 2 inches above the fire

INGREDIENTS (MAKES 6 SERVINGS)

3 slices bacon, finely chopped

2 pounds ground beef chuck, 85% lean

1 medium tomato, finely chopped (about $1/2$ cup)

3 cloves garlic, minced

$1/2$ cup freshly grated Parmigiano-Reggiano cheese

$1/4$ teaspoon kosher salt, or more to taste

$1/4$ teaspoon ground black pepper

Oil for coating grill grate

6 flatbread rolls such as ciabatta, split

DIRECTIONS

1. Heat the grill as directed.

2. Cook the bacon in a skillet over medium heat until crisp; remove with a slotted spatula and place on paper towels to drain.

3. Using your hands, mix the beef, tomato, garlic, cheese, salt, pepper, and the cooked bacon in a bowl until well blended; do not overmix. Using a light touch, form into 6 patties no more than 1 inch thick. Refrigerate the burgers until the grill is ready.

4. Brush the grill grate and coat it with oil. Put the burgers on the grill, cover, and cook for 7 minutes, flipping after about 4 minutes, for medium-done (150°F, slightly pink). Add a minute per side for well-done (160°F).

5. To toast the rolls, put them cut-sides down directly over the fire for the last minute of cooking.

6. If serving the burgers directly from the grill, serve on the rolls. If the burgers will sit, even for a few minutes, keep the rolls and burgers separate until just before eating.

SMOKED GOUDA AND BACON BURGERS

In this recipe we underscore the smoky flavor of bacon with smoked cheese. Again the flavorful ingredients are mixed right into the meat to spread the flavor around. We've chosen smoked Gouda, but any smoked cheese will give similar results.

THE GRILL

Gas: Direct heat, medium-high (425° to 450°F)
Clean, oiled grate

Charcoal: Direct heat, light ash
12-by-12-inch charcoal bed (about 3 dozen coals)
Clean, oiled grate on lowest setting

Wood: Direct heat, light ash
12-by-12-inch bed, 3 to 4 inches deep
Clean, oiled grate set 2 inches above the fire

INGREDIENTS (MAKES 6 SERVINGS)

4 slices bacon, finely chopped

2 pounds ground beef chuck, 85% lean

$1/4$ cup chopped fresh flat-leaf parsley

3 ounces smoked Gouda cheese, shredded

$1/4$ cup diced red onion

1 tablespoon Worcestershire sauce

$1/2$ teaspoon kosher salt

$1/4$ teaspoon ground black pepper

$1/4$ cup water

Oil for coating grill grate

6 hamburger buns, split

DIRECTIONS

1. Heat the grill as directed.

2. Cook the bacon in a skillet over medium heat until crisp; remove with a slotted spatula and place on paper towels to drain.

3. Using your hands, mix the beef, parsley, cheese, onion, Worcestershire, salt, pepper, water, and cooked bacon in a bowl until well blended; do not overmix. Using a light touch, form into 6 patties no more than 1 inch thick. Refrigerate the burgers until the grill is ready.

4. Brush the grill grate and coat it with oil. Put the burgers on the grill, cover, and cook for 7 minutes, flipping after about 4 minutes, for medium-done (150°F, slightly pink). Add a minute per side for well-done (160°F).

5. To toast the buns, put them cut-sides down directly over the fire for the last minute of cooking.

6. If serving the burgers directly from the grill, serve on the buns. If the burgers will sit, even for a few minutes, keep the buns and burgers separate until just before eating.

DEATH-DEFYING CAJUN BURGERS

TIMING
Prep: 10 minutes
   (plus 5 minutes for rub)
Grill: About 10 minutes

Screw cholesterol, sensible sodium, and saturated fat. Schedule your next bypass and bite into a burger with a heart of spiced butter that bleeds with flavor.

GRILL TOOLS AND EQUIPMENT
· Long-handled spatula

GETTING CREATIVE
· Stuffing a burger with seasoned butter adds unbelievable richness. The seasoning could be anything: herb butter, garlic butter, sun-dried tomato butter, lemon butter, curried butter. The choice is up to you.
· Because these burgers are a little messy (watch the butter drips), it is best to keep your garnishes tender: thin slices of ripe tomato or a mound of sautéed onions or mushrooms.
· If you are truly suicidal and insist on adding cheese to these burgers, make it something that goes with chiles, like Cheddar, Monterey Jack, or *queso fresco*.

THE GRILL

Gas: Direct heat, medium-high (425° to 450°F)
Clean, oiled grate

Charcoal: Direct heat, light ash
12-by-12-inch charcoal bed (about 3 dozen coals)
Clean, oiled grate on lowest setting

Wood: Direct heat, light ash
12-by-12-inch bed, 3 to 4 inches deep
Clean, oiled grate set 2 inches above the fire

INGREDIENTS (MAKES 6 SERVINGS)

4 tablespoons unsalted butter, finely chopped
2 tablespoons Cajun Blackening Rub (page 373)
1 1/2 teaspoons tomato paste

2 pounds ground beef chuck, 85% lean
Oil for coating grill grate
6 hamburger buns, split

DIRECTIONS

1. Heat the grill as directed.

2. Using a small knife or fork, mix the butter, 1 tablespoon of the Cajun rub, and the tomato paste on a plate, until blended. Divide the butter mixture into 6 balls and refrigerate.

3. Using your hands, mix the beef and the remaining 1 table-spoon Cajun rub in a bowl until well blended; do not overmix. Using a light touch, form into 12 patties no more than 1/2 inch thick.

4. Put a portion of the butter in the center of each of 6 patties; top with the remaining patties and press together, taking

care to seal the edges well. Refrigerate the burgers until the grill is ready.

5. Brush the grill grate and coat it with oil. Put the burgers on the grill, cover, and cook for 9 minutes, flipping after about 5 minutes, for medium-done (150°F, slightly pink). Add a minute per side for well-done (160°F).

6. To toast the buns, put them cut-sides down directly over the fire for the last minute of cooking.

7. If serving the burgers directly from the grill, serve on the buns. If the burgers will sit, even for a few minutes, keep the buns and burgers separate until just before eating.

HERB CHEESE–STUFFED GARLIC BURGERS

TIMING
Prep: 8 minutes
Grill: About 10 minutes

The widespread availability of herb-flavored cream cheeses makes this burger a snap. You can vary the results by moving between a mild, creamy Boursin, a more assertive goat cheese rolled in fresh herbs, or a Brie encased in herbs. The only essential thing when stuffing a burger with cheese is to make sure that the edges are sealed well, to keep the cheese from leaking out during cooking.

GRILL TOOLS AND EQUIPMENT
· Long-handled spatula

GETTING CREATIVE
· Because these burgers are stuffed and seasoned, it is best to keep your garnishes simple: a slice of ripe beef-steak tomato, a mound of sautéed onions, a leaf of romaine lettuce, a smear of honey mustard, or a few sprigs of fresh herbs.

THE GRILL

Gas: Direct heat, medium-high (425° to 450°F)
Clean, oiled grate

Charcoal: Direct heat, light ash
12-by-12-inch charcoal bed (about 3 dozen coals)
Clean, oiled grate on lowest setting

Wood: Direct heat, light ash
12-by-12-inch bed, 3 to 4 inches deep
Clean, oiled grate set 2 inches above the fire

2 pounds ground beef chuck, 85% lean

2 tablespoons chopped garlic

1/2 teaspoon kosher salt

1/4 teaspoon ground black pepper

3 tablespoons herbed garlic cream cheese such as Boursin

Oil for coating grill grate

6 hamburger buns, split

DIRECTIONS

1. Heat the grill as directed.

2. Using your hands, mix the beef, garlic, salt, and pepper in a bowl until well blended; do not overmix. Using a light touch, form into 12 patties no more than 1/2 inch thick.

3. Put a portion (about 1 1/2 teaspoons) of cheese in the center of each of 6 patties; top with the remaining patties and press together, taking care to seal the edges well. Refrigerate the burgers until the grill is ready.

4. Brush the grill grate and coat it with oil. Put the burgers on the grill, cover, and cook for 9 minutes, flipping after 5 minutes, for medium-done (150°F, slightly pink). Add a minute per side for well-done (160°F).

5. To toast the buns, put them cut-sides down directly over the fire for the last minute of cooking.

6. If serving the burgers directly from the grill, serve on the buns. If the burgers will sit, even for a few minutes, keep the buns and burgers separate until just before eating.

WILD MUSHROOM–STUFFED ROSEMARY BURGERS

The stuffing for these burgers could make shoe leather palatable. It combines inexpensive exotic mushrooms, like shiitake and cremini, with a little bit of dried wild mushrooms to boost the flavor. Don't let the price of dried wild mushrooms scare you; a little goes a long way, and you get the added benefit of a soaking liquid that can be reduced to the essence of mushroom-identity.

TIMING
Prep: 20 minutes
Grill: About 10 minutes

GRILL TOOLS AND EQUIPMENT
· Long-handled spatula

GETTING CREATIVE
· Garnish these savory burgers with rich, intense flavors, like caramelized onions or garlic, blue cheese, or a slice of fresh goat cheese.
· Season the surface of the burgers with an herb rub like Tuscan Rosemary Rub (page 375) or Provençal Herb Rub (page 373).

THE GRILL

Gas: Direct heat, medium-high (425° to 450°F)
Clean, oiled grate

Charcoal: Direct heat, light ash
12-by-12-inch charcoal bed (about 3 dozen coals)
Clean, oiled grate on lowest setting

Wood: Direct heat, light ash
12-by-12-inch bed, 3 to 4 inches deep
Clean, oiled grate set 2 inches above the fire

INGREDIENTS (MAKES 6 SERVINGS)

1/2 ounce dried wild mushrooms such as porcini, morels, and/or chanterelles

1/3 cup hot water

1 tablespoon olive oil

1/4 cup finely chopped onion

4 ounces fresh "wild" mushrooms such as oyster, cremini, and/or shiitake, sliced

1 tablespoon minced garlic

2 teaspoons finely chopped fresh rosemary leaves

1/4 cup red wine

1 tablespoon balsamic vinegar

3 tablespoons chopped flat-leaf parsley

1/2 teaspoon kosher salt, or more to taste

1/4 teaspoon ground black pepper, or more to taste

2 pounds ground beef chuck, 85% lean

Oil for coating grill grate

6 flatbread rolls such as ciabatta, split

DIRECTIONS

1. Soak the dried mushrooms in the hot water in a small bowl for 20 minutes, or until tender. Lift the mushrooms from the soaking liquid; don't discard the liquid. Chop the mushrooms finely and set aside.

2. Heat the grill as directed.

3. Heat the olive oil in a large skillet over medium-high heat. Add the onion and sauté until tender and lightly browned. Add the sliced fresh mushrooms and sauté until tender, about 4 minutes. Add the garlic and rosemary and cook for another minute. Add the wine, soaked mushrooms, and mushroom-

soaking liquid, being careful to leave behind any sediment at the bottom of the bowl. Boil until the liquid is almost all gone. Stir in the vinegar, parsley, and a pinch each of the salt and pepper; let cool.

4. Using your hands, mix the beef and the remaining salt and pepper in a bowl until well blended; do not overmix. Using a light touch, form into 12 patties no more than 1/2 inch thick.

5. Put a portion of the mushroom mixture in the center of each of 6 patties; top with the remaining patties and press together,

Photo: Herb Cheese–Stuffed Garlic Burger

taking care to seal the edges well. Refrigerate the burgers until the grill is ready.

6. Brush the grill grate and coat it with oil. Put the burgers on the grill, cover, and cook for 9 minutes, flipping after about 5 minutes, for medium-done (150°F, slightly pink). Add a minute per side for well-done (160°F).

7. To toast the rolls, put them cut-sides down directly over the fire for the last minute of cooking.

8. If serving the burgers directly from the grill, serve on the rolls. If the burgers will sit, even for a few minutes, keep the rolls and burgers separate until just before eating.

TIMING
Prep: 10 minutes
Grill: About 10 minutes

GRILL TOOLS AND EQUIPMENT
· Long-handled spatula

GETTING CREATIVE
· Garnish these burgers with anything you would use to garnish a chili: sour cream, avocado (or guacamole), sliced jalapeños, scallions, and so on.
· Substitute prepared barbecued beef or baked beans for the chili.

CHILI-STUFFED CHEESEBURGERS

This is a great use for leftover chili, or open a can if you don't have any leftovers. Because the chili is fluid, it needs to be solidified before you can stuff it into the burgers. This is done by adding cheese to make it cohesive. As the burger cooks, the cheese melts, leaving you with a chin of cheesy chili with every bite.

THE GRILL

Gas: Direct heat, medium-high (425° to 450°F)
Clean, oiled grate

Charcoal: Direct heat, light ash
12-by-12-inch charcoal bed (about 3 dozen coals)
Clean, oiled grate on lowest setting

Wood: Direct heat, light ash
12-by-12-inch bed, 3 to 4 inches deep
Clean, oiled grate set 2 inches above the fire

INGREDIENTS (MAKES 6 SERVINGS)

3/4 cup spicy leftover or canned chili, your favorite brand
1/2 cup shredded Cheddar cheese, or as needed
2 pounds ground beef chuck, 85% lean
1/2 teaspoon kosher salt

1/4 teaspoon ground black pepper
Oil for coating grill grate
6 hamburger buns, split

DIRECTIONS

1. Heat the grill as directed.

2. Mix the chili and cheese in a bowl. The mixture should be cohesive. If it's still runny, add a little more cheese.

3. Using your hands, mix the beef, salt, and pepper in a separate bowl until well blended; do not overmix. Using a light touch, form into 12 patties no more than 1/2 inch thick.

4. Put a portion of the chili mixture in the center of each of 6 patties; top with the remaining patties and press together, taking care to seal the edges well. Refrigerate the burgers until the grill is ready.

5. Brush the grill grate and coat it with oil. Put the burgers on the grill, cover, and cook for 9 minutes, flipping after about 5 minutes, for medium-done (150°F, slightly pink). Add a minute per side for well-done (160°F).

6. To toast the buns, put them cut-sides down directly over the fire for the last minute of cooking.

7. If serving the burgers directly from the grill, serve on the buns. If the burgers will sit, even for a few minutes, keep the buns and burgers separate until just before eating.

TIMING
Prep: 10 minutes
Grill: About 18 minutes
(8 minutes for stuffing ingredients,
10 minutes for burgers)

TURKEY BURGERS STUFFED WITH PEAR AND SAGE

Ground turkey is bland and dry. It needs help to become a succulent burger, which is why turkey burgers always have a lot more ingredients in them than burgers made from beef or pork. The secret to this one is apple butter, which gives the turkey a darker color and adds spices that make the meat taste richer. The burgers are also stuffed with sautéed pear, which releases moisture into the burgers as they cook.

Gas: Direct heat, medium-high (425° to 450°F) Clean, oiled grate **Charcoal:** Direct heat, light ash 12-by-12-inch charcoal bed (about 3 dozen coals) Clean, oiled grate on lowest setting	**Wood:** Direct heat, light ash 12-by-12-inch bed, 3 to 4 inches deep Clean, oiled grate set 2 inches above the fire

GRILL TOOLS AND EQUIPMENT
· Clean grill screen
· Long-handled spatula

GETTING CREATIVE
· Because these burgers have a slightly sweet flavor, it is best to keep your garnishes savory: sautéed onions and mushrooms, a leaf of romaine lettuce, some baby spinach, or a few slices of sweet pickle.
· If you want to add cheese, make it something that goes with fruit; an imported Swiss, some crumbled blue, or a sharp Cheddar work well.

INGREDIENTS (MAKES 4 SERVINGS)

Four ¹/₂-inch-thick slices onion 1 Bartlett pear, peeled cored, and cut into 8 wedges 1 tablespoon canola oil 6 fresh sage leaves, finely chopped ¹/₂ teaspoon kosher salt ¹/₄ teaspoon ground black pepper	1¹/₂ pounds ground turkey 2 tablespoons apple butter ¹/₂ teaspoon poultry seasoning 1 tablespoon chopped fresh flat-leaf parsley Oil for coating grill grate 4 hamburger buns, split

DIRECTIONS

1. Heat the grill as directed.

2. Put the grill screen on the grill to get hot. Coat the onion slices and pear wedges with the 1 tablespoon oil and put them on the grill screen. Grill until browned on both sides, about 4 minutes per side for the onion and 3 minutes per side for the pear.

3. Chop the grilled onion and pear into small pieces and mix with the sage and a pinch each of the salt and pepper in a small bowl; let cool.

4. Using your hands, mix the turkey, apple butter, poultry seasoning, parsley, and remaining salt and pepper in a separate bowl until well blended; do not overmix. Using a light touch, form into 8 patties no more than ¹/₂ inch thick.

5. Put a portion of the pear-sage mixture in the center of each of 4 patties; top with the remaining patties and press together, taking care to seal the edges well. Refrigerate the burgers until the grill is ready.

6. Brush the grill grate and coat it with oil. Put the burgers on the grill, cover, and cook for 9 minutes, flipping after about 5 minutes, for medium-done (150°F, slightly pink). Add a minute per side for well-done (160°F).

7. To toast the buns, put them cut-sides down directly over the fire for the last minute of cooking.

8. If serving the burgers directly from the grill, serve them on the buns. If the burgers will sit, even for a few minutes, keep the buns and burgers separate until just before eating.

GREEN PEPPERCORN BURGERS STUFFED WITH GORGONZOLA

It is best to make these burgers with a young Gorgonzola, like Gorgonzola dolce. Aged for about 3 months, Gorgonzola at this stage is not as flavorful as the longer-aged Gorgonzola *piccante,* but it is much softer and easier to form into a cohesive filling. The melting core of Gorgonzola and garlic is delicious with the glow of fresh peppercorns that permeate the burger.

TIMING
Prep: 10 minutes
Grill: About 10 minutes

THE GRILL

Gas: Direct heat, medium-high (425° to 450°F) Clean, oiled grate **Charcoal:** Direct heat, light ash 12-by-12-inch charcoal bed (about 3 dozen coals) Clean, oiled grate on lowest setting	**Wood:** Direct heat, light ash 12-by-12-inch bed, 3 to 4 inches deep Clean, oiled grate set 2 inches above the fire

GRILL TOOLS AND EQUIPMENT
· Long-handled spatula

MAKING SUBSTITUTIONS
· Any blue-veined cheese can be substituted for the Gorgonzola, but one with a creamy texture and mild flavor, like Cambozola, Montagnolo, or Danablu, will work best.
· If you don't have jarred (fresh) green peppercorns, you can substitute dried coarsely ground peppercorns, cutting the amount to ¹/₂ teaspoon or so.

GETTING CREATIVE
· Garnish these burgers with fresh produce that is enhanced by blue cheese, such as thin slices of apple or pear, or an assertive-tasting leaf like radicchio, endive, or spinach.

INGREDIENTS (MAKES 6 SERVINGS)

2 ounces Gorgonzola cheese, crumbled (about ¹/₂ cup) 5 cloves garlic, minced ¹/₂ teaspoon ground black pepper, or more to taste 2 pounds ground beef chuck, 85% lean	1¹/₂ tablespoons jarred green peppercorns, drained and rinsed ¹/₂ teaspoon kosher salt Oil for coating grill grate 6 flatbread buns such as ciabatta, split

1. Heat the grill as directed.

2. Mix the Gorgonzola, half of the garlic, and half of the black pepper in a bowl.

3. Using your hands, mix the beef, green peppercorns, salt, and remaining garlic and black pepper in a separate bowl until well blended; do not overmix. Using a light touch, form into 12 patties no more than $1/2$ inch thick.

4. Put a portion of the Gorgonzola mixture in the center of each of 6 patties; top with the remaining patties and press together, taking care to seal the edges well. Refrigerate the burgers until the grill is ready.

5. Brush the grill grate and coat it with oil. Put the burgers on the grill, cover, and cook for 9 minutes, flipping after about 5 minutes, for medium-done (150°F, slightly pink). Add a minute per side for well-done (160°F).

6. To toast the rolls, put them cut-sides down directly over the fire for the last minute of cooking.

7. If serving the burgers directly from the grill, serve on the rolls. If the burgers will sit, even for a few minutes, keep the rolls and burgers separate until just before eating.

TIMING
Prep: 10 minutes
Grill: 8 minutes

GRILL TOOLS AND EQUIPMENT
· Clean grill screen
· Long-handled tongs

GETTING CREATIVE
· Substitute drained chili for the sauerkraut.
· Replace the hot dog with chorizo, kielbasa, or any other smoked sausage.

HOT DOGS STUFFED WITH THE WORKS

You will need large hot dogs (knockwurst or foot-longs, take your choice) to hold all of the filling in this recipe. "The works" means anything and everything you like on a hot dog, so if there's something that works for you that we haven't included, bring it on; you can't mess it up. Whatever you do, the results will be over the top. One word of warning: Don't wrap the bacon too tightly, or it will break when the hot dogs swell during cooking.

THE GRILL

Gas: Direct heat, medium-high (425° to 450°F)
Clean, oiled grate

Charcoal: Direct heat, light ash
12-by-12-inch charcoal bed (about 3 dozen coals)
Clean, oiled grate on lowest setting

Wood: Direct heat, light ash
12-by-12-inch bed, 3 to 4 inches deep
Clean, oiled grate set 2 inches above the fire

INGREDIENTS (MAKES 6 SERVINGS)

2 teaspoons spicy brown mustard

2 tablespoons ketchup

1 cup refrigerated sauerkraut, drained, rinsed, and coarsely chopped

4 large hot dogs such as knockwurst

$1/2$ ounce Cheddar cheese, cut into 4 small sticks

4 slices bacon

Oil for coating grill screen

4 long hot-dog buns or small sub rolls, split

DIRECTIONS

1. Heat the grill as directed.

2. Mix the mustard, ketchup, and sauerkraut in a small bowl.

3. Slit the hot dogs lengthwise, forming a deep pocket end to end in each one. Fill the pockets halfway with the sauerkraut mixture. Put a stick of cheese in the center of each and top with the remaining sauerkraut mixture. Wrap a bacon slice around each hot dog to hold it together, and secure the ends of each bacon strip with wooden toothpicks.

4. Put the grill screen on the grill and coat it with oil. Wait a minute or two, until the surface is hot. Grill the hot dogs until the bacon is cooked through and the hot dogs are browned on all sides, about 2 minutes per side.

5. To toast the buns, put them cut-sides down directly over the fire for the last minute of cooking. Serve the hot dogs on the buns.

WHAT'S MUSTARD?

Mustard is a weed that grows wild in practically every region of the world. There are three types of mustard seed, categorized by color. Black mustard is the most pungent, followed by brown mustard, sometimes called Indian mustard, and then white mustard, which is the mildest.

Strong mustards from France and Germany are typically made with black or brown seeds. Yellow American mustard, which is relatively bland in comparison, is a mixture of white seeds and turmeric.

The production of prepared mustards is relatively uncomplicated. The seeds are soaked in water to soften their shells, and then they are ground. The pungency of mustard develops from essential oils in the seeds, which are activated when the ground seeds and soaking water are mixed together. Only then can enzymes present in the seeds activate the oils and create the strong, pungent aroma and flavor that characterize all fine mustards.

If the seeds are heated or exposed to strong acids early in this process, the enzymes will be destroyed and the mustard will lack its characteristic punch. For that reason, the addition of vinegars, wines, sugars, spices, or heat always takes place after the seeds have had a chance to release their oils. For whole seeds, this takes at least 3 hours of soaking. A finished mustard can either be finely ground, be coarsely ground, or include a proportion of whole seeds.

Mustards from different countries are flavored differently. French mustards often include wine, wine vinegar, sugar, and spices. German mustards are made from dark seeds, vinegar, and sugar, giving them a pronounced sweet-and-sour quality and strong aroma. Asian mustards usually have additional mustard oil, which makes them sharper and more pungent.

GRILL TOOLS AND EQUIPMENT
· Long-handled spatula

GETTING CREATIVE
· These burgers are great with a garnish of sautéed mushrooms or grilled onions. If you want to top them with cheese, try something a little nutty like Italian fontina, Emmental, or Grana Padano.
· Other liquors can be substituted for brandy. Scotch, bourbon, and port are logical choices.

FLAMING BRANDY BURGERS

These burgers are spectacular. The meat is inundated with onion, garlic, and the exotic aroma of allspice, but the extravagance comes just before serving. As soon as the burgers reach doneness, you douse them with a little brandy, which flames blue for a second as the alcohol evaporates and quickly burns off, leaving behind a sweet glaze, lightly caramelized edges, and an oaky, fruity aroma.

THE GRILL

Gas: Direct heat, medium-high (425° to 450°F)
Clean, oiled grate

Charcoal: Direct heat, light ash
12-by-12-inch charcoal bed (about 3 dozen coals)
Clean, oiled grate on lowest setting

Wood: Direct heat, light ash
12-by-12-inch bed, 3 to 4 inches deep
Clean, oiled grate set 2 inches above the fire

INGREDIENTS (MAKES 6 SERVINGS)

2 pounds ground beef chuck, 85% lean
$2/3$ cup finely chopped onion
3 cloves garlic, minced
$1/2$ teaspoon ground allspice
$1/2$ teaspoon kosher salt

$1/4$ teaspoon ground black pepper, or to taste
Oil for coating grill grate
$1/4$ cup brandy
6 kaiser rolls, split (optional)

DIRECTIONS

1. Heat the grill as directed.

2. Using your hands, mix the beef, onion, garlic, allspice, salt, and pepper in a bowl until well blended; do not overmix. Using a light touch, form into 6 patties no more than 1 inch thick. Refrigerate the burgers until the grill is ready.

3. Brush the grill grate and coat it with oil. Put the burgers on the grill, cover, and cook for 7 minutes, flipping after about 4 minutes, for medium-done (150°F, slightly pink). Add a minute per side for well-done (160°F).

4. Have the brandy in a small pitcher. Starting with the burgers farthest away from you, pour a small portion (about 2 teaspoons) over each burger. The brandy will flame up and flicker around the burgers for a few seconds.

5. To toast the rolls, if using, put them cut-sides down directly over the fire for the last minute of cooking.

6. If serving the burgers directly from the grill, serve on the rolls. If the burgers will sit, even for a few minutes, keep the rolls and burgers separate until just before eating.

GRILL TOOLS AND EQUIPMENT
· Long-handled spatula

MEATLOAF BURGERS

The meat for meatloaf (at least good meatloaf) is a mixture of two parts ground beef, one part ground pork, and one part ground veal, plus lots of other ingredients that give it flavor and help it to retain moisture. The pork makes it a little sweet, the veal makes it smooth, and everything makes it taste good. This burger is meatloaf on a bun; its base came from Andy's mom, who didn't cook much but made a killer meatloaf.

THE GRILL

Gas: Direct heat, medium-high (425° to 450°F)
Clean, oiled grate

Charcoal: Direct heat, light ash
12-by-12-inch charcoal bed (about 3 dozen coals)
Clean, oiled grate on lowest setting

Wood: Direct heat, light ash
12-by-12-inch bed, 3 to 4 inches deep
Clean, oiled grate set 2 inches above the fire

2 pounds meatloaf mix (1 pound ground beef, 8 ounces
 ground veal, and 8 ounces ground pork)

1/3 cup finely chopped onion

1/3 cup ketchup

1 1/2 teaspoons spicy brown mustard

1 tablespoon Worcestershire sauce

1/2 teaspoon kosher salt

1/4 teaspoon ground black pepper

Oil for coating grill grate

6 hamburger buns, split

DIRECTIONS

1. Heat the grill as directed.

2. Using your hands, mix the meatloaf mix, onion, ketchup, mustard, Worcestershire, salt, and pepper in a bowl until well blended; do not overmix. Using a light touch, form into 6 patties no more than 1 inch thick. Refrigerate the burgers until the grill is ready.

3. Brush the grill grate and coat it with oil. Put the burgers on the grill, cover, and cook for 7 minutes, flipping after about

4 minutes, for medium-done (150°F, slightly pink). Add a minute per side for well-done (160°F).

4. To toast the buns, put them cut-sides down directly over the fire for the last minute of cooking.

5. If serving the burgers directly from the grill, serve on the buns. If the burgers will sit, even for a few minutes, keep the buns and burgers separate until just before eating.

GETTING CREATIVE
· Top as you would a meatloaf, with a spicy tomato sauce or sautéed mushrooms.

TIP
· Like meatloaf, these burgers make better leftovers than your average burger.

GRILLED APPLE–SAUERKRAUT PORK BURGERS

The sweet, mild flavor of pork and the pungent salinity of sauerkraut are a classic combo. This simple pork burger, made richer with the addition of beef, mustard, and applesauce, is crowned with an elaborate sweet-sour-salty pickled cabbage prepared by simmering sauerkraut, apple, caraway, and bourbon until the flavors marry.

TIMING
Prep: 5 minutes
Grill: 7 minutes

GRILL TOOLS AND EQUIPMENT
· Clean grill screen
· Long-handled spatula

GETTING CREATIVE
· These burgers are too loaded to pick up. So in lieu of a roll, we suggest serving them with your choice of potatoes: mashed, hashed, baked, or scalloped (you can't go wrong).

THE GRILL

Gas: Direct heat, medium-high (425° to 450°F)
 Clean, oiled grate

Charcoal: Direct heat, light ash
 12-by-12-inch charcoal bed (about 3 dozen coals)
 Clean, oiled grate on lowest setting

Wood: Direct heat, light ash
 12-by-12-inch bed, 3 to 4 inches deep
 Clean, oiled grate set 2 inches above the fire

INGREDIENTS (MAKES SERVING 6)

1 large, crisp apple such as Granny Smith or Jonathan, peeled, cored, and cut into 8 wedges

1 tablespoon canola oil or other flavorless oil

1 tablespoon dark or light brown sugar

2 tablespoons bourbon

1/2 teaspoon caraway seed

2 cups (about 10 ounces) refrigerated sauerkraut, drained
 and finely chopped

1 tablespoon unsalted butter

1 1/2 pounds ground pork

8 ounces ground beef chuck, 85% lean

1 teaspoon Dijon-style mustard

1/4 teaspoon dried thyme

1/2 cup unsweetened applesauce

1/2 teaspoon kosher salt

1/4 teaspoon ground black pepper

Oil for coating grill grate

DIRECTIONS

1. Heat the grill as directed. Put the grill screen on the grill to get hot.

2. Coat the apple wedges with the 1 tablespoon oil, and grill them on the screen until browned on all 3 sides and tender, about 2 minutes per side. Remove the apple and screen. Chop the apple coarsely.

3. Combine the brown sugar, bourbon, caraway seed, and sauerkraut in a skillet. Cook over medium heat until heated through. Add the chopped apple and butter and stir until the butter melts; keep warm.

4. Using your hands, mix the pork, beef, mustard, thyme, applesauce, salt, and pepper in a bowl until well blended; do not overmix. Using a light touch, form into 6 patties no more than 1 inch thick.

5. Brush the grill grate and coat it with oil. Put the burgers on the grill, cover, and cook for 7 minutes, flipping after about 4 minutes, for medium-done (150°F, slightly pink). Add a minute per side for well-done (160°F).

6. Serve the burgers topped with some of the sauerkraut mixture.

GRILL TOOLS AND EQUIPMENT
· Long-handled spatula

GETTING CREATIVE
· If you want to enhance the Japanese character of these burgers, garnish them with pickled ginger or daikon, wasabi mayonnaise, or a drizzle of teriyaki sauce; or coat them in toasted sesame oil rather than canola.

MISO TUNA BURGERS

Raw tuna is one of the few fish that is both sturdy and fatty enough to form into a burger without the addition of binders and starches. The only requirement is that you chop the tuna finely enough so that the pieces adhere to one another, but not so finely so that the mixture becomes mushy. For that reason it is not a good idea to use a food processor to do your chopping. The danger of going too far is likely enough, and the results of misjudgment severe enough, that the convenience is not worth the risk.

THE GRILL

Gas: Direct heat, medium-high (425° to 450°F)
Clean, oiled grate

Charcoal: Direct heat, light ash
12-by-12-inch charcoal bed (about 3 dozen coals)
Clean, oiled grate on lowest setting

Wood: Direct heat, light ash
12-by-12-inch bed, 3 to 4 inches deep
Clean, oiled grate set 2 inches above the fire

INGREDIENTS (MAKES 4 SERVINGS)

1 1/2 pounds tuna steak, cut into small chunks
1 tablespoon miso paste
1/2 teaspoon prepared wasabi
1 teaspoon soy sauce

4 scallions, roots trimmed, cut into 1/2-inch pieces
Oil for coating grill grate
1 tablespoon mild-flavored oil such as canola
4 hamburger buns, split

DIRECTIONS

1. Heat the grill as directed.
2. Chop the tuna finely enough so that when you press some between your fingers it clings to itself, but not so finely that it becomes mushy.
3. Remove the fish to a bowl and mix in the miso, wasabi, soy sauce, and scallions until well blended; do not overmix. Using a light touch, form into 4 patties no more than 1 inch thick. Refrigerate the burgers until the grill is ready.
4. Brush the grill grate and coat it with oil. Coat the burgers with the 1 tablespoon oil, put them on the grill, cover, and cook

for 6 minutes, flipping halfway through, for medium-rare; do not cover the grill after flipping. Add a minute per side for medium-done.
5. To toast the buns, put them cut-sides down directly over the fire for the last minute of cooking.
6. If serving the burgers directly from the grill, serve on the buns. If the burgers will sit, even for a few minutes, keep the buns and burgers separate until just before eating.

TIMING
Soak wood chips: 1 hour
Prep: 10 minutes
     (plus 10 minutes for rub and dip)
Grill: 8 to 10 minutes

GRILL TOOLS AND EQUIPMENT
· 2 cups hardwood wood chips
· Smoker box or foil packet, if using a
  gas grill (see page 16)
· Clean grill screen
· Long-handled spatula

SMOKED CRAB BURGERS

The smoke in these burgers emanates from two sources: (1) wood chips and (2) hickory-smoked bacon strips that are tied around each crab cake like a ribbon. Make sure the wood chips go on a good 5 minutes before you put the burgers on the grill. Crab burgers cook so quickly that they will not absorb much smoky flavor unless the smoke is billowing vigorously before they come into contact with it. The recipe calls for back-fin crab, which isn't as impressive (or as expensive) as lump crab but will hold together on the grill much better than the high-priced stuff.

THE GRILL

Gas: Direct heat, medium-high (425° to 450°F)
Clean, oiled grate

Charcoal: Direct heat, light ash
12-by-12-inch charcoal bed (about 3 dozen coals)
Clean, oiled grate on lowest setting

Wood: Direct heat, light ash
12-by-12-inch bed, 3 to 4 inches deep
Clean, oiled grate set 2 inches above the fire

INGREDIENTS (MAKES 4 SERVINGS)

2 scallions, roots trimmed, thinly sliced
1/2 roasted red bell pepper, stemmed, seeded, and finely
   chopped (about 1/4 cup)
1 clove garlic, minced
2 tablespoons grated onion
2 tablespoons mayonnaise

1 teaspoon Cajun spice blend, Old Bay seasoning, or Cajun
   Blackening Rub (page 373)
1 pound canned back-fin crabmeat
4 slices center-cut hickory-smoked bacon, cut in
   half lengthwise
Oil for coating grill screen
1/4 cup Harissa Dip (page 396) or Lime-Cilantro Butter
   (page 393) (optional)

DIRECTIONS

1. Soak the wood chips in hot water in a medium bowl for at least 1 hour; heat the grill as directed. Drain the wood chips.
2. Mix the scallions, bell pepper, garlic, onion, mayonnaise, spice blend, and crabmeat in a bowl until well blended. Using a light torch, form into 4 patties about 1 1/4 inches thick, and wrap 2 strips of bacon around each burger so that the burgers look as though they have been tied with ribbons.

3. Put the soaked wood chips on the hot coals (see page 38), or set them in a smoker box of foil if using a gas grill (see page 39). Put the grill grate back in place and top with the grill screen. Coat the screen with oil, cover the grill, and wait for about 5 minutes, until the smoke is plentiful.
4. Put the burgers on the grill screen, cover, and cook for about 8 minutes, flipping halfway through, until the bacon and burgers are browned but still soft in the center.
5. Serve with Harissa Dip or cilantro butter, if desired.

SMOKED SALMON BURGERS

Like tuna, raw salmon has enough fat to form a burger. Chop the salmon by hand rather than in a food processor, which can give you mushy results if you accidentally process it a few seconds too long. The smoky flavor of these burgers comes from the addition of smoked salmon. A wide range of smoked salmon products are available, costing from $5 a pound to more than $40. We recommend using smoked salmon ends (available in any deli that hand-slices salmon), which will cost a fraction of the price of sliced salmon. Since you will be mincing it anyway, this will give you a higher-quality product for less money.

THE GRILL

Gas: Direct heat, medium-high (425° to 450°F)
Clean, oiled grate

Charcoal: Direct heat, light ash
12-by-12-inch charcoal bed (about 3 dozen coals)
Clean, oiled grate on lowest setting

Wood: Direct heat, light ash
12-by-12-inch bed, 3 to 4 inches deep
Clean, oiled grate set 2 inches above the fire

INGREDIENTS (MAKES 6 SERVINGS)

1 1/2 pounds skinned and boned salmon fillet, cut into small chunks

8 ounces smoked salmon, finely chopped

3 tablespoons finely chopped onion

1 tablespoon minced garlic

3 tablespoons chopped fresh chives

Four 1/4-inch-thick lemon slices

6 teaspoons extra-virgin olive oil

Oil for coating grill grate

DIRECTIONS

1. Heat the grill as directed.

2. Chop the salmon finely enough so that when you press some between your fingers it clings to itself, but not so finely that it becomes mushy.

3. Remove the fish to a bowl and mix in the smoked salmon, onion, garlic, and chives until well blended; do not overmix. Using a light touch, form into 4 patties no more than 1 inch thick. Refrigerate the burgers until the grill is ready.

4. Coat the lemon slices with 1 teaspoon of the olive oil; set aside.

5. Brush the grill grate and coat it with oil. Coat the burgers with 2 1/2 teaspoons of the olive oil and put them on the grill. Cover and cook for about 7 minutes for medium-rare, flipping after 4 minutes; do not cover the grill after flipping. Add a minute per side for medium-done (165°F).

6. When you flip the burgers, start grilling the lemon slices until browned on both sides, slightly softened, and oozing juice, about 1 minute per side.

7. Serve the burgers drizzled with the remaining 2 1/2 teaspoons olive oil, with the lemon slices on the side for squeezing.

GRILL TOOLS AND EQUIPMENT
- Long-handled spatula

GETTING CREATIVE
- Add chopped fresh dill to the burger mixture.
- Serve the burgers with minced red onion and capers on top.
- Serve on thinly sliced bagels smeared with cream cheese.

TURKEY SAUSAGES IN VINE LEAVES

Jarred grape leaves tend toward the insipid—drab, sodden, and tasting more of salt than anything else. But all of that changes on the grill. Their soaked texture dries and crisps, the brine intensifies, and the tobaccolike flavor of the leaf starts to bloom. Grilled grape leaves are a delicious foil to meaty, sweet Italian-style turkey sausage; the two are brought together in this elegant appetizer or light entrée with a drizzle of extra-virgin olive oil and lemon.

THE GRILL

Gas: Direct heat, medium-high (425° to 450°F)
Clean, oiled grate

Charcoal: Direct heat, light ash
12-by-12-inch charcoal bed (about 3 dozen coals)
Clean, oiled grate on lowest setting

Wood: Direct heat, light ash
12-by-12-inch bed, 3 to 4 inches deep
Clean, oiled grate set 2 inches above the fire

INGREDIENTS (MAKES 4 SERVINGS)

Oil for coating grill screen

1/3 cup extra-virgin olive oil

1 large clove garlic, minced

Juice of 1 lemon (about 3 tablespoons)

1/2 teaspoon dried oregano

1/4 teaspoon ground black pepper

6 fresh turkey sausages, preferably with garlic and/or feta, about 4 ounces each

12 jarred grape leaves, preferably early harvest

TIMING
Prep: 10 minutes
Grill: 8 minutes

GRILL TOOLS AND EQUIPMENT
- Clean grill screen
- Long-handled tongs

MAKING SUBSTITUTIONS
- These sausages are also delicious made with mint. You can either add a teaspoon of dried mint (or 1 tablespoon chopped fresh mint leaves) along with the oregano, or replace the oregano with mint.
- Use any mild, sweet sausage in place of turkey.

1. Heat the grill as directed. Put the grill screen on the grill and coat it with oil.

2. Mix the olive oil, garlic, lemon juice, oregano, and black pepper in a small bowl.

3. Brush the sausages with 2 tablespoons of the olive oil mixture, and roll each sausage in 2 grape leaves, securing the ends with wooden toothpicks.

4. Grill the sausages until the leaves are charred on all sides and the sausages feel firm to the touch, about 8 minutes, turning them a quarter turn every 2 minutes. Serve drizzled with the remaining olive oil mixture.

Photo: Turkey Sausages in Vine Leaves

CHICKEN AND ARTICHOKE KEBABS

TIMING

Prep: 10 minutes
(plus 5 minutes for rub)
Grill: About 10 minutes

Boneless chicken breast is not a natural for grilling. It cooks through quickly, and it's the right shape, but it is soooo lean that the harsh heat of an open flame can transform it to chicken jerky if you don't take precautions. One of the best things you can do is slip it onto a skewer with moister ingredients (such as the canned artichoke hearts used here) that will baste the chicken as it cooks, helping to replenish its moisture.

GRILL TOOLS AND EQUIPMENT

· Four 15-inch metal skewers,
  preferably flat or square
· Long-handled tongs

GETTING CREATIVE

· Use this recipe as a template for other two-ingredient kebabs: Try pork and par-cooked sweet potato; or canned pineapple chunks seasoned with Sweet Chimichurri Rub (page 380); or veal with artichokes or pears seasoned with Provençal Herb Rub (page 373).

THE GRILL

Gas: Direct heat, medium-high (425° to 450°F)
Clean, oiled grate

Charcoal: Direct heat, light ash
12-by-12-inch charcoal bed (about 3 dozen coals)
Clean, oiled grate on lowest setting

Wood: Direct heat, light ash
12-by-12-inch bed, 3 to 4 inches deep
Clean, oiled grate set 2 inches above the fire

INGREDIENTS (MAKES 4 SERVINGS)

1^1/$_2$ pounds boneless, skinless chicken breasts, cut into
  2-inch chunks (20 chunks)
^{1}/$_4$ cup extra-virgin olive oil
2 tablespoons Provençal Herb Rub (page 373)

1 can (about 14 ounces) artichoke hearts, drained and
  cut in half (16 halves)
Oil for coating grill grate
Juice of ^{1}/$_2$ lemon

DIRECTIONS

1. Heat the grill as directed.

2. Toss the chicken with half of the oil and half of the herb rub in a bowl. Toss the artichoke hearts with the remaining oil and herb rub in another bowl.

3. Skewer the chicken and artichoke hearts, alternating them and starting and ending with a piece of chicken. Be careful to leave a little space between the pieces.

4. Brush the grill grate and coat it with oil. Put the prepared skewers on the grill and cook until the chicken is browned on all sides and firm to the touch, about 10 minutes. Use tongs to grip the end of each skewer and rotate it a quarter turn after 3 minutes and then every 2 minutes after that; do not overcook.

5. Serve drizzled with the lemon juice.

TANDOORI CHICKEN KEBABS

TIMING

Prep: 10 minutes
(plus 5 minutes for marinade)
Grill: About 10 minutes

Tandoori originally meant any food cooked in an Indian clay oven, called a tandoor. Now it more often denotes a recipe with a currylike spice mixture that includes paprika, turmeric, coriander, and some sort of fermented dairy product to act as a marinade. In this recipe we've used yogurt for a thick, clinging marinade, which forms a crust around each chicken piece that is both flavorful and protective.

GRILL TOOLS AND EQUIPMENT

· Four 15-inch metal skewers,
  preferably flat or square
· Long-handled tongs

MAKING SUBSTITUTIONS

· As with most chicken breast recipes, turkey breast can be substituted for chicken without making any adjustments to cooking time or flavor.
· If you want a thinner marinade that adheres less spice to the surface of the chicken, replace the yogurt with buttermilk or with a mixture of yogurt and lemon or lime juice.

THE GRILL

Gas: Direct heat, medium-high (425° to 450°F)
Clean, oiled grate

Charcoal: Direct heat, light ash
12-by-12-inch charcoal bed (about 3 dozen coals)
Clean, oiled grate on lowest setting

Wood: Direct heat, light ash
12-by-12-inch bed, 3 to 4 inches deep
Clean, oiled grate set 2 inches above the fire

---

1 1/2 pounds boneless, skinless chicken breasts, cut into
   2-inch chunks (about 20 chunks)

1/2 cup Tandoori Yogurt Marinade (page 360)

Oil for coating grill grate

Juice of 1 lime

DIRECTIONS

1. Heat the grill as directed.

2. Toss the chicken with the marinade in a bowl, cover, and refrigerate for 10 minutes.

3. Skewer the chicken, being careful to leave a little space between the pieces.

4. Brush the grill grate and coat it with oil. Put the prepared skewers on the grill and cook until the chicken is browned on all sides and firm to the touch, about 10 minutes. Use tongs to grip the end of each skewer and rotate it a quarter turn after 3 minutes and then every 2 minutes after that; do not overcook.

5. Serve drizzled with the lime juice.

HABANERO–HONEY PORK KEBABS

Hot pepper and honey have a symbiotic relationship. Each tempers the excesses of the other, forming a partnership that is far more palatable than either can claim on its own. Habanero has the added effect of being so fiery that its aftereffect on the tongue is actually cooling. This happens more or less with all chiles. When capsaicin hits the tongue it damages surface tissue, causing the tongue to become more sensitive to its environment, in the same way that a cut on a finger makes you more aware of anything you touch. When you breathe in after eating chiles, especially strong ones like habanero, the sensitized skin on your tongue senses the flow of air through the mouth, which would normally have gone unnoticed, resulting in the feeling that the tongue is being fanned and cooled.

THE GRILL

Gas: Direct heat, medium-high (425° to 450°F)
         Clean, oiled grate

Charcoal: Direct heat, light ash
         12-by-12-inch charcoal bed (about 3 dozen coals)
         Clean, oiled grate on lowest setting

Wood: Direct heat, light ash
         12-by-12-inch bed, 3 to 4 inches deep
         Clean, oiled grate set 2 inches above the fire

INGREDIENTS (MAKES 4 SERVINGS)

1/4 cup honey

1/2 teaspoon habanero chile powder

1/4 cup Cuervo Gold tequila

3 teaspoons kosher salt

1 1/2 pounds boneless center-cut pork loin, cut into 2-inch
   chunks (about 20 chunks)

1/4 teaspoon ground black pepper

2 teaspoons garlic-flavored oil

Oil for coating grill grate

DIRECTIONS

1. Heat the grill as directed.

2. Mix the honey, habanero powder, tequila, and 2 1/2 teaspoons kosher salt in a small bowl; set aside.

3. Season the pork with the remaining 1/2 teaspoon kosher salt and the pepper, and toss with the garlic-flavored oil.

4. Skewer the pork, being careful to leave a little space between the pieces.

5. Brush the grill grate and coat it with oil. Put the prepared skewers on the grill and cook until the pork is browned on all sides and firm to the touch, about 10 minutes. Use tongs to grip the end of each skewer and rotate it a quarter turn after 3 minutes and then every 2 minutes after that; do not overcook. Brush with the honey mixture during the last 3 to 5 minutes of cooking.

6. Serve drizzled with the remaining honey mixture.

TIMING
Prep: 10 minutes
Grill: About 10 minutes

GRILL TOOLS AND EQUIPMENT
· Four 15-inch metal skewers, preferably flat or square
· Long-handled tongs
· Long-handled basting brush

MAKING SUBSTITUTIONS
· If you don't have garlic-flavored oil, substitute a similar amount of vegetable oil and 1/4 teaspoon minced garlic.
· You can reduce the heat by substituting a milder chile for the habanero. See the charts on page 82.

GETTING CREATIVE
· You can alternate pieces of fruit, like pineapple or apple, with the pork.
· Serve with yogurt or sour cream to help soothe the palate.

STEAK AND POTATO KEBABS

TIMING
Prep: 10 minutes
(plus 10 minutes for rub and glaze)
Grill: 8 to 10 minutes

This recipe offers yet another way to enjoy the perennial grilled pairing of steak and potatoes. Because the potatoes take longer to cook than the steak, it is necessary to precook them, which is done quickly and easily in a microwave oven.

GRILL TOOLS AND EQUIPMENT
· Four 15-inch metal skewers, preferably flat or square
· Long-handled tongs
· Long-handled basting brush

GETTING CREATIVE
· Use sweet potatoes in place of new potatoes.
· Replace half of the potatoes with baby onions or leeks.
· Replace the steak with any type of meat, and adjust the cooking time accordingly.

THE GRILL

Gas: Direct heat, medium-high (425° to 450°F)
Clean, oiled grate

Charcoal: Direct heat, light ash
12-by-12-inch charcoal bed (about 3 dozen coals)
Clean, oiled grate on lowest setting

Wood: Direct heat, light ash
12-by-12-inch bed, 3 to 4 inches deep
Clean, oiled grate set 2 inches above the fire

INGREDIENTS (MAKES 4 SERVINGS)

8 small, round potatoes, red or gold, halved
3 teaspoons garlic-flavored oil
1 pound trimmed sirloin steak, cut into 16 cubes

1 teaspoon store-bought steak seasoning blend or Ten-Pepper Rub (page 378)
Oil for coating grill grate
3/4 cup Steakhouse Glaze (page 389)

DIRECTIONS

1. Heat the grill as directed.

2. Toss the potatoes and 1 teaspoon of the garlic oil in a microwave-safe dish. Cover and microwave at full power for 4 minutes, until barely tender; let cool.

3. Toss the steak, par-cooked potatoes, remaining 2 teaspoons garlic oil, and steak seasoning in a large bowl until the potatoes and steak are uniformly coated.

4. Arrange 4 cubes of steak, alternating with 4 pieces of potato, on each skewer, being careful to leave a little space between the pieces.

5. Brush the grill grate and coat it with oil. Put the prepared skewers on the grill and cook until the beef is browned on all sides and firm to the touch, 8 to 10 minutes. Use tongs to grip the end of each skewer and rotate it a quarter turn after 3 minutes and then every 2 minutes after that; do not over-cook. Brush the kebabs with some of the glaze during the last 2 to 3 minutes of cooking.

6. Serve with the remaining glaze on the side.

THAI COCONUT SWORDFISH KEBABS

TIMING
Prep: 10 minutes
(plus 5 minutes for sauce)
Marinate: 30 minutes
Grill: About 10 minutes

These spectacular-looking kebabs are furred with coconut, fragrant with peanut sauce, and vibrantly colorful. Swordfish is a particularly meaty fish that holds up well on a skewer, but it could easily be replaced with tuna, salmon, or shark, if you wish. It is inevitable that some of the coconut will fall off as the fish grills. Don't worry about it; the amount in the recipe assumes some loss.

GRILL TOOLS AND EQUIPMENT
· Clean grill screen
· Four 15-inch metal skewers, preferably flat or square
· Long-handled tongs

NOTE:
Do not use sweetened shredded coconut. It will burn within seconds on the grill.

THE GRILL

Gas: Direct heat, medium-high (425° to 450°F)
Clean, oiled grate

Charcoal: Direct heat, light ash
12-by-12-inch charcoal bed (about 3 dozen coals)
Clean, oiled grate on lowest setting

Wood: Direct heat, light ash
12-by-12-inch bed, 3 to 4 inches deep
Clean, oiled grate set 2 inches above the fire

1 1/2 pounds swordfish steaks, skin trimmed,
   cut into 24 chunks
1 cup Thai Coconut Peanut Sauce (page 397)
Oil for coating grill screen

20 grape tomatoes
1 cup unsweetened shredded coconut (see note)
No-stick spray oil
1 lime, cut into 4 wedges

DIRECTIONS

1. Toss the swordfish chunks with 1/2 cup of the peanut sauce in a bowl. Cover and refrigerate for 30 minutes.

2. Heat the grill as directed. Put the grill screen on the grill and coat it with oil.

3. Arrange 6 pieces of swordfish, alternating with 5 grape tomatoes, on each of the 4 skewers, being careful to leave a little space between the pieces.

4. Spread the coconut on a sheet of foil in a thin layer. Roll the skewered swordfish in the coconut to coat it. Spray the coconut-coated fish liberally with oil.

5. Put the prepared skewers on the oiled grill screen and cook until the fish feels firm to the touch, about 10 minutes, turning once halfway through. Don't worry if some of the coconut burns or sticks to the screen.

6. Serve drizzled with some of the remaining 1/2 cup peanut sauce and a wedge of lime.

TIMING
Prep: 10 minutes
   (plus 5 minutes for sauce)
Marinate: 1 hour
   (soaking the skewers: 30 minutes)
Grill: About 6 minutes

GRILL TOOLS AND EQUIPMENT
- 12 long bamboo skewers
- 12 small pieces aluminum foil
- Long-handled tongs or grill mitts
- Long-handled basting brush

MAKING SUBSTITUTIONS
- The pineapple juice used to marinate the pork adds flavor, but it also helps to tenderize the meat due to a protein-cleaving enzyme in pineapple (bromelain). You can substitute papaya juice, which will give you a different flavor but a similar tenderizing effect, since papaya has its own protein-digesting enzyme (papain).

SWEET PORK SATAY

Satay came to Thailand via Indonesia, and although Thai satay sauce is always made with peanut butter and coconut milk, Indonesian satay doesn't always include coconut. This one is in the Indonesian style. It is made with pork, but you could just as easily use chicken or beef. Just make sure there is a generous amount of meat on the skewer so that it doesn't dry out before it browns.

THE GRILL

Gas: Direct heat, medium-high (425° to 450°F)
   Clean, oiled grate

Charcoal: Direct heat, light ash
   12-by-12-inch charcoal bed (about 3 dozen coals)
   Clean, oiled grate on lowest setting

Wood: Direct heat, light ash
   12-by-12-inch bed, 3 to 4 inches deep
   Clean, oiled grate set 2 inches above the fire

INGREDIENTS (MAKES 4 SERVINGS)

1 pound center-cut pork loin
1/2 cup pineapple juice
2 cloves garlic, minced
1/4 teaspoon kosher salt, or more to taste

1/4 teaspoon ground black pepper
1 to 2 tablespoons canola oil for coating pork
1 2/3 cups Indonesian Peanut Sauce (page 396)
Oil for coating grill grate

DIRECTIONS

1. Put the bamboo skewers in a roasting pan and add enough water to cover.

2. Cut the pork loin in half lengthwise. Cut into 1/4-inch-thick slices (about 24 slices) and place in a bowl. Season with the pineapple juice, garlic, salt, and pepper, and coat with the 1 to 2 tablespoons oil. Refrigerate for 1 hour.

3. Heat the grill as directed.

4. Arrange 2 pork slices on each skewer, threading the skewer through the length of each slice 2 to 3 times to secure it as

flat as possible. Wrap a piece of foil around the exposed end of each skewer.

5. Reserve 1 cup of the peanut sauce for serving.

6. Brush the grill grate and coat it with oil. Put the prepared skewers on the grill and cook until the pork is browned on all sides and firm to the touch, about 6 minutes. After the first 2 minutes of cooking, turn and brush with a thin layer of sauce every 1 to 2 minutes.

7. Serve 3 skewers per person, with the reserved sauce on the side.

VIETNAMESE BEEF SATAY BASTED WITH BASIL BUTTER

TIMING
Prep: 10 minutes
    (plus 5 minutes for sauce)
Marinate: 1 hour
Grill: 6 to 8 minutes

GRILL TOOLS AND EQUIPMENT
· 12 long bamboo skewers
· 12 small pieces aluminum foil
· Long-handled tongs or grill mitts
· Long-handled basting brush

Satay is typically served with peanut sauce, and many people think the sauce itself is "satay," when traditionally the name refers only to skewered marinated grilled meat. In this case the meat is beef and there is no dipping sauce at all. Rather, the meat is marinated in fish sauce and pineapple juice, which seasons and tenderizes the meat (pineapple contains bromelain, a natural meat tenderizer). After it is grilled, it is basted with basil butter, which glazes the crispy grilled beef with a delicate herbal perfume.

THE GRILL

Gas: Direct heat, medium-high (425° to 450°F)
Clean, oiled grate

Charcoal: Direct heat, light ash
12-by-12-inch charcoal bed (about 3 dozen coals)
Clean, oiled grate on lowest setting

Wood: Direct heat, light ash
12-by-12-inch bed, 3 to 4 inches deep
Clean, oiled grate set 2 inches above the fire

INGREDIENTS (MAKES 4 SERVINGS)

1 1/2 pounds boneless beef short ribs
1/4 cup pineapple juice
2/3 cup Vietnamese Dipping Sauce (page 398)
2 tablespoons salted butter

1/2 cup chopped fresh basil leaves (about 20), preferably
    Thai basil
Oil for coating grill grate

DIRECTIONS

1. Put the bamboo skewers in a roasting pan and add enough water to cover.

2. Cut the beef into 1/4-inch-thick slices (about 24 slices). Toss with the pineapple juice and 1/4 cup of the dipping sauce in a bowl. Cover and refrigerate for 1 hour.

3. Heat the grill as directed.

4. Arrange 2 beef slices on each skewer, threading the skewer through the length of each slice 2 to 3 times to secure it as flat as possible. Wrap a piece of foil around the exposed end of each skewer.

5. Brush the grill grate and coat it with oil. Put the prepared skewers on the grill, cover, and grill until browned on one side, about 2 minutes. Turn and brush with a thin layer of the remaining dipping sauce; grill for 2 minutes. Turn and brush with more sauce; grill for 1 minute. Turn and grill for 1 minute more. Transfer to a serving plate.

6. As soon as the beef is done cooking, melt the butter in a small skillet. Add the basil leaves and stir until wilted, a few seconds. Brush onto the beef. Serve 3 skewers per person.

Photo: Vietnamese Beef Satay Basted with
Basil Butter

TIMING
Prep: 10 minutes
   (plus 5 minutes for sauce)
Soaking the skewers: 30 minutes
Grill: 6 minutes

GRILL TOOLS AND EQUIPMENT
· 12 long bamboo skewers
· Clean grill screen
· 12 small pieces aluminum foil
· Long-handled tongs or grill mitts
· Long-handled basting brush

MAKING SUBSTITUTIONS
· This recipe can also be made with shrimp or pork.

GETTING CREATIVE
· Garnish the salad with toasted shredded coconut or chopped roasted peanuts.

GRILLED SATAY SALAD

In this satay, Thai peanut sauce is used both as a grilling sauce for chicken and as the base for a salad dressing that is tossed with baby greens, cucumber, scallions, and red peppers. The chicken strips are marinated and grilled on skewers and then served on top of the salad.

THE GRILL

Gas: Direct heat, medium-high (425° to 450°F)
Clean, oiled grate

Charcoal: Direct heat, light ash
12-by-12-inch charcoal bed (about 3 dozen coals)
Clean, oiled grate on lowest setting

Wood: Direct heat, light ash
12-by-12-inch bed, 3 to 4 inches deep
Clean, oiled grate set 2 inches above the fire

INGREDIENTS (MAKES 4 SERVINGS)

1 cup Thai Coconut Peanut Sauce (page 397)
2 tablespoons rice vinegar
2 tablespoons fresh lime juice
1 pound boneless, skinless chicken breasts
8 cups field greens or baby lettuce mix

$1/2$ small cucumber, cut into thin strips
2 scallions, roots trimmed, thinly sliced
1 red bell pepper, stem and seeds removed, cut into thin strips
Oil for coating the grill screen

DIRECTIONS

1. Put the bamboo skewers in a roasting pan and add enough water to cover; soak for at least 30 minutes. Heat the grill as directed. Put the grill screen on the grill.

2. Combine the peanut sauce, vinegar, and lime juice in a small bowl. Cut the chicken into $1/4$-inch-thick slices (about 24 slices). Toss with $1/4$ cup of the sauce in another bowl; set aside.

3. Wash your hands well and toss the greens, cucumber, scallions, and red pepper in a large bowl.

4. Arrange 2 chicken slices on each skewer, threading the skewer through the length of each slice 2 to 3 times to secure

it as flat as possible. Wrap a piece of foil around the exposed end of each skewer. Discard any sauce that has come into contact with the chicken.

5. Coat the grill screen with oil. Put the prepared skewers on the screen and grill, covered, until the chicken pieces are browned and firm, 2 to 3 minutes per side.

6. Toss $1/3$ cup of the remaining sauce with the salad and divide among 4 plates. Put 3 skewers on each plate and top with a small amount of the sauce. Serve the remaining sauce on the side for dipping.

TIMING
Prep: 10 minutes
Grill: 1 minute

GRILL TOOLS AND EQUIPMENT
· Flat-sided meat pounder
· Long-handled spatula

GRILLED CHICKEN PAILLARDS WITH ANCHOVY BUTTER

A *paillard* (pronounced pie-YARD) is a paper-thin fillet of meat that grills in seconds and is one of the quickest meals ever to slide onto a dinner plate. Preparing the meat is not difficult, but it does require some pounding. A wide, flat piece of meat (butterflied boneless chicken breast is a natural; see page 164 for butterflying instructions) is placed between sheets of plastic wrap and flattened until it spreads wide and thin (about $3/16$ inch). If you don't have a meat pounder or a flat-faced meat mallet, you can use the bottom of a heavy saucepan or skillet, but if you prepare boneless chicken breasts regularly (and who doesn't?), you should consider buying a good meat pounder. Paillards can be pounded hours ahead and stored in the refrigerator; they will be on the grill for no longer than 1 minute.

THE GRILL

Gas: Direct heat, high (500°F)
Clean, oiled grate

Charcoal: Direct heat, red hot
12-by-12-inch charcoal bed (about 3 dozen coals)
Clean, oiled grate on lowest setting

Wood: Direct heat, red hot
12-by-12-inch bed, 4 inches deep
Clean, oiled grate set 2 inches above the fire

INGREDIENTS (MAKES 4 SERVINGS)

4 boneless, skinless chicken breast halves, trimmed,
tenders removed

6 teaspoons extra-virgin olive oil

$1/4$ teaspoon kosher salt

$1/4$ teaspoon ground black pepper, plus more to taste

6 anchovy fillets, minced

2 cloves garlic, minced

3 tablespoons finely chopped flat-leaf parsley

Pinch of crushed red pepper flakes

2 tablespoons unsalted butter

Oil for coating grill grate

MAKING SUBSTITUTIONS

· Although boneless, skinless chicken
breast halves are the prime candidate
for paillardization, anything that can be
pounded thin enough can be turned into
a paillard. Unsoaked sea scallops make
elegant mini-paillards. Slices of boneless turkey breast and cross sections of
pork loin, beef tenderloin, or veal leg are
all viable options.

DIRECTIONS

1. Heat the grill as directed.

2. Coat the chicken breasts with 4 teaspoons of the olive oil.
Put one of them on a large sheet of plastic wrap, season it
with the $1/4$ teaspoon each salt and pepper, top with another
sheet of plastic wrap, and pound until uniformly $3/16$ inch thick
and the approximate dimensions of a dinner plate. This preparation is a paillard. Set aside. Repeat with the remaining
breast halves, using new sheets of plastic for each one.

3. Mash the anchovies, garlic, parsley, red pepper flakes, black
pepper to taste, and butter on a clean work surface with the
back of a fork until well combined. Divide into 4 equal portions.

4. Brush the grill grate and coat it liberally with oil. Remove
the plastic wrap from 2 of the flattened breasts and place
them on the grill so that they are spread out flat. The easiest
way is to support it with your open hand and flip it onto the
grill. Grill until the chicken looks opaque, about 30 seconds.
Flip with a spatula and grill for 15 seconds on the other side.
Remove to a platter, cover to keep warm, and repeat with the
other 2 paillards.

5. Top each paillard with a portion of anchovy butter;
serve immediately.

SKEWERED GRILLED SHRIMP WITH LIME, HONEY, AND MINT

TIMING

Prep: 5 minutes
Soaking the skewers: 10 minutes
Grill: About 4 minutes

These shrimp are the perfect pick-up with drinks (mojitos come to mind). They can be prepared from start
to finish in less than 10 minutes, ready in less time than it takes to preheat the grill.

GRILL TOOLS AND EQUIPMENT

· 8 long bamboo skewers
· 8 small pieces aluminum foil
· Clean grill screen
· Long-handled tongs or grill mitt

THE GRILL

Gas: Direct heat, medium-high (425° to 450°F)
Clean, oiled grate

Charcoal: Direct heat, light ash
12-by-12-inch charcoal bed (about 3 dozen coals)
Clean, oiled grate on lowest setting

Wood: Direct heat, light ash
12-by-12-inch bed, 3 to 4 inches deep
Clean, oiled grate set 2 inches above the fire

INGREDIENTS (MAKES 4 SERVINGS)

6 tablespoons honey

Juice and finely grated zest of 1 lime

1 tablespoon chopped fresh mint leaves

$1/4$ teaspoon kosher salt

1 pound extra-large (26–30 count) shrimp, shelled and cleaned

Oil for coating grill screen

DIRECTIONS

1. Put the bamboo skewers in a roasting pan and add
enough water to cover; soak about 10 minutes. Heat the grill
as directed.

2. Mix the honey, lime juice, lime zest, and mint, salt in a small
bowl. Toss about half of this mixture with the shrimp and
reserve the remainder for serving.

3. Arrange 3 or 4 shrimp on each skewer. Wrap a piece of foil
around the exposed end of each skewer.

4. Put the grill screen on the grill and coat it with oil; cover for
a few minutes to get the screen hot. Put the prepared skewers
on the hot screen and grill, covered, until the shrimp are lightly
browned and firm, about 2 minutes per side. Transfer to a serving plate, drizzle with the remaining sauce, and serve.

SZECHWAN SHRIMP WITH GRILLED MANGO CHUTNEY

TIMING
Prep: 5 minutes
 (plus 5 minutes for Szechwan salt
 and chutney)
Grill: 3 to 4 minutes

GRILL TOOLS AND EQUIPMENT
· Clean grill screen
· Long-handled tongs

The floral, lightly peppery scent of Szechwan pepper is a natural with tropical fruit. In this recipe, a Szechwan rub seasons quickly grilled shrimp that are served topped with a grilled fresh mango sauce. The vibrant colors (coral pink shrimp, sunset orange mango), disparate temperatures and textures (a pop of hot shrimp, a slurp of chilled sauce), and flavor (floral spice meets peppered fruit) are enough to cause swooning.

THE GRILL

Gas: Direct heat, medium-high (425° to 450°F)
Clean, oiled grate

Charcoal: Direct heat, light ash
12-by-12-inch charcoal bed (about 3 dozen coals)
Clean oiled grate on lowest setting

Wood: Direct heat, light ash
12-by-12-inch bed, 3 to 4 inches deep
Clean oiled grate set 2 inches above fire

INGREDIENTS (MAKES 4 SERVINGS)

Oil for coating grill screen
1 pound extra-large (26–30 count) shrimp, shelled and cleaned
2 teaspoons toasted sesame oil

1 teaspoon Sesame Szechwan Salt (page 380)
1 cup Grilled Mango Chutney (page 395)

DIRECTIONS

1. Heat the grill as directed. Put the grill screen on the grill and coat it with oil.
2. Toss the shrimp with the sesame oil in a bowl until coated. Spread the shrimp out on a sheet of foil and season with the Szechwan salt.

3. Grill the shrimp on the oiled screen, with the grill covered, 1 to 2 minutes per side, until firm and slightly browned.
4. Serve with the Grilled Mango Chutney as a dip.

PESTO-STUFFED JUMBO SHRIMP SKEWERED WITH GRAPE TOMATOES

TIMING
Prep: 10 minutes
 (plus 10 minutes for pesto)
Grill: About 8 minutes

GRILL TOOLS AND EQUIPMENT
· Four 15-inch metal skewers,
 preferably flat or square
· Long-handled tongs or grill mitts
· Long-handled basting brush

BASIL PESTO
Makes 3/4 cup (about 12 servings)

4-ounce bunch fresh basil, stems removed
4 cloves garlic, coarsely chopped
2 tablespoons toasted pine nuts
1/2 cup extra-virgin olive oil
1/3 cup freshly grated imported
 Parmesan cheese
Kosher salt and ground black pepper
 to taste

Chop the basil and garlic finely in a food processor. Add the pine nuts, olive oil, Parmesan, salt, and pepper and process in pulses until well blended. Use immediately or store in the refrigerator for up to 1 week.

Photo: Szechwan Shrimp with Grilled Mango Chutney

Choose the largest shrimp you can find for this recipe. The bigger they are, the longer they will take to cook, which means more time for them to absorb the basil fragrance from the pesto, and longer for the flame to singe their skins. The effect, as the parchment-crisp crust cracks between the teeth, releasing a burst of basil-scented juice across the palate, is ecstatic.

THE GRILL

Gas: Direct heat, medium-high (425° to 450°F)
Clean, oiled grill grate

Charcoal: Direct heat, light ash
12-by-12-inch charcoal bed (about 3 dozen coals)
Clean, oiled grate on lowest setting

Wood: Direct heat, light ash
12-by-12-inch bed, 3 to 4 inches deep
Clean, oiled grate set 2 inches above the fire

INGREDIENTS (MAKES 4 SERVINGS)

12 colossal (U-15) shrimp (about 1 pound),
 shelled and cleaned
3 tablespoons basil pesto, purchased or homemade
 (recipe at right)
16 underripe grape tomatoes

2 tablespoons extra-virgin olive oil
1/4 teaspoon kosher salt, or more to taste
1/4 teaspoon coarsely ground black pepper
Oil for coating grill grate

1. Heat the grill as directed.

2. Slit the shrimp along their backs, to open up the center crevice slightly. Fill the opening in each shrimp with about $1/2$ teaspoon pesto.

3. Arrange 3 shrimp on each skewer, alternating them with 4 grape tomatoes.

4. Mix the olive oil, salt, and peper with the remaining 1 tablespoon pesto in a small bowl. Brush the shrimp and tomatoes with some of this mixture.

5. Brush the grill grate and coat it with oil. Put the prepared skewers on the grill, cover, and cook for 8 minutes, turning and basting with some of the pesto oil every 2 minutes. Baste with any remaining oil mixture and serve.

TIMING
Prep: 10 minutes
  (plus 5 minutes for marinade)
Marinate: 20 minutes
Grill: 3 to 4 minutes

GRILL TOOLS AND EQUIPMENT
· Clean grill screen
· Long-handled tongs

STREAMLINING
Replace the canned artichoke hearts, garlic, and olive oil with a small jar of marinated artichokes and a small amount of the marinade from the jar.

GARLIC-BUTTERMILK SHRIMP WITH ARTICHOKE RELISH

In this recipe the Garlic-Buttermilk Marinade from Chapter 11 multitasks masterfully. It is the perfect marinade for shrimp because the protein and small amount of fat it contains help to protect the shrimp's delicate flesh from dehydrating as it takes on flavor. It also doubles as the sauce for an effortless, delicious, and sophisticated artichoke relish, spiked with a hefty dose of garlic and a pinch of crushed red pepper.

THE GRILL

Gas: Direct heat, medium-high (425° to 450°F)
  Clean, oiled grate

Charcoal: Direct heat, light ash
  12-by-12-inch charcoal bed (about 3 dozen coals)
  Clean, oiled grate on lowest setting

Wood: Direct heat, light ash
  12-by-12-inch bed, 3 to 4 inches deep
  Clean, oiled grate set 2 inches above the fire

INGREDIENTS (MAKES 4 SERVINGS)

1 pound extra-large (26–30 count) shrimp, shelled and cleaned
1 cup Garlic-Buttermilk Marinade (page 350)
Oil for coating grill screen
5 canned artichoke hearts (about half of a 14-ounce can), finely chopped

2 cloves garlic, minced
1 tablespoon extra-virgin olive oil
Pinch of crushed red pepper flakes
$1/4$ teaspoon kosher salt, or more to taste
$1/4$ teaspoon ground black pepper

DIRECTIONS

1. Toss the shrimp with $1/2$ cup of the buttermilk marinade. Cover and refrigerate for 20 minutes.

2. Heat the grill as directed. Put the grill screen on the grill and coat it with oil.

3. Combine the remaining $1/2$ cup buttermilk marinade, chopped artichokes, garlic, olive oil, red pepper flakes, salt, and black pepper in a small serving bowl; set aside.

4. Remove the shrimp from the marinade. Put them on the oiled screen, cover, and cook until firm and slightly browned, 3 to 4 minutes, turning halfway through.

5. Serve with the artichoke relish.

TIMING
Prep: 10 minutes
Marinate: 30 minutes
Grill: 6 to 8 minutes

GRILL TOOLS AND EQUIPMENT
· Clean grill screen
· Long-handled tongs

GRILLED GARLIC SCAMPI

This scampi recipe is one of the best we know. It takes a little bit of time to marinate, but once that is done it cooks in minutes. You start by marinating large shrimp in wine, garlic, and olive oil. Then grill the shrimp and boil the remaining marinade until it reduces to a glaze, mount it with butter, garnish with parsley, and toss with the lightly crusted shrimp as they emerge from the flames. You can serve the scampi over pasta, but if you do, you should double the amount of sauce.

Gas:	Direct heat, medium-high (425° to 450°F)	**Wood:**	Direct heat, light ash
	Clean, oiled grate		12-by-12-inch bed, 3 to 4 inches deep
Charcoal:	Direct heat, light ash		Clean, oiled grate set 2 inches above the fire
	12-by-12-inch charcoal bed (about 3 dozen coals)		
	Clean, oiled grate on lowest setting		

MAKING SUBSTITUTIONS
· The same preparation is delicious with large sea scallops, or use a combination of shrimp and scallops.

INGREDIENTS (MAKES 4 SERVINGS)

$1/4$ cup white wine

6 cloves garlic, minced

2 tablespoons olive oil

$1/2$ teaspoon kosher salt, or more to taste

$1/4$ teaspoon ground black pepper, or more to taste

1 pound colossal (U-15) shrimp, shelled and cleaned

Oil for coating grill screen

2 tablespoons unsalted butter, cut into pieces

2 tablespoons chopped fresh flat-leaf parsley

DIRECTIONS

1. Mix the wine, 2 cloves of the garlic, the olive oil, salt, and pepper in a medium bowl. Add the shrimp, toss to coat, cover, and refrigerate for 30 minutes.

2. Heat the grill as directed. Put the grill screen on the grill and coat it with oil.

3. Remove the shrimp from the marinade, reserving the marinade. Put the shrimp on the screen, cover, and cook until firm and slightly browned, about 6 minutes, turning halfway through.

4. While the shrimp are grilling, combine the reserved marinade and remaining garlic in a saucepan. Bring to a boil and boil for 1 minute. Remove from the heat and swirl in the butter and parsley. Adjust the seasoning with salt and pepper. Toss the grilled shrimp with the sauce and serve.

CHIPOTLE-DUSTED SOFT-SHELL CRABS WITH PINEAPPLE-MINT SALSA

Crustaceans, such as shrimp, lobsters, and crabs, have to shed their shells in order to grow. During the brief period that they are shell-less they are completely vulnerable to attack by other crustaceans, larger fish, and us. Soft-shell crabs have all of the succulence of blue crabs with none of the hassle. In this recipe the crabs are seasoned with chipotle pepper, a smoky spice that plays remarkably with their sweet, salty tang. Pineapple salsa is served alongside to help cool your palate.

TIMING
Prep: 20 minutes
Grill: 5 minutes

GRILL TOOLS AND EQUIPMENT
· Clean grill screen
· Long-handled tongs

THE GRILL

Gas:	Direct heat, medium-high (425° to 450°F)	**Wood:**	Direct heat, light ash
	Clean, oiled grate		12-by-12-inch bed, 3 to 4 inches deep
Charcoal:	Direct heat, light ash		Clean, oiled grate set 2 inches above the fire
	12-by-12-inch charcoal bed (about 3 dozen coals)		
	Clean, oiled grate on lowest setting		

INGREDIENTS (MAKES 4 SERVINGS, 2 CUPS SALSA)

For the crabs:

8 soft-shell crabs, about 5 ounces each

1 lime, halved

$1/4$ teaspoon ground chipotle pepper

$1/2$ teaspoon kosher salt

Oil for coating grill screen

No-stick spray oil

For the salsa:

1 cup (about 10 ounces) finely chopped fresh pineapple

1 cup finely chopped fresh tomato

$1/4$ cup finely diced red onion

$1/2$ to 1 serrano chile (depending on how hot you like it), seeds and stem removed, finely chopped

$1/2$ teaspoon kosher salt

$1/4$ teaspoon ground black pepper

2 tablespoons chopped fresh mint leaves

SOFT SHELLS: DRESSED TO GRILL

To prepare soft-shell crabs for grilling, you must remove any hard, tough, or inedible parts. This sounds more distasteful than it is. Think of yourself as a culinary surgeon, and you should do just fine. Although the job can be done with a small, sharp knife it is easier and less messy with scissors.

1. Place the crab on a plate to catch the juices. Snip off the eyes, removing as little of the top shell as possible. Snip off the hard manacles of the mouth on the beige underside of the crab, again removing as little as possible of the tender regions surrounding it.

2. Snip off the "apron" on the underside of the crab. In male crabs the apron is pointed. In female crabs it is shaped like a shield.

3. Flip the crab over so that its red side is facing up, and snip off the spongy, finger-shaped gills that lie under the top "shell" on either side of the crab's body.

4. Rinse the crabs and pat dry; discard all of the snipped-off parts.

DIRECTIONS

1. If the crabs have not been "dressed," you will have to trim them yourself (see "Soft Shells: Dressed to Grill," left).

2. Heat the grill as directed.

3. Put the crabs on a plate; squeeze the lime juice over the top and flip them over several times to coat. Mix the chipotle and salt and sprinkle over both sides of the crabs. Refrigerate.

4. Mix all of the salsa ingredients in a bowl.

5. Put the grill screen on the grill and coat it with oil. Spray the crabs on both sides with oil and grill for 3 minutes on the red side (top) and 2 minutes on the white side (bottom).

6. Serve topped with some of the salsa, with the remainder passed at the table.

Photo: Chipotle-Dusted Soft-Shell Crabs with Pineapple-Mint Salsa

GRILLED SOFT-SHELL CRABS WITH DILL BUTTER SAUCE

TIMING
Prep: 20 minutes
   (plus 5 minutes for marinade)
Marinate: 10 minutes
Grill: 5 minutes

Shrimp are easy to grill, lobsters are a little tricky, but crabs are impossible. They can be boiled first to kill them and finished on the grill, but you can always taste the deception. They never attain the fire-branded, concentrated flavor of shellfish cooked completely on the grill. But soft-shell crabs are another story; they can be cooked from start to finish over the fire, which doesn't take too long—about 5 minutes from start to finish. These are sauced in a classic manner with drawn butter infused with dill.

GRILL TOOLS AND EQUIPMENT
· Clean grill screen
· Long-handled tongs

THE GRILL

Gas: Direct heat, medium-high (425° to 450°F)
Clean, oiled grate

Charcoal: Direct heat, light ash
12-by-12-inch charcoal bed (about 3 dozen coals)
Clean, oiled grate on lowest setting

Wood: Direct heat, light ash
12-by-12-inch bed, 3 to 4 inches deep
Clean, oiled grate set 2 inches above the fire

INGREDIENTS (MAKES 4 SERVINGS)

8 soft-shell crabs, about 5 ounces each
1 cup Mignonette Marinade and Mop (page 352)
1/3 cup chopped fresh dill leaves

4 tablespoons (1/2 stick) unsalted butter, cut into pieces
Oil for coating grill screen
No-stick spray oil

DIRECTIONS

1. If the crabs have not been "dressed," you will have to trim them yourself (see "Soft Shells: Dressed to Grill," facing page).
2. Heat the grill as directed.
3. Put the crabs in a pie plate or other deep dish. Pour 2/3 cup of the mignonette sauce over the crabs and flip them over several times to coat. Refrigerate for at least 10 minutes.
4. Heat the remaining mignonette in a small skillet until boiling; boil until about 2 tablespoons of liquid are left. Add the dill and

stir to moisten. Reduce the heat to low and swirl in the butter until completely incorporated. Set aside.
5. Put the grill screen on the grill and coat it with oil. Spray the crabs on both sides with oil and grill for 3 minutes on the red side (top) and 2 minutes on the white side (bottom).
6. Rewarm the butter sauce if necessary (do not allow it to boil), and serve the crabs topped with sauce.

TEA-SMOKED CLAMS AND MUSSELS WITH SZECHWAN MIGNONETTE

TIMING
Prep: 10 minutes
   (plus 5 minutes for Szechwan salt)
Grill: 12 to 15 minutes

The acrid smoke from tea leaves seems destined for shellfish, and the cleanest, fastest, most trouble-free place to unite them is under a grill cover. Just throw soaked tea leaves onto the hottest fire you can make, perch some mussels and scallops above, and in a few minutes, the juices inside the shell will start to steam, the shells will pop open, and the tender meat will absorb whiffs of tea smoke and charcoal-grilled flavor. After that, they need only a dip in a bright bath of peppery mignonette to wash off any sand and send them on their way down the gullet.

GRILL TOOLS AND EQUIPMENT
· Large disposable aluminum pan
· Smoker box or foil packet,
   if using a gas grill (see page 39)
· Grill mitt

THE GRILL

Gas: Direct heat, medium-high (425° to 450°F)
Clean, oiled grate

Charcoal: Direct heat, light ash
12-by-12-inch charcoal bed (about 3 dozen coals)
Clean, oiled grate set on lowest setting

Wood: Direct heat, light ash
12-by-12-inch bed, 3 to 4 inches deep
Clean, oiled grate set 3 inches above the fire

$^1/_4$ cup loose tea, oolong, black, or green

$^1/_2$ cup boiling water

3 dozen clams, preferably steamers, cleaned

2 pounds mussels (about 3 dozen), cleaned

$^1/_2$ cup rice wine vinegar

1 tablespoon Sesame Szechwan Salt (page 380)

1 tablespoon chopped garlic

DIRECTIONS

1. Heat the grill as directed.

2. Mix the tea and boiling water in a small bowl; set aside for 10 minutes.

3. Discard any open shellfish. Make a layer of the remaining clams in the disposable pan; scatter the mussels over the clams; refrigerate.

4. Meanwhile, mix the vinegar, Szechwan salt, and garlic in a small bowl; set aside.

5. Scatter the soaked tea over the hot coals (if using a gas grill, put the tea in a foil packet or smoker box). Put a grate on the grill as close to the fire as possible. Set the pan of clams and mussels on the grate; cover the grill and smoke until all of the shellfish are open, about 15 minutes. Discard any shellfish that fail to open.

6. Transfer to a serving bowl, drizzle with the mignonette, and serve.

Photo: Tea-Smoked Clams and Mussels with
Szechwan Mignonette

CHARRED GARLIC SCALLOPS

TIMING
Prep: 5 minutes
   (plus 40 minutes for garlic paste)
Grill: 6 minutes

This dish is effortless, provided that your scallops are unsoaked. Cheap scallops are treated with sodium tripolyphosphate (STP) to force them to absorb water. When they cook, the bonds that hold the water in suspension break and the soaking liquid comes pouring out, causing the scallops to steam, which makes it impossible to sear them. To make sure that they have not been treated, look for scallops that are slightly gray, or beige, or pink—anything but pure white. Have your fire as hot as possible, and cook the scallops quickly. They should still be a little soft in the center when they come off the grill.

GRILL TOOLS AND EQUIPMENT
· Clean grill screen
· Long-handled tongs

THE GRILL

Gas: Direct heat, high (500°F)
Clean, oiled grate

Charcoal: Direct heat, red hot
12-by-12-inch charcoal bed (about 3 dozen coals)
Clean, oiled grate on lowest setting

Wood: Direct heat, red hot
12-by-12-inch bed, 4 inches deep
Clean, oiled grate set 2 inches above the fire

INGREDIENTS (MAKES 4 SERVINGS)

Oil for coating grill screen
1 1/4 pounds large, wild-caught sea scallops
   (about 16 scallops)

1/3 cup Roasted Garlic Paste (page 392)
1 tablespoon extra-virgin olive oil

DIRECTIONS

1. Heat the grill as directed. Put the grill screen on the grill and coat it with oil.
2. Toss the scallops with 2 tablespoons of the garlic paste and the olive oil in a small bowl until evenly coated.

3. Grill the scallops on the screen, uncovered, until they are lightly browned and feel springy to the touch but still a little soft in the center, about 6 minutes, turning halfway through.
4. Serve with a little of the remaining roasted garlic paste mixture spooned on top of each scallop.

SCALLOPS GRILLED WITH HORSERADISH AND PROSCIUTTO

TIMING
Prep: 10 minutes
Marinate: 30 minutes
Grill: 6 minutes

These are beautiful and delicious. The band of rosy prosciutto glows against the creamy white of the scallop as its sweet and salty hammy flavors permeate the edges of the fish. Meanwhile, the teary scent of horseradish that invades the scallop from its marinade plays off the flavor of the ham for a truly delicious effect.

GRILL TOOLS AND EQUIPMENT
· Clean grill screen
· Long-handled tongs

THE GRILL

Gas: Direct heat, high (500°F)
Clean, oiled grate

Charcoal: Direct heat, red hot
12-by-12-inch charcoal bed (about 3 dozen coals)
Clean, oiled grate on lowest setting

Wood: Direct heat, red hot
12-by-12-inch bed, 3 to 4 inches deep
Clean, oiled grate set 2 inches above the fire

1 tablespoon canola oil

Juice and finely grated zest of 1 lemon

2 cloves garlic, minced

2 tablespoons grated fresh horseradish, or 3 tablespoons
   jarred horseradish

1/2 teaspoon kosher salt

1/4 teaspoon ground black pepper

1 1/4 pounds large, wild-caught sea scallops
   (about 16 scallops)

Oil for coating grill screen

5 slices (1/2 ounce each) prosciutto, each cut lengthwise into
   3 or 4 strips about 1 inch wide

1 lemon or lime, cut into 4 wedges

DIRECTIONS

1. Mix the 1 tablespoon oil, lemon juice, lemon zest, garlic, horseradish, salt, and pepper in a medium bowl. Trim the scallops of any tough tissue from the sides, and toss them in the marinade until evenly coated. Cover and refrigerate for 30 minutes.

2. Heat the grill as directed. Put the grill screen on the grill and coat it with oil.

3. Wrap a strip of prosciutto around each scallop so that it looks like a little drum, and secure the end with a wooden toothpick speared through the scallop.

4. Grill the scallops on the screen, uncovered, until they are lightly browned and feel springy to the touch but still a little soft in the center, about 6 minutes, turning halfway through.

5. Serve with the wedges of lemon or lime.

TIMING

Prep: 10 minutes

Grill: 6 minutes

GRILL TOOLS AND EQUIPMENT

· Clean grill screen

· Long-handled tongs

GETTING CREATIVE

· This very special sauce can be used to add a touch of luxury to almost anything. Try it on grilled shrimp, an herb-brined chicken breast, or a mignonette-marinated veal chop.

GRILLED SCALLOPS WITH FOIE GRAS CREAM

Foie gras, the liver of a force-fed bird (or the pâté made from it), is so saturated with fat that it might as well be butter. The super-rich, utterly sophisticated sauce that tops these grilled scallops imagines that it is, using the pâté as the base for a riff on butter sauce. It sounds complex, but it really isn't. All of the sauce ingredients are simply whipped together in a food processor.

THE GRILL

Gas: Direct heat, high (500°F)
Clean, oiled grate

Charcoal: Direct heat, red hot
12-by-12-inch charcoal bed (about 3 dozen coals)
Clean, oiled grate on lowest setting

Wood: Direct heat, red hot
12-by-12-inch bed, 3 to 4 inches deep
Clean, oiled grate set 2 inches above the fire

INGREDIENTS (MAKES 4 SERVINGS)

Oil for coating grill screen

About 3 ounces (1/2 package) pâté de foie gras or other
   liver pâté

2 tablespoons aged balsamic vinegar

2 tablespoons orange juice

2 tablespoons extra-virgin olive oil, plus more for coating scallops

1/2 teaspoon minced garlic, fresh or jarred organic

1/2 teaspoon minced peeled gingerroot, fresh or jarred

1/4 teaspoon kosher salt, plus more to taste

1/8 teaspoon ground black pepper, plus more to taste

1 1/4 pounds large, wild-caught sea scallops
   (about 16 scallops)

DIRECTIONS

1. Heat the grill as directed. Put the grill screen on the grill and coat it with oil.

2. Purée the pâté, vinegar, orange juice, 2 tablespoons olive oil, garlic, ginger, 1/4 teaspoon salt, and 1/8 teaspoon pepper in a food processor or blender; set aside.

3. Coat the scallops with a little olive oil and season liberally with salt and pepper. Grill the scallops on the screen, uncovered, until they are lightly browned and feel springy to the touch, about 6 minutes, turning halfway through.

4. Top each scallop with a small dollop of the foie gras cream, and serve.

Photo: Scallops Grilled with Horseradish and Prosciutto

CHAPTER 6

MASTERING STEAKS, CHOPS, AND OTHER QUICK-COOKING CUTS

MASTERING TECHNIQUE

RECIPES

TIMING

Prep: 5 minutes

Rest before grilling: 1 to 8 hours

Grill: About 15 minutes

GRILL TOOLS AND EQUIPMENT
· Long-handled tongs

GETTING CREATIVE
· For smoky-tasting steaks, soak 1 cup of wood chips in water for 20 minutes. Add the soaked chips to the low-heat area of the grill until they begin to smolder. Grill the steaks as directed, covering the grill to trap the smoke.
· Use other sirloin steaks or rib-eye steaks in place of the strip steaks. Increase the cooking time slightly for bone-in steaks.
· For crosshatch marks, put the steaks at a 45-degree angle to the bars of the grill grate. Press on the steaks with a spatula periodically. Rotate the steaks 45 degrees on the grill grate and press down again. Flip and proceed with the recipe.

There are a few simple steps to a great grilled steak. First, buy the best grade of beef you can find, such as choice (see page 50 for more on grades of beef). Dry-aged beef will have a more concentrated flavor than your typical supermarket offerings. Second, bring the meat to room temperature before grilling. Warm meat sears better than cold meat; you'll get a better crust on your steak if you let it sit at room temperature for 30 minutes instead of taking it straight from the refrigerator to the grill. To keep steaming to a minimum—step three—pat the steaks dry before seasoning them or putting them on the grill. Add a raging hot fire and you will create a nice thick crust on the steak. But you don't want to burn it before the interior is done to your liking. So step four is to create a two-level fire with a high-heat area and a low-heat area. Sear the steak over high heat, then move it over low heat to finish cooking without burning. It also helps to let the meat rest off the heat before slicing. This brief resting period (5 to 10 minutes) allows moisture to redistribute throughout the meat so it tastes juicier. As with all the Mastering Technique boxes in this book, this recipe has only basic flavors (salt, pepper, and oil). It's mostly about the technique. To flavor the meat, use one of the marinades, rubs, or sauces you'll find beginning on page 350. Our favorite way to flavor steaks is to use a dry rub (such as Fragrant Chile Rub, page 372) and then set a pat of butter on the steak to melt at the table.

THE GRILL

Gas: Direct heat, high (500°F)
Clean, oiled grate on lowest setting

Charcoal: Direct heat, red hot
12-by-12-inch charcoal bed (about 3 dozen coals) with high- and low-heat areas
Clean, oiled grate on lowest setting

Wood: Direct heat, red hot
12-by-12-inch bed with a 4-inch-deep area for high heat and a 2-inch-deep area for low heat
Clean, oiled grate set 2 inches above the fire

INGREDIENTS (MAKES 6 SERVINGS)

4 boneless strip steaks, each 10 to 12 ounces and 1 to 1 1/2 inches thick
1 tablespoon kosher salt

1/2 teaspoon ground black pepper
Oil for coating grill grate
2 tablespoons olive oil

DIRECTIONS

1. Trim the fat on the steaks to about 1/4 inch. Pat the steaks dry with paper towels and sprinkle all over with the salt and pepper. Let rest at room temperature for 1 to 2 hours. Or cover and refrigerate for up to 8 hours if you have the time (this intensifies the flavors).

2. If you refrigerated the steaks, bring them to room temperature before grilling, about 1 hour.

3. Heat the grill as directed.

4. Brush the grill grate and coat it with oil. Rub the olive oil all over the steaks. Put the steaks on the grill over high heat and cook until darkly crusted, 3 to 5 minutes per side. Reduce the heat to medium-low (on a gas grill) or move the steaks to the low-heat area (on a charcoal or wood grill), cover, and grill for another 8 to 12 minutes for medium-rare to medium-done (135° to 140°F on an instant-read thermometer inserted into the thickest part). Transfer to a platter, cover loosely with foil, and let rest for 5 minutes before slicing.

MASTERING TECHNIQUE
BASIC PORK CHOPS

Grilling pork chops is similar to grilling steaks. We prefer thick chops (at least 1 inch thick, preferably 1½ inches). The best technique for grilling thick chops is searing them over high heat and then moving them over low to medium-low heat to finish cooking. Thinner chops can be grilled entirely over medium-high heat for a slightly shorter cooking time. As with steaks and other meat, the keys to a good grilled pork chop include letting the meat come to room temperature, patting the meat dry, using fairly high heat, and letting the meat rest off the heat before slicing. Today's pork is bred very lean, so it also pays to watch cooking times carefully. Cook the pork until it is still slightly pink in the center, and it will finish cooking off the heat as it rests. The basic technique below gives reliable results, but for the ultimate in juicy grilled chops, your best bet is to brine the chops first, as in Molasses-Brined Pork Chops with Roasted Corn Salsa (page 149). Brining goes a long way toward preventing pork chops from drying out on the grill.

THE GRILL

Gas: Direct heat, high (500°F)
Clean, oiled grate on lowest setting

Charcoal: Direct heat, red hot
12-by-12-inch charcoal bed (about 3 dozen coals)
with high- and low-heat areas
Clean, oiled grate on lowest setting

Wood: Direct heat, red hot
12-by-12-inch bed with a 4-inch-deep area for
high heat and a 2-inch-deep area for low heat
Clean, oiled grate set 2 inches above the fire

INGREDIENTS (MAKES 6 SERVINGS)

4 bone-in pork rib chops, each 1 to 1½ inches thick
(about 3 pounds total)
2 teaspoons kosher salt

½ teaspoon ground black pepper
Oil for coating grill grate
2 tablespoons olive oil

DIRECTIONS

1. Trim the fat on the chops to about ¼ inch. Pat the chops dry with paper towels and sprinkle all over with the salt and pepper. Let the chops rest at room temperature for 1 hour, or cover and refrigerate for up to 6 hours.

2. If you refrigerated the chops, bring them to room temperature before grilling, about 45 minutes.

3. Heat the grill as directed.

4. Brush the grill grate and coat it with oil. Rub the olive oil all over the chops. Put the chops on the grill, cover, and cook over

high heat until nicely grill-marked, 2 to 3 minutes per side. Reduce the heat under the chops to medium-low (on a gas grill) or move the chops to the low-heat area (on a charcoal or wood grill), cover, and grill for another 5 to 6 minutes for medium (145°F on an instant-read thermometer inserted into the thickest part).

5. Transfer to a platter or plates, cover loosely with foil, and let rest for 5 minutes before serving.

TIMING
Prep: 5 minutes
Rest before grilling: 1 to 6 hours
Grill: About 10 minutes

GRILL TOOLS AND EQUIPMENT
· Long-handled tongs

GETTING CREATIVE
· If you prefer boneless meat, replace the rib chops with boneless rib chops or center-cut loin chops and reduce the cooking time slightly.
· Try one of the dry rubs beginning on page 372, such as Cajun Blackening Rub, Jerk Rub, or Fragrant Chile Rub.
· For smoky-tasting chops, soak 1 cup of hickory or oak wood chips in water for 20 to 30 minutes. Add the soaked chips to the high-heat area of the grill until they begin to smolder. Grill the chops as directed, covering the grill to trap the smoke.

CHOP SHOP
Pork loin chops vary from market to market, but you'll probably find two basic choices: center-cut chops and rib chops. Center-cut loin chops are similar to T-bone beef steaks, with loin meat on one side, a smaller bit of very tender tenderloin meat on the other side, and a T-shaped bone in the middle. Rib chops are cut from the rib section of the loin and have a rib bone running along one edge of the chop and one large portion of loin meat on the other side. We generally like to grill rib chops because they have a bit more intramuscular fat, which helps keep them from drying out on the grill. You might also find two other pork chops at your market: sirloin chops and blade chops. These chops also make good choices for grilling. For more information and illustrations of various pork chops, see page 58.

MASTERING TECHNIQUE
BASIC BONE-IN CHICKEN PARTS

Here's our favorite way to make barbecued chicken pieces—brined to keep the meat moist. Use this as a base recipe and vary the flavors in the brine to suit your taste. We also recommend a dry rub and finishing sauce for flavor. Use any combination of the brines, dry rubs, and sauces beginning on page 362 that mention chicken as a suitable meat. Some of the marinades in that chapter can be used instead of a brine. One final step also helps to retain moisture in the meat: grilling the chicken with the skin on. If you prefer skinless chicken, the brine will help it hold on to moisture during grilling. Or you could grill the chicken with the skin on and then remove the skin before serving. If that's your preference, slather a finishing sauce onto the skinless chicken at the table rather than during grilling, because most of its flavor will be discarded with the skin.

TIMING
Prep: 5 minutes
(plus 5 minutes for sauce)
Brine: 2 to 3 hours
Grill: 30 to 40 minutes

GRILL TOOLS AND EQUIPMENT
· Long-handled tongs
· Long-handled basting brush

CUTTING A CHICKEN INTO PARTS

1. To save money, buy a whole chicken (3 1/2 to 4 pounds) and cut it into parts yourself. Put the chicken breast-side up, pull one of the legs away from the body, and cut through the skin and meat where the leg attaches to the body. Bend the leg away from the body until the ball of the thighbone pops out of the socket. Cut between the ball and socket to remove the leg from the body. Repeat with the other leg.

2. For each leg, cut the drumstick from the thigh by cutting down firmly through the joint.

3. Pull a wing away from the body and cut near the joint at the base of the wing to remove it from the body. Repeat with the other wing.

4. Pry the back away from the breast with your hands and cut the back from the breast. Save the backbone for stock, if you like.

5. Cut the breast lengthwise in half down the middle through the breastbone. If you like, cut each breast crosswise in half to make smaller pieces.

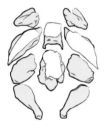

TIMING
Prep: 5 minutes
   (plus 5 minutes for sauce)
Brine: 1 to 2 hours
Grill: 10 to 14 minutes

GRILL TOOLS AND EQUIPMENT
· Long-handled tongs
· Long-handled basting brush

THE GRILL

Gas:	Indirect heat, medium (350°F)	**Charcoal:**	Indirect heat, medium ash
	3- or 4-burner grill–middle burner(s) off		Split charcoal bed (about 2 dozen coals per side)
	2-burner grill–1 side off		20 replacement coals
	Clean, oiled grate		Heavy-duty drip pan set between banks of charcoal
			Clean, oiled grate on medium setting

INGREDIENTS (MAKES 6 SERVINGS)

3 1/2 to 4 pounds bone-in chicken breasts, thighs, and drumsticks
1/2 cup sugar
1/2 cup kosher salt
1 cup hot (but not boiling) water

3 cups cold water
1/2 teaspoon ground black pepper
Oil for coating grill grate
1 1/4 cups Sweet, Hot, and Sour BBQ Sauce (page 391)

DIRECTIONS

1. Trim any excess fat from the chicken parts.

2. Put the sugar, salt, and hot water into a 2-gallon zipper-lock bag. Shake to dissolve the salt and sugar. Add the cold water and the chicken parts. Press the air out of the bag, seal, and refrigerate for 2 to 3 hours.

3. Remove the chicken from the brine and discard the brine. Pat the chicken dry with paper towels and sprinkle all over with the pepper. Let the chicken rest at room temperature before grilling, about 30 minutes.

4. Heat the grill as directed.

5. Brush the grill grate and coat it with oil. Put the chicken over the unheated part of the grill, cover, and cook, turning once or twice, until the chicken is no longer pink and the juices run clear (about 170°F on an instant-read thermometer inserted into the thickest part without touching bone), 30 to 40 minutes total. Breasts cook faster, so check them first. During the last 10 to 15 minutes of grilling, move the chicken over the heated part of the grill to brown all over. Brush with the barbecue sauce during the last 5 minutes. If your grill has a temperature gauge, it should stay at around 350°F.

6. Remove the chicken to a serving platter.

MASTERING TECHNIQUE
BASIC BONELESS CHICKEN PARTS

Boneless, skinless chicken parts—particularly chicken breasts—dry out quickly on the grill. Our solution is to brine the meat to retain moisture. If you skip the brine, be sure to baste the meat often with oil or basting sauce to keep it moist. This recipe mostly demonstrates technique. To add flavor, use any combination of the marinades, brines, rubs, and/or sauces beginning on page 350. For a triple shot of flavor, use a marinade or brine, then a dry rub, and finally a sauce, salsa, or chutney.

THE GRILL

Gas:	Direct heat, medium-high (450°F)	**Wood:**	Direct heat, light ash
	Clean, oiled grate		12-by-12-inch bed, 3 to 4 inches deep
Charcoal:	Direct heat, light ash		Clean, oiled grate set 2 inches above the fire
	12-by-12-inch charcoal bed (about 3 dozen coals)		
	Clean, oiled grate on lowest setting		

INGREDIENTS (MAKES 6 SERVINGS)

$1/2$ cup sugar

$1/2$ cup kosher salt

1 cup hot (but not boiling) water

3 cups cold water

4 boneless, skinless chicken breast halves or thighs, (about $1 1/2$ pounds total)

$1/2$ teaspoon ground black pepper

Oil for coating grill grate

$1 1/4$ cups Sweet, Hot, and Sour BBQ Sauce (page 391)

DIRECTIONS

1. Put the sugar, salt, and hot water into a 1-gallon zipper-lock bag. Shake to dissolve the salt and sugar. Add the cold water and the chicken pieces. Press the air out of the bag, seal, and refrigerate for 1 to 2 hours.

2. Remove the chicken from the brine and discard the brine. Pat the chicken dry with paper towels and sprinkle all over with the pepper. Let the chicken rest at room temperature before grilling, about 30 minutes.

3. Heat the grill as directed.

4. Brush the grill grate and coat it with oil. Put the chicken on the grill, cover, and cook until no longer pink and the juices run clear (about 170°F on an instant-read thermometer inserted into the thickest part), 5 to 7 minutes per side. Brush with the barbecue sauce during the last 5 minutes. If your grill has a temperature gauge, it should stay at around 450°F.

5. Remove the chicken to a serving platter.

GETTING CREATIVE

· Replace the barbecue sauce with one of the glazes beginning on page 384, such as Red-Cooking Lacquer, Peking Crackle, or Mustard-Molasses Glaze.

MASTERING TECHNIQUE
BASIC CHICKEN WINGS

Chicken wings have a lot of skin that drips fat into the fire. Keep a spray bottle handy to douse any flare-ups. It also helps to keep the grill covered to limit the oxygen supply, which kills the flames. We marinate the wings in Sweet, Hot, and Sour BBQ Sauce here as a basic flavor example, but you can flavor the wings however you like. See the marinades, brines, rubs, pastes, glazes, and sauces in Chapter 11. Garlic-Plum Barbecue Glaze, Hot Pepper–Bourbon Syrup, Mustard-Molasses Glaze, and Thai Coconut Peanut Sauce all make good sauces for tossing with the wings.

TIMING

Prep: 10 minutes
(plus 5 minutes for sauce)
Marinate: 2 to 8 hours
Grill: About 20 minutes

GRILL TOOLS AND EQUIPMENT

· Long-handled tongs
· Large disposable aluminum pan

THE GRILL

Gas: Direct heat, medium (350°F)
Clean, oiled grate on lowest setting

Charcoal: Direct heat, medium ash
12-by-12-inch charcoal bed (about 3 dozen coals)
Clean, oiled grate on lowest setting

Wood: Direct heat, medium ash
12-by-12-inch bed, 3 inches deep
Clean, oiled grate set 4 inches above the fire

INGREDIENTS (MAKES 4 SERVINGS)

2 pounds chicken wings (about 8 whole wings)

$1 1/4$ cups Sweet, Hot, and Sour BBQ Sauce (page 391)

Oil for coating grill grate

$1/2$ cup (1 stick) butter

DIRECTIONS

1. Cut off and discard the tips from the chicken wings. Cut the wings into 2 pieces through the central joint. Put the wings in a 1-gallon zipper-lock bag. Add $1/2$ cup of the sauce and reserve the rest. Press the air out of the bag and seal the top. Massage the sauce into the wings, then refrigerate for 2 to 8 hours.

2. Remove the wings from the refrigerator about 20 minutes before grilling.

3. Heat the grill as directed.

4. Brush the grill grate and coat it with oil. Put the wings on the grill and cook until well browned all over and no longer pink in the center near the bones, 10 to 12 minutes per side.

5. Meanwhile, melt the butter in a large disposable aluminum pan on the side of the grill (or in a saucepan over a separate burner). Stir in the remaining $3/4$ cup barbecue sauce until combined. Toss the grilled wings with the sauce in the pan. Or put the sauce and melted butter in a big bowl and toss with the wings until fully coated. Serve warm.

TIMING
Prep: 2 minutes
Grill: 4 to 8 minutes

GRILL TOOLS AND EQUIPMENT
· Long-handled tongs

TIP
· If using tuna steaks, grill them rare
  or medium-rare by reducing the cooking
  time just slightly. The tuna should still
  be red in the center.

MASTERING TECHNIQUE
BASIC FISH STEAKS

Fish steaks are among the most grill-friendly seafood. They can be grilled directly on the grill grate without falling apart, much like a beef steak or pork chop. We use salmon steaks here because they are so popular, but you can use this method for any fish steak you like. Keep in mind that salmon steaks are somewhat oily, and the fat keeps the steaks moist during grilling. Cod, tuna, and halibut steaks are a bit leaner and thus benefit from soaking in an oil-based marinade to keep the fish from drying out on the grill. Pair these or other lean fish steaks with any of the oily marinades in Chapter 11 that are suitable for fish. We've kept the flavorings ultra-simple here (just salt and pepper), but we recommend flavoring this salmon or any fish steak with one of the dry rubs, glazes, or sauces in Chapter 11.

THE GRILL

Gas: Direct heat, medium-high (450°F)
           Clean, oiled grate

Charcoal: Direct heat, light ash
           12-by-12-inch charcoal bed (about 3 dozen coals)
           Clean, oiled grate on lowest setting

Wood: Direct heat, light ash
           12-by-12-inch bed, 3 to 4 inches deep
           Clean, oiled grate set 2 inches above the fire

INGREDIENTS (MAKES 4 SERVINGS)

1 1/2 to 2 pounds salmon steaks, each about
    1 1/2 inches thick
1 teaspoon kosher salt
1/2 teaspoon ground black pepper

Oil for coating grill grate
2 tablespoons olive oil
4 lemon wedges

DIRECTIONS

1. Sprinkle the fish with the salt and pepper. Rest at room temperature before grilling, about 20 minutes.
2. Heat the grill as directed.

3. Brush the grill grate and coat it with oil. Rub the olive oil all over the fish and put the fish on the grill. Cover and cook until a bit filmy and moist in the center, 2 to 4 minutes per side.
4. Transfer to a platter or plates and serve with the lemon wedges for squeezing.

TIMING
Prep: 5 minutes
Grill: 6 to 10 minutes

GRILL TOOLS AND EQUIPMENT
· Fish-grilling basket or
  long-handled spatula
· Heat-resistant grill mitt

MASTERING TECHNIQUE
BASIC FISH FILLETS

Some fish fillets, such as catfish, red snapper, flounder (and other flatfish like sole), rockfish, and sea bass, are too thin to grill directly on the grill grate. For thin, delicate fillets, we use a fish-grilling basket to make turning the fillets easier. Other firm and thick fillets, such as grouper, striped bass, halibut, salmon, bluefish, and mackerel, can be grilled directly on the grill grate. Use any type of fish you like. Just be sure to keep the grill grate or grilling basket hot and well oiled to prevent sticking. Use heat-resistant gloves (preferably silicone) when handling a hot fish basket. Again, the flavors here are kept to a bare minimum. This recipe is meant to be a blank canvas on which you can build your favorite flavors. Choose from among the marinades, rubs, pastes, glazes, sauces, salsas, and chutneys in Chapter 11. Often a wet paste or thick glaze tastes best with fish fillets, but a dry rub and a chunky salsa works nicely too.

THE GRILL

Gas:	Direct heat, medium-high (450°F)	**Wood:**	Direct heat, light ash
	Clean, oiled grate		12-by-12-inch bed, 3 to 4 inches deep
Charcoal:	Direct heat, light ash		Clean, oiled grate set 2 inches above the fire
	12-by-12-inch charcoal bed (about 3 dozen coals)		
	Clean, oiled grate on lowest setting		

INGREDIENTS (MAKES 6 SERVINGS)

1¹/₂ pounds skinless red snapper fillets

1 teaspoon kosher salt

¹/₂ teaspoon ground black pepper

Oil for coating grill grate or fish basket

2 tablespoons olive oil

4 lemon wedges

DIRECTIONS

1. Heat the grill as directed. If using a fish grilling basket (which we recommend for thin, delicate fillets such as red snapper), preheat the basket on the grill.

2. Pat the fish dry with paper towels and sprinkle with the salt and pepper. Let rest at room temperature for 15 minutes.

3. Brush the grill grate and coat it with oil. If using a fish basket, coat the hot fish basket with oil. Rub the olive oil all over the fillets and put the fillets in the basket (if using). Put the basket on the grill (or put the fillets directly on the grate), cover, and cook until the fish is just slightly filmy and moist in the center, 3 to 5 minutes per side. If your grill has a temperature gauge, it should stay at around 450°F.

4. Serve the fillets with the lemon wedges for squeezing.

- -

PORTERHOUSE AU POIVRE

Here's the classic steak au poivre, done on the grill with a porterhouse steak. The steak is big, brawny, and rubbed with coarsely cracked peppercorns, but the Cognac cream sauce adds a touch of elegance, balancing out the dish nicely.

THE GRILL

Gas:	Direct heat, high (500°F)	**Wood:**	Direct heat, red hot
	Clean, oiled grate on lowest setting		12-by-12-inch bed with a 4-inch-deep area for
Charcoal:	Direct heat, red hot		high heat and a 2-inch-deep area for low heat
	12-by-12-inch charcoal bed (about 3 dozen coals)		Clean, oiled grate set 2 inches above the fire
	with high- and low-heat areas		
	Clean, oiled grate on lowest setting		

INGREDIENTS (MAKES 4 SERVINGS)

2 tablespoons mixed peppercorns, such as black, green, red, and white

1 large porterhouse or T-bone steak, 2¹/₂ to 3 pounds and at least 2 inches thick

2 tablespoons olive oil

Oil for coating grill grate

1 teaspoon kosher salt, plus more to taste for the sauce

3 tablespoons butter

1 large shallot or scallion, minced

¹/₂ cup Cognac

¹/₂ cup heavy cream

DIRECTIONS

1. Put the peppercorns in a zipper-lock bag, press out the air, seal, and coarsely crush with the bottom of a heavy skillet.

2. Pat the steak dry with paper towels and rub all over with the olive oil. Press the crushed pepper into both sides of the meat.

Cover loosely with foil and let the meat rest for 1 to 2 hours at room temperature.

3. Heat the grill as directed.

TIP

- This recipe is designed for skinless fillets. To grill skin-on fillets, create a crisp skin by brushing the skin with oil and grilling the fillet, skin-side down, directly on the grill grate over medium heat. Cover and cook for 10 to 12 minutes without flipping. This method works best with skin-on fillets that are less than 1 inch thick.

TIMING

Prep: 5 minutes

Rest before grilling: 1 to 2 hours

Grill: About 25 minutes

GRILL TOOLS AND EQUIPMENT

- Long-handled tongs

GETTING CREATIVE

- Watercress makes a nice garnish for the steak platter.
- For smoky-tasting steaks, soak 1 cup of wood chips in water for 20 minutes. Add the soaked chips to the low-heat area of the grill until they begin to smolder. Grill the steaks as directed, covering the grill to trap the smoke.

TIPS

- Most supermarkets don't usually cut steaks this thick. Call the meat department or your butcher ahead of time to order it.
- On this steak, the T-shaped bone separates the smaller and more tender tenderloin (or filet) from the larger and more flavorful top loin (strip). Make 4 servings by cutting the 2 pieces away from the bone and then cutting them into 4 pieces or by cutting all of the meat into ¹/₂-inch-thick slices and serving each guest a mix of tenderloin and top loin slices. The T-bone itself is up for grabs.

4. Brush the grill grate and coat it with oil. Sprinkle the salt over both sides of the steak. Put the steak on the grill over high heat and cook until darkly crusted, 4 to 6 minutes per side. Reduce the heat to medium-low (on a gas grill) or move the steaks to the low-heat area (on a charcoal or wood grill), cover, and grill for another 10 to 15 minutes for medium-rare to medium-done (135° to 140°F). Transfer to a platter, cover loosely with foil, and let rest for 5 to 8 minutes.

5. While the steak rests, put the butter in a medium heavy-gauge skillet and melt over medium-low heat, either on a stovetop or directly on the grill grate. Add the shallot and cook until softened, 1 to 2 minutes. Add the Cognac and move the pan over the high-heat area of the grill or raise the heat to high; the Cognac might flame. Boil until reduced to about 1/4 cup. Stir in the cream and any accumulated juices from the steak platter. Return to a boil and boil until slightly thickened, 2 to 3 minutes. Add salt to taste and serve with the steak.

BISTECCA ALLA FIORENTINA

TIMING
Prep: 8 minutes
Marinate: 8 to 24 hours
Soak wood chips: 30 minutes
Grill: About 25 minutes

The famous steak from Florence is essentially a grilled porterhouse. What makes it remarkable, however, is the Italian beef itself. Bistecca alla Fiorentina is traditionally made with steaks from Chianina cattle, a giant breed raised in the Val di Chiana near Arezzo. These enormous white oxen produce tender, flavorful steaks of considerable size—each steak can weigh upwards of 5 pounds. If you're interested in buying some of this extraordinary beef, contact the American Chianina Association, or try to find steaks from another high-quality breed such as Kobe. This simply seasoned and grilled steak is often served with lemon wedges for squeezing. We also put some lemon into the marinade to further flavor the meat.

GRILL TOOLS AND EQUIPMENT
- 1 cup oak or hickory wood chips or chunks
- Smoker box or foil packet, if using a gas grill (see page 39)
- Long-handled tongs

TIPS
- Most supermarkets don't usually cut steaks this thick. Call the meat department or your butcher ahead of time to order it.
- With these steaks, the T-shaped bone separates the smaller and more tender tenderloin (or filet) from the larger and slightly tougher top loin (strip). To cook both sections evenly, put the smaller, more tender section facing the low-heat area of the grill during the initial searing.
- Make 4 servings by cutting the 2 sections away from the bone and then cutting them into 4 pieces or by cutting all of the meat into 1/2-inch-thick slices and serving each guest a mix of tenderloin and top loin slices. The T-bone itself is up for grabs.

THE GRILL

Gas: Direct heat, high (500°F)
Clean, oiled grate on lowest setting

Charcoal: Direct heat, red hot
12-by-12-inch charcoal bed (about 3 dozen coals) with high- and low-heat areas
Clean, oiled grate on lowest setting

Wood: Direct heat, red hot
12-by-12-inch bed with a 4-inch-deep area for high heat and a 2-inch-deep area for low heat
Clean, oiled grate set 2 inches above the fire

INGREDIENTS (MAKES 4 SERVINGS)

1 large lemon
4 tablespoons extra-virgin olive oil
2 teaspoons kosher salt
1 teaspoon coarsely ground black pepper

1 large porterhouse or T-bone steak, 2 1/2 to 3 pounds and at least 2 inches thick
Oil for coating grill grate

DIRECTIONS

1. Cut the lemon in half lengthwise. Squeeze the juice from half of the lemon into a large zipper-lock bag. Reserve the other half. Add 3 tablespoons of the olive oil, 1 teaspoon of the salt, and 1/2 teaspoon of the pepper to the bag. Add the steak, press the air out of the bag, and seal the top. Massage the marinade into the meat and refrigerate overnight or up to 24 hours.

2. When ready to grill, remove the marinating steak from the refrigerator and let it rest at room temperature for 1 hour. Soak the wood chips in cold water for 30 minutes.

3. Heat the grill as directed, adding wood chips to the low-heat area of the grill until they smolder. If using a gas grill without a smoker box, put the chips in a packet of foil, poke holes in the foil, and put the foil directly over one of the gas burners.

4. Remove the steak from the marinade and discard the marinade. Brush and oil the grill grate, then grill the steak over high heat until darkly crusted, 4 to 6 minutes per side. Sprinkle all over with the remaining 1 teaspoon salt and 1/2 teaspoon pepper as you turn the steak. Reduce the heat to medium-low (on a gas grill) or move the steaks to the low-heat area (on a charcoal or wood grill), cover, and grill for another 10 to 15 minutes for medium-rare to medium-done (135° to 140°F). Transfer to a platter, cover loosely with foil, and let rest for 5 to 8 minutes.

5. While the steak rests, coat the reserved lemon half with a little of the remaining olive oil and grill, cut-side down, over medium-high heat until nicely grill-marked, 1 to 2 minutes. Cool slightly, then cut the lemon into 4 wedges.

6. Serve the steak with the grilled lemon wedges and the remaining olive oil for drizzling.

Photo: Porterhouse au Poivre

TIMING
Prep: 20 minutes
Grill: About 20 minutes

GRILL TOOLS AND EQUIPMENT
· Long-handled tongs

TIP
· To save time, use olive oil spray in
  place of the olive oil.

MUSHROOM-STUFFED FILET MIGNON WITH RED WINE SAUCE

Cut from the wide end of beef tenderloin, filet mignon ranks among the most tender cuts of meat available. It doesn't have a lot of flavor, however, so we like to cut a pocket in a thick filet and stuff it with grilled and seasoned mushrooms, scallions, and garlic. A simple red wine sauce adds moisture and flavor.

THE GRILL

Gas: Direct heat, high (500°F)
Clean, oiled grate on lowest setting

Charcoal: Direct heat, red hot
12-by-12-inch charcoal bed (about 3 dozen coals)
with high- and low-heat areas
Clean, oiled grate on lowest setting

Wood: Direct heat, red hot
12-by-12-inch bed with a 4-inch-deep area for
high heat and a 2-inch-deep area for low heat
Clean, oiled grate set 2 inches above the fire

INGREDIENTS (MAKES 4 SERVINGS)

4 filets mignons, each 8 to 10 ounces and 1 1/2 to
   2 inches thick
4 ounces (about 1 1/2 cups) fresh large-cap shiitake
   mushrooms
2 tablespoons olive oil
1 large scallion
1 large clove garlic, unpeeled

6 tablespoons (3/4 stick) butter, softened
3 teaspoons chopped fresh thyme, or 1 teaspoon dried
1 teaspoon kosher salt
1/2 teaspoon ground black pepper
Oil for coating grill grate
1 1/2 cups full-bodied red wine
1 teaspoon honey

DIRECTIONS

1. Heat the grill as directed.
2. Let the filets rest at room temperature, about 30 minutes.
3. Remove the stems from the mushrooms and brush clean if dirty in spots. Coat the mushroom caps all over with olive oil. Coat the scallion and unpeeled garlic clove with olive oil. If the garlic clove will fall through your grill grate, impale it on a skewer or toothpick.
4. Grill the mushrooms, scallion, and unpeeled garlic over medium heat until tender and grill-marked on both sides, 2 to 3 minutes total for the scallion and 5 to 8 minutes for the mushrooms and garlic. Peel the garlic, then chop it finely, along with the scallion and mushrooms. Toss the vegetables in a bowl with 2 tablespoons of the butter, 1 teaspoon of the chopped fresh thyme (or 1/4 teaspoon dried), 1/4 teaspoon of the salt, and 1/8 teaspoon of the pepper.
5. Cut a pocket through the side of the filets without cutting all the way through to the other side. Use a spoon to stuff each filet with the mushroom mixture (use about 2 tablespoons filling per filet). Gently press on the outside of the pocket to enclose the filling. Pat the outside of the steaks dry with paper

towels, then coat all over with the remaining olive oil and sprinkle with 1/2 teaspoon of the salt and 1/4 teaspoon of the pepper.
6. Brush and oil the grill grate, then grill the filets over high heat until nicely grill-marked, 2 to 3 minutes per side. Reduce the heat to medium-low (on a gas grill) or move the steaks to the low-heat area (on a charcoal or wood grill), cover, and grill for another 3 to 4 minutes per side for medium-rare to medium-done (135° to 140°F). Remove to warm plates and cover with foil to keep warm for 5 minutes. Avoid overcooking, as the steaks will continue to cook slightly off the heat.
7. As the steaks rest, bring the wine and remaining 2 teaspoons thyme (or 3/4 teaspoon dried) to a boil in a medium skillet or saucepan over medium-high heat (on your grill's side burner if it has one). Boil until the wine reduces to one-third of its volume, about 1/2 cup. Reduce the heat to low and stir in the honey and the remaining 4 tablespoons butter, 1/4 teaspoon salt, and 1/8 teaspoon pepper.
8. Serve the filets mignons with the wine sauce.

ESPRESSO-GLAZED RIB-EYE

TIMING
Prep: 5 minutes
    (plus 5 minutes for rub)
Rest before grilling: 30 minutes to 1 hour
Grill: About 10 minutes

GRILL TOOLS AND EQUIPMENT
· Long-handled tongs
· Long-handled basting brush

A rib-eye steak is nothing more then a boneless rib steak (a.k.a. Delmonico) cut from the rib section of the steer. These steaks include a fair amount of intramuscular fat that keeps the meat moist, so we like to flavor them with a dry rub and/or glaze rather than a marinade. This cut also stands up to fairly bold seasonings. Here, we dust the meat with a ground espresso rub and then glaze it with molasses-sweetened coffee. The flavors are strong and dark but don't overwhelm the meat itself.

THE GRILL

Gas: Direct heat, high (500°F)
Clean, oiled grate on lowest setting

Charcoal: Direct heat, red hot
12-by-12-inch charcoal bed (about 3 dozen coals)
    with high- and low-heat areas
Clean, oiled grate on lowest setting

Wood: Direct heat, red hot
12-by-12-inch bed with a 4-inch-deep area for
    high heat and a 2-inch-deep area for low heat
Clean, oiled grate set 2 inches above the fire

INGREDIENTS (MAKES 4 SERVINGS)

4 boneless beef rib-eye steaks, each 8 to 10 ounces and
    about 1 inch thick
1/2 cup Black Espresso Rub (page 379)
3 tablespoons butter, melted

2 tablespoons brewed espresso
1 tablespoon molasses
Oil for coating grill grate

DIRECTIONS

1. Pat the steaks dry with paper towels, then sprinkle all over with the espresso rub, patting it in with your fingertips. Let sit at room temperature for at least 30 minutes or up to 1 hour.
2. In a bowl, combine the melted butter, espresso, and molasses until blended.
3. Heat the grill as directed.
4. Brush the grill grate and coat it with oil. Grill the steaks over high heat until darkly crusted, 3 to 4 minutes per side. Reduce

the heat to medium-low (on a gas grill) or move the steaks to the low-heat area (on a charcoal or wood grill), cover, and grill for another 3 to 4 minutes for medium-rare to medium-done (135° to 140°F). Brush both sides with the espresso mixture as the steaks finish cooking over low heat. Transfer to a platter, cover loosely with foil, and let rest for 5 to 8 minutes before serving.

RIB-EYE STEAKS WITH FRAGRANT CHILE RUB AND SALSA BUTTER

TIMING
Prep: 5 minutes
    (plus 5 minutes for rub and
    salsa butter)
Grill: About 10 minutes

GRILL TOOLS AND EQUIPMENT
· Long-handled tongs

This cut of steak is so good for grilling that we decided to include a second recipe with a different flavor profile. As with the previous recipe, the rub here is rather assertive. But the heat of the chile peppers is tamed by the dairy fat in the butter sauce. We recommend getting the steak cut at least 1 inch thick and using the "sear and move" technique, as in the previous recipe. Sear the meat over high heat to develop a good crust, then move it over medium-low heat to gently cook the interior to medium-rare. Of course, you could cook the steaks for more or less time, according to how you like them done.

THE GRILL

Gas: Direct heat, high (500°F)
Clean, oiled grate on lowest setting

Charcoal: Direct heat, red hot
12-by-12-inch charcoal bed (about 3 dozen coals)
    with high- and low-heat areas
Clean, oiled grate on lowest setting

Wood: Direct heat, red hot
12-by-12-inch bed with a 4-inch-deep area for
    high heat and a 2-inch-deep area for low heat
Clean, oiled grate set 2 inches above the fire

➡

4 boneless beef rib-eye steaks, each 8 to 10 ounces and
    about 1 inch thick

1/2 cup Fragrant Chile Rub (page 372)

Oil for coating grill grate

1/2 cup Salsa Butter (page 393)

DIRECTIONS

1. Pat the steaks dry with paper towels, then scatter the chile rub over the steaks, patting it in with your fingers. Let the meat rest at room temperature as you heat the grill.

2. Heat the grill as directed.

3. Brush the grill grate and coat it with oil. Grill the steaks over high heat until darkly crusted, 3 to 4 minutes per side. Reduce the heat to medium-low (on a gas grill) or move the steaks to the low-heat area (on a charcoal or wood grill), cover, and grill for another 3 to 4 minutes for medium-rare to medium-done (135° to 140°F). Transfer to a platter, cover loosely with foil, and let rest for 5 to 8 minutes.

4. Serve with the Salsa Butter.

*Photo: Rib-Eye Steaks with Fragrant Chile Rub
and Salsa Butter*

BARBECUED LONDON BROIL

TIMING
Prep: 5 minutes
Marinate: 2 hours
Grill: 16 to 20 minutes

Flank steak is built for the grill. It's full of flavor, easy to cook, and because it is boneless and its fibers run parallel to one another, it is incredibly easy to slice. Flank steak is the original London broil (see "Will the Real London Broil Please Stand Up," sidebar at right, and no amount of marinating, pounding or wishful thinking can make another cut measure up to its potential for tenderness, flavor, or consistent quality. If you are cooking a London broil cut from the round, you will need to tenderize it through brining. Soak it in 1½ cups Red Wine–Rosemary Brine (page 366) or Steakhouse Brine (page 369) for at least 6 hours. If brining it, baste the meat with the barbecue sauce while it is grilling.

GRILL TOOLS AND EQUIPMENT
· Long-handled tongs

GETTING CREATIVE
· Try this recipe with a butterflied bone-less turkey breast; grill over medium heat for 10 to 12 minutes per side, until the meat bounces back when prodded.

KNOW YOUR INGREDIENTS
Will the Real London Broil Please Stand Up?
London broil is a scam. Fabricated by meat marketers as a cosmopolitan moniker for flank steak, it has come to mean any bone-less slab of meat resembling flank steak—flat and roughly rectangular in shape. Unfortunately, not every meat that looks like flank steak can be cooked like it.

The problem stems from the fact that flank steak is an unique cut of meat. Unlike other tough cuts, which need to be cooked in simmering liquid to soften their tough fibers, flank steak can be grilled just like a more tender loin steak, due to the structure of its muscle fiber.

The tough, thick-walled muscle fibers of flank steak are long and thin and run abso-lutely parallel to one another. Grilling or broiling does nothing to tenderize them. If you were to try to bite into a perfectly grilled flank steak before it is sliced, your teeth would barely make a dent, but when you slice the steak thinly, across the grain of its fiber, you automatically tenderize the meat.

That's why applying the name "London broil" to flank steak makes perfect sense. Even though the meat has nothing to do with Britain, it is a budget-priced piece of tough meat that can be broiled just like high-priced cuts. However, a problem arises when that same name is used for other tough cuts of meat.

These days, London broil is more com-monly butchered from the round, a cut composed of overlapping layers of muscle fiber that run perpendicular and diagonally to one another. Such variegated graining makes it impossible to slice across the grain with any uniformity, because although you may be cutting across the grain on the surface, you will be slicing with the grain in the next layer underneath.

No wonder London broil has a reputation for inconsistency. The problem is not a matter of good meat versus bad, but rather a question of identifying exactly what meat one is buying. For tried-and-true results, always use flank. But if you're shopping price and London broil is on sale, make sure you know where it comes from. Then you can take the proper measures to tenderize the steak through marinating or brining.

THE GRILL

Gas: Direct heat, high (500°F)
Clean, oiled grate on lowest setting

Charcoal: Direct heat, red hot
12-by-12-inch charcoal bed (about 3 dozen coals)
Clean, oiled grate on lowest setting

Wood: Direct heat, red hot
12-by-12-inch bed, 3 to 4 inches deep
Clean, oiled grate set 2 inches above the fire

INGREDIENTS (MAKES 6 SERVINGS)

1 cup ketchup
2 tablespoons steak sauce
1 teaspoon hot pepper sauce
1 tablespoon spicy brown mustard
3 tablespoons apple cider vinegar

2 tablespoons vegetable oil
Kosher salt and ground black pepper to taste
2 pounds flank steak
Oil for coating grill grate

DIRECTIONS

1. Combine the ketchup, steak sauce, hot pepper sauce, mus-tard, vinegar, 2 tablespoons oil, salt, and pepper in a gallon-size zipper-lock plastic bag; seal and shake to combine, about 30 seconds.

2. Add the flank steak and seal the zipper, leaving about an inch open; push on the bag to release any trapped air through the opening and close the zipper completely. Massage the liquid gently into the meat and refrigerate for at least 2 hours.

3. Heat the grill as directed. While the grill is heating, remove the steak from the bag and discard the marinade.

4. Brush the grill grate and coat it with oil. Put the steak on the grill and cook for 8 to 10 minutes per side for medium-rare to medium-done (135° to 140°F).

5. Let rest for 5 minutes before slicing. Cut across the grain in thin, diagonal slices and serve.

TIMING
Prep: 5 minutes
Marinate: 4 to 6 hours
Grill: 10 to 16 minutes

GRILL TOOLS AND EQUIPMENT
· Long-handled tongs

MAKING SUBSTITUTIONS
· If you can't find buffalo meat, use the same amount of beef skirt steak. You could also use flank steak.

SWEET BOURBON BUFFALO SKIRT STEAK WITH MINT

The skirt is a long, flat strip of meat cut from the chest area of the animal. This area is very well exercised, so the meat is dense and tough, yet full of rich flavor. The key thing to remember about buffalo meat is that it's quite lean compared to beef. Tenderize the meat with a somewhat acidic marinade and tend the steak carefully on the grill. It can cook to medium-rare in less than 10 minutes. When sliced across the grain into strips, it makes the perfect steak for fajitas.

THE GRILL

Gas: Direct heat, high (500°F)
Clean, oiled grate on lowest setting

Charcoal: Direct heat, red hot
12-by-12-inch charcoal bed (about 3 dozen coals)
Clean, oiled grate on lowest setting

Wood: Direct heat, red hot
12-by-12-inch bed, 4 inches deep
Clean, oiled grate set 2 inches above the fire

INGREDIENTS (MAKES 6 SERVINGS)

1 tablespoon dried thyme
3 tablespoons kosher salt
1 teaspoon ground black pepper
Finely grated zest and juice of 1 lemon
1/3 cup bourbon

2 cups water
1/4 cup honey
2 pounds buffalo skirt steak
Oil for coating grill grate
1/4 cup finely chopped fresh mint leaves

DIRECTIONS

1. Combine the thyme, salt, pepper, lemon zest, lemon juice, bourbon, water, and honey in a gallon-size zipper-lock plastic bag; seal and shake to dissolve the salt and honey, about 30 seconds.
2. Add the steak and seal the zipper, leaving about an inch open; push on the bag to release any trapped air through the opening and close the zipper completely. Massage the liquid gently into the meat and refrigerate for 4 to 6 hours.

3. Heat the grill as directed. While the grill is heating, remove the steak from the bag and discard the marinade. Skirt steak can be quite long; to ease handling, cut it into approximately 9- to 10-inch lengths. Brush the grill grate and coat it with oil. Put the steak(s) on the grill, cover, and grill for 5 to 8 minutes per side for medium-rare to medium-done (135° to 140°F).
4. Let rest for 5 minutes before slicing. Cut across the grain in thin, diagonal slices, and scatter the chopped mint leaves over the top.

TIMING
Prep: 10 minutes
   (plus 5 minutes for marinade)
Marinate: 2 hours or overnight
Grill: 16 to 20 minutes

GRILL TOOLS AND EQUIPMENT
· Long-handled tongs
· Long-handled basting brush

HORSERADISH FLANK STEAK WITH BALSAMIC BEURRE NOIR

Beef and horseradish make a heavenly match. Use prepared horseradish if you must, but you'll get much better results with fresh horseradish root. Most supermarkets carry it, and you need only grate it on a box grater to complete this recipe. Paired with a balsamic reduction sauce, this combination is bound to win you over. To avoid overwhelming the beef with vodka, use 1/2 cup vodka and 1/4 cup Worcestershire sauce when making the Horseradish Vodka Infusion.

THE GRILL

Gas: Direct heat, medium-high (400° to 450°F)
Clean, oiled grate on lowest setting

Charcoal: Direct heat, light ash
12-by-12-inch charcoal bed (about 3 dozen coals)
Clean, oiled grate on lowest setting

Wood: Direct heat, light ash
12-by-12-inch bed, 3 inches deep
Clean, oiled grate set 3 inches above the fire

INGREDIENTS (MAKES 4 TO 6 SERVINGS)

1 cup Horseradish Vodka Infusion (page 351)

2 tablespoons olive oil

1 large flank steak, about 1 1/2 pounds

1 1/2 teaspoons kosher salt

1/2 teaspoon ground black pepper

Oil for coating grill grate

1/2 cup (1 stick) butter, preferably unsalted

3 tablespoons balsamic vinegar

2 tablespoons minced fresh flat-leaf parsley

2 tablespoons grated fresh horseradish

DIRECTIONS

1. Put the horseradish infusion and olive oil in a gallon-size zipper-lock bag. Seal and shake to combine. Pour 2 tablespoons of the mixture into a small zipper-lock bag or bowl, seal or cover, and refrigerate.

2. Poke the flank steak all over with a fork or skewer to create holes. Add the steak to the large bag, press out the air, seal, and massage the liquid gently into the meat. Refrigerate for at least 2 hours or overnight.

3. Heat the grill as directed.

4. Remove the steak from the marinade and discard the marinade. Pat the steak dry with paper towels and sprinkle all over with the salt and pepper. Let the steak rest at room temperature before grilling, about 30 minutes.

5. Brush and oil the grill grate. Grill the steak for 8 to 10 minutes per side for medium-rare to medium-done (135° to 140°F), basting a few times with the reserved marinade.

6. Let the steak rest, loosely covered with foil, for 5 minutes before slicing. Cut across the grain in thin, diagonal slices.

7. As the steak cooks, melt the butter over medium heat in a small sauté pan. When the butter foams, reduce the heat to medium-low and cook until it turns from yellow to medium brown but not black, 5 to 7 minutes. Watch the butter carefully and do not let it become black or burnt. Pour the brown butter into a small, heatproof bowl, leaving the sediment in the pan. Raise the heat to medium and pour the balsamic vinegar into the pan, swirling it and letting it boil down to about half its volume. Remove from the heat and pour the browned butter back into the pan to combine.

8. Sprinkle the sliced steak with the parsley and horseradish. Drizzle with the balsamic brown butter and serve.

GRILL TOOLS AND EQUIPMENT
· Long-handled tongs

TIP
· The balsamic brown butter sauce can be prepared in advance, left in the pan, and gently reheated just before serving.

SHADES OF BEURRE
The beurre noir in this recipe is a classic French butter sauce made by cooking butter over low heat until it is dark brown, or *noir*, in color. As the butter darkens, it develops rich and heady aromas. The key is to brown the butter slowly so that it doesn't burn. If you cook the butter to a light brown color, it is called beurre noisette (hazelnut). Beurre blanc (white) is a butter sauce made by whisking cold butter into a mixture of wine, vinegar, and shallots.

SCOTCH STEAK IN THE COALS WITH STILTON BUTTER

David's friend Andrew Brubaker first raved to us years ago about this method of cooking steaks. He told us it was the best steak he had ever had, so we had to try it. At first, we didn't think putting meat directly onto hot coals would work; and in the first testing, it didn't. Our mistake was using charcoal briquettes, which have too fine an ash. The ashes stuck to the steak and made it taste like soot. But when we made the steak with lump charcoal and again with a wood fire, it worked beautifully. The steak chars quickly on the clean coals, developing a crisp crust, and there is no residual ash to speak of. The trick is to blow the ash off the coals before adding the steak. For this, you'll need a leaf blower, a hair dryer, a portable fan, or a magazine and a strong arm. It also helps to start with a relatively ash-free grill.

TIMING
Prep: 15 minutes
Marinate: 2 to 6 hours
Grill: 6 to 10 minutes

GRILL TOOLS AND EQUIPMENT
· Long-handled tongs

TIP
· Use a smoky-tasting Scotch like Laphroaig to enhance the smoke flavor in the steak.

SHORTCUT
· Make the Stilton butter ahead of time and refrigerate it for up to 1 week.

THE GRILL

Charcoal: Direct heat, red hot
12-by-12-inch lump charcoal bed (2 to 3 dozen pieces of lump charcoal, not briquettes)
No grill grate

Wood: Direct heat, red hot
12-by-12-inch bed, 4 inches deep
No grill grate

INGREDIENTS (MAKES 4 SERVINGS)

4 boneless strip steaks, preferably Angus, each 10 to 12 ounces and about 1 inch thick

1/2 cup Scotch

1 tablespoon kosher salt

1/2 teaspoon ground black pepper

4 ounces Stilton or other blue cheese, crumbled

4 tablespoons (1/2 stick) butter, softened

---

1. Trim the fat on the steaks to about ¹/₄ inch. Put the steaks and Scotch in a large freezer-weight zipper-lock bag, seal, and refrigerate for at least 2 hours or up to 6 hours, turning occasionally.

2. Remove the steaks from the Scotch and pat dry with paper towels. Sprinkle the salt and pepper all over the steaks, patting it in with your fingers. Let the meat sit at room temperature as you heat the grill.

3. Heat the grill as directed. Leave the grill grate off the grill so that the coals are accessible. Spread the coals to create a somewhat flat bed in the center where you will put the steaks. Blow the ashes off the coals with a leaf blower or hair dryer.

4. Grill the steaks directly on the flat bed of coals until nicely crusted, 3 to 5 minutes per side for medium-rare to medium-done (135° to 140°F). Remove to plates or a platter with tongs and pick off any loose ash. Let the meat rest off the heat, loosely covered with foil, for 5 minutes.

5. Mix together the cheese and butter. Melt about a table-spoon of the Stilton butter over each steak.

Photo: Scotch Steak in the Coals with Stilton Butter

APPLE-BOURBON-BRINED VENISON STEAKS

TIMING
Prep: 10 minutes
Brine: 2 to 6 hours
Grill: 10 to 14 minutes

Venison always tastes best in the fall, so we like to pair it with apples and bourbon—a classic American flavor combination. Like the meat of most game, deer meat can be fairly lean and tough, but a brine changes all that. It allows the proteins in finely grained deer meat to retain more moisture during cooking so that the meat tastes juicy when served.

GRILL TOOLS AND EQUIPMENT
· Long-handled spatula

WHAT IS VENISON?
For most people, venison means deer meat. But it can also refer to the meat of related animals, such as elk, caribou, moose, and reindeer. That's probably because the term "venison" comes from a Middle English word meaning "to hunt." Any type of venison meat will work here, and you could also use buffalo or antelope.

THE GRILL

Gas: Direct heat, medium-high (400° to 450°F)
Clean, oiled grate

Charcoal: Direct heat, light ash
12-by-12-inch charcoal bed (about 3 dozen coals)
Clean, oiled grate on lowest setting

Wood: Direct heat, light ash
12-by-12-inch bed, 3 to 4 inches deep
Clean, oiled grate set 2 inches above the fire

INGREDIENTS (MAKES 4 SERVINGS)

1 cup apple cider

1/2 cup bourbon

1/2 cup water

2 tablespoons kosher salt

1 tablespoon cracked black peppercorns

1 tablespoon dried thyme

2 teaspoons crushed dried rosemary

2 1/2 pounds venison leg steak, about 1 inch thick

1/4 cup hazelnut or walnut oil

Oil for coating grill grate

DIRECTIONS

1. Combine the cider, bourbon, water, salt, peppercorns, thyme, and rosemary in a gallon zipper-lock bag; seal and shake until the salt dissolves, about 30 seconds.

2. Place the bag in a bowl just large enough to hold it snugly. Open the bag and add the venison. Seal the zipper, leaving about an inch open; push on the bag to release any trapped air through the opening, and close the zipper completely. Massage the liquid gently into the meat and refrigerate for at least 2 hours and no more than 6 hours.

3. Heat the grill as directed.

4. Remove the venison from the marinade and discard the marinade. Pat the surface of the venison dry with paper towels and coat with the hazelnut oil.

5. Brush the grill grate and coat it with oil. Put the venison on the grill, cover, and cook until an instant-read thermometer inserted into the meat registers between 130° and 140°F, 5 to 7 minutes per side. If your grill has an external temperature gauge, it should stay at around 450°F.

SPICY INDONESIAN BEEF AND GRILL-TOASTED COCONUT SALAD

TIMING
Prep: 30 minutes
(plus 5 minutes for brine)
Brine: 2 to 4 hours
Grill: 16 to 20 minutes

If you like toasted coconut, you'll love this beef salad. Flank steak is marinated in a brine made with coconut milk, and then it is grilled, thinly sliced, and served on a bed of lettuce, cucumber, and onion garnished with cilantro and strips of grill-toasted fresh coconut. To cut the fresh coconut into strips, you crack the coconut, drain the liquid, and use a vegetable peeler to shave the coconut meat into strips. The coconut adds richness to the lean flank steak and creates a highly aromatic main dish salad.

GRILL TOOLS AND EQUIPMENT
· Long-handled tongs
· Grill skillet or vegetable grill tray
· Heat-resistant grill glove
· Long-handled basting brush

THE GRILL

Gas: Direct heat, medium-high (400° to 450°F)
Clean, oiled grate on lowest setting

Charcoal: Direct heat, light ash
12-by-12-inch charcoal bed (about 3 dozen coals)
Clean, oiled grate on lowest setting

Wood: Direct heat, light ash
12-by-12-inch bed, 3 inches deep
Clean, oiled grate set 3 inches above the fire

1. Use a hammer (or the back of a cleaver) to drive a clean screwdriver through the dark "eyes" of the coconut. Drain the liquid coconut "water" out the holes into a bowl. Taste the coconut water. If it tastes sweet, it is fine. If it tastes sour, the coconut is rotten and should be discarded. Set aside 3 tablespoons of the coconut water for the dressing and refrigerate or freeze the rest (add coconut water to drinks or rice cooking liquid for a subtle coconut flavor).

2. Hammer the coconut shell all around its middle until it cracks and breaks in half. Put the halves in a kitchen towel and hammer each into about 6 pieces. Use the screwdriver to separate any brown shell stuck to the white coconut meat on each piece.

3. Use a vegetable peeler to trim the thinner brown skin from the coconut meat. Reserve half of the trimmed coconut meat for another use (refrigerate for up to 2 days or freeze for up to 6 months). Use the vegetable peeler to shave thin, wide strips of coconut from each piece of the remaining coconut meat.

TIMING
Prep: 5 minutes
  (plus 25 minutes for peppers, rub, and sauce)
Rest before grilling: 1 to 6 hours
Grill: 14 to 20 minutes

GRILL TOOLS AND EQUIPMENT
- Long-handled tongs
- Long-handled basting brush

GETTING CREATIVE
- If you prefer boneless meat, replace the rib chops with boneless rib chops or center-cut loin chops and reduce the cooking time slightly. See sidebar on page 133 for a description of the various types of pork chops sold in most markets.
- For smoky-tasting chops, soak 1 cup of hickory or oak wood chips in water for 20 to 30 minutes. Add the soaked chips to the high-heat area of the grill until they begin to smolder. Grill the chops as directed, covering the grill to trap the smoke.

INGREDIENTS (MAKES 4 SERVINGS)

For the steak and coconut:
2 1/3 cups Javanese Coconut Brine (page 367)
1 large flank steak, about 1 1/2 pounds
1 coconut
3 tablespoons peanut oil or canola oil
1 teaspoon kosher salt
Oil for coating grill grate

For the dressing and salad:
1/4 cup rice vinegar
3 tablespoons sugar
3 tablespoons coconut liquid from the coconut
3 tablespoons peanut oil or canola oil
1 large clove garlic, crushed
1/2 to 1 teaspoon sriracha hot sauce or other hot sauce
1/2 teaspoon kosher salt
1 small head Boston or Bibb lettuce, separated into leaves
1 cup thinly sliced English cucumber
1 cup thinly sliced sweet onion such as Vidalia
2 tablespoons chopped fresh cilantro (optional)

DIRECTIONS

1. For the steak and coconut: Set aside 3 tablespoons of the coconut brine and refrigerate. Put the remaining coconut brine in a gallon-size zipper-lock bag. Poke the flank steak all over with a fork or skewer to create holes. Add the steak to the bag, press out the air, seal, and massage the liquid gently into the meat. Refrigerate for 2 to 4 hours.

2. Crack the coconut, saving 3 tablespoons of the liquid for the dressing. (See "Cracking a Coconut," left.) Shave the coconut meat into strips, using a vegetable peeler. You should have about 2 cups of strips. Toss the coconut strips in a bowl with 1 tablespoon of the peanut oil.

3. Remove the steak from the brine and discard the brine. Pat the steak dry with paper towels and rub all over with the remaining 2 tablespoons peanut oil. Sprinkle all over with the salt. Let the steak rest at room temperature before grilling, at least 30 minutes.

4. Heat the grill as directed.

5. Brush the grill grate and coat it with oil. Grill the coconut strips in a grill skillet or vegetable grill tray until lightly browned in spots, 10 to 15 minutes. Meanwhile, grill the steak directly over the heat for 8 to 10 minutes per side for medium-rare to medium-done (135° to 140°F), basting a few times with the reserved marinade.

6. Let the steak rest, loosely covered with foil, for 10 minutes before slicing. Cut across the grain into thin, diagonal slices.

7. For the dressing and salad: While the steak rests, whisk together the rice vinegar, sugar, reserved coconut liquid, peanut oil, garlic, hot sauce, and salt.

8. Line a platter or plates with the lettuce, cucumber, and onion. Drizzle with half of the dressing. Arrange the sliced steak and coconut strips on top. Drizzle with the remaining half of the dressing, garnish with the cilantro (if using), and serve.

PORK CHOPS WITH BARBECUED SWEET PEPPERS

Brining pork chops helps to keep them from drying out on the grill. But if you need to grill your chops without brining them, you can help keep them moist by searing them over high heat and then moving them over low heat to finish cooking. A spice rub adds flavor and a sauce adds moisture, all of which results in tender, juicy-tasting chops that require very little advance preparation before they go on the grill. Here's a basic example, using barbecue sauce and bell peppers.

THE GRILL

Gas: Direct heat, high (500°F)
Clean, oiled grate on lowest setting

Charcoal: Direct heat, red hot
12-by-12-inch charcoal bed (about 3 dozen coals) with high- and low-heat areas
Clean, oiled grate on lowest setting

Wood: Direct heat, red hot
12-by-12-inch bed with a 4-inch-deep area for high heat and a 2-inch-deep area for low heat
Clean, oiled grate set 2 inches above the fire

INGREDIENTS (MAKES 4 SERVINGS)

2 cups Marinated Fire-Roasted Peppers (page 276)

4 bone-in pork rib chops, each 1 to 1¹/₂ inches thick
(about 3 pounds total)

¹/₂ cup Sage and Savory Rub (page 375)

Oil for coating grill grate

³/₄ cup Sweet, Hot, and Sour BBQ Sauce (page 391), heated

TIPS

· To save time, use jarred roasted
peppers in place of the Marinated Fire-
Roasted Peppers.
· If you make the barbecue sauce ahead
of time, reheat it in the microwave or on
the stovetop. Cold sauce would delay
the cooking of the chops. Plus, the fire-
roasted peppers should be mixed with
warm rather than cold barbecue sauce.

DIRECTIONS

1. Prepare the fire-roasted peppers up to 1 week ahead, cutting the peppers into narrow strips.

2. Trim any excess fat from the chops. Scatter the rub over the chops, patting it in with your fingers. Let the chops rest at room temperature for 1 hour, or refrigerate in a zipper-lock bag for up to 6 hours.

3. Heat the grill as directed. If you refrigerated the rubbed chops, let them come to room temperature before grilling, about 30 minutes.

4. Brush the grill grate and coat it with oil. Put the chops on the grill, cover, and cook over high heat until nicely grill-marked, 2 to 3 minutes per side. Reduce the heat under the chops to medium-low (on a gas grill) or move the chops to the low-heat area (on a charcoal or wood grill), cover, and grill for another 5 to 6 minutes per side for medium (about 145°F). Brush with about ¹/₂ cup of the barbecue sauce during the last 5 minutes of cooking. Transfer to a platter, cover loosely with foil, and let rest for 5 minutes.

5. Just before serving, mix the peppers with the remaining ¹/₄ cup barbecue sauce. Serve with the chops.

MOLASSES-BRINED PORK CHOPS WITH ROASTED CORN SALSA

TIMING
Prep: 10 minutes
   (plus 5 minutes for brine)
Brine: 4 to 6 hours
Rest before grilling: 1 hour
Grill: 14 to 20 minutes

Modern breeding methods and consumer demand have resulted in lean pork with less intramuscular fat—the other white meat. That's great for reducing our overall calorie intake, but it presents a few challenges for grilling pork without drying it out. Here's where brining really shines. When you soak pork (or other lean meats) in salty water, the meat actually becomes juicier—a fact you can prove by weighing the meat before and after brining. The meat essentially absorbs the brining liquid, which increases its water weight. (This is one reason that commercial meats are often brined: You pay more for the meat because it weighs more, and producers can promote brining because it adds flavor and moisture. Of course, you can save money by brining fresh meat yourself at home.) Here's how it works: The salt in the brine causes protein strands in the meat to unravel, or "denature." As they unwind, the protein strands get caught up in one another, forming a sort of web, and the brining liquid gets caught in that web. Even when the protein strands firm up during cooking, liquid stays trapped in the newly formed web, resulting in moister grilled meat. And the technique couldn't be easier. As in marinating, you simply mix up a flavorful liquid (with the addition of extra salt and sometimes sugar) and then let the meat soak in the refrigerator for a few hours. See page 85 for more on the technique of brining.

GETTING CREATIVE
· If you prefer boneless meat, replace
the rib chops with boneless rib chops
or center-cut loin chops and reduce the
cooking time slightly. See sidebar on
page 133 for a description of the various types of pork chops sold in most
markets.
· For smoky-tasting chops, soak 1 cup of
hickory or oak wood chips in water for
20 to 30 minutes. Add the soaked
chips to the high-heat area of the grill
until they begin to smolder. Grill the
chops as directed, covering the grill to
trap the smoke.

THE GRILL

Gas: Direct heat, high (500°F)
             Clean, oiled grate on lowest setting

Charcoal: Direct heat, red hot
             12-by-12-inch charcoal bed (about 3 dozen coals)
                with high- and low-heat areas
             Clean, oiled grate on lowest setting

Wood: Direct heat, red hot
             12-by-12-inch bed with a 4-inch-deep area for
                high heat and a 2-inch-deep area for low heat
             Clean, oiled grate set 2 inches above the fire

2 cups Molasses Brine (page 371)

4 bone-in pork rib chops, each 1 to 1 1/2 inches thick (about 3 pounds total), trimmed of excess fat

2 tablespoons extra-virgin olive oil, plus more for oiling corn

1 tablespoon paprika, sweet, hot, or smoked

1 small tomato, seeded and finely chopped

1 jalapeño chile, seeded and finely chopped

1 small clove garlic, minced

2 tablespoons chopped red onion

2 tablespoons chopped fresh cilantro

Juice of 1/2 lime

1/4 teaspoon kosher salt

Oil for coating grill grate

3 ears fresh corn, husks removed

DIRECTIONS

1. Put the brine in a large zipper-lock bag. Add the chops, press out the air, seal, and refrigerate for 4 to 6 hours.

2. Remove the chops from the brine and pat dry with paper towels. Rub the chops with 1 tablespoon of the olive oil, then sprinkle them all over with the paprika. Cover loosely with foil and let the meat rest for about 1 hour at room temperature.

3. Heat the grill as directed.

4. Combine the tomato, jalapeño, garlic, onion, cilantro, lime juice, salt, and remaining 1 tablespoon olive oil in a bowl.

5. Brush the grill grate and coat it with oil. Coat the corn all over with additional oil or oil spray, then grill over medium to medium-high heat, turning often, until browned all over, about 10 minutes.

6. As the corn cooks, grill the chops over high heat until nicely grill-marked, 2 to 3 minutes per side. Reduce the heat under the chops to medium-low (on a gas grill) or move the chops to the low-heat area (on a charcoal or wood grill), cover, and grill for another 5 to 6 minutes per side for medium (about 145°F). Transfer to a platter, cover loosely with foil, and let rest for 5 minutes.

7. While the chops rest, cut the kernels from the corncobs and mix them into the salsa. Serve with the chops.

Photo: Molasses-Brined Pork Chops with Roasted Corn Salsa

TEQUILA PORK TENDERLOIN WITH SMOKY HOMINY

TIMING
Prep: 10 minutes (plus 10 minutes for brine and rub)
Brine: 2 to 3 hours
Rest before grilling: 1 hour
Grill: 16 to 20 minutes

The most tender meat on any animal comes from muscles that are rarely used. On four-legged animals, the least-used muscles run along the middle of the back and the inside of the rib cage. The muscles close to the rib cage yield the lean and aptly named tenderloin cut. While whole beef tenderloin is a rather large cut (about 5 pounds), whole pork tenderloins weigh less than a pound because they come from smaller animals. For this and other reasons, pork tenderloin has become extremely popular. Like boneless, skinless chicken breasts, pork tenderloins are easy to prepare, cook quickly, and marry well with a variety of flavors. They're especially good grilled. Here, we give the pork tenderloin moisture and flavor by soaking it in a brine of tequila, lime, cumin, and cilantro. A simple stew of hominy and chipotle salsa rounds out the textures and flavors.

THE GRILL

Gas: Direct heat, high (500°F)
Clean, oiled grate on lowest setting

Charcoal: Direct heat, red hot
12-by-12-inch charcoal bed (about 3 dozen coals) with high- and low-heat areas
Clean, oiled grate on lowest setting

Wood: Direct heat, red hot
12-by-12-inch bed with a 4-inch-deep area for high heat and a 2-inch-deep area for low heat
Clean, oiled grate set 2 inches above the fire

INGREDIENTS (MAKES 4 SERVINGS)

For the pork:
1 1/2 cups Tequila Brine (a variation of Cumin, Coriander, and Lime Brine, page 364)
2 pork tenderloins, 12 to 16 ounces each (see Tips)
1/2 cup Fragrant Chile Rub (page 372)
Oil for coating grill grate

For the hominy:
1 can (19 ounces) hominy, rinsed and drained
1/2 cup chicken or vegetable broth
1/2 cup chipotle salsa
1 tablespoon chopped fresh cilantro

DIRECTIONS

1. For the pork: Put the brine in a 2-gallon zipper-lock bag. Add the tenderloins, press out the air, seal, and refrigerate for 2 to 3 hours.

2. Remove the tenderloins from the brine and pat dry with paper towels. Rub the tenderloins all over with the chile rub. Cover loosely with foil and let the meat rest for about 1 hour at room temperature.

3. Heat the grill as directed.

4. Brush the grill grate and coat it with oil. Grill the tenderloins until browned all over, about 2 minutes on each of the 4 sides. Reduce the heat under the chops to medium-low (on a gas grill) or move the tenderloins to the low-heat area (on a charcoal or wood grill), cover, and grill until the meat is just firm when poked and an instant-read thermometer registers 145°F, another 2 to 3 minutes on each of the 4 sides. Transfer to a platter, cover loosely with foil, and let rest for 5 minutes.

5. For the hominy: While the tenderloins cook and rest, combine the hominy, broth, and salsa in a saucepan over medium heat. Cook until heated through, about 5 minutes.

6. Slice each tenderloin into 6 thick slices. Serve 3 slices per person, with some of the hominy and a sprinkling of chopped cilantro.

GRILL TOOLS AND EQUIPMENT
· Long-handled tongs

GETTING CREATIVE
· For smoky-tasting tenderloins, soak 1 cup of hickory or oak wood chips in water for 20 to 30 minutes. Add the soaked chips to the high-heat area of the grill until they begin to smolder. Grill the tenderloins as directed, covering the grill to trap the smoke.

TIPS
· Pork tenderloin is covered with a thin, shiny membrane called silver skin. If left on, the silver skin can cause the tenderloin to curl up during cooking. Remove the silver skin by grabbing it at the thick end of the meat and separating it from the meat with a small knife.

· If you don't have chipotle salsa, combine 1/2 cup salsa with 1/2 to 1 teaspoon ground chipotle powder or 1 to 2 teaspoons *adobo* sauce from canned *chipotles en adobo*. Try the Fire-Roasted Tomatillo Salsa on page 277.

· Hominy is whole, dried white or yellow corn kernels that have been treated with an alkali, such as lye, to remove the hull. They have a firm texture and a slightly sweet, earthy taste that's featured prominently in the Mexican stew known as *posole*. Sometimes whole hominy is labeled *posole* because it is used so often to make the stew and to differentiate whole hominy from hominy grits, which is hominy that has been ground coarse, medium, or fine.

TIMING

Prep: 40 minutes
   (plus 15 minutes for marinade and rub)
Marinate: 3 hours to 2 days
Rest before grilling: 1 hour
Grill: About 1 hour

GRILL TOOLS AND EQUIPMENT

- Long-handled tongs
- Sturdy, long-handled spatula

SHORTCUT

- To save time, replace the polenta with prepared polenta, which is sold in a cylindrical package in the refrigerated section of most grocery stores. Slice the cylinder of polenta crosswise about $3/8$ inch thick, and grill as directed.

CHOOSING A PORK LOIN ROAST

Cut from the same general area of the pig as pork tenderloin, center-cut pork loin is lean and fine grained in texture. It's the most popular pork roast sold. But other pork loin roasts can be used in any recipe calling for a center-cut roast. Here's some anatomy to help you visualize the differences among pork loin roasts. The entire loin runs along either side of the pig's back, from the shoulder to the hip. The loin muscles closer to the shoulder are worked more heavily and yield a slightly tougher and coarser roast called the blade roast. Loin muscles near the hip are also worked pretty hard and yield the similarly dense sirloin roast. While these bone-in loin roasts are slightly tougher than boneless center-cut pork loin, they're also juicy and full of flavor because the muscles are more developed. The bones provide a bit of juice and flavor as well.

CHILE-MARINATED PORK LOIN WITH GRILLED POLENTA CAKES

Lean, tender, and fine grained in texture, center-cut pork loin remains the most popular pork roast available (read more about pork loin roasts in "Choosing a Pork Loin Roast" at left). We love Latin American flavors with pork, so we've flavored this roast with a spicy beer marinade and then rubbed it with a coarse chimichurri paste inspired by Argentina's national table sauce. Grilled squares of polenta provide an earthy note of corn.

THE GRILL

Gas: Indirect heat, medium (350°F)
3- or 4-burner grill–middle burner(s) off
2-burner grill–1 side off
Clean, oiled grate

Charcoal: Indirect heat, medium ash
Split charcoal bed (about 2 dozen coals per side)
20 replacement coals
Heavy-duty drip pan set between banks of charcoal
Clean, oiled grate on medium setting

INGREDIENTS (MAKES 4 TO 6 SERVINGS)

For the polenta:
$3/4$ cup coarse yellow cornmeal
3 cups cold water
$1 1/4$ teaspoons kosher salt
$1/2$ cup crumbled *queso blanco* or grated Parmesan cheese
2 tablespoons chopped fresh cilantro or flat-leaf parsley
Oil for coating baking dish and polenta

For the pork:
$1 3/4$ cups Fire Beer Marinade (page 354)
1 boneless center-cut pork loin roast, $2 1/2$ to 3 pounds, surface fat trimmed to $1/4$ inch
$1/2$ cup Green Chimichurri Rub (page 381)
Oil for coating grill grate

DIRECTIONS

1. For the polenta: Put the cornmeal, water, and salt in a saucepan and whisk vigorously. Bring to a boil over high heat, stirring occasionally. Reduce the heat to medium-low and regulate it so that the mixture simmers gently until it is very thick and pulls away from the sides, 30 to 40 minutes, stirring almost constantly. It takes patience, but the stirring prevents the polenta from becoming gummy or burning on the bottom. When the polenta is thickened, stir in the cheese and cilantro.

2. Coat an 11-by-7-inch baking dish or other shallow 2-quart baking dish with a small amount of oil. Scrape the hot polenta into the dish and smooth the top. Let cool to room temperature, then cover and refrigerate until very firm, 2 to 3 hours or up to 2 days.

3. For the pork: Put the marinade and pork in a large zipper-lock bag. Press the air out of the bag, seal, and massage the marinade into the meat. Refrigerate for 3 hours or up to 2 days.

4. Remove the pork from the marinade and discard the marinade. Pat dry with paper towels and sprinkle the pork all over with the chimichurri rub, patting it in with your fingers. Let the meat rest at room temperature before grilling, about 1 hour.

5. Heat the grill as directed.

6. Brush the grill grate and coat it with oil. Put the pork on the grill away from the heat, cover, and cook until an instant-read thermometer inserted into the thickest part of the meat registers about 145°F, 50 to 60 minutes. If your grill has a temperature gauge, it should stay at around 350°F.

7. While the pork cooks, cut the polenta into 12 square "cakes." Coat the tops with oil or oil spray. When the pork is nearly done, grill the polenta cakes directly over the heat until nicely browned, 8 to 10 minutes per side.

8. Using tongs and a spatula for support, remove the pork to a large serving platter. Cover loosely with foil, and let rest for 10 to 15 minutes. Cut into slices $1/2$ to 1 inch thick and serve with the polenta cakes.

TIMING

Prep: 10 minutes
   (plus 5 minutes for marinade)
Marinate: 2 to 3 hours
Grill: About 10 minutes

VEAL LOIN CHOPS WITH WASABI BUTTER

We like both veal loin chops and rib chops for grilling. Loin chops are a bit leaner, so we add extra moisture and flavor by soaking them in a spicy vodka marinade. A pat of butter flavored with wasabi paste also adds a bit of fat, moisture, and flavor to the tender chops.

THE GRILL

Gas: Direct heat, medium-high (450°F)
Clean, oiled grate
Charcoal: Direct heat, light ash
12-by-12-inch charcoal bed (about 3 dozen coals)
Clean, oiled grate on lowest setting

Wood: Direct heat, light ash
12-by-12-inch bed, 3 to 4 inches deep
Clean, oiled grate set 2 inches above the fire

INGREDIENTS (MAKES 4 SERVINGS)

4 veal loin chops, each about 10 ounces and 1 to
1¹⁄₂ inches thick
1 cup Wasabi Vodka Infusion (a variation of Horseradish Vodka
Infusion, page 351)

1¹⁄₂ teaspoons wasabi powder or wasabi paste
4 tablespoons (¹⁄₂ stick) butter, softened
Oil for coating grill grate

DIRECTIONS

1. Trim the surface fat on the chops to about ¹⁄₄ inch. Put the chops in a large zipper-lock bag and add the vodka infusion. Press the air out of the bag, seal, and massage the liquid into the meat. Refrigerate for 2 to 3 hours.
2. Mix the wasabi powder with 1¹⁄₂ teaspoons water and let stand for 10 minutes to form a paste. Mix the rehydrated wasabi into the softened butter with a fork. If using prepared wasabi paste, just mix the paste directly into the softened butter without adding water.
3. Heat the grill as directed.

4. Remove the chops from the marinade and discard the marinade. Pat the chops dry with paper towels and let rest at room temperature, about 30 minutes.
5. Brush the grill grate and coat it with oil. Put the chops on the grill, cover, and cook for 4 to 6 minutes per side for medium-rare (135°F on an instant-read thermometer). If your grill has a temperature gauge, it should stay at around 450°F.
6. Remove the chops to a platter or plates, cover loosely with foil, and let rest for 5 minutes. Melt about a tablespoon of the wasabi butter over each chop.

VEAL RIB CHOPS WITH CUCUMBER RAITA

Although veal loin chops benefit from the extra moisture in a marinade, veal rib chops, which have more marbling, don't really need an infusion of liquid to keep them moist. We like to dry-rub rib chops and serve them with a chunky sauce. Veal chops take well to the warm spices in Indian garam masala and the cooling flavors of the traditional Indian cucumber-yogurt salad known as *raita*.

THE GRILL

Gas: Direct heat, medium-high (400° to 450°F)
Clean, oiled grate
Charcoal: Direct heat, light ash
12-by-12-inch charcoal bed (about 3 dozen coals)
Clean, oiled grate on lowest setting

Wood: Direct heat, light ash
12-by-12-inch bed, 3 to 4 inches deep
Clean, oiled grate set 2 inches above the fire

INGREDIENTS (MAKES 4 SERVINGS)

For the veal:
4 veal rib chops, each 10 to 12 ounces and 1 to
1¹⁄₂ inches thick
¹⁄₂ cup Garam Masala Rub (page 376)
¹⁄₄ teaspoon ground cayenne pepper, or more to taste
1 teaspoon kosher salt
Oil for coating grill grate

For the raita:
1 medium cucumber, peeled, seeded, and finely chopped
1 cup plain yogurt
1 tablespoon minced scallion (white part only)
3 tablespoons finely chopped fresh mint leaves
¹⁄₄ teaspoon kosher salt
¹⁄₈ teaspoon ground black pepper

GRILL TOOLS AND EQUIPMENT
· Long-handled tongs

TIPS
· If you can't find wasabi, replace it with 2 teaspoons finely grated fresh horseradish or well-drained prepared horseradish.
· For help with choosing veal chops, see below.

TIMING
Prep: 10 minutes
   (plus 5 minutes for rub)
Marinate: 1 to 8 hours
Grill: 8 to 12 minutes

GRILL TOOLS AND EQUIPMENT
· Long-handled tongs

TIPS
· Whole-milk yogurt tastes best in the *raita*, but low-fat yogurt will work.
· For a thicker texture in the *raita*, drain the yogurt in a cheesecloth-lined colander set over a bowl for about 1 hour. Or use a mixture of ³⁄₄ cup undrained yogurt and ¹⁄₄ cup sour cream.

VEAL CHOPS AND BEEF STEAKS
The best veal chops for grilling are rib chops and loin chops. These same cuts would be called steaks when cut from mature cattle. Veal rib chops look similar to a beef rib-eye steak with a bone running along the edge of the chop. Veal loin chops are the equivalent of a beef porterhouse steak with a small piece of the tenderloin and a larger piece of top loin separated by a T-shaped bone. Like the equivalent cuts from mature cattle, veal rib chops have a bit more intramuscular fat, a firmer texture, and more flavorful meat. Veal loin chops are more tender and have a bit less fat, but they are more apt to become dry and tough on the grill. A third option among veal chops is the top loin chop, the equivalent of a beef strip steak with relatively lean and tender meat. All three veal chops are interchangeable in the recipes given here. See page 55 for more on cuts of veal.

1. For the veal: Trim the surface fat on the chops to about $1/4$ inch. Scatter the garam masala and cayenne all over the chops, patting it in with your fingers. Let stand at room temperature for 1 hour, or cover and refrigerate for up to 8 hours.

2. For the *raita:* Combine all of the ingredients in a small bowl. Refrigerate for 1 hour or up to 8 hours to blend the flavors.

3. Heat the grill as directed.

4. If the seasoned chops were refrigerated, rest them at room temperature before grilling, about 45 minutes. Sprinkle the chops all over with the salt.

5. Brush the grill grate and coat it with oil. Put the chops on the grill, cover, and cook for 4 to 6 minutes per side for medium-rare (135°F on an instant-read thermometer). If your grill has a temperature gauge, it should stay at around 450°F.

6. Remove the chops to a platter or plates, cover loosely with foil, and let rest for 5 minutes. Serve with the *raita*.

GARLIC-BUTTERMILK LAMB CHOPS WITH HOT PEPPER HONEY

Loin lamb chops are a better buy than rib chops. First of all, there's less bone. The dirty secret of meat pricing is that whatever price per pound you're paying for meat, you're also paying for bone. Second, loin chops are more tender. They come from the center of the animal's back, and the farther you get from the fore and hind legs, the more tender the meat will be. Best of all, loin chops usually cost less. That's because rib chops look more familiar to most people, resembling the chop we know from cartoons and our dogs' squeaky toys, so they are more in demand and, therefore, higher priced.

THE GRILL

Gas: Direct heat, high (500°F)
Clean, oiled grate on lowest setting

Charcoal: Direct heat, red hot
10-by-10-inch charcoal bed (about 3 dozen coals)
Clean, oiled grate on lowest setting

Wood: Direct heat, red hot
10-by-10-inch bed, 1 inch deep
Clean, oiled grate set 2 inches above the fire

INGREDIENTS (MAKES 4 SERVINGS)

3 tablespoons coarse kosher salt
$1/2$ teaspoon coarsely ground black pepper
Big pinch (about $1/8$ teaspoon) crushed red pepper flakes
2 cups buttermilk
$1/4$ cup plus 2 tablespoons honey
3 tablespoons chopped garlic, jarred or fresh

1 tablespoon minced gingerroot, jarred or fresh
8 loin lamb chops, $1 1/2$ inches thick, about 6 ounces each
2 tablespoons extra-virgin olive oil
Oil for coating grill grate
1 tablespoon hot pepper sauce

DIRECTIONS

1. Combine the salt, black pepper and red pepper flakes, buttermilk, the 2 tablespoons honey, the garlic, and the ginger in a gallon-size zipper-lock plastic bag; seal and shake until the salt dissolves, about 30 seconds.

2. Add the lamb chops and seal the zipper, leaving about an inch open; push on the bag to release any trapped air through the opening, and close the zipper completely. Massage the liquid gently into the meat, and refrigerate for 2 hours.

3. Heat the grill as directed.

4. While the grill is heating, remove the lamb chops from the bag and discard the marinade. Pat the chops dry with paper towels and rub the outside of each chop with the olive oil.

5. Brush the grill grate and coat it with oil. Put the chops on the grill with plenty of room around each. Cover and grill for 4 to 8 minutes per side for medium-rare to medium-done (135° to 145°F).

6. In a bowl, combine the $1/4$ cup honey and hot sauce with a small whisk until well blended.

7. Serve the chops drizzled with the hot pepper honey.

TIMING
Prep: 5 minutes
Marinate: 2 hours
Grill: 8 to 16 minutes

GRILL TOOLS AND EQUIPMENT
· Long-handled tongs

GETTING CREATIVE
· Try this recipe with chicken parts, game hens, or pork chops.
· Vary the flavors in this recipe by replacing part of the buttermilk with coconut milk and adding curry to the marinade; or substitute puréed salsa for half the buttermilk and add cumin to the marinade.
· You can alter the punch of the hot pepper honey by using more hot sauce or a spicier variety, like habanero or Scotch bonnet.
· Garnish the chops with minced cilantro or with slices of grilled garlic (see the Vegetable-Grilling Guide on page 260).

TIPS
· The amount of marinating time given in the recipe is the minimum for getting the flavor of the marinade into the meat. Because the acid content of buttermilk is mild, it will not harm the meat if you marinate it longer, up to 12 hours.
· If you like your lamb more well-done, choose thinner chops or cook them over medium-high heat for 2 to 4 minutes longer.
· If your chops are very thick ($1 1/2$ to 2 inches), grill them for a few minutes on their edges in order to cook them through evenly. You may have to support the chops with tongs to keep them balanced on their sides.

Buttermilk: A Natural Marinade

The incredible versatility of buttermilk as an ingredient is due in large part to the fact that it is in flux itself. Buttermilk is made from low-fat milk to which a bacterial culture has been added. These bacteria feed off of the natural sugars in the milk and produce lactic acid as a by-product of that metabolism. As the acid builds up in the milk, it begins to clabber the milk protein into curds, causing the milk to thicken. The acidity of buttermilk makes it a natural base for marinades, but because it is less acidic than citrus juices or vinegars, it does its work more gently.

Photo: Garlic-Buttermilk Lamb Chops with Hot Pepper Honey

JAMAICAN JERK LAMB STEAKS

TIMING
Prep: 5 minutes
    (plus 5 minutes for jerk paste)
Marinate: 2 hours or overnight
Grill: 6 to 10 minutes

GRILL TOOLS AND EQUIPMENT
· Long-handled tongs
· Long-handled basting brush

GETTING CREATIVE
· You could use a dry rub instead of a wet paste for these steaks. Sprinkle the steaks all over with about 2/3 cup of Jerk Rub (page 377) or a commercial jerk rub. Marinate and grill as directed.

We prefer lamb leg meat for this dish, particularly leg "steaks" cut from the sirloin or center-cut lamb leg "chops." The sirloin steaks come from the larger, upper part of the leg, and the center-cut lamb leg "chops" are cut from the central portion of the leg. These two cuts have a rich flavor that stands up to the bold spiciness of the jerk paste.

THE GRILL

Gas: Direct heat, medium-high (450°F)
Clean, oiled grate
Charcoal: Direct heat, light ash
12-by-12-inch charcoal bed (about 3 dozen coals)
Clean, oiled grate on lowest setting

Wood: Direct heat, light ash
12-by-12-inch bed, 3 to 4 inches deep
Clean, oiled grate set 2 inches above the fire

INGREDIENTS (MAKES 4 SERVINGS)

2 1/2 cups Jerk Wet Paste (page 377)
4 lamb leg steaks, each 8 to 10 ounces and 3/4 to 1 inch thick

Oil for coating grill grate
2 tablespoons vegetable oil

DIRECTIONS

1. Spread the jerk paste all over the lamb steaks and put in a shallow baking dish. Cover and refrigerate for at least 2 hours or overnight.
2. Rest the lamb at room temperature before grilling, about 45 minutes.
3. Heat the grill as directed.

4. Brush the grill grate and coat it with oil. Put the steaks on the grill, cover, and cook for 3 to 5 minutes per side for medium-rare to medium (135° to 145°F on an instant-read thermometer). Brush both sides of the steaks with the 2 tablespoons oil when you flip them. If your grill has a temperature gauge, it should stay at around 450°F.
5. Remove the steaks to a platter or plates, cover loosely with foil, and let rest for 5 minutes before serving.

LEMON-ROSEMARY GRILLED LAMB WITH MEDITERRANEAN COUSCOUS

TIMING
Prep: 5 minutes
Marinate: 1 to 4 hours
Grill: 15 minutes

GRILL TOOLS AND EQUIPMENT
· Long-handled tongs

Here's a simple dish characteristic of Middle Eastern Mediterranean cooking. Cubes of marinated grilled lamb rest on a flavorful bed of couscous seasoned with cinnamon, coriander, and allspice. We prefer to grill large cubes of meat directly on the grill grate, but if you prefer, you can skewer the meat before grilling.

THE GRILL

Gas: Direct heat, medium (350°F)
Clean, oiled grate
Charcoal: Direct heat, medium ash
12-by-12-inch charcoal bed (about 3 dozen coals)
Clean, oiled grate on lowest setting

Wood: Direct heat, medium ash
12-by-12-inch bed, 3 to 4 inches deep
Clean, oiled grate set 4 inches above the fire

Juice of 1 large lemon

2 tablespoons olive oil

2 tablespoons chopped fresh rosemary leaves

3 cloves garlic, minced

1/2 teaspoon paprika

1/2 teaspoon kosher salt

1/2 teaspoon ground black pepper

1 1/2 pounds lamb leg meat, cut into 2-inch cubes

Oil for coating grill grate

1 1/4 cups low-sodium chicken broth

1 cup instant couscous

1/8 teaspoon ground cinnamon

1/8 teaspoon ground coriander

1/8 teaspoon ground allspice

DIRECTIONS

1. Combine the lemon juice, olive oil, rosemary, 2 of the garlic cloves, 1/4 teaspoon of the paprika, 1/4 teaspoon of the salt, and 1/4 teaspoon of the black pepper in a large zipper-lock bag. Add the lamb and press the air out of the bag. Seal and refrigerate for 1 to 4 hours.

2. Let the lamb rest at room temperature before grilling, about 20 minutes.

3. Heat the grill as directed.

4. Brush the grill grate and coat it with oil. Remove the lamb from the marinade and discard the marinade. Using tongs, put the lamb directly on the grill grate (or skewer the lamb for

a pretty presentation), cover, and cook for 12 to 15 minutes, turning often, for medium-rare meat. The lamb should be reddish pink in the center and will cook a bit further once removed from the heat.

5. While the lamb cooks, bring the broth to a boil in a medium saucepan. Stir in the couscous, cinnamon, coriander, allspice, and the remaining minced garlic, 1/4 teaspoon paprika, 1/4 teaspoon salt, and 1/8 teaspoon pepper. Cover, remove from the heat, and let stand for 5 minutes.

6. Fluff the couscous with a fork and divide among 4 plates. Top with the grilled lamb and serve.

CRANBERRY SWEET-AND-SOUR TURKEY LONDON BROIL

Tired of the same old holiday turkey year after year? Try this cranberry-orange alternative. The turkey isn't whole. Instead, it's a boneless butterflied turkey breast—perfect if you don't like carving the bird or if you prefer all white meat anyway. The meat is marinated in an orange-sage marinade and then served with a simple cranberry sauce made with the boiled marinade.

THE GRILL

Gas: Direct heat, medium (350°F)
Clean, oiled grate

Charcoal: Direct heat, light ash
12-by-12-inch charcoal bed (about 3 dozen coals)
Clean, oiled grate on lowest setting

Wood: Direct heat, light ash
12-by-12-inch bed, 3 to 4 inches deep
Clean, oiled grate set 2 inches above the fire

INGREDIENTS (MAKES 8 SERVINGS)

Juice and grated zest of 1 small orange

Juice and grated zest of 1 lemon

1/4 cup olive oil

2 teaspoons chopped or grated peeled gingerroot

2 cloves garlic, minced

2 teaspoons chopped fresh sage leaves, or 1/2 teaspoon dried

3/4 teaspoon kosher salt

1/4 teaspoon ground black pepper

1 turkey London broil, about 2 1/2 pounds (see "What Is Turkey London Broil?" right)

Oil for coating grill grate

2 cups (about 8 ounces) fresh cranberries, rinsed

3/4 cup sugar

4 tablespoons (1/2 stick) butter, cut into pieces

TIMING
Prep: 10 minutes
Marinate: 2 to 8 hours
Grill: 30 to 40 minutes

GRILL TOOLS AND EQUIPMENT
· Long-handled tongs

WHAT IS TURKEY LONDON BROIL?
Turkey sales spike during the holidays and drop off during the rest of the year. To attract health-conscious consumers year round, turkey producers have begun marketing turkey London broil as an alternative to beef London broil. Turkey London broil is simply a butterflied boneless turkey breast. This cut is tailor-made for the summer grilling season because it's boneless, easy to work with, cooks in about 30 minutes over direct heat, and feeds a crowd of 8 to 10 people. Plus you can flavor it in any number of ways. If you can't find turkey London broil, look for a skinless turkey breast half and butterfly it according to the directions on page 164.

1. Combine the orange juice and zest, lemon juice and zest, olive oil, ginger, garlic, sage, 1/2 teaspoon of the salt, and the pepper in a large zipper-lock bag. Add the turkey and press the air out of the bag. Seal and refrigerate for at least 2 hours or up to 8 hours.

2. Remove the turkey from the marinade and pat dry with paper towels. Save the marinade. Sprinkle the turkey all over with the remaining 1/4 teaspoon salt. Let the meat rest at room temperature before grilling, about 45 minutes.

3. Heat the grill as directed.

4. Brush the grill grate and coat it with oil. Put the turkey on the grill, cover, and cook for 30 to 40 minutes, or until just slightly pink in the center and the juices run clear (about 160°F

on an instant-read thermometer). Turn the turkey several times during grilling to brown it all over. If your grill has a temperature gauge, it should stay at around 350°F.

5. Remove to a platter, cover loosely with foil, and let rest for 10 minutes.

6. While the turkey cooks, pour the marinade into a small saucepan and boil for 5 minutes. Strain through a sieve and return to the saucepan. Add the cranberries and sugar, and cook over medium heat until the cranberries pop and the mixture thickens slightly, about 10 minutes. Whisk in the butter just before serving.

7. Slice the turkey thinly and serve with the cranberry sauce.

TIMING
Prep: 20 minutes
Marinate: 2 to 8 hours
Grill: 8 to 12 minutes

GRILL TOOLS AND EQUIPMENT
· Long-handled tongs
· Long-handled basting brush

TIP
· To peel and pit an avocado, cut it in halffrom top to bottom, through the peel and around the pit. Twist the halves apart and put the pitted half in your hand. Gently whack the knife blade into the pit and twist to remove the pit from the avocado (protect your hand with a kitchen towel if you're nervous). Knock the pit off the blade with a wooden spoon. Scoop the avocado from its peel with a spoon and mash as directed.

TURKEY FAJITAS WITH GUACAMOLE VINAIGRETTE

Fajitas are meant to be quickly cooked and wrapped finger foods. Beef and chicken are popular, but turkey works equally well. We marinate turkey tenderloins in a spicy lime marinade and then slice the grilled meat into strips. A simple vinaigrette of mashed avocado, lime juice, and olive oil adds moisture, richness, and flavor to the wraps.

THE GRILL

Gas: Direct heat, medium (350°F)
Clean, oiled grate on lowest setting

Charcoal: Direct heat, medium ash
12-by-12-inch charcoal bed (about 3 dozen coals)
Clean, oiled grate on lowest setting

Wood: Direct heat, medium ash
12-by-12-inch bed, 3 inches deep
Clean, oiled grate set 4 inches above the fire

INGREDIENTS (MAKES 8 FAJITAS/4 SERVINGS)

3 limes
1 cup olive oil
2 tablespoons chili powder
2 large cloves garlic, minced
1 3/4 teaspoons kosher salt
3/4 teaspoon black pepper
4 tablespoons chopped fresh cilantro
2 pounds turkey tenderloins

2 avocados, peeled and pitted
2 onions, peeled
1 small tomato, seeded and finely chopped
1 jalapeño or 2 serrano chiles, seeded and chopped
2 bell peppers, 1 red and 1 yellow
Oil for coating grill grate
8 large flour tortillas (8 to 10 inches in diameter)
1/2 cup sour cream

DIRECTIONS

1. Grate the zest from 2 of the limes into a large zipper-lock bag. Cut these limes in half and squeeze the juice into the bag. Reserve the remaining lime. Stir into the bag 1/4 cup of the olive oil, 1 tablespoon of the chili powder, 1 minced garlic clove, 1/2 teaspoon of the salt, 1/4 teaspoon of the pepper, and 2 tablespoons of the cilantro. Pour a few tablespoons of this marinade into a small zipper-lock bag or bowl, seal, and refrigerate. Add the turkey to the large bag, seal, and turn to coat completely. Refrigerate for at least 2 hours or up to 8 hours.

2. Heat the grill as directed.

3. For the vinaigrette, mash the avocadoes in a medium bowl with a whisk. Squeeze the juice from the reserved lime into the

bowl. Whisk in 1/2 cup of the remaining olive oil, 3/4 teaspoon of the remaining salt, 1/4 teaspoon of the remaining black pepper, the remaining minced garlic clove, and the remaining 2 tablespoons cilantro. Cut the onions lengthwise into quarters, leaving the root end intact to hold the quarters together as they grill. Finely chop 3 tablespoons of onion and stir into the vinaigrette along with the tomato and chile. Cover and set aside.

4. Mix the 1/4 cup olive oil, 1 tablespoon chili powder, 1/2 teaspoon salt, and 1/4 teaspoon pepper in a cup. Core, seed, and quarter the bell peppers. Brush the pepper slices and onion wedges with the seasoned oil and set aside.

5. Brush the grill grate and coat it with oil. Put the turkey on the grill and cover. Cook, turning and basting with the reserved marinade a few times, until nicely grill-marked and just slightly pink in the center, 4 to 6 minutes per side. Let rest for a few minutes, then slice the meat into thin strips and arrange on a platter.

6. While the turkey grills, grill the vegetables until almost tender and nicely grill-marked, 3 to 5 minutes per side. Remove from the grill, cut into thin strips, and arrange on the platter with the turkey.

7. Wrap the stack of tortillas in foil and warm over a very low-heat area of the grill, 3 to 4 minutes per side.

8. Allow guests to build their own fajitas by filling each tortilla with the turkey, vegetables, guacamole vinaigrette, and sour cream.

TIMING
Prep: 2 minutes
   (plus 10 minutes for brine and sauce)
Brine: 3 to 4 hours
Grill: 30 to 40 minutes

GRILL TOOLS AND EQUIPMENT
· Long-handled tongs
· Long-handled basting brush

MARGARITA-BRINED TURKEY BREAST WITH CHIPOTLE SAUCE

Turkey breasts make great roasts. If you use a boneless breast, you can grill it over direct heat and serve a crowd. Turkey breasts also take well to assertive flavors. The brine here keeps the lean meat moist on the grill and flavors it with tequila, orange, and lime. A chipotle sauce adds the dark, spicy flavors of smoked jalapeño chiles combined with mole (MOH-lay), Mexico's thick, rich concoction of spices, fruits, and a hint of chocolate.

THE GRILL

Gas: Direct heat, medium (350°F)
Clean, oiled grate

Charcoal: Direct heat, medium ash
12-by-12-inch charcoal bed (about 3 dozen coals)
Clean, oiled grate on lowest setting

Wood: Direct heat, medium ash
12-by-12-inch bed, 3 to 4 inches deep
Clean, oiled grate set 4 inches above the fire

INGREDIENTS (MAKES 8 SERVINGS)

1$^1/_3$ cups Margarita Brine (page 365)
1 boneless, skinless turkey breast half, about 2$^1/_2$ pounds
Oil for coating grill grate
2 tablespoons olive oil

$^1/_2$ teaspoon kosher salt
$^1/_4$ teaspoon ground black pepper
2 cups Chipotle Dipping Sauce (page 392)

DIRECTIONS

1. Put the brine in a large zipper-lock bag. Add the turkey and press the air out of the bag. Seal and refrigerate for 3 to 4 hours.

2. Remove the turkey from the brine and discard the brine. Let the meat rest at room temperature before grilling, about 45 minutes.

3. Heat the grill as directed.

4. Brush the grill grate and coat it with oil. In a bowl, stir together the olive oil, salt, and pepper and brush some of the mixture all over the turkey.

5. Put the turkey on the grill, cover, and cook for 30 to 40 minutes, or until just slightly pink in the center and the juices run clear (about 160°F on an instant-read thermometer). Turn the turkey several times during grilling, basting with the olive oil mixture to brown it all over. If your grill has a temperature gauge, it should stay at around 350°F.

6. Remove to a platter, cover loosely with foil, and let rest for 10 minutes. Slice thinly and serve with the chipotle sauce.

GARLIC-HAZELNUT CHICKEN BREASTS WITH MUSTARD GLAZE

TIMING
Prep: 25 minutes
  (plus 5 minutes for glaze)
Grill: 10 to 15 minutes

Here's a simple chicken dish that's impressive enough for company. You pound out a few chicken breasts, spread them with a simple hazelnut and parsley pesto, and then roll them up and grill them. A sweet-sour-salty glaze of mustard mixed with molasses creates a browned sheen on the chicken rolls.

GRILL TOOLS AND EQUIPMENT
· Long-handled tongs
· Long-handled basting brush

TIPS
· When pounding the chicken, sprinkle it with a few drops of water to prevent sticking. Begin pounding from the thickest part of the meat outward to encourage the meat to spread as it thins.
· To keep the toothpicks or skewers from burning on the grill, soak them in water for 20 minutes before using.
· To save time, buy skinless hazelnuts.

THE GRILL

Gas: Direct heat, medium (350°F)
Clean, oiled grate on lowest setting

Charcoal: Direct heat, medium ash
12-by-12-inch charcoal bed (about 3 dozen coals)
Clean, oiled grate on lowest setting

Wood: Direct heat, medium ash
12-by-12-inch bed, 3 to 4 inches deep
Clean, oiled grate set 4 inches above the fire

INGREDIENTS (MAKES 4 SERVINGS)

1/2 cup hazelnuts
6 cloves garlic
1/2 cup flat-leaf parsley leaves
1/2 cup extra-virgin olive oil
1/2 teaspoon kosher salt
1/4 teaspoon ground black pepper

4 boneless, skinless chicken breast halves, about
  1 1/2 pounds
No-stick spray oil
Oil for coating grill grate
1/2 cup Mustard-Molasses Glaze (page 386)

DIRECTIONS

1. Toast the hazelnuts in a skillet over medium heat, shaking the pan occasionally, until fragrant and lightly browned, about 5 minutes. If the nuts have skins, rub them in a kitchen towel to remove the skins.

2. Put the hazelnuts, garlic, parsley, olive oil, salt, and pepper in a small food processor and process until very finely chopped, scraping down the sides as necessary.

3. Put the chicken breasts, one at a time, between sheets of wax paper or plastic wrap, with the smooth side down. Pound with the flat side of a mallet or heavy skillet to an even 1/4-inch thickness, being careful not to tear the meat.

4. Spread the hazelnut mixture over the chicken, leaving a 1/4-inch border around the edges. Roll up jelly-roll style from a short side, pushing in the sides as you roll, to enclose the filling. Secure each roll with a wooden toothpick or short skewer and generously coat all over with spray oil.

5. Heat the grill as directed.

6. Brush and oil the grill grate, then grill the chicken until it is no longer pink and the filling is hot, 10 to 15 minutes total, turning often. Keep the grill lid down except to brush the chicken with the mustard glaze during the last 5 to 10 minutes of cooking. Cool slightly, then slice crosswise on a slight diagonal.

MINT-INFUSED CHICKEN WITH POMEGRANATE YOGURT

TIMING
Prep: 15 minutes
  (plus 5 minutes for marinade)
Marinate: 1 to 3 hours
Grill: 10 to 14 minutes

Don't fear the pomegranate. You simply break open this fruit and pluck out its garnet-colored, sweet-tart seeds. To easily extract the juice, we purée the pomegranate seeds in a food processor and then strain the juice into a bowl. Apart from marinating, this dish takes less than 30 minutes to make from start to finish.

GRILL TOOLS AND EQUIPMENT
· Long-handled tongs

TIP
· To create super-crisp skin and more even browning of the meat, weight down the chicken with a heavy cast-iron or other heatproof skillet as the chicken cooks. Fill the skillet with rocks or a brick if it needs more weight to press the chicken into the grill grate.

THE GRILL

Gas: Direct heat, medium-high (450°F)
Clean, oiled grate

Charcoal: Direct heat, light ash
12-by-12-inch charcoal bed (about 3 dozen coals)
Clean, oiled grate on lowest setting

Wood: Direct heat, light ash
12-by-12-inch bed, 3 to 4 inches deep
Clean, oiled grate set 2 inches above the fire

1 cup Lemon-Mint Marinade (page 358)

4 boneless, skinless chicken breast halves, about 1 1/2 pounds

1 pomegranate

1 scallion, roots trimmed, thinly sliced

1 cup plain yogurt

1 1/2 teaspoons honey

1/2 teaspoon kosher salt

1/8 teaspoon ground black pepper

Oil for coating grill grate

1 tablespoon chopped fresh mint or flat-leaf parsley (optional)

DIRECTIONS

1. Put the marinade and chicken in a large zipper-lock bag. Press out the air, seal the bag, and massage the liquid into the meat. Refrigerate for 1 to 3 hours. Remove from the refrigerator about 20 minutes before grilling.

2. Cut the pomegranate into quarters from stem to blossom end. Remove the seeds from the pale membranes. Put half of the seeds in an airtight container and reserve for another use (they can be frozen for up to 3 months). Set aside 2 tablespoons of the remaining seeds for garnish. Put the rest of the remaining seeds in a food processor and purée until the juice and seeds separate, 30 seconds to 1 minute. Strain the juice

into a medium bowl (you should have 3 to 4 tablespoons juice). Whisk in the scallion, yogurt, honey, salt, and pepper.

3. Heat the grill as directed.

4. Brush and oil the grill grate, then grill the chicken until no longer pink and the juices run clear (about 170°F on an instant-read thermometer), 5 to 7 minutes per side. Keep covered during grilling. If your grill has a temperature gauge, it should stay at around 450°F. Discard the marinade.

5. Serve the chicken with the pomegranate yogurt, and garnish with the reserved pomegranate seeds and mint or parsley, if using.

TANDOORI CHICKEN WITH VIDALIA CHUTNEY

A tandoor, the traditional oven of northern India, is essentially a bell-shaped charcoal grill lined with clay. The clay walls of the tandoor generate intense heat (up to 700°F) that creates a deep crust on the familiar tandoori chicken. You can get similar results in any charcoal grill using indirect heat; you can even use a gas grill. We like to brown the chicken over direct heat during the last 10 to 15 minutes to help develop a crust. What keeps the chicken from drying out? Using skin-on chicken pieces helps. So does an acidic marinade made with yogurt and lemon juice.

THE GRILL

Gas:	Indirect heat, medium (325° to 350°F)	**Charcoal:**	Indirect heat, medium ash
	3- or 4-burner grill–middle burner(s) off		Split charcoal bed (about 2 dozen coals per side)
	2-burner grill–1 side off		20 replacement coals
	Clean, oiled grate		Heavy-duty drip pan set between banks of charcoal
			Clean, oiled grate on medium setting

INGREDIENTS (MAKES 4 SERVINGS)

For the chicken:

2 cups Tandoori Yogurt Marinade (page 360)

3 1/2 to 4 pounds bone-in chicken breasts, thighs, and drumsticks

For the chutney:

Oil for coating grill grate

1 tablespoon golden raisins

2 thick slices Vidalia or other sweet onion

1/2 cup hot water

1 tablespoon sugar

2 tablespoons chopped fresh cilantro

1 tablespoon chopped fresh mint

1 teaspoon kosher salt

2 teaspoons concentrated tamarind paste,
   or 2 tablespoons freshly squeezed lime juice

2 serrano chiles or 1 jalapeño chile, stemmed and seeded

TIMING

Prep: 10 minutes
   (plus 5 minutes for marinade)

Marinate: 12 to 24 hours

Grill: 30 to 40 minutes

GRILL TOOLS AND EQUIPMENT

· Long-handled tongs

GETTING CREATIVE

· Use a whole, butterflied chicken instead of parts. To butterfly the bird, follow directions on page 169.

· To turn up the heat in the chutney, leave the seeds in the chile peppers.

1. For the chicken: Pour the marinade into a 2-gallon zipper-lock bag, two 1-gallon bags, or a glass baking dish. Add the chicken, massaging the marinade into the meat. Seal or cover and refrigerate for at least 12 hours and up to 24 hours.

2. For the chutney: Heat the grill as directed. Soak the raisins in the hot water until plump, about 15 minutes. Brush the grill grate and coat it with oil. Grill the onion slices directly over the heat until nicely grill-marked, 3 to 4 minutes per side. Pour the raisins with their soaking liquid into a food processor along with the onions and the remaining chutney ingredients. Pulse until chunky.

3. Put the chicken over the unheated part of the grill and put down the lid. Cook, turning once or twice, until the chicken is no longer pink and the juices run clear (about 170°F on an instant-read thermometer inserted into the thickest part without touching bone), 30 to 40 minutes total. Breasts cook faster, so check them first. During the last 10 to 15 minutes of grilling, move the chicken over the heated part of the grill to brown all over. If your grill has a temperature gauge, it should stay at around 350°F.

4. Remove the chicken to a large serving platter. Serve with the chutney.

SHORTCUT

· Fresh pomegranate juice tastes best, but in a pinch you can substitute bottled pomegranate juice, which is reconstituted from pomegranate concentrate.

Photo: Tandoori Chicken with Vidalia Chutney

TIMING

Prep: 10 minutes
(plus 10 minutes for rub and brine)
Brine: 4 to 6 hours
Grill: 20 to 30 minutes

GRILL TOOLS AND EQUIPMENT

· Long-handled spatula
· Long-handled tongs

TIP

· To create super-crisp skin and more even browning of the meat, weight down the chicken with a heavy cast-iron or other heatproof skillet as the chicken cooks. Fill the skillet with rocks or a brick if it needs more weight to press the chicken into the grill grate.

BUTTERFLYING A CHICKEN

1. Cut through the ribs on each side of the backbone with poultry shears or a heavy knife. If using shears, put the bird breast-side down so you can easily snip through the backbone on top. If using a knife, put the bird breast-side up so that you can use the work surface to get leverage as you cut through the rib bones. Cut from neck to tail on each side of the backbone and remove the backbone (save for stock if you like).
2. Turn the bird breast-side up and press down with your hands to flatten it out.
3. For a pretty presentation, make a 1/2-inch slit toward the bottom tip of each breast, about 1 inch from the end. Fold the legs around and tuck them into the slits.

SMOKED SALT–CRUSTED CHICKEN WITH OLIVE OIL DRIZZLE

The best way to develop a crisp skin on a whole chicken is to butterfly it so it lies flat on the grill. A butterflied (or split) chicken also cooks faster. But it still has a tendency to dry out, so we brine the bird first to keep it moist. Then we coat the chicken in a flavorful spice rub loaded with smoked salt. Even if you use a gas grill, you'll get wonderful smoked flavor in this chicken from the smoked salt. To intensify the smoke flavor even more, add a handful of soaked wood chips to the fire. Look for smoked salt at gourmet shops or through online sources.

THE GRILL

Gas: Direct heat, medium (350°F)
Clean, oiled grate

Charcoal: Direct heat, medium ash
12-by-12-inch charcoal bed (about 3 dozen coals)
Clean, oiled grate on lowest setting

Wood: Direct heat, medium ash
12-by-12-inch bed, 3 to 4 inches deep
Clean, oiled grate set 4 inches above the fire

INGREDIENTS (MAKES 4 SERVINGS)

1 whole chicken, 3 to 4 pounds
2 1/4 cups Orange-Fennel Brine (page 362)
1/2 cup Smoked Salt Rub (page 378)

Oil for coating grill grate
1/4 cup best-quality olive oil

DIRECTIONS

1. Trim any excess fat from the chicken, then rinse and pat dry with paper towels. Butterfly the chicken (see sidebar at left). Put the butterflied chicken in a 2-gallon zipper-lock bag so it lies flat in the bag. Add the brine and press the air out of the bag. Seal and refrigerate for 4 to 6 hours.
2. Remove the chicken from the brine and discard the brine. Sprinkle all over with the rub and let the meat rest at room temperature, about 45 minutes.

3. Heat the grill as directed.
4. Brush the grill grate and coat it with oil. Put the chicken flat on the grill with the skin side down. Cover and cook for 10 to 15 minutes per side, or until an instant-read thermometer registers about 170°F when inserted into the thickest part of a thigh.
5. Remove the chicken to a platter using tongs and a spatula for support, cover loosely with foil, and let rest for 5 minutes. Carve into servings and drizzle with the olive oil.

TIMING

Prep: 10 minutes
(plus 20 minutes for peppers and pesto)
Grill: 10 to 15 minutes

GRILL TOOLS AND EQUIPMENT

· Long-handled tongs

TIPS

· When pounding the chicken, sprinkle it with a few drops of water to prevent sticking. Begin pounding from the thickest part of the meat outward to encourage the meat to spread as it thins.
· To keep the toothpicks or skewers from burning on the grill, soak them in water for 20 minutes before using.

PESTO CHICKEN STUFFED WITH ARUGULA, ROASTED PEPPERS, AND CHÈVRE

Chicken rolls have an air of elegance about them, but they're dead-easy to make. This one reveals a beautiful spiral of green pesto, red bell peppers, and white goat cheese—the national colors of Italy. Serve it in spring or summer with a simple side of risotto or pasta.

THE GRILL

Gas: Direct heat, medium (350°F)
Clean, oiled grate on lowest setting

Charcoal: Direct heat, medium ash
12-by-12-inch charcoal bed (about 3 dozen coals)
Clean, oiled grate on lowest setting

Wood: Direct heat, medium ash
12-by-12-inch bed, 3 to 4 inches deep
Clean, oiled grate set 4 inches above the fire

Photo: Pesto Chicken Stuffed with Arugula, Roasted Peppers, and Chèvre

4 boneless, skinless chicken breast halves, about
   $1^1/_2$ pounds
$^1/_2$ teaspoon kosher salt
$^1/_4$ teaspoon ground black pepper
6 ounces soft goat cheese
1 ounce baby arugula (about 1 packed cup)

$^3/_4$ cup Marinated Fire-Roasted Peppers (page 276)
1 small scallion, roots trimmed, finely chopped
$^1/_4$ cup Tapenade Parsley Pesto (page 398) or prepared
   basil pesto
Oil for coating grill grate

DIRECTIONS

1. Put the chicken breasts, one at a time, between sheets of wax paper or plastic wrap, with the smooth side down. Pound with the flat side of a mallet or heavy skillet to an even $^1/_4$-inch thickness, being careful not to tear the meat.

2. Sprinkle the chicken with the salt and pepper, then spread the goat cheese over it, leaving a $^1/_4$-inch border around the edges. Top with the arugula, fire-roasted peppers, and scallions. Roll up jelly-roll style from a short side, pushing in the sides as you roll, to enclose the filling. Secure each with a wooden toothpick or short skewer. Brush the pesto over the surface of the chicken. To make ahead, cover and refrigerate for up to 8 hours. Rest at room temperature before grilling.

3. Heat the grill as directed. Brush the grill grate and coat it with oil. Grill the chicken, turning often, with the toothpicks in place and the grill lid down, until the chicken is no longer pink and the filling is hot, 10 to 15 minutes total. Cool slightly, then slice crosswise on a slight diagonal to reveal the filling, and serve.

Photo: Pesto Chicken Stuffed with Arugula, Roasted Peppers, and Chèvre

GRILLED PEKING-STYLE CHICKEN

TIMING
Prep: 10 minutes
Drying: 24 hours
Grill: 10 to 14 minutes

Peking duck, China's crowning achievement in the culinary arts, is an elaborate affair that begins by pumping air beneath the duck skin to help it crisp during roasting. For a fairly traditional Peking duck that's roasted on the grill, see page 246. If you want the signature flavors and presentation without the hassle, try this version, which uses skin-on chicken parts. We crisp the chicken by pouring boiling water over the skin and letting it dry out in the refrigerator before grilling. Like traditional Peking duck, the chicken is served with hoisin sauce, scallions, and mandarin pancakes. But we doctor up the hoisin with a little orange juice and chili garlic paste.

GRILL TOOLS AND EQUIPMENT
· Long-handled tongs
· Long-handled basting brush

TIP
· Packaged mandarin pancakes are available in Asian grocery stores and well-stocked supermarkets. If you can't find them and don't want to make the crêpes, use flour tortillas instead. Or skip the bread altogether; the chicken tastes great by itself.

GETTING CREATIVE
· Serve additional garnishes such as pickled ginger and chopped cilantro.

THE GRILL

Gas: Direct heat, medium (350°F)
Clean, oiled grate on lowest setting

Charcoal: Direct heat, medium ash
12-by-12-inch charcoal bed (about 3 dozen coals)
Clean, oiled grate on lowest setting

Wood: Direct heat, medium ash
12-by-12-inch bed, 3 inches deep
Clean, oiled grate set 4 inches above the fire

INGREDIENTS (MAKES 4 SERVINGS)

1 pound boneless, skin-on chicken thighs
1 pound boneless, skin-on chicken breasts
2 tablespoons toasted sesame oil
1 teaspoon Chinese five-spice powder
$1/2$ teaspoon kosher salt
$1/4$ teaspoon ground black pepper
1 cup hoisin sauce

$1/4$ cup honey
$1/4$ cup orange juice
1 to 2 tablespoons Chinese chili paste with garlic
(more if you like it hot)
Oil for coating grill grate
4 scallions, roots trimmed, thinly sliced
12 to 16 crêpes (page 246) or mandarin pancakes

DIRECTIONS

1. Bring 4 cups of water to a boil. Put the chicken thighs skin-side up in a colander in the sink. Slowly pour half of the water over the chicken skin. Remove the thighs to a rack set on a baking sheet. Put the chicken breasts in the colander in the sink and slowly pour the remaining hot water over the skin. Remove the breasts to the rack and refrigerate the rack of chicken, uncovered, for 24 hours (this blanching and drying process helps give the chicken a crisper skin).

2. Remove the chicken from the refrigerator and brush all over with the sesame oil. Sprinkle all over with the five-spice powder, salt, and pepper. Rest the chicken at room temperature before grilling, about 30 minutes.

3. Heat the grill as directed.

4. Mix together the hoisin sauce, honey, orange juice, and chili paste. Set aside $3/4$ cup for basting (the rest will be served with the chicken).

5. Brush the grill grate and coat it with oil. Put the chicken on the grill, cover, and cook until no longer pink in the center and the juices run clear, 5 to 7 minutes per side (170°F on an instant-read thermometer). Brush the chicken with the reserved $3/4$ cup hoisin mixture when you turn the pieces.

6. Remove the chicken to a platter and let rest for a few minutes. Thinly slice the chicken.

7. Serve the chicken with the remaining hoisin mixture, scallions, and pancakes for passing at the table. Allow guests to spread some sauce on a pancake, top with some chicken and scallions, and roll into a cone.

TIMING
Prep: 20 minutes
   (plus 5 minutes for sauce)
Marinate: 2 to 8 hours
Grill: 16 to 20 minutes

GRILL TOOLS AND EQUIPMENT
- Long-handled tongs
- Large disposable aluminum pan

TIPS
- Celery sticks make a great accompaniment to these wings.
- Keep a spray bottle of water at the grill to douse any flare-ups. Chicken skin tends to drip quite a bit of fat.

CHILE-GRILLED CHICKEN WINGS WITH CILANTRO-CHUTNEY DIP

In 1964, buffalo wings got their start in Buffalo, New York, when Teressa Bellissimo deep-fried some leftover chicken wings and served them with melted butter and hot sauce. From there, hot wings have traveled the world over, picking up every flavor imaginable. Here's a Southeast Asian rendition. The wing sauce is made with Thai hot sauce, lime juice, mustard, ginger, coriander, cumin, and cinnamon. The dipping sauce gets flavor from mango chutney and cilantro. The basic idea is the same, however. Hot wings dripping with sticky, spicy sauce and a simple dip to cool the flames.

THE GRILL

Gas: Direct heat, medium (350°F)
   Clean, oiled grate on lowest setting

Charcoal: Direct heat, medium ash
   12-by-12-inch charcoal bed (about 3 dozen coals)
   Clean, oiled grate on lowest setting

Wood: Direct heat, medium ash
   12-by-12-inch bed, 3 inches deep
   Clean, oiled grate set 4 inches above the fire

INGREDIENTS (MAKES 8 SERVINGS)

For the wings and sauce:
1¼ cups Sweet, Hot, and Sour BBQ Sauce (page 391)
2 cloves garlic, minced
Juice of 2 small limes or lemons
1 to 2 tablespoons Thai hot sauce (such as sriracha)
   or Tabasco
1 teaspoon mustard powder
1 teaspoon ground ginger
1 teaspoon ground coriander
½ teaspoon ground cumin
¼ teaspoon ground cinnamon
½ teaspoon kosher salt
¼ teaspoon ground black pepper
4 pounds chicken wings, about 16 whole wings
Oil for coating grill grate
¾ cup (1½ sticks) butter

For the dip:
¾ cup sour cream
¾ cup mayonnaise
¾ cup mango chutney, preferably mild
¼ cup chopped fresh cilantro
2 tablespoons minced onion
Juice of ½ lime
1 small clove garlic, minced
½ teaspoon kosher salt
¼ teaspoon ground black pepper
⅛ teaspoon ground cumin

DIRECTIONS

1. For the wings and sauce: In a small saucepan, combine the barbecue sauce, garlic, lime or lemon juice, hot sauce, mustard powder, ginger, coriander, cumin, cinnamon, salt, and pepper. Cook over medium heat, stirring occasionally, until heated through, about 5 minutes. Remove from the heat and let cool. (The sauce can be made up to 1 week ahead.)

2. Cut off and discard the tips from the chicken wings. Cut the wings into 2 pieces through the central joint. Put the wings in a 2-gallon freezer-weight zipper-lock bag (or 2 smaller bags). Add ½ cup of the wing sauce and reserve the rest. Press out the air from the bag and seal the top. Massage the sauce into the meat, then refrigerate for 2 to 8 hours.

3. For the dip: Stir together all of the ingredients in a medium bowl. Refrigerate for up to 4 days.

4. Heat the grill as directed. Remove the wings and dip from the refrigerator about 20 minutes before grilling.

5. Brush and oil the grill grate, then grill the wings until well browned all over and no longer pink in the center near the bones, 8 to 10 minutes per side.

6. Meanwhile, melt the butter in a large disposable aluminum pan on the side of the grill (or in a saucepan over a separate burner). Stir in the remaining wing sauce until combined. Toss the grilled wings with the sauce in the pan, or put the wing sauce in a big bowl and toss with the wings until fully coated. Serve warm.

SPICY THAI CHICKEN THIGHS

TIMING
Prep: 2 minutes
  (plus 10 minutes for brine and sauce)
Brine: 3 to 4 hours
Grill: 15 minutes

If you're wondering how to make chicken more interesting, try replacing plain ol' chicken breasts with chicken thighs. Thigh meat is richer and more flavorful but still cooks quickly on the grill. To make the meat super-moist, we soak bone-in, skin-on thighs in a flavorful brine and then brush them with a coconut-peanut sauce during the last few minutes of grilling. Apart from the brining time, this recipe comes together in about 15 minutes.

GRILL TOOLS AND EQUIPMENT
· Long-handled tongs
· Long-handled basting brush

THE GRILL

Gas: Direct heat, medium (350°F)
Clean, oiled grate on lowest setting

Charcoal: Direct heat, medium ash
12-by-12-inch charcoal bed (about 3 dozen coals)
Clean, oiled grate on lowest setting

Wood: Direct heat, medium ash
12-by-12-inch bed, 3 inches deep
Clean, oiled grate set 4 inches above the fire

INGREDIENTS (MAKES 4 SERVINGS)

1 1/2 cups Cumin, Coriander, and Lime Brine (page 364)
1 1/2 pounds skinless, bone-in chicken thighs
1 1/2 cups Thai Coconut Peanut Sauce (page 397)

1/4 teaspoon cayenne pepper, or more to taste
Oil for coating grill grate

DIRECTIONS

1. Put the brine in a 2-gallon zipper-lock bag (or 2 smaller bags). Add the chicken, press the air out of the bag, and seal the top. Refrigerate for 3 to 4 hours.

2. Heat the grill as directed.

3. Remove the chicken from the brine about 20 minutes before grilling.

4. Make the Thai sauce and stir in the cayenne pepper to taste. Remove half of the sauce to a serving bowl.

5. Brush the grill grate and coat it with oil. Put the chicken on the grill, cover, and cook until no longer pink in the center and the juices run clear, 6 to 8 minutes per side (170°F on an instant-read thermometer). Brush the chicken with the remaining half of the Thai sauce during the last 5 minutes of cooking. If your grill has a temperature gauge, it should stay at around 350°F.

6. Serve with the sauce you placed in the serving bowl.

BUTTERFLIED GAME HENS GRILLED WITH SICILIAN HERB BATH

TIMING
Prep: 10 minutes
  (plus 5 minutes for marinade)
Marinate: 4 to 6 hours
Grill: 20 to 30 minutes

Don't be put off by butterflying. You just cut the whole bird in half and open it up like a book. Butterflying allows you to quickly grill a whole chicken or game hen (rather than slowly grill-roasting it) because the bird lies flat on the grill. These game hens cook in less than 30 minutes and get deep flavor from soaking in a marinade made with fresh herbs.

GRILL TOOLS AND EQUIPMENT
· Long-handled tongs
· Long-handled basting brush

CORNISH HENS
A Rock Cornish hen (game hen) is a hybrid chicken small enough for a single serving. The diminutive bird is a cross between a Cornish chicken and a White Rock chicken. It's sold at 4 to 6 weeks old and weighs just a pound or two. You could substitute poussin (a similar young chicken), quail, or squab.

THE GRILL

Gas: Direct heat, medium (350°F)
Clean, oiled grate on lowest setting

Charcoal: Direct heat, medium ash
12-by-12-inch charcoal bed (about 3 dozen coals)
Clean, oiled grate on lowest setting

Wood: Direct heat, medium ash
12-by-12-inch bed, 3 inches deep
Clean, oiled grate set 4 inches above the fire

---

4 Cornish game hens, about 1¼ pounds each
1⅓ cups Sicilian Herb Bath (page 356)
Oil for coating grill grate

½ teaspoon kosher salt
½ teaspoon ground black pepper

DIRECTIONS

1. Rinse the game hens inside and out, then pat dry with paper towels. Butterfly the hens as directed on page 164. Put the butterflied hens in a large roasting pan so they lie flat in the pan. Reserve ⅓ cup of the herb bath, and brush the remaining 1 cup all over the hens. Cover and refrigerate for 4 to 6 hours.

2. Let the hens rest at room temperature before grilling, about 45 minutes.

3. Heat the grill as directed.

4. Brush the grill grate and coat it with oil. Put the hens flat on the grill, with the skin side down. Cover and cook for 20 to 30 minutes total, turning and basting frequently with the reserved herb bath and sprinkling with the salt and pepper. When done, the hens will be well browned all over and an instant-read thermometer will register about 170°F when inserted into the thickest part of a thigh.

5. Remove the hens to a platter, cover loosely with foil, and let rest for 5 minutes before serving.

SPICY BROWN SUGAR QUAIL STUFFED WITH CHEESE GRITS AND WRAPPED IN BACON

Quail are so small that they can dry out on the grill, especially if you're using wild quail, which have well-exercised muscles and less fat than farmed quail. To keep the birds moist, we marinate them in a buttermilk marinade and wrap them in bacon before grilling. The bacon fat melts into the bird, lending both flavor and moisture. The stuffing helps to plump up the birds so they can hold their original shape when grilled. It also fills out the meal.

THE GRILL

Gas: Direct heat, medium-high (400° to 450°F)
Clean, oiled grate on lowest setting

Charcoal: Direct heat, light ash
12-by-12-inch charcoal bed (about 3 dozen coals)
Clean, oiled grate on lowest setting

Wood: Direct heat, light ash
12-by-12-inch bed, 3 inches deep
Clean, oiled grate set 3 inches above the fire

INGREDIENTS (MAKES 4 SERVINGS)

For the birds:
1 cup Garlic-Buttermilk Marinade (page 350), made using thyme instead of dill
8 quail, preferably whole, rinsed and patted dry (see "Buying Quail," left)
Oil for coating grill grate

For the grits:
¾ cup water
½ cup milk
¼ teaspoon dried thyme
¼ teaspoon kosher salt
½ cup old-fashioned grits
¾ cup shredded sharp Cheddar cheese
½ teaspoon mild hot pepper sauce such as Frank's

For the rub:
¼ cup dark brown sugar
2 tablespoons paprika
2 tablespoons kosher salt
2 teaspoons mustard powder
1 teaspoon cayenne pepper
1 teaspoon garlic powder
1 teaspoon onion powder
½ teaspoon ground black pepper
8 slices bacon

TIMING
Prep: 15 minutes
(plus 5 minutes for marinade)
Marinate: 2 to 8 hours
Grill: 10 to 14 minutes

GRILL TOOLS AND EQUIPMENT
· Long-handled tongs

GETTING CREATIVE
· Add 2 tablespoons Southern Comfort to the buttermilk marinade to add peach and bourbon flavors.

BUYING QUAIL
Quail are sometimes sold semiboneless, meaning that only the wing bones and drumsticks are left intact. The backbone, rib bones, and thigh bones are removed, and a wire frame is often inserted into the bird to hold its shape. Remove the wire frame before working with these birds. The problem with semiboneless birds is that they have very few bones to hold up their original shape when cooked. We prefer working with whole quail. They retain their original shape better, look better when done, and hold stuffing better than semiboneless quail. But either will work for this recipe, and the preparation remains the same.

Photo: Spicy Brown Sugar Quail Stuffed with Cheese Grits and Wrapped in Bacon

1. Place the marinade in a large zipper-lock bag. Open up the quail cavities with your fingers and add the quail to the marinade, massaging the marinade into the meat and cavities. Seal the bag and refrigerate for at least 2 hours or up to 8 hours, turning the bag occasionally.

2. Remove the quail from the marinade and pat dry with paper towels. Discard the marinade.

3. For the grits, put the water, milk, thyme, and salt in a small saucepan. Bring to a boil over high heat. Gradually whisk in the grits and reduce the heat to medium-low so that the mixture simmers gently. Cover and simmer, stirring frequently, until the grits thicken enough to pull away from the sides of the pan, 8 to 10 minutes.

4. Remove from the heat and stir in the cheese and hot pepper sauce. Let cool slightly, then spoon the grits into the cavity of each prepared quail, stuffing each bird until full.

5. Combine the rub ingredients in a small bowl. Sprinkle the rub all over the birds, especially under the legs and wings, patting it in with your fingers. Wrap 1 slice of bacon over the wings and breast of each bird, overlapping the first end of the bacon to hold it down. Secure the second end of the bacon with a wooden toothpick. The legs will remain exposed.

6. Heat the grill as directed.

7. Brush the grill grate and coat it with oil. Put the birds on the grill on their sides with the legs slightly askew, as if they are sleeping on their sides. Cover and grill until nicely grill-marked on both sides, about 5 to 7 minutes per side for medium to medium-well (155° to 165°F). The meat will be a bit more pink than chicken when done.

8. Remove the toothpicks and serve the quail on a plate or platter on their sides (as they were grilled). Or position the birds breast-side up by pushing them gently onto the plate or platter on their backs.

TIMING

Prep: 15 minutes
  (plus 5 minutes for pesto)
Marinate: 2 to 4 hours (optional)
Soak wood chips: 1 hour
Grill: 40 to 50 minutes

GRILL TOOLS AND EQUIPMENT
· 1 cup wood chips (cherry, apple, or oak)
· Smoker box or foil packet if using a
  gas grill (see page 39)
· Long-handled spatula
· Long-handled tongs
· Long-handled basting brush

SMOKY TAPENADE GAME HENS

Game hens can be butterflied and quickly grilled or left whole and slowly grill-roasted via indirect heat. The latter method allows you to infuse smoky aromas deep into the meat with wood chips or chunks. We like to use cherry and apple wood with poultry. Hickory produces a rich smoke that overwhelms these delicate birds, but oak would work if you can't find cherry or apple.

THE GRILL

Gas: Indirect heat, medium (325° to 350°F)
3- or 4-burner grill–middle burner(s) off
2-burner grill–1 side off
Clean, oiled grate

Charcoal: Indirect heat, medium ash
Split charcoal bed (about 2 dozen coals per side)
20 replacement coals
Heavy-duty drip pan set between banks of charcoal
Clean, oiled grate on medium setting

INGREDIENTS (MAKES 4 SERVINGS)

4 Cornish game hens, about 1¼ pounds each
1½ cups Tapenade Parsley Pesto (page 398)

Oil for coating grill grate

DIRECTIONS

1. Rinse the game hens inside and out, then pat dry with paper towels. Rub 1 cup of the pesto evenly over the inside and outside of the birds. Cover and refrigerate for 2 to 4 hours if you have the time (this intensifies the flavor). Otherwise, let the hens rest at room temperature while you heat the grill.

2. Soak the wood chips in water for 1 hour. Heat the grill as directed, and add the wood chips to the coals. If using a gas grill without a smoker box, put the chips in foil, poke holes in the foil, and put the foil packet directly over one of the gas burners (see page 39).

3. Brush the grill grate and coat it with oil. Put the hens, breast-side down, on the grill away from the heat. Cover the grill and cook until an instant-read thermometer inserted into the thickest part of a thigh registers about 170°F, 40 to 50 minutes. Turn the hens frequently and baste with the remaining ½ cup pesto. The final turn should leave the hens breast-side up. If your grill has a temperature gauge, it should stay at around 350°F.

4. Remove the hens to a platter, cover loosely with foil, and let rest for 5 minutes before serving.

GRILLED DUCK BREAST WITH POMEGRANATE MOLASSES

TIMING
Prep: 5 minutes
   (plus 5 minutes for brine)
Brine: 2 to 4 hours
Grill: 4 to 6 minutes

Boneless, skinless duck breasts have become widely available in recent years. Check your supermarket's poultry case. If you can't find them, ask at the meat counter; they can probably get some duck breasts in. If you're starting with skin-on duck breasts, trim off most of the skin, but leave a long, narrow strip of skin attached, about 1 to 2 inches wide. Cut a few deep slits in the skin to help drain some of the excess fat. This little bit of left-on skin will add flavor and moisture to the meat. Grill the duck breast skin-side down for most of the grilling time to help crisp and dry out the skin. Then flip and finish grilling the other side for just a few minutes.

THE GRILL

Gas: Direct heat, medium-high (400° to 450°F)
   Clean, oiled grate

Charcoal: Direct heat, light ash
   12-by-12-inch charcoal bed (about 3 dozen coals)
   Clean, oiled grate on lowest setting

Wood: Direct heat, light ash
   12-by-12-inch bed, 3 to 4 inches deep
   Clean, oiled grate set 2 inches above the fire

INGREDIENTS (MAKES 4 SERVINGS)

4 boneless, skinless duck breast halves
1 3/4 cups Steakhouse Brine (page 369)
Juice of 2 pomegranates (about 2 cups; see Tips)
2 tablespoons butter
1/4 teaspoon sugar

1/2 teaspoon kosher salt
1/8 teaspoon ground black pepper
Oil for coating grill grate
2 tablespoons olive oil

DIRECTIONS

1. Put the duck breasts and brine in a large zipper-lock bag. Press the air out of the bag, seal, and refrigerate for 2 to 4 hours.

2. Remove the duck breasts from the brine and discard the brine. Rest the duck breasts at room temperature before grilling, about 30 minutes.

3. Meanwhile, put the pomegranate juice in a small saucepan and boil over high heat until syrupy and reduced to about 1/4 cup, 20 to 25 minutes. Reduce the heat to low and stir in the butter, sugar, salt, and pepper. Keep warm.

4. Heat the grill as directed.

5. Brush the grill grate and coat it with oil. Coat the duck breasts all over with the olive oil and put them on the grill. Cover and cook for 2 to 3 minutes per side for medium-rare (about 140°F on an instant-read thermometer). If your grill has a temperature gauge, it should stay at around 450°F.

6. Remove the duck breasts to a platter or plates, cover loosely with foil, and let rest for 5 minutes. Thinly slice on the diagonal and serve drizzled with the pomegranate sauce.

GRILL TOOLS AND EQUIPMENT
· Long-handled tongs

TIPS
· To juice a pomegranate, cut it into quarters from stem to blossom end. Remove the seeds from the pale membranes. Put the seeds in a food processor and purée until the juice and seeds separate, 30 seconds to 1 minute. Strain the juice into a medium bowl. One pomegranate yields about 1 cup juice.
· Save a few pomegranate seeds for garnish if you like.
· To save time, use bottled pomegranate juice. Most supermarkets carry it in the produce aisle. Or save even more time and look for bottled pomegranate molasses in place of juicing the pomegranates and cooking down the juice. Heat the pomegranate molasses in a small saucepan over medium heat before stirring in the remaining ingredients. Look for bottled pomegranate molasses in Middle Eastern markets.
· Duck should be cooked medium-rare because the meat is already firm and flavorful, like steak. It should still be rosy when you cut into it at the table.

ORANGE-ANISE DUCK BREAST WITH PLUM BUTTER SAUCE

TIMING
Prep: 5 minutes
   (plus 10 minutes for sauce and rub)
Rest before grilling: 2 to 24 hours (optional)
Grill: 4 to 6 minutes

In the previous recipe, we brine duck breasts to add flavor and moisture. Here, we simply rub the meat with Asian spices and serve it with a thick sauce made from plum preserves, fresh ginger, soy sauce, and tamarind paste. See the introduction to the previous recipe for information on using duck breasts.

THE GRILL

Gas: Direct heat, medium-high (400° to 450°F)
   Clean, oiled grate

Charcoal: Direct heat, light ash
   12-by-12-inch charcoal bed (about 3 dozen coals)
   Clean, oiled grate on lowest setting

Wood: Direct heat, light ash
   12-by-12-inch bed, 3 to 4 inches deep
   Clean, oiled grate set 2 inches above the fire

GRILL TOOLS AND EQUIPMENT
· Long-handled tongs

INGREDIENTS (MAKES 4 SERVINGS)

2/3 cup Hickory Orange-Anise Rub (page 383)

4 boneless, skinless duck breast halves

Oil for coating grill grate

2 tablespoons olive oil

1/2 cup Plum Ketchup (page 394)

3 tablespoons butter

1/4 teaspoon ground black pepper

DIRECTIONS

1. Scatter the rub all over the duck breasts, patting it in with your fingers. Cover and refrigerate for 2 hours or overnight if you have the time (this intensifies the flavors). Or let stand at room temperature while you heat the grill.

2. If refrigerated, bring the duck to room temperature before grilling, about 30 minutes.

3. Heat the grill as directed.

4. Brush the grill grate and coat it with oil. Coat the duck breasts all over with the olive oil and put them on the grill. Cover and cook for 2 to 3 minutes per side for medium-rare

(about 140°F on an instant-read thermometer). If your grill has a temperature gauge, it should stay at around 450°F.

5. Remove the duck breasts to a platter or plates, cover loosely with foil, and let rest for 5 minutes.

6. Meanwhile, heat the Plum Ketchup in a small saucepan over medium heat. Reduce the heat to low and stir in the butter and pepper until the butter is melted.

7. Thinly slice the duck on the diagonal and serve drizzled with the plum sauce.

TIMING

Prep: 10 minutes

    (plus 5 minutes for marinade)

Marinate: 1 to 2 hours

Grill: 8 to 10 minutes

GRILL TOOLS AND EQUIPMENT

• Long-handled spatula

GETTING CREATIVE

• To make Roasted Garlic Basil Oil, purée 1/4 cup roasted garlic (page 392) along with the basil and oil. Continue as directed, but use the oil within 2 days.

TIP

• If using 1 1/2 pounds of salmon fillet instead of steaks, marinate as directed and then grill in a fish basket.

SAFFRON-CITRUS SALMON STEAKS WITH BASIL OIL

We love the gorgeous orange-pink color of salmon. Why not enhance it with the golden glow and rich aromas of saffron? The juice and zest of oranges, limes, and lemons add even more flavor to the marinade. A simple drizzle of basil oil nicely finishes these salmon steaks. Aside from the marinating time, these salmon steaks can be prepped and grilled in about 20 minutes.

THE GRILL

Gas: Direct heat, medium-high (400° to 450°F)

Clean, oiled grate on lowest setting

Charcoal: Direct heat, light ash

12-by-12-inch charcoal bed (about 3 dozen coals)

Clean, oiled grate on lowest setting

Wood: Direct heat, light ash

12-by-12-inch bed, 3 inches deep

Clean, oiled grate set 3 inches above the fire

INGREDIENTS (MAKES 4 SERVINGS)

1 cup Saffron-Citrus Marinade (page 352)

4 salmon steaks, about 6 ounces each

1/2 cup olive oil

1/2 teaspoon kosher salt

1/4 teaspoon ground black pepper

1/2 cup packed fresh basil leaves

Oil for coating grill grate

4 lemon wedges

DIRECTIONS

1. Put the marinade and salmon in a large zipper-lock bag. Press the air out of the bag, seal, and refrigerate for 1 to 2 hours.

2. Remove the fish from the marinade and discard the marinade. Rub with 2 tablespoons of the olive oil and sprinkle with the salt and pepper. Let the fish rest at room temperature before grilling, about 20 minutes.

3. Heat the grill as directed.

4. Purée the basil and remaining olive oil in a blender or small food processor. Scrape into a small saucepan and bring to a

simmer over medium-high heat. Simmer for 2 to 3 minutes, then pass through a fine strainer into a heatproof bowl or jar and let cool. (The basil oil can be kept covered in a cool, dark place for 4 to 5 days.)

5. Brush the grill grate and coat it with oil. Put the fish on the grill, cover, and cook until it is just a bit filmy and moist in the center, 4 to 5 minutes per side. Avoid overcooking, as the fish will continue to cook slightly once removed from the grill.

6. Served drizzled with the basil oil, and pass the lemon wedges for squeezing.

MUSTARD-GLAZED PLANKED SALMON WITH HORSERADISH-DILL SAUCE

We like to grill salmon fillets on wood planks to enhance the woodsy aromas and to avoid problems with the skin sticking to the grill grate. Honey mustard creates a subtly sweet glaze on these light and summery fillets. A creamy dill sauce cools and balances the flavors. If you can, buy wild Alaskan salmon in season from May to September. It has a more complex flavor than most farmed salmon.

THE GRILL

Gas: Direct heat, medium-high (400° to 450°F)
Clean, oiled grate on lowest setting

Charcoal: Direct heat, light ash
12-by-12-inch charcoal bed (about 3 dozen coals)
Clean, oiled grate on lowest setting

Wood: Direct heat, light ash
12-by-12-inch bed, 3 inches deep
Clean, oiled grate set 3 inches above the fire

TIMING
Soak wood chips: 1 to 2 hours
Prep: 10 minutes
Grill: 10 to 15 minutes

GRILL TOOLS AND EQUIPMENT
· Wide, long-handled spatula or heat-resistant grill gloves
· 1 cedar or alder plank, about 6 by 12 by 1/4 inches

TIPS
· Look for cedar planks in well-stocked supermarkets and gourmet kitchen shops. You could also use untreated cedar shingles from a home center or lumberyard. Just be sure that the wood is untreated.
· We like to use skin-on fillets for flavor, but skinless fillets work just fine. Oil the bottom of skinless fillets before laying them on the plank.
· Be sure all the bones are removed from the fillet before grilling. Run your fingers down the flesh in both directions, feeling for tiny bones and pulling them out with needle-nose pliers or tweezers.
· If using 1 1/2 pounds of salmon steaks instead of a fillet, skip the cedar plank. Brush the steaks all over with the mustard glaze and grill on the oiled grill grate for 4 to 5 minutes per side.

Photo: Mustard-Glazed Planked Salmon with Horseradish-Dill Sauce

1 salmon fillet (about 1 1/2 pounds), bones removed

2 tablespoons honey mustard

1 tablespoon olive oil

2 tablespoons minced fresh dill

1/2 teaspoon kosher salt

1/4 teaspoon ground black pepper

1/2 cup sour cream

1/2 cup plain yogurt

1 large scallion, roots trimmed, finely chopped

1 tablespoon prepared horseradish

4 lemon wedges

DIRECTIONS

1. Soak the wood plank in cold water for 1 to 2 hours.

2. Heat the grill as directed. Remove the wood plank from the water and lay the fillet on it, skin-side down.

3. In a small bowl, combine the mustard, olive oil, 1 table-spoon of the dill, 1/4 teaspoon of the salt, and 1/8 teaspoon of the pepper. Brush over the top side of the salmon.

4. Put the planked fish on the grill, cover, and cook until the fish is just a bit filmy and moist in the center, 10 to 15 minutes. Lift the plank from the grill, using a wide spatula or grill

gloves. Avoid overcooking, as the fish will continue to cook slightly once removed from the grill.

5. In a medium bowl, combine the sour cream, yogurt, scallion, horseradish, and the remaining 1 tablespoon dill, 1/4 teaspoon salt, and 1/8 teaspoon pepper.

6. Cut the fish crosswise into 4 pieces and present the fish on the plank with the dill sauce on the side and lemon wedges for squeezing.

TIMING

Prep: 10 minutes
   (plus 5 minutes for rub)

Rest before grilling: 1 hour

Grill: 10 to 14 minutes

GRILL TOOLS AND EQUIPMENT

· Fish grilling basket

· Cast-iron or other heavy skillet

SHORTCUT

· Replace the Cajun Blackening Rub with your favorite commercial blackening rub or Cajun spice blend.

CAJUN PECAN CATFISH

With a sweet, mild flavor and juicy, flaky texture, catfish is among the five most popular fish fillets in American. They're particularly beloved in the South. We like to flavor the fillets with spicy seasonings, grill them, and serve them with a spoonful of buttered pecans. A fish grilling basket allows you to easily flip these delicate fillets. Preheating the basket on the grill also helps to prevent sticking.

THE GRILL

Gas: Direct heat, medium-high (450°F)
   Clean, oiled grate

Charcoal: Direct heat, light ash
   12-by-12-inch charcoal bed (about 3 dozen coals)
   Clean, oiled grate on lowest setting

Wood: Direct heat, light ash
   12-by-12-inch bed, 3 to 4 inches deep
   Clean, oiled grate set 2 inches above the fire

INGREDIENTS (MAKES 4 SERVINGS)

4 catfish fillets, 6 to 8 ounces each, rinsed and patted dry

1/4 cup Cajun Blackening Rub (page 373)

Oil for coating grill grate and fish basket

1/2 cup olive oil

4 tablespoons (1/2 stick) butter

2/3 cup chopped pecans

1/4 teaspoon kosher salt

1/8 teaspoon ground black pepper

1/8 teaspoon cayenne pepper

2 tablespoons fresh lemon juice

2 tablespoons minced fresh flat-leaf parsley

DIRECTIONS

1. Put the catfish in a large baking dish and scatter the rub all over them. Cover and refrigerate for 1 hour.

2. Heat the grill as directed. Brush the grill grate and coat it with oil. Put the fish basket on the grill to preheat it.

3. Coat the fish grilling basket with oil. Put the olive oil in a shallow dish. Dip each fillet in the olive oil and let the excess drip back in the dish. Put the fillets into the hot grill basket and put the basket on the grill. Cover and cook until the fish is just a bit filmy and moist in the center, 5 to 7 minutes per

side. If your grill has a temperature gauge, it should stay at around 450°F.

4. As the fish cooks, melt the butter in a cast-iron or other heavy skillet over medium heat (directly on the grill if you have room). When hot, add the pecans, salt, black pepper, and cayenne pepper. Cook, shaking the pan, until the nuts are toasted and fragrant, 3 to 5 minutes. Remove from the heat and stir in the lemon juice and parsley.

5. Serve each fillet topped with some of the pecan mixture.

BLACK BASS WITH FOIE GRAS VINAIGRETTE

TIMING
Prep: 5 minutes
Grill: 6 to 10 minutes

Black sea bass has pure white, delicate flesh that's sweet and flavorful. It pairs well with the rich taste of pâté de foie gras. We purée the foie gras with champagne vinegar, peach nectar, shallots, and fresh ginger to create a novel vinaigrette for the grilled fish.

GRILL TOOLS AND EQUIPMENT
· Fish grilling basket

WHAT IS FOIE GRAS?
Foie gras, or "fatty liver," is the enlarged liver of geese that have been continuously fed and fattened for several months. The goose liver is then soaked in a rich liquid such as port, generously seasoned, and baked. For pâté de foie gras, the fatty liver is puréed with other rich-tasting ingredients such as eggs and truffles. The texture is almost as remarkable as the flavor: silky smooth, with an unstoppable unctuousness that coats your palate long after the first taste. If you can't find pâté de foie gras, another liver pâté would suffice, although you'll miss out on the rich texture and flavor.

THE GRILL

Gas: Direct heat, medium-high (400° to 450°F)
Clean, oiled grate

Charcoal: Direct heat, light ash
12-by-12-inch charcoal bed (about 3 dozen coals)
Clean, oiled grate on lowest setting

Wood: Direct heat, light ash
12-by-12-inch bed, 3 to 4 inches deep
Clean, oiled grate set 2 inches above the fire

INGREDIENTS (MAKES 4 SERVINGS)

1 1/2 pounds sea bass fillets, about 3/4 inch thick
1 teaspoon kosher salt
1/2 teaspoon ground black pepper
About 3 ounces (1/2 package) pâté de foie gras or other liver pâté
2 tablespoons champagne vinegar

2 tablespoons peach nectar, or apple juice
4 tablespoons extra-virgin olive oil
1 teaspoon minced shallot
1/2 teaspoon minced peeled gingerroot
Oil for coating grill grate and fish basket

DIRECTIONS

1. Heat the grill as directed. Preheat the fish grilling basket on the grill.

2. Pat the fish dry and sprinkle with 1/2 teaspoon of the salt and 1/4 teaspoon of the pepper. Let rest at room temperature for 15 minutes.

3. Purée the pâté, vinegar, peach nectar, 2 tablespoons of the olive oil, the shallot, the ginger, and the remaining 1/2 teaspoon salt and 1/4 teaspoon pepper in a food processor or blender.

4. Brush the grill grate and coat it with oil. Coat the hot fish basket with oil. Coat the fillets with the remaining 2 tablespoons olive oil and put them in the basket. Put the basket on the grill, cover, and cook until the fish is just slightly filmy and moist in the center, 3 to 5 minutes per side. If your grill has a temperature gauge, it should stay at around 450°F.

5. Serve the fillets with the vinaigrette spooned over the top.

GRILLED FLOUNDER ESCABÈCHE

TIMING
Prep: 5 minutes
(plus 5 minutes for marinade)
Marinate: 2 to 24 hours
Grill: 4 minutes

Escabèche originated in Spain as a way of preserving fish. The marinade serves as a sort of pickle. Popular in Provence, Mexico, and Jamaica, *escabèche* can be served cold, warm, or at room temperature. We give this *escabèche* a more traditional Spanish treatment by grilling a mild white fillet and marinating it in Spanish *adobo,* a pungent blend of paprika, orange juice, vinegar, red wine, and green olives.

GRILL TOOLS AND EQUIPMENT
· Fish grilling basket

MAKING SUBSTITUTIONS
· Replace the flounder with any mild white fish fillets, such as sole, turbot, or dab.

THE GRILL

Gas: Direct heat, medium-high (450°F)
Clean, oiled grate

Charcoal: Direct heat, light ash
12-by-12-inch charcoal bed (about 3 dozen coals)
Clean, oiled grate on lowest setting

Wood: Direct heat, light ash
12-by-12-inch bed, 3 to 4 inches deep
Clean, oiled grate set 2 inches above the fire

1¹/₂ pounds flounder fillets, about ¹/₄ inch thick

¹/₄ teaspoon kosher salt

¹/₄ teaspoon ground black pepper

1¹/₄ cups Spanish Adobo Marinade (page 356)

2 tablespoons sherry vinegar or white wine vinegar

1 teaspoon sugar

¹/₄ teaspoon crushed red pepper flakes

Oil for coating grill grate and fish basket

2 tablespoons olive oil

DIRECTIONS

1. Heat the grill as directed. Preheat the fish grilling basket on the grill.

2. Pat the fish dry and sprinkle with the salt and pepper. Let rest at room temperature for 10 to 15 minutes.

3. Put the marinade, vinegar, sugar, and red pepper flakes in a small saucepan. Bring to a boil over high heat and simmer for 1 minute. Remove from the heat and set aside.

4. Brush the grill grate and coat it with oil. Coat the hot fish basket with oil and put the fillets in the basket. Put the basket on the grill, cover, and cook until the fish is just slightly filmy and moist in the center, about 2 minutes per side. If your grill has a temperature gauge, it should stay at around 450°F.

5. Put the fillets in a wide, shallow baking dish. Pour the marinade mixture over them, drizzle with the olive oil, and let cool to room temperature. Cover and refrigerate for 2 to 24 hours. Serve chilled, or bring to room temperature before serving.

TIMING

Prep: 10 minutes

Brine: 1 hour

Grill: 12 minutes

GRILL TOOLS AND EQUIPMENT

· Long-handled spatula or oiled grill basket

GETTING CREATIVE

· Try this recipe with boneless chicken breasts: Place the herbs on the outside of the chicken breasts and hold them in place with the slices of bacon.

· A thick salmon fillet can be cooked in the same way.

· Replace the orange juice with pineapple juice, or add other citrus juices. A few tablespoons of lemon or lime juice will intensify the flavor of the brine.

· Change the flavor of the brine to suit your taste: substitute minced ginger, cumin seed, coriander seed, or cardamom for the fennel.

· Vary the herbs to match the flavor in your brine. Tarragon tastes great with pineapple juice; cilantro is good with lime.

TIPS

· The amount of time needed for brining is approximate and can be adjusted to fit your schedule. Brining for too long will cause the fish to break down and absorb too much of the flavor of the brine. If that should occur, wash the brined fish in several changes of cold water before grilling.

· As the bacon grills, its fat helps to keep the fish moist, and it also adds flavor. If you don't want the bacon, reserve some of the olive oil to drizzle over the fish after it is cooked.

FENNEL-BRINED TROUT GRILLED WITH BACON AND HERBS

Brine doesn't just add moisture. As meat takes in liquid it also takes on flavor, making brining one of the most efficient ways to get the essence of herbs and spices deep into the interior of meat. This trout is a case in point; its flesh is permeated with the classic Provençal combination of orange and fennel. Be careful to limit the brining time to no more than 1 hour. The delicate flesh of trout quickly absorbs flavors and may get overpowered if left to brine any longer.

THE GRILL

Gas: Direct heat, medium-high (400° to 450°F)
Clean, oiled grate on lowest setting

Charcoal: Direct heat, light ash
10-by-10-inch charcoal bed (about 3 dozen coals)
Clean, oiled grate on lowest setting

Wood: Direct heat, light ash
10-by-10-inch bed, 1 inch deep
Clean oiled, grate set 2 inches above the fire

INGREDIENTS (MAKES 4 SERVINGS)

2 cups Orange-Fennel Brine (page 362)

4 boneless brook trout, about 6 ounces each

8 sprigs fresh dill, mint, sage, or rosemary

2 tablespoons olive oil

8 slices bacon

Oil for coating grill grate or basket

DIRECTIONS

1. Put the brine in a gallon-size zipper-lock bag.

2. The trout will be split down their bellies; open them up like a book to expose the interior to the brine. Place the fish in the brine and seal the zipper, leaving about an inch open; push on the bag to release any trapped air through the opening, and close the zipper completely. Massage the liquid gently into the fish and refrigerate for 1 hour.

3. Heat the grill as directed.

4. While the grill is heating, remove the fish from the brine and discard the brine. Place 2 herb sprigs in the cavity of each fish; close each fish around the herbs. Pat the fish skin until dry; rub the outside of each fish with olive oil.

5. Wrap 2 slices of bacon around each fish, allowing the ends of each strip to meet and overlap slightly. Secure each bacon slice with an oiled wooden toothpick.

6. Brush the grill grate and coat it with oil. If using a fish basket, coat the basket with oil. Put the fish in a single layer on the grill grate or in the grill basket and cover the grill. Cook until the bacon is cooked through and any exposed fish skin is crisp, about 6 minutes per side. Remove the toothpicks and serve.

WHY DOES BRINING WORK?

If salt dries out proteins, why does brining make meat moister?

During brining, the salt and acid in the brine make the tightly wound spiral structure of meat proteins unravel (denature). As the spiral opens up, the exposed bonds on the ribbons of protein bind with liquid in the brine, resulting in a 6 to 8 percent increase in the fluid content of the protein. When the meat is grilled, the structure of the protein reforms, trapping the absorbed juices inside. Be careful that you don't overcook brined meats. Excessive heat will cause the protein bonds to tighten, squeezing out all of the liquid that has been taken in.

LEMON-ROSEMARY SWORDFISH STEAKS WITH OLIVE AIOLI

These fish steaks have an incredible herbaceous aroma. Fresh garlic mayonnaise made with chopped green olives adds a rich counterpoint. There may appear to be a lot of ingredients here, but they are all quickly stirred together. Aside from the marinating time, the dish takes less than 15 minutes from start to finish. Fair warning: The fresh mayonnaise uses raw egg yolks in the traditional manner. If you're concerned about salmonella, buy your eggs from a trusted source. Or use prepared mayonnaise, as described in the shortcut.

TIMING

Prep: 5 minutes
Marinate: 1 to 3 hours
Grill: 6 to 8 minutes

GRILL TOOLS AND EQUIPMENT

· Long-handled spatula

Photo: Fennel-Brined Trout Grilled with Bacon and Herbs

Gas:	Direct heat, medium-high (400° to 450°F)	Wood:	Direct heat, light ash
	Clean, oiled grate		12-by-12-inch bed, 3 to 4 inches deep
Charcoal:	Direct heat, light ash		Clean, oiled grate set 2 inches above the fire
	12-by-12-inch charcoal bed (about 3 dozen coals)		
	Clean, oiled grate on lowest setting		

INGREDIENTS (MAKES 4 SERVINGS)

For the fish:

2 tablespoons fresh lemon juice

2 tablespoons chopped fresh rosemary

1 tablespoon chopped fresh flat-leaf parsley

1 tablespoon Dijon mustard

1 tablespoon olive oil

1 clove garlic, minced

1 1/2 pounds swordfish steaks, rinsed and patted dry

Oil for coating grill grate

For the aioli:

1 egg yolk

1 tablespoon fresh lemon juice

3 cloves garlic, minced

1/2 teaspoon mustard powder

1/2 teaspoon kosher salt

1/4 teaspoon ground black pepper

1/2 cup extra-virgin olive oil

2 tablespoons pitted, chopped green Spanish olives
    such as arauco, arbequina, or manzanilla

DIRECTIONS

1. For the fish: Combine the lemon juice, rosemary, parsley, mustard, olive oil, and garlic in a small bowl. Spread over the swordfish, cover, and refrigerate for 1 to 3 hours.

2. Rest the fish at room temperature before grilling, about 20 minutes.

3. Heat the grill as directed.

4. For the aioli: Whisk together the egg yolk, lemon juice, garlic, mustard, salt, and pepper in a medium bowl. When the mixture begins to thicken, whisk in the olive oil in a slow steady stream.

If it gets too thick, whisk in a little water to thin it. Whisk or stir in the chopped olives. (Let stand at room temperature until the fish is cooked. It can also be covered and refrigerated for 3 to 4 days.)

5. Brush the grill grate and coat it with oil. Put the swordfish on the grill, cover, and cook until just a bit filmy and moist in the center, 3 to 4 minutes per side.

6. Serve each swordfish steak with a dollop of the aioli.

SHORTCUT

· To save time, use 1/2 cup prepared mayonnaise to make the aioli. Stir in the garlic, olives, and 1 to 2 tablespoons extra-virgin olive oil. Omit the remaining ingredients.

LOBSTER TAILS WITH GARLIC-CITRUS BUTTER

Rock lobsters (spiny lobsters) have bigger tails than Maine lobsters, making them perfect for a meal of lobster tail. Butterflying the tails exposes more meat to the smoky flavors of the fire. It also makes a beautiful presentation. If you can't find rock lobsters for this recipe, use the tails from large Maine lobsters.

TIMING

Prep: 10 minutes

Grill: 8 to 11 minutes

GRILL TOOLS AND EQUIPMENT

· Long-handled tongs or long-handled spatula

· Long-handled basting brush

BUTTERFLYING LOBSTER TAILS

Split the lobster tail lengthwise through the rounded top shell and through the meat, but leave the flat bottom shell intact. (If the shell is too hard, use kitchen shears to cut through the shell and a knife to cut through the meat.) Gently open the lobster to expose the meat.

THE GRILL

Gas:	Direct heat, medium (350°F)	Wood:	Direct heat, medium ash
	Clean, oiled grate		12-by-12-inch bed, 3 inches deep
Charcoal:	Direct heat, medium ash		Clean, oiled grate set 4 inches above the fire
	12-by-12-inch charcoal bed (about 3 dozen coals)		
	Clean, oiled grate on lowest setting		

INGREDIENTS (MAKES 4 SERVINGS)

4 rock lobster tails, 8 to 10 ounces each, thawed if frozen

1 tablespoon olive oil

1 teaspoon kosher salt

1/2 teaspoon ground black pepper

1/2 cup (1 stick) butter, melted

3 cloves garlic, minced

1 tablespoon orange juice

1 tablespoon fresh lime juice

1 tablespoon chopped fresh cilantro, basil, or flat-leaf parsley

Oil for coating grill grate

4 lemon wedges

---

1. Heat the grill as directed.

2. Butterfly the lobster tails as directed on the facing page. Brush the meat with the olive oil and sprinkle with $1/4$ teaspoon of the salt and $1/4$ teaspoon of the pepper.

3. Mix together the butter, garlic, orange juice, lime juice, cilantro, remaining $3/4$ teaspoon salt, and remaining $1/4$ teaspoon pepper in a bowl.

4. Brush the grill grate and coat it with oil. Put the lobster tails, meat-side down, on the grill and cook until nicely grill-marked, 3 to 4 minutes. It may help to press the tails onto the grill using tongs or a spatula. Flip and grill until the meat is firm and white, basting generously with the garlic-citrus butter, 5 to 7 minutes more.

5. Remove to plates and serve with the lemon wedges and any remaining garlic-citrus butter.

TIP
· If you want to grill the whole "sea bug" (as lobsters are affectionately called) instead of just the tail, see Lobster Grilled with Seafood Butter (page 221).

GRILLED STUFFED SARDINES

This recipe, inspired by the Sicilian classic, *sarde alla beccafico alla palermitana,* is less elegant than its muse (a *beccafico* is a bird with a reputation of being a gourmand because it gorges on ripe figs whenever possible). But what it lacks in delicacy it makes up for with a dynamic contrast of crisp, charred skin; rich, oily fish; and the sweet and salty tang of the stuffing.

TIMING
Prep: 20 minutes
Grill: About 5 minutes

GRILL TOOLS AND EQUIPMENT
· Long-handled spatula
· Grill screen

THE GRILL

Gas: Direct heat, medium-high (400° to 450°F)
Clean, oiled grate

Charcoal: Direct heat, light ash
12-by-12-inch charcoal bed (about 3 dozen coals)
Clean, oiled grate on lowest setting

Wood: Direct heat, light ash
12-by-12-inch bed, 3 to 4 inches deep
Clean, oiled grate set 2 inches above the fire

SARDINES: OUT OF THE CAN
Fresh sardines are as different from their canned crammed counterparts as fresh tuna is from canned tuna fish. Fresh sardines are available year round, and it is mostly a matter of demand that dictates supply at your local fish store. Sardines are usually sold whole, gutted, with their heads on. If your fish seller will remove the bones for you, it will streamline your time in the kitchen, but if not, don't despair; the task is not difficult or time-consuming. As with all fish, look for fresh sardines that are firm and do not smell fishy.

INGREDIENTS (MAKES 4 TO 5 SERVINGS)

4 tablespoons extra-virgin olive oil
$1/4$ cup finely chopped onion
1 clove garlic, minced
$1/4$ cup pine nuts, coarsely chopped
1 teaspoon ground cumin
$1/4$ cup golden raisins, finely chopped
1 teaspoon capers, finely chopped

1 tablespoon dried breadcrumbs
$1/4$ cup chopped fresh flat-leaf parsley
Kosher salt and ground black pepper
2 pounds fresh sardines, cleaned, heads removed
Oil for coating grill screen
1 lemon, cut into 8 to 10 wedges

DIRECTIONS

1. Heat the grill as directed.

2. Heat 1 tablespoon of the olive oil in a small skillet over medium-high heat. Add the onion and sauté until tender, about 4 minutes. Stir in the garlic and pine nuts and sauté until the pine nuts are lightly toasted, about 2 minutes. Remove from the heat and stir in the cumin, raisins, capers, breadcrumbs, parsley, and salt and pepper to taste. Set aside.

3. Remove the bones from the sardines by grasping the backbone at the head end of the fish and pulling it toward the tail. The whole skeleton should separate from the flesh in one piece.

4. Place some of the stuffing inside each sardine, and mold the fillets around the stuffing to encase it. Coat the outside of the sardines with the remaining 3 tablespoons olive oil.

5. Place the grill screen on the grill, and coat it with oil. Place the sardines on the oiled screen, cover, and cook for 2 minutes. Flip, cover, and grill until the fish flakes to gentle pressure, about 2 minutes more. If your grill has an external temperature gauge, it should stay at around 450°F. Serve with the wedges of lemon.

CHAPTER 7

MASTERING ROASTS, RIBS, AND OTHER SLOW FOOD

MASTERING TECHNIQUE

BASIC GRILL-ROASTED CHICKEN 184
BASIC WHOLE FISH 184

RECIPES

TIMING
Prep: 5 minutes
Grill: About 1½ hours

GRILL TOOLS AND EQUIPMENT
· Kitchen twine
· Long-handled spatula
· Long-handled tongs

CARVING A CHICKEN

1. Remove the legs by holding the tip of a drumstick in one hand and pulling it away from the body. At the same time, cut through the skin between the leg and the body. Use the flat side of the knife to press the leg away from the body, and cut through the joint that joins the thigh to the hip. Separate the drumstick from the thigh by holding the tip of the drumstick in one hand with the V of the joint facing downward. Cut straight through the V, separating the drumstick from the thigh.

2. Remove the wings by cutting at a 45-degree angle through the joint where the wing joins the body, positioning the knife close into the body.

3. To remove the breast halves, make a slit through the skin along the crest of the breastbone. Remove one side at a time by working your knife down one side of the breastbone as you gently pull the breast half away from the body. Use the knife to help the breast separate from the rib cage. When the breast half is removed, serve it whole or cut into pieces or slices, depending on the size of the chicken.

Use this master recipe for grill-roasted chicken as a point of departure. Although the recipe will give you near-perfect results, it has not been built with flavor in mind. Feel free to use it as a template, but add flavor with one of the rubs, brines, marinades, or sauces from Chapter 11 if you want to use it for dinner.

THE GRILL

Gas: Indirect heat, medium (325° to 350°F)
3- or 4-burner grill–middle burner(s) off
2-burner grill–1 side off
Clean, oiled grate

Charcoal: Indirect heat, medium ash
Split charcoal bed (about 2 dozen coals per side)
20 replacement coals
Heavy-duty drip pan set between banks of charcoal
Clean, oiled grate on medium setting

INGREDIENTS (MAKES 4 SERVINGS)

1 chicken, about 4 pounds, washed and dried
½ teaspoon kosher salt
¼ teaspoon ground black pepper

1 tablespoon vegetable oil
Oil for coating grill grate

DIRECTIONS

1. Heat the grill as directed.

2. Season the interior cavity of the chicken with the salt and pepper. Tie the legs of the chicken together with kitchen twine. Rub the outside of the chicken with the 1 tablespoon oil.

3. Brush the grill grate and coat it with oil. Put the chicken on the grill away from the heat, cover the grill, and cook until an instant-read thermometer inserted into the thickest part of the breast registers about 170°F, about 1 hour and 20 minutes. If your grill has a temperature gauge, it should stay at around 350°F. If you are using charcoal, you may have to replenish the coals after the first hour.

4. Remove the chicken to a large serving platter, using tongs and a spatula for support. Let rest for 8 to 10 minutes; carve (left) and serve.

MASTERING TECHNIQUE
BASIC WHOLE FISH

TIMING
Prep: 5 minutes
Grill: About 15 minutes

GRILL TOOLS AND EQUIPMENT
· Long-handled fish spatula
· Grill screen or fish-grilling basket

Whether a fish is grill-roasted by direct or indirect heat is a question of size. Most whole fish weigh less than 2 pounds and serve 1 or 2 people. Fish of this size can be grilled directly over the fire. When doing this, it is a good idea to make several slashes in the flesh on both sides down to the bone to help the flesh cook through evenly. Fish that are thicker than 2 inches and/or weigh more than 2 pounds should be cooked with indirect heat.

THE GRILL

Gas: Direct heat, medium (350°F)
Clean, oiled grate

Charcoal: Direct heat, medium ash
12-by-12-inch charcoal bed (about 3 dozen coals)
Clean, oiled grate on medium setting

Wood: Direct heat, medium ash
12-by-12-inch bed, 3 inches deep
Clean, oiled grate set 4 inches above the fire

1 whole fish, about 1 1/2 pounds, gutted and cleaned

1/4 teaspoon kosher salt

1/8 teaspoon ground black pepper

1 tablespoon olive oil

Oil for coating grill screen or basket

1/2 lemon, cut into wedges

DIRECTIONS

1. Heat the grill as directed.

2. Scrape the dull side of a knife against the skin of the fish, running from tail to head, to remove excess moisture and fine scales. Cut 3 or 4 diagonal slices through the flesh of the fish on each side down to the bone. Season the fish inside and out with the salt and pepper, and rub the olive oil over the outside.

3. Oil the grill screen or fish basket liberally and put the fish on the screen or in the basket; place on the grill. Cover and cook until browned all over and an instant-read thermometer inserted into the thickest part of the fish registers 130°F, 7 to 8 minutes per side. If your grill has a temperature gauge, it should stay at around 375°F.

4. Serve the fish with the lemon wedges.

FIRE-ROASTED GARLIC-HERB CHICKEN

TIMING

Prep: 15 minutes
(plus 40 minutes for rub and garlic paste)

Grill: About 1 1/2 hours

Don't let the simplicity of this recipe fool you. It is destined to be one of the powerhouses of your culinary arsenal—a golden-crusted bird saturated with sweet butter and herbs and gilded with roasted garlic. If you don't have the herb rubs or garlic paste from Chapter 11, you can substitute jarred herbes de Provence and roasted garlic.

GRILL TOOLS AND EQUIPMENT

· Kitchen twine
· Long-handled spatula
· Long-handled tongs
· Long-handled basting brush

THE GRILL

Gas: Indirect heat, medium (325° to 350°F)

3- or 4-burner grill–middle burner(s) off

2-burner grill–1 side off

Clean, oiled grate

Charcoal: Indirect heat, medium ash

Split charcoal bed (about 2 dozen coals per side)

20 replacement coals

Heavy-duty drip pan set between banks of charcoal

Clean, oiled grate on medium setting

INGREDIENTS (MAKES 4 SERVINGS)

2 tablespoons Provençal Herb Rub (page 373) or Tuscan Rosemary Rub (page 375)

1 tablespoon salted butter, softened

1 chicken, about 4 pounds, washed and dried

1 tablespoon vegetable oil

1/2 cup Roasted Garlic Paste (page 392)

2 tablespoons fresh rosemary or thyme leaves

Oil for coating grill grate

DIRECTIONS

1. Heat the grill as directed.

2. Mix 1 tablespoon of the rub and the butter together by mashing them with a fork on a clean work surface until well blended.

3. Separate the skin from the breast and legs of the chicken, and gently but firmly insert your index finger under the skin at the neck end of the chicken. Move it around, separating the skin from the meat underneath. Gradually ease your whole hand under the skin, loosening the skin from the breast, legs, and drumsticks.

4. Spoon the herb butter under the skin and push it evenly over the breast and legs of the chicken by rubbing the skin to spread the butter.

5. Spoon the remaining 1 tablespoon rub into the interior of the chicken and rub it over the walls of the internal cavity.

Tie the legs of the chicken together with kitchen twine. Rub the outside of the chicken with the 1 tablespoon oil.

6. Mix the garlic paste and fresh herbs in a small bowl and set aside.

7. Brush the grill grate and coat it with oil. Put the chicken on the grill away from the heat, cover the grill, and cook until an instant-read thermometer inserted into the thickest part of the breast registers about 170°F, about 1 hour and 20 minutes. Baste twice with the garlic-herb mixture during the last 20 minutes of cooking. If your grill has a temperature gauge, it should stay at around 350°F. If you are using charcoal, you will probably have to replenish the coals after the first hour.

8. Remove the chicken to a large serving platter, using tongs and supporting the chicken with a spatula. Let rest for 8 to 10 minutes; carve (see facing page) and serve.

GRILL TOOLS AND EQUIPMENT
· Long-handled spatula
· Long-handled tongs
· Long-handled basting brush

GETTING CREATIVE
· Any of the sauces and rubs in Chapter 11 can be substituted for the chile rub and barbecue sauce to create endless variations. Try Provençal Herb Rub (page 373) with Orange Tapenade Dip (page 391); Garam Masala Rub (page 376) with Red Hots Syrup (page 387); or Habanero Zaa'tar Spice Rub (page 381) with Preserved Lemon Relish (page 394).

SWEET HEAT BARBECUED CHICKEN

Traditional barbecued chicken, made with chicken parts, takes frequent flipping and vigilance to ward off incineration. All of that changes when the chicken is whole. The entire process slows down. The flame is indirect, which means the threat of flare-ups disappears, and the chicken roasts on the grill while you relax. It takes a little longer, but the process is effortless, and incineration is out of the question.

THE GRILL

Gas: Indirect heat, medium (325° to 350°F)
3- or 4-burner grill–middle burner(s) off
2-burner grill–1 side off
Clean, oiled grate

Charcoal: Indirect heat, medium ash
Split charcoal bed (about 2 dozen coals per side)
20 replacement coals
Heavy-duty drip pan set between banks of charcoal
Clean, oiled grate on medium setting

INGREDIENTS (MAKES 4 SERVINGS)

1 chicken, about 4 pounds, washed and dried
2 tablespoons Fragrant Chile Rub (page 372)
2 teaspoons canola oil

Oil for coating grill grate
1¹/₄ cups Sweet, Hot, and Sour BBQ Sauce (page 391)

DIRECTIONS

1. Heat the grill as directed.
2. Tie the legs of the chicken together with kitchen twine. Rub the outside of the chicken with the chile rub and canola oil.
3. Brush the grill grate and coat it with oil. Put the chicken on the grill away from the heat, cover the grill, and cook until an instant-read thermometer inserted into the thickest part of the breast registers about 170°F, about 1 hour and 20 minutes.

Baste twice with the BBQ sauce during the last 20 minutes of cooking. If your grill has a temperature gauge, it should stay at around 350°F. If you are using charcoal, you will probably have to replenish the coals after the first hour.
4. Remove the chicken to a large serving platter with tongs, using a spatula for support. Let rest for 8 to 10 minutes; carve (see page 184) and serve.

GRILL TOOLS AND EQUIPMENT
· Kitchen twine
· Long-handled tongs
· Long-handled spatula

LEMON ROASTED CHICKEN STUFFED WITH SEAFOOD

This simple yet sophisticated roast chicken finds its culinary roots in Spain. The combination of seafood and poultry is pure Valencia (think paella), and the preserved lemon and Moroccan seasoning are Moorish. Preserved lemons are frequently available in fine gourmet shops and Mediterranean markets, or order them from www.mustaphas.com, a great Moroccan culinary Web site. If you want to make them yourself, there's a recipe on page 394, but you'll need to plan ahead, and if you don't want to do that you can cheat by simmering a lemon in heavily salted water for about 10 minutes.

THE GRILL

Gas: Indirect heat, medium (325° to 350°F)
3- or 4-burner grill–middle burner(s) off
2-burner grill–1 side off
Clean, oiled grate

Charcoal: Indirect heat, medium ash
Split charcoal bed (about 2 dozen coals per side)
20 replacement coals
Heavy-duty drip pan set between banks of charcoal
Clean, oiled grate on medium setting

INGREDIENTS (MAKES 4 SERVINGS)

2 tablespoons extra-virgin olive oil

8 ounces medium shrimp, shelled and cleaned

1 tablespoon Moroccan Rub (page 382)

3 tablespoons Preserved Lemon Relish (page 394)

1 chicken, about 4 pounds, washed and dried

Oil for coating grill grate

1 tablespoon fresh lemon juice

DIRECTIONS

1. Heat the grill as directed.

2. Heat 1 tablespoon of the olive oil in a skillet over medium-high heat. Add the shrimp and the rub, and sauté until the shrimp are firm and opaque. Stir in 1 tablespoon of the lemon relish. Set aside to cool.

3. Separate the skin from the breast and legs of the chicken, and gently but firmly insert your index finger under the skin at the neck end of the chicken. Move it around, separating the skin from the meat underneath. Gradually ease your whole hand under the skin, loosening the skin from the breast, legs, and drumsticks.

4. Spoon the remaining 2 tablespoons preserved lemon relish under the skin and push it evenly over the breast and legs of the chicken by rubbing the skin to spread it around.

5. Spoon the shrimp mixture into the cavity of the chicken. Tie the legs together with kitchen twine. Rub the outside of the chicken with the remaining 1 tablespoon olive oil.

6. Brush the grill grate and coat it with oil. Put the chicken on the grill away from the heat, cover the grill, and cook until an instant-read thermometer inserted into the thickest part of the breast registers about 170°F, about 1 hour and 20 minutes. Drizzle with the lemon juice during the last 20 minutes of cooking. If your grill has a temperature gauge, it should stay at around 350°F. If you are using charcoal, you will probably have to replenish the coals after the first hour.

7. Remove the chicken to a large serving platter with tongs, using a spatula for support. Let rest for 8 to 10 minutes; carve (see page 184) and serve.

MAKING SUBSTITUTIONS

· If the Moroccan rub, redolent of cinnamon and coriander, seems too exotic for your taste, the dish can be made a bit more mainstream by switching to Tuscan Rosemary Rub (page 375) instead.

· Gild this lily deliciously by mixing up a recipe of Lime-Cilantro Butter (page 393), substituting lemon juice for lime, and using it in place of the lemon juice on top of the chicken.

ROASTED CHICKEN GRILLED WITH HOT PEPPER PEARS AND HONEY

The crisp skin cracks like a single layer of Chinese lacquer as you carve into this savory, spicy, sweet roast chicken. The aromas of herbs swirl with the scent of soy sauce and honey, while the texture of the crackled skin, moistened by meaty steam and syrupy pears, is enough to make your head swim. Take a whiff and dive in.

TIMING

Prep: 15 minutes
   (plus 10 minutes for rub and
   Peking crackle)
Grill: About 1 1/2 hours

GRILL TOOLS AND EQUIPMENT

· Kitchen twine
· Long-handled spatula
· Long-handled tongs
· Long-handled basting brush

THE GRILL

Gas: Indirect heat, medium (325° to 350°F)	**Charcoal:** Indirect heat, medium ash
3- or 4-burner grill–middle burner(s) off	Split charcoal bed (about 2 dozen coals per side)
2-burner grill–1 side off	20 replacement coals
Clean, oiled grate	Heavy-duty drip pan set between banks of charcoal
	Clean, oiled grate on medium setting

INGREDIENTS (MAKES 4 SERVINGS)

2 tablespoons Tuscan Rosemary Rub (page 375)

2 tablespoons salted butter, softened

1 chicken, about 3 1/2 pounds, washed and dried

Oil for coating grill grate

1/2 cup Peking Crackle (page 385)

3 large Bartlett pears, firm but not hard

1 tablespoon vegetable oil

DIRECTIONS

1. Heat the grill as directed.

2. Mix 1 tablespoon of the rub with the butter by mashing them with a fork on a clean work surface until well blended.

3. Separate the skin from the breast and legs of the chicken, and gently but firmly insert your index finger under the skin at the neck end of the chicken. Move it around, separating the skin from the meat underneath. Gradually ease your whole

hand under the skin, loosening the skin from the breast, legs, and drumsticks.

4. Spoon the herb butter under the skin and push it evenly over the breast and legs of the chicken by rubbing the skin to spread the butter.

---

5. Spoon the remaining 1 tablespoon rub into the interior of the chicken and rub it over the walls of the internal cavity. Tie the legs of the chicken together with kitchen twine.

6. Brush the grill grate and coat it with oil. Put the chicken on the grill away from the heat, cover the grill, and cook until an instant-read thermometer inserted into the thickest part of the breast registers about 170°F, about 1 hour and 20 minutes. Baste with half of the glaze during the last 20 minutes of cooking. If your grill has a temperature gauge, it should stay at around 350°F. If you are using charcoal, you will probably have to replenish the coals after the first hour.

7. Meanwhile, cut the pears in half lengthwise, remove the core with a melon baller, and coat the pear halves with the 1 tablespoon oil.

8. During the last 10 minutes of cooking, put the pears directly over the heat, and cook until browned and tender, brushing with the remaining glaze and turning once.

9. Remove the chicken and pears to a large serving platter, lifting the chicken with tongs and using a spatula for support. Let rest for 8 to 10 minutes; carve (see page 184) and serve.

Photo, right: Rubbing butter under chicken skin
Photo, opposite: Roasted Chicken Grilled with Hot Pepper Pears and Honey

GRILL TOOLS AND EQUIPMENT
· Kitchen twine
· Rotisserie for grill
· Long-handled basting brush

THREE-GINGER ROTISSERIE CHICKEN

The triumvirate of ginger that dominates this chicken was divided in order to conquer. Fresh ginger minced with cardamom, garlic, and butter is rubbed under the skin. Ginger preserves mixed with soy sauce and balsamic vinegar form a piquant glaze, and the dish is served with a cool, clean combo of pickled ginger, scallions, and hot pepper.

THE GRILL

Gas: Indirect heat, medium (325° to 350°F)
3- or 4-burner grill–middle burner(s) off
2-burner grill–1 side off
Grate removed
Rotisserie set up

Charcoal: Indirect heat, medium ash
Split charcoal bed (about 2 dozen coals per side)
20 replacement coals
Heavy-duty drip pan set between banks of charcoal
Grate removed
Rotisserie set up

INGREDIENTS (MAKES 4 SERVINGS)

2 tablespoons grated peeled gingerroot
3 cloves garlic, minced
1/4 teaspoon ground cardamom
1/4 teaspoon dried thyme
1/4 teaspoon kosher salt, or more to taste
2 tablespoons unsalted butter, softened
1 chicken, about 4 pounds, washed and dried

1 teaspoon toasted sesame oil
1/2 cup ginger preserves
2 tablespoons plus 1 teaspoon soy sauce
1 teaspoon balsamic vinegar
1/3 cup pickled sushi ginger
3 scallions, roots trimmed, thinly sliced
Pinch of crushed red pepper flakes

DIRECTIONS

1. Heat the grill as directed.
2. Mix the ginger, 2 cloves of the garlic, the cardamom, thyme, salt, and butter by mashing them with a fork on a clean work surface until well blended.
3. Separate the skin from the breast and legs of the chicken, and gently but firmly insert your index finger under the skin at the neck end of the chicken. Move it around, separating the skin from the meat underneath. Gradually ease your whole hand under the skin, loosening the skin from the breast, legs, and drumsticks.
4. Spoon the spice butter under the skin and push it evenly over the breast and legs of the chicken by rubbing the skin to spread the butter.
5. Tie the legs of the chicken together with kitchen twine, rub the outside with the sesame oil, and slide onto the skewer of the rotisserie. Secure according to the rotisserie directions.

6. Combine the ginger preserves, 2 tablespoons soy sauce, and balsamic vinegar in a small saucepan. Heat until the preserves dissolve; set aside for glazing the chicken.
7. Put the skewered chicken into the rotisserie assembly. The chicken should be suspended away from direct heat and turn freely as the rotisserie rotates. Cover the grill and cook until an instant-read thermometer inserted into the thickest part of the breast registers about 170°F, about 1 1/2 hours, brushing the chicken with the glaze 3 times during the last 30 minutes of cooking. If your grill has an external thermometer, it should stay at around 350°F. If you are using charcoal, you will probably have to replenish the coals after the first hour.
8. Remove the chicken from the skewer to a large serving platter; let rest for 10 minutes. In a bowl, mix the pickled ginger, remaining clove of garlic, 1 teaspoon soy sauce, scallions, and red pepper flakes. Carve the chicken (see page 184), and serve with the pickled ginger mixture.

TIMING
Prep: 15 minutes
   (plus 5 minutes for brine)
Brine: 2 to 3 hours
Grill: About 1 1/2 hours

HOT PEPPER–COCONUT MILK CHICKEN

Coconut milk is sweet and rich, the perfect balm for a jolt of chile. In this recipe the two are infused deep into the flesh of a grill-roasted chicken. The result is subtle, radiating a peppery glow with every bite.

Gas: Indirect heat, medium (325° to 350°F)
3- or 4-burner grill–middle burner(s) off
2-burner grill–1 side off
Clean, oiled grate

Charcoal: Indirect heat, medium ash
Split charcoal bed (about 2 dozen coals per side)
20 replacement coals
Heavy-duty drip pan set between banks of charcoal
Clean, oiled grate on high setting

GRILL TOOLS AND EQUIPMENT
· Kitchen twine
· Long-handled tongs
· Long-handled spatula

INGREDIENTS (MAKES 4 SERVINGS)

3 cups Javanese Coconut Brine (page 367)
1 teaspoon ground habanero or other very hot ground chile
1 chicken, about 4 pounds, washed and dried
1 tablespoon toasted sesame oil

1/4 teaspoon Chinese chili paste with garlic
Oil for coating grill grate
Juice of 1 lime
2 tablespoons chopped fresh cilantro

DIRECTIONS

1. Set the zipper-lock bag containing the brine in a mixing bowl. Add the ground chile to the brine; stir to combine. Add the chicken and seal the zipper, leaving about an inch open; push on the bag to release any trapped air through the opening, and close the zipper completely. Massage the liquid gently into the chicken and refrigerate for 2 to 3 hours.

2. Heat the grill as directed.

3. Remove the chicken from the brine. Mix the sesame oil and chili paste and rub all over the outside of the chicken.

4. Brush the grill grate and coat it with oil. Put the chicken on the grill away from the heat, cover the grill, and cook until an

instant-read thermometer inserted into the thickest part of the breast registers about 170°F, about 1 hour and 20 minutes. If your grill has a temperature gauge, it should stay at around 350°F. If you are using charcoal, you will probably have to replenish the coals after the first hour.

5. Remove the chicken to a cutting board with tongs, using a spatula for support. Let rest for 8 to 10 minutes; carve (see page 184) and arrange the chicken pieces on a platter. Squeeze the lime juice over the chicken and scatter the cilantro over the top; serve.

SWEET RUMMY JERK CHICKEN

Don't confuse this tangy, sweet, and spicy grill-roasted chicken with authentic jerk. It is not nearly as incendiary, it doesn't take hours to prepare, and you don't cry with every bite. Think of it as G-rated jerk, or jerk for the whole family, or . . . okay, we admit it—it's wimpy, it's mainstream, and it's really good. What's more, the sauce is a great all-purpose barbecue sauce, good on ribs, pork, beef, and seafood, as well as chicken.

THE GRILL

Gas: Indirect heat, medium (325° to 350°F)
3- or 4-burner grill–middle burner(s) off
2-burner grill–1 side off
Clean, oiled grate

Charcoal: Indirect heat, medium ash
Split charcoal bed (about 2 dozen coals per side)
20 replacement coals
Heavy-duty drip pan set between banks of charcoal
Clean, oiled grate on medium setting

GRILL TOOLS AND EQUIPMENT
· Kitchen twine
· Long-handled tongs
· Long-handled spatula
· Long-handled basting brush

INGREDIENTS (MAKES 4 SERVINGS)

4 teaspoons Jerk Rub (page 377)
1 chicken, about 4 pounds, washed and dried
1 tablespoon vegetable oil
2 tablespoons dark rum
1 tablespoon ketchup

2 tablespoons dark brown sugar
1 tablespoon Worcestershire sauce
1 tablespoon apple cider vinegar
1 tablespoon canola oil
Oil for coating grill grate

1. Heat the grill as directed.

2. Sprinkle 1 teaspoon jerk rub into the interior cavity of the chicken. Rub 2 teaspoons over the outside, and coat the outside with the vegetable oil. Tie the legs of the chicken together with kitchen twine.

3. Mix the rum, remaining 1 teaspoon jerk rub, ketchup, brown sugar, Worcestershire sauce, vinegar, and canola oil in a bowl until blended; set aside.

4. Brush the grill grate and coat it with oil. Put the chicken on the grill away from the heat, cover the grill, and cook until an

instant-read thermometer inserted into the thickest part of the breast registers about 170°F, about 1 hour and 20 minutes. Baste 3 times with the rum mixture during the last 20 minutes of cooking. If your grill has a temperature gauge, it should stay at around 350°F. If you are using charcoal, you will probably have to replenish the coals after the first hour.

5. Remove the chicken to a large serving platter using tongs, with a spatula for support. Let rest for 8 to 10 minutes; carve (see page 184) and serve.

(see page 184)

TUSCAN ROASTED CHICKEN STUFFED WITH FRAGRANT GREENS

This gorgeous rustic chicken is Tuscan in the truest sense. It is simple and sophisticated, a blend of grilled meat, forest herbs, vibrant greens, toasted nuts, garlic, olive oil, and grapes, clouded and puckered from bursting. The stuffing can be made with any hearty green, although red chard is the most visually striking.

THE GRILL

Gas: Indirect heat, medium (325° to 350°F)
3- or 4-burner grill–middle burner(s) off
2-burner grill–1 side off
Clean, oiled grate

Charcoal: Indirect heat, medium ash
Split charcoal bed (about 2 dozen coals per side)
20 replacement coals
Heavy-duty drip pan set between banks of charcoal
Clean, oiled grate on medium setting

INGREDIENTS (MAKES 4 SERVINGS)

1 bunch red chard, kale, or broccoli rabe, cut into large bite-size pieces
1 cup (about 2 ounces) red seedless grapes
3 tablespoons extra-virgin olive oil
2 tablespoons mashed roasted garlic (page 392)

$1/2$ cup (about 2 ounces) walnut halves and pieces
1 chicken, about 4 pounds, washed and dried
2 teaspoons Tuscan Rosemary Rub (page 375)
Oil for coating grill grate

DIRECTIONS

1. Heat the grill as directed.

2. Bring a large pot of salted water to a boil. Add the chard and boil until barely tender, about 3 minutes; drain.

3. Meanwhile, toss the grapes with 1 teaspoon of the olive oil. Cook in a skillet over high heat on the stove, or in a grill skillet on the grill directly over the heat, until the grapes plump and a few pop.

4. Mix the chard, grapes, 1 tablespoon of the olive oil, 1 tablespoon of the roasted garlic, and the walnuts in a bowl.

5. Separate the skin from the breast and legs of the chicken, and gently but firmly insert your index finger under the skin at the neck end of the chicken. Move it around, separating the skin from the meat underneath. Gradually ease your whole hand under the skin, loosening the skin from the breast, legs, and drumsticks.

6. Mix the remaining tablespoon of roasted garlic with 1 teaspoon of the herb rub and 1 tablespoon olive oil in a small bowl. Spoon the garlic mixture under the skin and push it evenly

over the breast and legs of the chicken by rubbing the skin to spread it.

7. Spoon the remaining 1 teaspoon rub into the interior of the chicken and rub over the walls of the internal cavity. Spoon the chard and grape stuffing into the cavity, and tie the legs of the chicken together with kitchen twine. Rub the outside of the chicken with the remaining 2 teaspoons olive oil.

8. Brush the grill grate and coat it with oil. Put the chicken on the grill away from the heat, cover the grill, and cook until an instant-read thermometer inserted into the thickest part of the breast registers about 170°F, about 1 hour and 20 minutes. If your grill has a temperature gauge, it should stay at around 350°F. If you are using charcoal, you will probably have to replenish the coals after the first hour.

9. Remove the chicken to a large serving platter using tongs, with a spatula for support. Let rest for 8 to 10 minutes; carve (see page 184) and serve along with some of the stuffing.

TIMING
Prep: 15 minutes
(plus 40 minutes for roasted garlic and rub)
Grill: About $1 1/2$ hours

GRILL TOOLS AND EQUIPMENT
· Grill skillet (optional)
· Kitchen twine
· Long-handled spatula
· Long-handled tongs

Photo: Tuscan Roasted Chicken Stuffed with Fragrant Greens

BEAN BUTT CHICKEN

TIMING

Prep: 15 minutes
    (plus 5 minutes for rub)
Grill: About 1¹/₂ hours

GRILL TOOLS AND EQUIPMENT
· Long-handled tongs
· Long-handled spatula

THE GENIUS OF COOKING CHICKEN ON A CAN

Poultry has an engineering problem. The white meat is done at a temperature 10°F lower than the dark meat, resulting in roasted chickens with either desiccated breasts or wobbly thighs. The trick is to get the leg sections cooking faster or the breasts cooking slower, which is exactly what standing a chicken upright on a grill does. By perching a chicken on a can (or a vertical roaster), you lift the breast away from the fire and place the legs (especially the pesky hip joint, which is always the last part to get done) right next to the flame. The outcome is miraculous: No parts are dry and no parts are raw—perfect chicken every time.

We know you know about cooking chicken with a beer can stuffed up its butt. The sight of poultry compromised by brew has become a grilling icon, and it is the inspiration for this concoction, which attempts an improvement on the original by having something in the offending can that can actually be eaten (not just swilled). By grilling chicken on a can of baked beans, you get a perfectly roasted chicken, plus a side dish of baked beans flavored with chicken drippings and spice rub.

THE GRILL

Gas: Indirect heat, medium (325° to 350°F)
3- or 4-burner grill–middle burner(s) off
2-burner grill–1 side off
Clean, oiled grate

Charcoal: Indirect heat, medium ash
Split charcoal bed (about 2 dozen coals per side)
20 replacement coals
Heavy-duty drip pan set between banks of charcoal
Clean, oiled grate on medium setting

INGREDIENTS (MAKES 4 SERVINGS)

1 chicken, about 4 pounds, washed and dried
2 tablespoons plus 1 teaspoon Fragrant Chile Rub (page 372)

3 teaspoons canola oil
1 can (about 16 ounces) baked beans

DIRECTIONS

1. Heat the grill as directed.

2. Rub the chicken inside and out with the 2 tablespoons chile rub, and rub the outside of the chicken with 2 teaspoons of the oil.

3. Open the can of beans. Stir the 1 teaspoon chile rub into the beans. Remove the label from the can and coat the outside of the can with the remaining 1 teaspoon oil. Put on a plate or sturdy sheet pan. Lower the chicken onto the can, inserting the can into the internal cavity of the bird. Position the chicken so that the legs and the can form a tripod holding the chicken upright.

4. Put the chicken and can on the grill away from the heat, cover the grill, and cook until an instant-read thermometer inserted into the thickest part of a thigh registers about 170°F, about 1¹/₂ hours. If your grill has an external temperature gauge, it should stay at around 350°F. If you are using charcoal or wood, you will probably have to replenish after the first hour.

5. Transfer the chicken, still on the can, to a plate or tray, using tongs to hold the chicken and a spatula slipped under the can. Holding the can with tongs and gripping the chicken with a towel or silicone grill mitts, twist and lift the chicken off the can. Transfer to a carving board. Let rest for 8 to 10 minutes; carve (see page 184) and serve with the beans.

ARTICHOKE CHICKEN

TIMING

Prep: 15 minutes
    (plus 5 minutes for rub)
Grill: About 1¹/₂ hours

GRILL TOOLS AND EQUIPMENT
· Long-handled tongs
· Long-handled spatula

If you don't get enough occasions to ram a can into a chicken, this recipe provides a delicious opportunity to do so. Here a can of artichoke hearts flavored with herbs, garlic, wine, and lemon simmers on the grill while the chicken roasts regally above. The contents of the can become a light sauce and garnish for the finished chicken.

Gas:	Indirect heat, medium (325° to 350°F)	**Charcoal:**	Indirect heat, medium ash
	3- or 4-burner grill–middle burner(s) off		Split charcoal bed (about 2 dozen coals per side)
	2-burner grill–1 side off		20 replacement coals
	Clean, oiled grate		Heavy-duty drip pan set between banks of charcoal
			Clean, oiled grate on medium setting

INGREDIENTS (MAKES 4 SERVINGS)

1 chicken, about 4 pounds, washed and dried

2 tablespoons plus 1 teaspoon Tuscan Rosemary Rub (page 375)

3 teaspoons extra-virgin olive oil

1 tablespoon fresh lemon juice

$1/4$ cup white wine

1 can (about 14 ounces) artichoke heart quarters, drained

DIRECTIONS

1. Heat the grill as directed.

2. Rub the chicken inside and out with the 2 tablespoons rub, and rub the outside of the chicken with 2 teaspoons of the olive oil.

3. Stir the lemon juice, wine, and remaining 1 teaspoon rosemary rub into the artichokes, still in the can. Remove the label from the can and coat the outside of the can with the remaining 1 teaspoon olive oil. Put on a plate or sturdy sheet pan. Lower the chicken onto the can, inserting the can into the internal cavity of the bird. Position the chicken so that the legs and the can form a tripod holding the chicken upright.

4. Put the chicken and can on the grill away from the heat, cover the grill, and cook until an instant-read thermometer inserted into the thickest part of a thigh registers about 170°F, about $1 1/2$ hours. If your grill has an external temperature gauge, it should stay at around 350°F. If you are using charcoal or wood, you will probably have to replenish after the first hour.

5. Transfer the chicken, still on the can, to a plate or tray, using tongs to hold the chicken and a spatula slipped under the can. Holding the can with tongs and gripping the chicken with a towel or silicone grill mits, twist and lift the chicken off the can. Transfer to a carving board. Let rest for 8 to 10 minutes; carve (see page 184) and serve with the artichoke hearts, drizzling any liquid left in the can over the carved chicken.

ANCHO TURKEY BREAST STUFFED WITH CORN AND BLACK BEANS

Boneless turkey breasts are generally sold in one of four ways: as a whole breast with skin, as a half breast with skin, as a half breast without skin, or as a butterflied skinless breast, which can also be labeled "turkey London broil" (see page 157). Any of these forms will work for this recipe, although the last one will take the least amount of prep work on your part. Butterflying meat is not difficult. It involves slitting the meat through its thicker parts so that it opens out into a flat rectangle. The breasts of poultry, because they are relatively flat and rectangular to begin with, are very easy to butterfly. See the complete directions in the sidebar on page 196.

TIMING

Prep: 15 minutes
   (plus 5 minutes for rub)
Rest before grilling: About 45 minutes
Grill: About 1 hour and 15 minutes

GRILL TOOLS AND EQUIPMENT

· Kitchen twine
· Long-handled tongs

SHORTCUTS

· Replace the vegetables in the stuffing with $3/4$ cup purchased corn and black bean salsa and $1/3$ cup purchased black bean dip.
· Use any commercially prepared Southwest-flavored rub in place of the Fragrant Chile Rub.

THE GRILL

Gas:	Indirect heat, medium (325° to 350°F)	**Charcoal:**	Indirect heat, medium ash
	3- or 4-burner grill–middle burner(s) off		Split charcoal bed (about 2 dozen coals per side)
	2-burner grill–1 side off		Heavy-duty drip pan set between banks of charcoal
	Clean, oiled grate		Clean, oiled grate on medium setting

INGREDIENTS (MAKES 6 SERVINGS)

$1/4$ cup Fragrant Chile Rub (page 372)

1 boneless, skinless turkey breast half, about 3 pounds, butterflied

1 ear corn, with husk on

1 medium onion, unpeeled

1 whole jalapeño chile

1 whole tomato

1 can (10 ounces) black beans, rinsed and drained

1 dozen corn tortilla chips, crushed

Oil for coating grill grate

BUTTERFLYING BONELESS MEAT

Butterflying is a technique for cutting a thick, boneless piece of meat to make it flatter and wider so that it can be stuffed, or so that it will grill faster. The first step is to open the meat up like a book. This is done by placing the meat flat on a cutting board, slicing horizontally into the center of one of its long sides until you get all of the way across but not through the other side.

Open the two sides up like a book. If the meat is now an even thickness all the way across, you can proceed with the recipe; usually this is not the case, however. You can reduce the thickness in the thicker areas by making shallow slits wherever there is a bulge and pressing on that section to spread it out.

1. Heat the grill as directed.

2. Reserve 1 teaspoon of the chile rub, and rub the rest all over the turkey breast. Wrap in plastic or put in a plastic bag and refrigerate for at least 45 minutes.

3. Put the corn, onion, jalapeño, and tomato directly over the fire. Close the grill and cook until the surfaces of all are speckled, about 5 minutes. Turn and continue cooking until all of the vegetables are blackened all around. This will take about 8 minutes for the tomato and chile, 12 minutes for the onions and corn. Set the vegetables aside until they are cool enough to handle, about 10 minutes.

4. Remove the husk from the corn. Hold the ear of corn upright; cut off the kernels by slicing down the length of the ear with a slim-bladed knife. Discard the stem and seeds from the chile and dice the flesh finely (you may want to use rubber gloves to protect your hands). Core the tomato and peel the onion; chop both into small pieces.

5. Mash half of the black beans with the back of a fork in a medium bowl, adding enough water to make a smooth paste.

6. To make the stuffing, mix the vegetables with the mashed black beans, the whole black beans, the crushed tortilla chips, and the reserved teaspoon of rub.

7. If cooking over charcoal, replenish the coals.

8. Place three 12-inch lengths of kitchen twine side by side on a work surface. Remove the turkey from its wrapping and place it, butterflied-side up, on top of the twine. Spread the stuffing over the top of the turkey, and roll the turkey up into a log, encasing the stuffing in the center. Tie the twine to secure.

9. Brush the grill grate and coat it with oil. Put the rolled breast on the grill away from the heat, cover the grill, and cook until an instant-read thermometer inserted into the center registers about 170°F, about 1 hour, turning 2 to 3 times to help it cook evenly. If your grill has a temperature gauge, it should stay at around 350°F.

10. Remove to a cutting board; let rest for 8 to 10 minutes, then slice and serve.

Photo: *Lemon Turkey Breast Larded with Green Olive Tapenade*

LEMON TURKEY BREAST LARDED WITH GREEN OLIVE TAPENADE

TIMING
Prep: 20 minutes
  (plus 5 minutes for relish)
Grill: About 1 hour

GRILL TOOLS AND EQUIPMENT
· Long-handled spatula
· Long-handled tongs
· Long-handled basting brush

There are several ways of stuffing ingredients into a solid hunk of meat. You can cut a pocket in the center (see page 203), butterfly it (see page 196), or disperse the stuffing throughout the roast as is done here, a technique known as larding. Classically, larding is done to game meats to get fat (lardons) deep into the interior of meats that lack marbling (see page 47). In this recipe, you make holes all over a meaty turkey breast and then plug them up with a tangy paste of green olives, garlic, and lemon. Try to space the holes evenly so that every slice gets its share of the flavor.

THE GRILL

Gas: Indirect heat, medium (325° to 350°F)
3- or 4-burner grill–middle burner(s) off
2-burner grill–1 side off
Clean, oiled grate

Charcoal: Indirect heat, medium ash
Split charcoal bed (about 2 dozen coals per side)
Heavy-duty drip pan set between banks of charcoal
Clean, oiled grate on medium setting

INGREDIENTS (MAKES 6 TO 8 SERVINGS)

18 large pitted green olives, coarsely chopped (about 3/4 cup)
4 tablespoons extra-virgin olive oil
2 cloves garlic, minced
Kosher salt and ground black pepper

1 boneless turkey breast half, preferably with skin on, about
  3 1/2 pounds
Finely grated zest and juice of 1 lemon
1/4 teaspoon dried thyme
Oil for coating grill grate
1/2 cup Preserved Lemon Relish (optional; page 394)

DIRECTIONS

1. Heat the grill as directed.

2. Mix the olives, 1 tablespoon of the olive oil, the garlic, and salt and pepper to taste in a bowl.

3. Plunge a long, thin-bladed knife into the turkey breast and twist to make a hole. Stuff the hole with some of the green olive tapenade. Repeat until the turkey is uniformly punctuated with tapenade, making about 12 holes in all.

4. In another bowl, mix the lemon juice, 1 tablespoon of the olive oil, and salt and pepper to taste and coat the outside of the turkey with this mixture.

5. Mix the remaining 2 tablespoons olive oil, the lemon zest, the thyme, and salt and pepper to taste in another bowl; set aside.

6. Brush the grill grate and coat it with oil. Put the turkey on the grill away from the heat, cover the grill, and cook until an instant-read thermometer inserted into the thickest part of the breast registers about 165°F, about 1 hour. Baste twice with the olive oil–lemon zest mixture during the last 30 minutes of cooking. If your grill has a temperature gauge, it should stay at around 350°F.

7. Remove to a large serving platter, using tongs and a spatula for support. Let rest for 8 to 10 minutes; carve and serve with preserved lemon relish, if desired.

APPLE-SAGE BARBECUED TURKEY LEGS

TIMING
Prep: 15 minutes
  (plus 5 minutes for brine)
Brine: 2 to 6 hours
Grill: About 1 hour and 20 minutes

GRILL TOOLS AND EQUIPMENT
· Long-handled spatula or
  long-handled tongs
· Long-handled basting brush

Turkey legs are tough and stringy—and cheap. They typically sell for less than a third of the price of turkey breast, an opportunity you will have no problem taking advantage of once you have a recipe like this to turn the culinary challenges of a turkey leg into a flavorful asset. Remember, when it comes to meat, tough and stringy equals flavorful and moist. Brining helps to soften tough fibers, and in this case infuses the meat with chai spices and sweet apple. Low, slow grilling makes the meat melt off the bone. It takes a little time (about an hour and a half on the grill) but almost no attention, and the process is foolproof. There's no way to screw this one up.

Gas: Indirect heat, medium (325° to 350°F)
3- or 4-burner grill–middle burner(s) off
2-burner grill–1 side off
Clean, oiled grate

Charcoal: Indirect heat, medium ash
Split charcoal bed (about 2 dozen coals per side)
20 replacement coals
Heavy-duty drip pan set between banks of charcoal
Clean, oiled grate on medium setting

INGREDIENTS (MAKES 4 SERVINGS)

2 cups Apple-Chai Brine (page 371)
$1^{1}/_{4}$ teaspoons ground poultry seasoning
1 teaspoon dried sage
$^{1}/_{2}$ teaspoon crushed dried rosemary
4 turkey thighs and/or drumsticks, about 4 pounds

4 cups apple cider
2 cloves garlic, smashed
$^{1}/_{8}$ teaspoon kosher salt, or more to taste
$^{1}/_{8}$ teaspoon ground black pepper, or more to taste
Oil for coating grill grate

DIRECTIONS

1. Combine the brine, 1 teaspoon of the poultry seasoning, the sage, and the rosemary in a large zipper-lock bag, seal, and shake.

2. Put the bag in a bowl just large enough to hold it snugly. Open the bag and add the turkey. Seal the zipper, leaving about an inch open; push on the bag to release any trapped air through the opening, and close the zipper completely. Massage the liquid gently into the meat and refrigerate for at least 2 hours or as long as 6 hours.

3. To make the cider basting syrup, combine the cider, garlic, and remaining $^{1}/_{4}$ teaspoon poultry seasoning in a large skillet. Boil over high heat until reduced to one-quarter of its volume, about 1 cup. Season with the salt and pepper and set aside.

4. Heat the grill as directed.

5. Remove the turkey from the marinade and discard the marinade.

6. Brush the grill grate and coat it with oil. Put the turkey on the grill away from the heat, cover the grill, and cook until an instant-read thermometer inserted into the thickest part of a leg registers about 170°F, about 1 hour and 20 minutes, turning once in the first hour. In the last 20 minutes of cooking, turn and baste with the apple cider syrup every 5 minutes. If your grill has a temperature gauge, it should stay at around 350°F. If you are using charcoal or wood, you will probably have to replenish the coals or wood after the first hour.

7. Remove to a large serving platter, drizzle with any remaining cider syrup, and serve.

TIMING
Prep: 30 minutes
Dry: 2 hours
Grill: About 1 hour

GRILL TOOLS AND EQUIPMENT
· Small bicycle pump with a needle attachment, or a marinade injector
· Kitchen twine
· Electric fan
· Roasting rack
· Disposable aluminum foil roasting pan

TERIYAKI DUCK WITH DATE AND SCALLION CHUTNEY

When the first direction in a recipe calls for a bicycle pump, you know you're in for a good time. If anyone asks why you're laughing, your response will be that ducks have a fat problem. Which is true enough; they have a lot of it, and you want to get rid of most of it before anyone takes a bite, but you also want it to hang around long enough to flavor the duck and keep it moist. The best method is to create a channel between the fat and the meat that gives the fat an escape route as it melts and continually bastes the meat while it's cooking. That's where the bicycle pump comes in. By inserting the needle of the pump just under the fat in the skin, you can force air under the fat, and presto, you've got your channel. It is best to use a hand pump, since a standing pump is ungainly. If you have a marinade injector, that works too, although it takes a little longer.

THE GRILL

Gas: Indirect heat, medium (325° to 350°F)
3- or 4-burner grill–middle burner(s) off
2-burner grill–1 side off
Clean, oiled grate

Charcoal: Indirect heat, medium ash
Split charcoal bed (about 2 dozen coals per side)
20 replacement coals
Heavy-duty drip pan set between banks of charcoal
Clean, oiled grate on high setting

For the duck:

1 Long Island duckling, about 4 1/2 pounds, visible fat removed

3 tablespoons soy sauce

3 tablespoons honey

1/4 teaspoon Chinese chili paste with garlic

1 clove garlic, minced

For the chutney:

8 large, moist dates, such as Medjool, pits removed

1 clove garlic, minced

1 tablespoon peeled and minced ginger root

Finely grated zest and juice of 1 orange

1/4 teaspoon Chinese chili paste with garlic

1/4 teaspoon kosher salt, or more to taste

1/4 teaspoon ground black pepper

2 scallions, roots trimmed, thinly sliced

DIRECTIONS

1. Extend the plunger of the bicycle pump. Insert the needle just under the skin at the neck end of the duck. Depress the plunger, and the skin around the needle will puff up. Continue to pump air under the duck skin in the same way until the skin has been separated from the meat all over the breast and legs.

2. Heat a kettle of water to boiling. Put the duck, breast-side up, in a strainer set in a sink. Pour the boiling water over the duck. Hook a chopstick under the wings of the duck to hold them away from the body. Tie a string tightly around the neck and hang the duck over a sink or a large drip pan. Place an electric fan in front of the duck and blow air directly on it for about an hour to dry the skin.

3. Mix the soy sauce, honey, chili paste, and garlic in a small bowl. Brush over the duck and dry in front of the fan for another hour.

4. Heat the grill as directed.

5. Put the duck, breast-side up, on a rack set in the disposable roasting pan. Put on the grill away from the heat, cover the grill, and cook until an instant-read thermometer inserted into the thickest part of the breast registers 165°F, about 1 hour. If your grill has a temperature gauge, it should stay at around 350°F.

6. While the duck is grilling, prepare the chutney. Chop the dates finely and mix with the remaining ingredients. Set aside; the mixture will thicken as it sits.

7. Remove the duck to a large serving platter. Let rest for 8 to 10 minutes; carve as you would a chicken (see page 184) and serve with chutney.

ORANGE-ROSEMARY DUCK

TIMING

Prep: 30 minutes
     (plus 5 minutes for brine)
Brine: 2 to 8 hours
Grill: About 1 1/2 hours

GRILL TOOLS AND EQUIPMENT

· Roasting rack
· Disposable aluminum foil roasting pan
· Long-handled basting brush

Yet another way to rid a duck of fat is to pierce the skin around its fatty parts (the sides of the breast and the undersides of the thighs), making holes through which the fat can drain, and then pouring boiling water over the fatty areas to warm the fat and give it a head start. This method works better with a Muscovy duck, which is less fatty than the Long Island variety. The skin will not be as crisp as with the bicycle pump method (see the introduction to the recipe on the facing page), but the technique is much simpler and takes far less time. The flavors of orange and rosemary are classic with duck.

THE GRILL

Gas: Indirect heat, medium (325° to 350°F)
     3- or 4-burner grill–middle burner(s) off
     2-burner grill–1 side off
     Clean, oiled grate

Charcoal: Indirect heat, medium ash
     Split charcoal bed (about 2 dozen coals per side)
     20 replacement coals
     Heavy-duty drip pan set between banks of charcoal
     Clean, oiled grate on medium setting

1 duck, about 5 pounds, preferably Muscovy

2 cups Orange-Fennel Brine (page 362)

2 tablespoons crushed dried rosemary

2 tablespoons sherry vinegar

3 tablespoons maple syrup

1/4 teaspoon ground black pepper

1 orange, quartered

1 small onion, peeled and quartered

1. Wash the duck inside and out and poke the skin with a fork, especially where there are noticeable fat deposits under the skin, around the legs and along the sides of the breast.

2. Heat a kettle of water to boiling. Put the duck, breast-side up, in a strainer set in a sink. Pour the boiling water over the duck. Dry the duck and put it in a large (gallon-size) zipper-lock bag. Add the brine, 1 tablespoon of the rosemary, and 1 tablespoon of the sherry vinegar. Seal the zipper, leaving about an inch open; push on the bag to release any trapped air through the opening, and close the zipper completely. Massage the liquid gently into the duck and refrigerate for at least 2 hours and up to 8 hours.

3. Mix the maple syrup and remaining 1 tablespoon vinegar in a small bowl; set aside.

4. Heat the grill as directed.

5. Remove the duck from the marinade and discard the marinade. Pat dry. Rub the interior cavity of the duck with the remaining 1 tablespoon dried rosemary and the pepper. Put the orange and onion quarters in the interior cavity, and put the duck, breast-side up, on a rack set in the disposable roasting pan. Put the pan on the grill away from the heat, cover the grill, and cook until an instant-read thermometer inserted into the thickest part of the breast registers 165°F, about 1 1/2 hours. Baste the duck with the maple mixture 3 times during the last half hour. If your grill has an external thermometer, it should stay at around 375°F. If you are using charcoal, you will probably have to replenish the coals after the first hour.

6. Remove the duck to a large serving platter. Let rest for 8 to 10 minutes; carve as you would a chicken (see page 184) and serve. Do not serve the orange and onion that were stuffed into the duck.

SMOKY BARBECUED DUCK

There are two types of duck in the classic culinary world. Long Island duckling is the bird for a Chinese classic, like Peking duck. Muscovy duck is for European fare, like pressed duck. The main difference between the two is the size of the breast (Muscovy is meatier) and the amount of fat (Muscovy is leaner). Traditionally, Long Island ducks are more commonly available in the United States, but that is changing. Muscovy is easier to use in this recipe, but a Long Island will be fine; it just takes a little more work (see the box at left).

THE GRILL

Gas: Indirect heat, medium (325° to 350°F)
3- or 4-burner grill–middle burner(s) off
2-burner grill–1 side off
Heavy-duty drip pan set between banks of charcoal
Clean, oiled grate

Charcoal: Indirect heat, medium ash
Split charcoal bed (about 2 dozen coals per side)
20 replacement coals
Heavy-duty drip pan set between banks of charcoal
Clean, oiled grate on medium setting

INGREDIENTS (MAKES 4 SERVINGS)

3/4 cup Steakhouse Glaze (page 389)
1 teaspoon ground chipotle chile
1 Muscovy duck, about 5 pounds

2 1/2 tablespoons Jerk Rub (page 377)
Oil for coating grill grate

DIRECTIONS

1. Soak the wood chunks or chips for about 1 hour.

2. Heat the grill as directed. Mix the glaze and chipotle, and set aside.

3. Cut off the neck skin of the duck with scissors and remove any visible pockets of fat with your fingers. Wash the duck inside and out, and poke the skin deeply with a fork, especially where there are noticeable fat deposits, around the legs and along the sides of the breast. Sprinkle 1 tablespoon of the jerk rub into the cavity of the duck. Rub the rest of the rub over the skin.

4. Place the disposable pan in the opening of the fire bed and put the wood chunks directly over the coals. If using a gas grill, put the wood chips in a smoker box or in a foil packet directly over one of the heated burners.

5. Brush the grill grate and coat it with oil. Put the duck, breast-side down, on the grill directly over the fire; cover and grill for 10 minutes, until the breast skin browns. Douse any flare-ups with water from a spray bottle. Turn the duck over so that the breast side is facing up, and put it on the grill over the disposable pan away from direct heat. Cover the grill and cook until an instant-read thermometer inserted into the thickest

---

part of the breast registers about 165°F, about 1 hour and 20 minutes. Baste the duck with the glaze every 5 minutes during the last 20 minutes of cooking. If your grill has a temperature gauge, it should stay at around 350°F. If you are using charcoal, you will probably have to replenish the coals after the first hour.

6. Remove the duck to a large serving platter. Let rest for 8 to 10 minutes; carve and serve as you would a chicken (see page 184).

Photo: Smoky Barbecued Duck

TIMING
Prep: 15 minutes
Grill: About 2 hours

GRILL TOOLS AND EQUIPMENT
· Large, heavy-duty spatula or pair of
heat-resistant gloves

Some ingredients ask nothing more from us than a little privacy: an hour or two of solitude over a moderate fire, flanked by a flock of garlic, a glaze of extra-virgin oil, and a crusting of coarse salt and pepper. If you are smart enough to give such respect to a standing rib roast of beef, it will reward you beyond measure. If possible, have your butcher cut the meat from the bone along the ribs, leaving it attached at its widest end.

THE GRILL

Gas:	Indirect heat, medium (325° to 350°F)	Charcoal:	Indirect heat, medium ash
	3- or 4-burner grill–middle burner(s) off		Split charcoal bed (about 2 dozen coals per side)
	2-burner grill–1 side off		20 replacement coals
	Heavy-duty drip pan set between banks of charcoal		Heavy-duty drip pan set between banks of charcoal
	Clean, oiled grate		Clean, oiled grate on medium setting

INGREDIENTS (MAKES 6 SERVINGS)

3-bone standing rib roast of beef, about 3 pounds
6 cloves garlic, minced
2 tablespoons extra-virgin olive oil

1/2 teaspoon kosher salt
1 teaspoon ground black pepper

DIRECTIONS

1. Heat the grill as directed, placing the roasting pan away from the heat.

2. If the meat was not cut from the bone when you purchased it (see the recipe introduction), do this yourself, leaving it attached at its widest end.

3. Mix the garlic, olive oil, salt, and pepper in a small bowl and rub all over the meat, including the underside where it is sitting on the bones.

4. Put the roast, bone-side down, on the grill away from the heat (over the roasting pan), cover the grill, and cook until an

instant-read thermometer inserted into the thickest part registers about 130°F for medium-rare, about 2 hours. If your grill has a temperature gauge, it should stay at around 350°F. If you are using charcoal, you will probably have to replenish the coals after the first hour.

5. Remove the beef to a large carving board; let rest for at least 10 minutes. Carve and serve. Carving will have been made much easier by separating the roast from the bone before cooking.

TIMING
Prep: 30 minutes
     (plus 5 minutes for brine)
Brine: 2 to 6 hours
Grill: 16 to 20 minutes

GRILL TOOLS AND EQUIPMENT
· Long-handled spatula
· Metal or bamboo skewer

RED WINE–MARINATED FLANK STEAK STUFFED WITH WILD RICE

Wild rice is assertive, requiring other strong flavors to temper its influence. In this recipe the balance comes from the red wine brine, redolent with fruit, rosemary, and olive oil, permeating the flesh of the meat. Because wild rice can take a while to cook, you can streamline the recipe by boiling the rice and preparing the stuffing while the steak is marinating.

THE GRILL

Gas:	Direct heat, medium-high (400° to 450°F)	Wood:	Direct heat, light ash
	Clean, oiled grate		12-by-12-inch bed, 3 to 4 inches deep
Charcoal:	Direct heat, light ash		Clean, oiled grate set 2 inches above the fire
	12-by-12-inch charcoal bed (about 3 dozen coals)		
	Clean, oiled grate on lowest setting		

---

1 1/4 pounds flank steak, with pocket cut (see sidebar at right)

1 cup Red Wine–Rosemary Brine (page 366)

1/3 cup wild rice blend

1/2 teaspoon kosher salt, plus more to taste

1/4 teaspoon ground black pepper, plus more to taste

2 tablespoons olive oil

1/2 cup finely diced onion

1 rib celery, finely diced

1 clove garlic, minced

1 teaspoon fresh rosemary leaves

1 plum tomato, finely diced

Oil for coating grill grate

DIRECTIONS

1. Put the steak in a gallon zipper-lock bag with the brine. Seal the zipper, leaving about an inch open; push on the bag to release any trapped air through the opening, and close the zipper completely. Massage the liquid gently into the meat and refrigerate for at least 2 hours or as long as 6 hours.

2. Heat the grill as directed.

3. Bring at least 4 cups of water to a boil in a saucepan. Add the rice, 1/2 teaspoon salt, and 1/4 teaspoon pepper. Cover and cook over medium-low heat until the rice is tender, anywhere from 10 to 45 minutes, depending on the rice blend. Drain. This can be done while the steak is marinating.

4. Meanwhile, heat 1 tablespoon of the olive oil in a large skillet over medium-high heat. Add the onion and celery and sauté until tender, 3 to 4 minutes. Add the garlic, rosemary, and tomato, and cook until the tomato loses its raw look, about

3 minutes. Stir into the rice after it is cooked and drained, and adjust the seasoning with salt and pepper. Cool.

5. Remove the steak from the brine and discard the brine. Stuff the pocket with the rice mixture and use a skewer to hold the opening closed. Rub the outside of the steak with the remaining 1 tablespoon olive oil.

6. Brush the grill grate and coat it with oil. Put the steak on the grill, cover, and cook until an instant-read thermometer inserted into the thickest part of the steak registers about 140°F for medium, 16 to 20 minutes, turning halfway through. If your grill has a temperature gauge, it should stay at around 450°F.

7. Let rest for 3 to 5 minutes, then slice across the grain and serve.

CUTTING A POCKET IN A FLANK STEAK

Using a sharp, thin-bladed knife, cut a slit along the long, narrow edge of the steak. Keep the blade parallel to the steak, and work the knife into the center of the steak, opening up a pocket from one end of the steak to the other. Try to make the pocket as centered as possible, and at all costs do not cut through to the surface.

BARBECUED SHOULDER OF BEEF

A beef shoulder (chuck) is as tough and flavorful a cut of meat as you are likely to grill. It benefits from marinating and requires long, slow cooking, but taking those precautions causes its fat to infuse the muscle fibers, flavoring them and separating one from another, and turning it into one of the tenderest and most succulent of grilled meats. This chuck is marinated with hot peppers and chiles and rubbed with a sweet, aromatic chile rub. Slice it as a roast or serve it shredded on a sandwiched topped with your favorite barbecue sauce.

TIMING

Prep: 5 minutes
    (plus 15 minutes for marinade and rub)
Marinate: 12 to 24 hours
Grill: About 2 1/2 hours

GRILL TOOLS AND EQUIPMENT

· Long-handled tongs
· Long-handled spatula

THE GRILL

Gas: Indirect heat, medium (325° to 350°F)
    3- or 4-burner grill–middle burner(s) off
    2-burner grill–1 side off
    Clean, oiled grate

Charcoal: Indirect heat, medium ash
    Split charcoal bed (about 2 dozen coals per side)
    20 replacement coals
    Heavy-duty drip pan set between banks of charcoal
    Clean, oiled grate on medium setting

Wood: Indirect heat, medium ash
    12-by-12-inch bed, 3 inches deep
    Additional wood for replacement
    Clean, oiled grate set 4 inches above the fire

INGREDIENTS (MAKES 6 TO 8 SERVINGS)

3 pounds boneless beef chuck roast

1 3/4 cups Fire Beer Marinade (page 354)

1 tablespoon Fragrant Chile Rub (page 372)

2 teaspoons canola oil

Oil for coating grill grate

1. Put the beef in a gallon-size zipper-lock bag with the marinade. Seal the zipper, leaving about an inch open; push on the bag to release any trapped air through the opening, and close the zipper completely. Massage the liquid gently into the meat and refrigerate for at least 12 hours, turning about halfway through. Do not marinate any longer than 24 hours.

2. Heat the grill as directed.

3. Remove the beef from the marinade; discard the marinade. Pat dry and rub the chile rub all over the outside. Coat with the canola oil.

4. Brush the grill grate and coat it with oil. Put the beef on the grill away from the heat, cover the grill, and cook until an instant-read thermometer inserted into the thickest part of the meat registers about 155°F, about 2 1/2 hours, turning the meat 3 or 4 times during that time. If your grill has a temperature gauge, it should stay at around 350°F. If you are using charcoal or wood, you will probably have to replenish after the first hour.

5. Remove to a large serving platter, using tongs and a spatula for support. Let rest for 8 to 10 minutes; slice and serve.

PESTO-ROLLED BEEF TENDERLOIN WITH ROASTED PEPPER ROUILLE

TIMING
Prep: 40 minutes
Grill: About 35 minutes

GRILL TOOLS AND EQUIPMENT
· Grill screen
· Long-handled tongs

TIP
· If you want to cook the tenderloin more than medium-rare, move the meat out of direct heat. Cook for 10 minutes more and check the internal temperature (130°F for medium, 140°F or higher for well-done).

Tenderloin may be the tenderest cut of beef, but it is also the blandest. It needs help from a rich sauce, a fragrant rub, or (as in this recipe) a stuffing of grilled vegetables and a crust of aromatic pesto. If you need to prepare it in advance, you can stuff it and wrap it (steps 1 through 7) and refrigerate it for several hours before grilling. It's even great cold if you want to make the whole thing the day before.

THE GRILL

Gas: Direct heat, medium-high (400° to 450°F)
Clean, oiled grate

Charcoal: Direct heat, light ash
12-by-12-inch charcoal bed (about 3 dozen coals)
Clean, oiled grate on lowest setting

Wood: Direct heat, light ash
12-by-12-inch bed, 3 to 4 inches deep
Clean, oiled grate set 2 inches above the fire

INGREDIENTS (MAKES 8 SERVINGS)

For the beef:
1 red bell pepper
1 chile, such as jalapeño or serrano
Oil for coating grill screen and grate
1 beef tenderloin, about 3 pounds, trimmed and tied
2 cloves garlic, minced
1 anchovy fillet, finely chopped
2 tablespoons finely chopped fresh flat-leaf parsley
1/2 cup fresh breadcrumbs
2 tablespoons extra-virgin olive oil

1/4 teaspoon kosher salt, or more to taste
1/4 teaspoon ground black pepper

For the pesto:
2 ounces fresh basil leaves (about 2 cups)
2 cloves garlic, chopped
1 tablespoon pine nuts
1/4 cup extra-virgin olive oil
1/4 teaspoon kosher salt, or more to taste
1/4 teaspoon ground black pepper

DIRECTIONS

1. Heat the grill as directed.

2. Put an oiled grill screen on the grill and put the bell pepper and chile on the screen. Cook, covered, until they are charred on all sides, about 15 minutes for the bell pepper and 10 minutes for the chile. When charred, put in a covered bowl until cool enough to handle, about 10 minutes.

3. Meanwhile, prepare the pesto by chopping the basil, garlic, and pine nuts in a food processor until finely chopped. Add the olive oil and process in pulses to a smooth paste. Season with the salt and pepper. Set aside.

4. To make a hole down the center of the tenderloin, into which you can insert the stuffing, position a sharpening steel at the thicker end of the tenderloin and push it through until its tip comes out the other side. Remove the steel. Insert a thin,

long-bladed knife into the hole made by the steel several times, making shallow slits to enlarge the hole.

5. Peel the grilled peppers and discard the stem, core, and seeds. Dice finely and combine with the garlic, anchovy, parsley, breadcrumbs, olive oil, salt, and pepper in a bowl.

6. Stand the tenderloin on end and spoon the pepper mixture into the hole, packing it down with the steel or the handle of a wooden spoon. When about half of the stuffing is in the meat, turn the tenderloin over and fill the hole from the other side.

7. Put the beef on a sheet of plastic wrap and rub the exterior with the pesto. Wrap in the plastic and set aside for 10 minutes.

8. Brush the grill grate and coat it with oil. Put the tenderloin on the grill, cover, and cook until browned on all 4 sides, about

---

5 minutes per side. Check the temperature with an instant-read thermometer inserted into the thicker end; it should register 120°F for medium-rare. If your grill has a temperature gauge, it should stay at around 400°F.

9. Let rest for about 5 minutes; slice into 1/2-inch-thick slices and serve.

ORANGE—BLACK PEPPER BEEF TENDERLOIN WITH FRESH HERB WRAP

Compared to other cuts of beef, the tenderloin is tiny (a chuck can weigh 100 pounds; a whole tenderloin maxes out at around 7 pounds), yet it accounts for a lion's share of the potential value of the beef. This is because we will pay anything for tenderness, and a tenderloin is the tenderest of all cuts. At times it goes on sale, but beware. The sale price is usually for tenderloin that has not been trimmed, and the cut can lose 30 percent or more of its weight in unusable trimmings. This recipe makes the most of your investment, coating the beef in a fragrant, spicy rub and serving it with an orange-scented butter sauce. It is equally good served hot or at room temperature if you want to make it ahead.

TIMING
Prep: 20 minutes
Grill: About 20 minutes

GRILL TOOLS AND EQUIPMENT
· Long-handled tongs

THE GRILL

Gas:	Direct heat, medium-high (400° to 450°F)
	Clean, oiled grate
Charcoal:	Direct heat, light ash
	12-by-12-inch charcoal bed (about 3 dozen coals)
	Clean, oiled grate on lowest setting
Wood:	Direct heat, light ash
	12-by-12-inch bed, 3 to 4 inches deep
	Clean, oiled grate set 2 inches above the fire

Photo: Pesto-Rolled Beef Tenderloin with Roasted Pepper Rouille

INGREDIENTS (MAKES 8 SERVINGS)

For the beef:

$1/2$ teaspoon kosher salt

$1/2$ teaspoon ground dried orange peel

$1/2$ teaspoon coarsely ground black pepper

1 beef tenderloin, about 3 pounds, trimmed and tied

1 tablespoon extra-virgin olive oil

1 cup chopped fresh herbs (flat-leaf parsley, rosemary, oregano, thyme, chervil, and/or tarragon)

Oil for coating grill grate

For the sauce:

4 tablespoons ($1/2$ stick) butter, salted or unsalted

1 clove garlic, minced

1 teaspoon coarsely chopped fresh rosemary leaves

1 cup fresh orange juice

DIRECTIONS

1. Mix the salt, orange peel, and pepper in a small bowl. Set aside $1/4$ teaspoon for the sauce. Rub the remaining seasoning all over the tenderloin. Coat the tenderloin with the olive oil, and press the herbs into the surface. Wrap in plastic wrap and set aside for at least 10 minutes.

2. Heat the grill as directed.

3. Brush the grill grate and coat it with oil. Put the tenderloin on the grill, cover, and cook until browned on all 4 sides, about 5 minutes per side. Check the temperature with an instant-read thermometer inserted into the thicker end; it should

register 120°F for medium-rare. If your grill has a temperature gauge, it should stay at around 400°F. Transfer the tenderloin to a cutting board and let rest for about 5 minutes.

4. To make the sauce, heat 1 tablespoon of the butter and the garlic in a small skillet until you smell the garlic aroma, about 1 minute. Add the rosemary and orange juice and boil until reduced by half. Cut the remaining 3 tablespoons butter into pieces and swirl them into the sauce; keep warm.

5. Slice the tenderloin into $1/2$-inch-thick slices, pour the orange sauce over the top, and serve.

BALSAMIC–BLACK PEPPER BEEF SHORT RIBS

Black pepper hides in the background. We add it "to taste" so regularly that most of us have forgotten what it tastes like. These short ribs are destined to change all that. They are purposefully black peppered and glazed with a reduction of aged balsamic vinegar that makes the perfume of the pepper bloom across your palate.

TIMING
Prep: 5 minutes
Grill: About 30 minutes

GRILL TOOLS AND EQUIPMENT
· Long-handled tongs

SHORT RIBS
Short ribs are the last 3 inches of bone and meat on a primal beef rib that gets trimmed away when the primal cut is butchered down to a rib roast. They sell for a fraction of the cost of their high-priced brethren, even though they are essentially the same cut. Most people think short ribs need to be stewed or braised, but now that you know they are almost rib roast, you also know they are an excellent candidate for grilling. They don't need to be brined, marinated, pounded, or pulled. Like a standing rib roast, short ribs are ready to cook just the way they are.

THE GRILL

Gas: Indirect heat, medium (325° to 350°F)
3- or 4-burner grill–middle burner(s) off
2-burner grill–1 side off
Clean, oiled grate

Charcoal: Indirect heat, medium ash
Split charcoal bed (about 2 dozen coals per side)
20 replacement coals
Heavy-duty drip pan set between banks of charcoal
Clean, oiled grate on medium setting

INGREDIENTS (MAKES 4 TO 6 SERVINGS)

2 tablespoons olive oil

1 clove garlic, minced

12 pieces beef short ribs (about 3 pounds)

1 teaspoon kosher salt

1 teaspoon coarsely ground black pepper, or more to taste

Oil for coating grill grate

$1/2$ cup balsamic vinegar

DIRECTIONS

1. Heat the grill as directed.

2. Heat the olive oil and garlic in a small skillet over medium heat until the garlic starts to sizzle; do not let it brown. Transfer to a bowl; reserve the skillet. Rub half of the flavored oil over the meaty parts of the short ribs. Reserve the remaining garlic oil for the balsamic glaze. Season the ribs with the salt and pepper.

3. Brush the grill grate and coat it with oil. Put the short ribs on the grill away from the heat, cover the grill, and cook until

an instant-read thermometer inserted into the thickest section of the meat registers about 145°F, about 30 minutes, turning once halfway through. If your grill has a temperature gauge, it should stay at around 350°F.

4. While the short ribs are cooking, boil the balsamic vinegar in the same skillet you used to heat the olive oil, until the vinegar is reduced to about $1/4$ cup. Stir in the reserved garlic oil.

5. Remove the ribs to a serving platter; drizzle the balsamic glaze over the top and serve.

DINOSAUR RIBS

TIMING
Prep: 10 minutes
   (plus 10 minutes for rub and glaze)
Grill: 30 minutes

GRILL TOOLS AND EQUIPMENT
· Long-handled tongs
· Long-handled basting brush

These super-meaty ribs look as though they came from a primeval creature, but they are really just beef ribs. If your butcher cuts his own rib-eye roast or steaks, he will have the rib bones that he removed from the cut; that's what you want. For some reason the cut is unusual, and if you can't find them, more diminutive short ribs will work just as well. Just tell everyone it was a baby dinosaur.

THE GRILL

Gas: Indirect heat, medium-high (350° to 375°F)
3- or 4-burner grill–middle burner(s) off
2-burner grill–1 side off
Clean, oiled grate

Charcoal: Indirect heat, medium-light ash
Split charcoal bed (about 2 dozen coals per side)
20 replacement coals
Heavy-duty drip pan set between banks of charcoal
Clean, oiled grate on medium setting

INGREDIENTS (MAKES 4 SERVINGS)

8 beef back ribs, about 10 ounces each
1/4 cup Cajun Blackening Rub (page 373)
2 teaspoons garlic-flavored oil

Oil for coating grill grate
3/4 cup Steakhouse Glaze (page 389)
1 tablespoon ground chipotle chile

Photo: Dinosaur Ribs

1. Heat the grill as directed.

2. Rub the ribs with the Cajun rub and coat with the garlic-flavored oil.

3. Brush the grill grate and coat it with oil. Put the ribs on the grill away from the heat, cover the grill, and cook until you can pierce the meat of one of the thickest ribs easily with a fork, about 30 minutes, turning once after 10 minutes. Baste with the glaze and turn several times during the last 10 minutes of cooking.

4. Remove the ribs to a large platter and serve.

TIMING

Prep: 20 minutes
   (plus 5 minutes for rub)
Grill: About 1 hour

GRILL TOOLS AND EQUIPMENT

· Long-handled tongs

HERB-CRUSTED PORK LOIN WITH PISTACHIOS

The sweet, nutty, fragrant mixture of pistachios, garlic, lemon, and herbs runs through the heart of this pork loin. Try to buy roasted shelled pistachios. If you can't find them, you will have to shell about 30 nuts to make $1/3$ cup. The easiest way to toast them is in a microwave. Put the nuts on a plate and cook them at full power for 2 minutes. Stir and cook in 30-second intervals until they smell toasted.

THE GRILL

Gas: Indirect heat, medium-high (350° to 375°F)
3- or 4-burner grill—middle burner(s) off
2-burner grill—1 side off
Clean, oiled grate

Charcoal: Indirect heat, medium ash
Split charcoal bed (about 2 dozen coals per side)
20 replacement coals
Heavy-duty drip pan set between banks of charcoal
Clean, oiled grate on medium setting

INGREDIENTS (MAKES 4 SERVINGS)

$1/3$ cup shelled roasted pistachio nuts, coarsely chopped

3 tablespoons golden raisins, finely chopped

2 cloves garlic, minced

Finely grated zest and juice of 1 lemon

$1/4$ cup chopped fresh flat-leaf parsley

$1/4$ teaspoon kosher salt

$1/8$ teaspoon ground black pepper

2 tablespoons olive oil

1 center-cut pork loin, about 2 pounds, $7 1/2$ inches long and
   $2 1/2$ inches in diameter

3 tablespoons Tuscan Rosemary Rub (page 375)

Oil for coating grill grate

DIRECTIONS

1. Combine the pistachio nuts, raisins, garlic, lemon zest, parsley, salt, pepper, and 1 tablespoon of the olive oil in a bowl.

2. Heat the grill as directed.

3. Insert a long, thin-bladed knife into the center of one end of the roast until the tip comes out the other end. Enlarge the hole so that it is about 1 inch wide all the way through the roast. Stuff the hole with the pistachio mixture. Rub the outside with the remaining 1 tablespoon olive oil and the herb rub.

4. Brush the grill grate and coat it with oil. Put the roast on the grill away from the heat, cover the grill, and cook until an instant-read thermometer inserted into the center of the meat registers about 155°F, about 1 hour, turning it once halfway through. If your grill has a temperature gauge, it should stay between 350° and 375°F.

5. Remove to a large serving platter; drizzle with the lemon juice. Let rest for 8 to 10 minutes; slice and serve.

TIMING

Soak wood chips: 1 hour
Prep: 15 minutes
   (plus 10 minutes for rub and sauce)
Grill: About $2 1/2$ hours

SPICY MAPLE PORK SHOULDER

The picnic shoulder is a popular cut of pork for barbecue. That's because it's a little leaner than the butt portion of the shoulder but still has great flavor. The picnic comes from the upper foreleg, so it is smaller in circumference than the butt, and better for a smaller crowd. We like this recipe with some smoke, but if you don't have any wood, it's delicious smoke-free as well.

THE GRILL

Gas: Indirect heat, medium (325° to 350°F)
3- or 4-burner grill–middle burner(s) off
2-burner grill–1 side off
Clean, oiled grate

Charcoal: Indirect heat, medium ash
Split charcoal bed (about 2 dozen coals per side)
20 replacement coals
Heavy-duty drip pan set between banks of charcoal
Clean, oiled grate on medium setting

GRILL TOOLS AND EQUIPMENT
· 4 fruitwood chunks or 2 cups chips if using a smoker box
· Smoker box or foil packet, if using a gas grill (see page 39)
· Long-handled tongs
· Long-handled spatula
· Long-handled basting brush

INGREDIENTS (MAKES 6 SERVINGS)

1 boneless pork shoulder (picnic ham), about 2 3/4 pounds
2 tablespoons Fragrant Chile Rub (page 372)
1 tablespoon canola oil

3/4 cup Sweet, Hot, and Sour BBQ Sauce (page 391)
1/2 cup maple syrup
Oil for coating grill grate

DIRECTIONS

1. Soak the wood chunks or chips for about 1 hour.

2. Heat the grill as directed.

3. Rub the pork with the chile rub. Coat with the 1 tablespoon oil. Mix the barbecue sauce and maple syrup in a bowl; set aside.

4. Put the wood chunks directly over the coals. If using a gas grill, put the wood chips in a smoker box or in a foil packet directly over one of the heated burners.

5. Brush the grill grate and coat it with oil. Put the pork on the grill away from the heat, cover the grill, and cook until an instant-read thermometer inserted into the thickest part of the meat registers about 165°F, about 2 1/2 hours, turning the meat a quarter turn every 40 minutes or so for the first 2 hours. Baste with the barbecue sauce mixture every 5 minutes during the last 30 minutes of cooking. If your grill has a temperature gauge, it should stay at around 350°F. If you are using charcoal or wood, you will probably have to replenish the coals or wood after each hour.

6. Remove the pork to a serving platter, using tongs and a spatula for support. Let rest for 8 to 10 minutes; slice and serve.

PORK TENDERLOIN ROLLED WITH ROSEMARY AND PANCETTA

TIMING
Prep: 10 minutes
Grill: 8 minutes

GRILL TOOLS AND EQUIPMENT
· Long-handled tongs

Pancetta is cured pork belly. Often called Italian bacon, it is not much like bacon in either appearance or flavor. Pancetta is cured with salt, pepper, and other spices or herbs, but unlike bacon, it is not smoked. Bacon is from either the sides or the belly of the pig and is usually cut into slices; pancetta comes only from the belly and is generally sold rolled up into a sausage shape. Pancetta has a unique flavor that largely comes from its fatty parts, so don't trim it of fat. If you can't find it, you can substitute bacon, but the flavor will be completely different. You can mail-order high-quality pancetta from DiBruno Brothers at www.dibruno.com. It freezes well.

THE GRILL

Gas: Direct heat, medium-high (400° to 450°F)
Clean, oiled grate

Charcoal: Direct heat, light ash
12-by-12-inch charcoal bed (about 3 dozen coals)
Clean, oiled grate on middle setting

Wood: Direct heat, light ash
12-by-12-inch bed, 3 inches deep
Clean, oiled grate set about 4 inches above the fire

INGREDIENTS (MAKES 4 SERVINGS)

3 cloves garlic, minced
1 1/2 teaspoons minced fresh rosemary
1 ounce pancetta, finely chopped (about 1/4 cup)
1/4 teaspoon kosher salt, or more to taste

1/4 teaspoon ground black pepper
2 pork tenderloins, a little more than 1 pound each
1 tablespoon olive oil
Oil for coating grill grate

---

1. Heat the grill as directed.

2. Mix the garlic, rosemary, pancetta, salt, and pepper in a bowl.

3. Make a slit down the length of each tenderloin so that they open up like books (see "Butterflying Boneless Meat," page 196). Rub all over with the pancetta mixture and coat with the olive oil. Set aside for 5 minutes.

4. Brush the grill grate and coat it with oil. Put the tenderloins on the grill, cover the grill, and cook until an instant-read thermometer inserted into the thickest part of the meat registers about 155°F, about 8 minutes, turning halfway through. If your grill has a temperature gauge, it should stay at around 400°F.

5. Let rest for 8 to 10 minutes; slice and serve.

PULLED PORK THREE WAYS

Pork is the most common meat in the world, and every culture that eats it has a recipe involving long, slow cooking that ends up with the pork in shreds. Whether you are from South Carolina, southern Italy, or Southeast Asia, you know about pulled pork. The only difference is what you flavor the meat with after it cooks, and how you choose to present it. Here is a recipe to serve as an international guide. It includes enough to make 8 portions of pulled pork, and enough of three different sauces and accompaniments to flavor all of that pork. It is assumed that you will choose one way, but if you want to make all three, either you will need three times the amount of pork, or you will need to cut all of the sauce ingredients down by two-thirds.

THE GRILL

Gas: Indirect heat, medium (325° to 350°F)
3- or 4-burner grill–middle burner(s) off
2-burner grill–1 side off
Clean, oiled grate

Charcoal: Indirect heat, medium ash
Split charcoal bed (about 2 dozen coals per side)
80 replacement coals

Heavy-duty drip pan set between banks of charcoal
Clean, oiled grate on medium setting

Wood: Indirect heat, medium ash
12-by-12-inch bed, 3 inches deep
Additional wood for replacement
Clean, oiled grate set 4 inches above the fire

INGREDIENTS (MAKES 8 SERVINGS)

For the pork:
1 boneless pork shoulder, about 5 pounds
1/4 cup Fragrant Chile Rub (page 372)
2 tablespoons canola oil
Oil for coating grill grate

For the South Carolina Vinegar Mop:
3/4 cup apple cider vinegar
2 tablespoons sugar
2 teaspoons Tabasco hot pepper sauce
1/2 teaspoon kosher salt
1/2 teaspoon ground black pepper
8 hamburger rolls, for serving

For the Pungent Vietnamese Sauce:
1 cup Vietnamese Dipping Sauce (page 398)
8 leaves romaine lettuce, for serving
4 radishes, thinly sliced and cut into strips, for serving
1/2 cucumber, peeled, seeded, and cut into thin slices, for serving

For the Sicilian Bath:
1/4 cup extra-virgin olive oil
1/4 cup red wine vinegar
1/4 cup fresh lemon juice
1 tablespoon tomato paste
1 clove garlic, minced
1 teaspoon chopped fresh oregano leaves, or 1/4 teaspoon dried oregano
1 teaspoon chopped fresh rosemary leaves, or 1/4 teaspoon dried rosemary
1/2 teaspoon kosher salt
1/4 teaspoon ground black pepper
2 tablespoons chopped fresh flat-leaf parsley
8 sub rolls, for serving
2 large onions, cut into 1/2-inch-thick slices and grilled until tender, halved, for serving

TIMING
Prep: 30 minutes
(plus 10 minutes for rub and sauce)
Rest before grilling: 30 minutes to 1 hour
Grill: 3 to 4 hours

GRILL TOOLS AND EQUIPMENT
· Long-handled tongs
· Long-handled spatula
· Kitchen twine

Photo: Pulled Pork with Pungent Vietnamese Sauce

1. Rub the pork all over with the rub. Roll and tie the pork into a compact bundle, and rub it all over with the 2 tablespoons oil. Set aside for at least 30 minutes or up to 1 hour.

2. Heat the grill as directed.

3. Brush the grill grate and coat it with oil. Put the pork on the grill away from the heat, cover the grill, and cook until an instant-read thermometer inserted into the thickest part of the meat registers about 185°F, 3 to 4 hours. If your grill has a temperature gauge, it should stay at around 350°F. If you are using charcoal or wood, you will have to replenish the coals or wood every hour.

4. While the pork is cooking, make one of the sauces by combining the ingredients in a bowl; set aside.

5. Remove the pork to a cutting board, using tongs and a spatula for support, cover with foil, and let rest for at least 15 minutes. Untie and cut the meat into 1 1/2-inch-thick slices. Pull the slices apart with your fingers or 2 forks into shreds, discarding large pockets of fat as you proceed. Mix the pulled pork with one of the sauces. Serve South Carolina pulled pork on hamburger rolls. Serve Vietnamese pulled pork wrapped in lettuce leaves with slivers of radish and cucumber. Serve Sicilian pulled pork on sub rolls topped with grilled onions.

TIMING

Prep: 10 minutes
Grill: About 2 hours

GRILL TOOLS AND EQUIPMENT

· Long-handled tongs
· Long-handled spatula

MUSTARD-GLAZED RACK OF PORK WITH GRILLED PINEAPPLE

This is truly an impressive presentation. Like a standing rib roast of beef, a rack of pork is regal, with its bulging eye, crusted with spices, herbs, and mustard, perched atop an arch of bones. A 4-rib rack, weighing 3 1/2 pounds, will feed 6 people amply, but if you want to give each person a bone you will have to plan on almost a pound per person, which will come out to about 10 ounces of meat per serving. A roast of that size will not take any longer to cook, since it will have approximately the same circumference, but you will have to prepare about 50 percent more of the mustard coating.

THE GRILL

Gas: Indirect heat, medium (325° to 350°F)
3- or 4-burner grill—middle burner(s) off
2-burner grill—1 side off
Clean, oiled grate

Charcoal: Indirect heat, medium ash
Split charcoal bed (about 2 dozen coals per side)
20 replacement coals
Heavy-duty drip pan set between banks of charcoal
Clean, oiled grate on medium setting

INGREDIENTS (MAKES 6 SERVINGS)

2 tablespoons spicy brown mustard
1/4 teaspoon ground cinnamon
1/8 teaspoon ground allspice
1 teaspoon crushed dried rosemary
1/4 teaspoon ground black pepper
2 tablespoons canola oil

2 tablespoons dark brown sugar
4-rib rack of pork, about 3 1/2 pounds
Oil for coating grill grate
1/2 teaspoon kosher salt, or more to taste
1/8 teaspoon crushed red pepper flakes
4 pineapple slices, 1/2 inch thick, peeled, cored, and quartered

DIRECTIONS

1. Heat the grill as directed.

2. Mix the mustard, cinnamon, allspice, rosemary, black pepper, 2 teaspoons of the canola oil, and 1 tablespoon of the brown sugar in a bowl. Brush over the meaty parts of the pork.

3. Brush the grill grate and coat it with oil. Put the pork on the grill, bone-side down, away from the heat, cover the grill, and cook until an instant-read thermometer inserted into the thickest part of the meat registers about 150°F, about 2 hours. If your grill has a temperature gauge, it should stay at around 350°F. If you are using charcoal or wood, you will probably have to replenish the coals or wood after the first hour.

4. While the pork is cooking, mix the remaining 1 tablespoon brown sugar with the salt and red pepper flakes; set aside. Coat the pineapple slices with the remaining 1 tablespoon canola oil.

5. During the last 20 minutes of cooking the pork, put the pineapple on the grill directly over the heat and cook until browned on both sides, sprinkling with the salt–brown sugar mixture immediately after turning.

6. Remove the pork to a large serving platter, using tongs and a spatula for support, and surround it with grilled pineapple. Let rest for 8 to 10 minutes; carve as you would a rib roast and serve with some of the pineapple.

CAJUN CITRUS RIBS

TIMING
Prep: 5 minutes
  (plus 10 minutes for brine and syrup)
Brine: 6 to 12 hours
Grill: About 1 hour

Spareribs and citrus don't seem like a match made in barbecue heaven, but think about it. The acid in the citrus is a counterpoint to the rich fat of ribs, turning them from something slathered and gooey to something clean and spare. We finish them with a thin, spicy bourbon syrup just to make sure your fingers get sticky.

GRILL TOOLS AND EQUIPMENT
· Long-handled tongs
· Long-handled basting brush

THE GRILL

Gas: Indirect heat, medium (325° to 350°F)
3- or 4-burner grill–middle burner(s) off
2-burner grill–1 side off
Clean, oiled grate

Charcoal: Indirect heat, medium ash
Split charcoal bed (about 2 dozen coals per side)
20 replacement coals
Heavy-duty drip pan set between banks of charcoal
Clean, oiled grate on medium setting

INGREDIENTS (MAKES 4 SERVINGS)

2 racks ribs, about 4 pounds, St. Louis cut spareribs or
  baby back ribs (see page 215)
2 1/2 cups Spicy Citrus Brine (page 364)

Oil for coating grill grate
1 cup Hot Pepper–Bourbon Syrup (page 384)

DIRECTIONS

1. Cut the racks in half. Put them in a gallon-size zipper-lock bag with the citrus brine. Seal the zipper, leaving about an inch open; push on the bag to release any trapped air through the opening, and close the zipper completely. Massage the liquid gently into the meat and refrigerate for 6 to 12 hours.
2. Heat the grill as directed.
3. Brush the grill grate and coat it with oil. Put the ribs on the grill away from the heat, cover the grill, and cook until an

instant-read thermometer inserted into the thickest part of the ribs registers about 155°F, about 1 hour. If your grill has a temperature gauge, it should stay at around 350°F.
4. Brush the ribs with the bourbon syrup during the last 10 minutes, turning and basting until all of the syrup has been used up.
5. Remove the ribs to a large platter, cut into 1- or 2-rib sections, and serve.

CORIANDER RIBS WITH CILANTRO BUTTER

TIMING
Prep: 5 minutes
  (plus 10 minutes for brine and butter)
Brine: 6 to 12 hours
Grill: About 1 hour

You've never had ribs like these. Inundated with coriander, cumin, and lime, the meat is tenderized and moistened by brine and then glazed with a lime-butter vinaigrette that is flavored with cilantro (coriander leaf)—reflecting back on the coriander in the brine.

GRILL TOOLS AND EQUIPMENT
· Long-handled tongs
· Long-handled basting brush

THE GRILL

Gas: Indirect heat, medium (325° to 350°F)
3- or 4-burner grill–middle burner(s) off
2-burner grill–1 side off
Clean, oiled grate
Charcoal: Indirect heat, medium ash
Split charcoal bed (about 2 dozen coals per side)
20 replacement coals
Heavy-duty drip pan set between banks of charcoal
Clean, oiled grate on medium setting

Wood: Indirect heat, medium ash
12-by-12-inch bed, 3 inches deep
Clean, oiled grate set 4 inches above the fire

2 racks ribs, about 4 pounds, St. Louis cut spareribs or
   baby back ribs (see facing page)
2 1/2 cups Cumin, Coriander, and Lime Brine (page 364)

Oil for coating grill grate
1/3 cup Lime-Cilantro Butter (page 393)

DIRECTIONS

1. Cut the racks in half. Put them in a gallon-size zipper-lock bag with the brine. Seal the zipper, leaving about an inch open; push on the bag to release any trapped air through the opening, and close the zipper completely. Massage the liquid gently into the meat and refrigerate for 6 to 12 hours.
2. Heat the grill as directed.
3. Brush the grill grate and coat it with oil. Put the ribs on the grill away from the heat, cover the grill, and cook until an

instant-read thermometer inserted into the thickest part of the ribs registers about 155°F, about 1 hour. If your grill has a temperature gauge, it should stay at around 350°F.
4. When the ribs are done, brush them with half of the lime-cilantro butter, turn,
and brush with the rest of the butter.
5. Remove the ribs to a large platter, cut into 1- or 2-rib sections, and serve.

TIMING
Prep: 5 minutes
   (plus 10 minutes for brine and sauce)
Brine: 6 to 12 hours
Grill: About 1 hour

GRILL TOOLS AND EQUIPMENT
· Long-handled tongs
· Long-handled basting brush

SPICE-CURED BARBECUED RIBS

The trick to tender, succulent ribs is in the brine. The salt in the brine makes the twisted, ribbonlike proteins of meat unravel. As the proteins unwind, their newly opened bonds bind to the liquid in the brine, absorbing its moisture and flavor. When the meat cooks, the protein strands start to bond to one another, trapping the liquid. As long as you don't overcook the meat, this moisture will stay in it, causing brined meats to be 6 to 8 percent juicier than their unbrined counterparts.

THE GRILL

Gas: Indirect heat, medium (325° to 350°F)
   3- or 4-burner grill–middle burner(s) off
   2-burner grill–1 side off
   Clean, oiled grate
Charcoal: Indirect heat, medium ash
   Split charcoal bed (about 2 dozen coals per side)
   20 replacement coals
   Heavy-duty drip pan set between banks of charcoal
   Clean, oiled grate on medium setting

Wood: Indirect heat, medium ash
   12-by-12-inch bed, 3 inches deep
   Clean, oiled grate set 4 inches above the fire

INGREDIENTS (MAKES 4 SERVINGS)

2 racks ribs, about 4 pounds, St. Louis cut spareribs or
   baby back ribs (see facing page)
2 1/4 cups Ten-Pepper Brine (page 369)

Oil for coating grill grate
1 1/4 cups Sweet, Hot, and Sour BBQ Sauce (page 391)

DIRECTIONS

1. Cut the racks in half. Put them in a gallon-size zipper-lock bag with the brine. Seal the zipper, leaving about an inch open; push on the bag to release any trapped air through the opening, and close the zipper completely. Massage the liquid gently into the meat and refrigerate for 6 to 12 hours.
2. Heat the grill as directed.
3. Brush the grill grate and coat it with oil. Put the ribs on the grill away from the heat, cover the grill, and cook until an

instant-read thermometer inserted into the thickest part of the ribs registers about 155°F, about 1 hour. If your grill has a temperature gauge, it should stay at around 350°F.
4. Brush the ribs with half of the barbecue sauce, turn, cover, and cook for 3 minutes. Brush with the remaining sauce, turn, cover, and cook for another 3 minutes.
5. Remove the ribs to a large platter, cut into 1- or 2-rib sections, and serve.

CIDER-BRINED RIBS

TIMING
Prep: 5 minutes
    (plus 10 minutes for brine and glaze)
Brine: 6 to 12 hours
Grill: About 1 hour

Pork spareribs can come from the loin or the belly. Loin ribs are small and are therefore called "baby back." Belly ribs are larger, less meaty, and less expensive. There are at least 11 ribs in a rack of spareribs, and the cut includes portions of breast meat, sternum, and diaphragm. When these sections are trimmed, the rack takes on a rectangular shape and is sold as "St. Louis" ribs. We prefer the St. Louis cut because it is the same thickness from end to end, and so it cooks evenly. It is also easier to cut into serving portions.

GRILL TOOLS AND EQUIPMENT
· Long-handled tongs
· Long-handled basting brush

THE GRILL

Gas: Indirect heat, medium (325° to 350°F)
3- or 4-burner grill–middle burner(s) off
2-burner grill–1 side off
Clean, oiled grate

Charcoal: Indirect heat, medium ash
Split charcoal bed (about 2 dozen coals per side)

20 replacement coals
Heavy-duty drip pan set between banks of charcoal
Clean, oiled grate on medium setting

Wood: Indirect heat, medium ash
12-by-12-inch bed, 3 inches deep
Clean, oiled grate set 4 inches above the fire

INGREDIENTS (MAKES 4 SERVINGS)

2 racks ribs, about 4 pounds, St. Louis cut spareribs or baby back ribs
2½ cups Apple-Chai Brine (page 371)

Oil for coating grill grate
1 cup Ginger-Hoisin Balsamic Glaze (page 388)

DIRECTIONS

1. Cut the racks in half. Put them in a gallon-size zipper-lock bag with the brine. Seal the zipper, leaving about an inch open; push on the bag to release any trapped air through the opening, and close the zipper completely. Massage the liquid gently into the meat and refrigerate for 6 to 12 hours.

2. Heat the grill as directed.

3. Brush the grill grate and coat it with oil. Put the ribs on the grill away from the heat, cover the grill, and cook until an

instant-read thermometer inserted into the thickest part of the ribs registers about 155°F, about 1 hour. If your grill has a temperature gauge, it should stay at around 350°F.

4. Brush the ribs with half of the ginger-hoisin glaze, turn, cover, and cook for 3 minutes. Brush with the remaining glaze, turn, cover, and cook for another 3 minutes.

5. Remove the ribs to a large platter, cut into 1- or 2-rib sections, and serve.

OSSO BUCO NIÇOISE

TIMING
Prep: 15 minutes
    (plus 10 minutes for herb bath and dip)
Marinate: 6 to 12 hours
Grill: About 1 hour

Veal shanks are prized for their flavor and the nugget of marrow buried in the cross section of leg bone. This is not a cut that is typically grilled, but if you keep the fire indirect and low, the meat melts into a velvety mass. Brining helps, as it does with most tougher cuts. Don't be alarmed by the portion size (1 pound per person); the bone takes up more than half of that weight.

GRILL TOOLS AND EQUIPMENT
· Long-handled spatula or
  long-handled tongs

THE GRILL

Gas: Indirect heat, medium (325° to 350°F)
3- or 4-burner grill–middle burner(s) off
2-burner grill–1 side off
Clean, oiled grate

Charcoal: Indirect heat, medium ash
Split charcoal bed (about 2 dozen coals per side)
20 replacement coals
Heavy-duty drip pan set between banks of charcoal
Clean, oiled grate on medium setting

----

4 pieces veal shank, cut for osso buco, about 1 pound each

1$^1/_3$ cups Sicilian Herb Bath (page 356)

Oil for coating grill grate

1$^1/_2$ cups Orange Tapenade Dip (page 391)

$^1/_4$ cup chopped fresh flat-leaf parsley

DIRECTIONS

1. Put the veal shanks in a gallon-size zipper-lock bag with the herb bath. Seal the zipper, leaving about an inch open; push on the bag to release any trapped air through the opening, and close the zipper completely. Massage the liquid gently into the meat and refrigerate for 6 to 12 hours.

2. Heat the grill as directed.

3. Remove the shanks from the marinade; discard the marinade. Brush the grill grate and coat it with oil. Put the shanks on the grill away from the heat, cover the grill, and cook until an instant-read thermometer inserted into the thickest part of the shanks registers about 150°F, about 1 hour, turning halfway through. If your grill has a temperature gauge, it should stay at around 350°F.

4. Remove the shanks to a large serving platter; drizzle with some of the orange tapenade dip and sprinkle with the parsley. Serve with the remaining tapenade dip.

LEMON-GARLIC LAMB RIBLETS

Lamb ribs can be purchased as a rack of 7 or 8 ribs, or cut into individual ribs, called riblets. Either way they are a great and delicious alternative to pork ribs. Their one drawback is a tendency to be very fatty; soaking them in buttermilk and spices helps to counteract the fat and soothe their strong flavors. These ribs are served with a refreshing cucumber salad, tossed in some of the same buttermilk marinade.

THE GRILL

Gas: Indirect heat, medium-high (350° to 400°F)
Clean, oiled grate

Charcoal: Direct heat, medium ash
12-by-12-inch charcoal bed (about 3 dozen coals)
Clean, oiled grate on middle setting

INGREDIENTS (MAKES 4 SERVINGS)

3 pounds lamb riblets, cut into individual riblets

2 cups Garlic-Buttermilk Marinade (page 350)

Finely grated zest and juice of 1 lemon

1 large cucumber, peeled, seeded, and finely diced

1 teaspoon kosher salt

Pinch of crushed red pepper flakes

1 clove garlic, minced

Oil for coating grill grate

DIRECTIONS

1. Put the riblets in a gallon-size zipper-lock bag with the marinade, half of the lemon zest, and half of the lemon juice. Seal the zipper, leaving about an inch open; push on the bag to release any trapped air through the opening, and close the zipper completely. Massage the liquid gently into the meat and refrigerate for 6 to 12 hours.

2. Heat the grill as directed.

3. Toss the diced cucumber and salt in a bowl. Set aside for 10 minutes. Put the cucumber in a flat-woven dish towel. Wrap the towel around the cucumber and wring until most of the juice from the cucumber has drained through the towel. Toss the cucumber in a small serving bowl with the red pepper flakes, garlic, and remaining lemon zest and juice. Set aside.

4. Remove the riblets from the marinade; discard the marinade.

5. Brush the grill grate and coat it with oil. Put the riblets on the grill away from the heat, cover the grill, and cook until an instant-read thermometer inserted into the thickest rib registers about 145°F, about 30 minutes. If your grill has a temperature gauge, it should stay at around 375°F.

6. Serve the riblets with the cucumber relish.

TIMING

Prep: 5 minutes
(plus 5 minutes for marinade)
Marinate: 6 to 12 hours
Grill: 30 minutes

GRILL TOOLS AND EQUIPMENT

· Long-handled tongs

MOROCCAN BARBECUED LAMB SHANKS

TIMING
Prep: 15 minutes
(plus 5 minutes for rub)
Grill: About 1 hour

GRILL TOOLS AND EQUIPMENT
· Long-handled tongs
· Long-handled basting brush

Lamb shanks are not for the dainty. Because they are smaller than the shanks of veal or pork, they are not cut into delicate cross sections. Lamb shanks are served whole, a leg on a plate—think cave cuisine. These shanks are permeated with North African spices; they radiate cinnamon, thyme, coriander, and lemon—an exotic harmony.

THE GRILL

Gas: Indirect heat, medium (325° to 350°F)
3- or 4-burner grill–middle burner(s) off
2-burner grill–1 side off
Clean, oiled grate

Charcoal: Indirect heat, medium ash
Split charcoal bed (about 2 dozen coals per side)
20 replacement coals
Heavy-duty drip pan set between banks of charcoal
Clean, oiled grate on medium setting

Photo: Moroccan Barbecued Lamb Shanks

4 lamb shanks, about 12 ounces each

1/2 cup extra-virgin olive oil

3 tablespoons Moroccan Rub (page 382)

1/4 teaspoon kosher salt, or more to taste

1/4 teaspoon ground black pepper

1/4 cup fresh lemon juice

1/4 cup chopped fresh flat-leaf parsley

3 cloves garlic, chopped

1 tablespoon tomato paste

Oil for coating grill grate

DIRECTIONS

1. Heat the grill as directed.

2. Rub the lamb shanks with 1 tablespoon of the olive oil and the Moroccan rub, salt, and pepper.

3. Mix the remaining olive oil, the lemon juice, parsley, garlic, and tomato paste in a bowl; set aside.

4. Brush the grill grate and coat it with oil. Put the lamb shanks on the grill away from the heat, cover the grill, and cook until an instant-read thermometer inserted into the thickest part of a shank registers about 155°F, about 1 hour. Turn and baste with the parsley sauce 3 or 4 times. If your grill has a temperature gauge, it should stay at around 350°F.

5. Serve 1 shank per person.

TIMING

Prep: 15 minutes
(plus 40 minutes for garlic paste
and rub)

Grill: About 1 hour and 15 minutes

GRILL TOOLS AND EQUIPMENT

· Long-handled tongs

· Long-handled spatula

· Heavy-duty kitchen twine

DIGGING DEEPER

If you have a bone-in leg of lamb, you can remove the bone. You will need a butt-end leg weighing about 5 1/2 pounds to end up with a boneless 4-pound piece. To remove the bones:

1. Cut around the hip, or "aitch," bone with a slender knife, following its contours with the tip of the knife. When you get to the socket of the leg bone, cut between the socket and the ball of the leg bone. Remove the hipbone.

2. Cut through the side of the leg closest to the leg bone, opening it up as you cut until you have exposed the bone. Cut around the leg bone until it is released from the meat all the way around. Lift the bone and cut around the other ball joint of the knee until you can remove the bone.

Or you can leave the bone in and make 1-inch-deep slits all over the meat and stuff them with the herb and garlic paste mixture from step 2. Proceed with the recipe as written, but you will probably need to extend the cooking time to about 2 hours.

PROVENÇAL BONELESS LEG OF LAMB

A leg of lamb meets its destiny on the grill. Lacquered by fire, its gamy nuance is tamed and its affinity for the aromatics of forest herbs and garlic is enhanced. It is our opinion that lamb should never be cooked past medium-rare (135°F). Past that point it loses its moisture and succulence and begins to take on the livery flavors that folks who say they hate lamb think it tastes like.

THE GRILL

Gas: Indirect heat, medium (325° to 350°F)
3- or 4-burner grill–middle burner(s) off
2-burner grill–1 side off
Clean, oiled grate

Charcoal: Indirect heat, medium ash
Split charcoal bed (about 2 dozen coals per side)
20 replacement coals
Heavy-duty drip pan set between banks of charcoal
Clean, oiled grate on medium setting

INGREDIENTS (MAKES 10 TO 12 SERVINGS)

1/4 cup Roasted Garlic Paste (page 392)

1 tablespoon plus 1 teaspoon Provençal Herb Rub (page 373)

1 boneless leg of lamb (butt end), about 4 pounds

2 tablespoons extra-virgin olive oil

1/2 teaspoon kosher salt

1/2 teaspoon cracked black pepper

Oil for coating grill grate

DIRECTIONS

1. Heat the grill as directed.

2. Mix the garlic paste and the 1 teaspoon herb rub together in a small bowl and rub over the interior of the leg of lamb. Roll the lamb into a compact roast and tie it in place with heavy-duty kitchen twine.

3. Mix the 1 tablespoon herb rub with the olive oil in another small bowl and rub over the outside of the roast. Season with the salt and pepper.

4. Brush the grill grate and coat with oil. Put the lamb on the grill away from the heat, cover the grill, and cook until an instant-read thermometer inserted into the thickest part of the leg registers about 135°F for medium-rare, about 1 hour and 15 minutes. If your grill has a temperature gauge, it should stay between 350° and 375°F. If you are using charcoal, you will probably have to replenish the coals after the first hour.

5. Remove the lamb to a large serving platter, using tongs and a spatula for support. Let rest for 8 to 10 minutes; remove the twine, slice, and serve.

GRILLED SIDE OF SALMON IN CHILI PASTE

TIMING
Prep: 20 minutes
   (plus 5 minutes for glaze)
Grill: 10 to 16 minutes

GRILL TOOLS AND EQUIPMENT
· Long-handled fish spatula or
  2 regular offset spatulas
· Long-handled basting brush

The fat-rich flesh of salmon is built for the grill. It keeps the meat moist, even if it overcooks slightly, and it helps the fillet keep its shape, even if it sticks slightly. These attributes are enhanced in farmed salmon and diminished in wild-caught fish, which means that the two will have very different cooking times.

THE GRILL

Gas: Direct heat, medium (350°F)
         Clean, oiled grate
Charcoal: Direct heat, medium ash
         12-by-12-inch charcoal bed (about 3 dozen coals)
         Clean, oiled grate on medium setting

Wood: Direct heat, medium ash
         12-by-12-inch bed, 3 inches deep
         Clean, oiled grate set 4 inches above the fire

INGREDIENTS (MAKES 4 SERVINGS)

1/4 cup Ginger-Hoisin Balsamic Glaze (page 388)
1 to 1 1/2 tablespoons Chinese chili paste with garlic
1 side of salmon, about 1 1/2 inches thick, 1 1/2 pounds

2 teaspoons toasted sesame oil
Oil for coating grill grate
1 lime, cut into 4 wedges

DIRECTIONS

1. Heat the grill as directed.
2. Mix the glaze and chili paste (to taste); set aside. Coat the salmon with the sesame oil.
3. Brush the grill grate and coat it with oil. Put the salmon, flesh-side down, on the grill. Cover and cook until browned, about 5 minutes.
4. Flip the fish and baste with the chili paste mixture. Cover and grill until an instant-read thermometer inserted into the thickest part of the salmon registers 130°F, about 5 minutes

more for wild salmon, 10 to 12 minutes more for farm-raised (until the fish barely flakes when gently pressed). If your grill has a temperature gauge, it should stay between 375° and 400°F.
5. Transfer the fish to a serving platter by sliding the spatula(s) between the skin and the flesh. The skin will stick to the grill grate; let it stay there. You can scrape it off later. Serve with the lime wedges.

CUMIN-CRUSTED SEA BASS WITH LIME-CILANTRO BUTTER

TIMING
Prep: 5 minutes
   (plus 10 minutes for rub and butter)
Grill: About 15 minutes

GRILL TOOLS AND EQUIPMENT
· Long-handled fish spatula
· Grill screen or fish-grilling basket

Whole fish grilled over an open flame develops a crackled skin and concentrated moisture that is the essence of succulence. Unfortunately, the increased popularity of fish has not translated into an increase in the availability of whole fish. Almost everything you see is already filleted. This is a shame because the flesh of fish cooked whole has more flavor (from contact with the bone) and hangs on to its moisture better. If you don't want to serve the fish with its head on, remove it after cooking. Slashing the flesh in its thicker parts will help the fish cook more evenly and gets any seasoning closer to the meat, where it does the most good.

THE GRILL

Gas: Direct heat, medium (350°F)
         Clean, oiled grate
Charcoal: Direct heat, medium ash
         12-by-12-inch charcoal bed (about 3 dozen coals)
         Clean, oiled grate on medium setting

Wood: Direct heat, medium ash
         12-by-12-inch bed, 3 inches deep
         Clean, oiled grate set 4 inches above the fire

2 whole sea bass, about 1½ pounds each, gutted
   and cleaned
2 tablespoons Cumin Rub (page 382)

2 tablespoons olive oil
Oil for coating grill grate and screen or basket
⅓ cup Lime-Cilantro Butter (page 393), warmed

DIRECTIONS

1. Heat the grill as directed.
2. Scrape the dull side of a knife against the skin of the fish, running from tail to head, to remove excess moisture and fine scales. Cut 3 or 4 diagonal slices through the flesh of the fish on each side down to the bone. Season the fish inside and out with the cumin rub, and rub the olive oil over the outside.

3. Brush the grill grate and coat it with oil. Oil the grill screen or fish basket liberally and put the fish on the screen or in the basket; put it on the grill. Cover and cook until browned on both sides and an instant-read thermometer inserted into the thickest part of one of the fish registers 130°F, about 15 minutes. If your grill has a temperature gauge, it should stay at around 375°F.
4. Serve the fish with the warm butter sauce.

TIMING
Prep: 10 minutes
  (plus 10 minutes for rub and
  mop sauce)
Grill: About 12 minutes

GRILL TOOLS AND EQUIPMENT
· Long-handled tongs

GETTING CREATIVE
· Feel free to vary this recipe with other rubs and dipping sauces. Try Sesame Szechwan Salt (page 380), Ten-Pepper Rub (page 378), or Bedouin Dry Marinade (page 383), with Preserved Lemon Relish (page 394), Harissa Dip (page 396), or Vietnamese Dipping Sauce (page 398).

THAI BASIL ROASTED TUNA LOIN

If you are a fan of rare tuna, this recipe is for you. Most tuna steaks aren't thick enough to get much of a crust before the fish cooks through. By starting with a section of tuna loin (the muscle that tuna steaks are cut from), you have what looks like a small roast. Cook it directly over as hot a fire as you can get, crusting it on all 3 sides (because tuna loin is roughly cylindrical, turning it twice will brown it all around and give it a dynamic triangular profile), about 4 minutes per side. The center will stay raw, which means that you will have to test for doneness by taking its temperature both in the center and nearer to the edge. It should be well-done (140°F) at its edge, but not much warmer than refrigerator temperature in the center.

THE GRILL

Gas: Direct heat, high (500°F)
         Clean, oiled grate
Charcoal: Direct heat, red-hot
         12-by-12-inch charcoal bed (about 3 dozen coals)
         Clean, oiled grate on lowest setting

Wood: Direct heat, red-hot
         12-by-12-inch bed, 3 to 4 inches deep
         Clean, oiled grate set 2 inches above the fire

INGREDIENTS (MAKES 6 SERVINGS)

2 pounds tuna loin, 4½ inches long and 3 inches
   in diameter
1 ounce Thai basil or sweet basil leaves (about 1 cup)
1 tablespoon Moroccan Rub (page 382)

2 teaspoons olive oil
Oil for coating grill grate
1 cup Grapefruit Ponzu Marinade or Mop (page 359)

DIRECTIONS

1. Heat the grill as directed.
2. Stab the tuna with a knife about 2 dozen times, and stuff each slit with a leaf of basil. It's easiest to use the wide end of a chopstick to push the basil into the hole. Rub the outside with the Moroccan rub and coat with the olive oil.
3. Brush the grill grate and coat it with oil. Put the tuna on its long side on the grill, cover, and cook until browned on all 3 sides, about 12 minutes total. If your grill has a temperature gauge, it should stay between 425° and 450°F. It is important

that the center of the tuna remain raw; therefore, to judge doneness, imagine a target on one end of the tuna, with a bull's-eye in the center. An instant-read thermometer inserted into the bull's-eye should register 50°F, one ring out it should register around 70°F, farther toward the edge it should register about 100°F, and it should read 140°F at the surface.
4. Let the tuna rest for 5 minutes to set up. Slice into 6 steaks, and serve topped with the ponzu sauce.

LOBSTER GRILLED WITH SEAFOOD BUTTER

TIMING
Prep: 15 minutes
(plus 5 minutes for rub)
Grill: About 15 minutes

GRILL TOOLS AND EQUIPMENT
· Long-handled spatula or
long-handled tongs

It isn't easy to kill. Yet most of us do it one way or the other every time we cook. Few of us have pangs about taking a life when opening a can of tuna, but when it comes to grilling lobster it's a little harder to feign innocence. Lobsters must be cooked within minutes of dying (shellfish decompose quickly after death), so you have to either buy them cooked or do the deed yourself. It's easiest to boil them, but that leaves them with a steamed flavor that is antithetical to the intensity of the grill. We encourage you to follow the directions below, cooking the lobster completely on the grill, but if you really want to avoid the hand-to-hand combat required, you can boil the lobsters in a large pot of salted water just until they are bright red, split them in half lengthwise, and proceed with the rest of the recipe.

THE GRILL

Gas: Indirect heat, medium (325° to 350°F)
3- or 4-burner grill–middle burner(s) off
2-burner grill–1 side off
Clean, oiled grate

Charcoal: Indirect heat, medium ash
Split charcoal bed (about 2 dozen coals per side)
20 replacement coals
Heavy-duty drip pan set between banks of charcoal
Clean, oiled grate on medium setting

INGREDIENTS (MAKES 4 SERVINGS)

4 live lobsters, about 1 pound each
6 tablespoons Green Chimichurri Rub (page 381)
2 tablespoons chopped fresh dill
3 tablespoons unsalted butter

Finely grated zest and juice of 1 lime
1 teaspoon green hot pepper sauce
3 tablespoons extra-virgin olive oil
Oil for coating grill grate

DIRECTIONS

1. Heat the grill as directed.

2. Put a lobster on its belly on a rimmed sheet pan. Hold a sharp knife with the blade perpendicular to the length of the lobster. Insert the knife into the back of the lobster where the shell of the thorax meets the shell of the head (see the illustration on page 70). Remove the knife and turn the blade parallel to the length of the lobster. Starting at the place where you just inserted the knife, cut down the length of the lobster through the center of the thorax and the tail. Turn the lobster onto its back and cut it in half lengthwise. Remove and discard the sand sac from behind the head. Remove the light green tomalley from the body cavity and, if present, the long sac of dark green roe that runs down the back of the lobster, and put them in a small skillet or saucepan. Crack the claws by whacking them across the crest of their bulge with the back of a heavy knife. Put the lobster halves on a plate that will catch their juices. Repeat with the remaining lobsters.

3. Drain any liquid that has collected on the lobster plate into the pan holding the tomalley. Cook over medium-low heat just until the lobster drippings turn white and the tomalley brightens, about 1 minute. Cool.

4. In a food processor, purée the tomalley mixture with 2 tablespoons of the rub, the dill, the butter, about one-fourth of the lime zest and juice, and the hot pepper sauce until the mixture is smooth and thick; set aside.

5. Mix the olive oil with the remaining 4 tablespoons rub and spoon the mixture over the exposed lobster meat.

6. Brush the grill grate and coat it with oil. Put the lobsters, cut-sides down, on the grill directly over the heat. Cover and grill for about 4 minutes, until the edges start to brown. Turn the lobsters over and move them away from the heat. Cover and grill until an instant-read thermometer inserted into the meat registers about 140°F, about 10 minutes. If your grill has a temperature gauge, it should stay at around 350°F.

7. Remove the lobsters to a large serving platter. Drizzle the meat with the remaining lime zest and juice, and place a dollop of the seafood butter in the open space of each lobster half so that people can dip the lobster meat into it as they eat.

WILD SALMON GRILLED WITH LEEKS AND SALMON ROE SALSA

TIMING
Prep: 20 minutes
Grill: 20 minutes

GRILL TOOLS AND EQUIPMENT
· Long-handled fish spatula
· Grill screen or large fish-grilling basket

Whole farm-raised salmon is a little tricky to grill. The fish tend to be large and thick, making it difficult to cook them through before they dry out on the surface. Wild salmon are much leaner and cook through more quickly. This one is slashed and embedded with grilled leeks and herbs, and then served with a sophisticated salsa made from salmon roe (salmon caviar) and freshly grated horseradish root.

THE GRILL

Gas: Indirect heat, medium (325° to 350°F)
3- or 4-burner grill–middle burner(s) off
2-burner grill–1 side off
Clean, oiled grate

Charcoal: Indirect heat, medium ash
Split charcoal bed (about 2 dozen coals per side)
Clean, oiled grate on medium setting

INGREDIENTS (MAKES 6 SERVINGS)

3 small leeks (about 3 ounces each), dark greens removed
3 tablespoons extra-virgin olive oil
Oil for coating grill grate and screen or basket
2 lemons
1 tablespoon butter
2 tablespoons chopped fresh dill
2 cloves garlic, minced
$1/4$ teaspoon kosher salt, plus more to taste

$1/4$ teaspoon ground black pepper, plus more to taste
1 wild salmon, about 4 pounds, head, scales, and fins removed
1 ounce horseradish, freshly grated (about $1/4$ cup)
1 small cucumber, peeled, halved lengthwise, seeded, and finely diced
1 jar (4 ounces) salmon roe caviar
2 tablespoons thinly sliced chives

DIRECTIONS

1. Heat the grill as directed.

2. Cut the hairy roots from the ends of the leeks where they meet the bulb. Do not cut into the bulb of the leek or it will fall apart when you grill it. Cut the leeks in half lengthwise. Run cold water through the leek leaves to wash out sand deposits that tend to collect in the outer leaves. Pat dry and coat with 2 teaspoons of the olive oil.

3. Brush the grill grate and coat it with oil. Put the leeks, cut-side down, on the grill directly over the fire. Cover and cook until browned, about 5 minutes. Flip the leeks, cover, and cook for about 3 minutes more, until tender. Transfer to a cutting board and chop finely.

4. Remove the zest from the lemons with a fine grater; reserve half for the salsa. In a bowl, mix the remaining zest, leeks, butter, dill, 1 clove garlic, 1 tablespoon of the olive oil, $1/4$ teaspoon salt, and $1/4$ teaspoon pepper.

5. Scrape the dull side of a knife against the skin of the salmon, running from tail to head, to remove excess moisture and fine scales. Cut 6 diagonal slices through the flesh of the fish on each side down to the bone. Place on a rimmed

baking sheet. Fill the slits with the leek mixture and rub any excess into the interior cavity. Squeeze the juice from the lemons and pour half of it all over the fish; set aside.

6. Make the salsa by combining the horseradish, remaining lemon zest and lemon juice, cucumber, salmon roe, chives, and salt and pepper to taste in a bowl; keep refrigerated.

7. Coat the salmon on all sides with the remaining 4 teaspoons olive oil. Oil the grill screen or fish basket liberally. Put the screen or basket on the grill away from the heat, cover, and cook until an instant-read thermometer inserted into the thickest part of the salmon registers 130°F (until the fish barely flakes when gently pressed), about 20 minutes, turning halfway through. If your grill has a temperature gauge, it should stay at around 375°F.

8. If the skin should tear when you flip the fish, don't worry about it. Simply peel the skin off before serving. Use the slashes in the flesh to help portion the fish. Serve with the salsa.

CHAPTER 8

MASTERING THE BIG KAHUNA AND OTHER INCREDIBLE GRILL PROJECTS

RECIPES

GRILL TOOLS AND EQUIPMENT
- Heavy-duty aluminum foil
- Large needle, preferably curved (an upholstery needle works great)
- Heavy-duty thread
- Heavy-duty cotton kitchen twine
- Ti, palm, or banana leaves
- Large carving board

LOMI LOMI SALMON

This marinated salmon salad is a traditional luau side dish.

Makes about 15 servings

2 pounds salmon fillet, skin and bones removed
Kosher salt, as needed
4 tomatoes, stemmed and diced
1 small red onion, diced
3 scallions, trimmed and thinly sliced
Juice of 1 lime
1/4 to 1/2 teaspoon hot pepper sauce
Ground black pepper to taste

Slice the salmon thinly. Sprinkle generously with kosher salt, cover with plastic wrap, and refrigerate for 1 hour. Rinse and pat dry. Cut into small pieces and toss with the remaining ingredients.

PROCURING A PIG

A suckling pig is not just a small pig; it is an infant. The North American Meat Processors Association has developed guidelines for butchering and sizing animals, to which all butchers subscribe. Under these guidelines animals are categorized by size, A through D. Unless you have a gargantuan grill, you want to purchase a pig in the A weight range, which is 12 to 24 pounds. These will cost much more per pound than larger pigs, but you will end up paying about the same amount for the whole pig. Most supermarket meat departments will not be able to get an item this specific, so we suggest you look for a good-quality Italian or Hispanic butcher. You can order frozen suckling pigs online from www.mcreynoldsfarms.com.

The Hawaiian luau is an over-the-top eating extravaganza—the big kahuna of Hawaiian cooking. The centerpiece is kalua pig (*ka* meaning "the," and *lua* meaning "hole"), which refers to the method of cooking in an *imu*, a Polynesian pit oven. Digging the pit, constructing the *imu*, and cooking the pig is an all-day affair (literally all day, requiring about 18 hours). So we offer a modified mainland method that is impressive in its own right. Even so, your standard gas or kettle grill will not suffice. A big barrel-shaped smoker-grill or a premium gigantic gas grill will work well; otherwise, you will have to rent a large party grill.

THE GRILL (MINIMUM 36-INCH-WIDE BY 24-INCH-DEEP FIRE BED)

Gas: Indirect heat, low (225° to 250°F)
3- or 4-burner grill–middle burner(s) off
Clean, oiled grate

Charcoal: Indirect heat, heavy ash
Split charcoal bed (about 3 dozen coals per side)
60 to 80 replacement coals

Large, heavy-duty drip pan set between banks of charcoal
Clean, oiled grate on high setting

Wood: Indirect heat, heavy ash
2 beds, 8 by 8 inches, 2 inches deep
Additional wood for replacement
Clean, oiled grate set 6 to 8 inches above the fire

INGREDIENTS (MAKES ABOUT 15 SERVINGS)

For the pig:
2 tablespoons canola oil
2 cups unsweetened shredded coconut
2 cups long-grain rice
1 can (about 14 ounces) coconut milk
2 1/4 cups water
1/4 teaspoon crushed red pepper flakes
2 teaspoons kosher salt
1 1/2 cups coarsely chopped dried pineapple (6 ounces)
1/2 cup coarsely chopped crystallized ginger (2 ounces)
1 cup chopped dried apricots (4 ounces)
1 cup dried tart cherries
4 scallions, trimmed and thinly sliced
1 teaspoon vanilla extract
1 suckling pig, dressed, about 20 pounds (left)
2 cups Red-Cooking Lacquer (page 385)
1 lime (optional)

For the fruit and onions:
1 cup light brown sugar
1/2 cup dark rum
1 teaspoon ground cardamom
1 teaspoon toasted sesame oil
1 large pineapple, peeled, cored, and sliced into 1/2-inch-thick rings
1 papaya, peeled, seeded, and sliced into wedges
2 star fruit, cut into 1/4-inch slices
1 orange, thickly sliced
2 limes, sliced
2 large sweet onions, such as Maui, peeled and sliced into 1/2-inch-thick rings

Lomi Lomi Salmon (recipe at left; optional)

DIRECTIONS

1. For the pig, heat the oil in a large, heavy saucepan over medium-high heat. Add the coconut and stir until lightly toasted, about 3 minutes.

2. Add the rice and stir to coat with the oil. Add the coconut milk, water, red pepper flakes, and salt. Bring to a boil, stirring occasionally. Reduce the heat to a simmer, cover, and simmer until the rice is tender, about 15 minutes. Stir in the pineapple, ginger, apricots, cherries, scallions, and vanilla. Cool completely. The stuffing can be made a day ahead and refrigerated; bring to room temperature before continuing.

3. Brush the cavity of the pig with 1/2 cup of the Red-Cooking Lacquer. Loosely fill the pig with the rice stuffing and sew the cavity shut, using the needle and heavy-duty thread.

4. Position the legs under the pig. The front legs will rest under the chin (the pig might come this way from the butcher), and the back legs should be set forward, bent from the hip, not the

knee, so they extend along the belly. Tie the legs in place with several lengths of heavy-duty kitchen twine (see the illustration at left). Position the ears so that they cover the pig's eyes, and tie twine over the ears to hold them in place. Cover the snout and tail with aluminum foil. Place a double thickness of foil around the front feet and under the loin and the back feet in the center of the pig. Stuff a ball of foil (or a block of wood) in the pig's mouth if you are planning to serve it with a lime in its mouth.

5. Heat the grill as directed. Spread a double layer of aluminum foil on the grill grate, covering the area that is not directly over the heat. Line the foil with 2 to 3 layers of ti, palm, or banana leaves, and put the pig right-side up on top of the leaves. Cook, covered, for 2 hours, until the surface has begun to brown. If your grill has a temperature gauge, it should stay between 200° and 250°F. Replenish the charcoal or wood after the first hour.

6. Snip the twine and remove. Coat the outside of the pig with half of the remaining lacquer, cover the grill, and cook until an instant-read thermometer inserted into the thickest part of one of the thighs registers 160°F, making sure that the thermometer is not touching bone, about 1 1/2 hours longer. Brush with the remaining lacquer halfway through, and keep the temperature gauge at around 225°F.

7. For the fruit and onions, while the pig is roasting, mix the brown sugar, rum, cardamom, and sesame oil in a large saucepan; heat until the sugar dissolves. Cool. Add the fruit and onion slices just before the pig is done, and toss to coat.

8. Line a large carving board with ti, palm, or banana leaves. Remove the pig to the board and let it rest.

9. Grill the fruit and onion directly over the heat until browned on both sides, about 4 minutes per side, brushing several times with any extra glaze.

10. Pull the thread from the belly of the pig, and replace the wooden block or foil ball in the mouth with the lime, if desired; carve by cutting the pig into leg and shoulder sections and carving the meat from the bone. Cut the ribs into 2-rib sections. Serve the meat with the stuffing, grilled fruit and onions, and Lomi Lomi Salmon, if desired.

TIMING
Prep: 10 minutes
Brine: 1 hour
Grill: About 15 minutes

GRILL TOOLS AND EQUIPMENT
· Long-handled spatula
· Long-handled tongs
· Grill screen

MIXED GRILL WITH FENNEL AND FIGS

Mixed grill was probably the first cooked meal ever served. It's easy to imagine: a variety of meats from the day's hunt, cooked over the communal fire and eaten, not in courses, but all at once, juices and flavors mingling and enhancing one another. Our selection is largely poultry, mingling game hen, duck breast, and sausage with fresh figs, orange, and fennel.

THE GRILL

Gas: Direct heat, medium-low (300°F)
          Clean, oiled grate
Charcoal: Direct heat, medium ash
          12-by-12-inch charcoal bed (about 3 dozen coals)
          Clean, oiled grate on medium setting

Wood: Direct heat, medium ash
          12-by-12-inch bed, 3 inches deep
          Clean, oiled grate set 4 inches above the fire

INGREDIENTS (MAKES 6 SERVINGS)

3 game hens, about 1 1/2 pounds each, split lengthwise
3 boneless (but not skinless) Muscovy duck breast halves, about 8 ounces each, skin scored with 3 or 4 slashes
4 cups Orange-Fennel Brine (page 362)
1 ounce pancetta or bacon, finely chopped
1 cup white wine
1 cup orange juice

12 fresh figs, halved lengthwise
12 small fennel twigs (optional)
2 tablespoons extra-virgin olive oil
6 sausage links (your choice—anything from mild Italian to lamb with garlic)
Oil for coating grill grate
3 tablespoons unsalted butter, cut into pieces

DIRECTIONS

1. Put the game hen halves and duck breasts in a gallon-size zipper-lock bag with the brine. Seal the zipper, leaving about an inch open; push on the bag to release any trapped air through the opening, and close the zipper completely. Massage the liquid gently into the meat and refrigerate for about 1 hour.

2. Meanwhile, heat the pancetta in a small saucepan until the fat renders. Add the wine and orange juice and boil until reduced to 1 cup; set aside.

3. Heat the grill as directed.

4. Spear each fig half with a fennel twig (if desired) and coat the figs with the olive oil. Poke the sausages several times with a fork.

5. Remove the game hen halves and duck breasts from the brine; discard the brine. Pat dry. Brush the grill grate and coat it with oil; put the hens, skin-side down, on the grill. Cover and

cook for 5 minutes. Turn, and put the duck breasts, skin-side down, and the sausages on the grill. Cover and grill until an instant-read thermometer inserted into the thickest part of a game hen breast, a duck breast, or the end of a sausage registers 165°F, about 12 minutes, turning the sausages and duck breasts halfway through.

6. Remove everything to a large serving platter and keep warm. If using gas, turn the grill to high, put a grill screen on the grill, and heat for 1 minute. (If using charcoal or wood, place the grill screen over the hottest part of the fire.) Put the figs, cut-side down, on the grill screen, cover the grill, and cook until the figs have browned, about 3 minutes. Transfer to the platter.

7. Reheat the reduced wine and orange juice to boiling. Mix in the butter, stir until melted, and pour the sauce over everything. Serve immediately.

WHOLE BEEF TENDERLOIN STUFFED WITH FOIE GRAS AND MORELS

TIMING
Prep: 25 minutes
   (plus 5 minutes for rub)
Rest before grilling: 10 minutes
Grill: About 25 minutes

GRILL TOOLS AND EQUIPMENT
· Long-handled tongs
· Heavy-duty cotton kitchen twine

Under the assumption that nothing exceeds like excess, we offer this, our rendition of *übercarne*. If you can find fresh morels, the aroma will be heightened, but dried morels are wonderful as well and are a compromise only when compared to fresh. Plus they have the advantage of producing a concentrated soaking liquid that adds flavor to the stuffing when reduced. To get a jump on the meal, assemble the tenderloin ahead, refrigerate it for a day or more, and then grill it just before serving.

THE GRILL

Gas: Direct heat, medium-high (450°F)
        Clean, oiled grate

Charcoal: Direct heat, light ash
        12-by-12-inch charcoal bed (about 3 dozen coals)
        Clean, oiled grate on lowest setting

Wood: Direct heat, light ash
        12-by-12-inch bed, 3 to 4 inches deep
        Clean, oiled grate set 2 inches above the fire

INGREDIENTS (MAKES 8 SERVINGS)

6 ounces fresh morels, or 1 ounce dried morels, soaked in
    hot water and drained
4 tablespoons extra-virgin olive oil
2 shallots, finely chopped
1 clove garlic, minced
1 teaspoon chopped fresh rosemary leaves
1 plum tomato, finely chopped
1 cup beef broth or mushroom soaking liquid, if using
    dried morels

Kosher salt and ground black pepper to taste
4 ounces pâté de foie gras or goose liver pâté, broken or
    cut into pieces
1 trimmed beef tenderloin, about 5 pounds,
2 tablespoons Tuscan Rosemary Rub (page 375)
Oil for coating grill grate

DIRECTIONS

1. Heat the grill as directed.

2. Chop the morels coarsely. Heat 2 tablespoons of the olive oil in a large skillet over medium-high heat. Add the shallots, garlic, and rosemary and sauté until tender, about 2 minutes. Add the tomato and mushrooms and sauté until the vegetables soften, about 3 minutes. Add the broth or soaking liquid and simmer until the liquid is absorbed. Season with salt and pepper. Cool until barely warm, and stir in the pâté.

3. Make a lengthwise slit about halfway through the tail end of the tenderloin about 4 inches from the end, right where the meat tapers. Tie the wide end (butt end) with kitchen twine to make a neat, cylindrical shape. Fold in the tail end and tie it in place so that the tenderloin is uniformly shaped from end to end, to help it cook evenly.

4. To make a hole down the center of the tenderloin that you can stuff, position a sharpening steel at the thicker end of the tenderloin and push it through until its tip comes out the other side. Remove the steel. Insert a long, thin-bladed knife into the hole made by the steel several times, making short slits to enlarge the hole.

5. Stand the tenderloin on end and spoon the morel mixture into the hole, packing it down with the steel or the handle of a wooden spoon. When you've used about half of the stuffing, turn the tenderloin over and fill it from the other side.

6. Put the beef on a sheet of plastic wrap and rub the exterior with the remaining 2 tablespoons olive oil. Sprinkle with the rosemary rub and roll it around until coated. Wrap in the plastic and set aside for 10 minutes.

7. Brush the grill grate and coat it with oil. Put the tenderloin on the grill, cover, and cook until browned on 4 sides, 6 to 7 minutes per side. Check the temperature with an instant-read thermometer inserted into the thicker end; it should register 125°F for medium-rare. If your grill has an external temperature gauge, it should stay at around 400°F.

8. Transfer the beef to a carving board; let rest for 5 minutes. Slice into 1/2-inch-thick slices and serve.

GRILL TOOLS AND EQUIPMENT
· Long-handled tongs
· Long-handled spatula

GETTING CREATIVE
· Replace any of these recipes with another Mediterranean-style recipe in this book, such as Pesto-Stuffed Jumbo Shrimp Skewered with Grape Tomatoes (page 121), Grilled Stuffed Sardines (page 181), Roasted Onions with Gorgonzola Crumble (page 302), or Grilled Ratatouille (page 262).
· Substitute an appropriate seasonal vegetable if the vegetable called for is out of season.

TIP
· If you have fewer people to serve, prepare fewer recipes.

SHORTCUT
· Replace one or more of the recipes with fresh salads, cured sausages, or sliced cheeses.

ANTIPASTO GRIGLIATA GIGANTESCO

A grilled antipasto can be the precursor to an elaborate meal or a meal in itself. We have made a selection of grilled vegetables that could fit either scenario, but if you want to make it heartier you can add or substitute several grilled seafood dishes. Tackling all of this at once would require a detailed game plan and a level of oversight that would take all of the fun out of the activity, so we suggest you take your time. Any of these items can be grilled in advanced and served at room temperature.

THE GRILL

Gas: Direct heat, medium-high (400° to 450°F)
Clean, oiled grate

Charcoal: Direct heat, light ash
Clean, oiled grate on lowest setting

Wood: Direct heat, light ash
Clean, oiled grate set 2 inches above the fire

INGREDIENTS (MAKES 12 TO 15 SERVINGS)

Grilled Garlichokes (page 299)
Summer Squash Vinaigrette (page 266)
Grilled Tomatoes with Basil Butter (page 263)
Grilled Asparagus Wrapped in Prosciutto (page 299)
Marinated Fire-Roasted Peppers (page 276)
Grilled Caramelized Vidalia Onions (page 303)
Barbecued Balsamic Pears (page 312)

Grilled Polenta with Mediterranean Vegetable Compote (page 279)
1 loaf sourdough bread, sliced
1 cup of the best extra-virgin olive oil you can afford
1 small wedge (at least 4 ounces) well-aged (at least 1 year) Parmigiano-Reggiano cheese

DIRECTIONS

1. Prepare each of the recipes at any time, and serve at any temperature, from right off the grill to room temperature.
2. Just before serving, brush the bread slices with a thin film of olive oil and brown over direct high heat, about 20 seconds per side.

3. Arrange the antipasto recipes on a large platter and serve the toasted bread, olive oil, and cheese on the side, with a grater or cheese plane.

TIMING
Prep: 5 minutes (plus 20 minutes for rub, marinade, and sauce)
Rest before grilling: 9 to 24 hours
Soak wood chips: 1 hour
Grill: 6 to 7 hours

GRILL TOOLS AND EQUIPMENT
· 4 cups wood chunks or chips (hickory or oak)
· Smoker box or foil packet, if using a gas grill (see page 39)
· Long-handled tongs
· Large disposable aluminum foil pan

TEXAS BARBECUED BRISKET

Brisket is a tough slab of meat cut from the well-worked chest muscles of the steer. When cooked with low heat that's delivered slowly and steadily, tough brisket transforms into a tender, juicy slice of heaven. If you were to cook the same cut of meat quickly over high heat, you'd end up with chewy, dense shoe leather. It's all in the method. What you want to do is heat the meat very slowly to gradually dissolve the tough connective tissue (collagen) that surrounds the muscle fibers. Brisket has a high proportion of connective tissue to muscle fiber, so there's lots of dissolving to be done. And that takes time. Cooking slowly by the indirect heat of smoldering wood not only gives the collagen time to dissolve, it also infuses the meat with wonderful smoky aromas. This is the perfect recipe for days when you'll be outside all day anyway. Check on the meat every hour or so, drizzling it with beer and adding wood chips to the fire, and by the end of the day, you'll have enough deliriously good meat to please you and ten of your friends.

THE GRILL

Gas: Indirect heat, low (225°F)

3- or 4-burner grill–middle burner(s) off

2-burner grill–1 side off

Clean, oiled grate

Charcoal: Indirect heat, thick ash

Split charcoal bed (about 2 dozen coals per side)

60 replacement coals

Heavy-duty drip pan set between banks of charcoal

Clean, oiled grate on medium setting

Wood: Indirect heat, thick ash

12-by-12-inch bed, 1 inch deep

Additional wood for replacement

Clean, oiled grate set 6 inches above the fire

INGREDIENTS (MAKES 10 TO 12 SERVINGS)

$1/2$ cup Fragrant Chile Rub (page 372)

$2 1/2$ cups Fire Beer Marinade (page 354)

1 flat or center-cut beef brisket, 5 to 6 pounds, trimmed, with $1/4$ inch to $1/2$ inch of fat on one side

Oil for coating grill grate

$2 1/2$ cups Sweet, Hot, and Sour BBQ Sauce (page 391) or your favorite barbecue sauce (optional)

4 tablespoons ($1/2$ stick) butter (optional)

DIRECTIONS

1. Mix 1 tablespoon of the chile rub into the marinade and set aside. Scatter the remaining chile rub evenly over the brisket. Cover tightly and refrigerate for 8 to 24 hours.

2. Rest the meat at room temperature before grilling, about 1 hour.

3. Soak the wood chips in water for 1 hour. Heat the grill as directed.

4. Brush the grill grate and coat it with oil. Drain about 1 cup of wood chips and scatter $1/2$ cup over the coals on each side. If using a gas grill, drain all of the wood chips and put them in a smoker box or in a foil packet directly over one of the heated burners. Heat the gas grill to high until you see plenty of smoke, then turn the heat to low. Turn off the middle burner(s), or if you have only 2 burners, turn off the burner that doesn't have the foil over it.

5. Put the brisket, fatty-side up, on the grill away from the heat, cover the grill, and cook for 2 hours. Put the brisket in the disposable pan and set the pan on the grill away from the heat. (The pan helps to retain moisture in the brisket and keep it from drying out.) Cover the grill and continue cooking until severely browned and blackened in spots or very well-done

(about 190°F on an instant-read thermometer), 4 to 5 hours more. If using charcoal or wood, add fresh coals or wood and more wood chips when the old ones die out, about once an hour during cooking. Mop or drizzle the brisket with the marinade on both sides whenever the surface looks dry, every 40 to 60 minutes during the entire cooking time. Once the brisket is in the pan, you need to mop or drizzle only the top, fatty side. If your grill has a temperature gauge, it should stay between 250° and 300°F during the entire cooking time. If you can manage to keep it lower without the fire dying out, all the better.

6. Remove the pan of brisket from the heat and let rest for 20 minutes.

7. Heat the barbecue sauce and butter, if using, in a small saucepan over medium-low heat until the butter is incorporated into the sauce.

8. Remove the brisket to a cutting board. Trim any excess fat from the brisket and slice across the grain (don't trim too much fat, though; the crispy bits taste great). Serve with the barbecue sauce. Or skip the sauce and drizzle the sliced meat with the pan juices.

TIPS

· If using charcoal, keep the heat low by closing all the vents about three-fourths of the way immediately after adding fresh, hot coals each hour or so.

· If you use your own barbecue sauce, don't make it overly sweet, as a Kansas City sauce would be. It should be leaner and hotter, with more cider vinegar and chile pepper. You could doctor up your favorite bottled barbecue sauce by stirring in extra cider vinegar and Tabasco.

GETTING CREATIVE

· For Cajun Blackened Brisket, replace the Fragrant Chile Rub with Cajun Blackening Rub (page 373). Omit the barbecue sauce and serve only with the pan juices.

SMOKE RINGS

Brisket and other smoked meats often appear reddish-pink on the surface. When you slice into the meat, you'll see a pink ring on the surface contrasted by the familiar cooked color of the meat inside. These "smoke rings" are created by your heat source, which, in the case of barbecued brisket, is the smoldering wood and coals. According to food scientist Harold McGee, burning any organic fuel (wood, charcoal, or gas) will generate enough nitrogen dioxide (NO_2) to create pink smoke rings. The NO_2 first breaks down into nitrous acid (HNO_2) at the surface of the meat; it then transforms into nitric oxide (NO) as it penetrates the meat. When nitric oxide comes into contact with the raw meat's natural red pigment (myoglobin), it forms a pink molecule that remains pink throughout the cooking. But the nitric oxide penetrates only about $1/8$ inch into the meat. That's why the very interior of the muscle tissue on barbecued brisket has the familiar gray color of well-done meat, but the surface reveals an attractive pink smoke ring.

PIT SMOKERS

Traditionally, Texas brisket is barbecued in a pit smoker where the heat is in one chamber (an offset firebox) and the meat is in another. The meat is far enough away from the heat that it cooks not by the radiant heat of the coals, but by the relatively cool heat of the smoke. The temperature in the cooking chamber should remain a low 200° to 225°F throughout the entire cooking time. If you have a pit grill with an offset firebox, by all means use it for this recipe, and keep the heat as low as possible. Most people own gas or charcoal grills, however, so we've given the method for grill-roasting a brisket on these grills, using indirect heat and wood chips or chunks. The temperature is a bit higher than in a pit barbecue because the heat is closer to the meat. Nonetheless, you can still turn out a tender, juicy, smoky brisket from your average backyard grill. All it takes is time.

FISH STUFFED WITH FIVE-TREASURE JASMINE RICE ROASTED IN A LOTUS LEAF

Lotus is an olfactory orgasm; a deep whiff can lead to momentary swooning. The magic of cooking in lotus is that its intoxicating fragrance infuses anything it touches. Lotus leaves come dried and are available in Asian groceries. They are huge, spanning 2 feet or more. All you have to do is soak them in a sink (or large bowl) filled with warm water until they become pliable, about 10 minutes. The fish in this recipe is left whole, but its main skeletal bones are removed, making it easy to serve.

THE GRILL

Gas: Indirect heat, medium-high (350° to 375°F)
3- or 4-burner grill–middle burner(s) off
2-burner grill–1 side off
Clean, oiled grate

Charcoal: Indirect heat, medium ash
Split charcoal bed (about 2 dozen coals per side)
Clean, oiled grate on medium to low setting

Wood: Indirect heat, medium ash
12-by-12-inch bed, 3 inches deep
Clean, oiled grate set 4 inches above the fire

INGREDIENTS (MAKES 6 SERVINGS)

For the stuffing:

2 cups brewed jasmine tea made from 2 teabags or
2 tablespoons loose tea
1 1/2 cups sushi rice
2 teaspoons soy sauce
2 tablespoons chopped crystallized ginger
1 large dried fig, chopped
2 tablespoons shredded unsweetened coconut
1/2 teaspoon Sesame Szechwan Salt (page 380)
2 scallions, roots and wilted leaves trimmed, thinly sliced
2 tablespoons sliced or slivered almonds
2 tablespoons chopped fresh cilantro

For the fish:

2 whole red snappers or sea bass, about 2 pounds each, scales, gills, and fins removed
4 dried lotus leaves
2 tablespoons soy sauce
Juice of 1 lemon
2 teaspoons toasted sesame oil
Oil for coating grill grate and grill screen

DIRECTIONS

1. To make the stuffing, combine the brewed tea, rice, and soy sauce in a large saucepan; cover and heat to boiling over medium heat. Reduce the heat to low and simmer until the liquid is absorbed, about 15 minutes.

2. Add the crystallized ginger, fig, coconut, Szechwan salt, scallions, almonds, and cilantro to the pan (do not mix); cover and set aside for 5 minutes. Fluff with a fork, mixing the ingredients evenly into the rice.

3. While the rice is cooking, remove the central skeleton from the fish (see sidebar at right). Submerge the lotus leaves in a large bowl of hot water. Soak until pliable, about 10 minutes.

4. Heat the grill as described.

5. Brush the fish inside and out with the soy sauce, lemon juice, and sesame oil. Place 2 lotus leaves on top of one

another (dark-side down), and spread them out flat. Place a fish at one edge, and fill with half the stuffing. Fold the edges of the leaves over the ends of the fish and roll the fish up in the leaves until the package is completely encased; secure the loose end with a wooden toothpick. Repeat with the other fish and the remaining lotus leaves and stuffing. Oil the grill screen and put the lotus-wrapped fish on the screen, toothpick-side down.

6. Brush and oil the grill grate. Put the grill screen on the grill, positioning the fish away from the fire. Cover the grill and cook for 8 to 10 minutes per side; let rest for 5 minutes.

7. Slit open the lotus wrappers and serve.

TIMING
Prep: 40 minutes
(plus 5 minutes for Szechwan salt)
Grill: About 20 minutess

GRILL TOOLS AND EQUIPMENT
· Grill screen
· Long-handled spatula

REMOVING THE BONES FROM A WHOLE FISH
You will need:
· Clean cutting board
· Sharp, narrow-bladed knife (boning knife)
· Heavy-duty scissors

1. Lay the fish on its side on the cutting board, with its back facing the hand holding the knife. Make a slit through the skin just above and running along the central back ridge of the fish (see photo 2).

2. Using short strokes, work your knife along the bones supporting the dorsal fin (see the illustration), lifting the flesh from the bone down the length of the backbone, all the way from the head to the tail. As you are cutting, you should feel bone against one side of the knife at all times. This will ensure that you aren't leaving edible flesh on the carcass.

3. Continue cutting until the entire back-bone is exposed and you have cut over the ribs where the ribs end in the belly. One side of the rib cage should now be separate from the flesh of the fish (see photo 3).

4. To separate the flesh from the tail end of the fish, lay the flat side of the knife against the backbone, with the blade facing the tail. Hold the head end of the fish steady and cut back toward the tail, cutting through the skin connecting to the anal fin (see the illustration), but stopping before you get all the way to the tail. One side of the fish will now be separate from the skeleton but will still be attached at the head and tail.

5. Turn the fish over and fillet the other side in the same way.

6. Using scissors, cut the backbone where it connects to the head and again where it connects to the tail. Remove the skeleton. Use the tip of your knife to remove any small bones still remaining along the belly.

Photos:
1. Soaking lotus in sink
2. Beginning boning fish
3. Finishing boning fish
4. Wrapping stuffed fish
5. Fish on grill
6. Unwrapped and cut fish

GRILL TOOLS AND EQUIPMENT
· Large rimmed sheet pan
· 2 sturdy spatulas for lifting the roast

HERBED PRIME RIB WITH HORSERADISH YORKSHIRE PUDDING

Nothing surpasses the sight (and the smell) of prime rib encrusted with garlic and herbs emerging from the grill. Although this recipe is spectacular with any grade of beef, use it as an excuse to treat yourself to real prime rib. Only 2 percent of the beef in the United States is graded prime, and most of that never reaches the retail market, so you will have to seek it out. A trusted butcher can order it for you even if it is something he doesn't normally carry. Ask your butcher to cut the meat from the bone along the ribs, but leave it attached at its widest end. There are also many Internet sites that sell prime rib roasts, such as lobels.com and nfrnaturalbeef.com.

THE GRILL

Gas: Indirect heat, medium (325° to 350°F)
            3- or 4-burner grill—middle burner(s) off
            2-burner grill—1 side off
            Clean, oiled grate

Charcoal: Indirect heat, medium ash
              Split charcoal bed (about 2 dozen coals per side)
              30 replacement coals
              Heavy-duty drip pan set between banks of charcoal
              Clean, oiled grate on medium setting

INGREDIENTS (MAKES 14 SERVINGS)

For the beef:

7-bone prime rib roast of beef, about 7 pounds
1/2 cup chopped fresh herbs (rosemary, flat-leaf parsley, oregano, thyme, and/or basil)
8 cloves garlic, minced
2 tablespoons extra-virgin olive oil
2 teaspoons kosher salt
2 teaspoons ground black pepper

For the pudding:

6 eggs, large or extra-large
2 1/4 cups milk
1 teaspoon kosher salt
1/2 teaspoon ground black pepper
2 cups flour
1/3 cup drippings from the beef
2 tablespoons freshly grated horseradish or jarred horseradish, drained

DIRECTIONS

1. Heat the grill as directed.

2. If the meat was not cut from the bone when you purchased it (see the recipe introduction), do this yourself, leaving it attached at its widest end.

3. Mix the herbs, garlic, olive oil, salt, and pepper in a small bowl and rub all over the meat, including the underside where it is sitting on the bones.

4. Put the roast, bone-side down, on a large rimmed sheet pan and put it on the grill away from the heat. Cover the grill and cook for about 1 hour. Check the drippings in the pan; there should be about 1/2 cup. Remove the pan and keep the drippings in it. Return the beef to the grill away from the heat. Cover the grill and continue cooking until an instant-read

thermometer inserted into the thickest part registers about 130°F for medium-rare, about 1 1/2 more hours. If your grill has a temperature gauge, it should stay at around 350°F. If using charcoal, you may have to replenish coals after each hour.

5. Just before the beef is finished cooking, combine all of the ingredients for the Yorkshire pudding in a bowl and stir just until combined.

6. Remove the beef to a large carving board and keep warm. Return the sheet pan to the grill; cover and heat for a minute or two. Add the pudding batter, spreading it to cover the pan; cover and cook until puffed and browned at the edges, 10 to 15 minutes.

7. Slice the roast and cut the pudding into 14 pieces; serve.

CLAMBAKE ON THE GRILL

TIMING
Soak wood chips: 1 hour
Prep: 30 minutes
Grill: 1 to 1 1/2 hours

Seaside clambakes are a New England tradition. Native Americans are said to have taught the Pilgrims the technique, which is an all-day undertaking. For an authentic clambake on the beach, you dig a big pit in the sand about 2 to 3 feet deep and line the pit with rocks. Then you burn plenty of wood over the rocks for 2 to 3 hours, until the rocks are smoking hot (about 400°F). After you've raked away the coals, layers of seaweed, potatoes, corn, small clams, mussels, and sometimes sausages or other ingredients go directly over the hot rocks. Add some more seaweed, top with a huge, sea-soaked burlap tarp and more hot rocks, and let the whole shebang steam until the food is cooked through and infused with the briny aroma of the sea. If you don't have a beach nearby (or enough wood to burn for 3 hours), here's the backyard method. We use a covered kettle grill as the pit and rehydrated store-bought seaweed in place of fresh seaweed. The ingredients are layered in a large roasting pan, and the pan is put directly on the coals on the bottom of the grill. You could also do this on a gas grill with medium heat under the roasting pan, but we like the charcoal kettle grill because it's closer to the original method.

GRILL TOOLS AND EQUIPMENT
- Large roasting pan, such as a turkey roaster (heavy-duty if disposable)
- Heat-resistant grill mitts (preferably heatproof silicone)
- Long-handled tongs
- 40-by-15-inch piece of burlap
- 2 cups wood chunks or chips, preferably oak

TIPS
- Look for dried kombu seaweed in an Asian grocery store or large supermarket.
- Soaking mussels in salt water helps to rid them of any lingering sand. Mix 1/2 cup of salt in about a gallon of water in a large bowl. Add the mussels and let soak for 1 hour. Then scrub the mussels with a stiff brush under running water and yank off the mosslike "beard," using pliers if necessary.
- For the burlap, an old coffee sack works well. Ask for one at your local coffee shop. Some hardware stores also carry burlap.

THE GRILL

Gas: Indirect heat, medium (325° to 350°F)
3- or 4-burner grill–middle burner(s) on medium-low

Charcoal: Indirect heat, medium ash
Split charcoal bed (about 2 dozen coals per side), single layer of coals in center
20 replacement coals

INGREDIENTS (MAKES 10 TO 12 SERVINGS)

3 ounces dried kombu (kelp) seaweed (see Tips)
3 pounds small red-skinned or white potatoes, scrubbed
1 tablespoon crab boil seasoning, such as Old Bay, or sea salt
2 onions, peeled, leaving the root end intact, and cut lengthwise into eighths
12 ounces cured Portuguese linguiça or Spanish chorizo, sliced 1/2 inch thick

8 ears fresh corn, shucked and halved crosswise
3 dozen littleneck or small cherrystone clams
3 dozen mussels, scrubbed and debearded (see Tips)
1 small bunch flat-leaf parsley
6 live lobsters, 1 to 1 1/2 pounds each
1 cup (2 sticks) butter, melted
2 lemons, cut into wedges

DIRECTIONS

1. Heat the grill as directed. Soak the wood chunks or chips in water for 1 hour.

2. Bring a large pot of water to a boil. Remove from the heat and add the kombu, letting it soak until softened, about 5 minutes. Reserve the soaking liquid.

3. Put a thick layer of seaweed over the bottom of a large roasting pan such as a turkey roaster (heavy-duty if disposable), reserving some of the seaweed for the top layer. Put the potatoes in a single layer over the seaweed. Sprinkle the potatoes with a little of the crab boil seasoning, then add layers of onions, corn, sausage, clams, and mussels, in that order, sprinkling some crab boil seasoning and a few parsley sprigs over each layer. Pour about 1 cup of the seaweed soaking liquid over all of the ingredients. Arrange the remaining seaweed over the top. Soak the burlap in the remaining soaking liquid until saturated, 5 minutes. Fold the burlap to make a double thickness, then drape it over the seaweed, tucking the edges inside the roasting pan to cover the ingredients.

4. Rake a single layer of hot coals over the center of the grill, leaving the remaining hot coals banked on opposite sides. Put half of the soaked wood chunks or chips over the coals on the

sides. When the wood begins to smolder, put the roasting pan over the coals in the middle of the grill, cover the grill, and cook with the vents open until the potatoes are tender and the clams and mussels have opened, 1 to 1 1/2 hours. Test the potatoes by lifting up a corner of the cover, digging down with tongs, and poking the potatoes with a knife or fork. Add the replacement coals and the remaining wood chunks to both sides of the grill when the old ones begin to die out. If your grill has a temperature gauge, it should stay at around 350°F.

5. About 30 minutes before serving, bring 2 large pots of salted water to a boil. Add half the lobsters to each pot. Cover and cook until the shells are bright red, 8 to 12 minutes per batch. Remove and cover loosely with foil to keep warm.

6. Remove the roasting pan from the grill and transfer to a large trivet for serving. Or transfer the ingredients to a large serving platter. Discard the seaweed, parsley, and any clams or mussels that have not opened. Pour any juices from the bottom of the pan over the clambake. Sprinkle with a bit more crab boil seasoning. Cut the cooked lobsters in half lengthwise and arrange on top. Serve with the melted butter for drizzling or dipping, and lemon wedges for squeezing.

TIMING
Prep: 20 minutes
    (plus 5 minutes for rub and chimichurri)
Rest before grilling: 1 hour
Grill: About 1 1/4 hours

GRILL TOOLS AND EQUIPMENT
- Kitchen twine
- Spray bottle filled with water
- Heat-resistant gloves or
  2 large spatulas for lifting the roast

WORKING WITH A SMALLER GRILL

If your grill won't accommodate the entire roast in the center of the grill completely away from the heat, push all the coals to one side instead of banking them on either side of your charcoal grill. If you have a gas grill, heat the burners on only one side of the grill instead of heating the outside burners. This positions the meat opposite a single heated area rather than between two heated areas. Either way, there should be no heat directly beneath the roast.

DIFFERENT LINKS

Any cured or fully cooked sausages can be used in this recipe. We like long, skinny types such as chorizo because they are slender and long enough to stuff the whole length of the roast. You could replace the chorizo with *lap cheong*, a smoked Chinese sausage made with pork, soy sauce, and paprika. Or try another other long, skinny sausage. Any type will do. If you're using a smaller roast, shorter sausages work well too. Try slender *cervelat* (smoked German sausage made with pork and beef) or tender salami such as Hungarian salami or salami Genovese. The less firm the better, since the sausages won't soften much in the center of the roast.

CHILE-RUBBED STRIP ROAST LARDED WITH SAUSAGES

A strip roast is the whole loin of beef, also known as sirloin strip roast, shell roast, or top loin roast. This is the piece of meat that individual strip steaks are cut from. We're talking about 8 to 10 pounds of flavorful boneless beef. Look for this large roast sold whole in discount chain stores such as Costco. Or ask your butcher for one (it's a good idea to order ahead of time). The beauty of the whole top loin is that it can be cut into smaller roasts or steaks. If you want a smaller roast, cut some strip steaks as thick as you like and roast the rest. The cooking time won't vary much because the thickness of the roast remains the same. The flavor here is akin to prime rib and the meat is expensive, so serve this roast for a special occasion with a crowd. We burrow a few tunnels in the roast and stuff them with various sausages—pure indulgence. This whole roast can be cooked on your average-size kettle grill or gas grill. If your grill is on the small side, see "Working with a Smaller Grill" at left.

THE GRILL

Gas: Indirect heat, medium (325° to 350°F)
3- or 4-burner grill–middle burner(s) off
2-burner grill–1 side off
Clean, oiled grate

Charcoal: Indirect heat, medium ash
Split charcoal bed (about 2 dozen coals per side)
20 replacement coals
Heavy-duty drip pan set between banks of charcoal
Clean, oiled grate on medium setting

INGREDIENTS (MAKES 10 TO 12 SERVINGS)

1 whole boneless beef strip roast, about 10 pounds, surface fat trimmed to 1/4 to 1/2 inch
12 ounces long, skinny cured or cooked sausages, such as Spanish chorizo or Portuguese linguiça

1/2 cup Mild Chile Rub (a variation of Fragrant Chile Rub, page 372)
Oil for coating grill grate
2 cups Red Pepper Chimichurri (page 397)

DIRECTIONS

1. Make 3 tunnels in the center of the roast that you can stuff. To make each hole, push a sharpening steel through the meat on one side, then repeat in the same location on the other side so that the two tunnels meet to create one long tunnel. Insert a long, thin-bladed knife into the tunnel on both sides and cut slightly to enlarge the tunnel just enough to fit the sausages snugly.

2. Cut any pointed tips off the ends of the sausages. If the sausages are longer than the roast or are bent in the middle, cut the sausages in half. Stuff the sausages into each tunnel from either side so that the sausage pieces meet in the middle of each tunnel. You should have 3 tunnels completely stuffed with sausages.

3. Sprinkle the chile rub all over the roast, patting it in with your fingers. Let the meat rest at room temperature before grilling, about 1 hour.

4. Heat the grill as directed.

5. Brush the grill grate and coat it with oil. Put the roast on the grill grate directly over the heat to sear it briefly, 2 to 4 minutes per side. Douse any flare-ups with water from a spray bottle. Once it is grill-marked, move the roast to the unheated part of the grill with the fatty side up. There should be no heat directly beneath the roast. Cover the grill and cook until an instant-read thermometer inserted into the thickest part of the meat registers 125° to 130°F for medium-rare, about 60 to 80 minutes. For even browning, rotate the roast from end to end once during cooking. If the roast browns too much on the bottom sides, shield those sides with foil. If using charcoal, you'll probably need to add fresh coals after about an hour. If your grill has a temperature gauge, it should stay at around 350°F.

6. Remove the roast to a large serving platter, cover loosely, and let rest for 20 minutes. Carve the roast into slices no thicker than 1/2 inch.

7. Serve with the chimichurri.

HONEY-GLAZED ROAST SUCKLING PIG

TIMING

Soak wood chunks: 1 hour
Prep: 30 minutes
Grill: 3 to 4 hours

The glow on this pig is built in layers, like an Old World painting. First it is under-painted with a ruby-colored spice rub, after which transparent layers of golden smoke gild its surface. Finally, it is lacquered with honey for a crackled, crystalline skin that's as good as the melt-in-your-mouth meat beneath. Be strict about the size of the pig (see sidebar at right). Even a small suckling pig under 20 pounds will take up at least 2 feet of grill space, which means you will need a large, barrel-shaped grill or a gas grill with at least that much space between its outside burners to cook the pig correctly. If any part of the pig hangs directly over the fire, it will scorch; wrapping that part in heavy-duty foil will help, but it will not completely solve the problem. A big enough grill is key.

GRILL TOOLS AND EQUIPMENT

- 12 chunks apple or hickory wood (if not cooked on a wood fire)
- Heavy-duty aluminum foil
- Long-handled tongs
- Long-handled basting brush
- Large carving board

PROCURING A PIG

A suckling pig is not just a small pig; it is an infant. The North American Meat Processors Association has developed guidelines for butchering and sizing animals, to which all butchers subscribe. Under these guidelines animals are categorized by size, A through D. Unless you have a gargantuan grill, you want to purchase a pig in the A weight range, which is 12 to 24 pounds. These will cost much more per pound than larger pigs, but you will end up paying about the same amount for the whole pig. Most supermarket meat departments will not be able to get an item this specific, so we suggest you look for a good-quality Italian or Hispanic butcher. You can order frozen suckling pigs online from www.mcreynoldsfarms.com.

THE GRILL (MINIMUM 36-INCH-WIDE FIRE BED)

Gas: Indirect heat, low (225°F)
3- or 4-burner grill—middle burner(s) off
Clean, oiled grate

Charcoal: Indirect heat, heavy ash
Split charcoal bed (about 3 dozen coals per side)
Large, heavy-duty drip pan set between
    banks of charcoal

60 to 80 replacement coals
Clean, oiled grate on high setting

Wood: Indirect heat, heavy ash
2 beds, 8 by 8 inches and 2 inches deep
Additional wood for replacement
Clean, oiled grate set 6 to 8 inches above the fire

INGREDIENTS (MAKES 8 SERVINGS)

For the pig:
3 heads garlic, minced
1/3 cup honey
1/4 cup kosher salt
1 tablespoon ground black pepper
1/4 cup hot paprika
1 teaspoon ground cloves
1 tablespoon crushed dried rosemary
1/2 cup canola oil

1 suckling pig, dressed, about 20 pounds
    (see "Procuring a Pig," right)
Oil for coating grill grate
1 apple (optional)

For the glaze:
2 cups apple cider vinegar
2 cups honey
1 cup soy sauce
1/2 cup ketchup

DIRECTIONS

1. Heat the grill as directed. Soak the wood chunks in water for at least 1 hour.

2. Mix the garlic, honey, salt, black pepper, paprika, cloves, rosemary, and 1/2 cup oil in a bowl. Rub some of this mixture over the interior cavity of the pig.

3. Position the legs under the pig. The front legs will rest under the chin (the pig might come this way from the butcher), and the back legs should be set forward, bent from the hip, not the knee, so they extend along the belly. Tie the legs in place with several lengths of heavy-duty kitchen twine (see the illustration at right). Position the ears so that they cover the pig's eyes, and tie twine over the ears to hold them in place. Cover the snout and tail with aluminum foil. Place a double thickness of foil around the front feet, and under the loin and the back feet in the center of the pig. Stuff a ball of foil (or a block of wood) in the pig's mouth if you are planning to serve it with an apple in its mouth.

4. Put 3 chunks of soaked wood on each pile of charcoal, or on the grate right over the fire if using a gas grill. Brush the exposed grill grate and coat it with oil.

5. Put the pig right-side up on the grill, away from the heat. Coat with the remaining spice mixture, cover, and cook until the surface has begun to brown, about 2 hours. If your grill has a temperature gauge, it should stay between 200° and 250°F. If using charcoal or wood, you may have to replenish the coals after the first hour.

6. While the pig is cooking, mix the ingredients for the glaze in a bowl; reserve half. Snip the twine on the pig and remove. Brush the pig with the remaining glaze, being sure to get it spread evenly in all the nooks and crannies. Stoke the fire, add the remaining wood chunks, cover the grill, and cook the pig until an instant-read thermometer inserted into thickest part of one of the thighs registers 165°F, making sure that the thermometer is not touching bone, about another hour. The temperature gauge should stay between 200° and 250°F.

7. Remove the pig to a large carving board; let rest for 10 minutes. Replace the foil ball or block of wood in its mouth with an apple, if desired. Carve by cutting the pig into leg and shoulder sections and carving the meat from the bone. Cut the ribs into 2-rib sections. Serve with the reserved glaze for dipping.

TIMING
Prep: 45 minutes
   (plus 40 minutes for roasting garlic)
Grill: About 1 1/2 hours

GRILL TOOLS AND EQUIPMENT
· Heavy-duty aluminum foil
· Heavy-duty heat-resistant gloves

FIRE-ROASTED PUMPKIN FILLED WITH WILD MUSHROOM RISOTTO AND MASCARPONE

As we were looking for a mind-blowing vegetarian dish for this chapter, Andy's wife, Karen, was reading in bed and nudged him awake. "You've got to make this," she said as she read him the description of a Renaissance recipe for pumpkin baked with mushrooms, bread cubes, and cheese embedded in the text of *A Thousand Days in Venice,* by Marlena de Blasi. Three mouthwatering weeks and several failed experiments later, this beautiful and utterly romantic extravagance emerged from the grill.

THE GRILL

Gas: Indirect heat, medium (325° to 350°F)
   3- or 4-burner grill–middle burner(s) off
   2-burner grill–1 side off
   Clean, oiled grate

Charcoal: Indirect heat, medium ash
   Split charcoal bed (about 2 dozen coals per side)
   20 replacement coals
   Heavy-duty drip pan set between banks of charcoal
   Clean, oiled grate on middle setting

Wood: Indirect heat, medium ash
   12-by-12-inch bed, 3 inches deep
   Additional wood for replacement
   Clean, oiled grate set 4 inches above the fire

INGREDIENTS (MAKES 12 SERVINGS)

1 ounce dried porcini mushrooms
1 1/2 cups boiling water
2 tablespoons extra-virgin olive oil
1 large Spanish onion, finely chopped (about 2 1/2 cups)
1 1/2 pounds cremini mushrooms, halved or quartered, depending on size
1 teaspoon chopped fresh rosemary leaves
1 tablespoon coarsely chopped roasted garlic (page 392)
1 tablespoon truffle oil

Kosher salt and ground black pepper to taste
3/4 cup Arborio or Carnaroli rice
1 cup mascarpone
1 cup heavy cream
4 ounces Parmigiano-Reggiano cheese, grated (1 cup)
1/4 teaspoon grated nutmeg
1 pumpkin (flat rather than round and at least 12 pounds), with a stem
8 ounces Italian fontina cheese, shredded (2 cups)

DIRECTIONS

1. Soak the dried porcini mushrooms in the boiling water in a medium bowl until softened, about 10 minutes. Drain, retaining the soaking liquid, and chop coarsely.

2. Heat the olive oil in a large skillet over medium-high heat. Add the onion and sauté until tender, about 3 minutes. Add the cremini mushrooms and rosemary, and sauté until the mushrooms lose their raw look. Remove from the heat and stir in the roasted garlic, truffle oil, reserved soaked mushrooms, salt, and pepper; set aside.

3. Combine the reserved mushroom soaking liquid with enough water to measure 3 cups. Bring to a boil in a large saucepan, and add a big pinch of kosher salt and the rice. Boil until the rice is tender, about 10 minutes. Drain, and mix the rice with the mascarpone, cream, Parmigiano-Reggiano cheese, and nutmeg. Correct the seasoning with salt and pepper; set aside.

4. Heat the grill as directed.

5. Remove the stem end from the pumpkin and clean the interior cavity of seeds and pulp, just as you would if you were preparing to carve it as a jack-o'-lantern. Using a big spoon, scrape the flesh from the inside of the top half of the pumpkin, reducing its thickness by about half. Allow the scraped flesh to collect on the bottom, which will help the whole pumpkin roast more evenly. Cut a slice from the interior of the pumpkin's lid, reducing its thickness by half, and place the slice in the pumpkin, on the bottom.

6. Set the pumpkin on a sheet of heavy-duty foil folded in fourths to make a square large enough to cradle the bottom of the pumpkin. Season the interior of the pumpkin with salt and pepper and scatter half of the fontina over the bottom. Fill the pumpkin with alternating layers of rice mixture and mushrooms, ending with mushrooms. Top with the remaining fontina. Put the lid on the pumpkin and wrap the whole thing, including the folded foil base, in 2 layers of heavy-duty foil.

7. Put the whole thing on the grill away from the heat, cover, and cook until the pumpkin is tender to the touch, about 1 1/2 hours. If your grill has a temperature gauge, it should stay at around 350°F. If using charcoal or wood, you may have to replenish the coals after the first hour.

8. Remove the pumpkin and set it on a large platter; let rest for 10 minutes. Remove the foil from the top and sides of the pumpkin, tearing it around the base so that the pumpkin is still resting on foil but excess foil doesn't show. Remove the lid and serve portions of the rice and mushrooms along with pumpkin flesh scraped from the interior walls.

CROWN ROAST OF LAMB EMBEDDED WITH FIGS AND FOREST HERBS

TIMING

Prep: 30 to 45 minutes
  (plus 5 minutes for rub)
Grill: About 45 minutes

The gustatory folly known as crown roast, made by grafting two or more racks in a ring, forcing the ribs to arch up and out like the spikes of a crown, is more impressive than it is difficult, and it is one of the few grand celebratory presentations that feed a crowd and spend less than an hour roasting. The speedy cooking time is due to its form. Because of the center hole, heat is able to reach all sides of the meat, so regardless of how many racks you use to form the crown, the roast never takes much longer to cook than a single rack would. The only thing that will slow it down is stuffing the center, which blocks the heat circulation. For that reason we recommend grilling the stuffing around the roast and filling the center just before you bring it to the table.

GRILL TOOLS AND EQUIPMENT

- Grill screen or grill pizza pan
- Heavy-duty aluminum foil
- Heat-resistant bowl, about 6 inches in diameter, to support the center of the roast
- 2 sturdy long-handled spatulas

TIP

- A frenched rack of lamb is one in which the meat, fat, and membrane from the ends of the rib bones have been stripped away, exposing about 2 inches of cleaned bare bone, which can be used as a handle when eating the lamb chops.

THE GRILL

Gas: Indirect heat, medium (325° to 350°F)
3- or 4-burner grill–middle burner(s) off
2-burner grill–1 side off
Clean, oiled grate

Charcoal: Indirect heat, medium ash
Split charcoal bed (about 2 dozen coals per side)
20 replacement coals
Heavy-duty drip pan set between banks of charcoal
Clean, oiled grate on medium setting

TYING A CROWN

Most butchers will be happy to assemble a crown roast for you, but if you want to do it yourself, you will need:
- Heavy-duty thread (or thin, sturdy kitchen twine)
- Large needle with a large eye, preferably curved (an upholstery needle works great)
- Heavy-duty cotton kitchen twine
- 2 to 3 racks of lamb, frenched

INGREDIENTS (MAKES 9 TO 13 SERVINGS—2 TO 3 RIBS PER SERVING)

1 cup fresh flat-leaf parsley leaves
1/2 cup fresh mint leaves
2 tablespoons fresh rosemary leaves
1 head (about 25 cloves) garlic, coarsely chopped
1 tablespoon Provençal Herb Rub (page 373)
3/4 cup extra-virgin olive oil

5 Calimyrna figs, hard stem ends removed, coarsely chopped
3 racks of lamb, about 1 1/2 pounds each, frenched and tied into a crown roast (see Tip, and "Tying a Crown," right)
3 1/2 to 4 pounds fingerling or new potatoes, washed and dried, halved if large
Oil for coating grill grate and screen

1. On the nonmeaty side of the racks, make small slits into the meat (no more than 1/2 inch long and 1/4 inch deep) between the ends of the bones. These slits will spread open when the rack is curved into a crown.

2. Butt the end of one rack up to another. Using the bones as anchors, sew the ends together, using as few stitches as possible. Repeat with as many racks as you are using.

3. Stand the sewn racks so that the cleaned ends of the bones are pointing upward. Bend the meat into a ring, with the meaty side facing inward. As the ring forms, the rib bones will arch outward. To close the ring, tie the ends together, using the bones as anchors. Stitch as needed to secure them in place. When complete, the tied roast resembles a crown (see illustration).

DIRECTIONS

1. Put the parsley, mint, rosemary, and garlic in a food processor and chop finely (or you can chop them by hand). Add the herb rub and olive oil and process just until combined. Remove all but 2 tablespoons to a bowl. Add the figs and process until finely chopped. Put in another bowl.

2. Heat the grill as directed.

3. Using a thin-bladed knife, make a hole in the meaty part of the lamb right in front of each rib. Stick your pinky into the holes to widen them, and fill the holes with the fig mixture. Wrap small squares of foil around the exposed bones to keep them from scorching.

4. Toss the potatoes with 1/3 cup of the herb mixture and rub the remaining herb mixture all over the meaty parts of the lamb. Oil the grill screen and put the lamb in the center. Insert the heat-resistant bowl in the center of the crown to help it hold its shape.

5. Brush the grill grate and coat it with oil. Put the roast (on the screen) on the grill away from the heat, cover, and cook for 15 minutes. Put the potatoes around the roast directly over the fire, cover, and cook for 15 minutes more. Remove the bowl from the center of the crown, and turn the potatoes. Cover and cook until an instant-read thermometer inserted into a thick part of the meat registers about 130°F and the potatoes are browned and tender, about 15 minutes more. If your grill has a temperature gauge, it should stay between 350° and 375°F.

6. Using 2 spatulas, remove the roast to a large serving platter. Remove the string, and fill the center of the ring with the potatoes, if desired for presentation. Cut into chops, removing any string or thread from the lamb. Carve and serve.

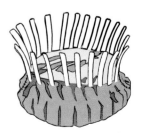

Prep: 5 minutes
(plus 10 minutes for marinade
and relish)
Rest before grilling: 1 to 2 hours
Grill: 1 to 1½ hours

GRILL TOOLS AND EQUIPMENT
- Rotisserie for grill
- Long-handled basting brush
- Heavy-duty heat-resistant gloves

TIPS
- If a whole leg of lamb is too big for your rotisserie (or just too much meat), use a half leg (4 to 5 pounds) and reduce the cooking time by 30 minutes or so. We prefer the sirloin or butt end (near the hip) because the meat is more tender. Of course, it doesn't have the classic protruding bone of the shank half.
- If you want to grill-roast only a half leg but think you'll use the rest of the leg meat for other meals, buy a whole leg and have your butcher cut a few thick lamb chops from the sirloin end of the leg. Then roast the rest of the leg.
- To carve a leg of lamb, slice off any bits of meat from the thicker sirloin end, then grip the shank (bone) with a kitchen towel and your hand. Run the knife from the bone end to the sirloin end as close to the bone as possible to loosen one side of the leg meat from the bone. Leave the meat attached to the bone and make thin slices down through the loosened leg meat. Repeat on the other side of the leg, and then cut any remaining meat from the bone.

GETTING CREATIVE
- For smoky-tasting leg of lamb, soak 1 to 2 cups of oak wood chunks or chips in water for 1 hour, then add half to the coals at the beginning of grilling and half after the first batch dies out. If using gas, put the chips in a smoker box or wrap them in perforated foil and put directly over one of the heated burners.
- You could serve the lamb without the lemon relish, but we like its tart, salty counterpoint. To make a pan sauce instead, spoon off almost all of the fat from the drip pan and then scrape the remaining contents of the drip pan into a small saucepan. Also add any juices from the platter on which the meat has been resting. Bring to a boil and add about ½ cup red wine and ½ cup chicken stock. Boil until the liquid is reduced to about ¾ cup. (Once the liquid boils, it also helps to pour the hot liquid into the drip pan and scrape the drip pan thoroughly. This deglazes extra flavor from the drip pan. Pour the contents back into the saucepan. If you know ahead of time that you'll be making a pan sauce, you could replace the aluminum drip pan with a shallow roasting pan that you can boil liquids in.)

BEDOUIN LEG OF LAMB ON A SPIT

No one knows lamb like the Greeks, Turks, and Arabs of the Middle East. Here's how a leg of lamb might be grilled over a live fire by bedouins (Arab nomads)—rubbed with saffron, caraway, and cardamom and served with a relish of preserved lemons and coriander. Although nomads would roast the lamb leg over a wood fire on a spit, we've given directions for backyard grilling using a charcoal or gas grill with a rotisserie setup. The beauty of rotisserie grilling is that the roast bastes itself as the surface fat melts and rolls around the meat. Lamb legs aren't always completely covered with fat, so even when using the rotisserie we like to baste the meat with some olive oil now and then to ensure even browning. If you don't have a rotisserie, cook the lamb on your grill using medium indirect heat, turning and basting every 20 minutes or so. Alternatively, you could roast the leg over a wood fire with a spit. See page 245 for information on spit-roasting, and set up the spit so that the meat rests about 2 feet above the heat.

THE GRILL

Gas: Indirect heat, medium (325° to 350°F)
3- or 4-burner grill–middle burner(s) off
2-burner grill–1 side off
Heavy-duty drip pan set between banks of charcoal
Grate removed
Rotisserie set up

Charcoal: Indirect heat, medium ash
Split charcoal bed (about 2 dozen coals per side)
20 replacement coals
Heavy-duty drip pan set between banks of charcoal
Grate removed
Rotisserie set up

Wood: Indirect heat, medium ash
12-by-12-inch bed, 3 inches deep
Additional wood for replacement
Rotisserie set up

INGREDIENTS (MAKES 8 TO 10 SERVINGS)

½ cup Bedouin Dry Marinade (page 383)
1 bone-in whole leg of lamb, 5 to 6 pounds, surface fat trimmed to ¼ inch

½ cup olive oil
2 cups Preserved Lemon Relish (page 394)

DIRECTIONS

1. Scatter the dry marinade all over the meat, patting it in with your fingers. Cover loosely and let rest at room temperature for 1 to 2 hours.

2. Heat the grill as directed, setting the drip pan(s) in the grill below the area where the lamb will rotate.

3. Slide the lamb leg onto the skewer of the rotisserie setup. Secure according to the manufacturer's directions.

4. Put the skewered lamb into the rotisserie assembly. The lamb should be suspended away from direct heat and turn freely above the drip pan(s) as the rotisserie rotates. Cover the grill and cook until an instant-read thermometer inserted into the thickest part of the leg (without touching the bone) registers about 125°F for medium-rare or 135°F for medium, 1 to 1½ hours total. Brush the lamb with the olive oil every 30 minutes or so. If your grill has an external thermometer, it should stay at around 350°F. If you are using charcoal, you will probably have to replenish the coals after the first hour.

5. Remove the rotisseried lamb to a large serving platter, cover loosely with foil, and let rest for 10 to 15 minutes. Remove the skewers.

6. Carve the lamb (see Tips), and serve with the lemon relish.

SPIT-ROASTED WHOLE SPRING LAMB OVERCOME BY GARLIC

TIMING
Soak wood chips: 1 hour (optional)
Prep: 1 1/2 hours
Grill: 5 to 5 1/2 hours

There is perhaps no greater culinary spectacle than a whole animal turning on a spit over hot coals. Roasting the whole beast also makes it easy to feed a crowd. The flavors here are some of lamb's favorites: rosemary, garlic, and lemon. The garlic and rosemary are inserted into slits in the meat to infuse the whole roast with their aromas. Plan to make a whole day out of the spit-roast. It takes a good hour or two to set up the spit-roaster, season the animal, and attach it to the spit-rod. Invite some friends over to help hoist the animal to and from the spit-roaster. After about 5 hours of slow roasting and tending the fire, you'll all be feasting on some of the finest meat you've ever tasted.

THE GRILL

Gas: Indirect, medium on a gas-fired spit roaster

Charcoal: Indirect, medium on a charcoal spit roaster, charcoal bed split into 4 corners (about 2 dozen coals per corner)

Wood: Indirect, medium on a wood-fired spit roaster, coal bed split into 4 corners

INGREDIENTS (MAKES 12 SERVINGS)

12 branches fresh rosemary
3 heads garlic, separated into cloves and peeled
1 small whole lamb, 25 pounds or so, dressed for spit-roasting
2 lemons, halved

1/2 cup olive oil, plus more if needed
3 tablespoons kosher salt
1 1/2 tablespoons ground black pepper
3 scallions, roots trimmed

DIRECTIONS

1. Strip the leaves from 8 of the rosemary branches and put the leaves in a food processor, along with the peeled cloves from 2 1/2 heads of garlic. Pulse until finely chopped. (Make and refrigerate up to 2 days ahead to get a jump on things.)

2. Put the lamb on a large work surface with the chest cavity up. Squeeze the juice from the lemons into a bowl, discarding the seeds but saving the rinds. Rub half of the lemon juice all over the inside of the lamb cavity and inner thighs. Rub the entire cavity with 1/4 cup of the olive oil. Sprinkle the cavity with one-third of the garlic mixture, 1 tablespoon of the salt, and 2 teaspoons of the pepper. Put the scallions, remaining 4 branches rosemary, remaining peeled garlic cloves, and the spent lemon rinds into the cavity.

3. Push the spit rod through the lamb's rear, along the cavity parallel to the backbone, and out through the neck or upper chest. Lay the lamb on its side with the cavity facing you so that you can wire the backbone to the spit rod. Position an 8-inch length of wire in the center of the cavity. Insert the wire through the inside of the lamb near the backbone and rod. When the wire pokes through the outside of the lamb, bend the wire around the outside of the backbone and push it back through the lamb so that the entire length of wire is wrapped around the backbone and rod. Use pliers to twist the two ends of the wire together, securing the wire very tightly around the spit rod. Repeat this process at roughly 4-inch intervals toward the rear and front of the animal until the backbone is securely fastened to the spit rod. (See Spit-Roasting 101, page 245.)

4. Slide the spit rod's skewers over the front and rear ends of the rod. Push the skewers firmly into the shoulders and thighs or hips of the lamb, then tighten the skewers onto the rod.

5. Attach the hind legs and forelegs to the rod with wire, twisting the ends of the wire until secured. Attach the neck to the rod in the same way.

6. Wire the lamb cavity shut by sewing from one end to the other with one long piece of wire. Twist each end of the wire with pliers to secure it. (You could also sew the cavity shut with kitchen twine or heavy cotton string and a large needle.)

7. Make 20 to 30 small, 1/2-inch-deep slits all over the outside of the lamb, especially around the shoulders and legs. Use your fingers to stuff each slit with the remaining garlic mixture (be mindful of the sharp ends of the wire as you work). Rub the remaining lemon juice all over the outside of the lamb. Rub all over with the remaining 1/4 cup olive oil, then sprinkle with the remaining 2 tablespoons salt and 2 1/2 teaspoons pepper.

8. If using wood chunks or chips, soak them in water for 1 hour. Heat the spit-roaster as directed. If using charcoal, light about 30 pounds (1 1/2 large bags) of charcoal. When the coals are just ashed over, rake them into 4 piles near the 4 corners of the firebox.

9. Attach the spitted lamb to the roaster so that the lamb rests 1 to 2 feet above the coals. If necessary, re-rake the coals to position the 4 piles just outside the shoulders and thighs so that the lamb cooks by indirect heat.

10. Roast over indirect heat for 5 to 5 1/2 hours, turning slowly but constantly. Add a few pounds of charcoal (about 2 dozen briquettes) to each pile when the old coals begin to burn low, about every hour, letting the charcoal ignite naturally. If using wood chunks or chips along with charcoal, add the soaked chunks to the hot coals every hour or so. After about 2 hours, re-rake the coals to position them directly beneath the lamb.

GRILL TOOLS AND EQUIPMENT
· Spit-roaster (see Tips)
· 60 pounds of charcoal, 5 hours' worth of gas, or about a quarter cord of wood
· 16 cups (4 quarts) wood chunks or chips, preferably oak or hickory (optional)
· Wire (18 to 20 gauge)
· Pliers
· Wire cutters
· Heat-resistant grill mitts (preferably heatproof silicone)
· Long-handled basting brush

TIPS

· Order the lamb several weeks ahead of your planned roasting day. A good country butcher or a farmer who sells at farmers' markets should be able to get you one. Order it dressed for spit-roasting, which means it will be gutted and skinned with the head and feet removed. Try to buy a lamb that's less than 30 pounds to keep it to a manageable size. If you can't find one locally, Jamison Farm in Latrobe, Pennsylvania, raises some of the country's best grass-fed lamb, and they ship small whole lambs year round.

· Let the lamb come to room temperature before firing up the spit-roaster. Otherwise, you'll waste some of your fuel just warming the meat up to room temperature. It may be easiest to get the lamb the day before you cook it.

· The lamb can be mounted on the spit with its fore and hind legs extended, as if the animal were flying through the air (as described in the recipe here). Or it can be positioned with the forelegs tucked under its chin and hind legs tucked up under its belly. This second position is a bit more dignified but less dramatic. Tell the butcher which way you want it, so the lamb can be positioned that way before rigor mortis sets in.

· Lambs have very thin ribs with very little meat. The shoulders and thighs are much thicker, which is why the heat is placed there (in the 4 piles of coals) and away from the rib cage. On the off chance that the rib cage begins to brown as much as the thighs and shoulders after only 1 to 2 hours of roasting, cover the rib cage with aluminum foil (shiny-side out) to help keep the rib meat from overcooking. Remove the foil during the last 30 minutes to 1 hour to finish cooking the ribs.

· You'll need a large work surface for preparing and serving the lamb. A picnic table works nicely. Cover the table with foil, a plastic dropcloth, or another cloth to protect it.

- If you can borrow a spit-roaster, that's the easiest way to go. Otherwise, you can rent one from a local all-purpose renter such as Taylor Rental. It'll cost $75 to $100 for the day.
- The spit rods for some spit-roasters have holes drilled into them every 6 inches or so. These holes make it much easier to attach the animal to the rod—and to remove it. Large skewers are pushed through one side of the animal, then through the holes in the rod, and then out through the other side of the animal. If you can find a spit-roaster of this sort, it will save you the trouble of tying the animal's backbone to the rod with wire and then removing the wire before serving.
- Some spit-roasters have skewers that mount onto the spit from the pointed end of the rod only. If that's the case with your spit-roaster, slide the rear skewer onto the rod before you push the rod through the lamb. After wiring the lamb to the rod, slide on the other skewer.
- Carving up the cooked whole lamb may seem like a daunting task, but it really isn't. A meat cleaver or other heavy, sharp knife makes the job go pretty quickly. First, make a few primal cuts. Remove the hind legs and forelegs/shoulders by driving the knife right through the primary joints. Each leg will serve 2 to 3 people. If you'd like to serve the ribs, cut them from the backbone by standing the lamb on its neck and driving the knife down as close to the backbone as possible to strip the ribs from the backbone. Cut each half of the rib cage into 2 or 3 sections before serving. There isn't much meat on the ribs of a 25-pound lamb, but those who love to lick the bones clean will enjoy them. Next, scrape the meat from the loin, back, and shoulder areas. The meat will be embedded all along the backbone. Finally, if you'd like to make lamb stock, hack off the neck with your cleaver. It can be frozen for a month before you toss it into the stockpot.

Make 2 large piles beneath the shoulders and legs, connected by a shallow, narrow strip of coals beneath the ribs. During the last hour of cooking, if the lamb is not browning sufficiently, baste it all over with additional olive oil. When done, the meat should be well browned on the outside and tender inside, with some pink meat only near the bones. An instant-read thermometer inserted into the thickest parts of the thighs and shoulders should register about 150° to 160°F.

11. Transfer the lamb to a large, clean work surface (see Tips) and let rest for 20 minutes. Using wire cutters and pliers, remove the wire from the legs and neck. Remove the wire that sewed the cavity shut and the wire from around the backbone (you may be able to cut it from outside the animal instead of inside). Remove the spit's skewers, then pull out the spit rod. Be sure all of the wire is removed before serving.

12. Carve the meat from the bones, or scrape it off in chunks, and serve.

Photos right and opposite: Spit-Roasted Whole Spring Lamb Overcome by Garlic

MASTERING THE GRILL

SPIT-ROASTING 101

This technique is no doubt one of the earliest methods of cooking meat. The entire animal, or a large cut of it, is suspended over a fire and rotated to cook it evenly. It's a convenient way to feed a crowd.

The trick with spit-roasting, as with any large roast, is to cook the meat through and brown the outside yet retain the flavorful juices inside the meat. It helps to think of these as two separate steps in the process. Each step requires a different type of heat. Browning the outside is best done over direct heat. Cooking the meat through to the bone, however, is best done by indirect heat to help prevent burning. Each step is simply a matter of managing the heat that reaches the animal. We prefer to cook whole animals slowly via indirect heat for at least half or, preferably, most of the cooking time. That means either (a) spreading out the coals so that the heat surrounds the animal instead of coming from directly beneath it, or (b) raising the animal high enough above the coals so that the meat heats slowly rather than quickly. When using charcoal or wood, we like to spread the coals so that the heat surrounds the animal. It's just easier to move the heat than to move the meat.

A note on marinating and basting. We believe that both marinating and basting are naturally achieved when spit-roasting a well-seasoned animal. If you include some lemon juice or another acidic ingredient along with your seasonings, the roasting time is long enough that the seasonings rubbed into the animal's surfaces penetrate and flavor the meat just as much as they would by marinating. So marinating is not strictly necessary. You could, for the sake of convenience, season the animal a day in advance of roasting it, and you may get a bit more flavor penetration that way.

As for basting, the animal should adequately baste itself on the spit. When turned steadily near the indirect heat of the coals, the animal's outer layers of fat slowly melt and roll around the meat, basting the meat and keeping it moist. If you happen to notice any dry areas on the surface of the animal during the last half of cooking, drizzle a little oil over the area to ensure even browning.

TIMING

Prep: 30 minutes
(plus 5 minutes for Peking crackle)
Dry: 2 hours
Grill: About 1 hour

GRILL TOOLS AND EQUIPMENT

- Small bicycle pump with a needle attachment, or a marinade injector
- Heavy-duty cotton kitchen twine
- Electric fan
- Roasting rack
- Disposable aluminum roasting pan
- Long-handled basting brush

SHORTCUT

- To make a simpler version of Peking duck, see the Grilled Peking-Style Chicken on page 167.

CRÊPES

Makes about 12 crêpes

3/4 cup flour
3/4 cup water
1/8 teaspoon kosher salt
3 eggs
No-stick spray oil for coating pan

1. Mix the flour, water, and salt with a whisk in a medium bowl until smooth. Beat in the eggs, one at a time. Set aside for at least 20 minutes.

2. Heat a small, nonstick skillet over medium-high heat until very hot. Spray very lightly with oil. Make crêpes in the hot skillet by pouring a few tablespoons of batter into the skillet. Swirl to cover the bottom of the skillet, and pour the excess batter back into the bowl. Cook for about 30 seconds; the edges of the crêpe will dry and it will be set across the surface. Flip the crêpe and cook for 5 or 10 seconds. Slip onto a plate and make another crêpe. Don't spray the skillet with more oil until the crêpes start to stick slightly, after about 6 crêpes. Keep the crêpes covered until ready to serve.

GRILLED PEKING DUCK

The pre-prep when making Peking duck, one of the epitomes of Chinese cuisine, includes pumping it with air, tying off the neck, and fanning it for hours as the skin dries. This process is so complex and arcane that culinary war stories hardly ever mention how the duck is roasted. This recipe doesn't skimp on any steps and will no doubt provide you with your own battle tales, but the difference here is what happens to the flavor when you roast the duck over coals. The skin crisps like a single layer of lacquer, and the meat gets a smoky nuance that deepens its traditional salty-sweet profile. The recipe calls for serving it traditionally with hoisin sauce and pancakes. If you want to skip that presentation, the duck is delicious all by itself.

THE GRILL

Gas: Indirect heat, medium-high (350° to 375°F)
3- or 4-burner grill–middle burner(s) off
2-burner grill–1 side off
Clean, oiled grate

Charcoal: Indirect heat, medium ash
Split charcoal bed (about 2 dozen coals per side)
Heavy-duty drip pan set between banks of charcoal
Clean, oiled grate on medium setting

Wood: Indirect heat, medium ash
12-by-12-inch bed, 3 inches deep
Clean, oiled grate set 4 inches above the fire

INGREDIENTS (MAKES 4 SERVINGS)

1 Long Island duckling, about 4 1/2 pounds, visible fat removed
1 cup Peking Crackle (page 385)
12 crêpes (recipe at left)

2 scallions, roots trimmed, thinly sliced
3 tablespoons hoisin sauce

DIRECTIONS

1. Extend the plunger of the bicycle pump and insert the needle just under the skin at the neck end of the duck. Depress the plunger, and the skin around the needle will puff up. Continue to pump air under the duck skin in the same way until the skin has been separated from the meat all over the breast and legs (see illlustration).

2. Heat a kettle of water to boiling. Put the duck, breast-side up, in a strainer set in a sink. Pour the boiling water over the duck. Hook a chopstick under the wings of the duck to hold them away from the body. Tie a string around the neck and hang the duck by the string over a sink or a large drip pan. Put an electric fan in front of the duck and blow air directly on it for about an hour to dry the skin.

3. Brush the duck with half of the Peking crackle and dry for another hour.

4. While the duck is drying, prepare the crêpes.

5. Heat the grill as directed.

6. Put the duck, breast-side up, on a rack set in a disposable roasting pan. Put the pan on the grill away from the heat, cover the grill, and cook until an instant-read thermometer inserted into the thickest part of the breast registers 165°F, about 1 hour, basting with the remaining glaze halfway through. If your grill has an external thermometer, it should stay at around 375°F during that time.

7. Remove the duck to a cutting board. Carve it as you would a chicken (see page 184). Lift the skin from the meat and cut it into strips. Cut the meat into large, bite-size chunks. Arrange the meat on a platter scattered with scallions and strips of crisp skin. Serve with the hoisin sauce and crêpes for rolling.

GRILLED THANKSGIVING

At first glance it seems iconoclastic to grill Thanksgiving dinner, but upon reflection it is ultimately fitting to have the definitive American meal prepared by the most American of cooking methods. Here you will find a completely grilled menu, including timetable and recipes. The recipes for four of the elements (turkey, sauce, stuffing, and cranberries) are right here. Recipes for the vegetables and dessert are from other chapters. When you bring it all to the table and gather around, we think you will find the spread so spectacular and each dish so delicious that you will wonder why grilling Thanksgiving wasn't part of your tradition long ago.

MENU TIMELINE

Day before: Grill vegetables for stuffing (refrigerate overnight).
Grill pears and prepare pear and cranberry compote (refrigerate overnight).
Roast chestnuts (keep covered at room temperature).
Caramelize milk for dulce de leche (refrigerate overnight).

6 hours ahead: Remove turkey from the refrigerator.
Remove everything prepared the day before from the refrigerator.
Prepare basting liquid for turkey.
Grill vegetables for harvest vegetables (keep covered at room temperature).
Prepare fennel bathed with riesling (keep covered at room temperature).

4 hours ahead: Inject basting liquid into turkey and start grilling turkey.

2 hours ahead: Assemble stuffing (keep warm in 200°F oven).
Put harvest vegetables in 200°F oven to warm up.
Put grilled fennel in 200°F oven to warm up.

Prepare fire-baked apples up to the point of grilling (keep at room temperature).
Finish dulce de leche sauce (keep covered at room temperature).

1 hour ahead: Check turkey temperature and adjust grill so that it will be done in 30 minutes.
Prepare sauce for harvest vegetables and keep warm.

30 minutes ahead: Remove turkey to a carving board and keep warm.
Prepare apple cider jus in pan from turkey and keep warm.
Cook apples.

Serving time: Carve turkey and serve with jus.
Serve stuffing.
Serve pear and cranberry compote.
Pour sauce over harvest vegetables and serve.
Serve fennel.
Check apples and remove from grill if ready (serve with dulce de leche for dessert).

Photo: Grilled-Roasted Turkey with Apple Cider Jus, Grilled Vegetable Stuffing, and Grilled Pear and Cranberry Compote

GRILL-ROASTED TURKEY WITH APPLE CIDER JUS

TIMING

Prep: 30 to 40 minutes
(plus 5 minutes for rub)
Grill: 3 to 4 hours

GRILL TOOLS AND EQUIPMENT

· Marinade injector
· Heavy-duty roasting pan with
  roasting rack
· Heat-resistant grill mitts
· Kitchen twine

Turkey gets burnished gold on the grill, and the method is effortless. You can literally put it on and forget about it (except for replenishing the charcoal every hour or so). The turkey is cooked in a roasting pan so that you can catch its drippings for the apple cider jus.

THE GRILL

Gas: Indirect heat, medium (325° to 350°F)
3- or 4-burner grill–middle burne(s)r off
2-burner grill–1 side off
Clean, oiled grate

Charcoal: Indirect heat, medium ash
Split charcoal bed (about 2 dozen coals per side)
60 to 80 replacement coals
Heavy-duty drip pan set between banks of charcoal
Clean, oiled grate on medium setting

INGREDIENTS (MAKES 12 TO 14 SERVINGS)

4 cups apple cider
1/2 cup chicken broth
5 tablespoons butter, salted or unsalted

3 teaspoons Tuscan Rosemary Rub (page 375)
1 fresh turkey, 12 to 14 pounds
Kosher salt and ground black pepper to taste

DIRECTIONS

1. Heat the grill as directed.

2. To make the basting liquid, heat 1/2 cup of the cider, the broth, 3 tablespoons of the butter, and 1 teaspoon of the Tuscan rub in a saucepan over medium heat until the butter melts. Cool to room temperature. This can be made a day ahead.

3. Wash the turkey inside and out with cold water and remove any visible pockets of fat. Pat dry. Rub 1 teaspoon Tuscan rub onto the walls of the interior cavity. Set on a roasting rack in a roasting pan.

4. Strain the basting liquid into a small bowl. Fill the injector with as much basting liquid as it will hold. Inject 1 ounce (30 cc) into each thigh and drumstick and each side of the breast, making several injections into each part. Pour and rub the remaining basting liquid over the outside of the turkey.

5. Put the roasting pan on the grill away from the heat, cover, and cook until an instant-read thermometer inserted into the thickest part of the breast registers about 170°F, 3 to 4 hours, depending on the turkey's weight. If your grill has a temperature gauge, it should register around 350°F during that time. If you are using charcoal, you will probably have to replenish the coals every hour.

6. When the turkey is done, use grill mitts to remove it to a carving board, and cover it with foil to keep warm. Remove the rack from the roasting pan and put the roasting pan on a burner heated to medium. Add the remaining 3 1/2 cups apple cider and 1 teaspoon Tuscan rub. Bring to a boil, scraping any brown bits clinging to the bottom of the pan into the jus. Boil for 2 minutes, remove from the heat, and swirl in the remaining 2 tablespoons butter. Adjust the seasoning with salt and pepper, and strain into a serving dish.

7. Carve the turkey and serve with the apple cider jus on the side.

GRILLED VEGETABLE STUFFING

TIMING

Prep: About 20 minutes
(plus 5 minutes for rub)
Grill: 10 to 14 minutes

GRILL TOOLS AND EQUIPMENT

· Long-handled tongs
· Long-handled spatula
· Grill screen

If you miss cooking the stuffing in the bird, you can get the same flavor by drizzling a little bit of the turkey drippings into the stuffing before serving. And if you insist on serving it directly from the carcass, stuff it into the turkey after it is cooked. But whatever you do, don't stuff the turkey when it is raw. You will lengthen the cooking time unnecessarily, and you will cause the surface to overcook before the interior ever reaches a safe temperature.

THE GRILL

Gas: Direct heat, medium-high (400° to 450°F)
Clean, oiled grate

Charcoal: Direct heat, light ash
Clean, oiled grate on medium setting

Oil for coating grill screen

2 large onions (about 12 ounces each), cut into 1/2-inch-thick slices

1 pound mushrooms, cleaned

4 ribs celery

1 large loaf (about 24 ounces) good-quality white sandwich bread, about 18 slices

4 large apples, peeled, cored, and halved

No-stick spray oil

2 cups chicken broth

1 cup apple cider

2 teaspoons Tuscan Rosemary Rub (page 375)

2 tablespoons butter, salted or unsalted, melted

DIRECTIONS

1. Heat the grill as directed. Oil the grill screen and put it on the grill.

2. Coat the onions, mushrooms, celery, apples, and bread slices on all sides with spray oil. Put the vegetables on the grill screen and grill until browned and tender, 3 to 4 minutes per side. Transfer to a large bowl. Grill the bread slices for 1 minute per side. Put in the bowl.

3. Cut the vegetables and bread into bite-size pieces, and toss with the chicken broth, apple cider, Tuscan rub, and butter until well combined. Put in an oven-to-table serving dish, cover, and keep warm in a 200°F oven for up to 2 hours.

GRILLED PEAR AND CRANBERRY COMPOTE

Pears and cranberries are an inspired combination in flavor (fragrant and milky versus tart and sharp), texture (velvet smoothness versus turgid pop), and color (creamy pale versus eye-popping scarlet). Adding a confetti of blackened flecks from the grill only increases the delight.

THE GRILL

Gas: Direct heat, medium-high (400° to 450°F)
Clean, oiled grate

Charcoal: Direct heat, light ash
Clean, oiled grate on medium setting

INGREDIENTS (MAKES 12 TO 14 SERVINGS)

Oil for coating grill screen

4 Bartlett pears or 12 Seckel pears

2 teaspoons vegetable oil

1 pound cranberries, fresh or frozen

1 1/3 cups sugar, plus more if needed

1 teaspoon vanilla vinegar (or 1 teaspoon red wine vinegar and 1/8 teaspoon vanilla extract)

DIRECTIONS

1. Heat the grill as directed. Oil the grill screen and put it on the grill.

2. Peel the pears, cut in half lengthwise, and remove the core with a small melon baller. If using Bartlett pears, cut each pear half in half again lengthwise. Toss the pears in a medium bowl with the 2 teaspoons oil until evenly coated.

3. Put the pears on the oiled grill screen; cover and cook until the pears are browned and barely tender, about 3 minutes per side (6 minutes total for Seckel pears, 9 minutes total for Bartlett pears).

4. Cut the pears into bite-size chunks; set aside.

5. Combine the cranberries and sugar in a large saucepan and cook, covered, over medium heat until the cranberries burst, about 4 minutes, stirring as needed. Taste for sweetness and add a little more sugar, if needed. Add the pears and simmer for a minute more. Stir in the vanilla vinegar. Serve warm or at room temperature.

TIMING
Prep: About 10 minues
Grill: 6 to 9 minutes

GRILL TOOLS AND EQUIPMENT
· Long-handled spatula
· Grill screen

Photo: Grilled Pear and Cranberry Compote

TIMING

Prep: 5 minutes
(plus 5 minutes for rub)
Rest before grilling: 2 hours or overnight
Grill: 1 1/2 to 2 hours

GRILL TOOLS AND EQUIPMENT

- Clean 20-gallon steel trash can, 2 1/2 to 3 feet tall
- 1 metal stake, 1 to 2 inches in diameter and 18 to 24 inches long (see Tips)
- Insulated grill mitts, preferably heat-resistant silicone

TIPS

- Leave plenty of time to thaw the turkey if it's frozen. A 10- to 12-pound turkey takes 1 to 2 days to thaw in the refrigerator or about 6 hours to thaw in continually replenished cold water in the sink.
- If you don't have a sturdy stake or you're on pavement or impervious ground, prop the bird up on a vertical roasting rack set on an inverted cast-iron or other heatproof Dutch oven.
- A 20-pound bag of charcoal should be plenty to cook the turkey. But if the weather is cold, the coals may burn out before the turkey is done. In that case, just add more hot coals until the turkey is finished cooking.
- We did some research into the safety of trash-can turkey because the FDA recommends against cooking any food on galvanized steel. The question is, can you safely cook *near* galvanized steel, as could happen with trash-can turkey? The answer, from Richard Tavoletti, executive director of the Can Manufacturers Institute (CMI), is yes. Some trash cans are made with galvanized steel and others aren't, so the easiest way to sidestep the issue is to use a can that's not galvanized. But even if you use a galvanized steel trash can, the zinc coating on the steel (the galvanizing material) will not get hot enough to become airborne and migrate from the can to the food. In the trash-can turkey method, the can never touches the food, so it is safe. Even if the trash can grazes the turkey slightly (which is unlikely), the food will not have been in contact with the hot steel long enough to impart any significant zinc residue to the food. We figured trash-can turkey was safe because Scoutmasters have been roasting birds this way for decades. But researching the issue gave us the reassurance we needed to pass the recipe along to you.

Boy Scouts are a resourceful bunch. David learned how to build a wood fire on Boy Scout camping trips when he was a kid, but he didn't hear about this Scout trick for cooking a whole turkey until he was in his late twenties. Trash-can turkey has since become a novel way to cook a whole bird at tailgates and other outdoor grill parties. The method's genius is its simplicity. Drive a stake into the ground, impale a turkey on the stake, then invert a metal trash can over the staked turkey to create an oven. All that's left to add is the heat. You burn a bag of charcoal, or use campfire coals, and shovel the hot coals on top of and around the metal trash can. The method is perfect for campfire cooking because it uses minimal equipment. Plus the turkey cooks quickly and stays moist due to the intense heat surrounding the can and the enclosed environment inside of this makeshift oven. Try this grill project at your next party. It's sure to impress your guests (and feed them well).

THE GRILL

Charcoal: Indirect heat, medium ash
20 pounds charcoal
No grill grate

Wood: Indirect heat, medium ash
8 to 10 quarts burning embers (from 6 to 10 split logs)
No grill grate

INGREDIENTS (MAKES 12 TO 14 SERVINGS)

1 turkey, 10 to 12 pounds, thawed if frozen, giblets removed
1/2 cup Sage and Savory Rub (page 375)

1 tablespoon vegetable oil

DIRECTIONS

1. Wash the turkey inside and out with cold water and remove any visible pockets of fat. Pat dry.

2. Rub a few tablespoons of the rub onto the walls of the bird's interior cavities. Rub the oil all over the skin of the turkey, then sprinkle with the remaining rub, patting it in with your fingers. Cover and refrigerate for 2 hours, or overnight for the best flavor. Or cook the bird right away if you're in a hurry.

3. Choose an area of level ground and clear a spot that's about 4 feet in diameter. Cover the area with aluminum foil. Drive the stake a few inches into the ground in the center of the foil so that about 15 to 20 inches are still visible above the ground.

4. Burn a wood fire as directed above or light all of the charcoal in a pyramid or in several chimney starters. If lighting batches of coals, they should be ready within 15 minutes of each other.

5. Lower the body cavity of the turkey over the top of the stake as you would lower it over a vertical roasting rack. Position the turkey so that it rests securely on the stake (the top of the

stake should be resting on bone rather than meat and skin alone).

6. Invert the trash can over the turkey, positioning it so that the turkey is in the center of the can. Put a few shovelfuls of hot coals on top of the inverted can. Shovel the rest of the coals around the bottom of the can, raking them as high up the sides of the can as possible (4 to 6 inches is fine).

7. Cook until an instant-read thermometer inserted into the thickest part of the turkey breast registers about 170°F, 1 1/2 to 2 hours, depending on the turkey's weight. To check the bird, rake or shovel away the coals from the top and sides of the can. Wearing insulated grill gloves (preferably silicone), carefully lift the hot can off the turkey, keeping the open end away from you to avoid steam burns. If the bird isn't done, replace the can and coals and continue cooking until it is nicely browned and cooked through to temperature.

8. When the turkey is done, use the grill gloves to lift it off the stake and remove it to a carving board. Cover loosely with foil and let rest for 10 to 15 minutes before carving and serving.

TURDUCKEN

TIMING
Prep: About 4 hours
Simmer: 3 hours
Cook: About 1 hour
Soak wood chips: 1 hour
Grill: About 8 hours

Books on medieval cooking abound in complicated recipes directing you to sew different animals together or stuff them inside larger animals. There's something oddly compelling about these cooking projects. It's not just their sheer novelty, it's to prove that such culinary feats taste great. Here's a contemporary version made with boneless birds: a turkey stuffed with a duck stuffed with a chicken. Turducken is wildly popular in Louisiana, and we've put Cajun flavors in the foreground of our grilled version. From the outside, the turducken looks like a relatively normal roasted turkey. But when you cut into the bird, you see three different meats and various stuffings. We use a sausage-cornbread stuffing and an oyster stuffing. And we've added to the fun by stuffing a few hard-cooked eggs in the very center. Traditional Cajun turducken is roasted in a low oven for several hours. But with that method, the duck and chicken are essentially steamed inside the turkey. On the grill, we experimented with searing the duck and chicken to develop more flavor in the meat. It worked wonders. We also decided to drain some of the excess fat from the duck before assembling the whole thing. Turducken makes a spicy—and impressive—alternative to the traditional holiday turkey. Start the recipe at least a day ahead so you have time to bone the birds, make the stuffings, and assemble the beast. Plus, it takes about 8 hours to cook on the grill. If you prep the entire day before, assemble the turducken very early the next morning, and get it on the grill by 8 a.m., you'll be carving the roast by 4 or 5 p.m.

GRILL TOOLS AND EQUIPMENT
- Heavy-duty thread and large needle, preferably curved (an upholstery needle works great)
- Heavy-duty roasting pan with roasting rack
- Heat-resistant grill mitts, preferably silicone
- 5 cups wood chunks or chips (apple and/or cherry)
- Smoker box or foil packet, if using a gas grill (see page 39)

TURDUCKEN TIMELINE
1 to 2 days ahead:
- Prick the duck skin.
- Debone and season the birds (refrigerate).
- Make the stock (refrigerate or freeze leftovers).
- Prepare the two stuffings (refrigerate).
- Layer the cornbread stuffing on the turkey (refrigerate).

12 hours ahead:
- Sear the chicken and duck.
- Assemble the turducken.

8 hours ahead:
- Grill-roast the turducken.

30 minutes ahead:
- Bake the extra stuffings.
- Make the gravy.

GETTING CREATIVE
- If you really want to go all out, cook the eggs on the grill instead of in boiling water. To allow steam to escape, poke a hole in the large end of each egg with a needle. Put the pricked whole eggs in their shells over direct medium heat on the grill. Cook until lightly browned all over and cooked through, 10 to 12 minutes, turning often. Spin an egg on a flat surface to test it. If it spins without wobbling, it's done. If it wobbles, grill for another minute or so.

THE GRILL

Gas: Direct heat, high (450° to 500°F), and
indirect heat, medium-low (250° to 300°F)
Large 3- or 4-burner grill–middle burner(s) off
2-burner grill–1 side off
Clean, oiled grate

Charcoal: Direct heat, red hot, and indirect heat, thick ash
Charcoal bed to one side (about 2 dozen coals on one side)
80 replacement coals
Heavy-duty drip pan set on empty side of grill
Clean, oiled grate on medium setting

INGREDIENTS (MAKES ABOUT 20 SERVINGS)

For the birds:
1 fresh chicken, 3 to 4 pounds
1 fresh Muscovy duckling, 5 to 6 pounds (see Tips, page 254)
1 fresh turkey, 16 to 20 pounds
1 1/2 cups Cajun Blackening Rub (page 373)
Oil for coating grill grate

For the stock:
Carcasses from boned turkey, duck, and chicken
1 large onion, quartered
1 large carrot, quartered
1 large rib celery, quartered
About 2 gallons water
8 sprigs flat-leaf parsley
8 sprigs thyme
2 bay leaves
2 teaspoons kosher salt

For the cornbread:
2 eggs
1 cup buttermilk
6 tablespoons (3/4 stick) butter, melted, or vegetable oil
2 tablespoons light brown sugar
1 teaspoon kosher salt
4 teaspoons baking powder
1 cup yellow cornmeal (stone-ground is best)
1 cup all-purpose flour

For the stuffings:
8 tablespoons (1 stick) butter
1 large loaf (1 to 1 1/2 pounds) Italian or French bread, cut into 1/4- to 1/2-inch cubes
2 cups pecans
1 1/2 pounds andouille or other fresh spicy pork sausage
5 onions, chopped
5 ribs celery, chopped
3 bell peppers (a mix of colors), seeded and chopped
4 cloves garlic, minced
3/4 cup chopped fresh flat-leaf parsley
2 teaspoons dried sage
2 teaspoons dried savory
2 teaspoons dried thyme
2 teaspoons paprika
1 1/2 teaspoons kosher salt
1 teaspoon ground black pepper
1/4 to 1/2 teaspoon cayenne pepper
2 dozen oysters, shucked (see Tips, page 254)
4 eggs, beaten

2 to 4 hard-cooked eggs (see Tips, page 255)

For the gravy:
1 1/2 tablespoons cornstarch dissolved in 1/3 cup cold water
Kosher salt and ground black pepper to taste

ASSEMBLING THE TURDUCKEN

1. Season the boneless birds.
2. Stuff the turkey legs and wings.
3. Put the duck on the turkey and spread with stuffing.
4. Put the chicken on the duck and spread with stuffing.
5. Center the hard-cooked eggs over the stuffing on the chicken.
6. Fold up the chicken.
7. Fold up the duck.
8. Fold up the turkey.
9. Sew up the back of the turkey.
10. Turn the turkey right-side up and truss with twine.

STRUCTURE OF THE TURDUCKEN

1. Turkey
2. Cornbread stuffing
3. Duck
4. Oyster stuffing
5. Chicken
6. Hard-cooked eggs

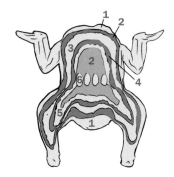

TIPS

- For information on types of ducklings, see the introduction to the Smoky Barbecued Duck recipe (page 200). Either a Long Island or Muscovy duck will work here, but a Muscovy is preferred because it is less fatty. If using a Long Island duck, dry out the skin according to the directions on page 200.
- This recipe calls for making poultry stock, since you have the bones anyway. But you could use about 10 cups (2 1/2 quarts) prepared chicken stock if you prefer.
- We make the two stuffings simultaneously in separate pans, since many of the same ingredients are used in both stuffings. If you have only one large sauté pan, make the two stuffings sequentially, wiping out the pan between batches.
- You'll have enough work to do in this recipe, so ask your fishmonger to shuck the oysters for you, saving the oyster juices or "liquor" so you can moisten the stuffing with it. Or to shuck the oysters yourself, cover your hand with a thick dish towel or oven mitt to protect it, and set a medium bowl on a work surface. Put an oyster in the towel in the palm of your hand and work over the bowl to catch the oyster juices. Dig the tip of an oyster knife or a pointy can opener deeply into the hinge of the oyster shell, then pry open and pop the two halves loose. Slide the oyster knife or a

DIRECTIONS

1. For the birds: The day before, remove the giblets from the chicken, duck, and turkey and reserve for another use. Remove any visible pockets of fat, especially from the duck, and rinse the birds inside and out. Pat the birds dry with paper towels. Heat a kettle of water to boiling. Poke the skin of the duck deeply with a fork, especially where there are noticeable fat deposits around the legs and along the sides of the breast. Put the duck, breast-side up, in a strainer set in a sink. Slowly pour the boiling water over the duck. This process helps remove some of the excess duck fat. Pat the duck dry.

2. Debone the birds according to the directions on page 256. The goal is to remove the bones without cutting through the skin. Debone the chicken and duck first to practice. Any mistakes there will be hidden inside the turkey. When deboning the turkey, debone the wings to the first joint only. Refrigerate each bird on a rimmed baking sheet before and after deboning.

3. Once they are deboned, open the birds up on their baking sheets and sprinkle about 1/4 cup of the blackening rub all over the chicken, 1/4 cup all over the duck, and 1/4 cup over just the exposed meat of the turkey (not the skin), patting the spices in with your fingers. Cover the turkey and chicken tightly. Leave the duck uncovered and refrigerate all the birds overnight. Leaving the duck uncovered, skin-side up, helps to dry out the skin.

4. For the stock, preheat the oven to 400°F. After boning the birds, put the bones in a large roasting pan along with the onion, carrot, and celery. Roast until the bones are deeply browned, about 30 minutes, stirring once or twice. Transfer the bones and vegetables to a large stockpot. Pour 1 cup water into the hot roasting pan and scrape the bottom to release the browned bits. Add the liquid to the stockpot along with enough water to cover the bones (about 2 gallons). Tie the parsley, thyme, and bay leaves with kitchen string, a clean twist tie, or in cheesecloth and add to the pot. Bring to a boil over high heat, then reduce the heat to medium-low and simmer until the liquid is reduced by nearly half its original volume, about 3 hours. Skim the surface occasionally. Strain, stir in the salt, and let cool. Pour into airtight containers and refrigerate for up to 3 days or freeze for up to 3 months. (Makes about 1 gallon total.)

5. For the cornbread: Preheat the oven to 400°F. Grease a 10-inch round cast-iron skillet or 1 1/2-quart baking dish. Whisk the eggs, buttermilk, melted butter, brown sugar, and salt in a large bowl until blended. Scatter the baking powder over the top and whisk until blended. Mix in the cornmeal and flour, gently stirring until the batter is almost free of lumps. Pour into the skillet or dish and bake until a knife inserted in the center comes out clean, 15 to 20 minutes. Cool completely on a rack.

6. For the stuffings: Melt 2 tablespoons of the butter in a large, deep sauté pan over medium heat. Melt another 2 tablespoons butter in another large, deep sauté pan over medium heat (if you have only one pan, see Tips at left). When melted and hot, crumble the cornbread into one pan and put the Italian or French bread cubes in the other. Toast the bread in the pans, shaking occasionally, until lightly browned, 10 to 12 minutes. Remove to separate large bowls.

7. Return one pan to medium heat and add the pecans. Toast the pecans in the pan, shaking occasionally, until fragrant and lightly browned, 5 to 7 minutes. Remove to a cutting board, let cool, and chop coarsely.

8. Return the pecan pan to medium-high heat. Cut the sausage into small cubes or remove from its casing (if necessary) and add to the pan. Cook, breaking up the meat with a spoon, until lightly browned all over and the fat begins to render, 5 to 7 minutes. Meanwhile, return the other sauté pan to medium-high heat so that you can prepare both stuffings simultaneously. Melt the remaining 4 tablespoons butter in that pan, then divide the onions, celery, bell peppers, and garlic between the 2 pans. Cook until the vegetables are tender, 8 to 12 minutes. Divide the parsley, sage, savory, thyme, paprika, salt, black pepper, and cayenne between the 2 pans. Stir until heated through, then remove the pans from the heat. Stir the sausage stuffing mixture into the cornbread crumbs in the bowl. Stir the other stuffing mixture into the Italian or French bread cubes in the other bowl. Stir the oysters into the bowl with the bread cubes. Add enough of the prepared poultry stock to the oyster juices to equal 1 cup. Drizzle the liquid over the oyster stuffing, stirring it in along with 2 of the beaten eggs. Drizzle about 1 cup of the poultry stock over the cornbread-sausage stuffing, stirring it in along with the remaining 2 beaten eggs.

9. Remove the turkey from the refrigerator and open up the bird as flat as possible. Stuff the leg and wing cavities with the cornbread-sausage stuffing, pushing it in with your hands and the handle of a wooden spoon or other narrow tool. Use enough stuffing so that the legs and wings are propped up and look as if they have bones, 1 to 2 cups per cavity. Spread 2 to 3 cups of the remaining cornbread stuffing over the exposed turkey meat, patting it into an even layer about 1/2 to 3/4 inch thick. You should have 6 to 8 cups of cornbread stuffing left over. Tightly cover the turkey and remaining stuffing and refrigerate overnight.

10. Ten to twelve hours before serving time: Heat the grill as directed for high direct heat. Remove the chicken, duck, and stuffings from the refrigerator about 20 minutes before grilling.

11. Brush the grill grate and coat it with oil. Put the boneless duck, skin-side down, on the grill directly over the heat. Cook just until the meat is seared on both sides but not cooked through, 2 to 3 minutes per side. Repeat with the boneless chicken. Remove the birds to foil-covered baking sheets.

12. To assemble the turducken, remove the stuffed turkey from the refrigerator. It should be flat, with the skin side down and the stuffing facing up. Put the seared boneless duck, skin-side down, over the stuffing on the turkey and spread the duck as flat as possible. Spread about 4 cups of oyster stuffing over the duck meat, patting it into an even layer about 1/2 to 3/4 inch thick. You should have 6 to 8 cups of oyster stuffing left over. Cover and refrigerate the remaining stuffing.

13. Put the seared boneless chicken, skin-side down, over the stuffing on the duck and spread the chicken as flat as possible. Spread 3 to 4 cups of the remaining cornbread-sausage stuffing over the chicken meat, patting it into an even layer about 1/2 to 3/4 inch thick. You should have 3 to 4 cups of cornbread-sausage stuffing left over; cover and refrigerate it. Peel the hard-cooked eggs under cool running water. Center the eggs on the chicken over the stuffing; the eggs should be in a horizontal row.

14. Grab one side of the chicken and stuffing and fold it tightly over the horizontal row of eggs. It should fold almost to the opposite side of the row of eggs. Repeat with the other side of the chicken, folding it tightly over the first side. Next, fold one side of the duck tightly over the chicken, holding the stuffed chicken firmly in place. Fold the other side of the duck tightly over the chicken, still holding the chicken firmly in place. Finally, fold one side of the turkey over the duck, holding the stuffed duck firmly in place. Fold the other side of the turkey over the duck, still holding the duck firmly in place. The two sides of the turkey should reach each other in the middle.

15. Sew up the back of the turkey, using a large, sturdy needle and heavy-duty thread, starting at the neck and ending at the tail. Stitch the openings as tightly as possible. Sprinkle with about $1/3$ cup of the remaining blackening rub, patting it in with your fingers. Turn the turkey breast-side up, then sprinkle with all but 1 tablespoon of the remaining rub; reserve the 1 tablesppon for the gravy. Tie the ends of the drumsticks together with kitchen twine and form the turkey into a natural turkey shape; tie lengths of twine around the middle of the turkey to secure it.

16. Soak the wood chips in water for 1 hour. Heat the grill as directed for medium-low indirect heat. Drain about 1 cup of wood chips and scatter them over the coals on the grill. If using gas, drain the wood chips and put them in a smoker box or in a perforated foil packet directly over one of the heated burners. Heat the gas grill to high until you see plenty of smoke, then turn the heat to low.

17. Put the turducken breast-side up on the roasting rack in the roasting pan. Put the roasting pan on the grill away from the heat, cover the grill, and cook until an instant-read thermometer inserted into the center of the turducken registers about 165°F, about 7 to 8 hours. If your grill has a temperature gauge, it should stay between 250° and 300°F. If you are using charcoal, you will have to replenish the coals every hour or so. Also replenish the wood chips or chunks every hour or so. For the most even browning, rotate the pan a few times during cooking. If the turducken browns too soon, lower the heat and cover the bird with foil.

18. About 15 minutes before the turkey reaches temperature, heat the oven to 350°F. Remove the extra stuffings from the refrigerator. Moisten the cornbread stuffing with $1/2$ to 1 cup poultry stock (more if you like very moist stuffing). Moisten the oyster stuffing with $1 1/2$ to 2 cups poultry stock. Scrape the cornbread stuffing into a 1-quart baking dish and the oyster stuffing into a 2-quart baking dish. Bake until the tops are browned and the stuffings are heated through, 15 to 30 minutes (less for the cornbread stuffing, more for the oyster stuffing).

19. When the turkey reaches doneness, use grill mitts to remove it to a carving board, and cover it with foil to keep warm. Let rest for about 30 minutes. Remove the rack from the roasting pan and spoon off or drain all but about $1/4$ cup of fat from the drippings (see Tips).

20. For the gravy, put the roasting pan of drippings on a burner heated to medium. Add 5 cups of the poultry stock and the reserved tablespoon of blackening rub. Bring to a boil, scraping up any brown bits clinging to the bottom of the pan. Boil for 5 minutes. Stir in the cornstarch mixture and boil for 1 minute, stirring constantly, until slightly thickened. Remove from the heat and adjust the seasoning with salt and pepper. Strain into a gravy boat.

21. To carve the turducken, remove the twine. Remove the legs and wings and cut into sections. Grab one end of the thread that is stitching up the back and pull; it will all come out. Cut the turducken in half lengthwise, then slice the breast crosswise in straight slices from one side to the other; because all of the bones have been removed, you will get perfect slices surrounding layers of meat and stuffing with a core of hard-cooked eggs. Serve with the gravy and extra baked stuffings.

dull knife such as a butter knife all the way under the oyster meat as close to the shell as possible, cutting the meat from the shell. Don't use a sharp knife here, since it could easily cut you. If you can't find fresh oysters in the shell, use about 1 pint raw oysters. Drain the raw oysters before adding them to the stuffing, and save the liquid for moistening the stuffing.

· Two to four hard cooked eggs will fit inside the chicken depending on the bird's size. To hard-cook the eggs for the center of the turducken, put the eggs in a single layer in a saucepan and cover with 1 inch of cold water. Bring to a boil over high heat. When the water begins to boil, remove the pan from the heat, cover, and let stand for 15 minutes. Drain and fill the pan with a few changes of cold water to stop the cooking. Refrigerate for up to 4 days.

· If you're using a kettle grill, position the grill lid so that its vents are directly over the food but opposite the coals. That way the smoke is drawn from the coals over the food on its way out the vents.

· To easily remove the excess fat from the drippings, use a fat separator (available in most grocery stores). The fat will rise to the top and you can pour the drippings out from the bottom. Barring that, siphon off the fat with a turkey baster or ladle it off with a spoon.

DEBONED WHOLE TURKEY STUFFED WITH KUMQUATS AND CHESTNUTS

This spectacular roast looks like a humble turkey when whole, but be ready to receive applause with grace and humility when you start to carve it. There are no bones to impede your progress as slice after perfect slice falls from your knife. The juxtaposition of sweet-tart kumquat, aromatic fennel, and velvety chestnuts in the stuffing is equally impressive.

THE GRILL

Gas: Indirect heat, medium (325° to 350°F)
3- or 4-burner grill–middle burner(s) off
2-burner grill–1 side off
Clean, oiled grate

Charcoal: Indirect heat, medium ash
Split charcoal bed (about 2 dozen coals per side)
20 replacement coals
Heavy-duty drip pan set between banks of charcoal
Clean, oiled grate on medium setting

TIMING
Prep: 1 hour
(plus 10 minutes for brine and rub)
Brine: Overnight
Grill: 3 to 4 hours

GRILL TOOLS AND EQUIPMENT
· Jumbo zipper-lock bag
· Grill screen
· Heavy-duty thread and large, sturdy needle, preferably curved (an upholstery needle works great)
· Kitchen twine
· Heavy-duty roasting pan with roasting rack
· Heat-resistant grill mitts

DEBONING A TURKEY (OR ANY OTHER BIRD)

1. Place the bird, backbone up, on a large, rimmed sheet pan. Make a slit through the skin running straight down the center of the backbone. If you are right-handed, start boning the left side of the turkey first. (Left-handed? Start on the right side.) Using short strokes, work your knife just under the skin, separating the meat from the bone all the way down the length of the backbone. As you are cutting, you should feel bone against one side of the knife at all times. This will ensure that you aren't leaving meat on the carcass. Use the illlustrations below as a guide to the bone structure of the bird.

2. After the meat is disengaged from the backbone, your knife will start to go over the outside of the rib cage. Continue to cut the meat from the rib cage in the same way that you disengaged it from the backbone. Soon you will come to where the leg joins the hip at one end of the turkey, and where the wing joins the shoulder at the other end. If you pull the limbs upward toward the backbone (in the opposite direction of the way they naturally move), the joints will pop out of their sockets. Cut through the tendons holding the joints in place, and the leg and wing will separate from the carcass.

3. In order to get the wing to disengage from the carcass, you will have to cut around the end of the wishbone and the thick bone that attaches the wing to the breast. In order to get the leg to disengage, you will have to cut around the hip bone and slit the membrane surrounding the internal cavity. The leg and wing will now fall away from the carcass.

4. To separate the breast from the carcass, continue to cut around the rib cage, still using short strokes and making sure that you feel bone against one side of the knife. Eventually you will get to the sternum (a large, flat bone that forms the arc of the breast). Scrape the meat from the sternum, stopping at its edge.

5. Turn the bird around and bone the other side in the same way. The bird will now be attached only along the edge of the sternum. Holding the carcass with one hand, and with the sharp edge of the knife angled toward the bone, make small slits down the edge of the sternum as you lift the carcass away from the meat. Be careful to avoid cutting through the skin; it lies right against the bone along the sternum.

6. If you wish, remove the leg and wing bones by grasping the hip bone (for the leg) and the shoulder bone (for the wing), then cutting around the bone with the tip of a knife, removing the meat from the bones. Be careful not to cut through the skin. When you reach the end of the leg, pull the bone from the skin by grasping both and stretching the bone and skin in opposite direction.

INGREDIENTS (MAKES 12 TO 14 SERVINGS)

For the turkey:

1 fresh turkey, 18 to 20 pounds
4 cups Orange-Fennel Brine (page 362)

For the stuffing:

6 dozen chestnuts
2 tablespoons olive oil
2 tablespoons butter
2 large onions, finely chopped
2 bulbs fennel, dark green stems and leaves removed, separated into stalks
2 teaspoons rubbed sage

2 teaspoons fresh rosemary leaves
3 cloves garlic, minced
3 cups chicken broth
30 kumquats (about 1½ pints), halved lengthwise, seeds removed, coarsely chopped

For the pan sauce:

1½ cups orange juice
1½ cups chicken or turkey broth
1 teaspoon herbes de Provence or Provençal Herb Rub (page 373)
2 tablespoons butter
Kosher salt and ground black pepper to taste

DIRECTIONS

1. The day before serving, debone the turkey (see "Deboning a Turkey," left).

2. Put the turkey in a jumbo-size zipper-lock bag with the brine. Seal the zipper, leaving about an inch open; push on the bag to release any trapped air through the opening, and close the zipper completely. Massage the liquid gently into the meat and refrigerate overnight, or for 6 to 12 hours.

3. Heat the grill as directed.

4. To make the stuffings, cut a small X just through the shell on the rounded side of each chestnut, using a serrated knife. Put a grill screen on the grill, away from the fire. Arrange the chestnuts, cut-side up, on the screen, close the grill, and cook until the cuts in the shells open wide, the chestnut meat is tender, and the bottom of the shells have browned, about 20 minutes. Let cool until comfortable to touch but still warm, about 10 minutes. Peel away the shells and the hairy skin underneath. Chop the chestnut meat finely.

5. Heat the olive oil and butter in a large, deep skillet over medium-high heat until the butter melts. Add the onions and fennel and sauté until tender, about 5 minutes. Add the sage, rosemary, and garlic and sauté for another minute. Add the chicken broth and boil until the liquid is almost all gone, stirring often. Stir in the kumquats. Cool.

6. Remove the turkey from the brine; discard the brine. Put the turkey, skin-side down, on a large, rimmed sheet pan. Sew up the back of the turkey, using a large, sturdy needle and heavy-duty thread, starting at the neck and ending at the tail. Turn the turkey right-side up. Stuff the cooled stuffing loosely into the cavity and stitch the opening shut. Tie the ends of the drumsticks together with twine and form the turkey into a natural turkey shape; tie lengths of twine around the turkey to secure it.

7. Put the turkey on a roasting rack in a roasting pan. Put the roasting pan on the grill away from the heat, cover the grill, and cook until an instant-read thermometer inserted into the thickest part of the breast registers about 170°F, about 3 hours. If your grill has a temperature gauge, it should stay between 350° and 375°F. If you are using charcoal, you will probably have to replenish the coals after the first hour.

8. When the turkey is done, use grill mitts to remove it to a carving board, and cover it with foil to keep warm. Remove the rack from the roasting pan and put the roasting pan on a burner heated to medium. Add the orange juice, broth, and herb blend. Bring to a boil, scraping any brown bits clinging to the bottom of the pan into the liquid. Boil for 5 minutes, remove from the heat, and swirl in the butter. Adjust the seasoning with salt and pepper, and strain into a serving dish.

9. To carve the turkey, remove the twine. Remove the legs and wings and cut into sections. Grab one end of the thread that is stitching up the back and pull; it will all come out. Slice the breast in straight slices from end to end; because all of the bones have been removed, you will get perfect slices surrounding a core stuffing. Serve with the pan sauce.

---

1. Sternum
2. Wishbone
3. Shoulder
4. Backbone
5. Wing
6. Ribcage
7. Hipbone
8. Thigh bone
9. Drumstick

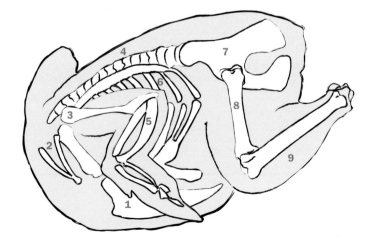

CHAPTER 9

MASTERING VEGETABLES AND OTHER SIDES

RECIPES

VEGGIES ON THE GRILL

Vegetables come in all shapes, sizes, and densities. Each one requires a slightly different preparation. And some vegetables can be grilled in more ways than one. For instance, eggplant can be sliced and grilled over direct heat to keep the slices intact, or whole eggplant can be grilled with indirect heat so you can scoop out the softened flesh from the skin. Sliced sweet potatoes can be grilled over direct heat, or you can bury whole sweet potatoes in the coals and eat them out of their skins like a baked potato.

In general, most vegetables should be grilled quickly over a medium-high fire. It helps to add some fat and flavor, so we recommend brushing or tossing most vegetables with oil and sprinkling them with salt and pepper or the spice rub of your choice (see Chapter 11 for various rubs). We prefer to grill whole vegetables or large pieces directly on the grill grate. This method works well for lengthwise slices of zucchini or eggplant, quartered bell peppers, quartered onions, and lengthwise slices of fennel. For smaller pieces, such as crosswise slices of zucchini or unpeeled garlic cloves, a grill screen coated with oil prevents the pieces from falling into the fire (see page 23 for more on grill screens and grill trays).

Here are general prep guidelines and cooking times for various vegetables. All cut vegetables should be washed, trimmed, and tossed with oil and the seasonings of your choice before grilling. For the larger vegetable pieces listed in the chart, we recommend grilling the vegetable and then cutting it into bite-size pieces after cooking. All vegetables listed below are cooked over direct medium to medium-high heat, turning once or twice during cooking, until just tender and grill-marked. Some whole vegetables are left unseasoned and are grilled by indirect heat; those are noted in the chart. Check out the recipes throughout this chapter for more creative ways to flavor and serve grilled vegetables.

VEGETABLE-GRILLING GUIDE

Vegetable	Prep	Grilling Time (in minutes)
Artichokes, sliced	Steam 25 minutes, slice in half lengthwise (remove fuzzy choke), oil, and season	10
Artichokes, whole	Trim, wrap in foil with liquid	Indirect heat, 40 to 50
Asparagus	Trim, oil, and season	5 to 8
Beets, sliced	Slice $1/4$ inch thick, oil, and season	15 to 20
Beets, whole	Prick skin in several places, oil, and season	Indirect heat, 40 to 50
Belgian endive	Halve lengthwise, oil, and season	8 to 10
Bok choy	Leave individual stalks whole, cut baby bok choy in half lengthwise; oil and season	8 to 10
Broccoli	Cut florets into small pieces, slice stems $1/4$ inch thick; oil and season	5 to 8
Carrots, baby	Leave whole, oil and season	8 to 10
Carrots, large	Cut into sticks or slabs, oil, and season	Medium to medium-low heat, 8 to 10
Corn, in the husk	Leave whole, grill until blackened all over, husk and season after cooking	15 to 18
Eggplant, sliced	Slice $1/4$ to $1/2$ inch thick, oil, and season	8 to 12
Eggplant, whole	Leave whole, prick skin in several places, season after cooking	Indirect heat, 30 to 40
Fennel, sliced	Trim, slice $1/4$ inch thick, oil, and season	10 to 12
Fennel, halved	Trim, halve lengthwise, oil, and season	Indirect heat, 18 to 20
Garlic, cloves	Leave unpeeled, oil, and squeeze from skin when soft	8 to 10
Garlic, whole head	Trim top to expose some cloves, oil, wrap in foil, squeeze from skin when soft	30 to 35
Green beans	Trim, oil, and season	5 to 8
Leeks	Trim, rinse, remove tough green tops, halve lengthwise, oil, and season	6 to 8
Mushrooms	Leave whole, slice, or grill caps only; oil and season	8 to 12
Okra	Oil and season	6 to 8
Onions	Cut into wedges with root end intact, or slice $1/4$ to $1/2$ inch thick and skewer slices through side to secure; oil and season	8 to 12
Peppers (bell or chile), sliced	Core, seed, and cut into large pieces; oil and season	8 to 12
Peppers (bell or chile), whole	Leave whole, grill until blackened all over, cover tightly for 15 minutes, then peel and seed before cutting	10 to 12
Potatoes, sliced	Slice $1/4$ inch thick, oil, and season	18 to 20

Potatoes, whole	Prick skin in several places, oil, and season	Indirect heat, 60 to 80
Radicchio	Cut into wedges, oil, and season	8 to 12
Scallions	Trim, leave whole, oil, and season	6 to 8
Squash, summer	Slice $1/4$ to $1/2$ inch thick, oil, and season	8 to 10
Squash, winter, sliced	Slice $1/2$ inch thick, steam 2 to 3 minutes, oil, and season	8 to 10
Squash, winter, whole	Halve, seed, oil and season hollows, wrap in foil	Indirect heat, 40 to 50
Sweet potatoes, sliced	Slice $1/4$ inch thick, oil, and season	18 to 20
Sweet potatoes, whole	Prick skin in several places, oil, and season	Indirect heat, 60 to 80
Tomatoes	Halve or slice $3/4$ inch thick, oil, and season	6 to 10

GRILLED SUMMER VEGETABLES WITH BROWN-BUTTER VINAIGRETTE

Vinaigrettes are simple. Made from two main ingredients, they differ largely in the proportions used—more oil or more vinegar? Will you add herbs this time, or just a clove of garlic? But occasionally something comes along that gives the old standby a whole new identity. In that vein, we give you Brown-Butter Vinaigrette. The oil is replaced with sautéed butter, creating a culinary hybrid—half vinaigrette, half butter sauce. It's vinaigrette deluxe.

TIMING
Prep: 10 minutes
Grill: 10 minutes

GRILL TOOLS AND EQUIPMENT
· Grill screen
· Long-handled spatula

GETTING CREATIVE
· Change the vegetables to fit what you have on hand, or pour this vinaigrette over a single vegetable, such as asparagus, potatoes, artichokes, or a variety of heirloom tomatoes.
· Add herbs to the vinaigrette, or replace part of the vinegar with lemon or lime juice.

THE GRILL

Gas: Direct heat, medium-high (400° to 450°F)
Clean, oiled grate

Charcoal: Direct heat, light ash
12-by-12-inch charcoal bed (about 3 dozen coals)
Clean, oiled grate on lowest setting

Wood: Direct heat, light ash
12-by-12-inch bed, 3 to 4 inches deep
Clean, oiled grate set 2 inches above the fire

INGREDIENTS (MAKES 6 SERVINGS)

Oil for coating grill screen
2 medium zucchini, cut lengthwise into $3/4$-inch slices
2 medium yellow squash, cut lengthwise into $3/4$-inch slices
1 red bell pepper, seeded and cut into strips
1 orange bell pepper, seeded and cut into strips
1 large onion, peeled and cut into wedges
3 large tomatoes, thickly sliced

$1/4$ cup olive oil
1 teaspoon kosher salt
$1/2$ teaspoon ground black pepper
4 tablespoons ($1/2$ stick) salted butter
$1/2$ cup red wine vinegar
$1/4$ cup capers

DIRECTIONS

1. Heat the grill as directed. Put the grill screen on the grill and coat it with oil.

2. Toss the vegetables with the olive oil, salt, and pepper in a large bowl. Place on the grill screen and grill until browned and tender, about 5 minutes per side. Watch carefully: Different vegetables cook at different rates. Turn as needed.

3. Put a large skillet over high heat. Add the butter and cook until it begins to brown lightly. Remove from the heat and stir in the vinegar and capers.

4. Cut the vegetables into large bite-size chunks, place in a serving bowl, and pour the brown butter vinaigrette over the top. Serve warm.

GRILL TOOLS AND EQUIPMENT
· Grill screen
· Long-handled spatula

GETTING CREATIVE
· Make golden gazpacho by using yellow tomatoes and yellow peppers in place of red.
· Vary the spiciness with the kind of hot sauce you use.
· Deepen the color and flavor of the gazpacho by using black bread in place of the white bread to thicken it.

STREAMLINING
· To get the gazpacho chilled faster, use ice cubes in place of water. As soon as they melt, the soup will be cold enough to serve.

GRILLED GAZPACHO

Sometimes all it takes to reinvent the very nature of a dish is a subtle shift, a change of ingredient, a slimmer slice, a different cooking method. In this recipe a classic gazpacho takes on a new personality. Grilling the vegetables for the soup deepens the flavors and heightens the spices, turning what was once a kind of liquid salad into a main attraction. Serve it as a substantial first course, a light meal, or a summer entrée by adding grilled shrimp, chicken, or sausage.

THE GRILL

Gas: Direct heat, medium-high (400° to 450°F)
Clean, oiled grate

Charcoal: Direct heat, light ash
12-by-12-inch charcoal bed (about 3 dozen coals)
Clean, oiled grate on lowest setting

Wood: Direct heat, light ash
12-by-12-inch bed, 3 to 4 inches deep
Clean, oiled grate set 2 inches above the fire

INGREDIENTS (MAKES 6 SERVINGS)

Oil for coating grill screen
1 red bell pepper, seeded and cut into strips
1 orange bell pepper, seeded and cut into strips
1 large onion, peeled and cut into wedges
3 large tomatoes, thickly sliced
5 tablespoons extra-virgin olive oil
1 teaspoon kosher salt, plus more to taste
$1/2$ teaspoon ground black pepper, plus more to taste

2 large cucumbers, peeled, seeded, and finely chopped
2 slices firm white bread, crusts removed, finely crumbled
$1^1/2$ cups vegetable broth
$1^1/2$ cups water
1 teaspoon hot pepper sauce
$1/4$ cup red wine vinegar
$1/4$ cup capers

DIRECTIONS

1. Heat the grill as directed. Put the grill screen on the grill and coat it with oil.

2. Toss the bell peppers, onion, and tomatoes in a large bowl with 2 tablespoons of the olive oil and the salt and pepper. Place on the grill screen and grill until browned and tender, about 5 minutes per side. Watch carefully: Different vegetables cook at different rates. Turn as needed.

3. Combine the cucumbers, bread, broth, water, hot pepper sauce, vinegar, capers, and remaining 3 tablespoons olive oil in a large serving bowl. Finely chop the grilled vegetables and add to the bowl. Adjust the salt and pepper to taste and chill thoroughly before serving.

GRILL TOOLS AND EQUIPMENT
· Grill screen
· Long-handled spatula

GRILLED RATATOUILLE

Here ratatouille, the symphonic vegetable stew of Provence, has been recast for the grill. In a traditional ratatouille, the vegetables are layered in a casserole with herbs and olive oil and simmered until their flavors mingle. Moving everything over a flame causes each vegetable to retain more of its distinctive flavor and texture and transforms the finished dish into a mountainous grilled salad, glistening with olive oil and radiating the aroma of fresh basil.

THE GRILL

Gas: Direct heat, medium-high (400° to 450°F)
Clean, oiled grate

Charcoal: Direct heat, light ash
12-by-12-inch charcoal bed (about 3 dozen coals)
Clean, oiled grate on lowest setting

Wood: Direct heat, light ash
12-by-12-inch bed, 3 to 4 inches deep
Clean, oiled grate set 2 inches above the fire

Oil for coating grill screen

1 medium eggplant, cut into 3/4-inch-thick rounds

1 medium zucchini, cut lengthwise into 3/4-inch slices

1 red bell pepper, seeded and cut into strips

1 large onion, peeled and cut into wedges

3 portobello mushrooms (about 6 ounces), trimmed and thickly sliced

4 tablespoons extra-virgin olive oil

2 cloves garlic, minced

1/2 teaspoon kosher salt, plus more to taste

1/4 teaspoon coarsely ground black pepper, plus more to taste

1 can (about 15 ounces) Italian-style diced tomatoes

1/4 cup chopped fresh basil leaves

Shredded or shaved Parmesan cheese

DIRECTIONS

1. Heat the grill as directed. Put the grill screen on the grill and coat it with oil.

2. Toss the eggplant, zucchini, bell pepper, onion, and mushrooms with 2 tablespoons of the olive oil, the garlic, and the salt and bell pepper in a large bowl. Place on the grill screen and grill until browned and tender, about 5 minutes per side.

Watch carefully: Different vegetables cook at different rates. Turn as needed.

3. Cut the vegetables into large bite-size chunks and place in a serving bowl. Toss with the tomatoes, basil, and remaining 2 tablespoons olive oil. Season with more salt and pepper, garnish with Parmesan, and serve.

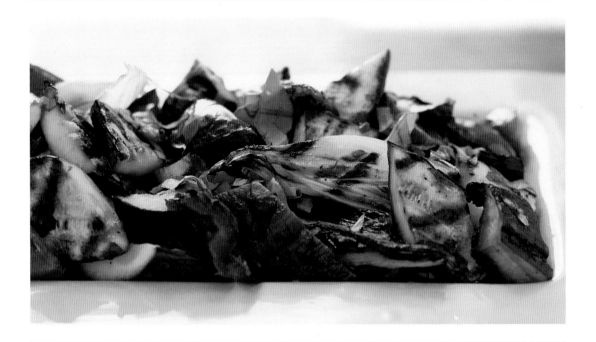

GRILLED TOMATOES WITH BASIL BUTTER

TIMING
Prep: 10 minutes
Grill: 6 minutes

GRILL TOOLS AND EQUIPMENT
· Grill screen
· Long-handled spatula

Grilling tomatoes brings out their juices and softens their fiber, so it is best to start with fruit that is not too ripe to ensure that the slices keep their shape. They are coated simply and elegantly with melted butter infused with fresh basil.

THE GRILL

Gas: Direct heat, medium-high (400° to 450°F)
Clean, oiled grate

Charcoal: Direct heat, light ash
12-by-12-inch charcoal bed (about 3 dozen coals)
Clean, oiled grate on lowest setting

Wood: Direct heat, light ash
12-by-12-inch bed, 3 to 4 inches deep
Clean, oiled grate set 2 inches above the fire

Photo: Grilled Ratatouille

MAKING SUBSTITUTIONS
· Almost any fresh herb can be substituted for basil. Tomatoes are equally
delicious with mint, tarragon, oregano,
or flat-leaf parsley.

INGREDIENTS (MAKES 4 SERVINGS)

3 to 4 large, barely ripe tomatoes (6 to 8 ounces each)

1 tablespoon extra-virgin olive oil

1/2 teaspoon kosher salt

1/4 teaspoon ground black pepper

Oil for coating grill screen

2 tablespoons salted butter

1/2 cup chopped fresh basil (about 20 leaves)

DIRECTIONS

1. Heat the grill as directed. Put the grill screen on the grill to heat up.

2. Cut the tomatoes into 1/2-inch-thick slices. Coat the slices with the olive oil, salt, and pepper.

3. Coat the grill screen with oil. Put the tomato slices on the grill screen and cook, uncovered, until browned and barely tender, about 6 minutes, turning halfway through.

4. Melt the butter in a small skillet. Add the basil leaves and stir until wilted, a few seconds. Arrange the tomato slices slightly overlapping on a serving platter, pour the basil butter over the top, and serve.

TIMING
Prep: 10 minutes
   (plus 5 minutes for rub)
Grill: 6 minutes

GRILL TOOLS AND EQUIPMENT
· Grill screen
· Long-handled spatula

GRILLED GREEN TOMATOES WITH CAJUN DRESSING

Green tomatoes are not just unripe red fruit. They are lemony tart and slightly crunchy, and when it comes to grilling they are the tomato of choice. Unlike ripe red tomatoes, which have a tendency to collapse on the grill, green tomatoes brown and crisp on the edges as their interior softens and swells with juice. In this recipe they are coated with a spicy rub and topped with a creamy dressing. If you don't have a garden, your biggest challenge could be finding green tomatoes to grill. They are most plentiful at the beginning and end of tomato season (summer), and are more common at farmers' markets than super-markets. Most farmers are happy to find customers for unripened tomatoes.

THE GRILL

Gas: Direct heat, medium-high (400° to 450°F)
Clean, oiled grate

Charcoal: Direct heat, light ash
12-by-12-inch charcoal bed (about 3 dozen coals)
Clean, oiled grate on lowest setting

Wood: Direct heat, light ash
12-by-12-inch bed, 3 to 4 inches deep
Clean, oiled grate set 2 inches above the fire

INGREDIENTS (MAKES 4 SERVINGS)

3 to 4 large green tomatoes (6 to 8 ounces each)

1 tablespoon canola oil

1 teaspoon Cajun Blackening Rub (page 373)

1/2 teaspoon kosher salt

1/4 cup sour cream

1/4 cup mayonnaise

1/4 cup mild hot pepper sauce such as Durkee Red Hot sauce

Oil for coating grill screen

DIRECTIONS

1. Heat the grill as directed. Put the grill screen on the grill to heat up.

2. Cut the tomatoes into 1/2-inch-thick slices. Coat the slices with the canola oil and sprinkle with the Cajun rub and salt; set aside.

3. Mix the sour cream, mayonnaise, and hot sauce in a bowl until blended; set aside.

4. Coat the grill screen with oil. Put the tomato slices on the grill screen and cook, uncovered, until browned, about 6 minutes, turning halfway through.

5. Serve the grilled tomato slices topped with dollops of the dressing.

Photo: Grilled Green Tomatoes with Cajun Dressing

SUMMER SQUASH VINAIGRETTE

Mild-tasting vegetables come to life on the grill. For instance, summer squash, such as zucchini, which tends to be watery and bland, takes on a nutty flavor and meaty texture after a few minutes on the grill. This recipe couldn't be simpler. Cut the squash lengthwise (rather than in rounds) to keep the slices from falling through the grate, and toss them with vinaigrette while they are still warm, to help them absorb its flavor.

THE GRILL

Gas: Direct heat, medium-high (400° to 450°F)
Clean, oiled grate

Charcoal: Direct heat, light ash
12-by-12-inch charcoal bed (about 3 dozen coals)
Clean, oiled grate on lowest setting

Wood: Direct heat, light ash
12-by-12-inch bed, 3 to 4 inches deep
Clean, oiled grate set 2 inches above the fire

INGREDIENTS (MAKES 6 SERVINGS)

2 tablespoons red wine vinegar
1/4 cup extra-virgin olive oil
2 tablespoons fresh lemon juice
1 clove garlic, minced
Pinch of cayenne pepper
1/4 teaspoon kosher salt

1/8 teaspoon ground black pepper
4 medium zucchini, stems removed, cut lengthwise into 1/2-inch-thick slices
Oil for coating grill grate
1 tablespoon chopped fresh flat-leaf parsley

DIRECTIONS

1. Heat the grill as directed.
2. Mix the vinegar, olive oil, lemon juice, garlic, cayenne, salt, and pepper in a small bowl. Toss 2 tablespoons of this mixture with the zucchini on a rimmed sheet pan until evenly coated.

3. Brush the grill grate and coat it with oil. Put the zucchini on the hot grill, cover, and cook until browned and barely tender, about 6 minutes, turning halfway through. Put on a serving platter.
4. Pour the remaining vinaigrette over the zucchini and serve.

TIMING
Prep: 5 minutes
(plus 5 minutes for rub)
Grill: 12 to 15 minutes

GRILL TOOLS AND EQUIPMENT
· Long-handled tongs

GRILLED CORN ON THE COB WASHED WITH CHIMICHURRI

The Argentinean herb mop *chimichurri* is typically basted on beef and gives one of the world's richest meats a fresh, piquant makeover. In this recipe, the same flavor of herbs and chiles souses ears of grilled corn, and the same phenomenon happens. What once was sweet and starchy is refreshed, perfumed with herbs, and cleansed with a scrub of hot chiles.

THE GRILL

Gas: Direct heat, medium-high (400° to 450°F)
Clean, oiled grate

Charcoal: Direct heat, light ash
12-by-12-inch charcoal bed (about 3 dozen coals)
Clean, oiled grate on lowest setting

Wood: Direct heat, light ash
12-by-12-inch bed, 3 to 4 inches deep
Clean, oiled grate set 2 inches above the fire

INGREDIENTS (MAKES 6 SERVINGS)

Oil for coating grill grate
6 ears unhusked corn
1 tablespoon olive oil

2 tablespoons fresh lime juice
1/4 cup Green Chimichurri Rub (page 381)

1. Heat the grill as directed.

2. Brush the grill grate and coat it with oil. Put the corn on the grill, cover, and cook until the husks are charred and you can hear the juices from the corn sputtering inside, 12 to 15 minutes, turning every 3 or 4 minutes.

3. Meanwhile, mix the olive oil, lime juice, and Chimichurri Rub in a small bowl.

4. Let the corn cool for a few minutes. Grasp each ear with a dish towel and peel off the husk. Serve the ears slathered with the chimichurri mixture.

GRILLED CORN AND CRAB SALAD WITH RASPBERRIES

TIMING
Prep: 15 minutes
Grill: 15 minutes
Chill: 2 hours

GRILL TOOLS AND EQUIPMENT
· Long-handled tongs

Who says light and delicate meals can't come off your grill? Try this refreshing crab salad on a hot summer day. The corn provides an earthy flavor (and picks up a hint of smoke if you peel back the husks toward the end of cooking), while the raspberries and dill have a cooling effect–all of which enhances the mild, sweet taste of crabmeat.

THE GRILL

Gas: Direct heat, medium (350°F)
Clean, oiled grate on lowest setting

Charcoal: Direct heat, light ash
10-by-10-inch charcoal bed (about 3 dozen coals)
Clean, oiled grate on lowest setting

Wood: Direct heat, medium ash
10-by-10-inch bed, 1 inch deep
Clean, oiled grate set 4 inches above the fire

Photo: Grilled Corn and Crab Salad with Raspberries

INGREDIENTS (MAKES 4 SERVINGS)

Oil for coating grill grate

4 medium ears corn

1 1/2 tablespoons raspberry vinegar

1/4 cup olive oil

3/4 teaspoon kosher salt

1/8 teaspoon ground white or black pepper

1 tablespoon chopped fresh dill

2 scallions, white and green parts, chopped

1 small red bell pepper, seeded and finely chopped

1 tomato, seeded and finely chopped

8 ounces fresh lump crabmeat, picked over to remove shells

6 ounces fresh raspberries

DIRECTIONS

1. Heat the grill as directed. Brush the grill grate and coat it with oil.

2. Put the corn on the grill, cover, and cook until the husks are charred and you can hear the juices from the corn spitting inside, 12 to 15 minutes, turning every 3 to 4 minutes. For more grilled flavor, peel back all but the last thin layer of husk for the last 5 minutes of grilling. Let cool enough to handle, then remove and discard the husks. Stand the corncobs upright on a cutting board and cut straight down the sides, slicing the kernels off the cobs.

3. Put the vinegar in a medium bowl. Whisk in the olive oil in a slow, steady stream until fully incorporated. Whisk in the salt and pepper, then stir in the dill, scallions, bell pepper, tomato, and corn. Gently stir in the crab. Chill for at least 2 hours or up to 1 day. Top with the raspberries just before serving.

GRILLED CORN WITH SPICY TOMATO BUTTER

In order to mix something moist, like a tomato, with butter (which is at least 80 percent fat), most of the juice has to be removed. You could squeeze it, but then you'd lose a lot of its flavor. You could cook it until it's dry, but that would take time and fairly constant attention. Or you could use a tablespoon of tomato paste, which is nothing more than ripe tomatoes simmered until most of the moisture is gone. The more a tomato cooks, the less it resembles fresh, and the more concentrated its flavor will be. Mixing a tomato concentrate with butter gives it dairy sweetness and a velvety texture that is delicious slathered over the charred kernels of an ear of grilled corn.

TOMATO PASTE
Tomato paste is made by cooking tomato purée until almost all of its liquid evaporates. It is too intense and too thick to be eaten alone; rather, it is best thought of as a flavoring agent. For grilling, its main role is as a component in barbecue glazes and sauces, but it can also infuse the flavor of tomato into a rub or a composed butter without the need to worry about adding extra moisture. The best-quality tomato paste is packaged in tubes and is double concentrated. Usually imported, these double tomato pastes are sweet, aromatic, and intensely flavored. Best of all, the tube keeps air away from any leftover paste, allowing it to stay fresh for months in a refrigerator. No more throwing out half-used cans of tomato paste.

THE GRILL

Gas: Direct heat, medium-high (400° to 450°F)
Clean, oiled grate

Charcoal: Direct heat, light ash
12-by-12-inch charcoal bed (about 3 dozen coals)
Clean, oiled grate on lowest setting

Wood: Direct heat, light ash
12-by-12-inch bed, 3 to 4 inches deep
Clean, oiled grate set 2 inches above the fire

INGREDIENTS (MAKES 6 SERVINGS)

Oil for coating grill grate

6 ears unhusked corn

4 tablespoons (1/2 stick) butter, softened

1 tablespoon corn or canola oil

1 1/2 tablespoons tomato paste

1/8 teaspoon Chinese chili paste with garlic

1/4 teaspoon garlic salt

DIRECTIONS

1. Heat the grill as directed.

2. Brush the grill grate and coat it with oil. Put the corn on the grill, cover, and cook until the husks are charred and you can hear the juices from the corn sputtering inside, 12 to 15 minutes, turning every 3 or 4 minutes.

3. Meanwhile, mix the butter, 1 tablespoon oil, tomato paste, chili paste, and garlic salt in a small bowl.

4. Let the corn cool for a few minutes. Grasp each ear with a dish towel and peel off the husk. Serve the ears slathered with the tomato butter.

GRILLED EGGPLANT ROLLATINE

TIMING
Prep: 15 minutes
Grill: About 30 minutes

Casseroles are built to be baked, and it is not usually worth the effort it takes to reinvent them for the grill, but in this case, the charred bits that speckle the eggplant and the flavor of fire that permeates the sauce give this traditional Italian vegetable casserole a whole new identity. The biggest effect comes from grilling the vegetables before they are layered in the casserole; cooking the casserole itself on the grill doesn't do much, although it does let you avoid having to heat up the oven.

GRILL TOOLS AND EQUIPMENT
· Long-handled spatula or tongs
· 9-by-13-inch grill-safe baking dish

BAKING INSTEAD OF GRILLING
· Instead of cooking the rollatine on the grill, you can finish them in a 350°F oven; bake for about 20 minutes.

THE GRILL

Gas: Direct heat, medium-high (350° to 400°F)
Clean, oiled grate

Charcoal: Direct heat, light ash
12-by-12-inch charcoal bed (about 3 dozen coals)
Clean, oiled grate on medium setting

INGREDIENTS (MAKES 8 SERVINGS)

2 large eggplants (about 1 pound each)
1/2 cup extra-virgin olive oil
5 cloves garlic, minced
1 1/4 teaspoons kosher salt
3/4 teaspoon ground black pepper
Oil for coating grill grate

1 can (28 ounces) crushed fire-roasted tomatoes
32 fresh basil leaves (about 1 cup)
12 ounces fresh mozzarella cheese, cut into 16 long, thin pieces
3 tablespoons (about 3/4 ounce) shaved imported Parmesan cheese

DIRECTIONS

1. Heat the grill as directed.

2. Cut both ends of both eggplants flat. One at a time, stand the eggplants on end and cut into lengthwise 1/4-inch-thick slices. You should get 8 per eggplant.

3. Mix 1/4 cup of the olive oil, 2 cloves of the garlic, 1/4 teaspoon of the salt, and 1/4 teaspoon of the pepper in a small bowl. Brush the eggplant slices with a thin film of the oil mixture. Season the slices with another 1/2 teaspoon salt and 1/4 teaspoon pepper.

4. Brush the grill grate and coat it with oil. Put the eggplant slices on the grill directly over the heat, cover, and cook until browned and tender, 6 to 8 minutes, turning halfway through. If your grill has a temperature gauge, it should stay at around 375°F.

5. If using a 3- or 4-burner grill, turn off the middle burner(s). If using a 2-burner grill, turn off one side; cover.

6. Mix the crushed tomatoes in a large bowl with 2 cloves of the garlic, 2 tablespoons of the olive oil, the remaining 1/2 teaspoon salt, and the remaining 1/4 teaspoon pepper. Chop 16 of the basil leaves finely and stir in.

7. Mix the pieces of mozzarella, the remaining 2 tablespoons olive oil, and the remaining clove of garlic in a separate bowl.

8. Spoon half of the tomato mixture into a 9-by-13-inch baking dish.

9. Place a basil leaf at one end of an eggplant slice. Top with a piece of cheese with the oil and garlic clinging to it and roll up the eggplant slice around the cheese. Put seam-side down on the tomato sauce. Roll up the remaining eggplant slices and cheese in the same way and pack them snugly into the baking dish. Top with the remaining tomato mixture, and scatter the Parmesan over the top.

10. Put the baking dish on the grill away from the direct heat, cover, and cook for about 20 minutes, until bubbling all around the edge. If your grill has a temperature gauge, it should stay at around 350°F.

11. Let rest for 5 minutes before serving. Serve 2 eggplant rolls to each person.

GRILLED ASIAN EGGPLANT WITH HOISIN AND VODKA

TIMING
Prep: 15 minutes
Grill: 6 to 8 minutes

GRILL TOOLS AND EQUIPMENT
· Grill screen
· Long-handled tongs

MAKING SUBSTITUTIONS
· If you don't want to use vodka, you can use water instead.
· Parsley can be substituted for the cilantro.

Asian eggplants are leaner, sweeter, and firmer than their more common Mediterranean counterparts. Their paper-thin skins don't toughen during cooking, and their dense flesh browns beautifully, making them the definitive eggplant for grilling. There are several types of Asian eggplant, but Chinese is preferred. It is more lavender than purple, and its flesh is creamy white. Japanese eggplant can also be used, but its flesh is more bitter.

THE GRILL

Gas: Direct heat, medium-high (400° to 450°F)
Clean, oiled grate

Charcoal: Direct heat, light ash
12-by-12-inch charcoal bed (about 3 dozen coals)
Clean, oiled grate on lowest setting

Wood: Direct heat, light ash
12-by-12-inch bed, 3 to 4 inches deep
Clean, oiled grate set 2 inches above the fire

INGREDIENTS (MAKES 4 SERVINGS)

1 pound Chinese or Japanese eggplant
4 tablespoons olive oil
2 tablespoons hoisin sauce
2 tablespoons vodka
1 medium tomato (about 8 ounces), cored and finely chopped

1 tablespoon chopped fresh cilantro leaves
1 tablespoon finely chopped peeled gingerroot
1 clove garlic, minced
2 tablespoons balsamic vinegar
Oil for coating grill screen

DIRECTIONS

1. Heat the grill as directed.
2. Slice the eggplants lengthwise in 3/8-inch-thick slices all the way to, but not through, the stem ends. Mix 2 tablespoons of the olive oil with the hoisin sauce and vodka in a deep-sided plate. Fan the eggplant slices and turn them in the sauce until thoroughly coated. Set aside for about 10 minutes.
3. Meanwhile, mix the tomato, cilantro, ginger, garlic, balsamic vinegar, and remaining 2 tablespoons olive oil in a small bowl.

4. Put the grill screen on the grill and coat it with oil. Put the fanned-out eggplant on the screen, cover, and cook until browned and tender, 3 to 4 minutes per side.
5. Transfer to a serving platter and top with the tomato mixture. Cover and keep warm for about 5 minutes to allow the flavors to mingle, then serve.

TIMING
Prep: 5 minutes
(plus 5 minutes for marinade)
Marinate: 15 minutes
Grill: 15 minutes

GRILL TOOLS AND EQUIPMENT
· Long-handled tongs

GRILLED TANDOORI EGGPLANT

Cooked eggplant isn't pretty. Cursed with the color of putty, and with pulp that's bland tasting at best, this perennial wallflower is crying out for a gilding of tandoori. Here a rich, thick tandoori marinade enrobes slices of eggplant with Indian spices in a rich yogurt mask. The eggplant emerges from the grill gleaming gold and heady with aromas. It is topped with a splash of orange juice and crisp fresh scallion for contrast.

THE GRILL

Gas: Direct heat, medium (350°F)
Clean, oiled grate

Charcoal: Direct heat, medium ash
12-by-12-inch charcoal bed (about 3 dozen coals)
Clean, oiled grate on medium setting

Wood: Direct heat, medium ash
12-by-12-inch bed, 3 inches deep
Clean, oiled grate set 4 inches above the fire

---

¹/₄ cup Tandoori Yogurt Marinade (page 360)

2 tablespoons olive oil

1 large eggplant (about 1 pound), ends cut off, peeled

Oil for coating grill grate

1 orange

¹/₈ teaspoon kosher salt, or more to taste

¹/₈ teaspoon ground black pepper, or more to taste

1 scallion, roots trimmed, thinly sliced

DIRECTIONS

1. Mix the marinade and olive oil in a medium bowl.

2. Cut the eggplant in half crosswise. Put each half on its widest cut side and cut into 1-inch-thick wedges. Toss with the tandoori mixture and set aside for 15 minutes.

3. Heat the grill as directed.

4. Brush the grill grate and coat it with oil. Put the eggplant wedges on the grill and cook until browned on all sides and tender, about 15 minutes, turning every 5 minutes. If your grill has a temperature gauge, it should stay at around 375°F.

5. While the eggplant is grilling, grate the zest from the orange and squeeze the juice; hold separately.

6. Transfer the grilled eggplant to a serving plate, season with salt and pepper, and top with the orange juice, scallion, and grated orange zest.

Photo: Grilled Asian Eggplant with Hoisin and Vodka

GRILL TOOLS AND EQUIPMENT

· 8 wooden skewers or 16 toothpicks, soaked in water for 1 hour
· Long-handled tongs

GETTING CREATIVE

· For a more substantial chili, grill about 1 pound of veggie burgers until cooked through. Pulse in a food processor until coarsely ground. Add to the soup pot along with the chopped vegetables.

TIPS

· To seed the tomatoes, dig out the seeds and pulp with your fingertips over a bowl.
· To seed the jalapeños, halve them lengthwise, leaving the stem attached. Hold the chile by the stem and scrape out the seeds with the small side of a melon baller.
· For a spicier chili, leave the seeds in the jalapeños and grill them whole. Remove the stems after grilling and chop the jalapeños along with the other vegetables.
· Some steak sauces, such as A1, are vegetarian. Others, like Worcestershire sauce, include anchovies but may be available in vegetarian versions.
· Freeze any leftover chili for up to 3 months. Defrost and reheat before serving.
· If you've added the tomato pulp and the chili is still too thick, add more broth, beer, or water.

GRILLED VEGETARIAN CHILI

As we were writing this book, we experimented with several grilled soups and stews. This chili was one of the winners. All of the vegetables are grilled instead of sautéed, giving them a darkly caramelized sweetness and a hint of smoke that enriches the heartiness of the stew. We kept the spiciness on the mild side, but feel free to add ground chiles or hot sauce to your tongue's content.

THE GRILL

Gas: Direct heat, medium-high (400° to 450°F)
Clean, oiled grate

Charcoal: Direct heat, light ash
12-by-12-inch charcoal bed (about 3 dozen coals)
Clean, oiled grate on lowest setting

Wood: Direct heat, light ash
12-by-12-inch bed, 3 to 4 inches deep
Clean, oiled grate set 2 inches above the fire

INGREDIENTS (MAKES 10 SERVINGS)

1/2 cup olive oil
2 large onions, each cut into 4 thick slices
1 small head garlic, unpeeled, top sliced off to reveal some garlic cloves
2 carrots, quartered lengthwise
2 bell peppers (red and/or green), seeded and quartered
2 to 4 large jalapeño chiles, halved lengthwise and seeded
3 pounds tomatoes (about 8 to 10 medium), halved crosswise and seeded, pulp and seeds reserved
6 portobello mushroom caps
Oil for coating grill grate
3 cups vegetable broth (or half broth and half beer)

3 tablespoons steak sauce (see Tips)
2 tablespoons chili powder
1 tablespoon ground cumin
1 tablespoon dried oregano
1 tablespoon sugar
1 teaspoon kosher salt
1/2 teaspoon ground black pepper
2 cans (15 ounces each) black beans, rinsed and drained
2 cans (15 ounces each) pinto beans or small red beans, rinsed and drained
Juice of 1 lime (about 2 tablespoons)
1/2 cup chopped fresh cilantro leaves

DIRECTIONS

1. Heat the grill as directed.

2. Rub or brush about a tablespoon of the olive oil all over the onion slices, head of garlic, carrot and bell pepper quarters, jalapeño halves, tomato halves, and mushroom caps. Push the skewers or toothpicks through the sides of the onion slices to keep them from separating on the grill.

3. Brush the grill grate and coat it with oil. Put all of the vegetables on the grill, cover, and cook, turning occasionally, until nicely grill-marked and softened, 5 to 20 minutes total. (The carrots will take 5 to 10 minutes. The onions, tomatoes, bell peppers, mushrooms, and jalapeños will take 10 to 15 minutes; don't worry if the peppers and tomatoes blacken in spots. The garlic will take 15 to 20 minutes and should be blackened in several places, and the garlic cloves should be soft.) If your grill has a temperature gauge, it should stay at around 450°F.

4. Let the vegetables cool slightly, then pop the garlic cloves out of their skins and put them in a blender or food processor. Add half of the grilled tomatoes and blend or process to a purée. Remove the skewers or toothpicks from the onions. Chop the onions and the remaining vegetables (including the remaining grilled tomatoes) and put them in a large soup pot. Add the garlic-tomato purée, broth, steak sauce, chili powder, cumin, oregano, sugar, salt, and black pepper. Bring to a boil over high heat, then reduce the heat to medium-low and simmer until thick like stew, 30 to 40 minutes. If you need to add liquid, stir in the reserved tomato pulp and seeds. Add the beans and heat through, 15 to 20 minutes.

5. Stir in the lime juice and cilantro and adjust the seasonings just before serving.

GRILLED VEGETABLE FAJITAS

TIMING
Prep: 10 minutes
    (plus 20 minutes for salsa and guac)
Marinate: 1 to 3 hours
Grill: 10 to 15 minutes

Plenty of good vegetarian fare can come off your grill. These fajitas get their satisfying chew from marinated and grilled portobello mushrooms. Other grilled vegetables, fire-roasted tomatillo salsa, and grilled guacamole fill out the wraps. These are somewhat mild. For more incendiary fajitas, add your favorite hot pepper sauce, ground cayenne pepper, chipotle pepper, or other hot chile peppers to the marinade.

GRILL TOOLS AND EQUIPMENT
- Long-handled tongs
- Long-handled basting brush
- Aluminum foil

HOW TO FOLD A FAJITA
1. To prevent any filling from falling out, position the filling in a column in the center near the top of the tortilla. Leave some empty space at the bottom of the tortilla.
2. Fold the bottom up partially over the filling, and then fold in the sides.

THE GRILL

Gas: Direct heat, medium (350°F)
Clean, oiled grate on lowest setting

Charcoal: Direct heat, medium ash
12-by-12-inch charcoal bed (about 3 dozen coals)
Clean, oiled grate on lowest setting

Wood: Direct heat, medium ash
12-by-12-inch bed, 3 inches deep
Clean, oiled grate set 4 inches above the fire

INGREDIENTS (MAKES 8 FAJITAS/4 SERVINGS)

1/3 cup olive oil

3 tablespoons Worcestershire sauce

4 cloves garlic, minced

2 tablespoons chili powder

1 tablespoon dried oregano

1 1/2 teaspoons ground cumin

1 1/2 teaspoons kosher salt

1 teaspoon ground black pepper

6 portobello mushroom caps

2 onions, cut in half from roots to tips

2 bell peppers (red and green or yellow), seeded and quartered

4 to 6 large jalapeño chiles, halved lengthwise and seeded

Oil for coating grill grate

8 large flour tortillas (8 to 10 inches in diameter)

3/4 cup sour cream (optional)

3/4 cup Fire-Roasted Tomatillo Salsa (page 277) or prepared salsa (optional)

3/4 cup Grilled Guac (page 276) or prepared guacamole (optional)

1 lime, cut into small wedges

DIRECTIONS

1. Put the olive oil, Worcestershire, garlic, chili powder, oregano, cumin, salt, and pepper in a 2-gallon zipper-lock bag. Shake to mix, then pour half of the mixture into another 2-gallon zipper-lock bag. Put the mushrooms caps in one bag and the onions, bell peppers, and jalapeños in the other. Press the air out of the bags, seal, and massage the marinade into the vegetables, especially the crevices of the mushroom caps. Let stand at room temperature for 1 to 3 hours.

2. Heat the grill as directed.

3. Brush the grill grate and coat it with oil. Put the vegetables on the grill and cover, positioning the jalapeños lengthwise across the bars of the grill grate (if you think they may fall through the grate, skewer them first to hold them in place).

Cook, turning and basting with the marinade a few times, until the vegetables are crisp-tender and nicely grill-marked. Plan on 5 to 10 minutes for the onions and peppers and 10 to 15 minutes for the mushrooms, which should be a bit softer in texture.

4. As the vegetables grill, wrap the stack of tortillas in foil and warm over a very low-heat area of the grill, 3 to 4 minutes per side.

5. Transfer the vegetables to a cutting board or platter and cut them into strips.

6. Allow guests to build their own fajitas by filling each tortilla with vegetables and dollops of the optional sour cream, salsa, and guacamole. Serve with the lime wedges for squeezing.

TIMING

Soak wood chips: 1 hour
Prep: 25 minutes
Grill: 20 to 30 minutes

GRILL TOOLS AND EQUIPMENT

· 2 cups apple or oak wood chips
  or chunks
· Smoker box or foil packet, if using
  a gas grill (see page 39)
· Long-handled tongs
  or long-handled spatula

GETTING CREATIVE

· Shaved ricotta salata cheese makes
  a good alternative to the Parmesan.

TIPS

· For 2 cups fresh corn kernels, you'll
  need 3 to 4 ears of corn. Remove the
  husks and silks, then stand the cobs
  upright on a cutting board with the fat
  end down. Cut straight downward all
  around the cob, cutting the kernels
  from the cob. For extra flavor, use the
  dull side of your knife blade to scrape
  the remaining corn and juices, or "milk,"
  from the cobs.
· Use a melon baller to quickly scrape
  the ribs from the bell peppers.
· Save time (but sacrifice some flavor)
  by replacing the breadcrumbs, herbs,
  salt, and pepper in the stuffing with
  seasoned dried breadcrumbs.

SMOKE-ROASTED BELL PEPPERS STUFFED WITH GARDEN VEGETABLES

This is one of the most colorful dishes that will ever grace your grill. Orange, yellow, red, and green bell peppers are stuffed with golden corn kernels, red tomatoes, green zucchini, and chopped fresh herbs. Breadcrumbs hold the filling together and develop a lightly toasted top crust as the stuffed peppers are grill-roasted via indirect heat. A few handfuls of wood chips infuse the vegetables with a subtle, smoky aroma.

THE GRILL

Gas: Indirect heat, medium (325° to 350°F)
3- or 4-burner grill—middle burner(s) off
2-burner grill—1 side off
Clean, oiled grate

Charcoal: Indirect heat, medium ash
Split charcoal bed (about 2 dozen coals per side)
Clean, oiled grate on medium setting

INGREDIENTS (MAKES 8 SMALL SERVINGS)

2 medium red bell peppers
3 medium mixed bell peppers (yellow, orange, green)
$3/4$ teaspoon kosher salt
$1/2$ teaspoon ground black pepper
3 tablespoons butter
1 onion, finely chopped
2 cloves garlic, minced
1 medium zucchini, cut into $1/4$-inch dice

1 medium yellow squash, cut into $1/4$-inch dice
2 cups fresh or frozen corn kernels (see Tips)
1 medium tomato, seeded and cut into $1/4$-inch dice
2 tablespoons chopped fresh herbs (such as parsley,
    oregano, basil, or a mix)
$1/4$ cup plain dried breadcrumbs
Oil for coating grill grate
2 tablespoons grated Parmesan cheese (optional)

DIRECTIONS

1. Heat the grill as directed. Soak the wood chips or chunks in water for 1 hour.

2. Seed, core, and cut one of the red bell peppers into $1/4$-inch dice. Cut the remaining bell peppers in half lengthwise right through the stem, leaving a bit of stem attached to each half. Cut out the cores, seeds, and ribs from the interiors of the peppers, leaving the stem intact. Sprinkle the insides of the peppers with $1/4$ teaspoon of the salt and $1/4$ teaspoon of the pepper.

3. Melt the butter in a large skillet over medium heat. Add the onion and sauté until almost tender, about 4 minutes. Add the garlic, chopped bell pepper, zucchini, and yellow squash. Sauté the vegetables until crisp-tender, about 4 minutes. Stir in the corn and tomato and cook until heated through, 1 to 2 minutes. Stir in herbs, breadcrumbs, and the

remaining $1/2$ teaspoon salt and $1/4$ teaspoon pepper. Cook and stir until the breadcrumbs soak up most of the liquid in the pan. Remove from the heat and spoon the filling equally into the pepper cavities.

4. When the grill is hot, put the soaked wood chips or chunks over the coals on both sides of the grill. If using gas, put the wood chips in a smoker box or in a perforated foil packet directly over one of the heated burners.

5. Brush the grill grate and coat it with oil. Put the stuffed peppers over the unheated part of the grill, cover, and cook until just tender, 20 to 30 minutes. If your grill has a temperature gauge, it should stay at around 350°F.

6. Remove the peppers to a large serving platter. Sprinkle with the Parmesan (if using) and serve.

TIMING
Prep: 15 minutes
Grill: 12 to 18 minutes
Rest: 15 to 20 minutes

GRILL TOOLS AND EQUIPMENT
· Long-handled tongs

MARINATED FIRE-ROASTED PEPPERS

Here's a homemade version of commercial marinated roasted peppers. Use a charcoal grill for the best flavor. We've doctored up the marinade with a few simple seasonings so these could be served as an appetizer with no further adornment. But mostly, we keep them in the fridge for other recipes, such as Grilled Polenta with Mediterranean Vegetable Compote (page 279), Pork Chops with Barbecued Sweet Peppers (page 148), and Pesto Chicken Stuffed with Arugula, Roasted Peppers, and Chèvre (page 164).

THE GRILL

Gas: Direct heat, medium-high (400° to 450°F)
Clean, oiled grate

Charcoal: Direct heat, light ash
12-by-12-inch charcoal bed (about 3 dozen coals)
Clean, oiled grate on lowest setting

Wood: Direct heat, light ash
12-by-12-inch bed, 3 to 4 inches deep
Clean, oiled grate set 2 inches above the fire

INGREDIENTS (MAKES 6 TO 8 SERVINGS—ABOUT 5 CUPS)

Oil for coating grill grate
4 mixed bell peppers (such as red, yellow, green, and orange)
2 tablespoons olive oil

1 teaspoon dried oregano
1/2 teaspoon kosher salt
1/4 teaspoon ground black pepper

DIRECTIONS

1. Heat the grill as directed.
2. Brush the grill grate and coat it with oil. Put the peppers on the grill and cook until bubbly and blackened all over, 4 to 6 minutes per side.
3. Transfer to a paper bag or shallow baking dish. Seal the bag or cover the dish and let rest for 15 to 20 minutes. When cool enough to handle, pull out the stems and cores with the seeds. Cut the peppers lengthwise and then gently scrape

away any lingering seeds or ribs from the pepper centers. Peel and discard the skin with your fingers or the edge of a paring knife. Cut the peppers lengthwise into halves, quarters, or narrow strips, as desired.
4. Combine the olive oil, oregano, salt, and pepper in a medium bowl or covered container. Add the peppers and any pepper juices from the cutting board. Mix briefly, then refrigerate for up to 1 week.

TIMING
Prep: 5 minutes
Grill: About 12 minutes

GRILL TOOLS AND EQUIPMENT
· Grill screen (optional)
· 2 skewers or 4 toothpicks (optional)
· Long-handled tongs
· Long-handled spatula

GRILLED GUAC

Grill an avocado? Blasphemy? Try this recipe before you dismiss the notion. Grilling the typical guacamole ingredients (onions, garlic, and jalapeño) develops their sweet flavor. Even the avocado benefits from a brief searing on the grill. The lightly caramelized flavors are a welcome addition to what is traditionally a very mild mash. Besides, guacamole is usually warmed up when added to hot dishes like fajitas anyway. Why not serve it warm in the first place? We love it served warm as a chip dip, too.

THE GRILL

Gas: Direct heat, medium (350°F)
Clean, oiled grate

Charcoal: Direct heat, medium ash
12-by-12-inch charcoal bed (about 3 dozen coals)
Clean, oiled grate on lowest setting

Wood: Direct heat, medium ash
12-by-12-inch bed, 3 inches deep
Clean, oiled grate set 4 inches above the fire

Oil for coating grill grate and screen
2 avocados, halved and pitted
1 small tomato
1 jalapeño or 2 serrano chiles
1 thick slice onion

2 cloves garlic, unpeeled
No-stick spray oil
3 tablespoons chopped fresh cilantro leaves
Juice of 1/2 lime
1/2 teaspoon kosher salt

DIRECTIONS

1. Heat the grill as directed.

2. Brush the grill grate and coat it with oil. Spray the avocados, tomato, jalapeño, onion, and garlic with oil. If not using a grill screen, push skewers or toothpicks through the jalapeño, onion, and garlic to keep them from falling through the grill or falling apart. Put the vegetables cut-sides down on the grill or on a heated, oiled grill screen and cook until nicely grill-marked, 6 to 12 minutes, turning a few times. The tomato and avocado should still be fairly firm and will be done first. The pepper skin should be blistered and will take the longest.

3. Scoop the avocado from its peel and mash in a medium bowl. Peel the grilled garlic, and remove the cores and seeds of the jalapeños (or leave in the seeds for more heat). Finely chop the garlic, jalapeños, tomato, and onion, and add to the bowl. Stir in the cilantro, lime juice, and salt. Serve immediately, or let cool and then cover with plastic wrap pressed onto the surface and refrigerate for up to 4 hours.

TIP
· To pit an avocado, cut it in half from top to bottom through the peel and around the pit. Twist apart the halves and put the half containing the pit in your palm or nest it in a towel. Whack the pit with the knife blade, then twist the knife to lift out the pit. Knock the pit off the knife with a spoon.

FIRE-ROASTED TOMATILLO SALSA

TIMING
Prep: 10 minutes
Grill: 5 to 10 minutes

Here's your basic salsa verde made with tomatillos, those wonderfully tart fruiting vegetables that resemble a small yellow-green tomato covered with a thin, papery husk. Be sure to remove the husks before grilling the tomatillos. The charred bits of tomatillo skin and jalapeño give this relish a well-rounded rustic flavor. Serve it as a chip dip or with grilled beef, lamb, pork, poultry, or fish.

GRILL TOOLS AND EQUIPMENT
· 5 or 6 skewers (optional)
· Long-handled tongs
· Long-handled spatula

THE GRILL

Gas: Direct heat, medium-high (400° to 450°F)
Clean, oiled grate on lowest setting

Charcoal: Direct heat, medium ash
10-by-10-inch charcoal bed (about 3 dozen coals)
Clean, oiled grate on lowest setting

Wood: Direct heat, light ash
10-by-10-inch bed, 1 inch deep
Clean, oiled grate set 3 inches above the fire

GETTING CREATIVE
· For Grilled Tomato Salsa, replace the tomatillos with 4 medium beefsteak tomatoes. Halve the tomatoes crosswise and dig out the seeds and pulp with your fingertips over a bowl. Grill as directed. Finely chop all of the vegetables by hand and combine with the remaining ingredients in a bowl, along with any accumulated juices. Add 2 to 3 teaspoons lime juice.
· Replace the jalapeños with 4 serrano chiles or 2 small canned chipotle chiles in adobo sauce. If using canned chipotle chiles, skip the grilling step and put the chipotles into the food processor along with the other grilled vegetables.
· For a thinner sauce to serve over grilled fish or pork, stir in a few tablespoons of water along with the cilantro.

INGREDIENTS (MAKES ABOUT 2 CUPS)

Oil for coating grill grate
1 pound tomatillos (10 to 12 medium), husked and rinsed
1 onion, peeled and cut crosswise into 4 thick slices
2 cloves garlic, unpeeled

2 small jalapeño chiles
1 tablespoon chopped fresh cilantro leaves
3/4 teaspoon kosher salt
1/2 teaspoon sugar

DIRECTIONS

1. Heat the grill as directed.

2. Brush the grill grate and coat it with oil. Grill the tomatillos, onion slices, garlic, and chiles directly on the grill grate until blistered and blackened all over, turning occasionally, 5 to 10 minutes total. Use a spatula and tongs to turn the onion slices to keep them from falling apart. Or you could skewer the slices through the side to hold them together. If the bars of your grill grate are far apart, skewer the garlic and jalapeños to keep them from falling into the fire.

3. Let the vegetables cool slightly, then peel the garlic and remove the stems from the chiles. For a mild salsa, cut the chiles in half lengthwise and scrape out the seeds and ribs with a spoon or knife. For a hotter salsa, leave the stemmed chiles intact.

4. Transfer all of the vegetables to a food processor with any accumulated juices. Pulse until a chunky purée forms. Pour into a bowl and stir in the cilantro, salt, and sugar.

GRILLED POTATO, ROASTED CORN, AND SMOKED PEPPER SALAD

TIMING
Prep: 15 minutes
Grill: 20 minutes

GRILL TOOLS AND EQUIPMENT
· Grill screen
· Long-handled spatula or tongs

This gutsy warm potato salad is studded with charred corn kernels and black-speckled roasted red pepper. Radiating with a pungent red wine and garlic vinaigrette, it is a perfect side dish for barbecued pork chops or a chile-rubbed sirloin steak.

THE GRILL

Gas: Direct heat, medium (350°F)
Clean, oiled grate

Charcoal: Direct heat, medium ash
12-by-12-inch charcoal bed (about 3 dozen coals)
Clean, oiled grate on lowest setting

Wood: Direct heat, medium ash
12-by-12-inch bed, 3 inches deep
Clean, oiled grate set 4 inches above the fire

INGREDIENTS (MAKES 4 SERVINGS)

For the salad:
Oil for coating grill grate and screen
1 pound new potatoes
2 ears corn, husked
1 tablespoon olive oil
1 red bell pepper
3 tablespoons chopped fresh flat-leaf parsley
1/2 cup chopped red onion

For the dressing:
3 tablespoons extra-virgin olive oil
2 tablespoons grapeseed oil
3 tablespoons fresh lemon juice
3 tablespoons red wine vinegar
1 clove garlic, minced
1/2 teaspoon kosher salt
1/4 teaspoon ground black pepper

DIRECTIONS

1. Heat the grill as directed.

2. Brush the grill grate and coat it with oil. Put the grill screen on the grill to one side, and coat it with oil.

3. For the salad, coat the potatoes and corn with the olive oil. Put the potatoes on the grill screen and the corn and bell pepper directly on the grate. Cover and cook until the vegetables are browned and tender. This will take about 20 minutes for the potatoes, turning halfway through; 15 minutes for the peppers, turning 3 or 4 times; and 15 minutes for the corn,

turning 3 or 4 times. If your grill has a temperature gauge, it should stay at around 375°F.

4. Peel the skin from the pepper with your fingers, discard the stem, core, and seeds, and dice the pepper finely.

5. Cut the potatoes into bite-size pieces, and cut the corn kernels from the cob (hold the corn vertically and cut down the cob with a small knife). Toss all of the vegetables in a bowl with the parsley and red onion.

6. Mix the dressing ingredients in a bowl with a small whisk and toss with the salad; serve.

GRILLED POLENTA WITH MEDITERRANEAN VEGETABLE COMPOTE

TIMING
Prep: 5 minutes
(plus 30 minutes for roasted peppers)
Simmer: 30 to 40 minutes
Chill: 2 to 3 hours
Grill: About 25 minutes

GRILL TOOLS AND EQUIPMENT
· Long-handled tongs
· Long-handled spatula

If you've got vegetarians to feed, this makes a satisfying main course that's mostly grilled. Or you could serve it as a first course when meat is on the menu. The dish has a few grilled items and a few sautéed items. If you're making it outdoors, it's easiest to use a grill with a side burner. Keep a cutting board nearby as well. Or you can go back and forth a few times from your indoor stovetop to the grill.

THE GRILL

Gas: Direct heat, medium (350°F)
Clean, oiled grate

Charcoal: Direct heat, medium ash
12-by-12-inch charcoal bed (about 3 dozen coals)
Clean, oiled grate on lowest setting

Wood: Direct heat, medium ash
12-by-12-inch bed, 3 inches deep
Clean, oiled grate set 4 inches above the fire

Photo: Grilled Potato, Roasted Corn, and Smoked Pepper Salad

· To save time, replace the homemade polenta with prepared polenta. You can find it sold in cylinder shapes in the refrigerated produce section of most supermarkets. Slice it into 12 rounds and coat each round with oil before grilling.
· To julienne basil, stack 2 to 3 leaves, roll them up from the short side, and then cut the roll crosswise to create long, thin strips.

GETTING CREATIVE
· To vary the flavor of the polenta, add chopped sun-dried tomatoes, chopped herbs, grated Parmesan cheese, or other seasonings after the polenta is cooked and thickened.
· Use a cookie cutter to cut the polenta into circles, stars, or other shapes instead of squares.

INGREDIENTS (MAKES 3 TO 4 SERVINGS)

For the polenta:

3/4 cup coarse yellow cornmeal

3 cups cold water

1 1/4 teaspoons kosher salt

Oil for coating baking dish

For the vegetable compote:

5 tablespoons extra-virgin olive oil

3 cloves garlic, halved lengthwise

1/3 cup chopped Marinated Fire-Roasted Peppers (page 276) or purchased roasted peppers

1 medium yellow tomato, finely chopped

Oil for coating grill grate

1 thick slice Vidalia or other sweet onion (about 1/2 inch thick)

3/4 cup crisp white wine (such as Pinot Grigio)

2 tablespoons butter, cut into pieces

3 tablespoons pitted kalamata olives, halved lengthwise

1/4 cup cooked or canned chickpeas

3 tablespoons julienned basil (see Tips)

1/4 teaspoon kosher salt

1/4 teaspoon ground black pepper

2 tablespoons crumbled feta or grated Parmesan cheese

DIRECTIONS

1. For the polenta: Put the cornmeal, cold water, and salt in a medium saucepan and whisk vigorously. Bring to a boil over high heat, stirring occasionally. Reduce the heat to medium-low and regulate it so that the mixture simmers gently until it is very thick and pulls away from the sides, 30 to 40 minutes, stirring almost constantly. It takes patience, but stirring every couple of minutes prevents the polenta from becoming gummy or burning on the bottom.

2. Coat an 11-by-7-inch baking dish or other shallow 2-quart baking dish with a small amount of oil. Scrape the hot polenta into the dish and smooth the top. Let cool to room temperature, then cover and refrigerate until very firm, 2 to 3 hours or up to 1 day.

3. Heat the grill as directed.

4. For the compote: Heat 2 tablespoons of the olive oil in a sauté pan over medium-low heat (preferably near your grill, as you'll be going back and forth a bit). Add the garlic, cut-side down, and cook until the bottoms are golden, 10 to 15 minutes, shaking the pan occasionally. Discard the garlic and add the tomato and peppers to the pan. Simmer over medium heat until the tomato is very soft, about 15 minutes.

5. As the compote cooks, cut the polenta into 12 squares. Coat the tops with 1 tablespoon of the remaining olive oil. Brush the grill grate and coat it with oil. Put the polenta on the grill and cook until nicely browned, 10 to 15 minutes per side.

6. Meanwhile, coat the onion slice with some of the remaining olive oil and grill near the polenta until softened and nicely browned, 5 to 7 minutes per side, turning once with a spatula to keep it from separating. Remove and chop finely.

7. When the tomatoes in the pan are soft, remove the compote with a slotted spoon and set aside. Add the wine to the pan and boil over medium-high heat until reduced to just a few tablespoons, swirling or stirring occasionally. Stir in the remaining 2 tablespoons olive oil, the butter, the reserved tomato mixture, the olives, and the chickpeas. Cook for 2 minutes, then stir in half of the basil, the salt, and the pepper.

8. Arrange the polenta on a platter or plates. Spoon the compote across the slices. Sprinkle with the onions, feta, and remaining basil and serve.

TIMING
Prep: 10 minutes
Grill: About 45 minutes

GRILL TOOLS AND EQUIPMENT
· Long-handled tongs
· Four 12-inch squares heavy-duty aluminum foil

GRILLED ACORN SQUASH STUFFED WITH APPLES

Here's a play on the medieval theme of whole animals stuffed into other whole animals. Why not stuff vegetables with fruits, or vice versa? Squash and apples have an affinity for one another and work beautifully when grilled together. Here, acorn squash halves are stuffed with apple halves and flavored with cinnamon-scented honey. Be sure to get medium to large squash and medium to small apples so that the apples will fit neatly into the hollows of the squash.

THE GRILL

Gas:	Indirect heat, medium (325° to 350°F)	**Wood:**	Indirect heat, medium ash
	3- or 4-burner grill–middle burner(s) off		12-by-12-inch bed, 3 inches deep
	2-burner grill–1 side off		Clean, oiled grate set 4 inches above the fire
	Clean, oiled grate		
Charcoal:	Indirect heat, medium ash		
	Split charcoal bed (about 2 dozen coals per side)		
	20 replacement coals		
	Heavy-duty drip pan set between banks of charcoal		
	Clean, oiled grate on medium setting		

Photo: Grilled Polenta with Mediterranean Vegetable Compote

4 tablespoons (1/2 stick) salted butter, softened

3 tablespoons honey

1/4 teaspoon ground cinnamon

2 medium to large acorn squash, halved, seeds and stringy pulp removed

Pinch of cayenne pepper

2 small apples, peeled, stemmed, halved, and core removed

Juice of 1/2 lemon

4 teaspoons raisins

DIRECTIONS

1. Heat the grill as directed.

2. Mash the butter with a fork on a clean work surface. Add the honey, cinnamon, and cayenne and mix until blended.

3. Put each squash half on a square of foil. Spread their interiors with half of the butter mixture. Put an apple half, flat-side up, in the hollow of each squash half. Drizzle with the lemon juice, and fill the hollow of each apple with raisins. Top with the remaining butter mixture. Wrap each loosely in a square of foil.

4. Put the squash on the grill away from the heat, cover, and cook for 45 minutes, until the squash and apples are tender enough to be easily pierced with a fork. If your grill has a temperature gauge, it should read between 350°F and 375°F. Unwrap and serve.

TIMING

Prep: 5 minutes

Grill: About 45 minutes

GRILL TOOLS AND EQUIPMENT

· Long-handled spatula or tongs

MAKING SUBSTITUTIONS

· Any orange-fleshed winter squash (such as acorn, buttercup, or sugar pumpkin) can be substituted for the butternut squash, but you will need a similar total weight to get 6 servings.

FIRE-ROASTED BUTTERNUT SQUASH WITH SPICY HONEY BUTTER

This hot-pepper-glazed squash depends on the flavor of fire for its success. To maximize the contact with flame, the squash is cut lengthwise. Each piece is charred on all 3 sides and washed with a mixture of sweet butter, hot pepper, lime juice, and honey. The combination gives you a wonderful sweet, hot, tart, bitter crust laminating the meaty flesh of the squash.

THE GRILL

Gas: Indirect heat, medium (325° to 350°F)

3- or 4-burner grill–middle burner(s) off

2-burner grill–1 side off

Clean, oiled grate

Charcoal: Indirect heat, medium ash

Split charcoal bed (about 2 dozen coals per side)

20 replacement coals

Heavy-duty drip pan set between banks of charcoal

Clean, oiled grate on medium setting

Wood: Indirect heat, medium ash

12-by-12-inch bed, 3 inches deep

Clean, oiled grate set 4 inches above the fire

INGREDIENTS (MAKES 6 SERVING)

4 tablespoons (1/2 stick) salted butter, softened

1 1/2 tablespoons honey

Pinch of ground cinnamon

1/2 teaspoon chili powder

1/2 teaspoon hot pepper sauce

1 large butternut squash (about 2 pounds)

1/4 teaspoon kosher salt

1/8 teaspoon ground black pepper

1 tablespoon olive oil

Juice of 1 lime

DIRECTIONS

1. Heat the grill as directed.

2. Mash the butter with a fork on a clean work surface. Add the honey, cinnamon, chili powder, and hot pepper sauce, and mix until blended. Set aside in a small bowl.

3. Slice the stem end off of the squash. Set it on a work surface, cut-side down, and cut into 6 long wedges. Scoop the seeds and stringy pulp from the interior of each squash wedge. Season with the salt and pepper, and coat with the olive oil.

4. Put the squash on the grill, skin-side down, away from the heat, cover, and cook for 30 minutes. If your grill has a temperature gauge, it should read between 350° and 375°F. Turn the squash wedges onto one of their cut sides, cover, and grill until browned, about 8 minutes. Turn onto the other cut side, cover, and grill for another 7 to 8 minutes. Check one of the larger pieces of squash; it should be tender enough to pierce easily with a fork.

5. Coat with the prepared butter, drizzle with the lime juice, and serve.

GRILLED HARVEST VEGETABLES WITH ROSEMARY–RED WINE SAUCE

TIMING
Prep: About 15 minutes
Grill: 20 minutes

GRILL TOOLS AND EQUIPMENT
· Grill screen
· Long-handled tongs
· Long-handled spatula

Plumed with herbs and rouged by a syrup of red wine and honey, this mountain of grilled vegetables would not be out of place at a Renaissance banquet. As vegetable side dishes go, this one is truly opulent. Make it with any selection of vegetables you want, but keep the volume close to what is described in the recipe (about 2 gallons of raw ingredient) so that the proportion of sauce to vegetable stays roughly the same.

THE GRILL

Gas: Direct heat, medium (350° to 375°F)
Clean, oiled grate

Charcoal: Direct heat, medium ash
12-by-12-inch charcoal bed (about 3 dozen coals)
Clean, oiled grate on lowest setting

INGREDIENTS (MAKES 12 TO 14 SERVING)

Oil for coating grill screen

2 large onions, cut into 1/2-inch-thick slices

2 sweet potatoes or yams, peeled and each cut into 8 chunks

14 small, unpeeled round potatoes (red or gold), washed and dried

2 large leeks, trimmed of dark green leaves, halved lengthwise, and washed

4 parsnips, peeled and cut in half lengthwise

1 celery root (about 1 pound), ends trimmed, deeply peeled, and cut into 1/2-inch-thick slices

1 large butternut squash, stem end removed, quartered lengthwise, seeds and pulp scooped out

1/4 cup olive oil

1/2 teaspoon kosher salt, plus more to taste

1/4 teaspoon ground black pepper, plus more to taste

3 cups fruity red wine, such as Merlot, Shiraz, or Grenache

2 tablespoons fresh rosemary leaves

1 tablespoon honey

1/2 cup (1 stick) unsalted butter

Photo: Grilled Harvest Vegetables with
Rosemary–Red Wine Sauce

1. Heat the grill as directed. Put the grill screen on the grill, and coat it with oil.

2. Toss the onions, sweet potatoes, round potatoes, leeks, parsnips, celery root, and butternut squash with the olive oil in a very large mixing bowl or roasting pan until evenly coated. Put the vegetables on the grill screen and grill until browned and tender on all sides, turning as needed. This will take about 10 minutes for onions and leeks; 15 minutes for sweet potatoes, round potatoes, parsnips, and celery root; and 20 minutes for butternut squash. Transfer the vegetables to a large bowl as they are done. If your grill has a temperature gauge, it should stay at around 375°F.

3. Cut the vegetables into large chunks, and toss with the salt and pepper.

4. Meanwhile, bring the wine and rosemary to a boil in a large skillet over medium-high heat. Boil until the wine reduces to one-third of its volume, about 1 cup. Reduce the heat to low and stir in the honey and butter until the butter melts. The sauce will be lightly thickened; if it is too watery, reduce more. Season to taste with the 1/2 teaspoon salt and the 1/4 teaspoon pepper.

5. To serve, mound the vegetables on a serving platter and pour the sauce over the top.

TIMING
Prep: 3 minutes
Grill: 23 minutes

GRILL TOOLS AND EQUIPMENT
· Large grill skillet or rimmed grill screen
· Long-handled spatula

GETTING CREATIVE
· Try this dish with a variety of colorful potatoes. Blue, yellow, and red-skinned potatoes are available as new potatoes, and many are sold as fingerlings.
· Several herbs are delicious with potatoes and could be used in this recipe. Try rosemary, thyme, basil, or tarragon.

FIRE-ROASTED NEW POTATOES WITH SIZZLED SAGE LEAVES

Snobbery accounts for almost as many mediocre recipes as sloth. It is a cardinal rule of snobby gastronomy that fresh herbs are superior to dried, when in truth the boldest flavor comes from the use of both in tandem. Dried herbs take time to release their flavor, but when they do their strength can grow for an hour or more. Fresh herbs, on the other hand, explode with flavor as soon as they hit the heat, but they spend themselves quickly. All of which explains why dried sage is rubbed on these roasted potatoes before they go on the grill and fresh sage leaves are added in the last few minutes. At last, something new to be snobby about!

THE GRILL

Gas: Direct heat, medium (350°F)
Clean, oiled grate

Charcoal: Direct heat, medium ash
12-by-12-inch charcoal bed (about 3 dozen coals)
Clean, oiled grate on lowest setting

Wood: Direct heat, medium ash
12-by-12-inch bed, 3 inches deep
Clean, oiled grate set 4 inches above the fire

INGREDIENTS (MAKES 4 SERVINGS)

1 pound new potatoes, cut in half if large
3 teaspoons extra-virgin olive oil
1/4 teaspoon dried sage
1/4 teaspoon kosher salt, or more to taste

1/4 teaspoon ground black pepper
Oil for coating grill skillet
2 tablespoons fresh sage leaves, cut into small pieces if large

DIRECTIONS

1. Heat the grill as directed.

2. Toss the potatoes, 2 teaspoons of the olive oil, the dried sage, salt, and pepper in a medium bowl until coated.

3. Put a large grill skillet on the grill and coat it with oil. Cover and heat for a minute. Add the potatoes and spread them out, leaving space between the pieces. Cover and cook for about 20 minutes, until browned and tender, turning halfway through. If your grill has a temperature gauge, it should stay at around 375°F.

4. Toss the sage leaves with the remaining 1 teaspoon olive oil. Scatter the sage leaves over the potatoes and cook until the sage starts to shrivel, about 2 minutes.

5. Transfer to a serving plate and serve.

GRILLED BUFFALO SPUDS

TIMING
Prep: 3 minutes
Grill: 18 minutes

GRILL TOOLS AND EQUIPMENT
· Grill screen or large grill skillet
· Long-handled spatula

The flavor of Buffalo chicken wings is even better on potatoes. These are grilled simply and then tossed with hot sauce and butter. They can be scattered with blue cheese, if you like. We suggest you serve them with burgers (anything but Buffalo wings; yes, you can get too much of a good thing).

THE GRILL

Gas: Direct heat, medium (350°F)
Clean, oiled grate

Charcoal: Direct heat, medium ash
12-by-12-inch charcoal bed (about 3 dozen coals)
Clean, oiled grate on lowest setting

Wood: Direct heat, medium ash
12-by-12-inch bed, 3 inches deep
Clean, oiled grate set 4 inches above the fire

INGREDIENTS (MAKES 4 SERVINGS)

1 1/2 pounds russet potatoes, cut into wedges
1 tablespoon canola oil
Oil for coating grill screen

2 tablespoons butter, melted
3 tablespoons mild hot sauce such as Durkee Red Hot
2 ounces blue cheese, crumbled (optional)

DIRECTIONS

1. Heat the grill as directed.
2. Toss the potatoes with the 1 tablespoon oil until coated.
3. Put the grill screen on the grill and coat it with oil. Cover and heat for a minute. Add the potatoes and spread them out, leaving space between the pieces. Cover and cook for about

18 minutes, turning halfway through. If your grill has a temperature gauge, it should stay at around 375°F.
4. Mix the butter and hot sauce in a serving bowl. Toss the potatoes in the sauce and serve. Scatter the blue cheese over the top while still warm, if desired.

GRILLED POTATO CHIPS

TIMING
Prep: 10 minutes
Grill: 6 minutes per batch

GRILL TOOLS AND EQUIPMENT
· Grill screen
· Long-handled spatula

Sometimes the packaged form of a food becomes so commonplace that it effectively wipes out the very notion of homemade—and such is the case with potato chips. We admit that frying them is messy and smelly, and it's hard to rationalize when perfectly good potato chips are just a ripped bag away. But grilled chips are something else. Not only are they spectacular with steaks and burgers, but the only way you're ever going to get your mitts on them is to grill some up yourself.

THE GRILL

Gas: Direct heat, medium-high (400° to 450°F)
Clean, oiled grate

Charcoal: Direct heat, light ash
12-by-12-inch charcoal bed (about 3 dozen coals)
Clean, oiled grate on lowest setting

Wood: Direct heat, light ash
12-by-12-inch bed, 3 to 4 inches deep
Clean, oiled grate set 2 inches above the fire

INGREDIENTS (MAKES 4 SERVINGS)

1 1/2 pounds russet potatoes, scrubbed
2 tablespoons canola oil
Oil for coating grill screen

Finely ground sea salt to taste
1/4 teaspoon freshly ground black pepper (optional)

1. Heat the grill as directed.

2. Slice the potatoes into slices that are as thin as you can make them, striving for less than $^{1}/_{16}$ inch. Toss with the 2 tablespoons oil.

3. Put the grill screen on the grill and coat it with oil. Grill the chips in batches until browned at the edges, about 3 minutes per side. Remove with a spatula to a bowl and season with salt and with pepper, if desired. Keep grilling the chips until all are cooked and seasoned. Serve.

Photo: Grilled Potato Chips

SWEET POTATOES IN THE COALS WITH LIME-CILANTRO BUTTER

TIMING
Prep: 1 minute
(plus 5 minutes for butter)
Grill: 45 minutes

You will no doubt be dubbed a grillmaster by anyone who watches you stick raw food directly into hot, burning embers. The simple truth is that any food that can be eaten out of its skin makes a good candidate for grilling right in the coals of a charcoal or wood fire. The skin will be left uneaten anyway, so who cares if it gets severely charred? That only adds to the smoky flavor within. Try this method with unpeeled baking potatoes or beets. The toppings are up to you, but we like to pair sweet potatoes with the Mexican flavors of lime, cilantro, and garlic.

GRILL TOOLS AND EQUIPMENT
· Long-handled tongs

TIP
· To make these on a gas grill, grill the sweet potatoes directly over high heat until blackened all over, 45 to 55 minutes, turning a few times.

THE GRILL

Charcoal: Direct heat, red hot
12-by-12-inch bed, 1 inch deep
No grate

Wood: Direct heat, red hot
12-by-12-inch bed, 4 inches deep
No grate

INGREDIENTS (MAKES 4 TO 6 SERVINGS)

4 orange-fleshed sweet potatoes (3 to 3 1/2 pounds total)

1/2 cup Sweet Lime-Cilantro Butter (a variation of Lime-Cilantro Butter, page 393)

DIRECTIONS

1. Heat the grill as directed. Leave the grill grate off the grill so that the coals are accessible.

2. Nestle the sweet potatoes directly in the coals, raking extra coals around each sweet potato. Cook until a skewer slides in and out of the centers easily, about 45 minutes, turning once or twice.

3. Brush off any loose ash, then remove the sweet potatoes to plates or a platter, using tongs. Let cool for a few minutes. Cut each sweet potato in half lengthwise and mash the flesh of each half with a fork. Drizzle evenly with the sweet cilantro butter. Allow guests to scoop the sweet potatoes from their jackets.

VANILLA CAULIFLOWER

TIMING
Prep: 5 minutes
Grill: 20 minutes

We tend to take vanilla for granted in ice cream and cake, but taste it out of context and its true exotic character blossoms. Vanilla is the fruit of a jungle orchid, and that's the tropical fragrance that surprises in this spicy, slightly floral, intriguingly crusty side dish of grilled cauliflower.

GRILL TOOLS AND EQUIPMENT
· Grill screen
· Long-handled tongs
or long-handled spatula

THE GRILL

Gas: Direct heat, medium-low (300°F)
Clean, oiled grate
Charcoal: Direct heat, medium ash
12-by-12-inch charcoal bed (about 3 dozen coals)
Clean, oiled grate on lowest setting

Wood: Direct heat, medium ash
12-by-12-inch bed, 2 inches deep
Clean, oiled grate set 5 inches above the fire

INGREDIENTS (MAKES 4 SERVINGS)

1 large cauliflower (about 2 pounds), leaves removed
2 tablespoons canola oil
1/4 teaspoon kosher salt
1/4 teaspoon ground black pepper

Oil for coating grill screen
2 tablespoons white balsamic vinegar or white wine vinegar
1/2 teaspoon vanilla extract
Small pinch ground habanero chile, or other hot ground chile

1. Heat the grill as directed.

2. Starting at the base, cut the large curds from the stalk of the cauliflower. When you get near the top, the curds will become smaller; cut them from the stalk in one piece. Discard the stalk and cut all of the pieces of cauliflower in half lengthwise. Coat with 1 tablespoon of the canola oil and season with the salt and pepper.

3. Put the grill screen on the grill and coat it with oil. Put the cauliflower on the screen, cut-side down. Cover and cook until browned and tender, about 20 minutes, turning halfway through. If your grill has a temperature gauge, it should stay at around 300°F.

4. While the cauliflower is grilling, mix the vinegar, remaining 1 tablespoon oil, vanilla, and ground chile in a serving bowl. Add the cooked cauliflower and toss to coat. Serve.

ORANGE-GLAZED BARBECUED CARROTS

Carrots aren't usually grilled. CCW (Conventional Culinary Wisdom) says they are too hard to ever soften in the harsh heat of direct flames. But if you keep the fire low and start dousing them with barbecue sauce the second they begin to brown, you will be astonished at how delicious a grilled carrot can be.

THE GRILL

Gas: Direct heat, medium-low (300°F)
Clean, oiled grill grate

Charcoal: Direct heat, medium ash
12-by-12-inch charcoal bed (about 3 dozen coals)
Clean, oiled grate on medium setting

Wood: Direct heat, medium ash
12-by-12-inch bed, 3 inches deep
Clean, oiled grate set 4 inches above the fire

INGREDIENTS (MAKES 4 SERVINGS)

1 pound carrots, peeled and cut into $1/2$-inch-thick slices
2 teaspoons canola oil
$1/4$ teaspoon kosher salt
$1/4$ teaspoon ground black pepper

$1/3$ cup Sweet, Hot, and Sour BBQ Sauce (page 391)
Finely grated zest and juice of 1 orange
Oil for coating grill screen

DIRECTIONS

1. Heat the grill as directed.

2. Toss the carrots with the 2 teaspoons oil and the salt and pepper in a bowl; set aside. Mix the barbecue sauce, orange zest, and orange juice in a small bowl; reserve.

3. Put the grill screen or wok on the grill and coat it with oil. Put the carrots on the screen in a single layer, cover, and cook until browned and tender, about 10 minutes, turning and coating with the barbecue sauce every 3 minutes. If your grill has a temperature gauge, it should stay at around 375°F.

4. Remove to a serving bowl or individual plates and serve.

GRILLED SESAME MUSHROOMS

Shiitake mushrooms have an earthy, woodsy aroma that's enhanced by grilling. Here, we grill the caps whole and then toss them with a teriyaki-like sauce for a simple side dish. Look for shiitake mushrooms with large caps so they can be grilled right on the grill grate. If you can find only small-capped shiitakes, use a grill screen, grill skillet, or grill wok.

TIMING
Prep: 5 minutes
(plus 5 minutes for sauce)
Grill: 10 minutes

GRILL TOOLS AND EQUIPMENT
· Grill screen or grill wok
· Long-handled spatula
· Long-handled basting brush

TIMING
Prep: 20 minutes
Grill: 5 to 8 minutes

GRILL TOOLS AND EQUIPMENT
· Grill screen, grill skillet, or grill wok (optional)
· Long-handled tongs

THE GRILL

Gas: Direct heat, medium-high (400° to 450°F)
Clean, oiled grate on lowest setting

Charcoal: Direct heat, light ash
12-by-12-inch charcoal bed (about 3 dozen coals)
Clean, oiled grate on lowest setting

Wood: Direct heat, light ash
12-by-12-inch bed, 3 to 4 inches deep
Clean, oiled grate set 3 inches above the fire

INGREDIENTS (MAKES 4 SERVINGS)

1 pound fresh large-capped shiitake mushrooms

2 tablespoons soy sauce

1 tablespoon rice vinegar or dry sherry

$1/2$ teaspoon honey

4 teaspoons toasted sesame oil

1 small scallion

3 tablespoons vegetable oil

1 teaspoon minced peeled gingerroot

$1/2$ teaspoon kosher salt

$1/4$ teaspoon ground black pepper

Oil for coating grill grate

1 teaspoon sesame seeds

DIRECTIONS

1. Remove the stems from the shiitake mushrooms. Brush the mushrooms clean if dirty in spots.

2. Heat the grill as directed.

3. Combine the soy sauce, rice vinegar, honey, and 2 teaspoons of the sesame oil in a small bowl. Set aside.

4. Cut the scallion in half crosswise, and thinly slice the whiter half. Put the slices in a large bowl. Reserve the green half. Add the remaining 2 teaspoons sesame oil, the vegetable oil, the ginger, and the salt and pepper to the slices in the bowl. Add the mushrooms and toss to coat.

5. Brush the grill grate and coat it with oil. Put the mushrooms directly on the grill grate and cook until they are nicely grill-marked and tender, turning once, 5 to 8 minutes total. If the mushroom caps are small, grill them on a heated, oiled grill screen or grill tray.

6. Remove the mushrooms to a platter and drizzle sparingly with the reserved sauce. Sprinkle with the sesame seeds. Slice the remaining scallion greens lengthwise into thin strips. Arrange the scallion strips on the platter and serve with the remaining sauce.

GETTING CREATIVE

· Replace the shiitakes with portobello mushroom caps. Combine all of the ingredients except the mushrooms, scallion greens, and sesame seeds. Let the portobellos marinate in this mixture for up to 6 hours, then grill until tender, 8 to 10 minutes, turning once or twice. Garnish with the scallion greens and sesame seeds.

Photo: Grilled Sesame Mushrooms

GRILL TOOLS AND EQUIPMENT
- Grill screen
- Long-handled spatula

GETTING CREATIVE
- Use portobello mushrooms to create entrée-size stuffed mushrooms. This amount of filling will be enough for 2 portobellos.

GRILLED STUFFED MUSHROOMS

Stuffed mushrooms are typically served as pick-up hors d'oeuvres, which might be the way you will choose to serve these, although they are also an elegant garnish for any roast (we suggest Fire-Roasted Garlic-Herb Chicken, page 185). The cooking is done in two parts. You start by grilling the mushrooms on the stem side. You then remove the stems, use them in the stuffing, stuff the caps, and return the mushrooms to the grill to cook the cap sides and warm up the filling. All of this can be done directly over the flame that surrounds a roast being grilled with indirect heat.

THE GRILL

Gas: Direct heat, medium-high (400° to 450°F)
Clean, oiled grate

Charcoal: Direct heat, light ash
12-by-12-inch charcoal bed (about 3 dozen coals)
Clean, oiled grate on lowest setting

Wood: Direct heat, light ash
12-by-12-inch bed, 3 to 4 inches deep
Clean, oiled grate set 2 inches above the fire

INGREDIENTS (MAKES 4 SERVINGS)

8 large mushrooms
1 tablespoon olive oil
2 slices bacon, finely chopped
1 clove garlic, minced
1 teaspoon chopped fresh herbs, such as rosemary, thyme, tarragon, or flat-leaf parsley

1 plum tomato, finely chopped
$1/4$ teaspoon kosher salt
$1/4$ teaspoon ground black pepper
1 tablespoon seasoned dried breadcrumbs
Oil for coating grill screen

DIRECTIONS

1. Heat the grill as directed.
2. Brush the stem and bottom side of each mushroom with the olive oil. Grill the mushrooms, stem side down, covered, for 5 minutes, shifting the mushrooms once if they do not sit flat, to help them cook evenly. Remove and let cool for a few minutes.
3. Remove the stem from each mushroom all the way down into the cap, using a small knife. Chop the stems finely.
4. Cook the bacon in a small skillet over medium heat until crisp. Add the garlic, tomato, herbs, and chopped mushroom

stems; sauté until the tomatoes soften, about 2 minutes. Season with salt and pepper and stir in the breadcrumbs.
5. Pour any liquid that has collected in the mushroom caps into the stuffing mixture. Fill the caps with the stuffing. Coat the grill screen with oil and put the stuffed mushroom caps on the screen.
6. Put the screen on the grill, cover, and cook until the caps are tender and bubbling around the edges, about 5 minutes. If your grill has a temperature gauge, it should stay at around 450°F.

TIMING
Soak wood chips: 1 hour
Prep: 5 minutes
    (plus 5 minutes for glaze)
Grill: 40 to 50 minutes

GRILL TOOLS AND EQUIPMENT
- 2 cups wood chips or chunks (apple, pear, or oak)
- Smoker box or foil packet, if using a gas grill (see page 39)
- Long-handled tongs

BARBECUED BEETS WITH ORANGE HONEY BUTTER

Beets are fantastic grilled. Like most root vegetables, beets are high in sugar, which melts and caramelizes on the grill and creates complex flavors. We like to grill these roots whole via indirect heat and then slice them, fan out the slices, and drizzle on a sauce. Lightly sweetened, honey-scented butter is just the ticket here.

THE GRILL

Gas: Indirect heat, medium-high (350° to 400°F)
3- or 4-burner grill–middle burner(s) off
2-burner grill–1 side off
Clean, oiled grate

Charcoal: Indirect heat, medium ash
Split charcoal bed (about 2 dozen coals per side)
Clean, oiled grate on medium setting

INGREDIENTS (MAKES 4 SERVINGS)

4 large beets, without leaves (about 1 pound), scrubbed

2 tablespoons vegetable oil

1/2 teaspoon kosher salt

1/4 teaspoon ground black pepper

1/2 cup Orange Honey-Butter Glaze (page 389)

1 scallion, thinly sliced

DIRECTIONS

1. Heat the grill as directed. Soak the wood chips or chunks in water for 1 hour.

2. Prick the scrubbed beets all over with a fork. Rub with the oil, then sprinkle the salt and pepper all over them.

3. When the grill is hot, put the soaked wood chips or chunks over the coals on both sides of the grill. If using gas, put the wood in a smoker box or in a perforated foil packet directly over one of the heated burners.

4. Put the beets over the unheated part of the grill, cover, and cook until tender, 40 to 50 minutes. A skewer should slide in and out of the centers very easily. If your grill has a temperature gauge, it should stay at around 350°F.

5. Let cool for a few minutes, then slice the beets crosswise and fan out the slices on plates or a platter. If you prefer, remove the peels before slicing, but it's a messy proposition. Plus, the peel should be tender enough to eat, and that's where the seasonings were sprinkled, so you'll lose some flavor if you remove it. That's three good reasons not to peel them.

6. Melt the glaze in a microwave oven or in a small saucepan over low heat for 10 to 20 seconds. Drizzle over the beets, then sprinkle with the scallions and serve.

TIP

· Buy beets with the leaves attached for the best flavor. Remove the leaves for this recipe. But don't throw them out! Cut the stems and leaves into 2-inch lengths and sauté them with some garlic, ginger, soy sauce, and a bit of sesame oil for a delicious side dish to an Asian meal.

BARBECUED GINGER-HOISIN BRUSSELS SPROUTS

Interesting vegetables always turn up at farmers' markets. Brussels sprouts aren't terribly unusual, but when you buy them on the stalk, at least one person will look at the 2-foot-long vegetable and say, "I didn't know that's how Brussels sprouts grew!" Here, the entire stalk of sprouts is slow-grilled via indirect heat and then brushed with a sweet-sour glaze. Impress your guests by carving individual sprouts from the stalk at the table.

THE GRILL

Gas: Indirect heat–medium (325° to 350°F)

3- or 4-burner grill–middle burner(s) off

2-burner grill–1 side off

Clean, oiled grate

Charcoal: Indirect heat–medium ash

Split charcoal bed (about 2 dozen coals per side)

20 replacement coals

Heavy-duty drip pan set between banks of charcoal

Clean, oiled grate on medium setting

TIMING

Soak wood chips: 1 hour

Prep: 2 minutes

(plus 5 minutes for glaze)

Grill: 15 minutes

GRILL TOOLS AND EQUIPMENT

· 1 cup hickory wood chips or chunks

· Smoker box or foil packet, if using a gas grill (see page 39)

· Long-handled tongs

· Long-handled basting brush

TIP

· If you're using precut sprouts (the way they're usually sold in supermarkets), you'll need 16 to 20 ounces. Put the sprouts on a large grill screen or tray and proceed with the recipe.

INGREDIENTS (MAKES 6 SERVINGS)

1 stalk Brussels sprouts (2 to 2 1/2 pounds)

2 tablespoons vegetable oil, or no-stick spray oil

1/2 cup Ginger-Hoisin Balsamic Glaze (page 388)

1 teaspoon sesame seeds (optional)

DIRECTIONS

1. Heat the grill as directed. Soak the wood chips in water for 1 hour.

2. Brush the Brussels sprouts with the oil, or spray them with oil (this is a bit quicker and easier).

3. When the grill is hot, put the soaked wood chips or chunks over the coals on both sides of the grill. If using gas, put the wood in a smoker box or in a perforated foil packet directly over one of the heated burners.

4. Put the Brussels sprouts over the unheated part of the grill, cover, and cook until the largest sprout is just tender when poked with a fork, about 15 minutes total, turning frequently and brushing with the glaze. If your grill has a temperature gauge, it should stay at around 350°F.

5. Remove the stalk to a large serving platter. Sprinkle with the sesame seeds and serve. For individual servings, cut the sprouts from the stalk and transfer to plates.

GRILLED FENNEL BATHED WITH RIESLING

TIMING
Prep: 5 minutes
Grill: About 20 minutes

GRILL TOOLS AND EQUIPMENT
· Long-handled spatula or tongs

Fennel (sometimes called anise) is a beautiful vegetable—a broad, white-green bulb that tapers into long, slim, celerylike stems topped with dark green, feathery fronds. The bulb is the only part that is cooked, but you can use the fronds as you would any other delicate herb such as dill. A fennel bulb is structured like a squat head of celery. For this recipe, it is sliced lengthwise into thick planks, leaving the white, pulpy end intact so that the ribs stay together. Because fennel is quite crisp, it needs to be basted with liquid as it browns to help it become tender. In this recipe, a fruity Riesling permeates the fennel's fibers as it cooks, marrying beautifully with the vegetable's natural licoricelike flavor.

THE GRILL

Gas: Indirect heat, medium (325° to 350°F)
3- or 4-burner grill–middle burner(s) off
2-burner grill–1 side off
Clean, oiled grate

Charcoal: Indirect heat, medium ash
Split charcoal bed (about 2 dozen coals per side)

20 replacement coals
Heavy-duty drip pan set between banks of charcoal
Clean, oiled grate on medium setting

Wood: Indirect heat, medium ash
12-by-12-inch bed, 3 inches deep
Clean, oiled grate set 4 inches above the fire

INGREDIENTS (MAKES 4 SERVINGS)

2 tablespoons extra-virgin olive oil
2 cloves garlic, minced
2 bulbs fennel, stems and leaves trimmed, cut lengthwise into
 1/2-inch-thick slices (see recipe introduction)
1/4 teaspoon kosher salt, or more to taste

1/4 teaspoon ground black pepper
Oil for coating grill grate
3/4 cup Riesling wine
4 sprigs rosemary, tied together at the stick end into a
 basting brush

DIRECTIONS

1. Heat the grill as directed.
2. Mix the olive oil and garlic in a small bowl, and coat the fennel slices with this mixture. Season with the salt and pepper.
3. Brush the grill grate and coat it with oil. Put the fennel on the grill away from the heat, cover the grill, and cook until

browned and tender, about 20 minutes, turning and basting with some of the Riesling, using the rosemary basting brush, about every 5 minutes. If your grill has a temperature gauge, it should stay at around 375°F.
4. Place on a serving platter or individual plates and serve.

SMOKY BLACK BEANS WITH CILANTRO AND LIME

TIMING
Prep: 10 minutes
 (plus 5 minutes for rub)
Soak: Overnight (or 8 hours)
Cook: 1 1/2 to 2 hours

GRILL TOOLS AND EQUIPMENT
· 20 pounds of charcoal or about an
 eighth cord of wood so that the fire
 can burn gently for about 2 hours
· Heavy pot, preferably cast iron, with
 a wire handle so it can be hung over
 the fire
· Heat-resistant grill mitt

Here's a Mexican take on barbecued baked beans. Black beans stand in for navy beans, and a sweet-hot spice mix replaces the molasses. Cilantro and lime perk up the flavors. Serve this as a side dish with fajitas, grilled pork, beef, or poultry.

THE GRILL

Charcoal: Indirect heat, medium ash
12-by-12-inch charcoal bed (about 3 dozen coals)
Clean, oiled grate on lowest setting or pot hanger
 and wire-handled pot

Wood: Indirect heat, medium ash
12-by-12-inch bed, 3 to 4 inches deep
Clean, oiled grate set 4 inches above the fire or
 pot hanger and wire-handled pot

Photo: Grilled Fennel Bathed with Riesling

GETTING CREATIVE

- For beans with a thick, soupy consistency similar to refried beans, cook them until the liquid evaporates and some beans cling to the bottom of the pan. Add about $1/2$ cup hot water before stirring in the salt, lime, and cilantro. Scrape up the bits stuck to the pan bottom and stir well.

TIP

- If you don't have enough fuel to cook the beans over an outdoor fire, you can cook them on the stovetop in a Dutch oven or large soup pot. The cooking directions remain the same.

TIMING

Prep: 10 minutes
    (plus 5 minutes for sauce)
Soak: Overnight (or 8 hours)
Cook: 4 to 5 hours

GRILL TOOLS AND EQUIPMENT

- 60 pounds of charcoal or about a quarter cord of wood so that the fire can burn gently for about 5 hours
- Heavy pot, preferably cast iron with a wire handle so it can be hung over the fire
- Heat-resistant grill mitt

TIP

- If you don't have enough fuel to cook the beans over an outdoor fire, you can cook them on the stovetop in a Dutch oven or large soup pot. The cooking directions remain the same.

INGREDIENTS (MAKES 6 SERVINGS)

10 ounces dried black beans, picked over and rinsed
2 tablespoons vegetable oil
1 small onion, finely chopped
3 cloves garlic, minced
2 bay leaves

$1/4$ cup Fragrant Chile Rub, made without the salt (page 372)
$1 1/2$ teaspoons kosher salt
Juice of $1/2$ lime
2 tablespoons chopped fresh cilantro leaves

DIRECTIONS

1. Put the beans in a large pot and cover with water by 2 inches. Let soak overnight.

2. Heat the grill as directed. Drain the beans in a colander and set aside. Heat the oil in the same bean pot directly over the heated part of the grill. Add the onion and cook until softened, about 5 minutes. Add the garlic and cook for 2 minutes. Add the beans and enough water to cover the beans by 1 inch. Stir in the bay leaves and the salt-free chile rub. Bring to a boil,

then move the pot to the unheated part of the grill and simmer gently, uncovered, until the beans are tender, 1 to $1 1/2$ hours, stirring now and then and adding hot water as necessary to keep the pan bottom from going dry.

3. Stir in the salt, lime juice, and cilantro. Cook for another 5 minutes, then taste and adjust the seasonings as necessary.

4. Remove the bay leaves before serving.

BARBECUED BAKED BEANS

American barbecue goes hand in hand with baked beans. Serve these traditional baked beans with any grilled pork, beef, or poultry. Slow-cooking the beans with bacon and molasses gradually infuses the entire stew with rich, sweet flavors. To make this dish over a low campfire, start the fire early and make sure you have enough wood for the fire to burn gradually for 5 hours (about a quarter of a cord of wood should do it). Set up the fire with a higher-heat area for adding wood and a medium-low-heat area for cooking. Rake coals into the cooking area as necessary. It also helps to have a camp grill with a pot hanger and a wire-handled pot, which allows you to suspend the pot over the cooking area and swing it toward you or over the heat as necessary. But a simple campfire grill grate will also work. Regulate the heat by raking more or fewer coals beneath the pot. The beans should simmer gently in the pot. If using a charcoal grill, put the pot of beans on a sturdy grill grate (make sure the grate can hold the weight of the beans), cover, and cook as directed, regulating the heat with the air vents and replenishing the coals as necessary.

THE GRILL

Charcoal: Indirect heat, medium ash
    12-by-12-inch charcoal bed (about 3 dozen coals)
    Clean, oiled grate on lowest setting or pot hanger
        and wire-handled pot

Wood: Indirect heat, medium ash
    12-by-12-inch bed, 3 to 4 inches deep
    Clean, oiled grate set 4 inches above the fire or
        pot hanger and wire-handled pot

INGREDIENTS (MAKES 8 SERVINGS)

10 ounces dried navy beans or other small white beans, picked over and rinsed
4 ounces thick-cut bacon, chopped
1 small onion, finely chopped

$1/3$ cup molasses
$1 1/4$ cups Sweet, Hot, and Sour BBQ Sauce (page 391)
$1/2$ teaspoon kosher salt
$1/4$ teaspoon ground black pepper

DIRECTIONS

1. Put the beans in a large pot and cover with water by 2 inches. Let soak overnight.

2. Heat the grill as directed. Drain the beans in a colander and set aside. Cook the bacon in the same bean pot directly over the heated part of the grill until crisp, about 10 minutes. Add the onion and cook until softened, about 5 minutes.

3. Add the beans and enough water to cover the beans by 1 inch. Stir in the molasses and barbecue sauce. Bring to a boil, then move the pot to the unheated part of the grill and simmer gently, uncovered, until the beans are tender, 4 to 5 hours, stirring now and then and adding hot water as necessary to keep the pan bottom from going dry.

4. Stir in the salt and pepper and serve.

-Photo: Barbecued Baked Beans

TIMING

Soak wood chips: 1 hour

Prep and press: 30 minutes
     (plus 15 minutes for paste)

Marinate: 2 to 6 hours

Grill: 30 minutes

GRILL TOOLS AND EQUIPMENT

· 1 cup wood chips, preferably hickory or
  oak, if using a gas or charcoal grill

· Smoker box or foil packet, if using a gas
  grill (see page 39)

· Long-handled spatula

· Long-handled basting brush

GETTING CREATIVE

· Use chicken parts or pork chops instead
  of the tofu. Smoke as directed, and then
  brown over the heated part of the grill
  until the juices run almost clear and an
  instant-read thermometer registers
  165°F for chicken or 155°F for pork.

· For a more traditional smoke aroma,
  use allspice wood (called pimento in
  Jamaica) instead of hickory or oak for
  the fire. A fruit wood such as apple also
  works well.

KNOW YOUR INGREDIENTS

What Is Tofu?

The process of making tofu is similar to
that of making soft cheese. But the "milk"
comes from soybeans instead of from
cows. First, soybeans are soaked, ground,
boiled, and mashed to extract their milky
liquid. A coagulant (usually calcium sulfate
or magnesium chloride) is added to separate the soymilk into curds and whey. Then
the curds are drained and pressed into
blocks of tofu, also known as bean curd or
Chinese tofu.

Depending on how much whey is
pressed out, tofu can be made into soft,
firm, or extra-firm textures. Extra-firm tofu
works best on the grill because it doesn't
fall apart on the grill grates. Look for extra-
firm tofu packed in tubs of water in grocery
store produce sections.

It might seem odd to grill something
akin to cheese, but cooks in Asia have
been grilling tofu for centuries. The porous
texture of tofu makes it especially good at
absorbing flavorful marinades and smoky
aromas from burning wood. For the best
texture, use the firmest tofu you can find,
press out the excess water under a heavy
weight (see page 298), and then marinate
or rub it with a spice mixture. It also helps
to smoke the tofu for 15 to 20 minutes
over indirect heat to draw out excess moisture and infuse the aroma of smoke into
the tofu. Then move the tofu over direct
heat and baste with a sauce as it cooks.
The flavor of tofu is very mild, so bring on
the bold-flavored marinades, and sauces.

You might also see another type of tofu
packaged in a small aseptic box. Known as
silken tofu or Japanese tofu, this creamy-
textured tofu is made by using thicker
soymilk that is carefully strained but not
pressed as densely as regular tofu. Silken
tofu can be used like yogurt or sour cream
to make creamy soups, dips, sauces, and
dressings. But its soft texture doesn't hold
up well on the grill. For live-fire cooking,
stick with extra-firm tofu.

SMOKED JERK TOFU

Jerk is Jamaican barbecue, and like American barbecue, it is both a dish and a method of cooking.
Typically done with chicken or pork that is marinated in an incendiary paste of Scotch bonnet peppers and
a litany of spices, it is a way of life in Jamaica, sold in fine restaurants as well as at roadside stands from
one end of the island to the other. Here, it is slathered on tofu. The initial step of pressing water from the
tofu before it is marinated is essential; if skipped, the sodium in the jerk paste will draw the moisture out
of the tofu, which will dilute the paste and soften its punch.

THE GRILL

Gas: Indirect heat, medium-high (375° to 400°F)	**Wood:** Indirect heat, light ash
Clean, oiled grate on lowest setting	Split bed of coals (1 inch deep per side)
Charcoal: Indirect heat, light ash	Clean, oiled grate set 3 inches above the fire
Split charcoal bed (about 2 dozen coals per side)	
Clean, oiled grate on lowest setting	

INGREDIENTS (MAKES 4 SERVINGS)

2 pounds extra-firm tofu	2 tablespoons vegetable oil
2 cups Jerk Wet Paste (page 377)	

DIRECTIONS

1. Cut each 1-pound block of tofu in half through the side to
make 2 thick slabs (for a total of 4 slabs). Press the slabs
under a heavy weight for 30 minutes (see page 298).

2. Spread a layer of the jerk paste over the bottom of a shallow 4-quart baking dish. Put the tofu over the paste and spread
the remaining paste evenly over the top and sides. Cover and
refrigerate for 2 to 6 hours.

3. Soak the wood chips in cold water for 1 hour.

4. Heat the grill as directed. If using a gas grill, put the wood
chips in the smoker box or in a perforated foil packet.

5. When ready to grill, if using a gas grill, turn off the middle
burner(s). If your gas grill has only 2 burners, turn off one side.
If using a charcoal grill, drain the wood chips and scatter them
over the coals. If using a wood grill, spread the coals to
opposite sides of the grill for indirect heat.

6. Put the tofu over the unheated part of the grill. Cover and
smoke for 20 minutes.

7. Using a basting brush, mix the oil into the jerk paste
remaining in the baking dish.

8. Move the tofu over the heated part of the grill and cook
until the underside is nicely browned, 3 to 5 minutes. Flip
with a spatula and baste the top side with the jerk paste.
Cook until nicely browned on the bottom, 3 to 5 minutes.

9. Cut each slab on the diagonal into 2 triangles per serving.
Serve warm.

ASIAN BARBECUED TOFU

TIMING
Prep: 5 minutes
   (plus 5 minutes for glaze)
Press: 30 minutes
Marinate: 2 hours
Grill: 8 to 12 minutes

GRILL TOOLS AND EQUIPMENT
· Long-handled spatula
· Long-handled basting brush

TIP
· For information on types of tofu, see "What is Tofu?", facing page.

In most meat grillery, the trick is to cook the meat without losing its precious juices. When grilling tofu, it's the opposite. You want to get rid of the excess liquid in the tofu to firm up its texture. So we cook it twice: first in a sauté pan and then on the grill. Double-cooking concentrates the tofu's texture, giving you a bit more to chew on. Try it—it's worth the tiny bit of extra effort. We also marinate and glaze the tofu for flavor.

THE GRILL

Gas: Direct heat, medium-high (400° to 450°F)
Clean, oiled grate

Charcoal: Direct heat, light ash
12-by-12-inch charcoal bed (about 3 dozen coals)
Clean, oiled grate on lowest setting

Wood: Direct heat, light ash
12-by-12-inch bed, 3 to 4 inches deep
Clean, oiled grate set 2 inches above the fire

INGREDIENTS (MAKES 4 SERVINGS)

2 pounds extra-firm tofu
2 tablespoons vegetable oil
2 tablespoons tamari or soy sauce
1 tablespoon rice vinegar
1 teaspoon toasted sesame oil

1 clove garlic, minced
1 scallion, sliced
1/2 cup Ginger-Hoisin Balsamic Glaze (page 388)
1/2 teaspoon sesame seeds (optional)
Oil for coating grill grate

DIRECTIONS

1. Cut each 1-pound block of tofu in half through the side to make 2 thick slabs (for a total of 4 slabs). Press the slabs under a heavy weight for 30 minutes (see page 298).

2. Heat 1 tablespoon of the vegetable oil in a large skillet or wok over medium-high heat. Add the pressed tofu and cook until golden brown on both sides, about 5 minutes per side, turning once. Combine the tamari, rice vinegar, sesame oil, garlic, and half of the scallion in a large zipper-lock bag. Let the tofu cool slightly, then add it to the bag. Let the tofu cool further with the bag open. When it approaches room temperature, press out the air and seal the bag. Gently massage the marinade into the tofu, then refrigerate for 2 hours or up to 2 days.

3. Heat the grill as directed.

4. Let the tofu rest at room temperature before grilling, about 30 minutes. Remove from the marinade and discard the marinade. Rub with the remaining 1 tablespoon vegetable oil.

5. Brush the grill grate and coat it with oil. Put the tofu on the grill and cook until nicely grill-marked, 4 to 6 minutes per side, brushing both sides with the glaze.

6. Cut each slab on the diagonal into 2 triangles per serving. Sprinkle with the reserved scallion and the sesame seeds (if using) and serve.

TOFU KEBABS WITH INDONESIAN PEANUT SAUCE

TIMING
Prep and press: 30 minutes
   (plus 5 minutes for sauce)
Stir-fry: 15 minutes
Marinate: 8 hours
Grill: 5 to 8 minutes

GRILL TOOLS AND EQUIPMENT
· 8 skewers, soaked in water for 20 minutes if bamboo
· Heat-resistant grill mitts

Everyone from vegetarians to steak lovers seems to like this recipe. The tofu is cooked twice to firm it up and give it a nice crust: First it's stir-fried and then it's grilled. The stir-frying can be done a day or two ahead, so when it comes time to grill, all you have to do is put the kebabs on the grill and baste them with sauce.

THE GRILL

Gas: Direct heat, medium (350°F)
Clean, oiled grate

Charcoal: Direct heat, medium ash
12-by-12-inch charcoal bed (about 3 dozen coals)
Clean, oiled grate on lowest setting

Wood: Direct heat, medium ash
12-by-12-inch bed, 3 inches deep
Clean, oiled grate set 4 inches above the fire

INGREDIENTS (MAKES 8 KEBABS)

2 tablespoons peanut oil or other vegetable oil

2 pounds extra-firm tofu, pressed (see Tips) and cut into 1-inch cubes

$1/4$ cup tamari or soy sauce

1 tablespoon rice vinegar

2 teaspoons toasted sesame oil

$3/4$ cup Indonesian Peanut Sauce (page 396)

1 large green bell pepper, cut into 1-inch chunks

16 cherry tomatoes

Oil for coating grill grate

1 tablespoon finely chopped cilantro

DIRECTIONS

1. Heat the peanut oil in a wok or large, nonstick skillet over medium-high heat. When hot, add the tofu and toss to coat it with oil. Cook, flipping the pieces every couple of minutes, until lightly golden all over, about 15 minutes. (Do this in batches if your pan isn't big enough to hold the tofu in a single layer.) Remove from the heat and let cool slightly.

2. Meanwhile, mix the tamari or soy sauce, rice vinegar, and sesame oil in a large bowl or plastic container. Add the tofu, cover, and toss until the tofu is well coated. Uncover to release any steam. Re-cover and refrigerate for 8 hours or overnight, tossing occasionally to coat the tofu.

3. Heat the grill as directed.

4. In a small saucepan, simmer the peanut sauce gently over medium-low heat until slightly thickened, about 5 minutes.

5. Thread the tofu, bell pepper, and tomatoes on the skewers, using 2 to 3 pieces of tofu for every piece of pepper and tomato. Brush the peanut sauce generously over the tofu and vegetables.

6. Brush the grill grate and coat it with oil. Put the skewers on the grill and cook until the vegetables are tender and the tofu is nicely grill-marked, turning often, 5 to 8 minutes total.

7. Serve with the chopped cilantro and any remaining peanut sauce.

Photo: Grilled Asparagus Wrapped in Prosciutto

GRILLED ASPARAGUS WRAPPED IN PROSCIUTTO

Slender stalks of asparagus are so elegant that the trick is to avoid doing too much to them. We like to grill them briefly, wrap them in thin sheets of prosciutto, and sprinkle them with shredded or grated Parmesan cheese.

THE GRILL

Gas: Direct heat, medium (350°F)
Clean, oiled grate on lowest setting

Charcoal: Direct heat, medium ash
12-by-12-inch charcoal bed (about 3 dozen coals)
Clean, oiled grate on lowest setting

Wood: Direct heat, medium ash
12-by-12-inch bed, 3 to 4 inches deep
Clean, oiled grate set 4 inches above the fire

INGREDIENTS (MAKES 8 SERVINGS)

2 1/2 pounds thin asparagus (40 to 45 thin spears), trimmed (see Tip)
1 tablespoon olive oil
Oil for coating grill grate

4 ounces sliced prosciutto (about 8 paper-thin slices)
1/4 teaspoon ground black pepper
1 tablespoon shredded or grated Parmesan cheese

DIRECTIONS

1. Heat the grill as directed.

2. Toss the asparagus with the olive oil on a rimmed baking sheet or in a zipper-lock bag until completely coated.

3. Brush the grill grate and coat it with oil. Put the asparagus on the grill, perpendicular to the bars of the grill grate. Grill until just tender but not limp, 4 to 5 minutes, rolling the asparagus once or twice with tongs.

4. Lay a slice of prosciutto horizontally on a work surface. Put 4 to 6 asparagus spears over the prosciutto near a short edge. Sprinkle the asparagus with some of the pepper. Tightly roll the prosciutto over the asparagus bundle on a slight diagonal, so that the prosciutto covers all but the tips of the spears. Sprinkle the tips with the Parmesan and serve.

TIMING
Prep: 12 minutes
Grill: 5 minutes

GRILL TOOLS AND EQUIPMENT
· Long-handled tongs

TIP
· To trim asparagus, hold a spear with the ends in each hand. Gradually bend the stalk. It will naturally snap where the stalk becomes tough. Discard the tough end. If the spears are very thick, peel them with a vegetable peeler by laying each spear on a work surface and peeling it with a vegetable peeler from the tip to the stem end.

GETTING CREATIVE
· For Grilled Asparagus with Barbecued Lemon Wedges, omit the prosciutto. Arrange the grilled asparagus on a platter and sprinkle with 2 teaspoons chopped fresh dill or tarragon, if you like. Cut 2 lemons into 4 wedges each. Put the wedges directly on the grill grate over a medium fire with the cut sides up. Thickly brush 1 to 2 tablespoons barbecue sauce over the cut sides. Grill until the peels are nicely grill-marked and the lemons are beginning to soften, 2 to 4 minutes. Remove with tongs and cool slightly on the platter. Pass the lemon wedges for squeezing over the asparagus.

GRILLED GARLICHOKES

There are two basic methods for grilling artichokes. You can precook them in liquid and finish them on the grill, which gives you a good roasted surface and tender, meaty leaves but a watery, steamed flavor. Or you can cook them completely over a flame, which concentrates their flavor but leaves the leaves slightly tougher. This recipe uses the latter method. The artichokes will keep warm in their foil wrappers for up to 30 minutes after being removed from the grill.

THE GRILL

Gas: Indirect heat, medium-high (350° to 400°F)
3- or 4-burner grill—middle burner(s) off
2-burner grill—1 side off
Clean, oiled grate

Charcoal: Indirect heat, light ash
Split charcoal bed (about 2 dozen coals per side)
20 replacement coals
Heavy-duty drip pan set between banks of charcoal
Clean, oiled grate on medium setting

TIMING
Prep: 15 minutes
Grill: About 45 minutes

GRILL TOOLS AND EQUIPMENT
· 4 squares heavy-duty aluminum foil
· Long-handled spatula or long-handled tongs

INGREDIENTS (MAKES 4 SERVINGS)

4 globe artichokes

2 lemons

1/4 cup minced garlic

4 tablespoons extra-virgin olive oil

1/2 teaspoon kosher salt

1/4 teaspoon coarsely ground black pepper

DIRECTIONS

1. Trim the artichokes with a thin-bladed stainless-steel knife; cut the stems flat to the bottoms and cut the thorny tips from the leaves by slicing off the top inch from the tapered end. Snip off the remaining tips with scissors.

2. Squeeze the juice from one of the lemons into a large bowl. Add the artichokes and turn to coat the cut surfaces with lemon. Add enough cold water to cover and put a plate on top to weigh down the artichokes so that they remain submerged; set aside for 10 minutes.

3. Remove the artichokes from the lemon water. Put a teaspoon of garlic in the center of each square of foil; top with an artichoke and spread the leaves gently. Work 2 teaspoons of garlic between the leaves of each artichoke. Drizzle 1 tablespoon oil over each artichoke and season them liberally with salt and pepper. Wrap each artichoke tightly in the foil.

4. Put the artichokes over the unheated part of the grill. Cover and cook for 45 minutes; let rest for 5 minutes. Remove the foil, and squeeze the juice of the remaining lemon over the artichokes; serve.

Photo: Grilled Garlichokes

GRILLED CHICORY WITH SOUR CHERRY VINAIGRETTE

TIMING
Prep: 8 minutes
Grill: 8 to 12 minutes

GRILL TOOLS AND EQUIPMENT
· Long-handled tongs

TIPS
· Save some fresh herbs to sprinkle over the top of the grilled chicory.
· Make the vinaigrette and refrigerate up to 2 days ahead of time.

Belgian endive and radicchio are both members of a leafy green family known as chicory. These bitter, tight-headed greens grill up beautifully. All they need is a quick glaze or drizzle of vinaigrette to flavor them up. A little sugar in this vinaigrette helps to balance the bitterness of the greens.

THE GRILL

Gas: Direct heat, medium-high (400° to 450°F)
Clean, oiled grate

Charcoal: Direct heat, light ash
12-by-12-inch charcoal bed (about 3 dozen coals)
Clean, oiled grate on lowest setting

Wood: Direct heat, light ash
12-by-12-inch bed, 3 to 4 inches deep
Clean, oiled grate set 2 inches above the fire

INGREDIENTS (MAKES 4 SERVINGS)

For the vinaigrette:
2 tablespoons raspberry vinegar or red wine vinegar
1/4 cup walnut oil or extra-virgin olive oil
1/2 cup sour cherry preserves
1/2 teaspoon Dijon mustard
1/2 clove garlic, minced
1/2 teaspoon kosher salt
1/4 teaspoon ground black pepper
1 tablespoon chopped fresh basil or flat-leaf parsley

For the chicory:
1 medium-large head radicchio, about 12 ounces
2 medium heads Belgian endive, about 12 ounces total
3 tablespoons olive oil
1/2 teaspoon kosher salt
1/4 teaspoon ground black pepper
Oil for coating grill grate

DIRECTIONS

1. Heat the grill as directed.

2. For the vinaigrette, put the vinegar in a bowl and whisk in the walnut oil in a thin, steady steam until incorporated. Whisk in the preserves, mustard, garlic, salt, pepper, and basil.

3. For the chicory, cut the radicchio through the core into eighths. Cut the endive in half lengthwise. Brush all over with the olive oil and sprinkle with the salt and pepper.

4. Brush the grill grate and coat it with oil. Put the radicchio and endive on the grill and cook until nicely grill-marked, 4 to 6 minutes per side (the endive will take slightly longer than the radicchio). If your grill has a temperature gauge, it should stay at around 450°F.

5. Put the radicchio and endive on plates or a platter, spoon the vinaigrette over the top, and serve. Pass any remaining vinaigrette at the table.

GRILLED GINGER AND GARLIC SCALLIONS

TIMING
Prep: 5 minutes
Grill: 2 to 6 minutes

GRILL TOOLS AND EQUIPMENT
· Long-handled tongs
· Long-handled basting brush

Nothing could be simpler than grilling scallions. Just toss the trimmed alliums across the bars of the grill grate for a minute or two per side. A basting sauce of sesame oil and soy sauce with fresh ginger and garlic makes these the perfect side dish for any grilled meat with an Asian flavor profile.

THE GRILL

Gas: Direct heat, medium-high (400° to 450°F)
Clean, oiled grate on lowest setting

Charcoal: Direct heat, light ash
12-by-12-inch charcoal bed (about 3 dozen coals)
Clean, oiled grate on lowest setting

Wood: Direct heat, light ash
12-by-12-inch bed, 3 to 4 inches deep
Clean, oiled grate set 3 inches above the fire

INGREDIENTS (MAKES 4 SERVINGS)

4 large scallions

1 tablespoon soy sauce

1 teaspoon rice vinegar or dry sherry

1 teaspoon toasted sesame oil

1/2 teaspoon honey

2 cloves garlic, minced

1 teaspoon minced peeled gingerroot

Oil for coating grill grate

DIRECTIONS

1. Trim the roots from the scallions and brush clean, if necessary.

2. Heat the grill as directed.

3. Combine the soy sauce, rice vinegar, sesame oil, honey, garlic, and ginger. Brush over the scallions.

4. Brush the grill grate and coat it with oil. Put the scallions on the grill and cook until nicely grill-marked, 1 to 3 minutes per side, basting with the soy sauce mixture.

5. Remove to plates or a platter, drizzle with any remaining soy sauce mixture, and serve.

ROASTED ONIONS WITH GORGONZOLA CRUMBLE

Few vegetables benefit from a sojourn on the grill as much as onions. Fire caramelizes an onion's ample sugars and concentrates its flavor. All the while, the onion's juices percolate deep inside, helping its crispy sections soften and its drier sections crisp. We recommend you use small cipolline onions (also spelled cipollini), which have an assertive flavor and lots of sugar. Most important, they're small enough to grill whole. Cipolline are increasingly available, although you may have to search. If you can't find them, any small onion will do. Or you could use small Vidalia and/or red onions, peeled and halved before grilling.

THE GRILL

Gas: Direct heat, medium (350°F)

Clean, oiled grate

Charcoal: Direct heat, medium ash

12-by-12-inch charcoal bed (about 3 dozen coals)

Clean, oiled grate on lowest setting

Wood: Direct heat, medium ash

12-by-12-inch bed, 3 inches deep

Clean, oiled grate set 4 inches above the fire

INGREDIENTS (MAKES 4 SERVINGS)

8 cipolline onions, about 3 ounces each

2 tablespoons extra-virgin olive oil

1/4 teaspoon kosher salt, plus more to taste

1/4 teaspoon ground black pepper, plus more to taste

1 ounce Gorgonzola cheese

2 tablespoons coarsely chopped fresh flat-leaf parsley

1 clove garlic, minced

Oil for coating grill grate

DIRECTIONS

1. Heat the grill as directed.

2. Trim the ends from the onions and peel. Coat with 1 tablespoon of the olive oil and season with the salt and pepper.

3. Crumble the Gorgonzola with your fingers into a small bowl. Toss with the remaining 1 tablespoon olive oil, the parsley, the garlic, and salt and pepper to taste.

4. Brush the grill grate and coat it with oil. Put the onions on the grill. Cover and cook until the onions are charred in spots and tender but not soft, about 18 minutes, turning halfway through. If your grill has a temperature gauge, it should stay at around 375°F.

5. Put the grilled onions in a serving bowl and scatter the Gorgonzola mixture over the top. Serve.

GRILLED CARAMELIZED VIDALIA ONIONS

We wondered whether you could caramelize onions on the grill. The answer: You can. While we normally prefer not to grill in foil packets, the foil is a necessity for this recipe. It traps the juices and keeps the onions moist. First we grill slices of onion to lightly char them. Then we break the charred onions into rings and sprinkle them with salt and sugar to help draw out the moisture. When wrapped in foil and returned to the grill, the onions soften in texture and deepen in sweetness. Serve them as a side dish or in a sandwich, or try them on Smoked Chorizo Pizza with Caramelized Onions and Arugula (page 332).

TIMING

Prep: 5 minutes

Grill: About 20 minutes

GRILL TOOLS AND EQUIPMENT

· Skewers (soaked in water for 1 hour, if bamboo)

· Aluminum foil

· Long-handled tongs

· Heat-resistant grill gloves

GETTING CREATIVE

· Add a splash of balsamic vinegar to the foil packet before sealing and finishing grilling.

· Replace the Vidalia with any sweet onion, such as Maui, Walla Walla, or Texas sweet onions.

TIPS

· When skewering the onion rounds, push the skewer across the grain of the rings to make sure the rounds will hold together on the grill.

· To keep the onions flat on the grill, put the skewers directly on the grill rather than hanging off the edge. Wear heat-proof gloves when turning the skewers.

THE GRILL

Gas: Direct heat, medium-high (400° to 450°F)
Clean, oiled grate on lowest setting

Charcoal: Direct heat, light ash
12-by-12-inch charcoal bed (about 3 dozen coals) with high- and low-heat areas
Clean, oiled grate on lowest setting

Wood: Direct heat, light ash
12-by-12-inch bed with a 3- to 4-inch-deep area for high heat and a 2-inch area for low heat
Clean, oiled grate set 3 inches above the fire

INGREDIENTS (MAKES 4 SERVINGS—ABOUT 1 CUP)

1 large Vidalia onion (about 1 1/2 pounds)

No-stick spray oil or olive oil

Oil for coating grill grate

1/2 teaspoon kosher salt

1/2 teaspoon sugar

DIRECTIONS

1. Heat the grill as directed.

2. Slice the onion into rounds about 1/4 inch thick. Skewer the rounds through the side so that they will lie flat on the grill. Generously coat them all over with oil.

3. Brush the grill grate and coat it with oil. Put the onion rounds on the grill directly over medium-high heat until nicely grill-marked, 2 to 4 minutes per side. Rotate the onions 45 degrees halfway through the cooking on each side to create crosshatch marks and more even browning.

4. Put the browned rounds on one side of a large piece of foil. Cut each round in half crosswise, if you like. Break the onions into rings with tongs and arrange in a single layer. Sprinkle all over with the salt and sugar, and spray or drizzle with a bit more oil. Fold the foil over the onions and crimp to seal. Reduce the heat to medium-low (on a gas grill) or put the foil over the medium-low-heat area (on a charcoal or wood grill). Cover and grill until the onions are very soft, 10 to 15 minutes, turning the sealed packet once or twice. Let rest, wrapped in foil, for 5 minutes before using.

CHAPTER 10

MASTERING FRUIT, DESSERT, DOUGH, AND EVERYTHING ELSE

RECIPES

FRUIT ON THE GRILL

If you enjoy fresh fruit, you'll love it grilled. Certain fruits, such as pineapple, caramelize beautifully on the grill because of their high concentration of sugars. You can grill many fruits much as you would grill vegetables. Slice or halve them and grill them fairly quickly over medium-high direct heat just until tender, turning once or twice. Just keep an eye on the fruit as it grills. The high sugar content can make fruits go from browned to burned in less than a minute. Most fruits have enough moisture and sugar to be grilled without oil or seasoning. But you can season some fruits, such as bananas, before grilling (see Grilled Mocha Bananas on page 308, for example). Some firm fruits, like apples and pears, can also be grill-roasted via indirect heat, just as you would bake them in an oven. However you grill them, fruits taste wonderful brushed with butter or a sweet glaze toward the end of cooking. Orange Honey Butter Glaze on page 389 is our all-purpose fruit glaze. You can also brush this glaze on grill-toasted sweet breads like pound cake, gingerbread, French toast, prepared waffles, or split croissants. See the recipes throughout this chapter for more ideas.

FRUIT-GRILLING GUIDE

Fruit	Prep	Grilling Time (in minutes)
Apples, sliced	Peel (or not), slice $1/4$ to $1/2$ inch thick	3 to 5
Apples, halved	Halve lengthwise and core	10 to 12
Apples, whole	Hollow out core, stuff with sweet filling	Indirect heat, 40 to 60
Apricots	Halve and pit	6 to 8
Bananas, peeled	Use slightly firm fruit, cut into 2- to 3-inch lengths, skewer	4 to 6
Bananas, unpeeled	Use slightly firm fruit, halve lengthwise, grill cut-side down	3 to 4
Figs, sliced	Halve lengthwise	2 to 3
Figs, whole	Skewer through side	6 to 8
Grapefruit	Halve crosswise, grill cut-side down	3 to 5
Grapes	Leave whole, skewer only if necessary	2 to 3
Lemons	Cut into wedges or slice $1/4$ inch thick	2 to 3
Limes	Cut into wedges or slice $1/4$ inch thick	2 to 3
Mangoes, sliced	Peel, pit, and slice $1/2$ inch thick	6 to 8
Mangoes, whole	Leave whole, peel and mash cooked fruit	8 to 10
Nectarines	Halve and pit	6 to 8
Oranges	Halve crosswise and grill cut-side down, or section and skewer the sections	3 to 5
Papayas, sliced	Peel, scoop out seeds, and slice $1/2$ inch thick	6 to 8
Papayas, halved	Halve lengthwise, scoop out seeds, eat from skin when cooked	8 to 10
Peaches	Halve and pit	6 to 8
Pears, halved	Halve lengthwise and core	10 to 12
Pears, whole	Hollow out core, stuff with sweet filling	Indirect heat, 40 to 60
Pineapples	Cut into rings or wedges	6 to 8
Plantains, unpeeled	Use very ripe (black) fruit, cut into 2- to 3-inch lengths	10 to 12
Plums	Halve and pit	4 to 6

GRILLED WAFFLES WITH GRILLED FRUIT AND MAPLE WHIPPED CREAM

TIMING
Prep: 15 minutes
Grill: 10 minutes

GRILL TOOLS AND EQUIPMENT
· Long-handled tongs

GETTING CREATIVE
· Try this recipe with French toast
  or croissants.

Give this dish a try on a whimsical summer morning. Grilled bananas and mangoes make a great accompaniment to waffles. The dish is meant to be easy, so we use prepared waffles. Any prepared waffles will do, but we prefer thick, square Belgian waffles. Grill the waffles until they are lightly toasted and grill-marked but not charred. If you don't have a sweet tooth in the morning, serve the waffles for dessert after dinner.

THE GRILL

Gas: Direct heat, medium (350°F)
Clean, oiled grate on lowest setting

Charcoal: Direct heat, medium ash
12-by-12-inch charcoal bed (about 3 dozen coals)
Clean, oiled grate on lowest setting

Wood: Direct heat, medium ash
12-by-12-inch bed, 3 inches deep
Clean, oiled grate set 4 inches above the fire

INGREDIENTS (MAKES 4 SERVINGS)

4 bananas

1 mango

1 tablespoon brown sugar

1/2 teaspoon ground cinnamon

Oil for coating grill grate

16 strawberries, hulled and quartered

8 prepared waffles

1 cup (1/2 pint) heavy cream

1/4 cup maple syrup, plus more for serving

2 teaspoons vanilla extract

DIRECTIONS

1. Heat the grill as directed.

2. Chill a medium bowl and a whisk or beaters for the whipped cream.

3. Cut the bananas in half lengthwise through the peel, following the arc of the curve, so that when they are cut the bananas will lie flat on the grill.

4. Stand the mango on its thick end and cut the sides off the center pit, curving the knife around the pit. Peel each half with a paring knife, then slice lengthwise into $1/2$-inch-thick slices.

5. Mix the brown sugar and cinnamon in a small bowl, then sprinkle over the cut sides of the banana and mango.

6. Brush the grill grate and coat it with oil. Put the bananas cut-side down on the grill and cook until nicely grill-marked,

3 to 4 minutes. Grill the mango until nicely grill-marked, 2 to 3 minutes per side. Remove from the grill and cut into bite-size pieces.

7. Grill the waffles until toasted and heated through, about 3 minutes per side.

8. Pour the cream into the chilled bowl and whisk vigorously or beat with an electric mixer on medium speed until the cream forms soft peaks when the whisk or beaters are lifted. Whisk or beat in the maple syrup and vanilla.

9. Arrange the waffles on a platter, with the grilled fruit and strawberries and maple whipped cream in small bowls. Allow guests to top their waffles with fruit, whipped cream, and additional maple syrup.

GRILLED MOCHA BANANAS

We love combining the dark flavors of the tropics: coffee and chocolate. Put that combination over a tropical fruit like bananas, and it's near nirvana. We've gilded the lily with mocha *dulce de leche,* but we didn't think you'd mind. Serve these richly spiced bananas with ice cream or pound cake. Or use them to make a tropical Grilled Banana Split (page 309).

THE GRILL

Gas: Direct heat, medium (350°F)
Clean, oiled grate on lowest setting

Charcoal: Direct heat, medium ash
12-by-12-inch medium charcoal bed
(about 3 dozen coals)
Clean, oiled grate on lowest setting

Wood: Direct heat, medium ash
12-by-12-inch bed, 3 inches deep
Clean, oiled grate set 4 inches above the fire

INGREDIENTS (MAKES 8 SMALL SERVINGS)

1 can (about 14 ounces) sweetened condensed milk
4 to 5 tablespoons brewed coffee
$1/8$ teaspoon baking soda
1 ounce bittersweet chocolate, broken into pieces
4 large, just-ripe bananas

2 teaspoons brown sugar
1 teaspoon finely ground espresso beans
1 teaspoon unsweetened cocoa powder
$1/4$ teaspoon ground cinnamon
Oil for coating grill grate

DIRECTIONS

1. Heat the grill as directed.

2. Mix the condensed milk and 2 tablespoons of the brewed coffee in a large cast-iron skillet or heavy-duty roasting pan until combined. Put the pan on the grill away from the direct heat, cover, and cook until the mixture boils, 8 to 10 minutes. Scrape the pan, especially the bottom, and stir the mixture with the scraper. Cover the grill and cook the *dulce de leche* until the mixture becomes thick and creamy, like pudding, about 15 minutes more, scraping every 5 minutes to make sure the bottom doesn't overcook.

3. Remove from the heat and stir in the baking soda. The mixture will bubble up; stir until the bubbles subside. Pass through a strainer into a bowl, and stir in 2 tablespoons of

the remaining brewed coffee and all of the chocolate. When the chocolate has melted, stir the *dulce de leche* until smooth. If the mixture is too thick, stir in another tablespoon or so of coffee. Set aside until ready to serve.

4. Meanwhile, cut the bananas in half lengthwise through the peel, following the arc of the curve, so that when they are cut they will lie flat on the grill.

5. Mix the brown sugar, espresso, cocoa powder, and cinnamon in a small bowl. Sprinkle over the cut sides of the bananas, pressing the mixture in gently with your fingertips.

6. Brush the grill grate and coat it with oil. Put the bananas cut-side down on the grill and cook until nicely grill-marked, 3 to 4 minutes. Serve with the mocha *dulce de leche.*

TIMING
Prep: 20 minutes
Grill: 25 to 30 minutes

GRILL TOOLS AND EQUIPMENT
· Large cast-iron skillet or heavy-duty roasting pan
· Heat-resistant silicone scraper
· Long-handled tongs

TIP
· Serve the bananas cut-side up in the skins, if you like. Or loosen the bananas from the skins and then scrape them onto a plate, cut-side up.

GRILLED BANANA SPLITS

TIMING
Prep: 5 minutes
    (plus 45 minutes for Mocha Bananas)
Grill: 10 to 15 minutes

GRILL TOOLS AND EQUIPMENT
· See recipe for Grilled Mocha Bananas
  (facing page).

SHORTCUT
· For simpler grilled banana splits, grill
  the bananas as directed in the Grilled
  Mocha Bananas recipe, but omit the
  topping and the *dulce de leche*. Proceed
  as directed.

This is really why we make Grilled Mocha Bananas. Sure, the grilled bananas and mocha *dulce de leche* are great on their own. But they're over the top in this banana split. Each serving gets three scoops of ice cream, a grilled mocha banana, a few generous ribbons of mocha *dulce de leche* and chocolate sauce, a dollop of fresh whipped cream, and a maraschino cherry. It's our grill-marked version of a time-honored American indulgence.

THE GRILL

Gas: Direct heat, medium (350°F)
          Clean, oiled grate on lowest setting
Charcoal: Direct heat, medium ash
          12-by-12-inch medium charcoal bed
              (about 3 dozen coals)
          Clean, oiled grate on lowest setting

Wood: Direct heat, medium ash
           12-by-12-inch bed, 3 inches deep
           Clean, oiled grate set 4 inches above the fire

INGREDIENTS (MAKES 4 LARGE SERVINGS)

For the chocolate sauce:
1/2 cup half-and-half
2 tablespoons light brown sugar
1 tablespoon light corn syrup
1 tablespoon butter
4 ounces bittersweet or semisweet chocolate, finely chopped
1 tablespoon rum or 1 teaspoon vanilla extract
Grilled Mocha Bananas (facing page)

For the whipped cream and ice cream:
1/2 pint (1 cup) heavy cream
2 tablespoons sugar
1 tablespoon rum, or 1 teaspoon vanilla extract
1/2 pint vanilla ice cream
1/2 pint chocolate ice cream
1/2 pint strawberry ice cream
4 maraschino cherries

DIRECTIONS

1. For the chocolate sauce, put the half-and-half, brown sugar, corn syrup, and butter in a medium saucepan. Bring to a boil over medium-high heat, stirring constantly. Remove from the heat and stir in the chocolate and rum. Cover and keep warm. Or cool, cover, and refrigerate for up to 1 week. Reheat over low heat until warm. If the sauce is too thick, stir in 1 teaspoon of water at a time until it thins.

2. Heat the grill as directed. Chill a medium bowl and a whisk or beaters for the whipped cream.

3. Prepare the Grilled Mocha Bananas.

4. For the whipped cream and ice cream: Pour the cream into the chilled bowl and whisk vigorously or beat with an electric mixer on medium speed until the cream barely forms soft peaks when the whisk or beaters are lifted. Whisk or beat in the sugar and rum.

5. To assemble the banana splits, mound a scoop (about 1/4 cup) of vanilla, a scoop of chocolate, and a scoop of strawberry ice cream in the center of each of 4 shallow dessert bowls, preferably oval-shaped. Loosen the grilled banana halves from their skins and slide 2 of each, cut-side up, into the bowls, with one on each side of the ice cream.

6. Drizzle generously with the chocolate sauce and *dulce de leche* from the mocha bananas. Dollop generously with the whipped cream, and top each serving with a maraschino cherry.

ORANGE-ESPRESSO PLANTAINS

TIMING
Prep: 5 minutes
    (plus 5 minutes for glaze)
Grill: 10 to 15 minutes

GRILL TOOLS AND EQUIPMENT
· Long-handled spatula

Unripe green plantains are starchy and firm. They're often thinly sliced into strips and fried to make snacks somewhat like long potato chips. Fully ripe black plantains are altogether different—sweeter, softer, and a little closer to bananas than potatoes in texture. Grilling them caramelizes the sugars in the fruit. Be sure to use plantains with skins that are completely black all over.

THE GRILL

Gas:	Direct heat, medium-high (400° to 450°F) Clean, oiled grate	**Wood:**	Direct heat, light ash 12-by-12-inch bed, 3 to 4 inches deep Clean, oiled grate set 2 inches above the fire
Charcoal:	Direct heat, light ash 12-by-12-inch charcoal bed (about 3 dozen coals) Clean, oiled grate on lowest setting		

INGREDIENTS (MAKES 4 SERVINGS)

4 ripe black plantains, unpeeled
Oil for coating grill grate

1/2 cup Orange-Espresso Glaze (page 387), made without the salt

DIRECTIONS

1. Heat the grill as directed.

2. Cut the plantains on the diagonal into 2- to 3-inch pieces. Cut off the ends from the end pieces.

3. Brush the grill grate and coat it with oil. Put the plantain pieces on the grill, cover, and cook, turning often, until the skins are blackened all over and the flesh feels very soft when

pressed, 10 to 15 minutes. If your grill has a temperature gauge, it should stay at around 450°F.

4. Remove the plantain pieces to serving plates. Slit the tops of the skins and peel back to expose the flesh. Brush the hot flesh generously with the glaze and serve.

TIMING
Prep: 15 minutes
(plus 5 minutes for glaze)
Grill: 5 to 8 minutes

GRILL TOOLS AND EQUIPMENT
· 6 skewers (soaked in water for 20 minutes if bamboo)
· Long-handled tongs

GETTING CREATIVE
· For a touch of anise flavor, add 1/8 teaspoon pure anise extract to the feta stuffing.

TIP
· To make these with dried figs, put the figs in a heatproof bowl, cover with boiling water, and soak until plump, 10 to 15 minutes. Proceed with the recipe. The figs will still be good, just not as good as fresh figs.

BUYING FIGS
Fresh figs are a fixture of Mediterranean culture. They come to American markets throughout the summer and fall. Among the hundreds of varieties, you'll find fig colors ranging from minty green to sunny yellow to dark purple. Inside, the soft, sweet flesh is usually pink or purple. Look for plump, unblemished fruits that barely yield to gentle pressure. Some of the more popular varieties include Mission, Kadota, Smyrna (from Turkey), Calimyrna (from California), Brown Turkey, Celeste, and Magnolia. Any variety can be grilled.

GRILLED FETA-STUFFED FIGS

Figs are more than 55 percent sugar. On the grill, that sugar caramelizes and creates complex flavors that complement a fig's natural floral aromas. We stuff the figs with a Greek mixture of feta cheese, honey, and oregano to heighten the flavors.

THE GRILL

Gas:	Direct heat, medium-low (300°F) Clean, oiled grate on lowest setting	**Wood:**	Direct heat, medium-light ash 12-by-12-inch bed, 2 inches deep Clean, oiled grate set 5 inches above the fire
Charcoal:	Direct heat, medium-light ash 12-by-12-inch charcoal bed (about 3 dozen coals) Clean, oiled grate on lowest setting		

INGREDIENTS (MAKES 6 SERVINGS)

18 large, fresh figs, stems trimmed
3 ounces feta cheese (about 3/4 cup crumbled), at room temperature
1 tablespoon honey

1 teaspoon finely chopped fresh oregano leaves
1 tablespoon olive oil
Oil for coating grill grate
3 tablespoons Orange Honey-Butter Glaze (optional; page 389)

DIRECTIONS

1. Heat the grill as directed.

2. Cut a narrow pocket into the blossom (bottom) end of each fig. Stick your pinky finger into the pocket and use it to press indentations into both sides of the pocket, creating a small cavity in the center of each fig.

3. Purée the feta, honey, oregano, and olive oil in a small food processor. The mixture will be thick. Alternatively, mash the cheese vigorously with a fork, then mix in the remaining ingredients.

4. Using a small spoon and your fingertips, stuff about 1 teaspoon of the feta mixture into each fig cavity. Or pipe the mixture from a pastry bag into the fig cavities. Gently squeeze the blossom ends together to enclose the filling.

5. Skewer 3 figs crosswise on each skewer (the stem end should be perpendicular to the skewer).

6. Brush the grill grate and coat it with oil. Put the fig skewers on the grill and cook until nicely grill-marked, turning once or twice, 5 to 8 minutes total.

7. Brush with the honey-butter glaze, if using.

Photo: Grilled Feta-Stuffed Figs

TIMING
Prep: 15 minutes
Grill: 30 to 40 minutes

GRILL TOOLS AND EQUIPMENT
· Small disposable aluminum foil pan
· Long-handled tongs
· Long-handled basting brush
· Long-handled spatula

TIP
· For a kiss of smoke in the pears, soak 1 cup apple or cherry wood chips or chunks in water for 30 minutes. (Hickory would be too harsh here.) Toss the chips on the coals and, when you see smoke, add the pan of pears to the grill. If using gas, put the chips in a smoker box or in a perforated foil packet directly over one of the heated burners.

GETTING CREATIVE
· To make Maple Grill-Roasted Pears, replace the water and sugar with 1 cup pure maple syrup (pancake syrup will be too thick). Mix the maple syrup with the vanilla extract and brush onto the pears as directed. Omit the balsamic vinegar sauce. Serve with any remaining maple syrup and vanilla ice cream.

PEAR VARIETIES
Pears are so soft that most varieties never make it to market. But a few common types are firm enough to be grilled. These include Bosc, Forelle, and Winter Nelis. Boscs have a golden or light brown skin with firm yet tender white flesh. Forelles are red-skinned and speckled with firm, grainy flesh. Winter Nelis pears are smaller and rounded, with green or red skin, but their firm flesh still makes them suitable for the grill. We call for Bosc pears here because they are widely available, but beautiful red Forelles are even better, especially for Grilled Pears Drizzled with Melted Stilton (below).

BARBECUED BALSAMIC PEARS

Here's a pyromaniac's version of poached pears. The whole, peeled fruit is cooked via indirect heat on the grill and frequently basted with sugar syrup to soften and sweeten the flesh. Drizzled with a buttered balsamic reduction sauce, the pears make a delightful fall dessert.

THE GRILL

Gas:	Indirect heat, medium (350°F)	Charcoal:	Indirect heat, medium ash
	3- or 4-burner grill—middle burner(s) off		Split charcoal bed (about 2 dozen coals per side)
	2-burner grill–1 side off		20 replacement coals
	Clean, oiled grate		Clean, oiled grate on medium setting

INGREDIENTS (MAKES 4 SERVINGS)

1 cup water plus hot water for the foil pan	Juice of 1/2 lemon
1/2 cup plus 1 teaspoon sugar	1/4 cup best-quality balsamic vinegar
1/2 teaspoon vanilla extract	1 tablespoon butter
4 just-ripe Bosc pears	Pinch of grated nutmeg

DIRECTIONS

1. Heat the grill as directed.

2. Put the 1 cup water and the 1/2 cup sugar in a small saucepan. Heat over medium heat, stirring once or twice, until the sugar dissolves, 3 to 5 minutes. Remove from the heat, stir in the vanilla, and let cool.

3. Peel the pears, but leave the stems intact. Cut a small slice from the bottom of each pear to make them stand upright. Cut out the core from the bottom of each pear, using a small, thin knife or the small side of a melon baller. Immediately brush the pears all over with the lemon juice, including the cavity.

4. Put the pears upright in a disposable aluminum pan large enough to hold them, and pour in enough hot water to just cover the bottom. Put the pan on the grill away from the heat, cover the grill, and cook until the pears are tender, 30 to 40 minutes. As they cook, baste the pears frequently with the sugar syrup, using tongs to steady them as you baste. If your grill has a temperature gauge, it should stay at around 350°F.

5. Meanwhile, put the balsamic vinegar and 1 teaspoon sugar in a small saucepan (on your grill's side burner if it has one). Bring to a boil over medium heat and cook until the liquid reduces to about 2 tablespoons. Stir in the butter and nutmeg. Remove from the heat.

6. Remove the pears to plates with tongs and a spatula. Drizzle with the balsamic sauce and serve.

GRILLED PEARS DRIZZLED WITH MELTED STILTON

Halved and cored pears can be briefly grilled and stuffed with any number of fillings, such as sweetened mascarpone. Pears and blue cheese have a particular affinity for each other, so we drizzle these grilled Boscs with Frangelico-scented warm Stilton. Serve this as a first course or dessert. It's excellent with port.

THE GRILL

Gas:	Direct heat, medium-low (300°F)	Wood:	Direct heat, medium ash
	Clean, oiled grate		12-by-12-inch bed, 3 inches deep
Charcoal:	Direct heat, medium ash		Clean, oiled grate set 4 inches above the fire
	12-by-12-inch medium charcoal bed		
	(about 3 dozen coals)		
	Clean, oiled grate on middle setting		

INGREDIENTS (MAKES 4 SERVINGS)

1 tablespoon butter

1 tablespoon Frangelico or amaretto

1 1/2 teaspoons sugar

8 ounces Stilton or other crumbly blue cheese

Oil for coating grill grate

4 just-ripe Bosc pears, halved lengthwise and cored

1 tablespoon vegetable oil

TIPS

· Core the pears with the small side of a melon baller.

· For information on pear varieties, see facing page.

DIRECTIONS

1. Heat the grill as directed.

2. Heat the butter, Frangelico, and sugar in a microwave or small saucepan over medium heat until melted (15 to 30 seconds in the microwave). Remove from the heat and stir in the Stilton until just beginning to melt. Heat briefly if necessary to break up the Stilton.

3. Brush the grill grate and coat it with oil. Coat the pears all over with the 1 tablespoon oil, then put them cut-side down on the grill. Cover and cook until tender and nicely grill-marked, about 5 minutes per side.

4. Remove the pears to plates, cut-sides up. Drizzle with the Stilton mixture and serve.

CHILE-SPICED PEACHES

Many fruits are served as dessert, but peaches pair well with pork, poultry, and game. We flavor these grilled peach halves with a mixture of ground ancho chile, ground chipotle chile, nutmeg, and brown sugar. Serve them alongside Smoky Barbecued Duck (page 200), Molasses-Brined Pork Chops with Roasted Corn Salsa (page 149), or Spicy Maple Pork Shoulder (page 208).

TIMING

Prep: 5 minutes

Grill: About 5 minutes

GRILL TOOLS AND EQUIPMENT

· Long-handled tongs

TIP

· For a novel dessert, serve the peaches with whipped cream that has been flavored with vanilla or maple syrup.

THE GRILL

Gas: Direct heat, medium-high (400° to 450°F) • Clean, oiled grate

Charcoal: Direct heat, light ash
12-by-12-inch charcoal bed
(about 3 dozen coals)
Clean, oiled grate on lowest setting

Wood: Direct heat, light ash
12-by-12-inch bed, 3 to 4 inches deep
Clean, oiled grate set 3 inches above the fire

INGREDIENTS (MAKES 4 SERVINGS)

4 large, ripe freestone peaches

1 tablespoon dark brown sugar

1 tablespoon ground ancho chile

1 teaspoon ground chipotle chile

1/2 teaspoon grated nutmeg

No-stick spray oil or vegetable oil

Oil for coating grill grate

DIRECTIONS

1. Heat the grill as directed.

2. Halve the peaches from the stem end to the blossom end and twist to separate the halves. Remove and discard the pits.

3. Combine the brown sugar, ground ancho, ground chipotle, and nutmeg. Coat the peaches all over with oil, then sprinkle all over with the chile mixture.

4. Brush the grill grate and coat it with oil. Put the peaches on the grill, cut-side down, cover, and cook until nicely grill-marked on both sides, 2 to 3 minutes per side.

5. Put the peaches cut-side up on plates and serve.

FIRE-BAKED APPLES WITH PRALINE CHESTNUTS AND BRANDY DULCE DE LECHE

TIMING

Prep: 15 minutes
Grill: About 1 hour

Baked stuffed apples work beautifully on the grill. You could fill the apples with a simple mixture of brown sugar, cinnamon, and butter. But when you want something more special, try this combination. We add roasted chestnuts and pecans to the stuffing, then drizzle the cooked apples with *dulce de leche,* a sweet and creamy dessert sauce made by cooking sweetened condensed milk until is thick and golden brown like butterscotch pudding.

GRILL TOOLS AND EQUIPMENT

· Large cast-iron skillet
  or heavy-duty roasting pan
· Heat-resistant silicone scraper
· Grill skillet, flat-bottomed grill wok,
  or grill screen
· Aluminum foil

TIPS

· When slitting the chestnut shells, take care not to cut through the nutmeats; otherwise, the nuts may break when you remove the shells.
· Remove the chestnut shells while they are still fairly warm (put them in a kitchen towel to protect your hands). If you let the chestnuts cool completely, the skins will adhere to the nuts, and shelling them will be more difficult.

THE GRILL

Gas: Indirect heat, medium-low (250°F)
3- to 4-burner grill–middle burner(s) off
2-burner grill–1 side off
Clean, oiled grate

Charcoal: Indirect heat, medium ash
Split charcoal bed (about 2 dozen coals per side)
20 replacement coals
Heavy-duty drip pan set between banks of charcoal
Clean, oiled grate on high setting

INGREDIENTS (MAKES 4 SERVINGS)

1 can (about 14 ounces) sweetened condensed milk
4 tablespoons brandy
3/4 teaspoon ground cinnamon
8 chestnuts
1/8 teaspoon baking soda
1/4 cup pecan pieces or chopped pecans

1 tablespoon flour
1/2 cup dark brown sugar
3 tablespoons cold unsalted butter, chopped
6 Rome apples or other large baking apples
1 cup apple cider

DIRECTIONS

1. Heat the grill as directed.

2. Mix the condensed milk, 2 tablespoons of the brandy, and 1/4 teaspoon of the cinnamon in a large cast-iron skillet or heavy-duty roasting pan until combined.

3. Slit through the chestnut shells on the rounded sides of the chestnuts, put them in a grill skillet, flat-bottomed grill wok, or grill screen, and put the pan or screen on the grill directly over the heat.

4. Put the skillet containing the milk mixture on the grill away from the direct heat, cover, and cook until the mixture boils, 8 to 10 minutes. Scrape the pan, especially the bottom, and stir the mixture with a heat-resistant scraper. At the same time, shake the pan of chestnuts and, if they have opened and smell toasty, remove from the grill. If not, cook for another 5 minutes and check again. Cover the grill and cook the *dulce de leche* until the mixture becomes thick and creamy, like pudding, about 15 minutes more, scraping every 5 minutes to make sure the bottom doesn't overcook.

5. Remove from the heat and stir in the baking soda. The mixture will bubble up; stir until the bubbles subside. Pass through a strainer into a bowl, and stir in the remaining 2 tablespoons brandy; set aside until serving. Wash out the skillet or roasting pan, but not too well.

6. Remove the shells from the chestnuts (see Tips) and chop the chestnuts coarsely. Combine in a bowl with the pecans, flour, brown sugar, and butter. Pinch with your fingers until the mixture is blended.

7. Cut the apples in half vertically and remove the core from each half with the large scoop of a melon baller. Put the apples in the cleaned pan, cut-sides up, and fill the center of each half with some of the chestnut mixture. Pour the apple cider around and over the apples, and sprinkle the remaining 1/2 teaspoon cinnamon over the top. Cover the pan with foil.

8. Put the pan on the grill away from direct heat, cover the grill, and cook for 20 minutes. Remove the foil and cook for another 20 minutes, until the apples are tender and the cider has reduced to a thin syrup.

9. Let cool for at least 10 minutes before serving. Serve half an apple per person, topped with a little of the apple cider syrup and drizzled with some of the brandy *dulce de leche.* You will probably have more *dulce de leche* than you need; store any extra in a covered container in the refrigerator and rewarm in a microwave before serving.

TIMING
Prep: 10 minutes
Grill: 2 to 4 minutes

GRILL TOOLS AND EQUIPMENT
· Long-handled tongs
· Long-handled basting brush

Whenever sugar meets heat, there's the potential for burning. Work quickly and watch these apple rings closely to keep them from becoming overly browned. If necessary, grill the apple rings in batches. They make the perfect accompaniment for grilled pork. Or serve them with ice cream for dessert. You could even serve them alongside pancakes or waffles.

THE GRILL

Gas: Direct heat, medium-high (400° to 450°F)
Clean, oiled grate

Charcoal: Direct heat, light ash
12-by-12-inch charcoal bed (about 3 dozen coals)
Clean, oiled grate on lowest setting

Wood: Direct heat, light ash
12-by-12-inch bed, 3 to 4 inches deep
Clean, oiled grate set 2 inches above the fire

INGREDIENTS (MAKES 6 SERVINGS—ABOUT 24 RINGS)

1 cup pure maple syrup
2 teaspoons vanilla extract
$1/2$ teaspoon ground cinnamon

$1/8$ teaspoon grated nutmeg
2 firm, crisp apples, such as Gala
Oil for coating grill grate

DIRECTIONS

1. Heat the grill as directed.
2. Heat the maple syrup, vanilla, cinnamon, and nutmeg in a small, shallow dish in a microwave or in a small saucepan over medium heat until just warm (15 to 30 seconds in the microwave).
3. Peel the apples. Using an apple corer or small, thin knife, core the apples from the stem through the blossom end. Cut the apples crosswise into rings about $1/4$ inch to $3/8$ inch thick.

Dip the apple rings into the syrup, then lay them on a foil-lined baking sheet.
4. Brush the grill grate and coat it with oil. Put the apple rings on the grill and cook until the apples are nicely grill-marked yet almost firm enough to hold their shape, 1 to 2 minutes per side. Baste the apples with any remaining maple syrup.
5. Remove the apples to a serving plate and serve.

TIMING
Prep: 30 minutes
Grill: About 10 minutes
Chill: About 10 minutes

GRILL TOOLS AND EQUIPMENT
· About 6 skewers (soaked in water for 20 minutes if bamboo)
· Long-handled spatula or tongs

GRILLED FRUIT COCKTAIL

If you're thinking canned fruit cocktail, think again. Almost any cut-up fruit can be tossed with syrup and chilled. Grilled fruits add a welcome flavor dimension in the form of caramelized sugar. Use any fruit you like, preferably a mix of acidic fruit such as citrus and sweet fruit such as pears. Here, we combine blood oranges, pineapple, peaches, pears, and sweet cherries in a ginger-almond-scented syrup. Whichever fruit you choose, grill it in large pieces and then cut it into smaller pieces before tossing it with the syrup.

THE GRILL

Gas: Direct heat, medium-high (400° to 450°F)
Clean, oiled grate

Charcoal: Direct heat, light ash
12-by-12-inch charcoal bed (about 3 dozen coals)
Clean, oiled grate on lowest setting

Wood: Direct heat, light ash
12-by-12-inch bed, 3 to 4 inches deep
Clean, oiled grate set 2 inches above the fire

INGREDIENTS (MAKES 8 TO 10 SERVINGS—ABOUT 6 CUPS)

2 to 3 blood oranges (10 to 12 ounces total)

2 cups water

2 2/3 cups sugar

One thumb-sized knob gingerroot, peeled and thinly sliced

1 teaspoon whole allspice berries

1/2 teaspoon almond extract

1 small pineapple (3 to 3 1/2 pounds)

2 fairly ripe freestone peaches

2 fairly ripe pears

Juice of 1/2 lemon

6 ounces sweet cherries, such as Royal Ann, stems removed

Oil for coating grill grate

8 mint leaves, for garnish

DIRECTIONS

1. Remove the zest from the oranges in strips, and put the zest in a small saucepan. Add the water, sugar, ginger, and allspice. Bring to a boil over medium heat, then reduce the heat to medium-low and simmer until slightly thickened and syrupy, 3 to 5 minutes. Remove from the heat, stir in the almond extract, and let cool to room temperature. Strain into a large bowl. At this point, the syrup can be refrigerated for up to a week or left at room temperature for several hours.

2. Heat the grill as directed.

3. Remove and discard the white pith from the oranges (your fingers or a paring knife will work best here). Break the oranges into segments and skewer them lengthwise so that the segments don't fall through the grill grate.

4. Cut off the spiky top and 1/2 inch from the base of the pineapple. Stand it upright and cut downward around the fruit to remove the peel and eyes. Cut lengthwise into quarters and slice off the core from each quarter. Set aside 2 of the quarters for another use (they can be refrigerated in a zipper-lock bag for up to 3 days and are great for snacking). Cut the remaining quarters crosswise into wedges about 1 inch thick.

5. Halve the peaches from the stem end to the blossom end and twist to separate the halves. Remove and discard the pits.

6. Peel, halve, and core the pears using a small melon baller. Immediately brush or rub with the lemon juice to prevent browning.

7. Pit and halve the cherries.

8. Brush the grill grate and coat it with oil. Put the skewered oranges and the pineapple, peaches, and pears on the grill (peaches and pears cut-side down). Cover and cook until nicely grill-marked on both sides, 2 to 6 minutes per side. The oranges will take less time; the peaches and pears should be tender and will take longer. If your grill has a temperature gauge, it should stay at around 450°F.

9. Remove the fruit to a cutting board. Dip the peaches in ice water for 1 minute, then peel off the skin while they are still warm. Let the fruit cool to room temperature, then cut into small pieces. Add the grilled fruit and cherries to the syrup in the bowl and toss gently to coat. Cover and refrigerate for at least 4 hours or up to 2 days.

10. Use a slotted spoon to transfer the fruit to martini or wine glasses and let stand for 20 minutes to take off the chill. Garnish with the mint leaves before serving.

GETTING CREATIVE

· Vary the fruit: Replace the oranges with other citrus like tangerines or pomelos. Replace the pineapples with kiwi and the peaches with plums, nectarines, or apricots. You could also make a more tropical fruit cocktail by using papaya and mango.

· If you can't find fresh cherries, use about 3/4 cup halved maraschino cherries (stems removed).

· If you can't find whole pineapple, use half of a peeled, cored golden pineapple. These are usually packed with pineapple juice in plastic tubs in the refrigerated produce section.

TIP

· After serving the fruit cocktail, use any leftover syrup to brush onto cakes or to serve with crêpes or pancakes.

GRILLED CHOCOLATE FONDUE

Fondue has the aura of sophisticated soirees in expensive dining rooms, but it's really just melted goo in a pot. Why not make it on the grill and serve it outside? Here, we toast cubes of pound cake on the grill and serve them with skewered bananas, kiwi, and strawberries as dippers for bittersweet chocolate fondue. The fondue itself is also cooked on the grill in a heavy-bottomed saucepan. If you prefer, you could heat the fondue mixture on the side burner of your grill or on a stovetop. Reheat the fondue over low heat on the grill (or stovetop) as necessary.

THE GRILL

Gas: Direct heat, medium (350°F)
Clean, oiled grate on lowest setting

Charcoal: Direct heat, medium ash
12-by-12-inch charcoal bed
(about 3 dozen coals)
Clean, oiled grate on lowest setting

Wood: Direct heat, medium ash
12-by-12-inch bed, 3 inches deep
Clean, oiled grate set 4 inches above the fire

TIMING

Prep: 20 minutes
(including soaking the skewers)
Grill: About 10 minutes

GRILL TOOLS AND EQUIPMENT

· Medium-heavy fondue pot, saucepan, or enameled iron pot, preferably with metal handles

· 64 short wooden skewers, soaked in water for 20 minutes

· Wide, long-handled spatula

MASTERING FRUIT, DESSERT, DOUGH, AND EVERYTHING ELSE

317

GETTING CREATIVE
· Try other dippers, such as pretzels, orange wedges, or pineapple wedges.
· Replace the rum with Cognac, orange liqueur such as Grand Marnier, or coffee liqueur such as Kahlúa.

TIP
· Instead of using so many wooden skewers, pick up reusable metal double skewers at a hardware or cookware store. Several manufacturers make them.

INGREDIENTS (MAKES 8 SERVINGS)

For the pound cake and fruit:

1 loaf prepared pound cake (1 pound)

No-stick spray oil or vegetable oil

4 ripe bananas, peeled

4 ripe kiwi fruit, peeled and ends removed

1 1/2 pints strawberries, hulled

Oil for coating grill grate

For the fondue:

3/4 cup heavy whipping cream

1/2 cup whole milk

1/4 cup light corn syrup

1 tablespoon dark rum

1 teaspoon vanilla extract

Pinch of kosher salt

12 ounces bittersweet chocolate, finely chopped

DIRECTIONS

1. Heat the grill as directed.

2. For the pound cake and fruit, cut the pound cake into 1-inch cubes. Using 2 short wooden skewers side by side, thread the pound cake cubes onto the double skewers. Coat all over with cooking spray or brush with oil.

3. Cut the bananas into 2-inch lengths and the kiwi fruit into quarters. Again using double skewers, alternately thread the bananas, strawberries, and kiwi fruit onto the double skewers, using about 2 pieces of each fruit per skewer. If you prefer, skip the skewers, arrange the cut fruit on a platter, and serve with fondue forks or other forks for dipping.

4. Brush the grill grate and coat it with oil.

5. For the fondue, stir together the cream, milk, corn syrup, rum, vanilla, and salt in a medium fondue pot or saucepan with metal handles. When combined, put the pot on the grill with the handle facing outward and not over the heat. Bring to a boil, then remove from the grill. Stir in the chocolate and let stand until almost melted, 2 to 3 minutes. Stir until combined and smooth.

6. While the fondue is on the grill, grill the skewered pound cake on the other side of the grill until nicely grill-marked on 2 sides, 2 to 3 minutes per side.

7. Lift the skewered grilled pound cake and skewered fruit from the grill with a wide spatula and arrange on a platter, allowing guests to dip them into the fondue. If the sauce gets too thick, gently reheat it by holding the pot a few inches above the coolest part of the grill and stirring constantly.

Photo: Grilled Chocolate Fondue

GRILLED GRAPEFRUIT WITH BROWN SUGAR GLAZE

TIMING
Prep: 2 minutes
Grill: About 5 minutes

GRILL TOOLS AND EQUIPMENT
· Long-handled tongs

We love to fire up the grill on summer mornings. And this recipe is simple enough for breakfast. It's just a halved grapefruit briefly grilled and glazed with cinnamon-scented brown sugar. Serve it alone or as an accompaniment to other grilled breakfasts, like Grilled Stuffed French Toast (page 329).

THE GRILL

Gas: Direct heat, medium-high (400° to 450°F)
Clean, oiled grate

Charcoal: Direct heat, light ash
12-by-12-inch charcoal bed (about 3 dozen coals)
Clean, oiled grate on lowest setting

Wood: Direct heat, light ash
12-by-12-inch bed, 3 to 4 inches deep
Clean, oiled grate set 2 inches above the fire

INGREDIENTS (MAKES 4 SERVINGS)

2 ripe grapefruits, halved crosswise
$1/2$ cup packed light brown sugar
$1/2$ teaspoon ground cinnamon

$1/8$ teaspoon grated nutmeg
Oil for coating grill grate

DIRECTIONS

1. Heat the grill as directed.

2. Cut a small slice off the bottom of the grapefruit halves to make them stand upright.

3. Combine the brown sugar, cinnamon, and nutmeg in a small bowl.

4. Spoon about a tablespoon of the brown sugar mixture over each grapefruit half, pressing the sugar into the flesh with the spoon.

5. Brush the grill grate and coat it with oil. Put the grapefruit halves on the grill, cut-side down, and cook until nicely browned, 3 to 4 minutes. Turn right-side up and press another tablespoon or so of the sugar into the cut side. Cover and let cook until the sugar melts, about a minute.

6. Remove to plates or shallow bowls and let cool to room temperature. Section the grapefruit and serve.

GRILLED PINEAPPLE WITH MOLASSES AND RUM

TIMING
Prep: 10 minutes
Grill: 6 to 10 minutes

GRILL TOOLS AND EQUIPMENT
· Long-handled tongs
· Long-handled basting brush

GETTING CREATIVE
· For Grilled Honey-Habanero Pineapple: Omit the molasses, rum, lime, allspice, and butter. Instead, mix together 1 cup honey (preferably orange blossom), 2 teaspoons grated orange zest, and 2 seeded and finely chopped habanero chiles. Proceed as directed.

Pineapple takes to the grill like no other fruit. It remains somewhat firm; develops a rich, browned sweetness; and can be flavored in any number of ways. The Caribbean flavors here go well with Jamaican jerk pork or chicken.

THE GRILL

Gas: Direct heat, medium-high (400° to 450°F)
Clean, oiled grate

Charcoal: Direct heat, light ash
12-by-12-inch charcoal bed (about 3 dozen coals)
Clean, oiled grate on lowest setting

Wood: Direct heat, light ash
12-by-12-inch bed, 3 inches deep
Clean, oiled grate set 3 inches above the fire

INGREDIENTS (MAKES 4 SERVINGS)

$1/3$ cup molasses
$1/4$ cup dark rum
Juice of $1/2$ lime
$1/2$ teaspoon ground allspice

3 tablespoons butter, cut into pieces
1 small pineapple
Oil for coating grill grate

---

1. Heat the grill as directed.

2. Put the molasses, rum, lime juice, and allspice in a small saucepan. Bring to a boil over high heat, then reduce the heat to medium-high and cook until reduced to about $1/3$ cup.

3. Remove from the heat and whisk in the butter. Set aside.

4. Cut off the spiky top and $1/2$ inch from the base of the pineapple. Stand it upright and cut downward around the fruit to remove the peel and eyes. Cut lengthwise into quarters and remove the core from each quarter by making a V-shaped cut

around the core. Cut each quarter crosswise into wedges about 1 inch thick.

5. Brush the grill grate and coat it with oil. Put the pineapple on the grill and cook until nicely grill-marked, 3 to 5 minutes per side. Brush with some of the glaze during the last 2 minutes of grilling.

6. Remove to plates and brush with the remaining glaze. Serve warm.

GRILLED FRUIT SKEWERS WITH GINGER–POPPY SEED LACQUER

Fruit kebabs make a colorful presentation and a fun dessert. Here, we skewer pineapple pieces, banana pieces, orange sections, and large blueberries, then briefly grill the fruit kebabs just until grill-marked. A clear, thin glaze flavored with fresh ginger, allspice, and poppy seeds gets brushed onto the fruit before and after grilling. Serve these kebabs with ice cream or slices of grilled pound cake.

THE GRILL

Gas:	Direct heat, medium-high (400° to 450°F)	**Wood:**	Direct heat, light ash
	Clean, oiled grate		12-by-12-inch bed, 3 inches deep
Charcoal:	Direct heat, medium ash		Clean, oiled grate set 3 inches above the fire
	12-by-12-inch charcoal bed (about 3 dozen coals)		
	Clean, oiled grate on lowest setting		

INGREDIENTS (MAKES 4 SERVINGS—2 SKEWERS PER SERVING)

1 cup brown sugar

$3/4$ cup water

4 slices gingerroot, each about $1/4$ inch thick

$1/2$ teaspoon whole allspice berries

$1/2$ teaspoon poppy seeds

1 small pineapple

2 large, firm, ripe bananas

1 seedless orange, peeled and sectioned

About $1/3$ cup large blueberries

Oil for coating grill grate

DIRECTIONS

1. If using wooden skewers, soak them in water for 20 minutes.

2. In a small saucepan, combine the brown sugar, water, ginger, and allspice. Bring to a boil over medium heat, then reduce the heat to medium-low and simmer until slightly thickened and syrupy, 3 to 5 minutes. Remove from the heat and let cool to room temperature. Strain into a small bowl and stir in the poppy seeds. At this point, the syrup can be refrigerated for up to a week or left at room temperature for several hours.

3. Heat the grill as directed.

4. Cut off the spiky top and $1/2$ inch from the base of the pineapple. Stand it upright and cut downward around the fruit to remove the peel and eyes. Cut lengthwise into quarters and remove the core from each quarter by making a V-shaped

cut around the core. Cut each quarter crosswise into wedges about $1 1/2$ inches thick. Peel the bananas and cut each crosswise into 4 pieces.

5. Arrange the pineapple wedges, banana pieces, and orange sections lengthwise on the skewers, putting a blueberry after each piece.

6. Brush the glaze generously over the fruit, reserving some to brush on after grilling.

7. Brush the grill grate and coat it with oil. Put the skewers on the grill and cook until nicely grill-marked, 2 to 3 minutes per side. Brush with the remaining glaze and serve warm, using a wide spatula to lift them from the grill.

Photo: Grilled Fruit Skewers with Ginger–Poppy Seed Lacquer

GRILLED FRUIT SKEWERS WITH HONEY MUSTARD

TIMING
Prep: 10 minutes
Grill: 6 to 8 minutes

GRILL TOOLS AND EQUIPMENT
· 8 large wooden or metal skewers
· Wide, long-handled spatula

You're probably familiar with the sweet-and-sour contrast of honey mustard on chicken or pork. It's great on grilled fruit, too. Here it's brushed on wedges of skewered peaches, plums, and blood oranges. A Mediterranean citrus, blood oranges have ruby or ruby-flecked flesh and a full orange flavor laced with plum or raspberry aromas. Serve these kebabs with grilled pork, chicken, or fish, such as Sicilian Pulled Pork (page 210), Tuscan Roasted Chicken Stuffed with Fragrant Greens (page 192), or Saffron-Citrus Salmon Steaks with Basil Oil (page 174).

THE GRILL

Gas: Direct heat, medium-high (400° to 450°F)
Clean, oiled grate

Charcoal: Direct heat, light ash
12-by-12-inch charcoal bed (about 3 dozen coals)
Clean, oiled grate on lowest setting

Wood: Direct heat, light ash
12-by-12-inch bed, 3 inches deep
Clean, oiled grate set 3 inches above the fire

INGREDIENTS (MAKES 4 SERVINGS—2 SKEWERS PER SERVING)

1/3 cup honey, preferably orange blossom

3 tablespoons coarse Dijon mustard

1 tablespoon orange juice

1/4 teaspoon grated nutmeg

2 small just-ripe freestone peaches

2 small just-ripe plums

2 blood oranges, peeled and sectioned

Oil for coating grill grate

DIRECTIONS

1. If using wooden skewers, soak them in water for 20 minutes.

2. Heat the grill as directed.

3. Combine the honey, mustard, orange juice, and nutmeg in a small bowl. Set aside.

4. Halve the peaches and plums from the stem end to the blossom end and twist to separate the halves. Remove and discard the pits. Cut the halved fruit into wedges about 1 inch thick at the wide end.

5. Arrange the peaches, orange sections, and plums on the skewers.

6. Brush the mustard glaze generously over the fruit, reserving some to brush on after grilling.

7. Brush the grill grate and coat it with oil. Put the skewers on the grill and cook until nicely grill-marked, 3 to 4 minutes per side. Brush with the remaining glaze and serve warm, using a wide spatula to lift them from the grill.

GRILLED PAPAYA WITH SWEET SAFFRON BUTTER AND LIME MASCARPONE CREAM

TIMING
Prep: 15 minutes
Grill: 9 to 12 minutes

GRILL TOOLS AND EQUIPMENT
· Long-handled tongs

Here's what might happen if southern Italians and southern Indians were to grill dessert together in Hawaii. Okay, maybe that's an unlikely scenario. But this is still a great flavor combination. We use lime oil here because the acidity of lime juice would curdle the mascarpone and make it grainy in texture. Pure lime extract works fine if you can't find lime oil.

THE GRILL

Gas: Direct heat, medium-high (400° to 450°F)
Clean, oiled grate

Charcoal: Direct heat, light ash
12-by-12-inch charcoal bed (about 3 dozen coals)
Clean, oiled grate on lowest setting

Wood: Direct heat, light ash
12-by-12-inch bed, 3 to 4 inches deep
Clean, oiled grate set 2 inches above the fire

INGREDIENTS (MAKES 4 SERVINGS)

2 tablespoons butter

1/4 teaspoon crushed saffron threads

1 teaspoon plus 2 tablespoons sugar

2 small papayas, about 1 pound each

Oil for coating grill grate

4 ounces (1/2 cup) mascarpone

1/2 cup very cold heavy cream

Grated zest of 1/2 lime

3 to 4 drops lime oil, or 3/4 teaspoon lime extract

1/8 teaspoon grated nutmeg (optional)

DIRECTIONS

1. Heat the grill as directed.

2. Put the butter, saffron, and the 1 teaspoon sugar in a small saucepan. Heat over low heat until melted and richly colored, 5 to 8 minutes, stirring occasionally.

3. Meanwhile, cut the papayas lengthwise and scoop out the seeds. Brush the cut sides of the papaya halves with the saffron butter.

4. Brush the grill grate and coat it with oil. Put the papaya halves, skin-side down, on the grill and cook until lightly grill-marked, 3 to 4 minutes. Flip and grill diagonally on the grill grate until grill-marked, 3 to 4 minutes. Turn 45 degrees and grill until grill-marked in a crosshatch pattern, 3 to 4 minutes more.

5. Put the papaya halves cut-side up on plates or a platter and brush with the remaining saffron butter.

6. Combine the mascarpone, 2 tablespoons of the heavy cream, the lime zest, and the lime oil or extract in a medium bowl.

7. Whip the remaining cream and 2 tablespoons sugar with an electric mixer on medium speed until soft peaks form, about 2 minutes. Fold the whipped cream into the mascarpone mixture.

8. Dollop the mascarpone cream in the center of each papaya half, sprinkle with the nutmeg, if using, and serve. Allow guests to scoop the papaya from its skin.

TIPS

· To whip the cream faster, chill the heavy cream and the bowl and beaters of the electric mixer in the freezer for 15 to 20 minutes.

· Save time by heating the sweet saffron butter in a microwave on low power for 3 to 4 minutes.

Photo: Grilled Papaya with Sweet Saffron Butter and Lime Mascarpone Cream

GRILL TOOLS AND EQUIPMENT
· Long-handled spatula
· Long-handled tongs

TIP
· To save time, replace the pound cake with store-bought pound cake. You'll lose a little flavor, but it will still be good.

HONEY-TOASTED POUND CAKE WITH GRILLED CANDIED BLOOD ORANGES

Pound cake is wonderful when toasted on the grill. We make this one with a touch of honey and orange zest to complement slices of candied blood oranges. The primary cooking here happens in the oven and on the stovetop. The grill is used merely to toast the pound cake and brown the candied oranges. Nonetheless, this double cooking deepens the caramelized flavors and adds a wisp of smoke if you use a charcoal grill. For more information on blood oranges, see the introduction to Grilled Fruit Skewers with Honey Mustard (page 322).

THE GRILL

Gas: Direct heat, medium (350°F)
Clean, oiled grate

Charcoal: Direct heat, medium ash
12-by-12-inch charcoal bed (about 3 dozen coals)
Clean, oiled grate on lowest setting

Wood: Direct heat, medium ash
12-by-12-inch bed, 3 inches deep
Clean, oiled grate set 4 inches above the fire

INGREDIENTS (MAKES 8 SERVINGS)

For the pound cake:
1 3/4 cups cake flour or all-purpose flour
1 1/2 teaspoons baking powder
1/2 teaspoon grated nutmeg
1/4 teaspoon kosher salt
1 cup (2 sticks) unsalted butter, at room temperature
1/2 cup sugar
1/2 cup honey, preferably orange blossom
4 eggs, at room temperature
2 teaspoons grated orange zest (blood orange or navel orange)

1 teaspoon vanilla extract
1/2 teaspoon almond extract
Oil for coating grill grate

For the candied oranges:
3 blood oranges, rinsed
3 cups water
1 1/2 cups sugar
1/4 cup light corn syrup

DIRECTIONS

1. For the pound cake: Preheat the oven to 350°F. Butter a 9-by-5-inch loaf pan.

2. Mix together the flour, baking powder, nutmeg, and salt in a medium bowl.

3. In a bowl, using an electric mixer on medium speed, beat the butter until creamy. Beat in the sugar and honey until light and fluffy, scraping down the sides of the bowl once or twice. Beat in the eggs, one at a time, beating thoroughly after each addition. Beat in the orange zest, vanilla extract, and almond extract. Mix in the dry ingredients on very low speed, or mix them in by hand just until incorporated.

4. Scrape the batter into the prepared pan and smooth the top. Bake until well browned on the top and a toothpick inserted into the center comes out clean, 45 to 55 minutes.

5. Let cool in the pan on a rack for 10 minutes. Run a thin knife around the edge to loosen the cake, then invert it onto the rack to cool completely. When cool, wrap in wax paper and store at room temperature for up to 2 days.

6. For the candied oranges: While the cake bakes, cut the oranges into slices about 1/8 inch thick. Put the water and sugar in a wide, shallow pan and cook over medium-high heat until the sugar dissolves. Stir in the corn syrup and bring to a boil. Add the orange slices and reduce the heat to low. Simmer until the slices are sugar-soaked and translucent, 45 minutes to 1 hour. Using tongs, transfer the slices to a wire rack set over foil or a baking sheet and cool completely. Reserve the syrup in the pan. To make ahead, cool the pan of orange slices and syrup, then cover and refrigerate for up to 2 days.

7. Heat the grill as directed.

8. Cut the pound cake into slices about 1 inch thick.

9. Brush the grill grate and coat it with oil. Put the pound cake and orange slices on the grill and cook until toasted and grill-marked, 2 to 4 minutes per side (less for the oranges, more for the pound cake).

10. Remove to plates and arrange the orange slices over the pound cake. Drizzle with some of the reserved orange syrup and serve.

GRILLED MANGO AND PAPAYA WITH CARDAMOM SHORTCAKES

TIMING
Prep: 30 minutes
Bake: 10 to 12 minutes
Grill: 6 to 10 minutes

Here's our tropical take on traditional strawberry shortcake. Grilled mango and papaya take the place of strawberries, and we add cardamom to the shortcakes, which are little more than sweet, rich biscuits. A rum-laced whipped cream completes the layers. This is a three-step recipe in which you bake the short-cakes, grill the fruit, and then layer the dessert with whipped cream, but if you take it one step at a time, it's fairly easy. The entire dessert can be made and served in just over 30 minutes. If you prefer, use other tropical fruit like pineapple, bananas, and/or oranges.

GRILL TOOLS AND EQUIPMENT
· Long-handled tongs

TIPS
· The key to tender, flaky shortcakes is keeping the butter cold. Start with cold butter, and when mixing up the dough, handle it very little and very gently. If you use your fingers to cut in the butter, work quickly so that the butter does not melt. You want the butter to stay cold so that when the dough hits the oven, the cold butter steams and puffs up the shortcakes. If the butter begins to melt before it hits the oven, it will not steam as much, and the shortcakes will not rise as high.
· For high-rising shortcakes, cut straight down and lift straight up with a sharp metal biscuit cutter when cutting the dough. Avoid twisting. Using a dull cutter such as an inverted drinking glass or twisting even just a bit will compress or twist the layers of the dough and prevent them from rising as high.
· If you don't have a biscuit or cookie cutter, pat the dough into a square and cut straight down with a sharp knife to make square shortcakes.

THE GRILL

Gas: Direct heat, medium (350°F)
Clean, oiled grate

Charcoal: Direct heat, medium ash
12-by-12-inch charcoal bed (about 3 dozen coals)
Clean, oiled grate on lowest setting

Wood: Direct heat, medium ash
12-by-12-inch bed, 3 inches deep
Clean, oiled grate set 4 inches above the fire

INGREDIENTS (MAKES 6 SERVINGS)

For the fruit:
1 mango
1 small papaya, about 1 pound
Oil for coating grill grate
1/4 cup sugar

For the shortcakes:
1 3/4 cups all-purpose flour
1 1/2 tablespoons sugar
2 1/2 teaspoons baking powder

1 teaspoon ground cardamom
3/4 teaspoon kosher salt
6 tablespoons cold butter, cut into pieces
3/4 cup half-and-half or light cream

For the whipped cream:
1 cup (1/2 pint) heavy whipping cream
2 tablespoons sugar
1 tablespoon rum
1 teaspoon vanilla extract

DIRECTIONS

1. For the fruit: Heat the grill as directed. Chill a medium bowl and a whisk or beaters for the whipped cream.

2. Stand the mango on its thick end and cut the sides off the center pit, curving the knife around the pit. Peel each half with a paring knife, then slice lengthwise into 1/2-inch-thick slices.

3. Cut the papaya lengthwise and scoop out the seeds. Peel each half with a paring knife or vegetable peeler, then slice the halves lengthwise into 1/2-inch-thick slices.

4. Brush the grill grate and coat it with oil. Put the mango and papaya on the grill and cook and until lightly grill-marked, 3 to 5 minutes per side.

5. Remove to a cutting board and cut into bite-size pieces. Transfer to a medium bowl and toss with the sugar until the sugar dissolves. Cover and keep warm.

6. For the shortcakes: Preheat the oven to 450°F.

7. Mix the flour, sugar, baking powder, cardamom, and salt in a large bowl. Cut in the butter with a pastry blender or 2 knives until the mixture looks like coarse breadcrumbs with some larger pieces. Pour in the half-and-half and stir just until the dough is moistened. Flour your hands and quickly gather the dough into a ball in the bowl, pressing and rolling it gently against the sides of the bowl a few times. Turn out onto a lightly floured work surface and quickly pat into a circle that's 1/2 inch to 3/4 inch thick. Cut straight down and lift straight up with a 3-inch round biscuit or cookie cutter. Transfer the shortcakes to a large baking sheet, keeping them about an inch apart. Gather up the scraps and quickly press together the dough to cut more shortcakes until the dough is used up.

8. Bake until the shortcakes are well browned on the bottom, 10 to 12 minutes.

9. For the whipped cream: While the shortcakes bake, pour the cream into the chilled bowl and whisk vigorously or beat with an electric mixer on medium speed until the cream forms very soft peaks when the whisk or beaters are lifted. Whisk or beat in the sugar, rum, and vanilla.

10. Split 6 of the shortcakes and arrange on plates (reserve any remaining shortcakes to spread with jam or for another use). Spread a thick layer (a couple of tablespoons) of whipped cream over the bottom half of the shortcakes. Layer on a large spoonful of the fruit and its liquid. Cover with the shortcake tops and spread with another thick layer of whipped cream. Spoon a few more tablespoons of the fruit and its liquid over the top. Serve warm.

TIMING
Prep: 25 minutes
  (plus 5 minutes for glaze)
Bake: 35 minutes
Grill: 10 minutes

GRILL TOOLS AND EQUIPMENT
· Long-handled spatula
· Long-handled tongs

GRILLED GINGERBREAD WITH HONEY-GLAZED PEACHES

Gingerbread always tastes best when served warm. Toasted is even better. Why not toast it on the grill and dress it up with grilled peaches? A dollop of whipped cream tops this late-summer dessert off nicely.

THE GRILL

Gas: Direct heat, medium-high (400° to 450°F)
Clean, oiled grate

Charcoal: Direct heat, light ash
12-by-12-inch charcoal bed (about 3 dozen coals)
Clean, oiled grate on lowest setting

Wood: Direct heat, light ash
12-by-12-inch bed, 3 to 4 inches deep
Clean, oiled grate set 2 inches above the fire

INGREDIENTS (MAKES 8 SERVINGS)

For the gingerbread:
2 cups all-purpose flour
1 teaspoon baking soda
1 tablespoon ground ginger
$1^1/_2$ teaspoons ground cinnamon
$1/_4$ teaspoon ground cloves
$1/_2$ teaspoon kosher salt
$1/_2$ cup (1 stick) unsalted butter, softened
$3/_4$ cup packed light brown sugar
2 large eggs
$3/_4$ cup light molasses

$1/_2$ cup hot water
$1/_4$ cup finely chopped crystallized ginger (optional)
Oil for coating grill grate
$1/_2$ cup Orange Honey-Butter Glaze (page 389)

For the whipped cream:
1 cup heavy cream (preferably not ultrapasteurized)
$1/_4$ cup confectioners' sugar
1 tablespoon vanilla extract

4 large, ripe freestone peaches

DIRECTIONS

1. For the gingerbread, set a rack in the middle of the oven and preheat to 350°F. Butter and flour a 9-inch square baking dish.

2. In a medium bowl, sift together the flour, baking soda, ginger, cinnamon, cloves, and salt.

3. In a large bowl, using an electric mixer on medium speed, beat the butter and brown sugar until well mixed, about 2 minutes. Beat in the eggs, one at a time, beating until smooth after each addition. The batter may look grainy, but it will become smooth again when the other ingredients are added. Beat in the molasses.

4. Reduce the speed to low and add the flour mixture and hot water alternately in 2 additions, mixing until smooth after each addition. You could also stir the flour and water in by hand. Fold in the crystallized ginger, if using.

5. Pour the batter into the prepared pan. Bake until a toothpick inserted in the center comes out clean, about 35 minutes. Cool in the pan on a rack for 10 minutes, then carefully unmold it to the rack and finish cooling right-side up. When cool, cut into 8 portions.

6. For the whipped cream, chill the bowl and beaters of an electric mixer in the freezer for 5 minutes. Whip the cream until beginning to thicken, 2 to 3 minutes. Add the confectioners' sugar and vanilla and beat until the cream holds soft peaks when the beaters are lifted, 1 to 2 minutes more. Cover and chill until serving time.

7. Heat the grill as directed.

8. Brush the grill grate and coat it with oil. Lightly brush the gingerbread pieces all over with some of the glaze. Put the gingerbread on the grill and cook until toasted on both sides, 1 to 2 minutes per side. Arrange on a platter or plates.

9. Halve the peaches from the stem end to the blossom end and twist to separate the halves. Remove and discard the pits. Brush the peaches all over with some of the glaze, and grill, cut-sides down, until nicely grill-marked on both sides, 2 to 3 minutes per side. Place a peach half, cut-side up, alongside or over the gingerbread. Drizzle with any remaining glaze, top with dollops of the whipped cream, and serve.

GRILL TOOLS AND EQUIPMENT
· Long-handled tongs

TIP
· To easily toast the pecans, put them on a baking sheet and toast them in the oven as it preheats. They should be fragrant and toasted in about 5 minutes. Or put them in the greased skillet and toast over medium heat for 5 minutes on the stovetop. Regrease the pan before adding the cake batter.

SHORTCUT
· Replace the corn cakes with store-bought corn cakes such as Thomas'. Brush with a mixture of 1/4 cup molasses and 1/4 cup melted butter before toasting on the grill. Serve with the whipped cream and toasted pecans as directed.

FIRE-TOASTED MOLASSES-PECAN CORN CAKES

Continuing with our theme of toasted breads on the grill, we give you a sweet cornbread that's a little closer to a cake than a bread. These corn cakes can be eaten warm out of the oven, but they taste even better when allowed to cool, toasted on the grill, and topped with molasses whipped cream and toasted pecans.

THE GRILL

Gas: Direct heat, medium (350°F)
Clean, oiled grate on lowest setting

Charcoal: Direct heat, medium ash
12-by-12-inch charcoal bed (about 3 dozen coals)
Clean, oiled grate on lowest setting

Wood: Direct heat, medium ash
12-by-12-inch bed, 3 inches deep
Clean, oiled grate set 4 inches above the fire

INGREDIENTS (MAKES 6 TO 8 SERVINGS)

For the corn cakes:
2 eggs, at room temperature
3/4 cup buttermilk, at room temperature
1/4 cup molasses (the darker the better)
1/2 cup (1 stick) butter, melted
1/4 cup packed light brown sugar
1 teaspoon kosher salt
4 teaspoons baking powder
1/2 teaspoon baking soda
1 cup yellow cornmeal (stone-ground is best)
1 cup all-purpose flour

1/2 teaspoon ground allspice
3/4 cup toasted chopped pecans (see Tip)
Oil for coating grill grate

For the whipped cream:
1 cup (1/2 pint) heavy cream
2 tablespoons molasses
1 tablespoon sugar
1 1/2 teaspoons vanilla extract

1/2 cup toasted chopped pecans (optional)

DIRECTIONS

1. For the corn cakes: Preheat the oven to 400°F. Grease a 10-inch round cast-iron skillet or other 1 1/2-quart baking dish.
2. Whisk the eggs, buttermilk, molasses, butter, brown sugar, and salt in a large bowl until blended. Scatter the baking powder and baking soda over the top and whisk until blended. Mix the cornmeal, flour, allspice, and 3/4 cup pecans in a small bowl. Gently stir the cornmeal mixture into the batter until the batter is almost free of lumps. Scrape into the skillet or dish and smooth the top. Bake until a knife inserted in the center comes out clean, 15 to 20 minutes. Cool completely on a rack.
3. Heat the grill as directed. Chill a medium bowl and a whisk or beaters for the whipped cream.

4. Brush the grill grate and coat it with oil. Cut the cornbread into 6 wedges, like a pizza, or into squares, depending upon the shape of your pan. Put the wedges or squares on the grill, top-side up. Grill until toasted on the bottom, sides, and top, 2 to 3 minutes per side (the top side will take less time, as it should already be somewhat browned).
5. Remove to plates and keep warm.
6. For the whipped cream, pour the cream into the chilled bowl and whisk vigorously or beat with an electric mixer on medium speed until the cream barely forms soft peaks when the whisk or beaters are lifted. Whisk or beat in the molasses, sugar, and vanilla.
7. Serve each corn cake with a dollop of molasses whipped cream. Garnish with the additional toasted pecans, if using.

TIMING
Prep: 1 minute
Grill: About 2 minutes

GRILL TOOLS AND EQUIPMENT
· Long-handled tongs

GRILLED PAIN AU CHOCOLAT WITH CHERRY GLAZE

Chocolate croissants are hard enough to resist. When you split them, toast them on the grill, and glaze them with cherry preserves, there's little reason to eat anything else. Except maybe some ginger ice cream on the side.

Gas:	Direct heat, medium-high (400° to 450°F) Clean, oiled grate	**Wood:**	Direct heat, light ash 12-by-12-inch bed, 3 to 4 inches deep Clean, oiled grate set 3 inches above the fire
Charcoal:	Direct heat, light ash 12-by-12-inch charcoal bed (about 3 dozen coals) Clean, oiled grate on lowest setting		

INGREDIENTS (MAKES 4 SERVINGS)

¹/₄ cup cherry preserves

¹/₄ teaspoon almond extract, or ¹/₂ teaspoon vanilla extract

¹/₈ teaspoon ground cinnamon

2 chocolate-filled croissants (pain au chocolat)

2 tablespoons butter, melted

Oil for coating grill grate

DIRECTIONS

1. Heat the grill as directed.

2. Combine the cherry preserves, almond extract, and cinnamon in a small bowl.

3. Halve the croissants through the side. Brush the cut sides with the melted butter.

4. Brush the grill grate and coat it with oil. Put the croissants on the grill, cut-side down, and cook until nicely grill-marked and toasted, 2 to 3 minutes. Turn them 45 degrees halfway through the cooking for crosshatch marks if you like. Turn cut-side up, glaze with the cherry mixture, and serve.

GRILLED STUFFED FRENCH TOAST

There is something luxuriantly daffy about cooking French toast outside. It's not just the reckless abandon of standing by an open fire in a robe and skivvies. Maybe it's the subtle fragrance of smoke that infuses the custard, or the extra crunch on the toast's blistered skin, or the slightly charred corner that is salved by a leak of liquefied cream cheese and blueberries . . . Nah, it's the skivvies.

THE GRILL

Gas:	Direct heat, medium (350°F) Clean, oiled grate on lowest setting	**Wood:**	Direct heat, medium ash 12-by-12-inch bed, 3 inches deep Clean, oiled grate set 4 inches above the fire
Charcoal:	Direct heat, medium ash 12-by-12-inch charcoal bed (about 3 dozen coals) Clean, oiled grate on lowest setting		

INGREDIENTS (MAKES 4 SERVINGS)

1 loaf Italian bread

8 ounces cream cheese, at room temperature

4 tablespoons confectioners' sugar

¹/₂ teaspoon almond extract

³/₄ cup blueberries

5 eggs

1¹/₂ cups half-and-half or milk

1 teaspoon vanilla extract

Pinch of kosher salt

Oil for coating grill grate

¹/₄ cup Orange Honey-Butter Glaze (page 389)

DIRECTIONS

1. Cut off and discard a small diagonal slice from each end of the bread. Cut the bread on the diagonal into about eight 1¹/₂-inch-thick slices. Cut a slit through the top crust of each slice to form a deep pocket.

2. In a medium bowl, mix together the cream cheese, 3 tablespoons of the confectioners' sugar, and the almond extract. Stir in the blueberries and spoon the filling equally into the

bread pockets. Lay the stuffed slices of bread in a shallow 4-quart baking dish, such as a 15-by-10-inch dish.

3. Clean and dry the bowl, then use it to whisk together the eggs, half-and-half, vanilla extract, salt, and remaining 1 tablespoon confectioners' sugar. Pour the mixture evenly over the bread. Carefully tilt the pan and swirl the egg mixture to completely coat the bread. Let sit for 30 minutes, or cover and refrigerate for up to 8 hours.

TIMING

Prep: 15 minutes
   (plus 5 minutes for glaze)

Soak: 30 minutes or up to 8 hours

Grill: 8 to 10 minutes

GRILL TOOLS AND EQUIPMENT

· Long-handled spatula

GETTING CREATIVE

· For a more full-flavored filling, use mascarpone cheese, a triple-cream Italian cream cheese.

· Replace the blueberries with chopped strawberries, or use a mixture of berries.

· Use ¹/₂ cup fruit jam or preserves in place of the fresh blueberries.

· Vary the flavor of the glaze by replacing the orange zest with lemon or lime zest.

TIPS

· Avoid the morning rush and make this recipe the night before, then refrigerate it until you are ready to grill.

· The butter glaze lends a touch of sweetness, but we like to serve the toast with pure maple syrup as well.

· Try the toast for dessert with a scoop of vanilla ice cream.

4. Heat the grill as directed.

5. Brush the grill grate and coat it with oil. Put the French toast on the grill and cook until nicely browned and crisp on the outside, about 5 minutes per side. Transfer to a platter and, using a pastry or basting brush, brush both sides with the Orange Honey-Butter Glaze.

STRAWBERRY PIZZA WITH ORANGE MASCARPONE

Pizza is an incredibly versatile flatbread, as you'll see in the next few recipes. And it's fabulous when grilled. The basic procedure is a little different than that for cooking a pizza in the oven. You put a small round of dough directly on a hot grill grate until browned on the underside. Then flip the dough so that the grilled side is up, and add your toppings. Slide the topped pizza back on the grill, cover, and cook until the cheese melts and the bottom browns. Grilled pizza develops a crisp crust and a smoky nuance that's even closer to charcoal-fired brick oven pizzas than today's typical pie. And there's no reason to stop at tomato sauce and cheese. These flatbreads can be topped with anything from fruit to vegetables to meat, as long as you don't pile on too much. We love making grilled fruit pizzas in the summer. Spread some sweetened mascarpone on the crust, maybe a swath of jam or preserves, and add the fresh-cut fruit of your choice. Strawberries with orange-scented mascarpone is one of our favorite combinations.

THE GRILL

Gas: Direct heat, medium-high (400° to 450°F)
Clean, oiled grate

Charcoal: Direct heat, light ash
12-by-12-inch charcoal bed (about 3 dozen coals) with medium-high- and medium-low-heat areas
Clean, oiled grate on lowest setting

Wood: Direct heat, light ash
12-by-12-inch bed, 1 inch deep, with medium-high- and medium-low-heat areas
Clean, oiled grate set 2 inches above the fire

INGREDIENTS (MAKES 4 SMALL PIZZAS— 8 APPETIZER SERVINGS, 4 DESSERT SERVINGS)

1 pint small strawberries

2 tablespoons Grand Marnier or other orange liqueur

4 tablespoons sugar

12 ounces (1 1/2 cups) mascarpone cheese

Finely grated zest of 1/2 orange

No-stick spray oil or vegetable oil

Basic Pizza Dough (page 332)

Oil for coating grill grate

2 tablespoons fruity, green extra-virgin olive oil

DIRECTIONS

1. Heat the grill as directed.

2. Hull the strawberries and halve them lengthwise.

3. Heat the Grand Marnier and 3 tablespoons of the sugar in a medium microwaveable bowl or small saucepan over medium heat until melted (15 to 30 seconds in the microwave). Stir in the mascarpone and orange zest. Set aside.

4. Cut 4 pieces of aluminum foil, each about 12 inches square. Coat one of the pieces with no-stick spray or oil. Divide the dough into 4 pieces. Put one piece of dough on the prepared foil, and cover the other pieces. Press and stretch the dough on the foil into a circle about 8 to 10 inches in diameter and 1/8 to 1/4 inch thick. Don't bother making a rim around the edge of the crust unless you like it for aesthetics. Coat the top of the dough round with spray or oil. Repeat with the remaining dough and foil, oiling each dough round well and stacking them up.

5. Brush the grill grate and coat it with oil. Invert each round of dough onto the grate over medium-high heat, carefully removing the foil. Do this in batches if all of the dough won't fit on the grill at once. Put down the lid and cook each dough round until bubbly on the top and nicely grill-marked on the bottom, 1 to 2 minutes.

6. Remove the dough rounds and invert them onto a cutting board so that the grilled side is up. Spread about 1/4 to 1/3 cup of the orange mascarpone on the top side of each dough round. Arrange the strawberries, cut-side down, over the mascarpone. Drizzle with the olive oil and sprinkle with the remaining 1 tablespoon sugar.

7. Slide the pizzas back onto the grill over medium-low heat, put down the lid, and grill until the bottom is browned, about 5 minutes, watching carefully so that the pizza doesn't burn.

8. Cut each pizza into 8 wedges and serve.

TIMING
Prep: 20 minutes
(plus 1 hour 20 minutes for dough)
Grill: 8 minutes

GRILL TOOLS AND EQUIPMENT
· Wide, long-handled spatula
· Aluminum foil

TIPS
· If the strawberries are large, slice them 1/4 to 1/2 inch thick.
· Any pizza dough can be grilled. The key is to use a well-oiled grill and to oil up the dough, too.
· For a lighter dough, punch it down after the first rising, then cover and let the dough rise until doubled in bulk again, about another hour.
· To save time, use prepared refrigerated pizza dough. If using the type sold in tubes near the tubes of biscuits, buy two 10-ounce tubes and cut each in half to make 4 rounds of dough.
· If your grill doesn't have a lid, cover the pizza with a large disposable aluminum pan to trap the heat and melt the cheese.

Photo: Grilled Stuffed French Toast

GRILL TOOLS AND EQUIPMENT
- Aluminum foil
- Wide, long-handled spatula

GETTING CREATIVE
- For Basic Grilled Pizza, omit the caramelized onions, chorizo, and arugula. Use only the Grilled Tomato Dip, and top the pizza with sliced mozzarella cheese.
- For Grilled Vegetable Pizza, replace the onions, chorizo, and arugula with your favorite grilled vegetables. Try the Marinated Fire-Roasted Peppers on page 276.

TIPS
- Any pizza dough can be grilled. The key is to use a well-oiled grill and to oil up the dough, too.
- For a lighter dough, punch it down after the first rising, then cover and let the dough rise until doubled in bulk again, about another hour.
- To save time, use prepared refrigerated pizza dough. If using the type sold in tubes near the tubes of biscuits, buy two 10-ounce tubes and cut each in half to make 4 rounds of dough.
- The onions can be made up to 2 days ahead and refrigerated.
- If your grill doesn't have a lid, cover the pizza with a large disposable aluminum pan to trap the heat and melt the cheese.
- Pepperoni or other cured sausage can stand in for the Spanish chorizo.
- To make the chorizo slices more crisp, grill them over medium-high heat in a grill skillet or vegetable grill tray until lightly browned, 3 to 5 minutes, flipping once or twice, before using as a pizza topping.

SMOKED CHORIZO PIZZA WITH CARAMELIZED ONIONS AND ARUGULA

This pizza should look a bit more familiar than the one before and after it. It's built with tomato sauce and soft, melting cheese. To enhance the basic pie, we add slices of smoked chorizo, caramelized onions, and fresh arugula leaves. We also mix things up by grilling the vegetables for the sauce, caramelizing the onions on the grill, and using Bel Paese cheese instead of mozzarella.

THE GRILL

Gas: Direct heat, medium-high (400° to 450°F)
Clean, oiled grate

Charcoal: Direct heat, light ash
12-by-12-inch charcoal bed (about 3 dozen coals) with medium-high- and medium-low-heat areas
Clean, oiled grate on lowest setting

Wood: Direct heat, light ash
12-by-12-inch bed with medium-high- and medium-low-heat areas
Clean, oiled grate set 2 inches above the fire

INGREDIENTS (MAKES 4 SMALL PIZZAS— 8 APPETIZER SERVINGS, 4 MAIN DISH SERVINGS)

For the Basic Pizza Dough:
1 cup warm water (110° to 115°F)
1 envelope active dry yeast (2 1/2 teaspoons)
1/2 teaspoon sugar
4 tablespoons olive oil
3 1/4 cups unbleached all-purpose flour, plus more if needed
2 teaspoons kosher salt
No-stick spray oil or vegetable oil
Oil for coating grill grate

For the toppings:
1 1/3 cups Grilled Tomato Dip (page 399) or prepared tomato sauce
12 ounces Bel Paese or fresh mozzarella cheese, thinly sliced
3/4 cup Grilled Caramelized Vidalia Onions (page 303)
4 ounces cured Spanish chorizo or Portuguese linguiça, thinly sliced
2 ounces baby arugula (about 1 1/4 cups)
2 tablespoons extra-virgin olive oil

DIRECTIONS

1. For the Basic Pizza Dough, combine the water, yeast, and sugar in a large bowl, stirring until mixed. Let sit until foamy, about 5 minutes. Stir in 3 tablespoons of the olive oil.

2. Put the flour and salt in a food processor fitted with the dough blade, or in a large bowl, and pulse or stir to mix. With the motor running, add the yeast mixture and process or stir until the dough forms a ball. Turn onto a lightly floured surface and knead until the dough is smooth and elastic, about 5 minutes. The dough should be only slightly sticky, not dry. If necessary, knead in more flour, 1 tablespoon at a time, to achieve that texture. Coat a large bowl with the remaining 1 tablespoon oil and add the dough, turning to coat it with the oil. Cover and let rise in a warm spot until doubled in bulk, about 1 hour.

3. Heat the grill as directed.

4. Cut 4 pieces of aluminum foil, each about 12 inches square. Coat one of the pieces with no-stick spray or oil. Divide the dough into 4 pieces. Put one piece of dough on the prepared foil, and cover the other pieces. Press and stretch the dough on the foil into a circle about 8 to 10 inches in diameter and 1/8 to 1/4 inch thick. Don't bother making a rim around the edge of the crust unless you like it for aesthetics. Coat the top of the dough round with spray or oil. Repeat with the remaining dough and foil, oiling each dough round well and stacking them up.

5. Brush the grill grate and coat it with oil. Invert each circle of dough onto the grate over medium-high heat, carefully removing the foil. Do this in batches if all of the dough won't fit on the grill at once. Put down the lid and cook each dough round until bubbly on the top and nicely grill-marked on the bottom, 1 to 2 minutes.

6. For the toppings, invert the dough rounds onto a cutting board so that the grilled side is up. Spread about 1/4 to 1/3 cup of the tomato dip on the top side of each dough round. Scatter the cheese over it, followed by the onions, chorizo, and arugula. Drizzle with the olive oil.

7. Slide the pizzas back onto the grill over medium-low heat, put down the lid, and grill until the cheese melts and the bottom is browned, about 5 minutes, watching carefully so that the pizza doesn't burn.

8. Cut each pizza into 8 wedges and serve.

TIMING
Prep: 15 minutes
    (plus 1 hour 20 minutes for dough
    and garlic paste)
Grill: 8 minutes

GRILL TOOLS AND EQUIPMENT
· Aluminum foil
· Wide, long-handled spatula

TIPS
· Any pizza dough can be grilled. The key
  is to use a well-oiled grill and to oil up
  the dough, too.
· For a lighter dough, punch it down after
  the first rising, then cover and let the
  dough rise until doubled in bulk again,
  about another hour.
· To save time, use prepared refrigerated
  pizza dough. If using the type sold in
  tubes near the tubes of biscuits, buy
  two 10-ounce tubes and cut each in half
  to make 4 rounds of dough.
· If your grill doesn't have a lid, cover
  the pizza with a large disposable aluminum pan to trap the heat and melt
  the cheese.

GRILLED PARMESAN PIZZA WITH CAESAR SALAD

You've seen fruit pizza (page 331); now get ready for salad pizza. The crust is grilled with roasted garlic paste and Parmesan, and then it is topped with Caesar salad while still hot. It's like having your bread and salad all in one handy slice of flavor. Traditional Caesar dressing is made by boiling whole eggs in the shell for a minute or two and then breaking them out of the shell and mixing them into the vinaigrette. Coddling the eggs like this helps to thicken the dressing, but the egg white ends up thinning it out too much for our taste. We prefer to just use egg yolks. Caution: We are using raw egg yolks here. If salmonella is a concern, look for pasteurized egg yolks in your supermarket.

THE GRILL

Gas: Direct heat, medium-high (400° to 450°F)
Clean, oiled grate

Charcoal: Direct heat, light ash
12-by-12-inch charcoal bed (about 3 dozen coals) with medium-high- and medium-low-heat areas
Clean, oiled grate on lowest setting

Wood: Direct heat, light ash
12-by-12-inch bed, 1 inch deep, with medium-high- and medium-low-heat areas
Clean, oiled grate set 2 inches above the fire

INGREDIENTS (MAKES 4 SMALL PIZZAS— 8 APPETIZER SERVINGS, 4 MAIN DISH SERVINGS)

1/3 cup best-quality extra-virgin olive oil
2 large egg yolks
2 tablespoons fresh lemon juice
1 to 3 teaspoons minced anchovy fillets
1 teaspoon Worcestershire sauce
3/4 teaspoon kosher salt
1/4 teaspoon ground black pepper

1 large head romaine lettuce, torn into bite-size pieces
No-stick spray oil or vegetable oil
Basic Pizza Dough (page 332)
Oil for coating grill grate
1 cup Roasted Garlic Paste (page 392)
2 cups grated Parmigiano-Reggiano cheese

DIRECTIONS

1. Heat the grill as directed.

2. In a large bowl, whisk together the olive oil, egg yolks, lemon juice, minced anchovy, Worcestershire, salt, and pepper. Add the romaine, toss, and set aside.

3. Cut 4 pieces of aluminum foil, each about 12 inches square. Coat one of the pieces with no-stick spray or oil. Divide the dough into 4 pieces. Put one piece of dough on the prepared foil, and cover the other pieces. Press and stretch the dough on the foil into a circle about 8 to 10 inches in diameter and 1/8 to 1/4 inch thick. Don't bother making a rim around the edge of the crust unless you like it for aesthetics. Coat the top of the dough round with spray or oil. Repeat with the remaining dough and foil, oiling each dough round well and stacking them up.

4. Brush the grill grate and coat it with oil. Invert each round of dough onto the grate over medium-high heat, carefully removing the foil. Do this in batches if all of the dough won't fit on the grill at once. Put down the lid and cook each dough round until bubbly on the top and nicely grill-marked on the bottom, 1 to 2 minutes.

5. Invert the dough rounds onto a cutting board so that the grilled side is up. Spread about 1/4 cup of the Roasted Garlic Paste on the top side of each dough round. Scatter about 6 tablespoons of the cheese onto each (use a total of about 1 1/2 cups), reserving the remaining 1/2 cup for the salad.

6. Slide the pizzas back onto the grill over medium-low heat, put down the lid, and grill until the cheese begins to melt and the bottom is browned, about 5 minutes, watching carefully so that the pizza doesn't burn.

7. Toss the remaining 1/2 cup cheese with the Caesar salad. Scatter the salad evenly over the hot pizzas.

8. Cut each pizza into 8 wedges and serve.

GRILLED TOMATO PIES

TIMING
Prep: 15 minutes
  (plus 1 hour 20 minutes for dough
  and dip)
Grill: 6 to 10 minutes

GRILL TOOLS AND EQUIPMENT
· Large perforated grill tray or grill topper
  (about 17 by 11 inches) or 2 grill
  skillets or pizza grills (10 to 12 inches
  in diameter)

TIP
· If using a round grill skillet, be sure that
  the handle will fit completely on the grill
  area so that you can close the grill lid.

We call these pies because they're grilled in a pan. They're also a bit thicker than grilled pizza and are built differently. The cheese goes on first so that it melts into the crust, kind of like the cheese scattered over the crust of a quiche before the filling goes in. The meld is wonderful and gives you something closer to a pie or tart than your average thin-crust pizza. The toppings? Three kinds of tomatoes: sauce, sun-dried, and fresh. Save this one for late summer when fresh tomatoes and basil are at their peak.

THE GRILL

Gas: Direct heat, medium-high (400° to 450°F)
Clean, oiled grate

Charcoal: Direct heat, light ash
12-by-12-inch charcoal bed (about 3 dozen coals)
  with medium-high- and medium-low-heat areas
Clean, oiled grate on lowest setting

Wood: Direct heat, light ash
12-by-12-inch bed with medium-high- and
  medium-low-heat areas
Clean, oiled grate set 2 inches above the fire

INGREDIENTS (MAKES 2 RECTANGULAR OR ROUND PIZZAS)

Oil for coating grill tray and grill grate
Basic Pizza Dough (page 332)
2 tablespoons extra-virgin olive oil, plus more for brushing
1 cup shredded provolone or mozzarella cheese
  (about 4 ounces)
1 cup grated Parmigiano-Reggiano or Asiago cheese

1 $1/3$ cups Grilled Tomato Dip (page 399) or your favorite
  tomato sauce
1 cup oil-packed sun-dried tomatoes, cut into thin strips
2 large, ripe tomatoes, thinly sliced
$1/2$ teaspoon kosher salt
$1/4$ teaspoon ground black pepper
20 to 30 whole basil leaves

DIRECTIONS

1. Heat the grill as directed. Oil a rectangular grill tray, round grill skillet, or pizza grill.

2. Divide the dough into 2 balls. Press and stretch one ball of dough to fit the oiled tray or skillet.

3. Brush the grill grate and coat it with oil. Put the pan of dough on the grill, cover, and cook until puffed on the top and nicely browned on the bottom, 2 to 4 minutes. Keep an eye on the dough, as it can quickly go from browned to burned.

4. Remove the pan of dough from the grill and brush or rub the top with a little olive oil. Invert the dough in the pan so that the browned side is up. Scatter $1/2$ cup of the provolone and $1/2$ cup of the Parmigiano-Reggiano over the browned side. Spread $2/3$ cup of the tomato dip or tomato sauce over the cheese. Scatter on $1/2$ cup of the sun-dried tomatoes, then arrange half of the ripe tomato slices over the top in overlapping circles. Sprinkle with $1/4$ teaspoon of the salt and $1/8$ teaspoon of the pepper. Scatter 10 to 15 basil leaves over the pie, and drizzle with 1 tablespoon of the olive oil.

5. Put the pan back on the grill, cover, and cook until the cheese melts and the crust is nicely browned on the bottom, 4 to 6 minutes. If the crust browns too much before the cheese is melted, move the pizza to a cooler part of the grill or turn down the heat.

6. Transfer the pizza to a cutting board or platter. Let cool slightly before cutting into wedges and serving.

7. Oil the pan again and repeat with the remaining dough and toppings.

TIMING
Prep: 15 minutes
    (plus 1 hour 20 minutes for dough
    and dip)
Grill: 6 to 10 minutes

GRILL TOOLS AND EQUIPMENT
· Aluminum foil
· Long-handled spatula

TIPS
· We call for dry-cured smoked ham here for smoky flavor. These hams also have a more complex flavor than wet-cured hams. Any Virginia ham such as Smithfield or Kentucky will do. If you can't find a Virginia ham, serrano or Iberico ham or prosciutto will also work, minus the smoke flavor. As a last resort, sliced deli ham wouldn't completely ruin the recipe.
· To save time, use prepared refrigerated pizza dough. If using the type sold in tubes near the tubes of biscuits, buy two 10-ounce tubes and cut each in half to make 4 rounds of dough.
· Save time by serving these calzones with your favorite prepared tomato sauce.

GRILLED HAM AND FONTINA CALZONES WITH GRILLED TOMATO DIP

Like many other sandwiches, calzones can be grilled directly on the grill grate. The dough develops a nicely browned crust with attractive grill marks, and the filling gets piping hot. We've used the traditional ham and cheese here (with fontina instead of mozzarella), but we encourage you to experiment with other fillings. Try cooked sausage, grilled cubed chicken, or grilled pulled pork.

THE GRILL

Gas: Direct heat, medium (350°F)
            Clean, oiled grate

Charcoal: Direct heat, medium ash
            12-by-12-inch charcoal bed (about 3 dozen coals)
                with medium- and low-heat areas
            Clean, oiled grate on medium setting

Wood: Direct heat, medium ash
            12-by-12-inch bed with medium- and low-heat areas
            Clean, oiled grate set 4 inches above the fire

INGREDIENTS (MAKES 4 CALZONES—4 TO 6 GENEROUS SERVINGS)

2 cups ricotta cheese

$1/2$ cup grated Parmesan cheese

$1/2$ teaspoon dried basil

$1/4$ teaspoon dried oregano

$1/4$ teaspoon dried thyme

No-stick spray oil or vegetable oil

Basic Pizza Dough (page 332)

6 ounces Virginia ham, thinly sliced

8 ounces fontina cheese, shredded or thinly sliced

Oil for coating grill grate

2 cups Grilled Tomato Dip (page 399)

Photo: Grilled Ham and Fontina Calzones
with Grilled Tomato Dip

DIRECTIONS

1. Heat the grill as directed.

2. Combine the ricotta, Parmesan, basil, oregano, and thyme in a medium bowl.

3. Cut 4 pieces of aluminum foil, each about 12 inches square. Coat each piece with no-stick spray or oil. Divide the pizza dough into 4 pieces. Put a piece of dough on each prepared sheet of foil. Press and stretch each piece of dough into a circle about 10 inches in diameter and $1/8$ to $1/4$ inch thick. Mound one -ourth of the ricotta mixture onto one side of each round of dough. Arrange one-fourth of the ham and fontina over the ricotta mixture on each round of dough. Pull the dough over the filling and seal the edges tightly with your fingers. Coat the tops with spray oil.

4. Brush the grill grate and coat it with oil. Carefully invert each calzone onto the grill over medium-low heat and remove the foil. Cover and grill until nicely browned, 3 to 5 minutes per side, flipping once with a long spatula. If necessary to prevent burning, reduce the heat to low or move the calzones to the low-heat area of the grill.

5. Remove to a cutting board and let rest for 5 minutes. Serve the calzones whole or cut them in half on the diagonal, with the tomato dip on the side.

GRILLED ROSEMARY AND PROSCIUTTO FOCACCIA

Focaccia is essentially a thick-crust pizza with minimal toppings—usually just olive oil and salt. When "baked" on the grill, the crust gets nice and crispy on the bottom and picks up a whiff of smoke aroma. To make it easier to handle the dough, we grill the focaccia in a large vegetable grill tray via indirect heat. A bit of prosciutto and fresh rosemary make this a satisfying snacking bread. Or cut the focaccia into sqare to use as sandwich bread.

THE GRILL

Gas: Indirect heat, medium (350° to 375°F)
Large 3- or 4-burner grill–middle burner(s) off
2-burner grill–1 side off
Clean, oiled grate

Charcoal: Indirect heat, medium to light ash
Charcoal bed to one side (about 2 dozen coals on one side)
Heavy-duty drip pan set on empty side of grill
Clean, oiled grate on medium setting

INGREDIENTS (MAKES 1 LARGE FOCACCIA—ABOUT 17 BY 11 INCHES)

For the Basic Focaccia:
$1/3$ cup olive oil
Basic Pizza Dough (page 332)
1 teaspoon kosher salt or coarse sea salt

For the toppings:
2 tablespoons chopped fresh rosemary leaves, or 2 teaspoons dried crumbled rosemary
2 tablespoons grated Parmigiano-Reggiano cheese
4 ounces thinly sliced prosciutto, chopped

DIRECTIONS

1. For the Basic Focaccia, use about a tablespoon of the oil to grease a large, perforated grill tray (about 17 inches by 11 inches).

2. After kneading the dough, coat it with oil and roll it into a rectangle. Put the rectangle of dough in the oiled pan, then press and stretch the dough to reach the edges of the pan. Stretch gently to avoid tearing the dough. If the dough shrinks back, let it rest for a few minutes, then press and stretch it again. Repeat until the dough reaches the edges of the pan and is about $1/2$ inch thick. Cover and let rise in a warm spot until puffy, about 1 hour.

3. Heat the grill as directed.

4. Dimple the dough all over with your fingertips. Drizzle with the remaining olive oil (3 to 4 tablespoons), and sprinkle with the salt. Scatter on the rosemary and Parmigiano-Reggiano.

5. Put the tray of focaccia on the grill away from the heat, cover the grill, and cook until golden, 20 to 30 minutes total. During the last 5 minutes, scatter the prosciutto over the focaccia. If your grill has a temperature gauge, it should stay at around 375° to 400°F.

6. Remove the focaccia to a cooling rack and let cool. Cut into squares and serve.

TIMING
Prep: 15 minutes
(plus 1 hour 20 minutes for dough)
Grill: 20 to 30 minutes

GRILL TOOLS AND EQUIPMENT
· Large perforated grill tray or grill topper (about 17 by 11 inches)

GETTING CREATIVE
· You can vary the toppings almost endlessly. Just keep them simple. Some ideas: Marinated Fire-Roasted Peppers (page 276), Grilled Caramelized Vidalia Onions (page 303), Tapenade Parsley Pesto (page 398), Roasted Garlic Paste (page 392), julienned sun-dried tomatoes, and/or your favorite chopped fresh herbs or hard grating cheese.

TIPS
· You'll need a rather large grill for this recipe. For even browning, be sure that the tray of focaccia is between the heated areas of the grill and not over any direct heat. If your grill is too small to have two heated areas and a large empty space in the middle, heat only one side of the grill, leaving a large unheated space on the other side of the grill for the focaccia.
· To make 2 small round focaccia, use two 10-inch grill skillets in place of the large grill tray.

TIMING
Prep: 15 minutes
    (plus 1 hour 40 minutes for focaccia,
    garlic paste, and roasted peppers)
Grill: About 20 minutes

GRILL TOOLS AND EQUIPMENT
· Long-handled spatula
· Heavy iron skillet or other weight

GETTING CREATIVE
· Sandwich fillings are limited only by your imagination. Use other grilled vegetables, grilled chicken paillards, thinly sliced prosciutto, or other sliced cured meats. For the cheese, use goat cheese, cream cheese, feta, provolone, mozzarella, or your favorite melting cheese. For the spread, try Tapenade Parsley Pesto (page 398) or the sandwich spread of your choice.

TIP
· Have everything at room temperature when making grilled sandwiches. That way the cheese will melt and the fillings will get warm before the bread burns on the outside.

EGGPLANT AND ROASTED PEPPER PANINI WITH SMOKED GOUDA

Panini, or "little breads," are sandwiches that are often made with focaccia as the bread. We grill the sandwiches under a heavy weight and add a triple shot of flavor with grilled eggplant, grilled peppers, and roasted garlic paste. A little smoked Gouda heightens the aromas.

THE GRILL

Gas: Direct heat, medium (350°F)
Clean, oiled grate

Charcoal: Direct heat, medium ash
12-by-12-inch charcoal bed (about 3 dozen coals)
Clean, oiled grate on lowest setting

Wood: Direct heat, medium ash
12-by-12-inch bed, 3 inches deep
Clean, oiled grate set 4 inches above the fire

INGREDIENTS (MAKES 4 SANDWICHES)

Basic Focaccia (page 337) or purchased focaccia
1 medium eggplant (about 1 pound), cut into
    $1/2$-inch-thick slices
2 tablespoons olive oil, plus more for brushing
$1/2$ teaspoon kosher salt
$1/4$ teaspoon ground black pepper
$1/2$ cup Roasted Garlic Paste (page 392) or purchased
    roasted garlic paste

Oil for coating grill grate
$1 1/2$ cups shredded smoked Gouda cheese (about 6 ounces),
    at room temperature
1 large, ripe tomato, thinly sliced
$2 1/2$ cups Marinated Fire-Roasted Peppers (page 276) or
    purchsed roasted peppers, at room temperature, cut into
    thin strips

DIRECTIONS

1. Prepare the focaccia as directed. When completely cool, cut into 4-to-5-inch squares or rectangles. Use 8 squares for the sandwiches, reserving any remaining squares for another use.
2. Heat the grill as directed.
3. Brush or rub the eggplant with the 2 tablespoons olive oil, then sprinkle with the salt and pepper.
4. Brush the grill grate and coat it with oil. Put the eggplant slices on the grill, cover, and cook until tender, 4 to 6 minutes per side. If your grill has a temperature gauge, it should stay at around 350°F.
5. Remove the eggplant to a cutting board or plate.
6. To assemble the sandwiches, spread the bottoms of each focaccia slice with some of the Roasted Garlic Paste. Sprinkle

half of the cheese over the bottoms of the sandwiches. Layer on the tomato slices, eggplant slices, and roasted peppers. Sprinkle with the remaining cheese and cover with the sandwich tops. Brush the outsides of the sandwiches with olive oil.
7. Put the sandwiches on the grill and compress them gently with a weight such as an iron skillet (the sandwiches should compress slightly, but the fillings should not be squeezed out). Fill the skillet with extra weight such as a rock or brick if necessary to gently compress the sandwiches. Grill until the cheese melts and the bread is toasted, about 5 minutes per side, using the weight on both sides.
8. Remove to a platter or plates and cut each panino in half on the diagonal before serving.

TIMING
Prep: 20 minutes
Marinate: 6 hours or up to 3 days
Grill: 10 to 15 minutes

GRILL TOOLS AND EQUIPMENT
· Heat-resistant grill mitts
· Aluminum foil

GRILLED MUFFULETTA

Here's a New Orleans specialty— a sandwich of cold cuts and olive salad layered in a round loaf and then pressed like a panino to compact the ingredients. The original is said to have been dreamed up at the New Orleans Central Grocery in 1906 by Salvatore Lupo. It's traditionally served cold, but muffuletta makes a damn fine hot sandwich off the grill. We grill-bake the whole shebang in foil until the cheese melts. We also use smoked cheese and smoked ham to enhance the grill flavors. This makes a great summer sandwich, especially when camping or lighting a fire that you can plan to let burn down slowly any way.

Gas:	Indirect heat, medium (325° to 350°F)		**Charcoal:**	Indirect heat, medium ash
	3- or 4-burner grill–middle burner(s) off			Split charcoal bed (about 2 dozen coals per side)
	2-burner grill–1 side off			Clean, oiled grate on medium setting
	Clean, oiled grate			

TIP
· Save time by replacing the olive salad with store-bought olive salad. Of course, you'll lose a bit of flavor this way.

INGREDIENTS (MAKES 6 SERVINGS)

For the olive salad:

1 jar (about 6 ounces) pimiento-stuffed Spanish olives, drained and finely chopped

1 cup pitted kalamata olives, drained and finely chopped

1 rib celery, finely chopped

1/2 cup extra-virgin olive oil

1/4 cup chopped fresh flat-leaf parsley

1 tablespoon red wine vinegar

1 large clove garlic, minced

1 teaspoon dried oregano

1/4 teaspoon ground black pepper

For the sandwich:

1 large round loaf Italian or French bread (1 1/4 to 1 1/2 pounds), preferably with sesame seeds

4 ounces thinly sliced smoked provolone or mozzarella cheese

3 ounces thinly sliced mortadella

3 ounces thinly sliced Genoa salami

2 ounces thinly sliced baked ham, preferably smoked Virginia ham

1/2 cup oil-packed sun-dried tomatoes, drained and thinly sliced

DIRECTIONS

1. For the olive salad, combine all of the ingredients in a small bowl, cover, and refrigerate for 6 hours or up to 3 days.

2. Remove the olive salad from the refrigerator about 30 minutes before assembling the sandwich, to let it warm up a bit.

3. For the sandwich, cut the bread in half through the side and remove some of the inner bread to create a hollow for the stuffing; leave about 1 inch of soft bread attached to the crust. Reserve the removed bread for breadcrumbs or another recipe.

4. Drain the olive salad and reserve the liquid. Dip a basting brush into the liquid and brush the interior of the bread with it.

5. Layer half of both cheeses on the bottom of the bread. Layer on half of the olive salad, then the mortadella, salami, ham, and sun-dried tomatoes. Add the remaining half of the

olive salad and the remaining half of the cheese. Cover with the top of the bread and compress the sandwich with your hands. Wrap in foil and weight down the foil-wrapped sandwich with a heavy skillet filled with canned goods or another heavy weight. Let stand for 30 minutes or until the grill is ready.

6. Heat the grill as directed.

7. Put the foil-wrapped sandwich on the grill away from the heat, and weight it down with the skillet and a rock or brick if necessary to keep the sandwich compressed. Cover the grill and cook until the cheese melts, 10 to 15 minutes. If your grill has a temperature gauge, it should stay at around 350°F.

8. Remove the sandwich to a cutting board. Unwrap, cut into wedges, and serve.

SMOKY BLACK BEAN QUESADILLAS

Like grilled cheese sandwiches, quesadillas are meant to be simple little snacks. But you don't have to stop at just tortillas and cheese. You can add beans, vegetables, or shredded chicken or pork along with the cheese. Just don't fill them up too much or the fillings will get squeezed out when you cut them into wedges. Here we fill the tortillas with some Smoky Black Beans with Cilantro and Lime.

TIMING
Prep: 5 minutes
(plus 10 hours for beans)
Grill: 6 to 10 minutes

GRILL TOOLS AND EQUIPMENT
· Long-handled spatula

SHORTCUT
· To save time, drain a can (15 ounces) of black beans and mash the beans along with about 1/2 cup jarred or well-drained refrigerated salsa. Use this mixture instead of the smoky black beans.

THE GRILL

Gas:	Direct heat, medium (350°F)		**Wood:**	Direct heat, medium ash
	Clean, oiled grate			12-by-12-inch bed, 3 inches deep
Charcoal:	Direct heat, medium ash			Clean, oiled grate set 4 inches above the fire
	12-by-12-inch charcoal bed (about 3 dozen coals)			
	Clean, oiled grate on lowest setting			

- As with most sandwiches, the fillings here are endlessly variable. Replace the beans with the grilled vegetables from Grilled Vegetable Fajitas (page 273). Use some shredded chicken from Bean Butt Chicken (page 194), some shredded duck from Smoky Barbecued Duck (page 200), or a bit of pulled pork from Pulled Pork Three Ways (page 210). If you have leftover rotisseried chicken in the fridge, shred it and use that. It's a sandwich after all. Fill it with what you like.
- For a rich flourish, brush the quesadillas with melted butter right when they come off the grill and before cutting them into wedges. They're a bit messier to eat when brushed with butter, but they taste great.

1½ cups Smoky Black Beans with Cilantro and Lime (page 293)

2 cups shredded pepper Jack or Cheddar cheese

8 flour tortillas (8 to 10 inches in diameter)

Oil for coating grill grate

1 cup salsa, for dipping

DIRECTIONS

1. Heat the grill as directed.

2. Put the beans in a medium bowl and mash with a fork.

3. For each quesadilla, scatter about ¼ cup of cheese over a tortilla. Spread about one-fourth of the beans over the cheese, then scatter another ¼ cup of cheese on top. Top with another tortilla.

4. Brush the grill grate and coat it with oil. Put the quesadillas on the grill (use a spatula to help transfer them), cover, and cook until nicely grill-marked and the cheese melts, 3 to 5 minutes per side. If your grill has a temperature gauge, it should stay at around 350°F.

5. Remove to a cutting board and let cool slightly. Cut into wedges like a pizza and serve.

TIMING

Prep: 1 minute
Grill: 2 to 4 minutes

GRILL TOOLS AND EQUIPMENT

- Long skewers or thin sticks

TIPS

- Packaged shortbread comes in all shapes and sizes, including rounds, rectangles, and triangular wedges. We tested these s'mores with round shortbread Sandies made by Keebler because they're widely available and the round shape is perfect for marshmallows.
- To prepare several s'mores at once, spread several cookies with chocolate spread and impale as many marshmallows onto your skewer or stick as it will comfortably hold, toasting the marshmallows all at once.

SHORTBREAD S'MORES

One of David's pet peeves about s'mores is that the toasted marshmallows are rarely hot enough to melt the chocolate from a typical chocolate bar. So we skip the chocolate bar and use spreadable chocolate instead. Nutella is a widely available brand of chocolate-hazelnut spread with a rich, creamy texture and subtle hazelnut flavor. Europeans eat it like peanut butter. Look for Nutella near the peanut butter or other chocolate in your grocery store. David's *other* pet peeve is that when you make a sandwich out of s'mores and bite down, the hot, melted marshmallow squishes out. So we use only one cookie per serving to make open-face s'mores. Shortbread cookies make the perfect bed for these campfire snacks.

THE GRILL

Gas: Direct heat, medium-high (400° to 450°F)

Charcoal: Direct heat, light ash
12-by-12-inch charcoal bed (about 3 dozen coals)

Wood: Direct heat, light ash
12-by-12-inch bed, 3 to 4 inches deep

Photo, right: Shortbread S'mores
Photo, opposite: Toasted marshmallow

1 pound purchased round shortbread cookies (about 28)

$^2/_3$ cup chocolate-hazelnut spread such as Nutella

28 marshmallows (about 8 ounces)

DIRECTIONS

1. Heat the grill as directed.

2. For each s'more, spread the flat side of a cookie with about 1 teaspoon of the chocolate spread. Impale a marshmallow on a long skewer or stick and toast over the fire until golden brown all over and gooey inside, turning often, 2 to 4 minutes. Pull the marshmallow onto the prepared cookie and let cool for a minute before taking a bite.

TIMING
Prep: 20 minutes
Grill: 15 to 20 minutes

GRILL TOOLS AND EQUIPMENT
· Grill skillet or wok, grill tray, or grill screen
· Heavy skillet or saucepan

GETTING CREATIVE
· To make Chocolate-Coated Fire-Roasted Chestnuts, omit the butter and use 5 to 6 ounces of chocolate. Melt the chocolate over very low heat in the pan on the grill with the lid down, stirring often. When almost melted, remove from the heat and stir in the peeled chestnuts. Remove the chestnuts to a cookie sheet lined with waxed paper. Chill until the chocolate is firm.

Chocolate and roasted chestnuts marry well. They're both buttery smooth yet nutty tasting. Serve these chocolate-drizzled chestnuts with vanilla ice cream, or coat the chestnuts in pure chocolate and then chill them until firm (see "Getting Creative" on this page). Chocolate-coated chestnuts make an irresistible snack. You could also chop them up and mix them into brownie batter.

THE GRILL

Gas: Direct heat, medium (350°F)
Clean, oiled grate

Charcoal: Direct heat, medium ash
12-by-12-inch charcoal bed (about 3 dozen coals)
Clean, oiled grate on lowest setting

Wood: Direct heat, medium ash
12-by-12-inch bed, 3 inches deep
Clean, oiled grate set 4 inches above the fire

INGREDIENTS (MAKES 4 SERVINGS)

1 pound Italian chestnuts (about 20)
3 tablespoons butter

3 ounces bittersweet or semisweet chocolate, chopped (about ½ cup)

Photo: Roasted chestnuts

DIRECTIONS

1. Heat the grill as described.

2. Slit the nuts on the rounded sides of the shells (see Tips) and put them in a grill skillet. Put the skillet on the grill directly over the heat and roast until the chestnuts have opened and smell toasty, turning or shaking a few times, 15 to 20 minutes. Remove the shells from the chestnuts while still warm (see Tips).

3. Put the butter in a cast-iron or other heavy skillet and melt it over a low-heat part of the grill. When melted, remove from the heat, add the chocolate, and stir until smooth.

4. Add the chestnuts to the chocolate, tossing to coat. Serve drizzled with any remaining chocolate butter.

TIPS
- When slitting the chestnut shells, take care not to cut through the nutmeats; otherwise, the nuts may break when you remove the shells.
- Remove the chestnut shells while they are still fairly warm (put them in a kitchen towel to protect your hands). If you let the chestnuts cool completely, the skins will adhere to the nuts, and shelling them will be more difficult.

GRILLED NAAN

About fifteen years ago, David threw himself into Indian cuisine, making everything he could, from curries to dumplings. He also experimented with naan, the soft Indian flatbread traditionally cooked in a tandoor, that magical clay-lined open-air charcoal oven best known for turning out tandoori chicken. To make naan, a simple wheat flour dough is stretched into an oval or teardrop shape and then slapped onto the hot walls of the tandoor, where the dough bubbles and browns almost instantly. You can get the dough to puff and crisp up pretty well on a pizza stone in your oven, but it's even better on a charcoal grill. Some naan dough is leavened with yeast, and some isn't. Here's the simpler version without yeast. For yeasted naan, check out the recipe for Grilled Cardamom Flatbread (page 344).

TIMING
Prep: 15 minutes
Rest: 30 minutes to 24 hours
Grill: 2 minutes

GRILL TOOLS AND EQUIPMENT
- Long-handled tongs

TIP
- For a more crisp, evenly browned crust, preheat a pizza stone directly on your grill grate as you heat the grill. Let it heat for at least 20 minutes. It should be quite hot. Cook the naan directly on the hot stone, which absorbs moisture from the dough and makes the bread crisper.

THE GRILL

Gas: Direct heat, medium-high (400° to 450°F)
Clean, oiled grate

Charcoal: Direct heat, light ash
12-by-12-inch charcoal bed (about 3 dozen coals)
Clean, oiled grate on lowest setting

Wood: Direct heat, light ash
12-by-12-inch bed, 3 to 4 inches deep
Clean, oiled grate set 2 inches above the fire

INGREDIENTS (MAKES 4 FLATBREADS)

3 cups all-purpose flour
2 teaspoons baking powder
1 teaspoon kosher salt
About $3/4$ cup milk, at room temperature

3 tablespoons vegetable oil
2 teaspoons sugar
Oil for coating bowl, dough rounds, and grill grate
2 tablespoons butter, melted

DIRECTIONS

1. Put the flour, baking powder, and salt in a food processor fitted with the dough blade or in a large bowl, pulsing or stirring to mix.

2. In a small bowl, mix together $3/4$ cup of the milk, the 3 tablespoons oil, and the sugar until blended. Slowly pour the milk mixture into the food processor with the motor running or into the bowl and process or stir until a soft dough forms. Add more milk, 1 tablespoon at a time, if the dough is too dry.

3. Turn out onto a lightly floured surface and knead until the dough is smooth and pliable, about 5 minutes. Coat a large bowl lightly with oil and add the dough, turning to coat it with the oil. Cover and let rest at room temperature for 30 minutes or refrigerate for up to 24 hours. Return the dough to room temperature before rolling it out.

4. Heat the grill as directed.

5. Divide the dough into 4 pieces and roll each piece into a ball. Cover and let rest for 20 minutes as the grill heats up. Lightly oil a work surface and roll each ball out to an oval or teardrop shape, about 8 inches in diameter and $1/4$ inch thick. Lightly oil both sides of each round of dough and stack them on a plate.

6. Brush the grill grate and coat it with oil. Put the dough rounds on the grill, cover, and cook until browned on the bottom and puffed on top, 1 to 2 minutes. Turn with tongs and brown the other side for 30 seconds or so. Watch the breads carefully, as they can quickly go from browned to burned (a few little burnt spots are okay).

7. Remove the flatbreads to a plate and brush with the melted butter. Serve immediately and cover to keep warm. To eat the flatbread, tear pieces from it.

GRILL TOOLS AND EQUIPMENT
· Long-handled tongs

TIP
· For a more crisp, evenly browned crust, preheat a pizza stone directly on your grill grate as you heat the grill. Let it heat for at least 20 minutes. It should be quite hot. Cook the flatbread directly on the hot stone, which absorbs moisture from the dough and makes the bread crisper.

GRILLED CARDAMOM FLATBREAD

This yeasted version of naan is slightly sweeter and redolent with the spicy-sweet aromas of cardamom. See facing page for a description of naan and an unyeasted recipe.

THE GRILL

Gas: Direct heat, medium-high (400° to 450°F)
Clean, oiled grate

Charcoal: Direct heat, light ash
12-by-12-inch charcoal bed (about 3 dozen coals)
Clean, oiled grate on lowest setting

Wood: Direct heat, light ash
12-by-12-inch bed, 3 to 4 inches deep
Clean, oiled grate set 2 inches above the fire

INGREDIENTS (MAKES 4 FLATBREADS)

2 1/4 cups all-purpose flour
1 1/2 tablespoons sugar
1 1/2 teaspoons active dry yeast
3/4 teaspoon ground cardamom
1/2 teaspoon kosher salt

About 1 cup buttermilk, at room temperature
2 tablespoons vegetable oil, plus more for coating bowl, dough rounds, and grill grate
2 tablespoons butter, melted

DIRECTIONS

1. Put the flour, sugar, yeast, cardamom, and salt in a food processor fitted with the dough blade or in a large bowl, pulsing or stirring to mix.

2. Slowly pour in 3/4 cup of the buttermilk and the 2 tablespoons vegetable oil and process or stir until a soft dough forms. Add more buttermilk, 1 tablespoon at a time, if the dough is too dry.

3. Turn out onto a lightly floured surface and knead until the dough is smooth and pliable, 5 to 10 minutes. Coat a large bowl lightly with oil and add the dough, turning to coat it with the oil. Cover and let rise at room temperature until doubled in bulk, about 1 1/2 hours.

4. Heat the grill as directed.

5. Punch down the dough and divide into 4 pieces. Roll each piece into a ball, then cover and let rest for 15 to 20 minutes

as the grill heats up. Lightly oil a work surface and roll each ball out to an oval or teardrop shape, about 8 inches in diameter and 1/4 inch thick. Lightly oil both sides of each round of dough and stack them on a plate.

6. Brush the grill grate and coat it with oil. Put the dough rounds on the grill, cover, and cook until browned on the bottom and puffed on top, 1 to 2 minutes. Turn with tongs and brown the other side for 30 seconds or so. Watch the breads carefully, as they can quickly go from browned to burned (a few little burnt spots are okay).

7. Remove the flatbreads to a plate and brush with the melted butter. Serve immediately and cover to keep warm. To eat the flatbread, tear pieces from it.

TIMING
Prep: 10 minutes
Grill: 2 minutes

GRILL TOOLS AND EQUIPMENT
· Long-handled tongs

GRILLED GARLIC BREAD

Italy's most famous toast, bruschetta, is a form of grilled garlic bread in which slices of bread are toasted over hot coals, rubbed with a cut clove of garlic, and then drizzled with olive oil. Here's a version that's closer to the buttered garlic bread served with pasta in most Italian-American restaurants. It's quick and simple.

THE GRILL

Gas: Direct heat, medium-high (400° to 450°F)
Clean, oiled grate

Charcoal: Direct heat, light ash
12-by-12-inch charcoal bed (about 3 dozen coals)
Clean, oiled grate on lowest setting

Wood: Direct heat, light ash
12-by-12-inch bed, 3 to 4 inches deep
Clean, oiled grate set 2 inches above the fire

INGREDIENTS (MAKES 8 SERVINGS (ABOUT 2 SLICES EACH)

1 large loaf French or Italian bread (about 1 pound)

3/4 cup (1 1/2 sticks) butter, softened

3 to 4 cloves garlic, minced

2 teaspoons dried oregano

1/2 teaspoon ground black pepper

1/8 teaspoon kosher salt

Oil for coating grill grate

DIRECTIONS

1. Heat the grill as directed.

2. Cut the bread on the diagonal into slices about 1/2 to 3/4 inch thick, and put the slices on a baking sheet or tray.

3. Put the butter, garlic, oregano, pepper, and salt in the bowl of an electric mixer and beat on medium speed until light, fluffy, and blended, scraping the sides as necessary.

4. Spread the flavored butter over both sides of the bread slices.

5. Brush the grill grate and coat it with oil. Put the buttered bread slices on the grill and cook until toasted and lightly grill-marked, 1 to 2 minutes per side, turning with tongs (watch carefully; toast can burn quickly). Serve immediately.

GRILLED BRIE WRAPPED IN GRAPE LEAVES

This makes a fabulous fall appetizer. You slather a wheel of Brie with roasted garlic paste, wrap it in grape leaves, and then grill it directly on the grill rack until the cheese begins to ooze. Serve it with your favorite crackers for scooping up the cheese, or use sliced baguettes. If you can't wait to slice the bread, just rip off small hunks to dip into the melting cheese. The Brie will start to firm up after 10 to 15 minutes, depending upon the ambient temperature. To prolong the ooze, preheat your cheese plate. The grape leaves can also be eaten. They develop wonderfully crisp edges on the grill.

THE GRILL

Gas: Direct heat, medium (350° to 400°F)
Clean, oiled grate

Charcoal: Direct heat, medium ash
12-by-12-inch charcoal bed (about 3 dozen coals)
Clean, oiled grate on lowest setting

Wood: Direct heat, medium ash
12-by-12-inch bed, 3 inches deep
Clean, oiled grate set 4 inches above the fire

INGREDIENTS (MAKES 6 TO 8 SERVINGS)

5 to 7 brined grape leaves, drained

1/2 cup Roasted Garlic Paste (page 392)

1 small wheel Brie cheese (8 ounces), ripe but still firm

2 tablespoons olive oil

Oil for coating grill grate

DIRECTIONS

1. Lay the grape leaves out in a circle about 12 inches in diameter. Spread the garlic paste all over the Brie—top, bottom, and sides. Lay the Brie in the middle of the grape leaf circle. Fold the grape leaves over the Brie toward the middle of the top. Pat the leaves all around the Brie to secure them over the surface. Rub the outside of the grape leaves all over with the olive oil.

2. Heat the grill as directed. Warm a large cheese plate in the microwave or oven.

3. Brush the grill grate and coat it with oil. Put the wrapped Brie on the grill with the folded side down, cover, and cook for 1 to 2 minutes. Turn, cover, and cook until the Brie is just beginning to melt, about 1 to 2 minutes more. To check for

doneness, press the center of the cheese—it should feel like warm, softened butter. If your grill has a temperature gauge, it should stay at around 375°F.

4. Using tongs and/or a spatula, remove the Brie to the warmed cheese plate (the folded side should be up). Fold back the leaves to expose the top of the cheese. Let the leaves rest on the plate. Make a cut from the center to the edge of the wheel of Brie and spread it slightly to let the cheese begin to melt out. If the cheese isn't yet melted, fold the leaves back up and put the cheese back on the grill for a minute or so. It's perfectly safe (and encouraged) to eat the white rind of the Brie.

GETTING CREATIVE

· Add grated Parmesan, crumbled Gorgonzola, minced scallions, and/or fresh herbs to the butter.

TIMING

Prep: 10 minutes
    (plus 40 minutes for garlic paste)
Grill: About 2 minutes

GRILL TOOLS AND EQUIPMENT

· Long-handled tongs
· Long-handled spatula

TIP

· Grape leaves are widely available packed in brine in 1-pound jars. Look for them in Greek and Middle Eastern markets or well-stocked supermarkets.

GRILLED CHÈVRE WITH POPPED GRAPES

TIMING
Prep: 15 minutes
   (plus 5 minutes for rub)
Grill: About 10 minutes

This dish gives new meaning to the phrase "grilled cheese." A small disk of chilled goat cheese is coated with herbs and grilled directly on the grill grate just until the cheese begins to melt. The warm cheese is served with grilled grapes and toasted baguette slices. It's a remarkable combination. Be sure to chill the cheese before grilling so that it doesn't completely melt and fall into the fire. A generous coating of oil on the surface also helps to create darker grill marks on the disk of herb-rubbed cheese.

GRILL TOOLS AND EQUIPMENT
- Grill screen or tray (optional)
- Long-handled tongs

GETTING CREATIVE
- To save time, use store-bought herbed goat cheese in place of the goat cheese rolled in Provençal Herb Rub.
- If you can't find a hockey puck–sized piece of goat cheese, unwrap your goat cheese and lay it on fresh plastic wrap. Let it come to room temperature and then wrap it loosely and reshape it into a disk about 3 1/2 inches in diameter and 1 1/2 inches thick, like a hockey puck. Coat with the herb rub and chill well before grilling.
- If you like, rub the baguette slices with the cut sides of halved garlic cloves before coating with oil and grilling.
- Fresh grape leaves make a nice garnish for the platter.

THE GRILL

Gas: Direct heat, medium-high (400° to 450°F)
Clean, oiled grate

Charcoal: Direct heat, light ash
12-by-12-inch charcoal bed (about 3 dozen coals)
Clean, oiled grate on lowest setting

Wood: Direct heat, light ash
12-by-12-inch bed, 3 to 4 inches deep
Clean, oiled grate set 2 inches above the fire

INGREDIENTS (MAKES 8 SERVINGS)

1 thick round of firm goat cheese, about 3 1/2 inches in diameter and 1 1/2 inches thick (roughly 8 ounces), chilled
2 tablespoons Provençal Herb Rub (page 373)
3 tablespoons olive oil, preferably in a spray bottle

1 baguette, cut into 1/4- to 1/2-inch-thick slices (16 to 20 pieces)
Oil for coating grill grate
16 to 20 seedless red or green grapes (one for each bread slice; 4 to 6 ounces)

DIRECTIONS

1. Put the goat cheese on a piece of plastic wrap and coat all over with the herb rub, patting it in with your fingers. Wrap and chill until cold and firm, about 15 minutes.

2. Heat the grill as directed.

3. Spray or brush about 2 tablespoons of the olive oil on the bread slices. Spray or drizzle the remaining olive oil all over the herb-rubbed cheese.

4. Brush the grill grate and coat it with oil. Put the grapes directly on the grill grate and cook until grill-marked and just beginning to split or pop, 2 to 3 minutes, turning once. If your grapes may fall through the grill grate, grill them on a heated, oiled grill screen or tray. Remove the popped grapes and arrange on a platter.

5. Meanwhile, grill the bread until toasted, 1 to 2 minutes per side. Remove and arrange on the platter.

6. Put the oil-coated herb-rubbed cheese directly on the grill grate. Cook until lightly grill-marked, 1 to 2 minutes per side, turning once with tongs. The cheese should begin to melt on the grilled sides yet be rather firm in the center. Remove with tongs to the center of the platter (avoid using a spatula, as it will smear the melting cheese).

7. Allow guests to scoop some warm goat cheese onto each baguette slice and top with a popped grape.

CHAPTER 11

MASTERING MARINADES, MOPS, BRINES, RUBS, WET PASTES, GLAZES, SAUCES, AND DIPS

RECIPES

General Marinating Tips

- The amount of time needed for marinating is approximate and can be adjusted to fit your schedule; 30 minutes to an hour more will not be disastrous, but marinating for too long will cause the flesh to break down and absorb too much of the flavor of the brine. If that should occur, wash the marinated food in several changes of cold water and pat it dry before grilling.
- If the meat is done marinating but you are not ready to cook it, remove it from the marinade, wipe off any excess, and store it, tightly wrapped, in the refrigerator for up to 24 hours.
- Part of a marinade can be set aside and mopped on the grilled item as it cooks, to keep it moist and increase the infusion of flavor.

GARLIC-BUTTERMILK MARINADE

Buttermilk works magic in a marinade. It not only delivers the needed acid to tenderize tough fibers, but it relaxes the structure of proteins, allowing them to absorb flavors more readily. And unlike harsh vinegars and citrus juices, low-fat buttermilk contains just enough fat to help prevent meats from dehydrating.

TIMING
Prep: 5 minutes

GETTING CREATIVE
- For a thicker, clingier, more sour marinade, substitute yogurt for the buttermilk.
- For a different flavor profile, substitute mint, basil, or a Greek spice blend for the dill.
- Turn this recipe into a buttermilk ranch marinade by adding 1 tablespoon onion powder and 2 additional cloves of garlic, minced.

KNOW YOUR INGRDIENTS
Buttermilk is made from fat-free or low-fat milk to which a bacterial culture is added. The bacteria feed off of the natural sugars in the milk and produce lactic acid as a by-product of their metabolism. As the acid builds up in the milk, it begins to coagulate the milk protein, causing the milk to thicken. Some brands of buttermilk are thicker than others, but this thickness usually comes from additions of starches and gums, rather than an increase in acid. When the acidity in the milk reaches about 4.5 pH, the fermentation is stopped. In most commercial buttermilk, the bacteria are then made inactive, but some regional brands are sold with active cultures in them. Active-culture buttermilk will increase in acidity as it ages and therefore can be a bit stronger in a marinade. Unlike other acids used in marination, buttermilk contains proteins and a small amount of fat, which tend to protect meat from dehydrating on its surface as it marinates.

MARINATING TIME | GOOD WITH

Marinating **small seafood** and **thin fish:** 30 minutes
Marinating **thick fish** and **boneless poultry:** 1 hour
Marinating **bone-in poultry, chops,** and **steaks:** 2 to 3 hours
Marinating **roasts:** 3 to 8 hours (depending on size)

Seafood: shrimp, scallops, salmon, any white-fleshed fish
Poultry: chicken, turkey, game hen
Meat: lamb, pork, veal

INGREDIENTS (MAKES ABOUT 1 CUP)

2 cloves garlic, minced
3/4 cup low-fat buttermilk
1 tablespoon olive oil
1 tablespoon chopped fresh dill, or 1 teaspoon dried

Pinch crushed red pepper flakes
2 teaspoons kosher salt
1 teaspoon ground black pepper, or to taste

DIRECTIONS

1. Combine the ingredients in a gallon-size zipper-lock bag; seal and shake.
2. Put the bag in a bowl just large enough to hold it snugly. Open the bag and add the meat. Seal the zipper, leaving about an inch open; push on the bag to release any trapped air through the opening, and close the zipper completely. Massage the liquid gently into the meat, and refrigerate for the suggested marinating time.

HORSERADISH VODKA INFUSION

This marinade is inspired by horseradish aquavit, the killer schnapps that Marcus Samuelson serves at his landmark Scandinavian restaurant. All we've done is substituted vodka for aquavit and added salt and citrus to help the marinade permeate the meat more effectively. The vodka delivers a pure, flavorless base that intensifies the other flavors in the marinade. It's especially good with seafood.

MARINATING TIME

Marinating **small seafood** and **thin fish**: 30 minutes
Marinating **thick fish** and **boneless poultry**: 1 hour
Marinating **bone-in poultry, chops,** and **steaks**: 2 to 3 hours
Marinating **roasts**: 3 to 8 hours (depending on size)

GOOD WITH

Seafood: shrimp, scallops, soft-shell crabs, any fish
Poultry: chicken, turkey, game hen, duck, goose
Meat: beef, lamb, pork, veal

INGREDIENTS (MAKES ABOUT 1 CUP)

1 lemon
3 tablespoons grated horseradish, purchased or fresh
1 cup vodka

1 fresh jalapeño chile, stem removed, chopped
2 tablespoons kosher salt
1 medium onion, thinly sliced

DIRECTIONS

1. Grate the zest from the lemon with a fine grater. Trim the white pith from the fruit, and slice the lemon into thin rounds.
2. Combine the lemon zest, lemon slices, and remaining ingredients in a gallon-size zipper-lock bag; seal and shake.

3. Put the bag in a bowl just large enough to hold it snugly. Open the bag and add the meat. Seal the zipper, leaving about an inch open; push on the bag to release any trapped air through the opening, and close the zipper completely. Massage the liquid gently into the meat and refrigerate for the suggested marinating time.

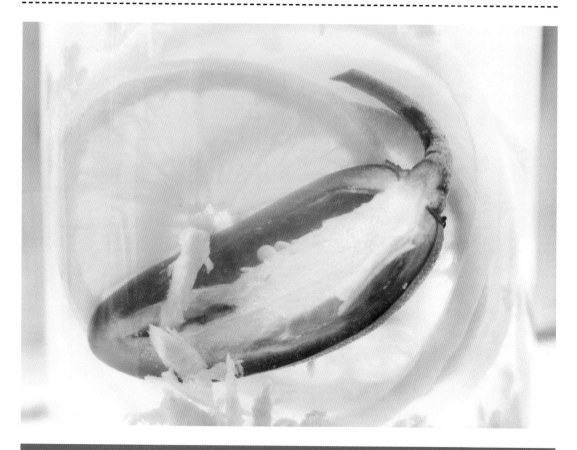

TIMING
Prep: 5 minutes

TIP
· You can substitute hot pepper vodka for the vodka and omit the jalapeño.

GETTING CREATIVE
· Replacing the lemon with a small grapefruit or a lime will give you a completely different flavor.
· For Wasabi Vodka Infusion, replace the horseradish with prepared wasabi paste (sold in a tube), and replace the jalapeño with a Japanese red pepper (togorashi), which is similar to cayenne pepper. Add a tablespoon of minced peeled gingerroot.
· For a spicier marinade, add a chopped habanero or Scotch bonnet chile; do not omit the jalapeño.

KNOW YOUR INGREDIENTS
Horseradish, *Armoracia rusticana,* is native to eastern Europe and western Asia. It is related to the mustard family, which is obvious the minute you encounter its biting flavor and aroma. Its volatile, mustardlike oil deteriorates rapidly once the horseradish is cut or grated and exposed to air, and heat processing reduces both its aroma and pungency, which is why freshly grated horseradish is much stronger than prepared horseradish from a jar. Fresh horseradish root is available year round in most markets, but it is most abundant from late fall into early spring. The roots are usually sold in 2-inch-long sections (although the whole root can range up to 20 inches), measuring 1 to 2 inches in diameter. Choose roots that are very hard and are free of spongy spots. Over-the-hill horseradish roots will look shriveled and dry. Bottled prepared horseradish is readily available in the refrigerated condiment section of grocery stores. Prepared horseradish is preserved in vinegar and salt.

Photo: Horseradish Vodka Infusion

MIGNONETTE MARINADE AND MOP

TIMING

Prep: 5 minutes (plus cooling time)

GETTING CREATIVE

· Make a red wine mignonette to use with beef or lamb by substituting red wine for white and red wine vinegar for white wine vinegar.

· Adjust the pepper flavor by substituting different types of peppercorns and/or chile peppers for the black pepper.

· Add a tablespoon or two of lemon or lime juice if using this marinade with seafood.

TIP

· For better pepper flavor, crack whole peppercorns right before you use the marinade. This can be done with a mallet, a mortar and pestle, or (Andy's favorite) a small iron skillet. *Thwack!*

Mignonette is French for a cracked peppercorn, and the flavor of freshly bruised pepper is the raison d'être of this marinade, which is delicious with seafood, chicken, and light meats. It can also be used as a dip or table sauce.

MARINATING TIME	GOOD WITH
Marinating **small seafood** and **thin fish:** 30 minutes	**Seafood:** shrimp, scallops, any fish
Marinating **thick fish** and **boneless poultry:** 1 hour	**Poultry:** chicken, turkey, game hen, duck
Marinating **bone-in poultry, chops,** and **steaks:** 2 to 3 hours	**Meat:** pork, veal
Marinating **roasts:** 3 to 8 hours (depending on size)	

INGREDIENTS (MAKES ABOUT 1 1/2 CUPS)

1 cup white wine	1 teaspoon kosher salt
1 cup diced onion	1/3 cup white wine vinegar
1 tablespoon cracked black pepper	1 tablespoon chopped fresh flat-leaf parsley
1/4 teaspoon crushed red pepper flakes	

DIRECTIONS

1. Cook the white wine and onion in a medium skillet over medium-high heat until the liquid is reduced to 1/4 cup. Remove from the heat and cool.

2. Combine the cooled onion-wine mixture and the remaining ingredients in a gallon-size zipper-lock bag; seal and shake.

3. Put the bag in a bowl just large enough to hold it snugly. Open the bag and add the meat. Seal the zipper, leaving about an inch open; push on the bag to release any trapped air through the opening, and close the zipper completely. Massage the liquid gently into the meat and refrigerate for the suggested time.

SAFFRON-CITRUS MARINADE

TIMING

Prep: 5 minutes (plus cooling time)

This crystalline liquid glows gold and has a subtle aroma of citrus blossoms. Reserve this marinade for delicate meats, and especially for seafood. If you don't want to spring for the cost of saffron, we'd suggest you move on to another marinade. Someone might say that you can substitute turmeric and get the same effect, but the flavor is completely different, the clarity will be lost, and the turmeric's yellow is closer to mustard than gold.

MARINATING TIME	GOOD WITH
Marinating **small seafood** and **thin fish:** 30 minutes	**Seafood:** shrimp, scallops, salmon, tuna, any white-fleshed fish
Marinating **thick fish** and **boneless poultry:** 1 hour	**Poultry:** chicken, turkey, game hen
Marinating **bone-in poultry, chops,** and **steaks:** 2 to 3 hours	**Meat:** pork, veal
Marinating **roasts:** 3 to 8 hours (depending on size)	

INGREDIENTS (MAKES ABOUT 1 CUP)

1/4 teaspoon saffron threads

1/4 cup vodka

1/4 cup extra-virgin olive oil

1 medium onion, sliced into thin rings

Juice and finely grated zest of 1 lemon

Juice and finely grated zest of 1/2 lime

Juice and finely grated zest of 1/2 orange

1 teaspoon dried basil

1 tablespoon kosher salt

DIRECTIONS

1. Combine the saffron and vodka and set aside.

2. Heat the olive oil in a saucepan over medium heat. Add the onions and sauté for 5 minutes, until tender; let cool.

3. Combine the saffron mixture, cooled onion, citrus juices and zests, basil, and salt in a gallon-size zipper-lock bag; seal and shake.

4. Put the bag in a bowl just large enough to hold it snugly. Open the bag and add the meat. Seal the zipper, leaving about an inch open; push on the bag to release any trapped air through the opening, and close the zipper completely. Massage the liquid gently into the meat and refrigerate for the suggested time.

GETTING CREATIVE

· Try substituting tarragon or dill for the basil.

· The total amount of juice in the marinade is about 1/3 cup. The balance of citrus juices can be altered to fit what you have on hand or to change the flavor profile of the marinade; more lemon or lime juice will make the marinade stronger and more piquant; increasing the proportion of orange juice will make the marinade sweeter and milder.

CITRUS ZEST

The skin of oranges, lemons, limes, and grapefruit is composed of two layers. The outer colorful epidermis (called the zest) is filled with thousands of aromatic oil glands that each hold a small amount of citrus oil. The thicker white, spongy underlayer contains bitter phenols that need to be removed before the skin is palatable. There are many methods of leaching the phenols from the skin, but the easiest way is to separate the zest from the underlayer with a vegetable peeler, a fine grater, or a specialized kitchen gadget called a zester that peels the epidermis from the fruit in thread-thin strips. However you do it, make sure not to dig too deep. If any of the underlayer is attached to the zest, the results will be bitter rather than aromatic. When a recipe calls for both citrus juice and zest, remove the zest first. It is virtually impossible to grate the zest from a squeezed lemon.

Photo: Saffron-Citrus Marinade

GRILL TOOLS & EQUIPMENT
· Long-handled tongs

GETTING CREATIVE
· Vary the amount of the chiles for different effects: Use more chipotle for intense smoke, more habanero for more heat, or all ancho for mild sweetness.
· Vary the beer depending on what you are cooking (see the "Beer Primer" below).

TIP
· If you don't have molasses, brown sugar will give similar results.

BEER PRIMER
There are two major categories of beer, lagers and ales, which account for most of the beer you will encounter, except for the dozens of idiosyncratic boutique beers that don't fit into either category. You can choose the beer you want to drink by your personal taste, but you should choose the beer you grill with as you would any ingredient—by its intrinsic flavors. Here's an overview to get you started.

All beers get their flavor and consistency from three primary ingredients:

Malted barley Malting is a process of sprouting barley so that it develops the sugars and soluble starches needed for fermentation, and then drying and mashing it to extract the sugars and starches from the grain. Roasted malt is used to produce dark beers.

Hops Not all of the sugar in barley ferments during malting, which causes beer that is made completely from barley to be decidedly sweet. Hops (1-inch-long green cone-shaped flowers) are added to beer to balance the sweetness. Mature hops contain bitter-tasting lupulin, which counteracts sweetness, gives beer a "hoppy" aroma, and acts as mild sedative.

Yeast Yeast is a living organism that feeds off of the sugars in the malt, converting them to alcohol and carbon dioxide in a process called fermentation. The yeast also affects the taste and mouth-feel of beer.

How these ingredients are combined with water to produce beer yields brews with different characteristics, which are described in the chart on the facing page.

FIRE BEER MARINADE

The yeasty, bittersweet, slightly acidic character of beer makes it a natural base for a marinade. We have inundated it with mild, sweet ancho chile (dried poblano); a spicy, smoky chipotle chile (smoked jalapeño); and the hottest chile of all, a habanero. Starting with a whole ancho pepper and toasting it on the spot, rather than starting with ground ancho chile, makes a huge difference in flavor. Because the chipotle is already smoked, it doesn't benefit from toasting.

MARINATING TIME

Marinating **small seafood** and **thin fish**: 30 minutes
Marinating **thick fish** and **boneless poultry**: 1 hour
Marinating **bone-in poultry, chops,** and **steaks**: 2 to 3 hours
Marinating **roasts**: 3 to 8 hours (depending on size)

GOOD WITH

Seafood: shrimp, any dark-fleshed fish
Poultry: chicken, turkey, duck, goose
Meat: lamb, beef, pork

INGREDIENTS (MAKES ABOUT 1 3/4 CUPS)

1 dried ancho chile, or 2 tablespoons ground ancho chile
1 dried chipotle pepper, stem and seeds removed (keep the seeds if you like it hot), chopped, or 2 teaspoons ground chipotle chile
1 habanero chile, stem and seeds removed (keep the seeds if you like it hot), chopped

1 can (12 ounces) beer
1 cup diced onion
2 tablespoons molasses
1 tablespoon kosher salt
1/4 cup aged balsamic vinegar
1/4 cup apple cider vinegar

DIRECTIONS

1. To toast the ancho chile, hold it with long-handled tongs directly over the open flame of a stove top, or on the grill using direct high heat. Turning it once or twice to ensure even cooking, toast it until the chile gets pliable and puffs slightly. Let cool until comfortable to touch. Remove the stem and tear into small pieces. If using ground ancho chile, skip this step.
2. Combine the ancho chile and the remaining ingredients in a saucepan; cover and bring to a boil. Reduce the heat and sim-

mer for 5 minutes; cool to room temperature. Strain out the onions and chiles.
3. Put an open gallon-size zipper-lock bag in a bowl just large enough to hold it snugly. Add the cooled liquid and the meat. Seal the zipper, leaving about an inch open; push on the bag to release any trapped air through the opening, and close the zipper completely. Massage the liquid gently into the meat and refrigerate for the suggested time.

Category	Style	Description	Statistics*	Good with
Lager	Pilsner	Light colored, sweet caramel flavors, medium to high bitterness, hoppy aroma, high carbonation, clean, crisp	IBU: 35–45 ABV: 4.0–5.0 FG: 1.014–1.020 SRM: 3–5	Seafood, chicken, pork
Lager	American lager	Pilsner-type beer with sugars added, sweet, less hoppy, watery, clean, crisp	IBU: 5–17 ABV: 3.5–4.5 FG: 1.006–1.010 SRM: 2–4	Fish, chicken
Lager	Bock	Hearty, pronounced malt flavor, light hops, heavy mouth-feel	IBU: 35–45 ABV: 4.0–5.0 FG: 1.018–1.024 SRM: 3–5	Pork, lamb, beef, sausage
Lager	Marzen	Amber, heavy mouth-feel, malty sweet, low to medium bitterness, high alcohol	IBU: 18–25 ABV: 5.0–6.0 FG: 1.012–1.020 SRM: 15–35	Shellfish, oily fish, pork, lamb, beef
Lager	Helles	Pale color, low alcohol, low hop flavor and aroma, clean	IBU: 18–25 ABV: 4.0–5.0 FG: 1.008–1.012 SRM: 3–5	Fish, chicken, pork
Ale	English bitter	Three styles—ordinary, special, and extra special: range from pale through medium gold to dark copper color, low carbonation, medium to strong bitterness, low to high hop flavor, light to full body	IBU: 20–65 ABV: 3.0–6.2 FG: 1.008–2.000 SRM: 6–14	Shellfish, veal, dark-meat poultry, beef, lamb, sausage
Ale	Pale ale	Very little malted sweetness, high hoppy bitterness, pale to amber color, light to medium body, high alcohol	IBU: 40–60 ABV: 5.0–7.6 FG: 1.012–1.018 SRM: 8–14	Shellfish, veal, dark-meat poultry, beef, lamb, sausage
Ale	Scottish ale	Dark, malty sweet, mild bitterness, light to medium body, high alcohol, can have smoky character	IBU: 12–20 ABV: 5.0–7.6 FG: 1.010–1.014 SRM: 10–18	Dark-meat poultry, beef, lamb, game, sausage
Ale	Porter	Very dark, sweet malt balanced by hops, medium body	IBU: 25–40 ABV: 4.5–6.0 FG: 1.008–1.016 SRM: 30+	Dark-meat poultry, beef, lamb, game, sausage
Ale	Stout	Almost black, strong malt sweetness and hoppy bitterness, medium body, high alcohol	IBU: 50–80 ABV: 7.0–9.0 FG: 1.020–1.030 SRM: 40+	Dark-meat poultry, beef, lamb, game, sausage

* IBU = International Bittering Units; ABV = alcohol percentage by volume; FG = finished gravity (body); SRM = Standard Reference Method (color intensity)

SICILIAN HERB BATH

TIMING
Prep: 5 minutes

MAKING SUBSTITUTIONS

- Make the marinade spicy by adding a pinch of crushed red pepper flakes or substituting a tablespoon of hot pepper oil for a tablespoon of the olive oil.
- If you really don't like anchovies, you can substitute a few chopped-up dried wild mushrooms, but we'd suggest giving the anchovies a try.
- You can substitute a tablespoon of anchovy paste for the anchovies.

The key to this all-purpose Italianesque marinade isn't the extra-virgin olive oil, wine vinegar, oregano, or tomato—it's the anchovies. If you don't like them, you've probably taken too big a bite. Anchovies are fermented, like stinky cheese and pungent fish sauce. No one wants a mouthful, but taken in slivers, as seasoning rather than the main attraction, anchovies add a depth of flavor that a list of a dozen "fresh" ingredients couldn't duplicate.

MARINATING TIME

Marinating **small seafood** and **thin fish**: 30 minutes

Marinating **thick fish** and **boneless poultry**: 1 hour

Marinating **bone-in poultry, chops,** and **steaks**: 2 to 3 hours

Marinating **roasts**: 3 to 8 hours (depending on size)

GOOD WITH

Seafood: shrimp, scallops, salmon, tuna, or any oily fish

Poultry: chicken, turkey, duck, goose, squab, game hen

Meat: beef, lamb, veal

INGREDIENTS (MAKES ABOUT 1 1/4 CUPS)

1/3 cup extra-virgin olive oil

2 tablespoons crushed tomato, or 1 tablespoon tomato paste

1/4 cup red wine

1/4 cup red wine vinegar

1 clove garlic, minced

1 teaspoon dried oregano

1/2 cup fresh basil leaves, torn into pieces

4 canned anchovy fillets, mashed with a fork

1 teaspoon kosher salt

DIRECTIONS

1. Combine the ingredients in a gallon-size zipper-lock bag; seal and shake.

2. Put the bag in a bowl just large enough to hold it snugly. Open the bag and add the meat. Seal the zipper, leaving about

an inch open; push on the bag to release any trapped air through the opening, and close the zipper completely. Massage the liquid gently into the meat and refrigerate for the suggested time.

ADOBO MARINADES: SPANISH, MEXICAN, AND FILIPINO

TIMING
Prep: 5 minutes

Adobo is a pungent marinade in Spain, a hearty chile-laden stew in Mexico, and a pickled dish of chicken, pork, and/or fish in the Philippines. The Spanish version is the original one, and there are many variations on the theme. What they all have in common is paprika, preferably *pimentón* (the smoked paprika of Andalucia), and lots of olive oil. The main recipe here is a Spanish *adobo* marinade; ours adds sweetness and pungency with some orange juice, vinegar, red wine, and green olives. We also offer Mexican and Filipino variations.

MARINATING TIME

Marinating **small seafood** and **thin fish**: 30 minutes

Marinating **thick fish** and **boneless poultry**: 1 hour

Marinating **bone-in poultry, chops,** and **steaks**: 2 to 3 hours

Marinating **roasts**: 3 to 8 hours (depending on size)

GOOD WITH

Seafood: shrimp, scallops, salmon, any white-fleshed fish

Poultry: chicken, turkey, game hen

Meat: lamb, pork, veal

Spanish Adobo Marinade

2 cloves garlic, minced

2 tablespoons tomato sauce

1/4 cup orange juice

1/4 cup red wine

1/4 cup red wine vinegar

1/4 cup chopped green olives (about 6 large olives)

2 teaspoons paprika, preferably pimentón (smoked paprika)

1 tablespoon extra-virgin olive oil

1 teaspoon kosher salt

Mexican Adobo Marinade

1/4 cup Spanish-style tomato sauce

1/4 cup tequila

1/4 cup stemmed, seeded, and chopped chiles
  (fresh jalapeño or poblano, or rehydrated guajillo or ancho)

1 tablespoon cider vinegar

2 tablespoons finely chopped onion

1 tablespoon chopped fresh cilantro leaves

1 teaspoon ground cumin

1/4 teaspoon ground cinnamon

1 teaspoon kosher salt

Filipino Adobo Marinade

1/4 cup cider vinegar

1/4 cup red wine

1/4 cup water

1 tablespoon minced garlic

1 teaspoon kosher salt

1 teaspoon ground black pepper

2 bay leaves

2 tablespoons brown sugar, light or dark

1 teaspoon hot pepper sauce

2 tablespoons soy sauce

2 tablespoons brown sugar

DIRECTIONS

1. Combine the ingredients in a zipper-lock bag; seal and shake

2. Put the bag in a bowl just large enough to hold it snugly. Open the bag and add the meat. Seal the zipper, leaving about an inch open; push on the bag to release any trapped air through the opening, and close the zipper completely. Massage the liquid gently into the meat and refrigerate for the suggested time.

ADOBO VARIATIONS

In Mexico, adobo is a stew made with meat, vegetables, and chiles. This thicker adobo marinade gives you the flavor of Mexican adobo. Use it in the same way you would use the basic adobo marinade.

Photo: Spanish Adobo Marinade

GETTING CREATIVE
· To make a Middle Eastern–style marinade, replace the olive oil with $1/4$ cup plain yogurt, and substitute $1/4$ teaspoon ground coriander and $1/4$ teaspoon ground cumin for the green olives.

SHORTCUT
· Use 1 tablespoon purchased green olive tapenade in place of the chopped olives.

LEMON-MINT MARINADE

Lemon and mint should be a standard flavor combo in every cook's arsenal. Citric acid brightens the flavors of anything it touches, and the menthol in the mint delivers a cooling afterglow that refreshes the palate, enticing another bite, and another, and another . . .

MARINATING TIME	GOOD WITH
Marinating **small seafood** and **thin fish:** 30 minutes	**Seafood:** shrimp, scallops, soft-shell crabs, any fish
Marinating **thick fish** and **boneless poultry:** 1 hour	**Poultry:** chicken, turkey, game hen
Marinating **bone-in poultry, chops,** and **steaks:** 2 to 3 hours	**Meat:** lamb, pork, veal
Marinating **roasts:** 3 to 8 hours (depending on size)	

INGREDIENTS (MAKES ABOUT 1 CUP)

$2/3$ cup fresh lemon juice

1 tablespoon olive oil

1 tablespoon chopped green olives (about 3 olives)

$1/4$ cup chopped fresh mint leaves

2 teaspoons kosher salt

$1/2$ teaspoon cracked black pepper

Photo: Lemon-Mint Marinade

DIRECTIONS

1. Combine the ingredients in a gallon-size zipper-lock bag; seal and shake.

2. Put the bag in a bowl just large enough to hold it snugly. Open the bag and add the meat. Seal the zipper, leaving about an inch open; push on the bag to release any trapped air through the opening, and close the zipper completely. Massage the liquid gently into the meat and refrigerate for the suggested time.

GRAPEFRUIT PONZU MARINADE OR MOP

TIMING
Prep: 5 minutes

Ponzu is a Japanese mainstay that is served with light, clean foods, like sashimi. Traditional *ponzu* is a mixture of soy sauce, lemon juice, and mirin (sweet rice wine); this variation is a little brighter (from the grapefruit) and a little stronger (from the vodka). It is a perfect marinade for seafood of any type, or for white meats.

MARINATING TIME

Marinating **small seafood** and **thin fish:** 30 minutes
Marinating **thick fish** and **boneless poultry:** 1 hour
Marinating **bone-in poultry, chops,** and **steaks:** 2 to 3 hours
Marinating **roasts:** 3 to 8 hours (depending on size)

GOOD WITH

Seafood: shrimp, scallops, any fish
Poultry: chicken, turkey, game hen
Meat: lean pork, veal

GETTING CREATIVE
Use this recipe as a template for a wide variety of ponzu sauces:

· Substitute lemon or lime juice for the grapefruit juice.
· Use other tart juices, such as cranberry or pomegranate juice; these are especially good when pairing the marinade with poultry or meat.
· Traditional Japanese ponzu sauce is often flavored with seaweed. This requires cooking, but you can streamline the process by adding a teaspoon of kelp granules, which are available in Asian and health-conscious food stores.
· For a richer marinade, add 1 tablespoon miso paste.

INGREDIENTS (MAKES ABOUT 1 1/4 CUPS)

3/4 cup grapefruit juice
2 tablespoons soy sauce
1/4 cup sake or vodka

1 tablespoon minced pickled sushi ginger
2 teaspoons kosher salt

DIRECTIONS

1. Combine the ingredients in a gallon-size zipper-lock bag; seal and shake.

2. Put the bag in a bowl just large enough to hold it snugly. Open the bag and add the meat. Seal the zipper, leaving about an inch open; push on the bag to release any trapped air through the opening, and close the zipper completely. Massage the liquid gently into the meat and refrigerate for the suggested time.

PAPAYA MARINADE

TIMING
Prep: 5 minutes

Papaya is the source of papain, a protein-cleaving enzyme that is the main ingredient in many commercial meat tenderizers, which makes this tropical fruit the perfect base for a meat marinade. Not only does it tenderize tough fibers, but by unraveling the protein bonds it encourages absorption of other flavors from the marinade into the meat. See the next page for more information on natural meat tenderizers.

MARINATING TIME

Marinating **small seafood** and **thin fish:** 30 minutes
Marinating **thick fish** and **boneless poultry:** 1 hour
Marinating **bone-in poultry, chops,** and **steaks:** 2 to 3 hours
Marinating **roasts:** 3 to 8 hours (depending on size)

GOOD WITH

Seafood: shrimp, scallops, salmon, any fish
Poultry: chicken, turkey, game hen, duck
Meat: beef, pork, veal, lamb

MAKING SUBSTITUTIONS
· Papaya is not the only tropical fruit that contains a natural meat tenderizer. There are enzymes in pineapple that also soften meat fibers. You can replace pineapple juice for the papaya to very similar effect.

TIMING
Prep: 5 minutes

GETTING CREATIVE
· For the brilliant red hue sometimes seen on tandoori chicken, add ¼ teaspoon red food coloring to the marinade.

MAKING SUBSTITUTIONS
· For a less viscous marinade, replace the yogurt with buttermilk or kefir.

INGREDIENTS (MAKES ABOUT 2 CUPS)

1 ½ cups (12-ounce can) papaya juice

Juice of 1 lemon (about ¼ cup)

1 clove garlic, minced

1 tablespoon white wine vinegar

2 teaspoons sriracha hot pepper sauce or other hot pepper sauce

2 tablespoons Thai fish sauce, preferably Tiparos

¼ teaspoon crushed red pepper flakes

½ cup finely chopped red onion

⅓ cup coarsely chopped fresh basil leaves

1 tablespoon kosher salt

DIRECTIONS

1. Combine the ingredients in a gallon-size zipper-lock bag; seal and shake.

2. Put the bag in a bowl just large enough to hold it snugly. Open the bag and add the meat. Seal the zipper, leaving about an inch open; push on the bag to release any trapped air through the opening, and close the zipper completely. Massage the liquid gently into the meat and refrigerate for the suggested time.

TANDOORI YOGURT MARINADE

Tandoori is the name for foods that are cooked in a tandoor, a cylindrical clay oven that is the secret behind tandoori chicken and Indian naan. The distinct flavors of food cooked in a tandoor result from oils and fats dripping from the marinated ingredients onto the hot charcoal lying on the floor of the oven, a phenomenon that is easily duplicated in a charcoal grill.

MARINATING TIME	GOOD WITH
Marinating **small seafood** and **thin fish:** 30 minutes	**Seafood:** shrimp, scallops, salmon, any fish
Marinating **thick fish** and **boneless poultry:** 1 hour	**Poultry:** chicken, turkey, game hen
Marinating **bone-in poultry, chops,** and **steaks:** 2 to 3 hours	**Meat:** beef, pork, lamb
Marinating **roasts:** 3 to 8 hours (depending on size)	

INGREDIENTS (MAKES ABOUT 1 CUP)

¾ cup (6 ounces) plain yogurt

2 tablespoons fresh lemon juice

1 tablespoon minced peeled gingerroot

1 tablespoon minced garlic

2 teaspoons ground coriander

1 teaspoon ground cumin

2 teaspoons garam masala

½ teaspoon crushed red pepper flakes

½ teaspoon ground turmeric

1 tablespoon ground paprika

1½ teaspoons kosher salt

½ teaspoon ground black pepper

DIRECTIONS

1. Mix the ingredients in a bowl until blended.

2. Add the ingredients to be marinated, toss to coat, and cover. Refrigerate for the suggested time.

MOJITO MARINADE OR MOP

A mojito is a marinade waiting to happen. It's got acid (lime juice and rum), sweetness (sugar and rum), and aromatics (mint, lime zest, rum). All that's needed is a little salt. This marinade is the essence of summer (there's something about the combination of fresh lime, fresh mint, and tropical rum); it also makes a good basting sauce.

MARINATING TIME

Marinating **small seafood** and **thin fish:** 30 minutes
Marinating **thick fish** and **boneless poultry:** 1 hour
Marinating **bone-in poultry, chops,** and **steaks:** 2 to 3 hours
Marinating **roasts:** 3 to 8 hours (depending on size)

GOOD WITH

Seafood: shrimp, scallops, any fish
Poultry: chicken, turkey, game hen
Meat: pork, veal

INGREDIENTS (MAKES ABOUT 1 CUP)

$1/4$ cup chopped fresh mint leaves
$1/4$ cup white rum
2 tablespoons kosher salt

Finely chopped zest of 1 lime
Juice of 2 limes (about $1/2$ cup)
$1/3$ cup sugar

DIRECTIONS

1. Combine the ingredients in a gallon-size zipper-lock bag; seal and shake until the salt and sugar dissolve, about 30 seconds.
2. Put the bag in a bowl just large enough to hold it snugly. Open the bag and add the meat. Seal the zipper, leaving about an inch open; push on the bag to release any trapped air through the opening, and close the zipper completely. Massage the liquid gently into the meat and refrigerate for the suggested time.

TIMING
Prep: 5 minutes

GETTING CREATIVE
· Add different herbs in addition to, or in place of, the mint. We have tried cilantro, basil, and/or tarragon with great success.
· This is not a spicy marinade, but it can handle a bit of heat if you want. We suggest a habanero, for its clean, crisp quality.
· If you want more perfume, replace the sugar with honey or add a little vanilla extract.

DR PEPPER'S MAGIC ELIXIR

The magic of this mixture is that it is both a marinade and a barbecue sauce. Folks have been using soda pop in barbecue sauce for as long as anyone can remember, and Dr Pepper was likely one of the first to generate experimentation. Its fruity base is ripe for spicing. This one embellishes the doctor with a head of caramelized garlic, a hefty shake of Tabasco, a tart hit of tamarind, a dose of salt, and the piney aroma of fresh rosemary.

MARINATING TIME

Marinating **small seafood** and **thin fish:** 30 minutes
Marinating **thick fish** and **boneless poultry:** 1 hour
Marinating **bone-in poultry, chops,** and **steaks:** 2 to 3 hours
Marinating **roasts:** 3 to 8 hours (depending on size)

GOOD WITH

Seafood: shrimp, scallops, salmon, swordfish
Poultry: chicken, turkey, game hen, duck
Meat: beef, lamb, pork

TIMING
Prep: 5 minutes
(plus 45 minutes for roasting garlic)

MAKING SUBSTITUTIONS
· If you don't have Dr Pepper, substitute any fruity, sugar-laden soft drink, such as root beer or cola.
· Orange marmalade can be used in place of the plum preserves.

For the marinade:

1 head roasted garlic (page 392)

1 teaspoon olive oil

1 tablespoon Tabasco hot pepper sauce

1 bottle (17 ounces) Dr Pepper

1 tablespoon tamarind paste

2 tablespoons kosher salt

1/4 cup plum preserves or prune paste (*lekvar*)

1 cup minced onion

2 teaspoons crushed dried or fresh rosemary leaves

For the sauce:

1/4 cup ketchup

DIRECTIONS

1. In a bowl, mash the roasted garlic cloves with a fork. Add the remaining marinade ingredients; stir to combine. Pour half (about 1 1/2 cups) into a gallon-size zipper-lock bag.

2. Put the bag in a bowl just large enough to hold it snugly. Open the bag and add the meat. Seal the zipper, leaving about an inch open; push on the bag to release any trapped air through the opening, and close the zipper completely. Massage the liquid gently into the meat and refrigerate for the suggested time.

3. To make the barbecue sauce, mix the ketchup into the reserved marinade.

BRINES

General Brining Tips

The amount of time needed for brining is approximate and can be adjusted to fit your schedule; 30 minutes to an hour more will not be disastrous, but brining for too long will cause the flesh to break down and absorb too much of the flavor of the brine. If that should occur, wash the brined food in several changes of cold water before grilling.

If the meat is done brining but you are not ready to cook it, remove it from the brine, wipe off any excess, and store it, tightly wrapped, in the refrigerator for up to 24 hours.

ORANGE-FENNEL BRINE

TIMING
Prep: 5 minutes

GETTING CREATIVE
- Replace the orange juice with pineapple juice, or add other citrus juices. A few tablespoons of lemon or lime juice will intensify the flavor of the brine.
- Change the flavor of the brine to suit your taste, substituting minced ginger, cumin seed, coriander seed, or cardamom for the fennel.
- Vary the herbs to match the flavor in your brine. Tarragon tastes great with pineapple juice; cilantro is excellent with lime.

This medium-strength brine is built to infuse seafood, poultry, and veal with the aromas and flavors of Provence. Fennel, anise, and licorice all have a similar base flavor (see "Why Do Fennel, Anise, and Licorice Taste Alike?" on facing page) and can be interchanged in this brine, although fennel seed will give you the most authentic Provençal flavor. Do not substitute fresh fennel or anise bulb for the seed; their flavor is not nearly intense enough.

BRINING TIME	GOOD WITH
Brining **small seafood** and **thin fish**: 30 minutes	**Seafood:** shrimp, scallops, salmon, any white-fleshed fish
Brining **thick fish** and **boneless poultry**: 1 hour	**Poultry:** chicken, turkey, game hen
Brining **bone-in poultry, chops,** and **steaks**: 2 to 3 hours	**Meat:** beef, lamb, veal
Brining **roasts**: 3 to 8 hours (depending on size)	

INGREDIENTS (MAKES ABOUT 2 CUPS)

2 cups orange juice

2 tablespoons sugar

3 tablespoons kosher salt

$1/2$ teaspoon coarsely ground black pepper

2 tablespoons fennel seed or anise seed

DIRECTIONS

1. Combine the ingredients in a gallon-size zipper-lock bag; seal and shake until the salt and sugar dissolve, about 30 seconds.

2. Put the bag in a bowl just large enough to hold it snugly. Open the bag and add the meat. Seal the zipper, leaving about

an inch open; push on the bag to release any trapped air through the opening, and close the zipper completely. Massage the liquid gently into the meat and refrigerate for the suggested time.

WHY DO FENNEL, ANISE, AND LICORICE TASTE ALIKE?

Fennel, anise, and licorice are not related botanically, but they do have some similarities in flavor chemistry. All but one contains the same flavor component—anethole. In addition to tasting like anise, anethole is exceptionally sweet, about 13 times sweeter than table sugar, ounce for ounce, which is why in Southeast Asia and the Middle East spices like star anise, anise seed, and fennel are chewed as breath fresheners. Anise seed has the purest anise flavor because its flavor comes solely from anethole. In star anise the anethole is modified by some floral aromas, and in fennel seed the anethole is mitigated by the presence of pine and lemon components. The flavor of licorice is similar to that of anise and fennel, but it comes from a different chemical compound, paeonol, which has a musky nuance. That is why anethole is sometimes added to licorice candy to lend a sweeter, purer anise flavor. Anethole is also part of the flavor profile of the herb sweet cicely.

Photo: Trout soaking in Orange-Fennel Brine

SPICY CITRUS BRINE

Acids and salts both have the ability to denature proteins, which is why they are used to tenderize meats and infuse them with flavor. Marinades usually depend on acids, and brines use salt, but a partnership can be helpful. By flavoring this brine with citrus juice, we have been able to cut back on the amount of salt needed without sacrificing the brine's ability to tenderize, flavor, and moisten.

BRINING TIME	GOOD WITH
Brining **small seafood** and **thin fish**: 30 minutes	**Seafood:** shrimp, scallops, salmon, any fish
Brining **thick fish** and **boneless poultry**: 1 hour	**Poultry:** chicken, turkey, game hen
Brining **bone-in poultry, chops,** and **steaks**: 2 to 3 hours	**Meat:** pork, veal
Brining **roasts**: 3 to 8 hours (depending on size)	

INGREDIENTS (MAKES ABOUT 1 1/4 CUPS)

Juice of 2 oranges (about 2/3 cup)	1 1/2 tablespoons kosher salt
Juice of 1 lemon (about 1/4 cup)	1 teaspoon dried thyme
Juice of 1 lime (about 2 tablespoons)	1 tablespoon crushed red pepper flakes

DIRECTIONS

1. Pour the juices into a 2-cup measuring cup, and add enough water to make 1 1/4 cups. Pour into a gallon-size zipper-lock bag and add the salt, thyme, and red pepper flakes; seal and shake until the salt dissolves, about 30 seconds.

2. Put the bag in a bowl just large enough to hold it snugly. Open the bag and add the meat. Seal the zipper, leaving about an inch open; push on the bag to release any trapped air through the opening, and close the zipper completely. Massage the liquid gently into the meat and refrigerate for the suggested time.

CUMIN, CORIANDER, AND LIME BRINE

GETTING CREATIVE
- This versatile brine can be made Mexican with the addition of dried or fresh chiles; Moroccan with some cinnamon and turmeric; Middle Eastern with mint and garlic; and Indian with some ginger, cardamom, and crushed red chile flakes.
- For Tequila Brine, replace the water with tequila.

THE TWO CORIANDERS

Both the leaves and dried fruit of the parsley-like herb coriander are common in world cuisines, and although they come from the same plant, they couldn't be more different in flavor or in how they are used culinarily.

The dried fruit, which is round, pale brown, and about the size of a peppercorn, has a citrusy, floral fragrance that is the base of the Indian spice blend garam masala, is a standard ingredient in pickling spices, and is one of the distinctive flavors in hot dogs.

The combination of cumin and coriander may be exotic in mainstream America, but it is one of the most common pairings in world cuisine, helping to define the flavors of North Africa, the Middle East, India, and Latin America. This brine infuses whatever it touches with a fragrant base that can be made spicy, sweet, floral, or cooling by adding a chile pepper to the mix, substituting honey for the sugar, or replacing the cilantro with freshly chopped mint.

BRINING TIME	GOOD WITH
Brining **small seafood** and **thin fish**: 30 minutes	**Seafood:** shrimp, scallops, salmon, any white-fleshed fish
Brining **thick fish** and **boneless poultry**: 1 hour	**Poultry:** chicken, turkey, game hen
Brining **bone-in poultry, chops,** and **steaks**: 2 to 3 hours	**Meat:** beef, pork
Brining **roasts**: 3 to 8 hours (depending on size)	

1 tablespoon ground cumin

1 tablespoon ground coriander

2 tablespoons kosher salt

1 teaspoon ground black pepper

1 tablespoon sugar

1 cup water

Juice of 1 lime

2 tablespoons chopped fresh cilantro leaves

DIRECTIONS

1. Combine the ingredients in a gallon-size zipper-lock bag; seal and shake until the salt and sugar dissolve, about 30 seconds.
2. Put the bag in a bowl just large enough to hold it snugly. Open the bag and add the meat. Seal the zipper, leaving about an inch open; push on the bag to release any trapped air through the opening, and close the zipper completely. Massage the liquid gently into the meat and refrigerate for the suggested time.

MARGARITA BRINE

With a bit less salt, this brine would be drinkable! With the classic margarita flavors—tequila, lime, and orange—it is perfect for poultry and quite good on pork and fish as well. Use it whenever you want to infuse meat, poultry, or fish with a Mexican flair.

BRINING TIME

Brining **small seafood** and **thin fish:** 30 minutes

Brining **thick fish** and **boneless poultry:** 1 hour

Brining **bone-in poultry, chops,** and **steaks:** 2 to 3 hours

Brining **roasts:** 3 to 8 hours (depending on size)

GOOD WITH

Seafood: shrimp, scallops, salmon, any white-fleshed fish

Poultry: chicken, turkey, game hen

Meat: beef, pork

INGREDIENTS (MAKES 1 1/3 CUPS)

1/2 cup water

1/2 cup tequila

Juice of 1 lime

2 tablespoons triple sec

2 tablespoons kosher salt

1 tablespoon sugar

1 tablespoon grated tangerine or orange zest

DIRECTIONS

1. Combine the ingredients in a gallon-size zipper-lock bag; seal and shake until the salt and sugar dissolve, about 30 seconds.
2. Put the bag in a bowl just large enough to hold it snugly. Open the bag and add the meat. Seal the zipper, leaving about an inch open; push on the bag to release any trapped air through the opening, and close the zipper completely. Massage the liquid gently into the meat and refrigerate for the suggested time.

The leaf, which is called cilantro in Hispanic markets, Chinese parsley in Asian groceries, and fresh coriander around the Mediterranean, looks like flat-leaf parsley but is paler green and has a more delicate leaf with a rounded edge. It is highly fragrant and needs very little cooking to release its flavor. If you don't like cilantro (some people think it tastes soapy), you can substitute flat-leaf parsley; the results won't taste the same, but if you don't like cilantro that could be seen as a benefit.

Coriander is only sold dried; the leaf is sold both fresh and dried, although dried coriander does not have much fragrance. Cilantro (the leaf) is also available frozen and as a paste sold in a tube. Both of these products have good flavor.

TIMING

Prep: 5 minutes

TAMARIND AND MANGO BRINE

Tamarind is the intensely tart pulp that surrounds the seeds in a tamarind pod. You can buy fresh tamarind pods in most Asian markets. Inside the reddish-brown, bulgy, smooth skin you will find several large seeds and a lot of brown-black viscous pulp. Soak the pulp in water and squeeze the fibrous mass from the seeds. Then strain off the flavored water. It is easier to buy already extracted pulp in paste form, which is sold in Asian and Caribbean markets, both frozen and in shelf-stable form.

BRINING TIME

Brining **small seafood** and **thin fish:** 30 minutes
Brining **thick fish** and **boneless poultry:** 1 hour
Brining **bone-in poultry, chops,** and **steaks:** 2 to 3 hours
Brining **roasts:** 3 to 8 hours (depending on size)

GOOD WITH

Seafood: shrimp, scallops, salmon, any white-fleshed fish
Poultry: chicken, turkey, game hen
Meat: lamb, pork, veal

INGREDIENTS (MAKES ABOUT 2 1/2 CUPS)

1 large, ripe mango (about 1 pound)
1 tablespoon tamarind paste (see headnote)
1 cup water

1 teaspoon ground dried lemon grass
3 tablespoons kosher salt
2 tablespoons sugar

DIRECTIONS

1. Light a medium-hot fire in a charcoal grill, or heat a gas grill to medium-high. Put the mango on the grill, cover, and grill for about 10 minutes, turning the mango every 3 minutes or so, until the fruit feels soft and the skin is moderately charred. Remove to a bowl; cover and set aside for 10 minutes.
2. Peel the skin from the mango with your fingers, scraping any flesh clinging to the skin into the bowl. Holding the skinned mango over the bowl, squeeze it with your hands, allowing the soft flesh to squish between your fingers (see photos on page 395). Keep squeezing and rubbing until all that is left is the pit; discard the pit.

3. Dissolve the tamarind paste in enough water to soften.
4. Combine the mango mush, tamarind mixture, and the remaining ingredients in a gallon-size zipper-lock bag; seal and shake until the salt and sugar dissolve, about 30 seconds.
5. Put the bag in a bowl just large enough to hold it snugly. Open the bag and add the meat. Seal the zipper, leaving about an inch open; push on the bag to release any trapped air through the opening, and close the zipper completely. Massage the liquid gently into the meat and refrigerate for the suggested time.

RED WINE–ROSEMARY BRINE

Here's the classic brine for tenderizing and flavoring wild game. The piney aroma of rosemary is a natural for animals that fed on forest vegetation, and the red wine complements gamy flavors well. The olive oil adds needed fat.

BRINING TIME

Brining **small seafood** and **thin fish:** 30 minutes
Brining **thick fish** and **boneless poultry:** 1 hour
Brining **bone-in poultry, chops,** and **steaks:** 2 to 3 hours
Brining **roasts:** 3 to 8 hours (depending on size)

GOOD WITH

Seafood: salmon or any other oily fish
Poultry: turkey, duck, game hen
Meat: beef, lamb, pork

TIMING
Prep: 5 minutes
Grill: 10 minutes

GRILL TOOLS AND EQUIPMENT
· Long-handled tongs

MAKING SUBSTITUTIONS
· Substitute 1 1/2 cups mango nectar or orange juice for the mango, and omit the sugar.
· Substitute 1 tablespoon each lemon juice and balsamic vinegar for the tamarind.
· Substitute finely shredded lemon zest for the lemon grass.

TIMING
Prep: 5 minutes

GETTING CREATIVE
· Vary the red wine with the meat being brined. Try a Zinfandel with oily fish or lamb, or a Burgundy (or Pinot Noir) with beef or dark-meated game.

TIP
· The flavor of shallots, onion, and leek are almost interchangeable. Feel free to substitute an equal amount of one for another.

2 cups red wine

2 tablespoons extra-virgin olive oil

2 tablespoons fresh rosemary leaves (from about 3 sprigs)

1 tablespoon chopped shallot (about 1 large shallot)

1 teaspoon cracked black pepper

4 teaspoons kosher salt

2 tablespoons balsamic vinegar

1 bay leaf, crushed

3 tablespoons sugar

DIRECTIONS

1. Combine the ingredients in a gallon-size zipper-lock bag; seal and shake until the salt and sugar dissolve, about 30 seconds.

2. Put the bag in a bowl just large enough to hold it snugly. Open the bag and add the meat. Seal the zipper, leaving about an inch open; push on the bag to release any trapped air through the opening, and close the zipper completely. Massage the liquid gently into the meat and refrigerate for the suggested time.

JAVANESE COCONUT BRINE

This amalgam of coconut, hot peppers, lemongrass, soy sauce, seaweed, and lime is pure South Sea island. It is especially good with seafood and chicken or turkey breast, where the richness of the coconut milk adds needed fat. You can substitute light coconut milk for regular, but it will have less flavor and less richness. Make sure you don't use sweetened coconut milk, also called coconut cream. See the sidebar at right to make your own coconut milk. Granulated kelp and other seaweed are sold in most health food stores.

BRINING TIME	GOOD WITH
Brining **small seafood** and **thin fish**: 30 minutes	**Seafood:** shrimp, scallops, any white-fleshed fish
Brining **thick fish** and **boneless poultry**: 1 hour	**Poultry:** chicken, turkey
Brining **bone-in poultry, chops**, and **steaks**: 2 to 3 hours	**Meat:** lamb, pork, veal
Brining **roasts**: 3 to 8 hours (depending on size)	

INGREDIENTS (MAKES ABOUT 3 CUPS)

1 can (about 14 ounces) coconut milk

2 teaspoons ground dried lemongrass

2 teaspoons sriracha hot pepper sauce or other hot pepper sauce

2 teaspoons onion powder

1 tablespoon kelp or other seaweed granules

Juice of 2 limes (about 1/4 cup)

1 tablespoon soy sauce

2 1/2 tablespoons kosher salt

1 large clove garlic, minced

2/3 cup water

DIRECTIONS

1. Combine the ingredients in a gallon-size zipper-lock bag; seal and shake until the salt dissolves, about 30 seconds.

2. Put the bag in a bowl just large enough to hold it snugly. Open the bag and add the meat. Seal the zipper, leaving about an inch open; push on the bag to release any trapped air through the opening, and close the zipper completely. Massage the liquid gently into the meat and refrigerate for the suggested time.

TIMING

Prep: 5 minutes

FRESH COCONUT MILK

It's easy to open a can of coconut milk, but making it fresh is a fun project and easy in its own right. The results are less thick but taste fresher than the canned version.

Makes about 4 cups

1 coconut, heavy for its size

1. Preheat the oven to 375°F.

2. Punch holes into 2 of the coconut's eyes with a Phillips-head screwdriver. Drain the liquid from the coconut into a bowl; drink or discard.

3. Put the coconut in the oven and bake for 20 minutes; remove and let cool. Lay the coconut on a sturdy surface and hit it with a hammer until the shell cracks into several large pieces.

4. Hold one of the pieces of coconut in your palm, protecting your hand with a folded kitchen towel. Pry the coconut meat from its shell with a flat-head screwdriver.

5. Using a vegetable peeler, peel the dark skin from the shelled coconut meat, and cut the pieces into small chunks. Grind in a food processor until the coconut meat turns into pulp. Add 1 cup very hot water and process for 30 seconds.

6. Put the mixture in a large mixing bowl and add 3 cups hot water. Massage the pulp with your hands, milking its contents into the water, until the water turns opaque, about 100 strokes. Strain out the pulp and use the milk as needed; discard the pulp.

DRIED CHILE CHARTS

Name	Color	Size	Heat (Flavor)	Where Grown	Dried Form of:
Ancho	Brick red to mahogany	5 inches long, 3 inches wide	Medium to hot (sweet/fruity)	Mexico/ Southwestern U.S.	Poblano; also known as poblano, pasilla
Arbol	Red-orange	3 inches long, 1/2 inch wide	Very hot	Mexico/ Southwestern U.S.	Cayenne
California	Burgundy	6 inches long, 2 inches wide	Medium (sweet)	California/ Southwestern U.S.	Anaheim
Cascabel	Red-brown	1 1/2 inches round	Medium-hot (fruity)	Mexico/ Southwestern U.S.	Cascabel; confused with guajillo
Chinese red	Red-brown	1 1/2 inches long, 1/4 inch wide	Hot	Worldwide	Cayenne
Chipotle	Tan-brown	2 1/2 inches long, 3/4 inch wide	Very hot (very smoky)	Americas	Jalapeño, smoked
Guajillo	Burgundy	5 inches long, 1/2 inch wide	Hot (fruity/tobacco finish)	Americas	Mirasol
Mulato	Black-red	5 inches long, 3 inches wide	Medium to hot (smoky/fruity)	Mexico/ Southwestern U.S.	Poblano; also known as poblano, ancho
New Mexico	Brick red	5 inches long, 1 inch wide	Medium (fruity, hint of tomato)	New Mexico/ Southwestern U.S.	New Mexico
Pasilla	Purple-black	5 inches long, 1 inch wide	Hot (smoky tobacco)	Americas	Pasilla (like ancho)
Pequin	Orange	1/4 inch round	Fiery (like cayenne)	Worldwide	Any small chile

FRESH CHILE CHARTS

Name	Color	Size	Heat (Flavor)	Where Grown	Uses/Substitutes:
Anaheim	Pale green	6 inches long, 2 inches wide	Mild	California/ Southwestern U.S.	Rellenos, stews
Cayenne	Bright red	6 inches long, 1/2 inch wide	Fiery	Worldwide	Hot sauce, all-purpose
Cubanelle	Yellow	5 inches long, 2 inches wide	Very mild	Eastern U.S.	Sub for anaheim; similar to pepperoncini
Fresno	Red	2 inches long, 2 inches wide	Very hot	Southwestern U.S.	Sub for jalapeño
Güero	Pale yellow	5 inches long, 2 inches wide	Mild to hot	Americas	Pickled, sauces; also known as banana pepper
Habanero	Green, yellow, orange	2 inches long, 2 inches wide	Inferno	Yucatan/Americas	Hot sauce, stews; sub for Scotch bonnet
Jalapeño	Dark green	2 inches long, 1 inch wide at shoulders	Hot	Mexico/Americas	Pickled, salsas, tacos, soups, all-purpose
New Mexico	Green to red	5 inches long, 2 inches wide	Medium to very hot	New Mexico	Roasted; sub for anaheim
Poblano	Green	5 inches long, 4 inches wide	Medium to hot	Mexico/ Southwestern U.S.	Rellenos; also known as ancho
Serrano	Green or red	2 inches long, 1 inch wide	Hot	Mexico/ Southwestern U.S.	Roasted, pickled, salsa
Scotch bonnet	Green, yellow, orange	2 inches long, 2 inches wide	Inferno	Caribbean/Americas	Hot sauce, stews; sub for habanero
Thai	Green or red	4 inches long, 3/4 inch wide	Very hot	Southeast Asia	Soups, stews; sub for serrano or jalapeño

TEN-PEPPER BRINE

TIMING
Prep: 10 minutes

GRILL TOOLS AND EQUIPMENT
· Long-handled tongs

The aroma of peppers is often overshadowed by their heat, but that's not so here. Capturing the range of peppers, from hot to sweet, dried to fresh, peppercorns to pepper fruits, balances the sharp edges of one pepper with the floral fragrance of another and rounds the whole to a radiating glow. Unlike in a peppery rub, the fragrance of pepper in a brine permeates every bite.

BRINING TIME

Brining **small seafood** and **thin fish:** 30 minutes
Brining **thick fish** and **boneless poultry:** 1 hour
Brining **bone-in poultry, chops,** and **steaks:** 2 to 3 hours
Brining **roasts:** 3 to 8 hours (depending on size)

GOOD WITH

Seafood: shrimp, scallops, salmon, any white-fleshed fish
Poultry: chicken, turkey, game hen
Meat: lamb, pork, veal

INGREDIENTS (MAKES ABOUT 2 1/4 CUPS)

1 dried ancho chile pepper
1 green bell pepper, stemmed, seeded, and coarsely chopped
1 red bell pepper, stemmed, seeded, and coarsely chopped
1 fresh or dried Scotch bonnet or habanero chile, stem and seeds removed
1 fresh serrano chile, stem and seeds removed
1 canned chipotle pepper *en adobo*

1 tablespoon cracked Szechwan pepper
1 tablespoon cracked black pepper
1 teaspoon crushed red pepper flakes
1 teaspoon Chinese chili paste with garlic
1 cup water
2 tablespoons kosher salt
1 tablespoon sugar

DIRECTIONS

1. Toast the ancho chile by holding it with long-handled tongs directly over the open flame of a stovetop, or on the grill using direct high heat. Turning it once or twice to ensure even cooking, toast it until the chile gets pliable and puffs slightly. Let cool until comfortable to touch. Remove the stem and tear into small pieces.
2. Put the toasted ancho chile, green and red bell peppers, Scotch bonnet chile, serrano chile, and chipotle chile in a food processor and pulse until roughly chopped.

3. Combine the pepper mixture, Szechwan red pepper, black pepper, pepper flakes, chili paste, water, salt, and sugar in a gallon-size zipper-lock bag; seal and shake until the salt and sugar dissolve, about 30 seconds.
4. Put the bag in a bowl just large enough to hold it snugly. Open the bag and add the meat. Seal the zipper, leaving about an inch open; push on the bag to release any trapped air through the opening, and close the zipper completely. Massage the liquid gently into the meat and refrigerate for the suggested time.

STEAKHOUSE BRINE

TIMING
Prep: 5 minutes

GETTING CREATIVE
· Add a smoky redolence to this brine by using a chipotle steak sauce, or by adding a little chipotle hot sauce.

If you like the flavor of steak sauce with grilled meat, you'll like this brine. It will infuse its essence deep into the fibers of a steak or roast.

BRINING TIME

Brining **boneless poultry:** 1 hour
Brining **bone-in poultry, chops,** and **steaks:** 2 to 3 hours
Brining **roasts:** 3 to 8 hours (depending on size)

GOOD WITH

Poultry: duck, goose, game hen
Meat: beef, lamb, pork

1 tablespoon kosher salt

2 tablespoons sugar

1/4 cup steak sauce such as A1

3 tablespoons purchased steak seasoning

1/4 cup ketchup

1 cup water

DIRECTIONS

1. Combine the ingredients in a gallon-size zipper-lock bag; seal and shake until the salt and sugar dissolve, about 30 seconds.

2. Put the bag in a bowl just large enough to hold it snugly. Open the bag and add the meat. Seal the zipper, leaving about an inch open; push on the bag to release any trapped air through the opening, and close the zipper completely. Massage the liquid gently into the meat and refrigerate for the suggested time.

TIMING
Prep: 5 minutes

HOT PEPPER–CHAI BRINE

Chai, a blend of black tea, honey, and spices, usually cardamom, ginger, cinnamon, cloves, and pepper, is served with warm milk throughout Southeast Asia. About ten years ago, chai started to be manufactured commercially in the Unites States. Now it is available in teabags and as liquid tea, instant tea, and most commonly as a tea concentrate. The concentrate is an instant flavor source, and all you have to do is add salt and water to turn it into brine. Chai has a distinctly Asian profile; pair a chai-brined chicken breast with Garam Masala Rub (page 376), Moroccan Rub (page 382), or Ginger-Hoisin Balsamic Glaze (page 388).

BRINING TIME

Brining **small seafood** and **thin fish:** 30 minutes

Brining **thick fish** and **boneless poultry:** 1 hour

Brining **bone-in poultry, chops,** and **steaks:** 2 to 3 hours

Brining **roasts:** 3 to 8 hours (depending on size)

GOOD WITH

Seafood: shrimp, scallops, any fish

Poultry: chicken, turkey, game hen, duck

Meat: beef, lamb, pork, veal

INGREDIENTS (MAKES ABOUT 1 CUP)

1/2 teaspoon ground ancho chile

1 jalapeño chile, stemmed, seeded, and finely chopped

1/2 cup chai tea concentrate such as Oregon Chai

1/2 cup plain yogurt, whole milk or low-fat

2 tablespoons kosher salt

1 teaspoon ground cinnamon

1/2 teaspoon ground allspice

1 teaspoon ground black pepper

1/2 teaspoon cayenne pepper

1 tablespoon sugar

DIRECTIONS

1. Combine the ingredients in a gallon-size zipper-lock bag; seal and shake until the salt and sugar dissolve, about 30 seconds.

2. Put the bag in a bowl just large enough to hold it snugly. Open the bag and add the meat. Seal the zipper, leaving about an inch open; push on the bag to release any trapped air through the opening, and close the zipper completely. Massage the liquid gently into the meat and refrigerate for the suggested time.

APPLE-CHAI BRINE

TIMING
Prep: 5 minutes

This simple, sweetly aromatic four-ingredient brine is a favorite for flavoring the Thanksgiving turkey. Its essence of fruit and mulled spices is the perfect counterpoint to the savory herbs of a classic stuffing. See the introduction to the right for Hot Pepper–Chai Brine (facing page) for information on the ten blend chai.

GETTING CREATIVE
- Vary the fruit with different types of cider, juice, and fruit nectar. Try apricot, pear, peach, pineapple, mango, or papaya.

BRINING TIME

Brining **small seafood** and **thin fish:** 30 minutes
Brining **thick fish** and **boneless poultry:** 1 hour
Brining **bone-in poultry, chops,** and **steaks:** 2 to 3 hours
Brining **roasts:** 3 to 8 hours (depending on size)

GOOD WITH

Seafood: shrimp, scallops, any fish
Poultry: chicken, turkey, game hen, duck, goose
Meat: beef, lamb, pork, veal

INGREDIENTS (MAKES ABOUT 2 CUPS)

1 cup apple cider
1 cup chai tea concentrate such as Oregon Chai

$1^{1}/_{2}$ tablespoons kosher salt
$^{1}/_{2}$ teaspoon cracked black pepper

DIRECTIONS

1. Combine the ingredients in a gallon-size zipper-lock bag; seal and shake until the salt dissolves, about 30 seconds.
2. Put the bag in a bowl just large enough to hold it snugly. Open the bag and add the meat. Seal the zipper, leaving about an inch open; push on the bag to release any trapped air through the opening, and close the zipper completely. Massage the liquid gently into the meat and refrigerate for the suggested time.

MOLASSES BRINE

TIMING
Prep: 5 minutes

Here's your best defense against dry grilled pork chops. Molasses, brown sugar, apple cider vinegar, and ketchup make this sweet-and-sour brine perfect for pork. But try it also with duck or other poultry. The brine itself is fairly simple, so you may want to add a dry rub or sauce to further flavor the meat.

TIPS
- Unsulfured molasses has a lighter, cleaner flavor than sulfured molasses, which is preserved with sulfur dioxide. Most supermarkets carry the unsulfured type.
- To dissolve the ingredients faster, mix them with $^{3}/_{4}$ cup hot water until dissolved, and then add the remaining 1 cup cold water to cool the mixture.

BRINING TIME

Brining **small seafood** and **thin fish:** 30 minutes
Brining **thick fish** and **boneless poultry:** 1 hour
Brining **bone-in poultry, chops,** and **steaks:** 4 to 6 hours
Brining **roasts:** 8 to 10 hours (depending on size)

GOOD WITH

Seafood: salmon or any other oily fish
Poultry: duck, chicken, turkey, game hen
Meat: pork, beef, lamb

INGREDIENTS (MAKES ABOUT 2 CUPS)

$1^{3}/_{4}$ cups water
2 tablespoons apple cider vinegar
2 tablespoons kosher salt

2 tablespoons unsulfured molasses
1 tablespoon light brown sugar
1 tablespoon ketchup

1. Combine the ingredients in a gallon-size zipper-lock bag; seal and shake until the salt and sugar dissolve, about 30 seconds.
2. Put the bag in a bowl just large enough to hold it snugly. Open the bag and add the meat. Seal the zipper, leaving about an inch open; push on the bag to release any trapped air through the opening, and close the zipper completely. Massage the liquid gently into the meat and refrigerate for the suggested time.

TIMING
Prep: 5 minutes (plus cooling time)

BROWNING—THE FLAVOR OF THE GRILL

When meat browns, complex chemical reactions take place that result in the formation of hundreds of flavorful by-products that are sweet, sour, bitter, fruity, nutty, chocolaty, savory, meaty, floral, and caramelized (to name a few). These reactions (called the Maillard reactions after Louis Maillard, a French physician who discovered and described their effects around 1910; see page 17) occur with any speed only when the temperature of meat gets above 250°F, which is why grilled meat browns only on the outside. The temperature of water can't get above 212°F at sea level. So as long as moisture is present, as is the case inside a juicy steak or roast, the meat can't get hot enough to brown. But on the outside, the moisture in the meat rapidly evaporates, raising the surface temperature well over 300°F, creating a rich, caramelized color; a dense, concentrated crust; and a complex "browned" flavor.

ESPRESSO JOLT

Espresso-roasted coffee is browned to the verge of being burnt, giving it a flavor complexity that has more kinship to charcoal than to a cup of cappuccino. When it comes to cooking meat, browning is not just a color; it is an essential part of our perception of succulence, which is why a brine built from the dark, roasted flavors of coffee beans and molasses has the surprising effect of making a roast taste meatier, rather than like dessert.

BRINING TIME	GOOD WITH
Brining **small seafood** and **thin fish**: 30 minutes	**Seafood:** salmon or any other oily fish
Brining **thick fish** and **boneless poultry**: 1 hour	**Poultry:** duck, chicken, turkey, game hen
Brining **bone-in poultry, chops,** and **steaks**: 2 to 3 hours	**Meat:** beef, lamb, pork
Brining **roasts**: 3 to 8 hours (depending on size)	

INGREDIENTS (MAKES ABOUT 3 CUPS)

1 lemon
2 cups strong coffee, preferably espresso roast
$1/2$ teaspoon crushed red pepper flakes

3 tablespoons kosher salt
$1/4$ cup molasses
2 tablespoons aged balsamic vinegar

DIRECTIONS

1. Peel the zest from the lemon with a vegetable peeler; squeeze the juice from the lemon.
2. Combine the lemon zest, lemon juice, and the remaining ingredients in a saucepan and bring to a boil. Reduce the heat, cover, and simmer for 5 minutes; let cool and pour into a gallon-size zipper-lock bag.

3. Put the bag in a bowl just large enough to hold it snugly. Open the bag and add the meat. Seal the zipper, leaving about an inch open; push on the bag to release any trapped air through the opening, and close the zipper completely. Massage the liquid gently into the meat and refrigerate for the suggested time.

RUBS AND WET PASTES

FRAGRANT CHILE RUB

TIMING
Prep: 5 minutes

This all-purpose rub is the one you want for an all-American barbecue. Slightly sweet, a little bit spicy, smoky, and highly aromatic, it makes almost anything it touches taste great. Pair it with Sweet, Hot, and Sour BBQ Sauce (page 391).

GOOD WITH

Seafood: any fish or shellfish
Poultry: chicken, turkey, game hen, duck

Meat: beef, lamb, pork

INGREDIENTS (MAKES ABOUT ¹/₂ CUP)

2 tablespoons kosher salt
2 tablespoons paprika
1 tablespoon dark brown sugar
1 tablespoon ground ancho chile

1 to 3 teaspoons ground chipotle chile
¹/₂ teaspoon ground cumin
¹/₂ teaspoon ground black pepper

DIRECTIONS

1. Combine all of the ingredients.

2. Use as directed in a recipe; can be stored in a tightly closed container at room temperature for up to 1 month.

GETTING CREATIVE
· For Mild Chile Rub, omit the ground chipotle.

STORING RUBS
When a rub contains only dry ingredients, it can be kept in a tightly closed container for up to a month. But if there is any moisture (from fresh herbs, oils, freshly grated citrus zest, or juice), the rub is best used right away. It can be kept tightly sealed in the refrigerator for a day or two, but even then its flavors will diminish and merge as it sits.

PROVENÇAL HERB RUB

The hot, dry landscape of Provence produces herbs of particular intensity, and the cuisine of that region is inundated with them. Fennel, rosemary, thyme, and basil mixed with citrus and lots of garlic flavors everything from Provençal fire-roasted lamb to *loup de mer* (a Mediterranean bass) grilled over fennel twigs.

TIMING
Prep: 5 minutes

GOOD WITH

Seafood: shrimp, scallops, salmon, any white-fleshed fish
Poultry: chicken, turkey, game hen

Meat: lamb, pork, veal

INGREDIENTS (MAKES ABOUT 3 TABLESPOONS)

1 tablespoon fennel seed, crushed
1 teaspoon dried thyme
1 teaspoon dried rosemary, crushed
2 teaspoons garlic salt

1 teaspoon ground black pepper
1 teaspoon ground dried orange peel
2 tablespoons dried basil
¹/₂ teaspoon kosher salt

DIRECTIONS

1. Combine all of the ingredients.

2. Use as directed in a recipe; can be stored in a tightly closed container.

GETTING CREATIVE
· Replace the basil with 1 tablespoon dried tarragon for a subtle anise flavor.
· Team this rub with Orange-Espresso Glaze (page 387), Roasted Garlic Paste (page 392), Mignonette Marinade and Mop (page 352), or Orange-Fennel Brine (page 362).

TIP
· Crush the fennel seed in a mortar and pestle or in a zipper-lock bag with a heavy skillet. Crush the rosemary between your fingers.

CAJUN BLACKENING RUB

The Cajun technique of blackening food in a super-heated iron skillet shares the same flavor challenges as grilling over a roaring flame. The bitterness of charring has to be met with assertive seasoning. This rub is built for fire. It is not hot, but it is aggressively aromatic, able to hold its own against the highest flame.

TIMING
Prep: 5 minutes

MASTERING MARINADES, MOPS, BRINES, RUBS, WET PASTES, GLAZES, SAUCES, AND DIPS

GOOD WITH

Seafood: shrimp, scallops, salmon, any white-fleshed fish

Poultry: chicken, turkey, game hen

Meat: lamb, pork, veal

INGREDIENTS (MAKES ABOUT ¹/₄ CUP)

1 teaspoon garlic powder

1 teaspoon onion powder

1 teaspoon cayenne pepper

¹/₂ teaspoon mustard powder

³/₄ teaspoon ground white pepper

³/₄ teaspoon ground black pepper

¹/₂ teaspoon dried thyme

¹/₂ teaspoon dried oregano

1 tablespoon sweet paprika

1 tablespoon kosher salt

DIRECTIONS

1. Combine all of the ingredients.

2. Use as directed in a recipe; can be stored in a tightly closed container.

GETTING CREATIVE

· Team this rub with Dr Pepper's Magic Elixir (page 361), Steakhouse Brine (page 369), Ten-Pepper Brine (page 369), Hot Pepper–Bourbon Syrup (page 384), or Salsa Butter (page 393).

TUSCAN ROSEMARY RUB

TIMING

Prep: 5 minutes

Simple and straightforward, this all-purpose herb rub is perfect for anything from artichokes to potatoes to steak (hmm, not a bad menu!).

GETTING CREATIVE

· Pair this rub with Orange Tapenade Dip (page 391), Roasted Garlic Paste (page 392), or Red Wine–Rosemary Brine (page 366).

GOOD WITH

Seafood: shrimp, scallops, salmon, any white-fleshed fish

Poultry: chicken, turkey, game hen

Meat: lamb, pork, veal, beef

INGREDIENTS (MAKES ABOUT ¹/₄ CUP)

2 tablespoons dried rosemary, crushed

2 cloves garlic, minced

1 teaspoon kosher salt

¹/₄ cup finely chopped fresh flat-leaf parsley

1 tablespoon ground black pepper

DIRECTIONS

1. Combine all of the ingredients.

2. Use as directed in a recipe; can be stored in a tightly closed container in the refrigerator for up to 2 weeks.

SAGE AND SAVORY RUB

TIMING

Prep: 5 minutes

If you're grilling poultry, try this dried herb rub. The flavors are similar to commercial poultry seasoning. It's also great on pork. For a simple basting liquid, mix the rub with olive oil. Or grind the rub very finely and mix it with other liquids, such as apple cider and olive oil, to use as an injector marinade for poultry.

Seafood: any fish or shellfish
Poultry: any poultry

Meat: lamb, pork, veal

INGREDIENTS (MAKES ABOUT 1/2 CUP)

2 tablespoons dark brown sugar
2 tablespoons kosher salt
1 tablespoon paprika
2 teaspoons mustard powder
2 teaspoons dried sage
2 teaspoons dried savory

2 teaspoons dried thyme
1 teaspoon dried marjoram
1 teaspoon dried rosemary, crushed
1 teaspoon garlic powder
1 teaspoon onion powder
1 teaspoon ground black pepper

DIRECTIONS

1. Combine all of the ingredients in a small bowl.

2. Use as directed in a recipe; can be stored in a tightly closed container for up to 1 month.

TIMING
Prep: 5 minutes

GETTING CREATIVE
· Team this rub with Saffron-Citrus Marinade (page 352), Tamarind and Mango Brine (page 366), Red Hots Syrup (page 387), or Grilled Mango Chutney (page 395).

SPICES VS. HERBS
Spices are the hard parts of aromatic plants—the seeds, the roots, the bark, the petrified berries. They are tropical, and they are always dried. Whole dried spices last longer than ground spices, which, depending on how picky you are, could be anywhere from a minute to several months. Most of us have a collection of over-the-hill spices. To judge whether yours are still good, take a whiff. If they have little or no aroma, they have little or no flavor.

Herbs are the soft parts of aromatic plants—mostly leaves and flowers. They are temperate, and they can be dried or fresh. Fresh herbs should be treated like fresh greens. They need very little cooking; once they are wilted they have given all they have. Dried herbs need a little moisture and some time to release their flavor.

As a rule of thumb, dried herbs are about three times as strong as the same herb fresh, except for rosemary, which is equal in strength. But strength isn't the whole story. Dried herbs have more concentrated aromatic oils, but they lack the fresh chlorophyll greenness of fresh herbs, making them more one-dimensional.

You can store fresh herbs in the refrigerator in a loosely closed plastic bag for several days. Dried herbs will last longer, but they have the same perishability issues as spices. Always buy dried herbs in as whole a form as possible, and crush them with your fingers as you use them.

GARAM MASALA RUB

Masala is a blend of spices. *Garam* means warm or hot, and garam masala is the basic spice blend in northern India. There are as many formulas for garam masala as there are households. This one is meant to be generic, allowing you to add hot peppers or other aromatics as you wish. It is important to start with whole spices so that they can be toasted to bring out their maximum flavor.

GOOD WITH

Seafood: any fish or shellfish
Poultry: any poultry

Meat: lamb, pork, veal

INGREDIENTS (MAKES ABOUT 1/2 CUP)

2 cinnamon sticks, each about 3 inches long
18 green cardamom pods
2 teaspoons whole cloves

3 tablespoons black peppercorns
1/3 cup cumin seed
1/4 cup coriander seed

DIRECTIONS

1. Smash the cinnamon sticks with a hammer into small shards; crack the cardamom pods with the hammer, remove the seeds, and discard the pods.
2. Heat a skillet over high heat for 2 minutes. Add the cinnamon, cardamom, cloves, peppercorns, cumin, and coriander and stir until the spices are lightly toasted and aromatic, about 1 minute.

3. Transfer to a spice grinder or mini-chopper and grind to a powder. Pass through a coarse strainer to remove any large pieces.
4. Use as directed in a recipe; can be stored in a tightly closed container for up to 1 month.

JERK RUB

Jerk is to Jamaicans what barbecue is to Southerners—something to eat, a way to cook, and a lifestyle. This rub is for cooking, and you might find it addictive enough to turn it into a lifestyle. It is best with chicken and pork, but, as you will see, it's pretty good on most anything.

GOOD WITH

Seafood: any fish or shellfish
Poultry: chicken, turkey, game hen, duck

Meat: lamb, pork, veal

INGREDIENTS (MAKES ABOUT 1/3 CUP)

1 tablespoon sugar
1 tablespoon onion powder
1 tablespoon dried thyme
2 teaspoons ground allspice
2 teaspoons ground black pepper
1/2 teaspoon cayenne pepper

1 teaspoon kosher salt
1/2 teaspoon ground nutmeg
1/4 teaspoon ground cloves
1/2 teaspoon ground ginger
1/2 teaspoon ground Scotch bonnet, habanero,
    or other super-hot chile

DIRECTIONS

1. Combine all of the ingredients.

2. Use as directed in a recipe; can be stored in a tightly closed container for up to 1 month.

TIMING
Prep: 5 minutes

GETTING CREATIVE
· Match this rub with
   Fire Beer Marinade (page 354),
   Hot Pepper–Chai Brine (page 370),
   Hot Pepper– Bourbon Syrup (page 384),
   or Lime–Cilantro Butter (page 393).

JERK WET PASTE

Here's another style of jerk seasoning: a wet paste made with ground spices plus a healthy dose of fresh chiles, scallions, garlic, ginger, and lime. Use this wet mixture on lean foods like chicken to help them retain more moisture on the grill.

GOOD WITH

Seafood: any fish or shellfish
Poultry: chicken, turkey, game hen, duck

Meat: lamb, pork, veal
Other: tofu

INGREDIENTS (MAKES ABOUT 2 1/2 CUPS)

12 scallions, trimmed and coarsely chopped
3 to 10 Scotch bonnet chiles, seeded and coarsely chopped
3 cloves garlic, chopped
2 tablespoons chopped peeled gingerroot
1/3 cup fresh thyme leaves
1/3 cup packed dark brown sugar
2 teaspoons ground allspice
1 teaspoon ground cinnamon

1 teaspoon ground nutmeg
1 teaspoon ground coriander
1 teaspoon salt
1 teaspoon ground black pepper
1/4 cup vegetable oil
2 tablespoons soy sauce
2 tablespoons fresh lime juice
1 tablespoon dark rum

TIMING
Prep: 15 minutes

SHORTCUT
· Replace the jerk paste with 2 cups of your favorite store-bought jerk marinade. Or use 1/4 cup of Jerk Rub (previous recipe) or store-bought dry jerk seasoning (available in the spice aisle of most grocery stores) mixed with the brown sugar, oil, soy sauce, lime juice, and rum called for in the recipe.

TIP
· This jerk paste is smoking hot from the Scotch bonnet chiles. If you want even more heat, include the seeds. Capsaicin, the heat-producing oil in chile peppers, tends to concentrate in the seeds and ribs of chile peppers. To avoid getting the hot chile oil on your skin, wear kitchen gloves when chopping. This is especially important if you wear contact lenses, since the hot oil can be extremely painful if it touches your eyes. Another option: Skip the gloves and hold the chile by its stem. Cut the pepper flesh off the core and chop the flesh with your knife, never touching the cut part of the chile with your hands.

1. Put the scallions, Scotch bonnet chiles, garlic, ginger, thyme, brown sugar, allspice, cinnamon, nutmeg, coriander, salt, and black pepper in a food processor. Process to a rough paste, about 20 seconds. Add the oil, soy sauce, lime juice, and rum, and process to a loose paste, about 20 seconds. Scrape down the sides of the food processor bowl, if necessary.

2. Use as directed in a recipe; can be refrigerated in an airtight container for up to 3 months.

SMOKED SALT RUB

To make this rub, we first tried smoking salt ourselves on the grill. But we couldn't get sufficient smoke flavor into the salt to make the process worthwhile. Plus, richly aromatic smoked salt is available commercially, so why reinvent the wheel? Our favorite commercial smoked salt is Danish Viking smoked salt. The crystals are chunky, moist, and overwhelmingly smoky. But it is expensive. Fortunately, the smoke flavor is so strong that you can mix this smoked salt with kosher salt to make the smoked salt last longer in your cupboard.

GOOD WITH

Seafood: any fish or shellfish
Poultry: any poultry

Meat: lamb, pork, veal

INGREDIENTS (MAKES ABOUT 1/2 CUP)

2 tablespoons smoked salt
2 tablespoons kosher salt
2 tablespoons paprika
1 tablespoon dark brown sugar

2 teaspoons ground black pepper
1 teaspoon mustard powder
1 teaspoon garlic powder
1 teaspoon onion powder

DIRECTIONS

1. Combine all of the ingredients.

2. Use as directed in a recipe; can be stored in a tightly closed container in the refrigerator for up to 2 weeks.

TEN-PEPPER RUB

Fiery and nose-runningly, eye-wateringly aromatic, this is the rub for steaks. Since the recipe calls for a lot of different peppers, you might want to make up one giant batch to avoid having a lot of jars hanging around. Freeze what you won't use within two weeks; spices will keep frozen nearly forever.

GOOD WITH

Seafood: any fish or shellfish
Poultry: chicken, turkey, game hen, duck

Meat: beef, lamb, pork, veal

1 teaspoon cracked green peppercorns

1 tablespoon cracked black peppercorns

1 teaspoon ground white pepper

1 tablespoon cracked Szechwan pepper

1 teaspoon ground ancho chile

1 teaspoon ground chipotle chile

1 teaspoon ground habanero chile

1 teaspoon crushed red pepper flakes

1/2 teaspoon cayenne pepper

1 tablespoon sweet paprika

2 tablespoons kosher salt

2 tablespoons sugar

DIRECTIONS

1. Combine all of the ingredients.

2. Use as directed in a recipe; can be stored in a tightly closed container in the refrigerator for up to 2 weeks.

BLACK ESPRESSO RUB

TIMING
Prep: 5 minutes

This super-dark rub has a deeply roasted aroma that is delicious with rich meats, like lamb, beef, and dark-fleshed poultry, especially duck.

GOOD WITH

Seafood: salmon or any other oily fish

Poultry: duck, dark meat of chicken or turkey, goose, squab

Meat: beef, lamb, pork

INGREDIENTS (MAKES ABOUT 2/3 CUP)

1/4 cup finely ground espresso beans

2 teaspoons finely grated lemon zest

3 tablespoons sugar

2 tablespoons kosher salt

2 teaspoons garlic powder

1 teaspoon ground coriander

2 teaspoons coarsely ground black pepper

1 teaspoon ground chipotle chile

DIRECTIONS

1. Combine all of the ingredients.

2. Use as directed in a recipe; can be stored in a tightly closed container in the refrigerator for up to 1 month.

SESAME-MISO WET RUB

TIMING
Prep: 5 minutes

Miso is made by fermenting soybeans and salt in cedar vats for one to three years, until the mixture is rich and pungent. Sometimes other grains or beans are added, creating a variety of colors and flavors, such as barley miso, red miso, brown rice miso, and so on. In this rub you can use any style, but be careful—a little bit goes a long way. The pungency of the miso is balanced by dark aromatic sesame oil, garlic, lemon, and honey. The rub is especially suited to seafood.

GOOD WITH

Seafood: shrimp, scallops, salmon, any white-fleshed fish

Poultry: chicken, turkey, game hen, duck

Meat: lamb, pork, veal

---

2 cloves garlic, finely chopped

2 tablespoons miso (any type), thinned with 1 tablespoon warm water

3 tablespoons toasted sesame oil

Juice and finely grated zest of 1 lemon

2 tablespoons honey

1 tablespoon kosher salt

1/8 teaspoon cayenne pepper

1 tablespoon soy sauce

DIRECTIONS

1. Combine all of the ingredients.

2. Use as directed in a recipe; can be stored in a tightly closed container in the refrigerator for up to 1 month.

SESAME SZECHWAN SALT

This delicious, fragrant salt and pepper blend is wonderful on plain grilled shellfish and poultry; it needs nothing more than a drizzle of ponzu sauce (such as Grapefruit Ponzu Marinade or Mop, page 359) or a wedge of lime.

GOOD WITH

Seafood: any fish or shellfish

Poultry: chicken, turkey, game hen

Meat: lamb, pork, veal

INGREDIENTS (MAKES ABOUT 1/3 CUP)

1 tablespoon sesame seeds

2 tablespoons cracked Szechwan pepper

2 tablespoons kosher salt

2 teaspoons cracked black pepper

1 teaspoon ground ginger

DIRECTIONS

1. Heat a small, heavy skillet over high heat for 1 minute. Add the sesame seeds and stir until the seeds start to pop. Remove from the heat and add the cracked Szechwan pepper; stir until aromatic. Add the salt, black pepper, and ginger.

2. Use as directed in a recipe; can be stored in a tightly closed container in the refrigerator for up to 2 weeks.

SWEET CHIMICHURRI RUB

Chimichurri, the Argentinean marinade of herbs and peppers, is the inspiration for this citrus and parsley concoction. Even though *chimichurri* is traditionally used with beef, this rendition is lighter and sweeter, giving it an affinity for light meats and seafood. Try to use this rub quickly; the parsley deteriorates within a few days. Dried citrus peel is readily available in the spice aisles of most grocery stores.

GOOD WITH

Seafood: any fish or shellfish

Poultry: chicken, turkey, game hen, duck

Meat: lamb, pork, veal

INGREDIENTS (MAKES ABOUT 1/2 CUP)

1 tablespoon ground dried lemon peel

1 tablespoon ground dried orange peel

1 tablespoon sugar

1/2 cup chopped fresh flat-leaf parsley

1 teaspoon dried oregano

2 teaspoons kosher salt

1 teaspoon ground black pepper

1/4 teaspoon cayenne pepper

DIRECTIONS

1. Combine all of the ingredients.

2. Use as directed in a recipe; can be stored in a tightly closed container in the refrigerator for a day.

GREEN CHIMICHURRI RUB

TIMING
Prep: 5 minutes

Here's a rub that delivers the traditional flavors of *chimichurri* without having to wait for a marinade to seep into the meat. It's instantly flavorful and can be used as a seasoning at the table or as a rub for grilling. As with any rub that has a high proportion of fresh ingredients, you should try to use it all right away.

GOOD WITH

Seafood: shrimp, scallops, salmon, any white-fleshed fish

Poultry: chicken, turkey, game hen

Meat: lamb, pork, veal, beef

INGREDIENTS (MAKES ABOUT 1/2 CUP)

2/3 cup finely chopped fresh flat-leaf parsley

2 cloves garlic, minced

2 tablespoons grated onion

2 teaspoons kosher salt

1/4 teaspoon ground black pepper

1/2 teaspoon dried marjoram

1/2 teaspoon crushed red pepper flakes

DIRECTIONS

1. Combine all of the ingredients.

2. Use as directed in a recipe; can be stored in a tightly closed container in the refrigerator for a day.

HABANERO ZAA'TAR SPICE RUB

TIMING
Prep: 5 minutes

Zaa'tar is a traditional Arab spice blend of sour sumac berries and thyme leaves. In the Middle East it is often combined with sesame seeds and served as a table condiment or sprinkled on flatbreads right before they are baked. Ours is ignited with a hit of habanero chile, which helps to transform it from a seasoning into a rub. Sumac is a gorgeous maroon-red powder that delivers a pleasant sour flavor and a floral fragrance without adding acid. It is sold in Middle Eastern groceries, or you can order it online from www.zamourispices.com or www.penzeys.com.

Seafood: shrimp, scallops, salmon, any white-fleshed fish | **Meat:** lamb, pork, veal
Poultry: chicken, turkey, game hen

INGREDIENTS (MAKES ABOUT 1/3 CUP)

2 tablespoons sesame seeds	1 teaspoon ground black pepper
1 tablespoon sumac	1 teaspoon kosher salt
1 tablespoon dried thyme	1/2 teaspoon ground habanero chile

DIRECTIONS

1. Grind the sesame seeds with a mortar and pestle or spice grinder.

2. Combine the ground sesame seeds with the remaining ingredients.

3. Store in a tightly closed container at room temperature for up to 1 month.

MOROCCAN RUB

TIMING
Prep: 5 minutes

GETTING CREATIVE
· Pair this rub with Garlic-Buttermilk Marinade (page 350), Cumin, Coriander, and Lime Brine (page 364), or, most impressively, with Harissa Dip (page 396).

Morocco food smells of cinnamon, coriander, and thyme; it's stained yellow with turmeric and rouged with paprika. This fragrant sweet and savory rub attempts to capture the cacophony. Although it looks drab brown before cooking, it blooms gold when subjected to heat.

GOOD WITH

Seafood: shrimp, scallops, salmon, any dark-fleshed fish | **Meat:** lamb, beef, pork, veal
Poultry: chicken, turkey, game hen, duck

INGREDIENTS (MAKES ABOUT 1/2 CUP)

2 teaspoons ground cinnamon	1 teaspoon ground turmeric
2 tablespoons dried thyme	2 tablespoons sugar
1 teaspoon ground dried lemon peel	2 teaspoons kosher salt
2 teaspoons ground coriander	1 teaspoon ground black pepper

DIRECTIONS

1. Combine all of the ingredients.

2. Use as directed in a recipe; can be stored in a tightly closed container in the refrigerator for up to 1 month.

CUMIN RUB

TIMING
Prep: 15 minutes

Cumin is so easy to love. Nutty, with a hint of pine, it is the aroma that most Americans identify with chili. But in the world of cooking its redolence permeates cuisines around the globe, from Morocco to Mexico (traveling clockwise, of course). The aroma of toasted cumin dominates this rub, yet it takes on complexity with the addition of fresh gingerroot and cilantro. Like all rubs that include fresh ingredients, this one is perishable and should be used within a few days.

GOOD WITH

Seafood: shrimp, scallops, salmon, any white-fleshed fish
Poultry: chicken, turkey, game hen, duck

Meat: lamb, beef, pork, veal

INGREDIENTS (MAKES ABOUT ²/₃ CUP)

3 tablespoons cumin seeds
2 tablespoons minced garlic
2 tablespoons minced peeled gingerroot
1 tablespoon kosher salt

½ cup chopped fresh cilantro leaves
1 tablespoon sugar
1 teaspoon ground dried lemon peel or 1 tablespoon
   grated fresh lemon zest

DIRECTIONS

1. Heat a medium, heavy skillet over high heat for 1 minute. Add the cumin seeds and stir until the seeds are lightly toasted, about 1 minute. Grind in a spice grinder or mini-chopper into a fine powder. Combine with the remaining ingredients.

2. Use as directed in a recipe; can be stored in a tightly closed container in the refrigerator for a day.

TOASTING SPICES
The flavor of any spice comes from aromatic oils. When the spice is whole, the oils remain relatively inert, trapped inside rigid cell walls. But once the spice is ground, the cells break and the oils are released, which is why the flavors of spices are at their height right after grinding and diminish rapidly after that. Toasting enhances most spices by browning the sugars and proteins in the cells, creating darker and richer flavor components, and by liquefying the oil, which makes more of it emerge during grinding.

HICKORY ORANGE-ANISE RUB

Orange and anise are delicious together: bright and pungent, fruity and earthy, playing off each other's differences so naturally that their coupleness becomes a more intriguing entity than either one could possibly be alone. The addition of hickory smoke flavor helps to reinforce the pungency of the anise.

TIMING
Prep: 5 minutes

GOOD WITH

Seafood: salmon or any other oily fish
Poultry: duck, goose, chicken, turkey, game hen

Meat: beef, lamb, pork

INGREDIENTS (MAKES ABOUT ¹/₃ CUP)

1 tablespoon ground dried orange peel
1 tablespoon kosher salt
2 tablespoons sugar

1 tablespoon ground anise seed
½ teaspoon dried thyme
½ teaspoon liquid smoke (see sidebar)

DIRECTIONS

1. Combine all of the ingredients.

2. Use as directed in a recipe; can be stored in a tightly closed container in the refrigerator for up to 1 month.

WHAT IS LIQUID SMOKE?
Liquid smoke is made by burning hardwood chips (like hickory, mesquite, and fruit and nut woods) in a sealed environment that is inundated with moisture, causing the wood to smolder and generate vapor permeated with smoke. As in making distilled liquor, this vapor is trapped and chilled in condensers that precipitate the gas back into liquid. The liquid is filtered to remove impurities, mixed with vinegar, molasses, and caramel color, and aged to help the flavors mellow.

There is some evidence that liquid smoke has antimicrobial abilities that kill bacteria on the surface of meats, and its antioxidant properties help it to counteract the off flavors resulting from the oxidation of fat associated with warming leftovers. Liquid smoke is very strong and should be used with caution. Overdoing it makes food taste as though it's been slathered with soot.

BEDOUIN DRY MARINADE

This gorgeous, wonderfully fragrant rub gilds anything it touches with a golden glow and the heady, aromatic combination of black pepper, cardamom, and caraway. It is delicious on chicken.

TIMING
Prep: 5 minutes

GOOD WITH

Seafood: any fish or shellfish
Poultry: chicken, turkey, game hen, duck

Meat: beef, lamb, pork, veal

INGREDIENTS (MAKES ABOUT 1/3 CUP)

$1^1/_2$ tablespoons coarsely ground black pepper
1 tablespoon caraway seed
1 teaspoon ground cardamom
$^1/_2$ teaspoon saffron threads

1 teaspoon ground turmeric
2 teaspoons kosher salt
1 teaspoon sugar

DIRECTIONS

1. Combine all of the ingredients.

2. Use as directed in a recipe; can be stored in a tightly closed container in the refrigerator for up to 1 month.

GLAZES

HOT PEPPER–BOURBON SYRUP

This spicy, not-so-sweet hard sauce is splendid with any roast: turkey, chicken, lamb, and especially pork. Notice that there are two types of pepper in this recipe: red and black. The reason is not for color (although the contrasting specks do look nice together); it is because different peppers hit the palate at different places. Red pepper (cayenne) tends to warm the back of the throat, jalapeño heats the lips, and black pepper radiates around the center of the mouth. When food tastes painfully peppery, it is not usually because there is too much pepper; rather, the types of pepper are out of balance. The remedy is to add more pepper of a different sort to redirect the heat.

GOOD WITH

Seafood: salmon or any other oily fish
Poultry: chicken, turkey, game hen

Meat: lamb, pork, veal

INGREDIENTS (MAKES ABOUT 1 CUP)

1 cup bourbon whiskey
$^1/_2$ cup dark brown sugar
2 teaspoons kosher salt

$^1/_2$ teaspoon crushed red pepper flakes
1 teaspoon ground black pepper
2 tablespoons butter

DIRECTIONS

1. In a small saucepan, heat the bourbon with the sugar, salt, and red and black peppers. Whisk in the butter until incorporated.

2. Serve warm. Refrigerate in a tightly closed container for up to 2 weeks; rewarm before serving.

TIMING
Prep: 5 minutes

TAKE CARE WHEN YOU GLAZE
Most glazes include a significant amount of sweeteners to help them lacquer a food with a crispy crust and a beautiful sheen, but it also makes them scorch easily. For that reason, always use glazes in the last 5 minutes of cooking, and don't turn your back on them.

RED-COOKING LACQUER

TIMING
Prep: 5 minutes

In Chinese cuisine, "red-cooking" means simmering in soy sauce until whatever is being cooked, usually chicken or pork, turns a deep mahogany red. The same way that brine adds moisture and flavor (page 85), seasoned soy sauce has the potential to relax proteins and invade them with whatever flavorful ingredients are infused into it. This glaze includes floral-scented Szechwan pepper and sweet anise seed.

GOOD WITH

Seafood: salmon or any other oily fish

Poultry: chicken, turkey, duck, game hen

Meat: lamb, pork, beef

INGREDIENTS (MAKES ABOUT 1 CUP)

$1/2$ cup dark brown sugar

$1/4$ cup soy sauce

1 teaspoon cracked Szechwan pepper

1 teaspoon anise seed

1 tablespoon sherry

2 tablespoons ketchup

1 teaspoon kosher salt

DIRECTIONS

1. Mix all of the ingredients in a small saucepan and heat until the brown sugar dissolves.

2. Serve at room temperature. Refrigerate in a tightly closed container for up to 2 weeks. Bring back to room temperature before serving.

PEKING CRACKLE

TIMING
Prep: 5 minutes

Based on the glaze that gives Peking duck its crackling skin, this salty, sweet, and savory glaze is delicious on any poultry. It is best used with indirect grilling. If used directly over a flame, watch its progress very carefully. It can reduce to a blackened sheen in a few untended seconds.

GOOD WITH

Seafood: salmon

Poultry: chicken, duck, turkey, game hen

Meat: lamb, pork

INGREDIENTS (MAKES ABOUT $1/2$ CUP)

3 tablespoons hoisin sauce

3 tablespoons honey

1 clove garlic, crushed

1 teaspoon Chinese chili paste with garlic

1 teaspoon toasted sesame oil

$1/2$ teaspoon kosher salt

DIRECTIONS

1. Combine all of the ingredients.

2. Serve at room temperature. Refrigerate in a tightly closed container for up to 1 month. Bring back to room temperature before serving.

MUSTARD-MOLASSES GLAZE

The combination of mustard and molasses is magical–similar to honey mustard, yet darker, richer, and more pungent. This glaze is especially good on salmon, where it develops a meaty richness that the fish has been alluding to its entire culinary life. Make up a double batch and keep the extra on hand to glaze everything from shrimp to chicken to burgers; nothing in this recipe is perishable, which means that you will go bad long before the glaze does.

GOOD WITH

Seafood: salmon or any other oily fish
Poultry: chicken, turkey, game hen, duck

Meat: lamb, pork, beef

INGREDIENTS (MAKES ABOUT 1 CUP)

1/2 cup dark molasses
1/4 cup prepared brown mustard
2 tablespoons cider vinegar

1 teaspoon ground black pepper
2 teaspoons kosher salt

DIRECTIONS

1. Combine all of the ingredients.

2. Use as directed in a recipe; can be stored in a tightly closed container in the refrigerator forever.

GARLIC-PLUM BARBECUE GLAZE

Some fruits are generic. Apple, for instance, when mixed with other fruits, hides its identity, becoming a base flavor over which berries and peaches claim star status. Pear juice and white grape juice do the same thing in fruit juice blends, and when it comes to fruit and meat combinations, it is the plum that takes on the all-important and thankless supporting role. Plums are the meatiest of fruits, and when they are mixed with savory flavors they form a delicious sweet-tart pulp that everyone savors but no one can quite identify. In this glaze, plum butter or plum preserves are overshadowed by ketchup, garlic, and Worcestershire sauce.

GOOD WITH

Seafood: shrimp, salmon or any other oily fish
Poultry: chicken, turkey, game hen, duck

Meat: lamb, pork

INGREDIENTS (MAKES ABOUT 2/3 CUP)

1/3 cup plum butter or other plum preserves
3 tablespoons ketchup
3 cloves garlic, minced

2 tablespoons Worcestershire sauce or soy sauce
1 teaspoon kosher salt

DIRECTIONS

1. Combine all of the ingredients.

2. Use as directed in a recipe; can be stored in a tightly closed container in the refrigerator for up to 1 month.

ORANGE-ESPRESSO GLAZE

TIMING
Prep: 5 minutes

Like the other espresso mixtures in this chapter, this glaze underscores the charcoal roasted flavor of whatever grilled item it touches. The orange marmalade adds a bittersweet, fruity aftertaste that reciprocates and mellows the bitter flavor of the coffee.

GOOD WITH

Seafood: shrimp, scallops, salmon or any other oily fish
Poultry: chicken, turkey, game hen, duck

Meat: lamb, pork, veal, beef

INGREDIENTS (MAKES ABOUT 1 $^1/_3$ CUPS)

1 cup strong brewed coffee
$^1/_2$ teaspoon ground cloves
1 teaspoon kosher salt

$^1/_4$ cup plus 2 tablespoons orange marmalade
$^1/_4$ cup honey

DIRECTIONS

1. Combine all of the ingredients.

2. Use as directed in a recipe; can be stored in a tightly closed container in the refrigerator for up to 2 weeks.

RED HOTS SYRUP

TIMING
Prep: 5 minutes

This syrup tastes exactly like those teeny red cinnamon candies that burned holes into your childhood tongue (what exquisite agony) during your virginal introduction to the pain-pleasure sensation that is the adult allure of hot chiles and strong horseradish. The secret to the syrup is Vietnamese (or Saigon) cinnamon, which is from the same cassia family as regular cinnamon but has three times the volatile oils. It gives the spice a reddish cast and a sweet, pungent flavor that other cinnamons can't match. Vietnamese cinnamon is sold as a gourmet spice in most supermarkets, and it is available online from penzeys.com and thespicehouse.com

GOOD WITH

Seafood: shrimp, salmon or any other oily fish
Poultry: chicken, turkey, game hen, duck

Meat: lamb, pork

INGREDIENTS (MAKES ABOUT $^1/_3$ CUP)

$^1/_3$ cup honey
1 tablespoon Vietnamese (or Saigon) cinnamon

1 teaspoon Tabasco hot pepper sauce
2 teaspoons kosher salt

DIRECTIONS

1. Combine all of the ingredients.

2. Use as directed in a recipe; can be stored in a tightly closed container in the refrigerator for up to 1 month.

GINGER-HOISIN BALSAMIC GLAZE

Thick, red-brown, sweet, and spicy, hoisin sauce is a mainstay of Chinese cooking. It is often used as a barbecue glaze on its own, but thinning it with orange juice and balsamic vinegar and spicing it up with freshly grated ginger makes a big improvement.

GOOD WITH

Seafood: shrimp, scallops, salmon or any other oily fish
Poultry: chicken, turkey, game hen, duck

Meat: lamb, pork, beef

INGREDIENTS (MAKES ABOUT $^1/_2$ CUP)

1 tablespoon grated peeled gingerroot
$^1/_4$ cup hoisin sauce

2 tablespoons aged balsamic vinegar
1 tablespoon orange juice

DIRECTIONS

1. Combine all of the ingredients.

2. Use as directed in a recipe; can be stored in a tightly closed container in the refrigerator for up to 2 weeks.

ASIAN SAUCES

Unlike their Western counterparts, who let flavors emerge from the cooking process, Asian cooks have been adding instant flavor with bottled sauces for centuries. Most of them keep indefinitely in the refrigerator. Here's an overview.

Chili oil (also called hot pepper oil): This incendiary seasoning should be used as a seasoning, not as a cooking oil. It is made by steeping chiles in oil; sometimes toasted sesame oil is used, in which case the product is called hot sesame oil.

Chinese chili paste (also called chili sauce): This cayenne pepper paste is a mainstay of Chinese cooking, and there are several different styles. It can either be made totally from hot peppers (the hottest) or combined with fermented bean paste (still hot). It is frequently seasoned with garlic.

Fish sauce (also called *nam pla*): Made by fermenting salted fish, fish sauce is an ancient and important flavoring in Southeast Asian dishes. Fish sauces vary widely in quality, and cheaper ones can have an off-putting aroma. Those made in China and Thailand are the best. Fresh fish sauce is a light amber color (the color of tea). It will darken with age. When it turns brown, discard it.

Hoisin sauce: A thick, fermented soybean sauce, hoisin is dark reddish brown, slightly sweet, and subtly spicy. It is a common seasoning in Chinese dishes and is best known as the sauce that you are served in Chinese restaurants with Peking duck. It is sold in jars and cans.

Oyster sauce: Originally made by fermenting oysters, oyster sauce is now a thickened, subtly sweet-salty brown sauce flavored with oyster extracts. It is not fishy, nor as aromatic as fish sauce, but it is slightly more pungent than hoisin sauce, which it closely resembles.

Peanut sauce: Thai peanut sauce is a blend of coconut milk, peanuts, fish sauce, and spices, usually including tamarind, chiles, lemongrass, and coriander. It comes dried in a packet or jarred.

Ponzu sauce: This Japanese dipping sauce is a mixture of soy sauce and citrus juice. It is very light and fresh and a good substitute for soy sauce when you want something more subtle.

Soy sauce: There are two types of soy sauce, thin and thick. Most of the soy sauces you will find are thin. They are watery, dark brown, and salty. You will see thick soy sauce (also called dark soy sauce) only in Asian markets. It is a thick paste, more fermented tasting and less salty. Of the thin soy sauces, buy only those that say they are naturally brewed. They can be labeled premium, superior, or light.

Stir-fry sauce: Asian stir-fry sauces are all-purpose, flavored sauces that are similar to teriyaki, combining soy sauce, sugar, vinegar, ginger, garlic, and sugar. They are a way of simplifying the list of ingredients one would have to assemble to make a typical stir-fry.

Teriyaki: A traditional Japanese marinade, grilling, and dipping sauce, teriyaki is a combination of soy sauce, sugar, vinegar, ginger, and garlic.

STEAKHOUSE GLAZE

TIMING
Prep: 5 minutes

This souped-up steak sauce transforms the ubiquitous steakhouse condiment into a glaze. Added sugar from ketchup helps the sauce to caramelize on the surface of meat as it browns. The sauce is pungent and should be reserved for richly flavored meats.

GOOD WITH

Seafood: salmon or any other oily fish
Poultry: chicken, turkey, duck breast

Meat: beef, pork

INGREDIENTS (MAKES ABOUT $3/4$ CUP)

$1/2$ cup A1 steak sauce
1 tablespoon brown mustard

1 tablespoon garlic-flavored oil
2 tablespoons ketchup

DIRECTIONS

1. Combine all of the ingredients.

2. Use as directed in a recipe; can be stored in a tightly closed container in the refrigerator for up to 1 month.

ORANGE HONEY-BUTTER GLAZE

TIMING
Prep: 5 minutes

This simple glaze is nothing more than butter sweetened with honey and flavored with orange zest and nutmeg. Brush it on almost any grilled fruit, pound cake, or other grilled bread for a final lick of flavor. It also lends a sweet kiss to pork and chicken.

GOOD WITH

Seafood: shrimp, scallops, salmon, any white-fleshed fish
Poultry: chicken, turkey, game hen
Meat: lamb, pork

Other: Firm fruits such as apples, pineapples, mangoes, papaya, bananas; plain cakes and breads like pound cake or naan; sweet vegetables such as beets, carrots, and yams

INGREDIENTS (MAKES ABOUT $1/4$ CUP)

2 tablespoons butter, well softened
1 tablespoon honey

1 tablespoon grated orange zest
Pinch of grated nutmeg

DIRECTIONS

1. In a small bowl, mix all ingredients until creamy and spreadable like icing. Refrigerate for up to 2 weeks.

2. Soften to a spreadable consistency before using.

SAUCE CAUTION

For the most part, grilling sauces are meant to be used as condiments at the table or mixed with shredded grilled meats after cooking. You will find that we do cook with them throughout the book, but when we do they are given a minimal amount of heat. Even if you are brushing them on during the last few minutes on the grill, you usually want to save some to serve at the table as well.

Clockwise from top: Sweet, Hot, and Sour BBQ Sauce; Harissa Dip; Lime-Cilantro Butter Sauce; Grilled Mango Chutney; Vietnamese Dipping Sauce; Preserved Lemon Relish.

SWEET, HOT, AND SOUR BBQ SAUCE

TIMING
Prep: 5 minutes

If you're looking for a delicious all-purpose barbecue sauce, look no further. As with all sweet sauces, you must be careful during cooking. Use this sauce only during the last 5 minutes when grilling over direct heat; for indirect grilling, the sauce will be fine on the grill for up to half an house without burning.

GOOD WITH

Seafood: salmon or any other oily fish
Poultry: chicken, turkey, game hen

Meat: beef, pork

INGREDIENTS (MAKES ABOUT 1 1/4 CUPS)

1/2 cup ketchup
1/4 cup honey mustard
2 tablespoons apple cider vinegar

1/4 cup light brown sugar
2 tablespoons Tabasco hot pepper sauce
1/2 teaspoon ground black pepper

DIRECTIONS

1. Combine all of the ingredients.

2. Use as directed in a recipe; can be stored in a tightly closed container in the refrigerator for up to 1 month.

GETTING CREATIVE
- For a smoky aroma, add 1 teaspoon liquid smoke.
- For a richer sauce, add 2 tablespoons melted butter.
- For a sweeter sauce, add 1 to 2 tablespoons molasses.

BARBECUE SAUCE STYLES
Much fuss has been made over regional styles of barbecue sauce, but such distinctions are general at best, comprising so many variations that the differences tend to blur in actual practice. With that in mind, here's the general lay of the land:
- Carolina: spicy and sour
  - Eastern North Carolina: vinegar, peppers, and a little sugar
  - Western North Carolina: the same thing with ketchup
  - Central South Carolina: the same thing with mustard
- Memphis: sweet, hot, and smoky, with a ketchup base
- Texas: savory, smoky, made with thinned ketchup
- Kansas City: sweet, sour, hot, thick ketchup base
- Urban coastal: lots of ketchup, very sweet, thick, a little sour, not so hot

ORANGE TAPENADE DIP

TIMING
Prep: 5 minutes

The flavor of olives seems older than time. And in Provence, where time seems to stand still, the flavor of olives permeates everything, even dessert. This pungent table sauce is based on tapenade, a paste of oil-cured olives, garlic, anchovies, and olive oil that is the ketchup of Provence. It is delicious on almost anything, from grilled asparagus to grilled steak.

GOOD WITH

Seafood: shrimp, scallops, any fish
Poultry: chicken, turkey, game hen, duck

Meat: lamb, pork, veal, beef

INGREDIENTS (MAKES ABOUT 1 CUP)

1/2 cup pitted oil-cured black olives, finely chopped
1 anchovy fillet, finely chopped
4 cloves garlic, minced
1/3 cup extra-virgin olive oil
Juice and finely grated zest of 1 orange

1 tablespoon chopped fresh rosemary leaves
2 teaspoons kosher salt
Pinch of crushed red pepper flakes
2 teaspoons honey

DIRECTIONS

1. Combine all of the ingredients.

2. Use as directed in a recipe; can be stored in a tightly closed container in the refrigerator for up to 1 month.

ROASTED GARLIC

Makes about 16 cloves, or about 1/4 cup

1 head garlic
1 teaspoon olive oil

1. Preheat the oven to 400°F or heat a grill to medium for direct heat. Cut the pointed end off the garlic head, exposing most of the cloves. Put the garlic cut-side up on a 6-inch square of aluminum foil, top with the oil, and wrap the foil around the garlic so that it is completely enclosed. Place near the middle of the oven or directly on the grill grate and roast until the cloves are soft, 30 to 35 minutes.
2. Unwrap and let cool for 10 minutes. For individual cloves, peel the papery skin from each roasted garlic clove. Or cut the whole head in half lengthwise and squeeze the roasted garlic from the skins. Refrigerate the roasted cloves in a tightly closed container for up to 2 weeks. Use in any preparation calling for roasted garlic.

SHORTCUT
Good-quality roasted garlic is sold as whole cloves, chopped, or pureed in jars.

ROASTED GARLIC PASTE

When garlic is roasted, its sugars caramelize, and what was pungent and sharp becomes sweet and mellow. This luscious poultice is little more than puréed roasted garlic. It is a welcome complement to almost any grilled meat, fish, or vegetable. If you want to thin it into a sauce, simply add more water and olive oil.

GOOD WITH

Seafood: shrimp, scallops, any fish
Poultry: chicken, turkey, game hen

Meat: lamb, pork, veal

INGREDIENTS (MAKES ABOUT 3/4 CUP)

3 heads roasted garlic (at left)
3 tablespoons extra-virgin olive oil
1 teaspoon kosher salt
1/8 teaspoon ground black pepper

1/4 cup packed chopped fresh flat-leaf parsley
Pinch of cayenne pepper, or more to taste
1 tablespoon sugar
3 to 4 tablespoons water

DIRECTIONS

1. Mash the roasted garlic with a fork. Add the olive oil, salt, pepper, parsley, red pepper, sugar, and water and mix to combine.

2. Serve at room temperature or refrigerate in a tightly closed container for up to 2 weeks. Let return to room temperature before serving.

CHIPOTLE DIPPING SAUCE

The discovery of chipotle peppers by salsa manufacturers and Mexican chain restaurants has steered this relatively esoteric pepper (a smoked jalapeño) into the mainstream. We have chipotle-flavored bean dip, taco chips, and mayonnaise. The best chipotle flavor still comes from canned chipotles *en adobo*, which has been around for decades. This easy dip flavors canned chipotle chiles with mole paste, a concentrate of spices and fruits available in the Mexican area of your supermarket. Use it as a pour-over sauce, too.

GOOD WITH

Seafood: shrimp, scallops, salmon or any other oily fish
Poultry: chicken, turkey, game hen, duck

Meat: beef, lamb, pork

INGREDIENTS (MAKES ABOUT 1 CUP)

1/4 cup jarred mole paste
2 canned chipotle peppers *en adobo*, finely chopped
2 tablespoons adobo sauce from chipotles *en adobo*
1/3 cup orange juice

1/3 cup V-8 juice
1 teaspoon kosher salt
1 teaspoon toasted ground cumin

DIRECTIONS

1. Combine all of the ingredients. Serve at room temperature.

2. Use as directed in a recipe; can be stored in a tightly closed container in the refrigerator for up to 2 weeks. Bring back to room temperature before serving.

LIME-CILANTRO BUTTER

TIMING
Prep: 5 minutes

The pairing of lime and cilantro is commonplace—probably because it is so good. It's imperative that you use both the zest and juice of the lime, or else the mixture will be too tart and the flavor of the cilantro will dominate. We call for unsalted butter to control the salt level, but if all you have is salted butter, just eliminate the salt in the recipe and the flavor will be fine. You can make the sauce ahead, but it will have to be reheated just before serving.

GETTING CREATIVE
· To make Sweet Lime-Cilantro Butter, add 1/2 teaspoon brown sugar along with the lime zest and juice.

GOOD WITH

Seafood: shrimp, scallops, any fish
Poultry: chicken, turkey, game hen

Meat: lamb, pork, veal

INGREDIENTS (MAKES ABOUT 1/3 CUP)

4 tablespoons (1/2 stick) unsalted butter
1 clove garlic, minced
Finely grated zest and juice of 1 lime

1/4 cup finely chopped fresh cilantro leaves
1/2 teaspoon kosher salt
1/4 teaspoon ground black pepper

DIRECTIONS

1. Heat the butter and garlic in a small skillet until the garlic sizzles; stir in the lime zest and juice and heat to boiling.

2. Remove from the heat and stir in the cilantro, salt, and pepper.
3. Serve warm as a dip or table sauce.

SALSA BUTTER

TIMING
Prep: 5 minutes

What is salsa but a jar of lightly cooked, already chopped vegetables? To turn it into a super-rich sauce for grilled meat, boil away the liquid and replace it with butter. The butter gives the salsa a velvety texture, and the piquant character of the salsa balances the butter's richness.

GETTING CREATIVE
· For the salsa, use Fire-Roasted Tomatillo Salsa or its variation, Grilled Tomato Salsa (both on page 277).

GOOD WITH

Seafood: shrimp, scallops, salmon, any white-fleshed fish
Poultry: chicken, turkey, game hen

Meat: lamb, pork, veal

INGREDIENTS (MAKES ABOUT 1 1/2 CUPS)

1 1/2 cups salsa, any heat level

3 tablespoons unsalted butter, cut into pieces

DIRECTIONS

1. Bring the salsa to a boil in a small saucepan or skillet, and cook until most of the liquid is gone.

2. Remove from the heat and whisk in the butter until the sauce is smooth. Serve warm as a dip or sauce.

PLUM KETCHUP

It used to be that there were scores of ketchups in the American larder: mushroom ketchup, oyster ketchup, and ketchups made from every kind of fruit imaginable. Since ketchup originally was an Indian condiment akin to chutney, fruit ketchups don't seem far-fetched. Use this one made from plums as you would tomato ketchup. Think of it as the reemergence of an extinct culinary species.

GOOD WITH

Seafood: salmon or any other dark-fleshed fish
Poultry: chicken, turkey, duck, goose

Meat: lamb, beef, pork

INGREDIENTS (MAKES ABOUT 1 CUP)

1/2 cup plum preserves, preferably damson plums
6 pitted prunes, finely chopped, or 1/4 cup jarred prune
    paste (*lekvar*)
2 cloves garlic, minced
1 teaspoon grated peeled gingerroot

1/4 cup soy sauce
1 tablespoon tamarind paste or concentrate, or 1 tablespoon
    lemon juice
1/2 teaspoon kosher salt

DIRECTIONS

1. Combine all of the ingredients in a small saucepan and warm over medium heat until the ingredients have blended.

2. Use as a dip or condiment or as directed in a recipe; can be stored in a tightly closed container in the refrigerator for up to 1 month.

**MAKING YOUR OWN
PRESERVED LEMONS**

If you can't find preserved lemons in a local market, you can make them yourself.

Makes 1 quart

10 lemons, scrubbed clean
Kosher salt
Fresh lemon juice, as needed

1. Cut the tips off the ends of the lemons. Slice into quarters lengthwise, leaving the slices attached at one end. Pack the lemons with as much salt as they will hold.
2. Put the lemons in a sterilized wide-mouth quart jar, packing them in as tightly as possible. As you push the lemons into the jar, some juice will be squeezed from them. When the jar is full, the juice should cover the lemons; if it doesn't, add some fresh lemon juice.
3. Seal the jar and set aside for 3 to 4 weeks, until the lemon rinds are soft, shaking the jar every day to keep the salt distributed. The lemons should be covered with juice at all times; add more as needed.
4. Rinse before using.

PRESERVED LEMON RELISH

Preserved lemons are one of the indispensable ingredients in Moroccan cooking. They are wonderfully aromatic and are one of the only ways you ever get to use whole lemons in a recipe. Both the preserved lemons and this relish made from them will keep for a month or more in the refrigerator. If you can't find preserved lemons at your local food store, they are easy to make (see sidebar), but they take weeks to cure. You can order several brands of jarred preserved lemons from www.mustaphas.com and other online sources.

GOOD WITH

Seafood: shrimp, scallops, salmon, any white-fleshed fish
Poultry: chicken, turkey, game hen

Meat: lamb, pork, veal

INGREDIENTS (MAKES ABOUT 1 CUP)

2 preserved lemons, coarsely chopped, seeds discarded
1/2 cup fresh cilantro leaves and stems

4 cloves garlic, coarsely chopped
1/4 cup olive oil

DIRECTIONS

1. Place all of the ingredients in a food processor and process until finely chopped.

2. Use as directed in a recipe; can be stored in a tightly closed container in the refrigerator for up to 1 month.

GRILLED MANGO CHUTNEY

TIMING
Prep: 20 minutes

GRILL TOOLS AND EQUIPMENT
· Clean, oiled grill grate
· Long-handled tongs

In this novel recipe, the mango is grilled as one would grill a tomato or bell pepper, charring the skin while the flesh insides smokes and softens. Not only does it give the mango a wonderful flavor, but it makes the fruit a cinch to peel. Grilling the fruit also makes it easy to force the flesh of the fruit from its pesky pit, a hairy task if you're using a knife and raw fruit. The finished chutney is vibrant in color and very flavorful. It's particularly good as a condiment for seafood.

GOOD WITH

Seafood: shrimp, scallops, any fish

Poultry: chicken, turkey, game hen, duck

Meat: lamb, pork, veal

INGREDIENTS (MAKES ABOUT 1 3/4 CUPS)

1 large, ripe mango, about 1 pound

1 large onion, peeled and cut into 1/2-inch-thick slices

1 tomato, seeded and finely chopped

1/2 teaspoon kosher salt

1 teaspoon sugar

1 tablespoon minced peeled gingerroot

1 serrano chile, stem and seeds removed, minced

Finely grated zest and juice of 1 lime

2 tablespoons chopped fresh cilantro leaves

1 teaspoon vanilla vinegar or other sweet-flavored vinegar

DIRECTIONS

1. Light a medium-hot fire in a charcoal grill, or heat a gas grill to medium-high. Put the mango and onion slices on the grill; grill the mango until the skin is spotty with burnt marks and the fruit inside feels soft, about 10 minutes, turning 3 times; grill the onions for 3 minutes per side. Put both in a bowl, cover, and let rest for 10 minutes.

2. Meanwhile, combine the remaining ingredients in a separate bowl.

3. Peel the skin from the mango with your fingers, scraping any flesh clinging to the skin into the bowl it's been resting in. Holding the skinned mango over the bowl, squeeze it with your hands, allowing the soft flesh to squish between your fingers. Keep squeezing and rubbing until all that is left is the pit; discard the pit. Add the mashed mango to the tomato-onion mixture, and mix to combine

4. Use as directed in a recipe; can be stored in a tightly closed container in the refrigerator for up to 1 month.

Photo: Making Grilled Mango Chutney

HARISSA DIP

Harissa, the aromatic Moroccan chile sauce, is easy to make from scratch now that ground chiles are readily available. We use a combination of a mild chile (like ancho), a sweet pepper (like smoked paprika), and a just hint of fire from habanero for a harissa that is more aromatic and less painful on the palate than jarred harissa. Use harissa exclusively as a table sauce; it gets bitter when cooked on the grill.

GOOD WITH

Seafood: shrimp, scallops, salmon, any fish
Poultry: chicken, turkey, game hen, duck

Meat: lamb, pork, veal

INGREDIENTS (MAKES ABOUT 1 1/2 CUPS)

1/4 cup ground ancho chile
1 teaspoon spicy ground chile, such as habanero
1 teaspoon kosher salt
1 teaspoon ground coriander
1 teaspoon ground cumin

2 tablespoons *pimentón* (smoked paprika)
1/2 cup olive oil
1 tablespoon tomato paste
About 1/2 cup boiling water

DIRECTIONS

1. Mix the ground ancho chile, spicy ground chile, salt, coriander, cumin, *pimentón,* and olive oil in a small skillet. Heat over medium heat until the mixture loosens and forms bubbles around the edge of the pan; do not allow to brown.

2. Remove from the heat and mix in the tomato paste and 1/2 cup boiling water. The mixture should be the texture of ketchup; add more water if needed.
3. Use as directed in a recipe; can be stored in a tightly closed container in the refrigerator for up to 1 month.

INDONESIAN PEANUT SAUCE

There are two peanut sauces in this chapter. This one is spicier, more garlicky, and thicker. It is best for meat. For a richer, more mellow peanut sauce, see the next recipe.

GOOD WITH

Poultry: chicken, turkey, game hen

Meat: pork, beef

INGREDIENTS (MAKES ABOUT 1 2/3 CUPS)

1 clove garlic, minced
3/4 cup peanut butter, chunky or smooth
1 cup chicken broth or vegetable broth
2 to 3 teaspoons sriracha hot pepper sauce or other hot pepper sauce

1 teaspoon toasted sesame oil
2 teaspoons sugar
1 tablespoon soy sauce

DIRECTIONS

1. Combine all of the ingredients in a saucepan and heat over medium heat until well combined and heated through.

2. Serve as a dip or use as directed in a recipe; can be stored in a tightly closed container in the refrigerator for up to 1 week.

THAI COCONUT PEANUT SAUCE

TIMING
Prep: 5 minutes

This peanut sauce is mild, sweet, aromatic, and just a bit pungent. It's best for fish and chicken.

MAKING SUBSTITUTIONS
· If you don't have any fresh mint, replace it with another fragrant herb, such as basil or cilantro.

GOOD WITH

Seafood: shrimp, scallops, any fish
Poultry: chicken, turkey, game hen

Meat: pork, veal

INGREDIENTS (MAKES ABOUT 1 CUP)

3/4 cup coconut milk
1/2 cup peanut butter, chunky or smooth
1 tablespoon Thai fish sauce (nam pla)
2 teaspoons ground ginger

1 clove garlic, minced
1 teaspoon sriracha hot pepper sauce or other hot pepper sauce
2 tablespoons minced fresh mint leaves

DIRECTIONS

1. Combine all of the ingredients.

2. Use as a dip or sauce, or as directed in a recipe; can be stored in a tightly closed container in the refrigerator for up to 1 week.

RED PEPPER CHIMICHURRI

TIMING
Prep: 5 minutes

The inspiration for this absolutely vivid vegetable and herb relish is Argentinean *chimichurri,* although the two bear very little resemblance to each other. This sauce is thick with vegetables and is special enough to transform even the plainest grilled meat into an extravagance. Take your time chopping; perfect, even pieces add to the beauty of the sauce.

GOOD WITH

Seafood: shrimp, scallops, any fish
Poultry: chicken, turkey, game hen

Meat: pork, veal

INGREDIENTS (MAKES ABOUT 2 CUPS)

1/2 cup very finely chopped red bell pepper
1/4 cup very finely chopped carrot
1/2 cup very finely chopped red onion
1 clove garlic, minced
1/2 cup very finely chopped fresh flat-leaf parsley
2 tablespoons very finely chopped fresh tarragon leaves

3 tablespoons apple cider vinegar
3 tablespoons ketchup
1/2 teaspoon crushed red pepper flakes
1/4 teaspoon ground black pepper
1 teaspoon kosher salt

DIRECTIONS

1. Combine all of the ingredients.

2. Use as a dip or table sauce, or as directed in a recipe; can be stored in a tightly closed container in the refrigerator for up to 3 days.

VIETNAMESE DIPPING SAUCE

TIMING
Prep: 5 minutes

Thai fish sauce (*nam pla*) is made by fermenting salted fish for weeks, giving it a pungent aroma somewhere between musky-sexy and putrid-rotten. How you perceive it depends on who you are and your mood of the moment. Many people are repulsed by their first whiff and then warm up to its charms after a taste or two. This dipping sauce rounds out the pungency of fish sauce with lime juice, vinegar, and the sweetness of freshly grated carrot. It is delicious with grilled seafood and makes distinctive pulled pork.

GOOD WITH

Seafood: shrimp, scallops, any fish
Poultry: chicken, turkey, game hen

Meat: pork, veal

INGREDIENTS (MAKES ABOUT 1 CUP)

1/4 cup fresh lime juice
1/4 cup Thai fish sauce (*nam pla*)
1/4 cup water
1 tablespoon rice wine vinegar

1 clove garlic, minced
1 hot chile pepper, such as bird chile, habanero, cayenne, or Scotch bonnet
1/4 cup shredded carrot

DIRECTIONS

1. Combine all of the ingredients.

2. Use as a dip or as directed in a recipe; can be stored in a tightly closed container in the refrigerator for up to 2 weeks.

TAPENADE PARSLEY PESTO

TIMING
Prep: 5 minutes

If you find tapenade a little too intense, this might be the alternative you've been looking for. It has the pungency of cured black olives and the aroma of garlic and extra-virgin olive oil, but it has been refreshed with an invasion of fresh parsley.

GOOD WITH

Seafood: shrimp, scallops, any fish
Poultry: chicken, turkey, game hen

Meat: lamb, pork, veal

INGREDIENTS (MAKES ABOUT 1/2 CUP)

2 ounces (1/2 cup) pitted kalamata olives, finely chopped
2 cloves garlic, minced
1/3 cup chopped fresh flat-leaf parsley

1 teaspoon tomato paste
1/4 teaspoon ground black pepper
1/4 cup extra-virgin olive oil

DIRECTIONS

1. Combine all of the ingredients.

2. Use as a dip or as directed in a recipe; can be stored in a tightly closed container in the refrigerator for up to 1 month.

GRILLED TOMATO DIP

Why settle for plain tomato sauce when you can easily make fire-roasted tomato sauce? Grilling the tomatoes, onions, and garlic adds a whole new flavor dimension. Use this tomato condiment as a dip, sauce, or glaze just as you would use traditional simmered tomato sauce.

GRILL TOOLS AND EQUIPMENT
· Long-handled tongs
· Long-handled spatula
· About 6 skewers (soaked in water for 30 minutes if bamboo)

GOOD WITH

Seafood: shrimp, scallops, any fish
Poultry: any poultry

Meat: beef, pork, lamb, veal

GETTING CREATIVE
· Vary the flavor by stirring in $1/2$ cup pitted kalamata olives, $1/2$ teaspoon crushed red pepper flakes, and/or 6 mashed anchovy fillets (or $1 1/2$ tablespoons anchovy paste).

TIP
· For a smoother sauce, pass it through a food mill or fine sieve.

THE GRILL

Gas: Medium heat (350°F)
Clean, oiled grate
Charcoal: Direct heat–medium ash
12-by-12-inch charcoal bed (about 3 dozen coals)
Clean, oiled grate on lowest setting

Wood: Direct heat–medium ash
12-by-12-inch bed, 3 inches deep
Clean, oiled grate set 4 inches above the fire

INGREDIENTS (MAKES ABOUT 4 CUPS)

1 onion
No-stick spray oil
5 unpeeled garlic cloves
3 pounds ripe tomatoes (8 to 12 medium)
$1/4$ cup tomato paste
$1/4$ cup extra-virgin olive oil, or more to taste

3 tablespoons chopped fresh oregano leaves, or $1 1/2$ teaspoons dried, or more to taste
1 teaspoon kosher salt, or more to taste
$1/2$ teaspoon sugar, or more to taste
$1/2$ teaspoon ground black pepper, or more to taste

DIRECTIONS

1. Heat the grill as directed.
2. Peel the onion and slice it crosswise into rounds about $1/4$ inch thick. Skewer the rounds through the side so that they will lie flat on the grill. Generously coat all over with spray oil.
3. Skewer the unpeeled garlic cloves and coat all over with spray oil. Grill the whole tomatoes and skewered onions and garlic until softened and nicely grill-marked all over, turning occasionally, about 5 minutes per side. The tomatoes should

be blistered and blackened all over; they may take a few minutes more.
4. Let cool slightly, then peel the tomatoes and garlic. Put the peeled tomatoes and garlic in a food processor along with the grilled onions, tomato paste, olive oil, oregano, salt, sugar, and pepper. Purée until smooth. Taste and add more olive oil, oregano, salt, sugar, and/or pepper as necessary.

parsley
ketchup
onions
cardamom
olive oil
lamb chops
bell pepper
scallions
sriracha

INDEX

Aidells, Bruce, and Denis Kelly. *The Complete Meat Cookbook*. Houghton Mifflin, 1998.

Beard, James. *Cook It Outdoors*. M. Barrows and Company, 1941.

———. *James Beard's American Cookery*. Little, Brown and Company, 1972.

Bittman, Mark. *Fish: The Complete Guide to Buying and Cooking*. Macmillan, 1994.

Brillat-Savarin, Jean-Anthelme. *The Physiology of Taste*. Counterpoint, 1949.

Chesman, Andrea. *The Vegetarian Grill*. Harvard Common Press, 1998.

Corriher, Shirley O. *Cookwise*. William Morrow, 1997.

Davidson, Alan, *Seafood: A Connoisseur's Guide and Cookbook*. Simon & Schuster, 1989.

———. *The Oxford Companion to Food*. Oxford University Press, 1999.

Fearnley-Whittingstall, Hugh. *The River Cottage Meat Book*. Hodder and Stoughton, 2004.

Griffith, Dottie. *Celebrating Barbecue*. Simon & Schuster, 2002.

Hillman, Howard. *The New Kitchen Science (Revised Edition)*. Houghton Mifflin, 2003.

Jamison, Cheryl Alters and Bill Jamison. *Smoke & Spice*. Harvard Common Press, 1994.

———. *Texas Home Cooking*. Harvard Common Press, 1993.

Joachim, David. *The Food Substitutions Bible*. Robert Rose, 2005.

———. *The Tailgater's Cookbook*. Broadway, 2005.

———. *A Man, A Can, A Grill*. Rodale, 2003.

Kirk, Paul. *Paul Kirk's Championship Barbecue*. Harvard Common Press, 2004.

———. *Paul Kirk's Championship Barbecue Sauces*. Harvard Common Press, 1998.

Labensky, Sarah R. and Alan M. Hause. *On Cooking (Third Edition)*. Prentice Hall, 2003.

McGee, Harold. *On Food and Cooking (revised edition)*. Scribner, 2004.

———. *The Curious Cook*. North Point Press, 1990.

Raichlen, Steven. *BBQ USA*. Workman, 2003.

———. *How to Grill*. Workman, 2001.

———. *The Barbecue! Bible*. Workman, 1998.

Schlesinger, Chris and John Willoughby. *How to Cook Meat*. William Morrow, 2000.

———. *The Thrill of the Grill*. William Morrow, 1990.

Schulz, Stephen Philip. *Cooking with Fire & Smoke*. Simon and Schuster, 1986.

Sinnes, A. Cort. *The Gas Grill Gourmet*. Harvard Common Press, 1996.

Thorne, John, with Matt Lewis Thorne. *Serious Pig*. North Point Press, 1996.

Walsh, Robb. *Legends of Texas Barbecue Cookbook*. Chronicle Books, 2002.

Wolke, Robert L. *What Einstein Told His Cook*. W.W. Norton & Company, 2002.

———. *What Einstein Told His Cook 2*. W.W. Norton & Company, 2005.

TABLE OF EQUIVALENTS

LIQUID/DRY MEASURES

U.S.	Metric
1/4 teaspoon	1.25 milliliters
1/2 teaspoon	2.5 milliliters
1 teaspoon	5 milliliters
1 tablespoon (3 teaspoons)	15 milliliters
1 fluid ounce (2 tablespoons)	30 milliliters
1/4 cup	60 milliliters
1/3 cup	80 milliliters
1/2 cup	120 milliliters
1 cup	240 milliliters
1 pint (2 cups)	480 milliliters
1 quart (4 cups, 32 ounces)	960 milliliters
1 gallon (4 quarts)	3.84 liters
1 ounce (by weight)	28 grams
1 pound	454 grams
2.2 pounds	1 kilogram

LENGTH

U.S.	Metric
1/8 inch	3 millimeters
1/4 inch	6 millimeters
1/2 inch	12 millimeters
1 inch	2.5 centimeters

OVEN TEMPERATURE

Fahrenheit	Celsius	Gas
250	120	1/2
300	150	2
325	160	3
350	180	4
375	190	5
400	200	6
425	220	7
450	230	8
475	240	9
500	260	10